God's
Prophets
Speak

3,300 Statements on
97 Doctrines and Practices
by the Presidents of
The Church of Jesus Christ
of Latter-day Saints

God's Prophets Speak

3,300 Statements on
97 Doctrines and Practices
by the Presidents of
The Church of Jesus Christ
of Latter-day Saints

Compiled by
Stanley E. & Amydee M. Fawcett

The following topics are presented in this book:

Secind Printing: July 2004

International Standard Book Number:
0-88290-644-5

Horizon Publishers' Catalog and Order Number:
H1096

Printed and distributed
in the United States of America by

Mailing Address:
925 North Main Street
Springville, Utah 84663

Local Phone: (801) 489-4084
Toll Free: 1 (800) SKYBOOK
FAX: (800)489-1097

E-mail: skybook@cedarfort.com
www.cedarfort.com

CONTENTS

GOD AND MAN'S DESTINY

THE PLAN OF SALVATION

PRINCIPLES AND ORDINANCES

THE COMMANDMENTS

RIGHTEOUS LIVING

FAMILY

THE PRIESTHOOD

LEADERSHIP

CHURCH HISTORY AND MISSION

THE CHURCH AND THE WORLD

FOREWORD

Several years ago, while working on my doctorate in business administration at Arizona State University, I found myself seriously considering the value and relevance of some of the material at hand. Over the years, I have discovered that most doctoral students spend at least some time thinking about this same topic—which of the various topics of study are of most worth. My barren upstairs cubicle in the business building provided an appropriate setting to contemplate my scholarly focus, especially since the inventory models I was then examining seemed quite uninteresting. On this particular autumn day, a somewhat novel thought came into my mind. The impression was that as a member of The Church of Jesus Christ of Latter-day Saints, I should take some time to find out what the Lord's latter-day prophets had taught since the restoration of the gospel. As I concluded my studies for the day, I resolved that if I were going to wholeheartedly sustain each of the presidents in their own time as the Lord's mouthpiece and living representative, then I would need to carefully study their teachings.

I later discussed these feelings with my wife, Dee, and we agreed that we would both begin to study the teachings of the latter-day prophets. I was to begin with Joseph Smith Jr. and she was to start with Ezra Taft Benson. In effect, we embarked on a race to see who could complete the study of the prophets' teachings first. The loser would be spending time in the kitchen baking the victor a cherry pie for each set of teachings not completed. Once the journey began, I found the teachings of each prophet to be remarkable and most appropriate to resolving the challenges that my growing family faced in our modern and hectic world. Of course this new appreciation should not have come as a surprise given that prophets are called to help each of us "Come unto Christ" and overcome the hurdles that impede our return to Heavenly Father's presence. President Benson highlighted the need to be familiar with the teachings of the living prophet when he said,

> The living prophet is more important to us than a dead prophet. The living prophet has the power of TNT. By that I mean "Today's News Today." God's revelations to Adam did not instruct Noah how to build the ark. Noah needed his own revelation. Therefore, the most important prophet, so far as you and I are concerned, is the one living in our day and age to whom the Lord is currently revealing His will for us. (ETB, p. 335.)

Interestingly, President Benson also answered my earlier question regarding "the knowledge of greatest value." He noted, "Knowledge is power, but all knowledge is not of equal value. That knowledge which deals with the personality and attributes of God the Father and man's relationship to Him is of supreme importance." (ETB, p. 3.) Not surprisingly, as my course of study proceeded, question after question was answered. But perhaps more importantly, I began to feel that I knew each prophet personally—almost as if each prophet was speaking directly to me. The end result of this effort was that our testimonies were greatly strengthened. We came to respect and love each of the prophets for their dedication and consecration before the Lord. The conviction that each was called to lead the restored church at a specific point in history and that each was endowed with unique and appropriate characteristics to provide guidance and stand as a witness of the Savior became firmly established in our hearts and minds.

This understanding and knowledge has proven invaluable in making daily decisions as well as in teaching a year-long institute course on the teachings of latter-day prophets. The encouragement of the young men and women in this course led us to put the compilations together in their present form. We recognize that the selected quotes are certainly not exhaustive, but an effort was made to include representative selections, especially as they relate to the challenge of righteous living in today's world. We express appreciation to each of the prophets for the lives they have lived and the words they have taught. We are grateful to all the teachers that influenced them in their development. We hope that those who read this work come to feel what we know—that God leads His children today through living prophets.

While we appreciate the encouragement, insight, and assistance of many friends who have helped bring this effort to fruition, we must accept the responsibility for any mistakes or errors which may have inadvertently occurred in the compilation and publication of this work.

Stanley E. Fawcett
Amydee M. Fawcett

REFERENCES CITED

BYU   Talk given at Brigham Young University

CN   *Church News*

CP   *In the Company of Prophets*, (1993) Heidi S. Swinton, Deseret Book: Salt Lake City.

IE   *Improvement Era*

JD   *Journal of Discourses*, (1854-1886) Vols. 1-26.

JI   *Juvenile Instructor*

KRL   *I Know that my Redeemer Lives*, (1990) Deseret Book: Salt Lake City.

LPS   *Latter-day Prophets Speak*, (1948) Compiled by Daniel H. Ludlow, Bookcraft, Salt Lake City.

LTT   *Latter-day Prophets—Their Lives, Teachings, and Testimonies*, (1997) Emerson Roy West, Covenant Communications, Inc.

NE   *New Era*

PC   *The Presidents of the Church*, (1971) Compiled by Preston Nibley, Deseret Book: Salt Lake City.

PCE   *Presidents of the Church: Biographical Essays*, (1986) Edited by Leonard J. Arrington, Deseret Book: Salt Lake City.

PCM   *Presidents of the Church* (1979) Student Manual (Rel. 345) The Church of Jesus Christ of Latter-day Saints: Salt Lake City.

Gordon B. Hinckley

BTE   *Be Thou an Example*, (1981) Deseret Book: Salt Lake City.

FETR   *Faith, the Essence of True Religion*, (1989) Desert Book: Salt Lake City.

Howard W. Hunter

WMJ   *That We Might Have Joy*, (1994) Deseret Book: Salt Lake City.

Ezra Taft Benson

AWW   *A Witness and a Warning*, (1988) Deseret Book: Salt Lake City.

CLP   *Come, Listen to a Prophet's Voice*, (1990) Desert Book: Salt Lake City.

CUC   *Come Unto Christ*, (1983) Deseret Book: Salt Lake City.

ETB   *The Teachings of Ezra Taft Benson*, (1988) Bookcraft: Salt Lake City.

GFC   *God, Family, Country*, (1974), Deseret Book: Salt Lake City.

Spencer W. Kimball

FPM   *Faith Precedes the Miracle* (1972) Deseret Book: Salt Lake City.

MF   *The Miracle of Forgiveness*, (1969) Bookcraft: Salt Lake City.

SWK   *The Teachings of Spencer W. Kimball*, (1982) Edited by Edward L. Kimball, Bookcraft: Salt Lake City.

Harold B. Lee

DSL   *Decisions for Successful Living*, (1973) Deseret Book: Salt Lake City.

HBL   *The Teachings of Harold B. Lee*, (1996) Edited by Clyde J. Williams, Bookcraft: Salt Lake City.

SHP   *Stand Ye in Holy Places*, (1976) Deseret Book: Salt Lake City.

YLW   *Ye Are the Light of the World*, (1974) Deseret Book: Salt Lake City.

Joseph Fielding Smith

DS1   *Doctrines of Salvation*, Vol. 1, (1954) Compiled by Bruce R. McConkie, Bookcraft: Salt Lake City.

DS2   *Doctrines of Salvation*, Vol. 2, (1955) Compiled by Bruce R. McConkie, Bookcraft: Salt Lake City.

DS3   *Doctrines of Salvation*, Vol. 3, (1956) Compiled by Bruce R. McConkie, Bookcraft: Salt Lake City.

David O. McKay

GI   *Gospel Ideals*, (1953) Improvement Era, Salt Lake City.

TF   *True to the Faith*, (1966) Compiled by Llewelyn R. McKay, Bookcraft: Salt Lake City.

TL   *Treasures of Life*, (1962) Compiled by Clare Middlemiss, Deseret Book: Salt Lake City.

George Albert Smith

GAS   *The Teachings of George Albert Smith*, (1996) Edited by Robert and Susan McIntosh, Bookcraft: Salt Lake City.

SGO   *Sharing the Gospel with Others*, (1948) Compiled by Preston Nibley, Deseret Book: Salt Lake City.

Heber J. Grant

GS   *Gospel Standards*, (1941) Compiled by Dr. G. Homer Durham, Improvement Era Publication: Salt Lake City.

Joseph F. Smith

GD   *Gospel Doctrine*, (1952) Deseret Book: Salt Lake City.

Lorenzo Snow

LS   *The Teachings of Lorenzo Snow*, (1984) Compiled by Clyde J. Williams, Bookcraft: Salt Lake City.

Wilford Woodruff

WW   *The Discourses of Wilford Woodruff*, (1946) Edited by G. Homer Durham, Bookcraft: Salt Lake City.

John Taylor

GK   *The Gospel Kingdom*, (1987) Edited by G. Homer Durham, Bookcraft: Salt Lake City.

Brigham Young

BY   *Discourses of Brigham Young*, (1957) Arranged by John A. Widtsoe, Deseret Book: Salt Lake City.

Joseph Smith Jr.

HC   *History of the Church of Jesus Christ of Latter-day Saints*, (1980) Deseret Book: Salt Lake City.

LF   *Lectures on Faith*, (1985) Deseret Book: Salt Lake City.

STJS *Scriptural Teachings of the Prophet Joseph Smith*, (1993) Arranged by Joseph Fielding Smith, Desert Book: Salt Lake City.

GOD AND MAN'S DESTINY

1. GOD AND MAN'S DESTINY

The experience of Joseph Smith in a few moments in the grove on a spring day in 1820, brought more light and knowledge and understanding of the personality and reality and substance of God and his Beloved Son than men had arrived at during centuries of speculation. —*Gordon B. Hinckley* (CR, Apr. 1960, 82)

We approach the Father through the Son. He is our intercessor at the throne of God. How marvelous it is that we may so speak to the Father in the name of the Son, and come to know by the power of the Holy Ghost, as a divine gift, of the living reality of these three who constitute the Godhead. —*Gordon B. Hinckley* (FETR , 27)

All nature portrays the existence of a supreme being. In this material world, we have learned that every building has a builder and everything that is made has a maker. . . . All of nature whispers to my reasoning that there was a creator. I know this to be God. —*Howard W. Hunter* (CR, Oct. 1968, 139)

In order to find God as a reality, we must follow the course which he pointed out for the quest. The path is one that leads upward; it takes faith and effort, and is not the easy course. For this reason many men will not devote themselves to the arduous task of proving to themselves the reality of God. —*Howard W. Hunter* (IE, June 1970, 33)

Musicians, mathematicians, scientists, athletes, and skilled people in many fields spend years in study, practice, and hard work to acquire their ability. Can others who are not willing to make the effort say there are no such things as music, mathematics, science, or athletics? It is just as foolish for man to say there is no God simply because he has not had the inclination to seek him. —*Howard W. Hunter* (IE, June 1970, 34)

The greatest quest is a search for God—to determine his reality, his personal attributes, and to secure a knowledge of the gospel of his Son Jesus Christ. —*Howard W. Hunter* (CR, Oct. 1974, 138)

Our Heavenly Father is not far away. He can be very close to us. God lives, I know that He lives. He is our Father. Jesus Christ, the Redeemer of the world, watches over this earth. He will direct all things. Be unafraid, keep His commandments, love one another, pray for peace and all will be well. —*Ezra Taft Benson* (ETB, 666)

Apart from God we cannot succeed, but as a partner with God we cannot fail. —*Ezra Taft Benson* (ETB, 413)

Of all the treasure of knowledge, the most truly vital is the knowledge of God, of his existence, his powers, his love, and his promises. Through this knowledge, we learn that our great objective in life is to build character. In fact, we learn that the building of faith and character is paramount, for character is higher than intellect, and perfect character will be continually rewarded with increased intellect. —*Spencer W. Kimball* (Ensign, Sept. 1983, 3-4)

I say to you that I know as though I have seen, that He lives, that He is real, that God the Father and His Son are living realities, personalities with bodies, parts, and passions—glorified beings. If you believe that, then you are safe. If you don't believe it, then struggle for that witness, and all will be well with you. —*Harold B. Lee* (KRL, 177)

There is nothing which a man can possess in this world, which will bring more hope and faith than a testimony of the existence of a Heavenly Father who loves us, or of the reality of Jesus Christ, his Only Begotten Son, that those two heavenly personages appeared to the Prophet Joseph and established the Church of Jesus Christ, and that men are officially authorized to represent Deity. —*David O. McKay* (CR, Oct. 1953, 88)

We accept what the Bible teaches with reference to God the Father and Jesus Christ, His Son, and what the Book of Mormon teaches with reference to the same Godhead. We believe that in our own time they have again appeared, so that all doubts as to their existence has been removed. —*George Albert Smith* (CR, Apr. 1940, 85)

What the world needs today more than anything else is an implicit faith in God, our Father, and in Jesus Christ, His Son, as the Redeemer of the world. The message of the Church of Jesus Christ of Latter-day Saints to the world is that God lives, that Jesus Christ is His Son, and that They appeared to the boy Joseph Smith, and promised him that he should be an instrument in the hands of the Lord in restoring the true gospel to the world. —*Heber J. Grant* (CR, Apr. 1935, 9)

I do not believe that any man has discovered any principle of science, or art, in mechanism, or mathematics, or anything else, that God did not know before man did. Man is indebted to the source of all intelligence and truth, for the knowledge that he possesses; and all who will yield obedience to the promptings of the Spirit, which lead to virtue, to honor, to the love of God and man, and to the love of truth and that which is ennobling and enlarging to the soul, will get a cleaner, a more expansive, and a more direct and conclusive knowledge of God's truths than anyone else can obtain. —*Joseph F. Smith* (CR, Apr. 1902, 85-86)

The thing I want to impress upon you is that God is real, a person of flesh and bones, the same as you are and I am. Christ is the same, but the Holy Ghost is a person of spirit. —*Joseph F. Smith* (LPS, 274)

There is no man that knows the truth of this work more than I do. I know it fully; I know it distinctly. I know there is a God just as well as any man knows it, because God has revealed Himself to me. I know it positively. I shall never forget the manifestations of the Lord; I never will forget them as long as memory endures. It is in me. —*Lorenzo Snow* (CR, Oct. 1897, 55)

We believe that the spirit which enlightens the human family proceeds from the presence of the Almighty, that it spreads throughout all space, that it is the light and life of all things, and that every honest heart possesses it in proportion to his virtue, integrity, and his desire to know the truth and do good to his fellow men. —*Lorenzo Snow* (LS, 107)

It is necessary that we suffer in all things, that we may be qualified and worthy to rule, and govern all things, even as our Father in Heaven and His eldest son, Jesus. —*Lorenzo Snow* (LS, 119)

God is God. Christ is Christ. The Holy Ghost is the Holy Ghost. That should be enough for you and me to know. If we want to know any more, wait till we get where God is in person. —*Wilford Woodruff* (WW, 236)

These two principles do exist, good and evil, God and the Devil. Whatever leads to good and to do good is of God. Whatever leads to evil and to do evil is of the devil. God has labored from the creation of man to lead him to keep the celestial law, that he may inherit a celestial glory and partake of eternal life, the greatest of all the gifts of God to man; while the devil, with all the fallen angels, has labored from the creation to lead man astray, to lead him down to the perdition of ungodly men, that he may have dominion over him. —*Wilford Woodruff* (WW, 239)

If I am a being that came into the world yesterday, and leaves it again tomorrow, I might as well have one religion as another, or none at all . . . If I am an eternal being, I want to know something about that eternity with which I am associated. I want to know something about God, the devil, heaven, and hell. If hell is a place of misery, and heaven a place of happiness, I want to know how to escape the one, and obtain the other. . . . as an intelligent being, if I have a mind capable of reflection, I wish to contemplate the works of nature, and to know something of nature's God, and my destiny. —*John Taylor* (GK, 16-17)

When we are able to comprehend things as God does, we shall comprehend a great many principles that have never entered into our hearts to conceive of. —*John Taylor* (GK, 69-70)

If there is anything that is great and good and wise among men, it cometh from God. If there are men who possess great ability as statesmen, or as philosophers, or who possess remarkable scientific knowledge and skill, the credit thereof belongs to God, for he dispenses it to his children whether they believe in him or not, or whether they sin against him or not; it makes no difference; but all will have to account to him for the way and manner in which they have used the talents committed unto them. —*Brigham Young* (BY, 19)

The difference between God and the devil is that God creates and organizes while the whole study of the devil is to destroy. —*Brigham Young* (JD, 13:4)

[W]e should . . . state the spirit is a substance; that it is material, but that it is more pure, elastic and refined matter than the body; that it existed before the body, can exist in the body; and will exist separate from the body, when the body will be mouldering in the dust; and will in the resurrection be again united with it. —*Joseph Smith, Jr.* (STJS, 235-236)

I would just remark, that the spirits of men are eternal . . . that they are organized according to that Priesthood which is everlasting . . . that they all move in their respective spheres, and are governed by the law of God; that when they appear upon the earth they are in a probationary state, and are preparing, if righteous, for a future and greater glory; that the spirits of good men cannot interfere with the wicked beyond their prescribed bounds . . .

It would seem also, that wicked spirits have their bounds, limits, and laws by which they are governed or controlled, and know their future destiny. —*Joseph Smith, Jr.* (STJS, 235-236)

I have always declared God to be a distinct personage, Jesus Christ a separate and distinct personage from God the Father, and the Holy Ghost was a distinct personage and a Spirit: and these three constitute three distinct personages and three Gods. If this is in accordance with the New Testament, lo and behold! we have three Gods anyhow, and they are plural; and who can contradict it?—*Joseph Smith, Jr.* (STJS, 417)

Where was there ever a son without a father? And where was there ever a father without first being a son? Whenever did a tree or anything spring into existence without a progenitor? And everything comes in this way. . . . Hence if Jesus had a Father, can we not believe that He had a Father also? I despise the idea of being scared to death at such a doctrine, for the Bible is full of it. —*Joseph Smith, Jr.* (STJS, 421)

Everlasting covenant was made between three personages before the organization of this earth, and relates to their dispensation of things to men on the earth; these personages, according to Abraham's record, are called God the first, the Creator; God the second, the Redeemer; and God the third, the witness or Testator. —Joseph Smith, Jr. (STJS, 215)

2. HEAVENLY FATHER

I believe without equivocation or reservation in God, the Eternal Father. He is my Father, the Father of my spirit, and the Father of the spirits of all men. He is the great Creator, the Ruler of the universe. He directed the creation of this earth on which we live. In his image man was created. He is personal. He is real. —*Gordon B. Hinckley* (FETR , 21)

God is weaving his tapestry according to his own grand design. All flesh is in his hands. It is not our prerogative to counsel him. It is our responsibility and our opportunity to be at peace in our minds and in our hearts, and to know that he is God, that this is his work, and that he will not permit it to fail. —*Gordon B. Hinckley* (Ensign, May 1983, 6)

To fully understand this gift of agency and its inestimable worth, it is imperative that we understand that God's chief way of acting is by persuasion and patience and long-suffering, not by coercion and stark confrontation. He acts by gentle solicitation and by sweet enticement. He always acts with unfailing respect for the freedom and independence that we possess. He wants to help us and pleads for the chance to assist us, be he will not do so in violation of our agency. He loves us too much to do that, and doing so would run counter to his divine character. —*Howard W. Hunter* (WMJ, 78)

To countermand and ultimately forbid our choices was Satan's way, not God's; the Father of us all simply never will do that. He will, however, stand by us forever to help us see the right path, find the right choice, respond to the true voice, and feel the influence of his undeniable Spirit. —*Howard W. Hunter* (WMJ, 79)

Knowledge is power, but all knowledge is not of equal value. That knowledge which deals with the personality and attributes of God the Father and man's relationship to Him is of supreme importance. —*Ezra Taft Benson* (ETB, 3)

Our doctrine of God is clear. He is our Heavenly and Eternal Father. We are His literal children. Through righteous living according to His plan we can see God and Become like Him. —*Ezra Taft Benson* (ETB, 4-5)

Our Heavenly Father is the supreme scientist of the universe. He is the supreme authority of the humanities. God is the supreme authority on politics, on economics, on sociology. He knows what works best in human relations. He is the master teacher, with a glorious plan based on freedom of choice, for the building of godlike men and women. He stands today ready to help us reach out and tap that great unseen power as we heed the counsel of His living mouthpiece, a true prophet of God. —*Ezra Taft Benson* (ETB, 5)

Men may deceive each other, but God does not deceive men. —*Ezra Taft Benson* (CR, Oct. 1984, 6)

God, our Heavenly Father—Elohim—lives. That is an absolute truth. All four billion of the children of men on the earth might be ignorant of him and his attributes and his powers, but he still lives. All the people on the earth might deny him and disbelieve, but he lives in spite of them. They may have their own opinions, but he still lives, and his form, powers, and attributes do not change according to men's opinions. In short, opinion alone has no power in the matter of an absolute truth. He still lives. —*Spencer W. Kimball* (Ensign, Sept. 1978, 3)

We only find God by searching for Him. —*Harold B. Lee* (HBL, 5-6)

Do we believe that God has all "wisdom"? If so, in that, he is absolute. If there is something he does not know, then he is not absolute in "wisdom," and to think such a thing is absurd. Does he have all "power"? If so then there is nothing in which he lacks. If he is lacking in "wisdom" and in "power" then he is not supreme and there must be something greater than he is, and this is absurd. —*Joseph Fielding Smith* (DS1, 5)

It is not because the Lord is ignorant of law and truth that he is able to progress, but because of his knowledge and wisdom. The Lord is constantly using his knowledge in his work. And his great work is in bringing to pass the immortality and eternal life of man. By the creation of worlds and peopling them, by building and extending, he progresses, but not because the fulness of truth is not understood by him . —*Joseph Fielding Smith* (DS1, 10)

When we sincerely accept God as our Father and make him the center of our being, we become conscious of a new aim in life. No longer is the chief end of daily life merely to nourish and to pamper the body as all animals do. Spiritual attainment, not physical indulgence, becomes the chief goal. God is not viewed from the standpoint of what we may get from him, but what we may give to him. —*David O. McKay* (CR, Apr. 1948, 67)

The chief tragedy in the world at the present time is its disbelief in God's goodness, and its lack of faith in the teachings and doctrines of the gospel. To all who believe in a Living, Personal God and his divine truth, life can be so delightful and beautiful. —*David O. McKay* (CR, Oct. 1961, 8-9)

Our Heavenly Father loves us, and he loves our lives when they conform to his teachings. —*George Albert Smith* (CR, Apr. 1944, 31)

If we have the confidence of our Heavenly Father, if we have his love, if we are worthy of his blessings, all the armies of the world cannot destroy us, cannot break down our faith, and cannot overcome the church that is named for the Son of God. —*George Albert Smith* (CR, Apr. 1943, 92)

Our Heavenly Father will not coerce or compel mankind, but in loving kindness has given to them from the age when the world was first peopled until now, opportunity to know the truth. —*George Albert Smith* (CR, Oct. 1928, 93)

I think it is marvelous to know how close we are to our Heavenly Father, and I also think it is deplorable that some of us do not appreciate how near he is, for the reason that we have failed to measure up in many cases to his wise counsels. —*George Albert Smith* (CR, Apr. 1946, 4-5)

We are the children of God. He is an eternal being, without beginning of days or end of years. He always was, he is, he always will be. We are precisely in the same condition and under the same circumstances that God our heavenly Father was when he was passing through this or a similar ordeal. —*Joseph F. Smith* (GD, 32-33)

Every unfoldment of the nineteenth century in science, in art, in mechanism, in music, in literature, in poetic fancy, in philosophical thought, was prompted by His Spirit which before long will be poured out upon all flesh that will receive it. He is the Father of us all and He desires to save and exalt us all. —*Lorenzo Snow* (PC , 171)

The more I can know of God, the dearer and more precious he is to me, and the more exalted are my feelings towards him. —*Brigham Young* (BY, 18)

I want to tell you, each and every one of you, that you are well acquainted with God our Heavenly Father, or the great Elohim. You are all well acquainted with him, for there is not a soul of you but what has lived in his house and dwelt with him year after year; and yet you are seeking to become acquainted with him, when the fact is, you have merely forgotten what you did know. —*Brigham Young* (BY, 50)

If any of us could now see the God we are striving to serve—if we could see our Father who dwells in the heavens, we should learn that we are as well acquainted with him as we are with our earthly father; and he would be as familiar to us in the expression of his countenance, and we should be ready to embrace him and fall upon his neck and kiss him, if we had the privilege. And still we, unless the vision of the Spirit is opened to us, know nothing about God. You know much about him, if you did but realize it. And there is no other one item that will so much astound you, when your eyes are opened in eternity, as to think that you were so stupid in the body. —*Brigham Young* (JD, 8:30)

I want to ask this congregation, every man, woman and child, to answer the question in their own heart, what kind of a being God is? Ask yourselves; turn your thought into your hearts, and say if any of you have seen, heard, or communed with him. This is a question that may occupy your attention for a long time. I again repeat the question—What kind of a being is God? . . .

God himself was once as we are now, and is an exalted man, and sits enthroned in yonder heavens! That is the great secret. If the veil were rent today, and the great God who holds this world in its orbit, and who upholds all worlds and all things by his power, was to make himself visible,—I say, if you were to see him today, you would see him like a man in form—like yourselves in all the person, image, and very form as a man. —*Joseph Smith, Jr.* (STJS, 388-390)

It is the first principle of the Gospel to know for a certainty the Character of God, and to know that we may converse with him as one man converses with another, and that he was once a man like us. —*Joseph Smith, Jr.* (STJS, 392)

We here observe that God is the only supreme governor and independent being in whom all fullness and perfection dwell; who is omnipotent, omnipresent, and omniscient . . . and he is the object in whom the faith of all other rational and accountable beings center for life and salvation. —*Joseph Smith, Jr.* (LF, 10)

Previous to the time that any of Adam's posterity had obtained a manifestation of God to themselves, Adam, their common father, had testified unto them of the existence of God, and of his eternal power and Godhead. . . .

From the foregoing it is easily to be seen, not only how the knowledge of God came into the world, but upon what principle it was preserved; that from the time it was first communicated, it was retained in the minds of righteous men, who taught not only their own posterity but the world; so that there was no need of a new revelation to man, after Adam's creation to Noah, to give them the first idea or notion of the existence of a God; and not only of a God, but the true and living God. —*Joseph Smith, Jr.* (LF, 18-20)

3. HEAVENLY MOTHER

Logic and reason would certainly suggest that if we have a Father in Heaven, we have a Mother in Heaven. That doctrine rests well with me.

However, in light of the instruction we have received from the Lord Himself, I regard it as inappropriate for anyone in the Church to pray to our Mother in Heaven. . . .

The fact that we do not pray to our Mother in Heaven in no way belittles or denigrates her. —*Gordon B. Hinckley* (Ensign, Nov. 1991, 100)

God made man in his own image and certainly he made woman in the image of his wife-partner. You [women] are daughters of God. You are precious. You are made in the image of our heavenly Mother. —*Spencer W. Kimball* (SWK, 25)

[W]hen we sing that doctrinal hymn and anthem of affection, 'O My Father,' we get a sense of the ultimate in maternal modesty, of the restrained, queenly elegance of our Heavenly Mother, and knowing how profoundly our mortal mothers have shaped us here, do we suppose her influence on us as individuals to be less if we live so as to return there?—*Spencer W. Kimball* (Ensign, May 1978, 6.)

Women can become like our mother in heaven. You sisters, I suppose, have read that poem which my sister composed years ago, and which is sung quite frequently now in our meetings. It tells us that we not only have a Father in "that high and glorious place," but that we have a Mother too; and you will become as great as your Mother, if you are faithful. —*Lorenzo Snow* (LS, 7-8)

We are the offspring of God. He is our Father, and we have a Mother in the other life as well. —*Lorenzo Snow* (CR, Oct. 1898, 56)

4. THE SON—JESUS CHRIST

I believe in the Lord Jesus Christ, the Son of the eternal, living God. . . . I believe that in his mortal life he was the one perfect man to walk the earth. I believe that in his words are to be found that light and truth which, if observed, would save the world and bring exaltation to mankind. I believe that in his priesthood rests divine authority—the power to bless, the power to heal, the power to govern in the earthly affairs of God, the power to bind in the heavens that which is bound upon the earth.

I believe that through his atoning sacrifice, the offering of his life on Calvary's hill, he expiated the sins of mankind, relieving us from the burden of sin if we will forsake evil and follow him. I believe in the reality and the power of his resurrection. I believe in the grace of God made manifest through Jesus' sacrifice and redemption, and I believe that through his atonement, without any price on our part, each of us is offered the gift of resurrection from the dead. I believe further that through that sacrifice there is extended to every man and woman, every son and daughter of God, the opportunity for eternal life and exaltation in our Father's kingdom, as we hearken to and obey his commandment. —*Gordon B. Hinckley* (FETR , 23-24)

Some modern theologians have attempted to strip the Lord of his divinity and then they wonder why men do not worship him. They have tried to take from Jesus the mantle of Godhood and have left only a man in the eyes of their followers. They have tried to accommodate him to their own narrow thinking. In the process they have robbed the Lord of his divine sonship and have taken from the world its rightful King. —*Gordon B. Hinckley* (Ensign, Apr. 1983, 4)

It is important to remember that Jesus was capable of sinning, that he could have succumbed, that the plan of life and salvation could have been foiled, but that he remained true. Had there been no possibility of his yielding to the enticement of Satan, there would have been no real test, no genuine victory in the result. . . . He was perfect and sinless, not because he had to be, but because he clearly and determinedly wanted to be. —*Howard W. Hunter* (Ensign, Nov. 1976, 17-19)

I give to you my solemn witness that Jesus Christ is in fact the Son of God. . . .
It is by the power of the Holy Ghost that I bear my witness. I know of Christ's reality as if I had seen with my eyes and heard with my ears. I know also that the Holy Spirit will confirm the truthfulness of my witness in the hearts of all those who listen with an ear of faith. —*Howard W. Hunter* (Ensign, Jan. 1984, 70)

Too many men have worshiped at the shrine of Christ's attributes and ethics but have denied the divinity of their redeemer. —*Howard W. Hunter* (Ensign, Jan. 1984, 70)

The first task Christ did as a perfect, sinless Son was to redeem all mankind from the Fall, providing an atonement for Adam's sin and for our own sins if we will accept and follow him. The second great thing he did was to set a perfect example of right living, of kindness and mercy and compassion, in order that all of the rest of mankind might know how to live, know how to improve, and know how to become more Godlike. —*Howard W. Hunter* (WMJ, 4)

As we search for the shore of safety and peace, whether we be individual women and men, families, communities, or nations, Christ is the only beacon on which we can ultimately rely. —*Howard W. Hunter* (WMJ, 17)

In this age, as in every age before us and in every age that will follow, the greatest need in all the world is an active and sincere faith in the basic teachings of Jesus of Nazareth, the living Son of the living God. Because many reject those teachings, that is all the more reason why sincere believers in the gospel of Jesus Christ should proclaim its truth and show by example the power and peace of a righteous, gentle life. —*Howard W. Hunter* (WMJ, 17)

Jesus was a God in the premortal existence. —*Ezra Taft Benson* (ETB, 6)

What think we of Christ? Whose Son is He?
We accept Him as the divine Son of God.
We believe Him to be the promised Messiah.
We rely on His atonement for personal salvation.
We declare His literal bodily resurrection.

Yes, we believe in Jesus Christ, but more. We look to Him, we trust Him, and we strive to emulate His attributes. —*Ezra Taft Benson* (CUC , 10)

A testimony of Jesus means that we accept the divine mission of Jesus Christ, embrace His gospel, and do His works. —*Ezra Taft Benson* (CUC , 11-12)

To qualify as the Redeemer of all our Father's children, Jesus had to be perfectly obedient to all the laws of God. —*Ezra Taft Benson* (CUC , 128)

No other single influence has had so great an impact on this earth as the life of Jesus the Christ. We cannot conceive of our lives without His teachings. Without Him we would be lost in a mirage of beliefs and worships born in fear and darkness where the sensual and materialistic hold sway. We are far short of the goal He set for us, but we must never lose sight of it, nor must we forget that our great climb toward the light, toward perfection, would not be possible except for His teaching, His life, His death, and His resurrection. —*Ezra Taft Benson* (Ensign, Aug. 1991, 4)

I add my own testimony. I know that Jesus Christ is the Son of the living God and that he was crucified for the sins of the world.
He is my friend, my Savior, my Lord, my God. —*Spencer W. Kimball* (CR, Nov. 1978, 4)

Jesus stands on the horizon of human experience as the only one who cannot be improved. —*Spencer W. Kimball* (SWK, 9)

Think of the individual who impresses you most as perfection in chastity . . .
Now think of the one who is most unselfish . . .
Now let pass in review one who is your ideal in kindliness . . .
Now . . . who is the individual whom you admire most as one who is obedient . . .
And now consider the person whom you most admire . . .
And now, the one who exhibits the greatest degree of love . . .
And now . . . combine all these heroic people with all their monumental virtues into one composite figure and you still have an inferior to the Lord, Jesus Christ, who had all virtues at their best, than whom there is no peer except His Father, God. —*Spencer W. Kimball* (KRL, 184-185.)

Before we can feel kinship to our Savior and be influenced by His teachings in all our thoughts and deeds, we must be impressed by the reality of His existence and the divinity of His mission. —*Harold B. Lee* (SHP, 27)

Christ came not only into the world to make an atonement for the sins of mankind, but to set an example before the world of the standard of perfection of God's law and of obedience to the Father. —*Harold B. Lee* (SHP, 342)

Today we should ask ourselves the question, . . . "What think ye of Christ?" (Matthew 22:42) We ought to ask as we would say it today, "What think we of Christ?" and then make it a little more personal and ask, "What think I of Christ?" Do I think of Him as the Redeemer of my soul? . . . Do I accept him as the Savior of this world? Am I true to my covenants, . . . that I would stand as a witness of Him at all times, and in all things, and in all places, wherever I would be, even until death?—*Harold B. Lee* (HBL, 8)

All revelation since the fall has come through Jesus Christ, who is the Jehovah of the Old Testament. . . . The Father has never dealt with man directly and personally since the fall, and he has never appeared except to introduce and bear record of the Son. —*Joseph Fielding Smith* (DS1, 27)

Our Savior was a God before he was born into this world, and he brought with him that same status when he came here. —*Joseph Fielding Smith* (DS1, 32)

Christ, who is the firstborn in the Spirit of the children of God, was elevated to Godhood . . . . He was chosen. . . as the Lamb slain from before the foundation of the earth. When the plan of salvation and the mortal existence were discussed, he was chosen to be the Only Begotten Son of God on the earth. This was his divine right by birth and appointment of the Father. —*Joseph Fielding Smith* (KRL, 158-159)

With my whole soul I accept Jesus Christ as the personification of human perfection— as God made manifest in the flesh, as the Savior and Redeemer of mankind. Accepting him as my Redeemer, Savior, and Lord, I accept his gospel as the plan of salvation, as the one perfect way to human happiness and peace. There is not a principle which was taught by him but seems to me to be applicable to the growth, development, and happiness of mankind. Every one of his teachings seems to me to touch the true philosophy of living. I accept them with all my heart. —*David O. McKay* (CR, Oct. 1965, 144)

No man can sincerely resolve to apply in his daily life the teachings of Jesus of Nazareth without sensing a change in his whole being. The phrase "born again" has a deeper significance than what many people attach to it. This changed feeling may be indescribable, but it is real. Happy is the person who has truly sensed the uplifting, transforming power that comes from this nearness to the Savior, this kinship to the living Christ. I am thankful that I know that Christ is my Redeemer. —*David O. McKay* (CR, Apr. 1966, 59)

A mere belief in Jesus as a great teacher or even as the greatest man that ever lived has proved inadequate in combating the ills of the world. —*David O. McKay* (KRL, 135)

What you sincerely think in your heart of Christ will determine what you are, will largely determine what your acts will be. No person can study His divine personality, can accept His teachings, or follow His example, without becoming conscious of an uplifting and refining influence within himself. —*David O. McKay* (KRL, 141)

To my fellowmen I commend the life of Jesus of Nazareth as the profoundest ideal of the ages. —*George Albert Smith* (SGO, 32-33)

It is unexplainable to me that men expect to know of the divinity of the Redeemer's mission when they make so little effort to discover what that mission was. Many men decry him and repudiate him, who have never read the messages of life and salvation contained in the Bible, as well as in latter-day revelation. —*George Albert Smith* (SGO, 53-54)

Christ, the ideal, has been falsely portrayed so much by word and brush that he is thought of as being weak, and effeminate; whereas, he was vigorous, active, and courageous. The basis of his doctrine was individual responsibility, which calls forth the best and most virile attributes of man. —*George Albert Smith* (KRL, 118)

Jesus Christ was a man without sin. By reason of his purity, his uprightness and his virtue, he was able to unlock the doors of the prison, to overcome death and the grave, and pioneer the way for his fellow creatures unto that heaven where we expect to go. —*George Albert Smith* (CR, Apr. 1905, 60)

Among those who claim to believe in Christianity, comparatively few of them really believe in the divine mission of Jesus Christ. —*George Albert Smith* (CR, Apr. 1948, 179)

The Redeemer of mankind was more than a good man who came into the world to teach us ethics. . . . He was indeed the Son of God, the Only Begotten of God in the flesh. —*George Albert Smith* (CR, Oct. 1921, 39)

Any individual who does not acknowledge Jesus Christ as the Son of God, the Redeemer of the world, has no business to be associated with the Church of Jesus Christ of Latter-day Saints. *—Heber J. Grant* (CR, Oct. 1924, 6-7)

We all know that no one ever lived upon the earth that exerted the same influence upon the destinies of the world as did our Lord and Savior Jesus Christ; and yet He was born in obscurity, cradled in a manger. He chose for His apostles poor, unlettered fishermen. More than nineteen hundred years have passed and gone since His crucifixion, and yet all over the world, in spite of all strife and chaos, there is still burning in the hearts of millions of people a testimony of the divinity of the work that He accomplished. *—Heber J. Grant* (GS, 22-23)

We believe absolutely that Jesus Christ is the Son of God, begotten of God, the first-born in the spirit and the only begotten in the flesh; that He is the Son of God just as much as you and I are the sons of our fathers. *—Heber J. Grant* (LPS, 280)

Now, my brethren and sisters, I know that my Redeemer lives. I feel it in every fiber of my being. I am just as satisfied of it as I am of my own existence. I cannot feel more sure of my own being than I do that my Redeemer lives, and that my God lives, the Father of my Savior. *—Joseph F. Smith* (GD, 69)

If any man object to Christ, the Son of God, being King of Israel, let him object, and go to hell just as quick as he please. *—Joseph F. Smith* (CR, Oct. 1906, 9)

Christ came not only to atone for the sins of the world, but to set an example before all men, and to establish the standard of God's perfection, of God's law, and of obedience to the Father. *—Joseph F. Smith* (IE, 21:104)

Let us follow in the footsteps of our Master, the Lord Jesus Christ. He alone is the perfect example for mankind. He is the only infallible rule and law, way and door into everlasting life. Let us follow the Son of God. Make him our exemplar, and our guide. Imitate him. Do his work. Become like unto him, as far as it lies within our powers to become like him that was perfect and without sin. *—Joseph F. Smith* (CR, Apr. 1907, 118)

Jesus, the Son of God, was sent into the world to make it possible for you and me to receive these extraordinary blessings. He had to make a great sacrifice. It required all the power that He had and all the faith that He could summon for Him to accomplish that which the Father required of Him. Had He fallen in the moment of temptation, what do you suppose would have become of us? Doubtless at some future period the plan would have been carried out by another person. But He did not fail, though the trial was so severe that He sweat great drops of blood. *—Lorenzo Snow* (LS, 98)

When Jesus lay in the manger, a helpless infant, He knew not that He was the Son of God, and that formerly He created the earth. When the edict of Herod was issued, He knew nothing of it; He had not power to save Himself; and His father and mother had to take Him and fly into Egypt to preserve Him from the effects of that edict. Well, He grew up to manhood, and during His progress it was revealed unto Him who He was, and for what purpose He was in the world. The glory and power He possessed before He came into the world was made known unto Him. *—Lorenzo Snow* (CR, Apr. 1901, 3)

The revelations of Jesus Christ teach us that the Savior was born in the flesh; and the Father said that he did not give him a fulness at first, but continued from grace to grace until he had received a fulness, and was called the Son of God because he did not receive a fulness at first. We in like manner should seek with all our souls to grow in grace, light, and truth, that in due time we may receive a fulness. *—Wilford Woodruff* (WW, 20)

If he was the firstborn and obedient to the laws of his Father, did he not inherit the position by right to be the representative of God, the Savior and Redeemer of the world? And was it not his peculiar right and privilege as the firstborn, the legitimate heir of God, the Eternal Father, to step forth, accomplish, and carry out the designs of his Heavenly Father pertaining to the redemption, salvation, and exaltation of man? And being himself without sin (which no other mortal was), he took the position of Savior and Redeemer, which by right belonged to him as the firstborn. And does it not seem that in having a body specially prepared, and being the offspring of God, both in body and spirit, he stood preeminently in the position of the Son of God, or in the place of God, and was God, and was thus the fit and only personage capable of making an infinite atonement?—*John Taylor* (GK, 115)

I testify that Jesus is the Christ, the Savior and Redeemer of the world; I have obeyed his sayings, and realized his promise, and the knowledge I have of him, the wisdom of this world cannot give, neither can it take away. —*Brigham Young* (BY, 26)

The Lord has revealed to us a plan by which we may be saved both here and hereafter. God has done everything we could ask, and more than we could ask. The errand of Jesus to earth was to bring his brethren and sisters back into the presence of the Father; he has done his part of the work, and it remains for us to do ours. There is not one thing that the Lord could do for the salvation of the human family that he has neglected to do; and it remains for the children of men to receive the truth or reject it; all that can be accomplished for their salvation, independent of them, has been accomplished in and by the Savior. —*Brigham Young* (BY, 27)

What shall we say, will not Jesus reign and subdue the world? . . . He is my master, my elder brother. He is the character I look to, and the one I try to serve to the best of my ability. —*Brigham Young* (JD, 1:40)

Jesus treads in the tracks of his Father, and inherits what God did before; and God is thus glorified and exalted in the salvation and exaltation of all his children. —*Joseph Smith, Jr.* (STJS, 392)

After a person has faith in Christ, repents of his sins, and is baptized for the remission of his sins and receives the Holy Ghost, (by the laying on of hands), which is the first Comforter, then let him continue to humble himself before God, hungering and thirsting after righteousness, and living by every word of God, and the Lord will soon say unto him, Son, thou shalt be exalted. When the Lord has thoroughly proved him, and finds that the man is determined to serve Him at all hazards, then the man will find his calling and his election made sure, then it will be his privilege to receive the other Comforter, which the Lord hath promised the Saints. . . .

Now what is this other Comforter? It is no more nor less than the Lord Jesus Christ Himself; and this is the sum and substance of the whole matter; that when any man obtains this last Comforter, he will have the personage of Jesus Christ to attend him, or appear unto him from time to time, and even He will manifest the Father unto him, and they will take up their abode with him, and the visions of the heavens will be opened unto him, and the Lord will teach him face to face, and he may have a perfect knowledge of the mysteries of the Kingdom of God. —*Joseph Smith, Jr.* (STJS, 171-172)

And now, after the many testimonies which have been given of him, this is the testimony, last of all which we give of him: That he lives! For we saw him, even on the right hand of God; and we heard the voice bearing record that he is the Only Begotten of the Father— That by him, and through him, and of him, the worlds are and were created, and the inhabitants thereof are begotten sons and daughters unto God. —*Joseph Smith, Jr.* (D&C 76:23)

5. THE HOLY GHOST

The Holy Ghost stands as the third member of the Godhead, the Comforter promised by the Savior, who would teach his followers all things and bring all things to their remembrance . . .

The Holy Ghost is the Testifier of truth, who can teach mankind things they cannot teach one another. —*Gordon B. Hinckley* (FETR , 26)

We must always be responsive to the whisperings of the spirit. These promptings most often come when we are not under the pressure of appointments and when we are not caught up in the worries of our day-to-day life. —*Ezra Taft Benson* (ETB, 76)

There is one major question we should ask ourselves. Assuming we are living a life so we can know, then what does the Holy Ghost have to say about it?—*Ezra Taft Benson* (ETB, 77)

The veil is very thin, brothers and sisters. Impressions may and do come to us when we are in tune with the spirit. —*Ezra Taft Benson* (ETB, 114)

A testimony is to have current inspiration to know the work is true, not something we receive only once. The Holy Ghost abides with those who honor, respect, and obey God's laws. And it is that Spirit which gives inspiration to the individual. —*Ezra Taft Benson* (CR, May 1983, 53)

The people of the world have the light of Christ to help guide them, but members of the Church are entitled to the gift of the Holy Ghost. For the Holy Ghost to be fully operative in our lives, we must keep our channels clear of sin. The clearer our channels, the easier it is for us to receive and follow, the greater will be our joy. If our channels are not clear of sin, then we may think we have received inspiration on a matter when it is really promptings from the devil. —*Ezra Taft Benson* (Ensign, Sept. 1988, 6)

If one does not receive the great gift of the Holy Ghost, then it is his fault, that he hasn't been spiritual enough or close enough to Heavenly Father. —*Spencer W. Kimball* (SWK, 12)

The sin against the Holy Ghost requires such knowledge that it is manifestly impossible for the rank and file to commit such a sin. —*Spencer W. Kimball* (SWK, 12)

The Holy Spirit of Promise is the Holy Ghost, which searches the hearts of men, one who reads our thoughts and our doings, and until he gives His sealing approval, then only will our blessings be efficacious and of full force when we are out of this world. —*Harold B. Lee* (HBL, 15-16)

No man can receive the gift of the Holy Ghost without receiving revelations, for the Holy Ghost is a revelator . . . And every baptized member of the Church, who lives worthy of it, may have the greatest of all gifts that can come to mankind, the gift of the Holy ghost. —*Harold B. Lee* (HBL, 16)

The Holy Ghost is a personage of Spirit, and has a spirit body only. His mission is to bear witness of the Father and the Son and of all truth.

As a Spirit personage the Holy Ghost has size and dimensions. He does not fill the immensity of space, and cannot be everywhere present in person at the same time. He is also called the Holy Spirit, the Spirit of God, the Spirit of the Lord, the Spirit of Truth, and the Comforter. —*Joseph Fielding Smith* (DS1, 38)

I have never troubled myself about the Holy Ghost whether he will sometime have a body or not because it is not in any way essential to my salvation. He is a member of the Godhead, with great power and authority, with a most wonderful mission which must be performed by a spirit. This has satisfied me without delving into mysteries that would be of no particular benefit. —*Joseph Fielding Smith* (DS1, 39)

Every man can receive a manifestation of the Holy Ghost, even when he is out of the Church, if he is earnestly seeking for the light and for the truth. The Holy Ghost will come and give the man the testimony he is seeking, and then withdraw; and the man does not have a claim upon another visit or constant visits and manifestations from him. —*Joseph Fielding Smith* (CN, Apr. 27, 1935, 7)

The Spirit of God speaking to the spirit of man has power to impart truth with greater effect and understanding than the truth can be imparted by personal contact even with heavenly beings. Through the Holy Ghost the truth is woven into the very fibre and sinews of the body so that it cannot be forgotten. —*Joseph Fielding Smith* (DS1, 47-48)

What is the gift of the Holy Ghost? Nothing more nor less than the right to the companionship of the Holy Ghost. —*Joseph Fielding Smith* (CN, Apr. 27, 1935, 7)

The man who is confirmed receives, in addition to this Spirit of Christ, the companionship of the third member of the Godhead. Therefore, he is back again in the presence of God, through the gift of the Holy Ghost. —*Joseph Fielding Smith* (CN, Apr. 27, 1935, 7)

What the sun is to the earth, so that Holy Spirit is to man, . . . each individual is entitled to that glorious light of the Holy Spirit. —*David O. McKay* (CR, Oct. 1961, 90)

If we so live to be worthy of the companionship of the Holy Spirit, he will guide us unto all truth; he will show us things to come, he will bring all things to our remembrance; he will testify of the divinity of the Lord Jesus Christ and restoration of the gospel. —*David O. McKay* (CR, Apr. 1967, 88)

If we are living as we know that we should we are entitled to the whispering of a still small voice calling attention to danger saying this is the pathway of safety, walk ye in it. —*George Albert Smith* (CR, Oct. 1937, 52)

The Holy Ghost is a personage in the Godhead, and is not that which lighteth every man that cometh into the world. It is the Spirit of God which proceeds through Christ to the world, that enlightens every man that comes into the world, and that strives with the children of men, and will continue to strive with them, until it brings them to a knowledge of the truth and the possession of the greater light and testimony of the Holy Ghost. —*Joseph F. Smith* (GD, 67-68)

The presentation or "gift" of the Holy Ghost simply confers upon a man the right to receive at any time, when he is worthy of it and desires it, the power and light of truth of the Holy Ghost, although he may often be left to his own spirit and judgment. —*Joseph F. Smith* (LPS, 117)

[W]e must be worthy of the companionship of the Holy Ghost to aid us in the work of righteousness all the day long, to enable us to sacrifice our own will to the will of the Father, to battle against our fallen nature, and to do right for the love of doing right, keeping our eye single to the honor and glory of God. —*Lorenzo Snow* (LS, 38)

We are all dependent upon the Holy Ghost. And what is the Holy Ghost? . . . It is one of the Godhead—God the Father, God the Son, and God the Holy Ghost. Will the Holy Ghost deceive any man? It will not. When a man speaks as he is moved upon by the Holy Ghost, it is the spirit of inspiration; it is the word of God; it is the will of God. It cannot lie; it cannot deceive. It leads into all truth and reveals to man the will of his Maker. —*Wilford Woodruff* (WW, 5)

Now we have no right, power nor authority to seal the gifts of the Holy Ghost upon anybody, they are the property of the Holy Ghost itself. . . .
We lay hands upon the heads of those who embrace the gospel and we say unto them, "In the name of the lord Jesus Christ receive ye the Holy Ghost." We seal this blessing upon the heads of the children of men, just as Jesus and his apostles and the servants of God have done in every age when preaching the gospel of Christ. But the gifts of the Holy Ghost are his property to bestow as he sees fit. —*Wilford Woodruff* (WW, 6-7)

You may have the administration of angels, you may see many miracles; you may see many wonders in the earth; but I claim that the gift of the Holy Ghost is the greatest gift that can be bestowed upon man. —*Wilford Woodruff* (WW, 5)

I have been blessed at times with certain gifts and graces, certain revelations and ministrations; but with them all I have never found anything that I could place more dependence upon than the still small voice of the Holy Ghost. —*Wilford Woodruff* (JD, 21:195-196)

The special gift of the Holy Ghost is obtained, as I have said, through obedience to the first principles of the gospel. Its province is to lead us into all truth, and to bring to our remembrance things past, present, and to come. It contemplates the future and unfolds things we had not thought of heretofore. —*John Taylor* (GK, 43)

When men obey the gospel with pure hearts—when they are baptized in the name of Jesus Christ for the remission of sins, and have hands laid upon them for the gift of the Holy Ghost, and have received that Spirit and live in obedience to the dictates of that Spirit, it will bring things past and present to their remembrance, lead them into all truth, and show them things to come. This is part and parcel of our belief. —*John Taylor* (JD, 6:106)

Not a desire, act, wish, or thought does the Holy Ghost indulge in contrary to that which is dictated by the Father. —*Brigham Young* (BY, 30)

I have proven to my satisfaction, according to the best knowledge I can gather, that man can be deceived by the sight of the natural eye, he can be deceived by the hearing of the ear, and by the touch of the hand; that he can be deceived in all of what is called the natural senses. But there is one thing in which he cannot be deceived. What is that? It is the operations of the Holy Ghost, the Spirit and power of God upon the creature. It teaches him of heavenly things; it directs him in the way of life. —*Brigham Young* (BY, 31)

This first Comforter or Holy Ghost has no other effect than pure intelligence. . . . [T]he effect of the Holy Ghost upon a Gentile, is to purge out the old blood, and make him actually of the seed of Abraham. —*Joseph Smith, Jr.* (STJS, 170-171)

We believe that the Holy Ghost . . . being a comforter and a witness bearer, that it brings things past to our remembrance, leads us into all truth, and shows us of things to come; we believe that "no man can know that Jesus is the Christ, but by the Holy Ghost." We believe in it [this gift of the Holy Ghost] in all its fullness, and power, and greatness, and glory. —*Joseph Smith, Jr.* (STJS, 271-272)

No man can receive the Holy Ghost without receiving revelations. The Holy Ghost is a revelator. —*Joseph Smith, Jr.* (STJS, 370)

6. MAN AND WOMAN

Woman is God's supreme creation. —*Gordon B. Hinckley* (Ensign, Sept. 1988, 11)

Of all the creations of the Almighty, there is none more beautiful, none more inspiring than a lovely daughter of God who walks in virtue with an understanding of why she should do so, who honors and respects her body as a thing sacred and divine, who cultivates her mind and constantly enlarges the horizon of her understanding, who nurtures her spirit with everlasting truth. God will hold us accountable if we neglect His daughters. He has given us a great and compelling trust. —*Gordon B. Hinckley* (Ensign, Sept. 1988, 11)

He [God] then created man in His own likeness and image. Then as His final creation, the crowning of His glorious work, He created woman. I like to regard Eve as His masterpiece after all that had gone before, the final work before He rested from His labors.

I do not regard her as being in second place to Adam. She was placed at his side as an helpmeet. They were together in the Garden, they were expelled together, and they labored together in the world into which they were driven. —*Gordon B. Hinckley* (Ensign, Nov. 1991, 98-99)

My beloved sisters, I greet you in love and respect, knowing that you are daughters of our Heavenly Father and knowing what each of you has the potential to become. . . .

We thank God for the refining influence you have upon our world through your service, sacrifice, compassion, and striving for that which is beautiful and ennobling.

Thank you for making our lives so much better because of who you are. Your steady example of righteousness stands in contrast to the ways of the world. —*Howard W. Hunter* (Ensign, Nov. 1992, 95)

Recognize your divine birthright as daughters of our Heavenly Father. Be one who heals with your words as well as your hands. Seek to know the will of the Lord in your life, and then say, as did that wonderful exemplar Mary, the mother of Jesus, "Behold the handmaid of the Lord; be it unto me according to thy word. (Luke 1:38)—*Howard W. Hunter* (Ensign, Nov. 1994, 97)

The conventional wisdom of the day would have you [women] be equal with men. We say, we would not have you descend to that level. More often than not the demand for equality means the destruction of the inspired arrangement that God has decreed for man, woman, and the family. Equality should not be confused with equivalence. —*Ezra Taft Benson* (ETB, 548)

Men and women who turn their lives over to God will discover that He can make a lot more out of their lives than they can. He will deepen their joys, expand their vision, quicken their minds, strengthen their muscles, lift their spirits, multiply their blessing, increase their opportunities, comfort their souls, raise up friends, and pour out peace. Whoever will lose his life in the service of God will find eternal life. —*Ezra Taft Benson* (Ensign, Dec. 1988, 4)

Bear in mind, dear sisters, that the eternal blessing which are yours through membership in The Church of Jesus Christ of Latter-day Saints are far, far greater than any other blessings you could possible receive. No greater recognition can come to you in this world than to be known as a woman of God. —*Spencer W. Kimball* (Ensign, Nov. 1979, 102)

If a woman will preserve and properly maintain her God-given identity, she can captivate and hold the true love of her husband and the admiration of those who admire natural, pure, lovely womanhood. What I am saying to sisters first of all, then, is to be what God intends you to be, a true woman. —*Harold B. Lee* (YLW, 281-282)

May God render our wives, our sweethearts, our mothers even more perfect in order to hold the bearers of the priesthood, under their influence, to a truer course of happiness here and eternal joy in the world to come, for which I humbly pray. —*Harold B. Lee* (YLW, 318-319)

Adam was placed on the earth after all other creatures were here. He came when the earth was prepared for him. The Lord speaks of his becoming the first "flesh," or mortal, because of his fall. He was, of course, the first man on the earth, contrary to the teachings of our evolutionists. His name means "many," in reference to the greatness of his posterity as the human father of mankind. —*Joseph Fielding Smith* (DS1, 92)

Do you think that Adam, this great and important prince, the archangel before the presence of God, was a half-breed monkey? In other words, that he had just developed gradually from the animal kingdom, from some animal form, so that the Lord could put a spirit in him and call him a man? Do you think that? There are people who do believe that. That is why I ask you that question.

Of course, I think those people who hold to the view that man has come up through all these ages from the scum of the sea through billions of years do not believe in Adam. —*Joseph Fielding Smith* (CN, Apr. 15, 1939, 6)

I believe that there is in every human soul a something good calling for something better . . . So there is in the human soul that divine element which is calling, striving, urging the person up to a higher, to a better life. —*David O. McKay* (CR, Oct. 1920, 42-43)

He approaches nearest the Christ spirit who makes God the center of his thoughts; and he who can say in his heart, "Not my will, but thine be done," approaches most nearly the Christ ideal. —*David O. McKay* (CR, Oct. 1953, 10)

Man is a spiritual being, and sometime or another every man is possessed with a longing, an irresistible desire, to know his relationship to the Infinite. He realizes that he is not just a physical object to be tossed for just a short time from bank to bank, only to be submerged finally in the ever-flowing stream of life. There is something within him that urges him to rise above himself, to control his environment, to master the body and all things physical, and to live in a higher and more beautiful world. —*David O. McKay* (CR, Apr. 1968, 91-92)

In showing this relationship, by a symbolic representation, God didn't say that woman was to be taken from a bone in the man's head that she would rule over him, nor from a bone in his foot that she should be trampled under his feet, but from a bone in his side to symbolize that she was to stand by his side, to be his companion, his equal, and his help-meet in all their lives together. —*George Albert Smith* (YLW, 284)

Do we realize that every man is in the image of God and is a son of God, and every woman his daughter?—*George Albert Smith* (CR, Apr. 1935, 46)

Talk about sacrifice! Why, the sacrifice of the women of this Church and their devotion are beyond the power of pen and tongue of man to pay proper tribute. —*Heber J. Grant* (CR, Apr. 1934, 17)

Just as surely as failing to eat will cause our physical frames to shrink and die, just so sure neglect to supply our spiritual natures will bring death to them. —*Heber J. Grant* (LPS, 361)

I do not expect that any of us will ever become in mortality quite so perfect as God is perfect; but in the spheres in which we are called to act, and according to the capacity and breadth of intelligence that we possess, in our sphere, and in the existence of the talent, the ability, and intelligence that God has given to us, we may become as perfect in our sphere as God is perfect in his higher and more exalted sphere. I believe that. —*Joseph F. Smith* (CR, Apr. 1916, 6-7)

We are called mortal beings because in us are seeds of death, but in reality we are immortal beings, because there is also within us the germ of eternal life. Man is a dual being, composed of the spirit which gives life, force, intelligence and capacity to man, and the body which is the tenement of the spirit and is suited to its form, adapted to its necessities, and acts in harmony with it, and to its utmost capacity yields obedience to the will of the spirit. —*Joseph F. Smith* (JD, 23:169)

Thousands and thousands of years hence we will be ourselves, and nobody else, so far as our individuality is concerned. That never dies from all eternity to all eternity. —*Lorenzo Snow* (CR, Apr. 1898, 63)

Our identity will always remain the same. . . . Our identity is insured. We will be ourselves and nobody else. Whatever changes may arise, whatever worlds may be made or pass away, our identity will always remain the same; and we will continue on improving, advancing, and increasing in wisdom, intelligence, power, and dominion, worlds without end. Our present advancement is simply a starting out, as it were, on this path of immortality. —*Lorenzo Snow* (CR, Apr. 1898, 12)

These children are now at play, making mud worlds, the time will come when some of these boys, through their faithfulness to the gospel, will progress and develop in knowledge, intelligence and power, in future eternities, until they shall be able to go out into space where there is unorganized matter and call together the necessary elements, and through their knowledge of and control over the laws and powers of nature, to organize matter into worlds on which their posterity may dwell, and over which they shall rule as gods. —*Lorenzo Snow* (PCM, 142)

We know that we are created in the image of God, both male and female; and whoever goes back into the presence of God our Eternal Father, will find that he is a noble man, a noble God, tabernacled in a form similar to ours, for we are created after his own image; they will also learn that he has placed us here that we may pass through a state of probation and experience, the same as he himself did in his day of mortality. —*Wilford Woodruff* (WW, 3)

How does God feel towards the human family? He feels that they are his children. What, all? Yes, the white, the black, the red, the Jew, the gentile, the heathen, the Christian, and all classes and grades of men. He feels interested in all. He has done so from the beginning and will continue to do so to the end. He will do all that lies in his power for the benefit, blessing, and exaltation of the human family, both in time and eternity. —*John Taylor* (GK, 63)

Man is an intelligent being, but how far does his intelligence fall short of that which regulates the world! He cannot even govern himself; he never was able to do it, and never will be able until he receives that wisdom and intelligence of that kind, and from that source, which governs the world . . . If he can receive it from God, as his instructor, he is then able to govern himself, possessing intelligence which he now knows nothing about, an intelligence which indeed is worthy of God and man. —*John Taylor* (GK, 66)

But if a man is a man of God, he has his eyes upon eternal things and is aiming to accomplish the purposes of God, and all will be well with him in the end. —*John Taylor* (GK, 317)

We are not our own rulers. We are all the children of God. He is our Father and has a right to direct us, not only us, but has a perfect right to direct and control the affairs of all the human family that exist upon the face of the earth for they are all his offspring. —*John Taylor* (GK, 79)

My doctrine is—that there never was a son and daughter of Adam and Eve born on this earth whose names were not already written in the Lamb's book of life, and there they will remain until their conduct is such that the angel who keeps the record is authorized to blot them out and record them elsewhere. —*Brigham Young* (BY, 7)

When I am left to myself, I have no power, and my wisdom is foolishness; then I cling close to the Lord, and I have power in his name. I think I have learned the Gospel so as to know, that in and of myself I am nothing. —*Brigham Young* (BY, 84)

No man can know himself unless he knows God, and he cannot know God unless he knows himself. —*Brigham Young* (BY, 426)

If men do not comprehend the character of God, they do not comprehend themselves. —*Joseph Smith, Jr.* (STJS, 387-388)

7. OUR BIRTHRIGHT AND POTENTIAL

The whole design of the gospel is to lead us onward and upward to greater achievement, even, eventually, to Godhood. . . .

This lofty concept in no way diminishes God the Eternal Father. He is the Almighty. He is the Creator and Governor of the universe. He is the greatest of all and will always be so. But just as any earthly father wishes for his sons and daughters every success in life, so I believe our Father in Heaven wishes for his children that they might approach him in stature and stand beside him resplendent in Godly strength and wisdom. —*Gordon B. Hinckley* (Ensign, Nov. 1994, 48)

My great plea is that we all try a little harder to live up to the stature of divinity that is within us, my brethren and sisters. We can do better than we are doing. We can be better than we are. If we would hold before us that image constantly of divine inheritance, of the fatherhood of God and the brotherhood of man as realities, we would be a little more tolerant, a little more kindly, a little more outreaching to lift and help and sustain those among us, we would be less prone to stoop to those things which clearly are unbecoming us. —*Gordon B. Hinckley* (CN, Apr. 27, 1996, 4)

We are creatures of the flesh as well as the spirit, and the great striving in life is to develop the spirit as well as the physical body. True growth is dependent upon our conscious effort in lifting our awareness above and beyond those things which are physical. —*Howard W. Hunter* (CR, Oct. 1968, 139)

We have a divine pedigree; every person is a spiritual child of God. —*Howard W. Hunter* (WMJ, 59)

Just as teachings that do not conform to Christ's doctrine are false, so a life that does not conform to Christ's example is misdirected, and may not achieve its high potential destiny. —*Howard W. Hunter* (Ensign, Sept. 1994, 2)

If you endure to the end, and if you are valiant in the testimony of Jesus, you will achieve true greatness and will live in the presence of our Father in Heaven. —*Howard W. Hunter* (CN, March 11, 1995, 7)

As God's offspring, we have His attributes in us. We are gods in embryo, and thus have an unlimited potential for progress and attainment. —*Ezra Taft Benson* (ETB, 21)

We cannot know about God and Jesus without studying about them and then doing their will. This course leads to additional revealed knowledge which, if obeyed, will eventually lead us to further truths. If we follow this pattern, we will receive further light and joy, eventually leading into God's presence where we, with Him, will have a fullness. —*Ezra Taft Benson* (Ensign, Sept. 1988, 2)

Man alone, of all creatures of earth, can change his thought pattern and become the architect of his destiny.

Man can transform himself and he must. Man has in himself the seeds of godhood, which can germinate and grow and develop. As the acorn becomes the oak, the mortal man becomes a god. It is within his power to lift himself by his very bootstraps from the plane on which he finds himself to the plane on which he should be. It may be a long, hard lift with many obstacles, but it is a real possibility. —*Spencer W. Kimball* (SWK, 27-28)

I have little patience with persons who say, "Oh, nobody is perfect," the implication being: "so why try?" Of course no one is wholly perfect, but we find some who are a long way up the ladder. —*Spencer W. Kimball* (SWK, 165)

The great calamity, as I see it, is when you or I with so much potential grow very little. That is the calamity—when I could be so much and I am so little; when I am satisfied with mediocrity in proselyting, in dentistry, in teaching, in whatever I am going to do with my life. —*Spencer W. Kimball* (SWK, 173)

It is impossible for us here in mortality to come to that state of perfection of which the Master spoke, but in this life we lay the foundation on which we will build in eternity; therefore, we must make sure that our foundation is laid on truth, righteousness and faith. In order for us to reach that goal we must keep God's commandments and be true to the end of our lives here, and then beyond the grave continue in righteousness and knowledge until we become as our Father in Heaven. —*Harold B. Lee* (DSL, 41)

If the children of the Lord, which includes all who are upon this earth, regardless of nationality, color, or creed, will heed the call of the true messenger of the gospel of Jesus Christ, . . . each may in time see the Lord and know that He is, as the Lord has promised, and then their calling and election will be made sure. —*Harold B. Lee* (SHP, 237)

It was not until man forsook the divine guidance which the Lord was always willing to extend to him, that retrogression set in. The "cave-man" and the savage are products of transgression and sin; for, in the beginning man was intelligent, and directed by light and truth, even by the Savior, Jesus Christ, who is the Mediator between man and God. The destiny of man is to become, through stages of progression, like unto his Father. —*Joseph Fielding Smith* (IE, 23: 393)

Our Father in heaven is infinite; he is perfect; he possesses all knowledge and wisdom. However, he is not jealous of his wisdom and perfection, but glories in the fact that it is possible for his children who obey him in all things and endure to the end to become like him. —*Joseph Fielding Smith* (DS2, 35)

Man is a dual being—he is human, physical, of the earth, earthy, but he is, also, divine the offspring of God. —*David O. McKay* (CR, Oct. 1953, 9)

Spirituality is the consciousness of victory over self, the consciousness of being above the passions, whether in anger or jealousy, or envy, or hatred. . . . Man is spirit, the son of his Father, and has within him that which will cause him to yearn and to aspire to become dignified as a son of God should be dignified. —*David O. McKay* (CR, Oct. 1969, 135)

We came not from some menial order of life, but our ancestor is God our Heavenly Father. —*George Albert Smith* (LPS, 5)

We are the children of God. He is the Father of our spirits. We have not come from some lower form of life, but God is the Father of our spirits, and we belong to the royal family, because he is our Father. —*George Albert Smith* (LPS, 275)

The spirit of man, the intelligent ego, is the offspring of God; therefore men and women of all races and kindreds and tribes and tongues on the face of the earth are brothers and sisters. —*Heber J. Grant* (PC, 240)

[If] Jesus, the Son of God, and the Father of the heavens and the earth in which we dwell, received not a fulness at the first, but increased in faith, knowledge, understanding and grace until he received a fulness, is it not possible for all men who are born of women to receive little by little, line upon line, precept upon precept, until they shall receive a fulness, as he has received a fulness, and be exalted with him in the presence of the Father?—*Joseph F. Smith* (GD, 68)

[W]e are to understand that only resurrected and glorified beings can become parents of spirit offspring. Only such exalted souls have reached maturity in the appointed course of eternal life; and the spirits born to them in the eternal worlds will pass in due sequence through the several stages or estates by which the glorified parents have attained exaltation. —*Joseph F. Smith* (IE, 19:942)

Man is the child of God, formed in the divine image and endowed with divine attributes, and even as the infant son of an earthly father and mother is capable in due time of becoming a man, so the undeveloped offspring of celestial parentage is capable, by experience through ages and aeons, of evolving into a God. —*Joseph F. Smith* (LPS, 73)

As man now is, God once was; As God now is, man may be. —*Lorenzo Snow* (LS, 2)

Now, we are the sons and daughters of God. He has begotten us in His own image. He has given us faculties and powers that are capable of enlargement until His fulness is reached which He has promised. —*Lorenzo Snow* (LS, 3)

We were born in the image of God our Father; He begot us like unto Himself. There is the nature of deity in the composition of our spiritual organization; in our spiritual birth our Father transmitted to us the capabilities, powers and faculties which He Himself possessed—as much so as the child on its mother's bosom possesses, although in an undeveloped state, the faculties, powers, and susceptibilities of its parent. —*Lorenzo Snow* (LS, 4)

There is a spirit in man, possessed of so much "divinity, that it will discover truth by its own light; no matter whether it is covered with a "sectarian cloak," or thrown among the rubbish of scoffers. —*John Taylor* (GK, 6)

If we take man, . . . he did not originate from a chaotic mass of matter, moving or inert, but came forth possessing, in an embryonic state, all the faculties and powers of a God. And when he shall be perfected, and have progressed to maturity, he will be like his Father—a God, being indeed his offspring. As the horse, the ox, the sheep, and every living creature, including man, propagates its own species and perpetuates its own kind, so does God perpetuate his. —*John Taylor* (GK, 52)

The principles of justice, righteousness, and truth, which have an endless duration, can alone satisfy the capacious desires of the immortal soul. [W]hen the man comes to reflect, when the saint of God considers, and the visions of eternity are open to his view and the unalterable purposes of God are developed to his mind when he contemplates his true position before God, angels, and men, then he soars above the things of time and sense and bursts the cords that bind him to earthly objects. He contemplates God and his own destiny in the economy of heaven and rejoices in a blooming hope of an immortal glory. —*John Taylor* (GK, 63)

I expect, if I am faithful, with yourselves, that I shall see the time, with yourselves, that we shall know how to prepare to organize an earth like this—know how to people that earth, how to redeem it, how to sanctify it, and how to glorify it, with those who live upon it who hearken to our counsels. —*Brigham Young* (BY, 97)

After men have got their exaltations and their crowns—have become gods, even the sons of God—are made kings of kings and lords of lords, they have the power then of propagating their species in spirit. Power is then given to them to organize the elements, and then commence the organization of tabernacles. —*Brigham Young* (BY, 98)

We consider that God has created man with a mind capable of instruction, and a faculty which may be enlarged in proportion to the heed and diligence given to the light communicated from heaven to the intellect; and that the nearer man approaches perfection, the clearer are his views, and the greater his enjoyments, till he has overcome the evils of his life and lost every desire for sin; and like the ancients, arrives at that point of faith where he is wrapped in the power and glory of his Maker and is caught up to dwell with Him. But we consider that this is a station to which no man ever arrived in a moment: he must have been instructed in the government and laws of that kingdom by proper degrees, until his mind is capable in some measure of comprehending the propriety, justice, equality, and consistency of the same. —*Joseph Smith, Jr.* (STJS, 63-64)

[Y]ou have got to learn how to be Gods yourselves, and to be kings and priests to God, the same as all Gods have done before you, namely, by going from one small degree to another, and from a small capacity to a great one; from grace to grace, from exaltation to exaltation, until you attain to the resurrection of the dead, and are able to dwell in everlasting burnings, and to sit in glory, as do those who sit enthroned in everlasting power. —*Joseph Smith, Jr.* (STJS, 391)

THE PLAN OF SALVATION

8. THE PLAN OF SALVATION

The marvelous thing to me is that the Lord never asks us to do anything that He does not attach to it a blessing. It is not a sacrifice to live the gospel of Jesus Christ. It is never a sacrifice when you get back more than you give. It is an investment. And the living of the gospel of Jesus Christ becomes a greater investment than any of which we know because its dividends are eternal and everlasting. —*Gordon B. Hinckley* (CN, Aug. 26, 1995, 4)

When all is said and done, the most precious thing you have is the gospel of Jesus Christ. —*Gordon B. Hinckley* (CN, Dec. 2, 1995, 2)

The most satisfying experience I have is to see what this gospel does for people. It gives them a new outlook on life. It gives them a perspective that they have never felt before. It raises their sights to things noble and divine. Something happens to them that is miraculous to behold. They look to Christ and come alive. —*Gordon B. Hinckley* (CR, May 1997, 48)

Philosophy and theology may be interesting and give us lofty concepts, and we may become inspired by profound thinking, but Christian faith is based upon the simplicity of the gospel, the example, the life, and the teachings of Jesus Christ. —*Howard W. Hunter* (CR, Apr. 1969, 138)

The gospel is often referred to as the good news, or glad tidings of salvation. The plan of salvation therefore, is the gospel of Jesus Christ. —*Howard W. Hunter* (CR, Apr. 1973, 174)

The gospel is the way of life. It is practical, plain, and simple. It is a gospel of action, even to the tiny day-to-day actions that make up the art of living. —*Howard W. Hunter* (WMJ, 134)

Our inability to explain a thing in terms of our materialism does not disprove its reality. —*Ezra Taft Benson* (ETB, 68)

This master plan, if lived, will build men of character, men of strength, men of deep spirituality, godlike men. —*Ezra Taft Benson* (ETB, 80)

The gospel is a program, a way of life, the plan of personal salvation, and is based upon personal responsibility. —*Spencer W. Kimball* (SWK, 28)

Expertise in religion comes from personal righteousness and from revelation. —*Spencer W. Kimball* (Ensign, Sept. 1978, 3)

This life we speak of did not begin with mortal birth. This life does not end with mortal death. There is something that is not created or made. The scriptures called it "intelligence," which at a certain stage in the pre-existence was organized into a "spirit." After that spirit had grown to a certain stature it then was given the opportunity by an all-wise Father to come into another stage for its development. It was added upon, and after having lived its span and having attained to its purpose in mortality, another change took place. We go, not into another life, in fact, but into another stage of the same life. —*Harold B. Lee* (HBL, 74)

The plan of salvation, or code of laws, which is known as the gospel of Jesus Christ, was adopted in the heavens, before the foundation of the world was laid. —*Joseph Fielding Smith* (DS1, 121)

Some members of the Church have an erroneous idea that when the millennium comes all of the people are going to be swept off the earth except righteous members of the Church. That is not so. There will be millions of people, Catholics, Protestants, agnostics, Mohammedans, people of all classes, and of all beliefs, still permitted to remain upon the face of the earth, but they will be those who have lived clean lives, those who have been free from wickedness and corruption. All who belong, by virtue of their good lives, to the terrestrial order, as well as those who have kept the celestial law, will remain upon the face of the earth during the millennium. —*Joseph Fielding Smith* (DS1, 86-87)

The Lord is not going to wait for us to get righteous. When he gets ready to come, he is going to come—when the cup of iniquity is full—and if we are not righteous then, it will be just too bad for us, for we will be classed among the ungodly, and we will be as stubble to be swept off the face of the earth. —*Joseph Fielding Smith* (CN, May 4, 1935, 8)

All those who have died in Christ shall come forth from the dead at his coming and shall dwell upon the earth as Christ shall be upon the earth during this millennium. They shall not remain here all the time during the thousand years, but they will mingle with those who are still here in mortal life. These resurrected saints and the Savior himself, shall come to give instruction and guidance; to reveal unto us the things we ought to know; to give us information concerning the work in the temples of the Lord so we may do the work which is essential to the salvation of worthy men. —*Joseph Fielding Smith* (DS3, 59)

What the sun in the heavenly blue is to the earth struggling to get free from winter's grip, so the gospel is to sorrowing souls yearning for something higher and better than mankind has yet found. —*David O. McKay* (CR, Oct. 1947, 121)

The gospel bids the strong bear the burdens of the weak, and to use the advantages given them by their larger opportunities in the interest of the common good that the whole level of humanity may be lifted, and the path of spiritual attainment opened to the weakest and most unlearned as well as to the strong and intelligent. —*David O. McKay* (CR, Apr. 1962, 7)

I bear you my witness that the teachings of our Lord and Savior Jesus Christ contain the true philosophy of living. I make no exception. I love them. There are men who say that they are not applicable to this day, but I say they are as applicable today as they were when he spoke them; and, because they contain eternal truths, they will be applicable through all time. —*David O. McKay* (CR, Oct. 1969, 9)

Individual happiness and world-wide peace will not be permanent until those who dwell on the earth accept the gospel and conform their lives to its precepts. It is the power of God unto salvation to all who believe and obey. It is the kind advice of a loving Father, who, seeing the end from the beginning, says, this is the path, walk ye in it, and eternal life and eternal progress and eternal happiness shall be your reward. —*George Albert Smith* (SGO, 50-51)

It would seem, as you look over the conditions in the world, that men generally have lost all understanding of the purpose of life. A great majority of the people of the world do not know why we are here; but the Lord, in the beginning, starting with our first parents who were placed upon the earth, began teaching His children the purpose of life, and gave them rules of conduct, which, if observed, would have enriched their lives, brought happiness in mortality, and enjoyment of eternal life in the Celestial Kingdom. —*George Albert Smith* (CR, Apr. 1944, 27)

The purpose of the Gospel of Jesus Christ is to prepare us for the Celestial kingdom. —*George Albert Smith* (CR, Apr. 1934, 28)

What is this gospel to which we refer? It is the only power of God unto salvation, it is the only plan that will enable man to go back into the presence of his Maker and enjoy the celestial kingdom. It is the only plan that will bring peace and happiness to all the children of men, of every race and creed. —*George Albert Smith* (CR, Oct. 1928, 93)

Time and time again my heart has been melted, my eyes have wept tears of gratitude for the knowledge that He lives and that this gospel called Mormonism is in very deed the plan of life and salvation, that it is the only true gospel upon the face of the earth, that it is in very deed the gospel of the Lord Jesus Christ. That God may help you and me and everyone to live it, is my constant and earnest prayer. —*Heber J. Grant* (CR, Oct. 1918, 23-25)

I think that the spirit, before and after this probation, possesses greater facilities, aye, manifold greater, for the acquisition of knowledge, than while manacled and shut up in the prison-house of mortality. —*Joseph F. Smith* (GD, 13)

We must, therefore, learn the laws of heaven, which are the laws of the gospel, live and obey them with all our hearts, and in faith abide in them, perfecting ourselves thereby, in order to receive the fulness of the glory of that kingdom. —*Joseph F. Smith* (GD, 440)

In God's plans, there is no such thing as idleness. God is not pleased with the thought of idleness. He is not idle, and there is no such thing as inertia in the providences and in the purposes of God. We are either growing and advancing, or are retrograding. We are not stationary. We must grow. The principles of everlasting growth and development tend to glory, to exaltation, to happiness, and to a fulness of joy. —*Joseph F. Smith* (GD, 459)

In the first place every person should know that the gospel is true, as this is everyone's privilege who is baptized and receives the Holy Ghost. —*Joseph F. Smith* (GD, 43)

The gospel is perfect in its organization. It is for us to learn the gospel, and to become acquainted with the principles of truth, to humble ourselves before God that we may bring ourselves into subjection to his laws, and be continually willing to listen to the counsels of those whom the Lord has appointed to guide us. —*Joseph F. Smith* (GD, 82)

I dare say that in the spirit world, when it was proposed to us to come into this probation, and pass through the experience that we are now receiving, it was not altogether pleasant and agreeable; the prospects were not so delightful in all respects as might have been desired. Yet there is no doubt that we saw and understood clearly there that, in order to accomplish our exaltation and glory, this was a necessary experience; and however disagreeable it might have appeared to us, we were willing to conform to the will of God, and consequently we are here. —*Lorenzo Snow* (LS, 92-93)

The Lord knew our natures and dispositions, and He knew exactly what to place before us in order to stimulate us to that course of action which will enable us to overcome the various difficulties that arise in our path of progress. —*Lorenzo Snow* (LS, 124)

Those who endure to the end will receive all things. . . . Those who endure unto the end shall sit upon thrones, as Jesus hath overcome and sat down upon His Father's throne. All things shall be given unto such men and women, so we are told in the revelations we have received. In view of these prospects, what should we not be willing to sacrifice when duty requires?—*Lorenzo Snow* (CR, Oct. 1898, 55-56)

We have received the gospel, and if we are true to the principles of that gospel as long as we live, we shall be made partakers of immortality, exaltation and glory. —*Wilford Woodruff* (WW, 250)

We have but a little time to spend on earth even though we live to be a hundred years of age, and we have no time to waste. We should live in such a manner that the Spirit and blessing of God may attend us; and then when we cease our labors here we shall pass hence to continue them in the same cause of salvation and redemption, and all will be well with us. —*Wilford Woodruff* (WW, 260)

According to our ideas of things as they have been revealed to us, we had an existence before we came here. We came here to accomplish a certain purpose which was decreed by the Almighty before the world was. We came to receive bodies or tabernacles, and in them to pass through a certain amount of trial in what is termed a probationary state of existence, preparatory to something to be developed hereafter. Hence this world is the state of our probation, and we look forward to the future as something with which we are as much connected as we are with anything pertaining to time. We look forward to another state of existence with that degree of certainty and confidence that we do when we go to bed in the evening expecting to see the light of the sun in the morning. —*John Taylor* (GK, 11)

We, as Latter-day Saints, believe, first, in the gospel, and that is a great deal to say, for the gospel embraces principles that dive deeper, spread wider, and extend further than anything else that we can conceive. The gospel teaches us in regard to the being and attributes of God. It also teaches us our relationship to that God and the various responsibilities we are under to him as his offspring. It teaches us the various duties and responsibilities that we are under to our families and friends, to the community, to the living and the dead. It unfolds to us principles pertaining to futurity. —*John Taylor* (GK, 93)

Never serve God because you are afraid of hell; but live your religion, because it is calculated to give you eternal life. —*Brigham Young* (BY, 96)

Everything in heaven, on earth, and in hell is organized for the benefit, advantage, and exaltation of intelligent beings. —*Brigham Young* (BY, 53)

The things of God are of deep import; and time, and experience, and careful and ponderous and solemn thoughts can only find them out. —*Joseph Smith, Jr.* (HC 3:295)

The great plan of salvation is a theme which ought to occupy our strict attention, and be regarded as one of heaven's best gifts to mankind. —*Joseph Smith, Jr.* (STJS, 82)

Christ and the resurrected Saints will reign over the earth during the thousand years. They will not probably dwell upon the earth, but will visit it when they please, or when it is necessary to govern it. There will be wicked men on the earth during the thousand years. The heathen nations who will not come up to worship will be visited with the judgments of God, and must eventually be destroyed from the earth. —*Joseph Smith, Jr.* (STJS, 303)

The principle of knowledge it the principle of salvation. This principle can be comprehended by the faithful and diligent; and every one that does not obtain knowledge sufficient to be saved will be condemned. The principle of salvation is given us through the knowledge of Jesus Christ. —*Joseph Smith, Jr.* (STJS, 331)

There is no such thing as immaterial matter. All spirit is matter, but is more fine or pure, and can only be discerned by purer eyes. We cannot see it, but when our bodies are purified, we shall see that it is all matter. —*Joseph Smith, Jr.* (STJS, 337)

The punishment of the devil was that he should not have a habitation like men. The devil's retaliation is, he comes into this world, binds up men's bodies, and occupies them himself. When the authorities come along, they eject him from a stolen habitation. —*Joseph Smith, Jr.* (STJS, 341)

Intelligence is eternal and exists upon a self-existent principle. It is a spirit from age to age, and there is no creation about it. All the minds and spirits that God ever sent into the world are susceptible of enlargement. —*Joseph Smith, Jr.* (STJS, 397)

9. AGENCY

There has never been a time when man has been forced to do good or forced to obey the commandments of God. He has always been given his free choice—his free moral agency. If one looks back through the events of history, there come into view the results of the greatness of men who kept the commandments of the Lord and made the choice on His side. One also sees strewn along the wayside the ruins that stand as silent reminders of those who chose otherwise. Both had their free moral agency. —*Howard W. Hunter* (CR, Apr. 1966, 47)

Given the freedom to choose, we may, in fact, make wrong choices, bad choices, hurtful choices. And sometimes we do just that, but that is where the mission and the mercy of Jesus Christ come into full force and glory. He has taken upon himself the burden of all the world's risk. —*Howard W. Hunter* (WMJ, 79)

Satan would have coerced us, and he would have robbed us of that most precious of gifts if he could: our freedom to choose a divine future and the exaltation we all hope to obtain. —*Howard W. Hunter* (WMJ, 77-78)

Free agency is an eternal principle. We enjoyed freedom of choice in the spirit world as spirit children. . . . The right of choice—free agency—runs like a golden thread throughout the gospel plan of the Lord for the blessing of His children. —*Ezra Taft Benson* (ETB, 80-81)

And I say to you that no one can imagine the condemnation that will come upon men who deliberately take away from their fellowmen their freedom of choice. It goes contrary to everything that the gospel stands for. —*Ezra Taft Benson* (ETB, 656-657)

We are free to choose, but we are not free to alter the consequences of those choices. —*Ezra Taft Benson* (CUC, 40)

You cannot avoid the responsibility of your acts! Think that through clearly. Do not fool yourself. Your own life is too precious! The lives of your posterity are too priceless! You will receive the rewards of right thinking, righteous doing, conforming attitudes; and wholly beyond your own controls, you will pay penalties—not that God will punish you but that you, yourself, will bring down upon yourself the judgments. —*Spencer W. Kimball* (SWK, 160)

Yes, every soul has his agency. We can have all the blessings Christ lived and died to give us. But Christ's death and plan are in vain if we do not take advantage of them. —*Spencer W. Kimball* (Ensign, Dec. 1984, 2-4)

Freedom of choice, free agency, next to life itself, is the greatest endowment of God to His children. —*Harold B. Lee* (YLW, 230)

Next to life itself, free agency is God's greatest gift to mankind, providing thereby the greatest opportunity for the children of God to advance in this second estate of mortality. —*Harold B. Lee* (SHP, 235)

The spirits of men were not equal. They may have had an equal start, and we know they were all innocent in the beginning; but the right of free agency which was given to them enabled some to outstrip others, and thus, through the eons of immortal existence, to become more intelligent, more faithful, for they were free to act for themselves, to think for themselves, to receive the truth or rebel against it. —*Joseph Fielding Smith* (IE, 19:319)

No person is ever predestined to salvation or damnation. Every person has free agency. —*Joseph Fielding Smith* (DS1, 61)

If there had been no free agency, there could have been no rebellion in heaven; but what would man amount to without this free agency? He would be no better than a mechanical contrivance. He could not have acted for himself, but in all things would have been acted upon, and hence unable to have received a reward for meritorious conduct. He would have been an automaton . . . and such could hardly be called existence. Under such conditions there could have been no purpose in our creation. —*Joseph Fielding Smith* (DS1, 64-65)

God gave to man part of his divinity. He gave man the power of choice, and no other creature in the world has it. So he placed upon the individual the obligation of conducting himself as an eternal being. You cannot think of any greater gift that could come to a man or woman than the freedom of choice. You alone are responsible, and by wielding and exercising that freedom of choice, you grow in character, you grow in intelligence, you approach divinity, and eventually you may achieve that high exaltation. That is a great obligation. Very few people appreciate it. The roads are clearly marked—one offering animal existence, the other life abundant. Yet, God's greatest creation—man—often is content to grovel on the animal plane. —*David O. McKay* (CR, Oct. 1969, 6-7)

Freedom of choice is more to be treasured than any possession earth can give. It is inherent in the spirit of man. It is a divine gift to every normal being. Whether born in abject poverty or shackled at birth by inherited riches, everyone has this most precious of all life's endowments—the gift of free agency, man's inherited and inalienable right.
Free agency is the impelling source of the soul's progress. It is the purpose of the Lord that man become like him. In order for man to achieve this it was necessary for the Creator first to make him free. —*David O. McKay* (CR, Apr. 1950, 32-33)

Next to faith as an essential to man's advancement is free agency. —*David O. McKay* (CR, Apr. 1940, 116)

Only by the exercising of Free Agency can the individual even approach perfection. —*David O. McKay* (CR, Apr. 1940, 118)

To decide one's own relationship to the Creator and to his creations is the natural and inalienable right of all. —*David O. McKay* (CR, Oct. 1961, 5)

Without this divine power to choose, humanity cannot progress. —*David O. McKay* (CR, Oct. 1965, 8)

What you make of yourself depends upon you as an individual. You are in this world to choose the right or the wrong, to accept the right or yield to temptation. Upon that choice will depend the development of the spiritual part of you. That is fundamental in the gospel of Jesus Christ. —*David O. McKay* (CR, Apr. 1967, 134-135)

God has given us our agency. He will not take it from us, and if I do that which is wrong and get into the devil's territory, I do it because I have the will and power to do it. I cannot blame anybody else, and if I determine to keep the commandments of God and live as I ought to live and stay on the Lord's side of the line I do it because I ought to do it, and I will receive my blessing for it. It will not be the result of what somebody else may do. —*George Albert Smith* (CR, Oct. 1932, 27)

In coming here, we forgot all, that our agency might be free indeed, to choose good or evil, that we might merit the reward of our own choice and conduct. —*Joseph F. Smith* (GD, 13-14)

God has given to all men an agency and has granted to us the privilege to serve him or serve him not, to do that which is right or that which is wrong, and this privilege is given to all men irrespective of creed, color or condition. . . . This agency has been given to all. This is a blessing that God has bestowed upon the world of mankind, upon all his children alike. But he will hold us strictly to an account for the use that we make of this agency. —*Joseph F. Smith* (GD, 49)

It is part of the divine economy not to force any man to heaven, not to coerce the mind, but to leave it free to act for itself. He lays before his creature man the everlasting gospel, the principles of life and salvation, and then leaves him to choose for himself or to reject for himself, with the definite understanding that he becomes responsible to him for the results of his acts. —*Wilford Woodruff* (WW, 9-10)

There is a law given unto all kingdoms, and all things are governed by law throughout the whole universe. Whatever law anyone keeps, he is preserved by that law, and he receives whatever reward that law guarantees unto him. It is the will of God that all his children should obey the highest law, that they may receive the highest glory that is ordained for all immortal beings. But God has given all his children an agency, to choose what law they will keep. —*Wilford Woodruff* (WW, 10)

I wish to say that God has given unto all of his children of this dispensation, as he gave unto all of his children of previous dispensations, individual agency. This agency has always been the heritage of man under the rule and government of God. . . . By virtue of this agency you and I and all mankind are made responsible beings, responsible for the course we pursue, the lives we live, the deeds we do in the body. —*Wilford Woodruff* (WW, 8-9)

Free agency and direct individual accountability to God are among the essentials of our church doctrine. —*Wilford Woodruff* (LPS, 156)

It was necessary and proper that there should be good and evil, light and darkness, sin and righteousness, one principle of right opposed to another of wrong, that man might have his free agency to receive the good and reject the evil, and by receiving the good . . . they might be saved and exalted to the eternal Godhead, and go back to their Father and God, while the disobedient would have to meet the consequences of their own acts. —*John Taylor* (GK, 98-99)

We talk sometimes about free will. Is that a correct principle? Yes. And it is a principle that has always existed, and proceeded from God, our Heavenly Father. —*John Taylor* (GK, 59)

Every intelligent being must have the power of choice. —*Brigham Young* (JD, 11:272)

God rules and reigns, and has made all his children as free as himself, to choose the right or the wrong, and we shall then be judged according to our works. —*Brigham Young* (BY, 55)

Man can produce and control his own acts, but he has no control over their results. —*Brigham Young* (BY, 63)

The children of men are made as independent in their sphere as the Lord is in His, to prove themselves, pursue which path they please, and choose the evil or the good. For those who love the Lord, and do His will, all is right, and they shall be crowned, but those who hate His ways shall be damned, for they choose to be damned. —*Brigham Young* (JD, 1:49)

[Y]ou stand then in these last days, as all have stood before you, agents unto yourselves, to be judged according to your works. —*Joseph Smith, Jr.* (STJS, 17)

10. THE PREEXISTENCE

Part of our reassurance about the free, noble, and progressing spirit of man comes from the glorious realization that we all existed and had our identities, and our agency, long before we came to this world. —*Howard W. Hunter* (WMJ, 77)

In a great premortal existence . . . we developed our identities and increased our spiritual capabilities by exercising our agency and making important choices. We developed our intelligence and learned to love the truth, and we prepared to come to earth to continue our progress. —*Howard W. Hunter* (WMJ, 77)

The calling of men to sacred office is not confined to earth life only. There is organization, direction, and assignment in pre earth life and in postearth life also. —*Ezra Taft Benson* (ETB, 21)

The war that began in heaven is not yet over. The conflict continues on the battlefield of mortality. —*Ezra Taft Benson* (ETB, 24)

I testify that all those who come into mortality accepted our Father's plan. Having proved faithful in their first estate in heaven, they are now subject to the test of mortality in this second estate. That test entails doing all things whatsoever the Lord requires. Those who prove faithful in this second estate will have glory added upon their heads forever and ever. —*Ezra Taft Benson* (Ensign, Nov. 1988, 86)

Long before this world was created, all of the spirits of the men and women who were assigned to this earth lived in a spiritual existence. —*Spencer W. Kimball* (SWK, 30)

Remember, in the world before we came here, faithful women were given certain assignments while faithful men were foreordained to certain priesthood tasks. While we do not now remember the particulars, this does not alter the glorious reality of what we once agreed to. —*Spencer W. Kimball* (Ensign, Nov. 1979, 102)

There is no truth more plainly taught in the Gospel than that our condition in the next world will depend upon the kind of lives we live here. . . . Is it not just as reasonable to suppose that the conditions in which we now live have been determined by the kind of lives we lived in the pre-existent world of spirits?—*Harold B. Lee* (DSL, 164-165)

May I ask each of you again the question, "Who are you?" You are all the sons and daughters of God. Your spirits were created and lived as organized intelligences before the world was. You have been blessed to have a physical body because of your obedience to certain commandments in that premortal state. You are now born into a family to which you have come, into the nations through which you have come, as a reward for the kind of lives you lived before you came here. —*Harold B. Lee* (SHP, 9-11)

Every creature had a spiritual existence. The spirits of men, beasts, and all animal life, existed before the foundations of the earth were laid, and are living entities. —*Joseph Fielding Smith* (CN, Feb. 15, 1941, 1)

Environment and many other causes . . . have great influence on the progress and destiny of man, but we must not lose sight of the fact that the characteristics of the spirit, which were developed through many ages of a former existence, play a very important part in our progression through mortal life. —*Joseph Fielding Smith* (IE, 19:313-316)

We believe in a pre-existence. The Lord has taught us that doctrine in the scriptures, but there are millions of those who profess belief in the Holy Bible, who do not believe in, or at least do not understand, what pre-existence really means. They do not realize that we lived before we came here; they do not comprehend that this body has been given to us as a reward for faithfulness in the spirit world. —*George Albert Smith* (CR, Oct. 1923, 70)

The fact that we are living in the flesh is evidence that we did keep our first estate. —*George Albert Smith* (CR, Oct. 1906, 48)

We believe that we are harvesting the fruits of our pre-existent lives, and earning here the reward we expect to reap when we go hence. —*George Albert Smith* (CR, Apr. 1907, 18-19)

The doctrine of pre-existence pours a wonderful flood of light upon the other wise mysterious problem of man's origin. It shows that man, as a spirit, was begotten and born of heavenly parents and reared to maturity in the eternal mansions of the Father, prior to coming upon the earth in a temporal body to undergo an experience in mortality. —*Heber J. Grant* (LPS, 4)

The labors that we performed in the sphere that we left before we came here have had a certain effect upon our lives here, and to a certain extent they govern and control the lives that we lead here, just the same as the labors that we do here will control and govern our lives when we pass from this stage of existence. —*Heber J. Grant* (LPS, 4)

Had we not known before we came the necessity of our coming, the importance of obtaining tabernacles, the glory to be achieved in posterity, the grand object to be attained by being tried and tested—weighed in the balance, in the exercise of the divine attributes, god-like powers and free agency with which we are endowed; whereby, after descending below all things, Christ-like, we might ascend above all things, and become like our Father, Mother and Elder Brother, Almighty and Eternal!—we never would have come; that is, if we could have stayed away. —*Joseph F. Smith* (GD, 13)

Where did we come from? From God. Our spirits existed before they came to this world. They were in the councils of the heavens before the foundations of the earth were laid. We were there. We sang together with the heavenly hosts for joy when the foundations of the earth were laid, and when the plan of our existence upon this earth and redemption were mapped out. We were there; we were interested, and we took a part in this great preparation. —*Joseph F. Smith* (GD, 93-94)

Pre-earth life affects relations here. We have not come into this world accidentally. It is my opinion that there has been an inspiration to bring about certain relations that we are forming here in this life, and most likely they arise because of certain relations that existed in our previous life. —*Lorenzo Snow* (LS, 93)

We have learned that we existed with God in eternity before we came into this life, and that we kept our estate. Had we not kept what is called our first estate and observed the laws that governed there, you and I would not be here today. We are here because we are worthy to be here. —*Lorenzo Snow* (LPS, 7)

Every man who has a calling to minister to the inhabitants of the world was ordained to that very purpose in the Grand Council of heaven before this world was. I suppose I was ordained to this very office in that Grand Council. —*Joseph Smith, Jr.* (STJS, 411)

11. THE CREATION

She wondered about the creation because she had read the theories of the scientists, and the question that she was really asking was: How do you reconcile science with religion? The answer must be, If science is not true, you cannot reconcile truth with error. —*Harold B. Lee* (Ensign, December 1972, 2)

The account of the creation in the Book of Abraham is "The Lord's Blueprint of Creation." By this I mean Abraham gives an account of the planning in heaven for this earth and its inhabitants, before the work of building was done. —*Joseph Fielding Smith* (DS1, 75)

The Lord pronounced the earth good when it was finished. Everything upon its face was called good. There was no death in the earth before the fall of Adam. I do not care what the scientists say in regard to dinosaurs and other creatures upon the earth millions of years ago, that lived and died and fought and struggled for existence. When the earth was created and was declared good, peace was upon its face among all its creatures. Strife and wickedness were not found here, neither was there any corruption. —*Joseph Fielding Smith* (DS1, 108)

Things upon the earth, so far as they have not been perverted by wickedness, are typical of things in heaven. Heaven was the prototype of this beautiful creation when it came from the hand of the Creator, and was pronounced "good."—*Joseph F. Smith* (GD, 21)

The spirit of man is not a created being; it existed from eternity, and will exist to eternity. Anything created cannot be eternal; and earth, water, etc., had their existence in an elementary state, from eternity. —*Joseph Smith, Jr.* (STJS, 179)

The elements are eternal. That which has a beginning will surely have an end; take a ring, it is without beginning or end—cut it for a beginning place and at the same time you have an ending place. . . .

So it is with God. If the soul of man had a beginning it will surely have an end. In the translation "without form and void" it should be read, empty and desolate. The word created should be formed, or organized. —*Joseph Smith, Jr.* (STJS, 205)

Now, the word create came from the word *baurau* which does not mean to create out of nothing; it means to organize; the same as a man would organize materials and build a ship. Hence, we infer that God had materials to organize the world out of chaos—chaotic matter, which is element, and in which dwells all the glory. Element had an existence from the time he had. The pure principles of element are principles which can never be destroyed; they may be organized and re-organized, but not destroyed. They had no beginning, and can have no end. —*Joseph Smith, Jr.* (STJS, 393-395)

12. THE FALL

Just as a man does not really desire food until he is hungry, so he does not desire the salvation of Christ until he knows why he needs Christ.

No one adequately and properly knows why he needs Christ until he understands and accepts the doctrine of the Fall and its effect upon all mankind. And no other book in the world explains this vital doctrine nearly as well as the Book of Mormon. —*Ezra Taft Benson* (AWW, 33)

Besides the Fall having had to do with Adam and Eve, causing a change to come over them, that change affected all human nature, all of the natural creations, all of the creation of animals, plants—all kinds of life were changed. The earth itself became subject to death that it might be cleansed likewise. How it took place no one can explain, and anyone who would attempt to make an explanation would be going far beyond anything the Lord has told us. —*Harold B. Lee* (HBL, 33-35)

Let us honor in our minds and in our teachings the great legacy which Adam and Eve gave to us when, through their experience, by the exercise of their own agency, they partook of fruit which gave them the seeds of mortal life and gave to us, their descendants down through the generations of time, that great boon by which we too can receive the joy of our redemption, and in our flesh see God, and have eternal life. —*Harold B. Lee* (HBL, 33-35)

When Adam was in the Garden of Eden he was in the presence of the Father and was taught by him. He learned his language. He was as familiar with our Eternal Father in that garden as we are with our fathers in mortal life. . . .

After he partook of the forbidden fruit, Adam and Eve were cast out of that garden and likewise out of the presence of the Father. He was banished because of his transgression, and became spiritually dead—that is, he was shut out from the presence of God. —*Joseph Fielding Smith* (DS1, 26)

The fall of man came as a blessing in disguise, and was the means of furthering the purposes of the Lord in the progress of man, rather than a means of hindering them. —*Joseph Fielding Smith* (CR, Apr. 1945, 48)

If there was no fall; if death did not come into the world as the scriptures declared that it did—and to be consistent, if you are an evolutionist, this view you must assume—then there was no need for a redemption, and Jesus Christ is not the Son of God, and he did not die for the transgression of Adam, nor for the sins of the world. Then there has been no resurrection from the dead! Consistently, logically, there is no other view, no alternative that can be taken. Now, my brethren and sisters, are you prepared to take this view?—*Joseph Fielding Smith* (IE, 23:390)

Was it known that man would fall? Yes. We are clearly told that it was understood that man should fall, and it was understood that the penalty of departing from the law would be death, death temporal. And there was a provision made for that. Man was not able to make that provision himself, and hence we are told that it needed the atonement of a God to accomplish this purpose; and the Son of God presented himself to carry out that object. —*John Taylor* (GK, 97)

Mother Eve partook of the forbidden fruit. We should not have been here today if she had not; we could never have possessed wisdom and intelligence if she had not done it. It was all in the economy of heaven . . . We should never blame Mother Eve, not the least. —*Brigham Young* (BY, 103)

[T]hough our first parents were driven out of the garden of Eden, and were even separated from the presence of God by a veil, they still retained a knowledge of his existence, and that sufficiently to move them to call upon him. And further, that no sooner was the plan of redemption revealed to man, and he began to call upon God, than the Holy Spirit was given, bearing record of the Father and Son. —*Joseph Smith, Jr.* (LF, 12-15)

13. Mortal Life

There will be a day of reckoning. There will be a time of confession and accounting. Each day in mortality we are writing the text of that accounting. —*Gordon B. Hinckley* (Ensign, Jan. 1989, 4)

Life is a mission, not just the sputtering of a candle between a chance lighting and a gust of wind that blows it out forever. —*Gordon B. Hinckley* (Ensign, Jan. 1994, 4)

We are on the road that leads to immortality and eternal life and today is a part of it. Let us never forget it. —*Gordon B. Hinckley* (CN, Nov. 4, 1995, 2)

Will we wear the victor's crown? Satan may have lost Jesus, but he does not believe he has lost us. He continues to tempt, taunt, and plead for our loyalty. We should take strength for this battle from the fact that Christ was victorious not as a God but as a man. —*Howard W. Hunter* (Ensign, Nov. 1976, 17-19)

This life is the schoolroom of our journey through eternity. There is work to do and lessons to learn that we might prepare and qualify ourselves to go into the spiritual existence to follow. —*Howard W. Hunter* (CR, Oct. 1961, 109)

We came to mortal life to encounter resistance. It was part of the plan for our eternal progress. Without temptation, sickness, pain, and sorrow, there could be no goodness, virtue, appreciation for well-being, or joy. —*Howard W. Hunter* (WMJ, 98)

Life—every—life has a full share of ups and downs. Indeed, we see many joys and sorrows in the world, many changed plans and new directions, many blessings that do not always look or feel like blessings, and much that humbles us and improves our patience and our faith. We have all had those experiences from time to time, and I suppose we always will. —*Howard W. Hunter* (WMJ, 122)

Doors close regularly in our lives, and some of those closings cause genuine pain and heartache. But I do believe that where one such door closes, another opens (and perhaps more than one), with hope and blessings in other areas of our lives that we might not have discovered otherwise. —*Howard W. Hunter* (WMJ, 123)

Coming to earth was part of God's plan for eternal progress. . . . We are here to learn self-mastery. By learning to govern our natures, our appetites and passions, we draw closer to the divine nature of God. —*Ezra Taft Benson* (CUC , 74-75)

Give God your best, and His best will come back to you. —*Ezra Taft Benson* (Ensign, Dec. 1988, 2)

Our affections are often too highly placed upon the paltry, perishable objects. Material treasures of earth are merely to provide us, as it were, room and board while we are here at school. It is for us to place gold, silver, houses, stocks, lands, cattle, and other earthly possessions in their proper place.
This is but a place of temporary duration. We are here to learn the first lesson toward exaltation—obedience to the Lord's gospel plan. —*Ezra Taft Benson* (Ensign, Aug. 1991, 2)

You will arise about the way you die. You will not change very much. You cannot repent on the Word of Wisdom violation in the spirit world because you have no body which you must change. You can hardly change its urges and desires and its pleadings and pullings in the spirit world. This is the time to put your lives in order. —*Spencer W. Kimball* (SWK, 41)

Today is, for all we know, the opportunity and occasion of our lives. Let us lay hold on happiness today; for know this, if you are not happy today, you may never be happy. Today is given you to be patient, unselfish, purposeful, strong, and eager to work mightily. —*Spencer W. Kimball* (SWK, 173)

Who knows but that many of those with seemingly inequalities in this life, if they do everything possible with their limited opportunities, may not receive greater blessings than some of those rewarded by having been born to a noble lineage and to superior social and spiritual opportunities who fail to live up to their great privileges?—*Harold B. Lee* (DSL, 166)

Only when our lives are measuring up to the best we know, despite unfortunate and trying situations, only then have we conquered self and are we realizing the joy of living which is the purpose of existence. —*Harold B. Lee* (YLW, 264)

We were duly formed that in this mortal life we would have to walk by faith. Previously we had walked by sight, but now was to come a period of trial to see if by faith we would be true to every covenant and commandment our Father required at our hands. We were informed that many would fail. Those who rebelled against the light which would be revealed to them should be deprived of exaltation. They could not come back to dwell in the presence of God, but would have to take a place in some other sphere where they would be blessed according to their works, and likewise restricted in their privileges. —*Joseph Fielding Smith* (CN, June 12, 1949, 12)

Mortality is the testing or proving ground for exaltation to find out who among the children of God are worthy to become Gods themselves. —*Joseph Fielding Smith* (DS1, 69-70)

No man wants to be cursed with mortal life and live forever. No, that would be a calamity. Mortal life is all right for the little space of time that we spend here in this world. It is necessary. It is a mighty important part of our existence, because it is here that we prove ourselves. It is here that we prepare ourselves for that which is to come. *—Joseph Fielding Smith* (DS2, 284)

The house is not the family. The wind may tear the roof off, blow out the windows; the hurricane may even sweep the house away; but the family remains, that which makes the home. Nor is the body the life itself. It is but the house in which the spirit lives. Sickness may waste the body, but the true life is the spirit within, that which thinks and feels and loves and suffers and wills and chooses, aspires, and achieves. The purpose in life is to beautify, ornament, develop that something within. To develop a more radiant and lovely character is the true purpose in life. *—David O. McKay* (GI, 357)

The true aim of life is seeking the spiritual development rather than physical enjoyment or the acquisition of wealth. *—David O. McKay* (GI, 394)

Man's earthly existence is but a test as to whether he will concentrate his efforts, his mind, his soul upon things which contribute to the comfort and gratification of his physical nature or whether he will make as his life's purpose the acquisition of spiritual qualities. *—David O. McKay* (CR, Apr. 1958, 6)

We are not here to while away the hours of this life and then pass to a sphere of exaltation; but we are here to qualify ourselves day by day for the positions that our Father expects us to fill hereafter. *—George Albert Smith* (CR, Apr. 1905, 62)

There is no doubt in the mind of a Latter-day Saint as to the purpose of our earth life. We are here to prepare ourselves and develop ourselves and qualify ourselves to be worthy to dwell in the presence of our Heavenly Father. We must learn to overcome our passions, our evil tendencies. We must learn to resist temptations. That is why we are here. *—George Albert Smith* (CR, Oct. 1926, 102)

I am thankful that there has been revealed to us and made plain in this latter-day that this life is not the end, that this is but a part of eternity, and that if we take advantage of our privileges here, that this is but the stepping stone to greater and more desirable conditions. *—George Albert Smith* (CR, Oct. 1923, 71)

Our Father has given us the knowledge that this life is a probation, that we are building for the future, and how grateful we ought to be for this assurance, and Oh, how sad we would be if we thought that death terminated our career. If, when our life's labor on earth was finished, we had no opportunity to go on developing, there would be little to inspire us to live as we should here. The knowledge that all the good we accomplish here, and all development we make, will enhance our happiness eternally, encourages us to do our best. *—George Albert Smith* (CR, Oct. 1921, 41)

We are in a school, fitting, qualifying, and preparing ourselves that we may be worthy and capable of going back and dwelling in the presence of our Heavenly Father. *—Heber J. Grant* (GS, 40)

We are the architects of our own lives, not only of the lives here, but the lives to come in the eternity. We ourselves are able to perform every duty and obligation that God has required of men. No commandment was ever given to us but that God has given us the power to keep that commandment. If we fail, we, and we alone, are responsible for the failure, because God endows His servants . . . with all the ability, all the knowledge, all the power that is . . . to discharge every duty and every obligation that rests upon them, and we, and we alone, will have to answer if we fail in this regard. *—Heber J. Grant* (CR, Apr. 1943, 4)

The important consideration is not how long we can live, but how well we can learn the lessons of life, and discharge our duties and obligations to God and to each other. One of the main purposes of our existence is that we might conform to the image and likeness of Him who sojourned in the flesh without blemish—immaculate, pure, and spotless!—*Joseph F. Smith* (IE, 21:104)

The object of our being here is to do the will of the Father as it is done in heaven, to work righteousness in the earth, to subdue wickedness and put it under our feet, to conquer sin and the adversary of our souls, to rise above the imperfections and weaknesses of poor, fallen humanity, by the inspiration of Almighty God and his power made manifest, and thus become indeed the saints and servants of the Lord in the earth. —*Joseph F. Smith* (CR, Apr. 1902, 85)

We are precisely in the same condition and under the same circumstances that God our Heavenly Father was when He was passing through this or a similar ordeal. We are destined to come forth out of the grave as Jesus did, and to obtain immortal bodies as He did . . . This is the object of our existence in the world. —*Joseph F. Smith* (JD, 25:58-59)

Our trials and sufferings give us experience, and establish within us principles of godliness. —*Lorenzo Snow* (LS, 6)

All men and women who are worthy to be called Latter-day Saints should live hour by hour in such a way that if they should be called suddenly from this life into the next they would be prepared. The preparation should be such that we should not fear to be called away suddenly into the spirit life. It is our privilege to so live as to have the spirit of light and intelligence to that extent that we shall feel satisfied that all will be well if we should be called away at any hour. —*Lorenzo Snow* (CR, Oct. 1899, 2)

The Lord has determined in His heart that He will try us until He knows what He can do with us. He tried His Son Jesus. Thousands of years before He came upon earth, the Father had watched His course and knew that He could depend upon Him when the salvation of worlds should be at stake; and He was not disappointed. So in regard to ourselves. He will try us, and continue to try us, in order that He may place us in the highest positions in life and put upon us the most sacred responsibilities. —*Lorenzo Snow* (LS, 93)

It is our duty to desire to live long upon the earth, that we may do as much good as we possibly can. I esteem it a great privilege to have the opportunity of living in mortality. The Lord has sent us here "for a wise and glorious purpose," and it should be our business to find out what that purpose is and then to order our lives accordingly. —*Lorenzo Snow* (LS, 94)

A strong character is an asset in the spirit world. I am under the strongest impression that the most valuable consideration, and that which will be of the most service when we return to the spirit world, will be that of having established a proper and well-defined character as faithful and consistent Latter-day Saints in this state of probation. —*Lorenzo Snow* (LS, 23)

If there was a point where man in his progression could not proceed any further, the very idea would throw a gloom over every intelligent and reflecting mind. . . . We are in a probation, which is a school of experience. —*Wilford Woodruff* (WW, 3)

We are in a great school; and it is a profitable one, in which we are receiving very important lessons from day to day. We are taught to cultivate our minds, to control our thoughts, to thoroughly bring our whole being into subjection to the spirit and law of God, that we may learn to be one and act as the heart of one man, that we may carry out the purposes of God upon the earth. —*Wilford Woodruff* (WW, 10-11)

We would not be worthy of salvation, we would not be worthy of eternal lives in the kingdom of our God, if anything could turn us away from the truth or from the love of it. —*Wilford Woodruff* (WW, 23)

I want to live as long as I can do good; but not an hour longer than I can live in fellowship with the Holy Spirit, with my Father in heaven, my Savior, and with the faithful Latter-day Saints. To live any longer than this, would be torment and misery to me. When my work is done I am ready to go; but I want to do what is required of me. —*Wilford Woodruff* (WW, 274)

We came on this earth, and obtained tabernacles, that, through taking possession of them, and passing through a scene of trial, and tribulation, and suffering, we might be exalted to more glory, dignity, and power than would have been possible for us to obtain had we not been placed in our present position. —*John Taylor* (GK, 14)

It is also necessary that we should learn the principles of order and government, but we must first learn how to govern ourselves, then how to govern our families, and lastly, learn how to be governed, which is the most difficult lesson that can be set us—it is infinitely worse than governing others. —*John Taylor* (GK, 17-18)

It is the crowns, the principalities, the powers, the thrones, the dominions, and the associations with the Gods that we are after, and we are here to prepare ourselves for these things—this is the main object of existence. —*John Taylor* (GK, 343)

We have learned many things through suffering, we call it suffering; I call it a school of experience . . . Why is it that good men should be tried? Why is it, in fact, that we should have a devil? Why did not the Lord kill him long ago? Because He could not do without him. He needed the devil and a great many of those who do his bidding just to keep men straight, that we may learn to place our dependence upon God and trust in Him, and to observe His laws and keep His commandments. —*John Taylor* (JD, 23:336)

Our mortal existence is a school of experience. —*Brigham Young* (BY, 56)

We are now in a day of trial to prove ourselves worthy or unworthy of the life which is to come. —*Brigham Young* (BY, 345)

There is no life more precious than the present life which we enjoy; there is no life that is worth any more to us than this life is. It may be said that an eternal life is worth more. We are in eternity, and all that we have to do is to take the road that leads into the eternal lives. Eternal life is an inherent quality of the creature, and nothing but sin can put a termination to it. —*Brigham Young* (BY, 15)

The object of this existence is to learn, which we can only do a little at a time. —*Brigham Young* (BY, 87)

We are placed on this earth to prove whether we are worthy to go into the celestial world, the terrestrial, or the telestial or to hell, or to any other kingdom, or place, and we have enough of life given to us to do this. —*Brigham Young* (BY, 87)

We came to this earth that we might have a body and present it pure before God in the celestial kingdom. The great principle of happiness consists in having a body. —*Joseph Smith, Jr.* (STJS, 206)

14. DEATH

What a wonderful thing is death, really, when all is said and done. It is the great reliever. It is a majestic, quiet passing on from this life to another life, a better life, I'm satisfied of that. We go to a place where we will not suffer as we have suffered here, but where we will continue to grow, accumulating knowledge and developing and being useful under the plan of the Almighty made possible through the atonement of the Son of God. —*Gordon B. Hinckley* (CN, Feb. 13, 1996, 2)

The death of a righteous individual is both an honorable release and a call to new labors. —*Ezra Taft Benson* (ETB, 33)

It is my feeling that every good and righteous person has a specific time to go. I don't think it applies to everyone. —*Ezra Taft Benson* (ETB, 35)

The great plan of salvation is operating, not only . . . on this side of the veil but on the other side also. The Church is organized over there. The priesthood is functioning over there. The missionary work is going on over there. It makes very little difference whether we serve on one side of the veil or the other, so long as our service is actuated by a spirit of devotion, a spirit of loyalty, a spirit of love, and is in line with these eternal principles which our Heavenly Father has been kind enough to reveal unto us. —*Ezra Taft Benson* (ETB, 22)

There were two grand divisions in the world of spirits. Spirits of the righteous (the just) had gone to paradise, a state of happiness, peace, and restful work. The spirits of the wicked (the unjust) had gone to prison, a state of darkness and misery. (See Alma 40:12-15) Jesus went only to the righteous—to paradise. —*Ezra Taft Benson* (CUC , 118)

The spirit world is not far away. From the Lord's point of view, it is all one great program on both sides of the veil. Sometimes the veil between this life and the life beyond becomes very thin. Our loved ones who have passed on are not far from us. —*Ezra Taft Benson* (Ensign, Apr. 1993, 4)

Yes, men die—all men die. Millions have died unheard, unsung, unknown. The question is, when they die have they fulfilled the measure of their mortal creation? Certainly it is not so much that men die, or when they die, but that they do not die in their sins. —*Spencer W. Kimball* (Ensign, Dec. 1980, 3)

In death do we grieve for the one who passes on, or is it self-pity? To doubt the wisdom and justice of the passing of a loved one is to place a limitation on the term of life. It is to say that it is more important to continue to live here than to go into other fields. Do we grieve when our son is graduated from the local high school and is sent away from home to a university of higher learning? Do we grieve inconsolably when our son is called away from our daily embrace to distant lands to preach the gospel? To continue to grieve without faith and understanding and trust when a son goes into another world is to question the long-range program of God, life eternal with all its opportunities and blessings. —*Spencer W. Kimball* (IE, May 1945, 3)

Death of a loved one is the most severe test that you will ever face, and if you can rise above your griefs and if you will trust in God, then you will be able to surmount any other difficulty with which you may be faced. —*Harold B. Lee* (YLW, 257)

Beautifully and dramatically, Easter morning in the springtime proclaims that divine truth that "death is not the end—it is but a beginning!—*Harold B. Lee* (YLW, 238)

Death is just as essential as birth. Who would want to live in this world in this mortal condition, forever, with all the pain and the suffering and the anguish of soul that come? None of us would wish it, and especially if we understood that this is only a temporary probation and that by passing on we should come to a glorious condition of eternal life. We would not want to stay here. And so we have before us the plan of salvation. —*Joseph Fielding Smith* (DS1, 68)

There is no information given by revelation in regard to the status of stillborn children. However, I will express my personal opinion that we should have hope that these little ones will receive a resurrection and then belong to us. I cannot help feeling that this will be the case. —*Joseph Fielding Smith* (DS2, 280)

Personality is persistent, and that is the message of comfort, that is the real way in which death is conquered. Death cannot touch the spirit of man. —*David O. McKay* (GI, 55)

It is disobedience that brings death. Obedience to Christ and his laws brings life. —*David O. McKay* (CR, Apr. 1939, 115)

There is no cause to fear death; it is but an incident in life. It is as natural as birth. Why should we fear it? Some fear it because they think it is the end of life and life often is the dearest thing we have. Eternal life is man's greatest blessing. —*David O. McKay* (CR, Apr. 1966, 58)

That the spirit of man passes triumphantly through the portals of death into everlasting life is one of the glorious messages given by Christ, our Redeemer. To him this earthly career is but a day, and its closing but the setting of life's sun; death, but a sleep, is followed by a glorious awakening in the morning of an eternal realm. —*David O. McKay* (CR, Oct. 1968, 5)

We come here and sojourn in the flesh a little season and then we pass away. Every soul that is born into the world will die. . . . We shall all die. But is that the end of our being? If we had an existence before we came here we certainly shall continue that existence when we leave here. The spirit will continue to exist as it did before, with the additional advantages derived from having passed through this probation. —*Joseph F. Smith* (GD, 31-32)

We are living for eternity and not merely for the moment. Death does not part us from one another, if we have entered into sacred relationships with each other by virtue of the authority that God has revealed to the children of men. Our relationships are formed for eternity. —*Joseph F. Smith* (GD, 277)

[W]ith little children who are taken away in infancy and innocence before they have reached the years of accountability, and are not capable of committing sin, the gospel reveals to us the fact that they are redeemed, and Satan has no power over them. Neither has death any power over them. They are redeemed by the blood of Christ, and they are saved just as surely as death has come into the world through the fall of our first parents. —*Joseph F. Smith* (GD, 452)

Death lies along the road of eternal progress; and though hard to bear, no one who believes in the gospel of Jesus Christ, and especially in the resurrection, would have it otherwise. Children should be taught early in life that death is really a necessity as well as a blessing, and that we would not and could not be satisfied and supremely happy without it. —*Joseph F. Smith* (GD, 297)

I cannot help but think that in every death there is a birth; the spirit leaves the body dead to us, and passes to the other side of the veil alive to that great and noble company that are also working for the accomplishment of the purposes of God, in the redemption and salvation of a fallen world. . . . I have always felt with regard to faithful Latter-day Saints, when they have finished their work and gone behind the veil that there are none of them that would return to their earthly bodies if they had the opportunity. —*Wilford Woodruff* (WW, 245)

Some labor this side of the veil, others on the other side of the veil. If we tarry here we expect to labor in the cause of salvation, and if we go hence we expect to continue our work until the coming of the Son of Man. The only difference is, while we are here we are subject to pain and sorrow, while they on the other side are free from affliction of every kind. —*Wilford Woodruff* (WW, 246)

It certainly does require a good deal of the Spirit of the Lord to give comfort and consolation to a father and mother mourning for the loss of their children; and without the gospel of Christ the separation by death is one of the most gloomy subjects it is possible to contemplate; but just as soon as we obtain the gospel and learn the principle of the resurrection, the gloom, sorrow, and suffering occasioned by death are, in a great measure, taken away. —*Wilford Woodruff* (WW, 249-250)

We struggle sometimes while we are occupants of these mortal bodies, for riches and position, for fame and honor. We jostle one against another, entertaining various conflicting sentiments, ideas, and theories, but they are all leveled with the balance in the grave. Such has been, and such is the position of the human family. —*John Taylor* (GK, 11)

We believe in a religion that will make a man go down to the grave with a clear conscience, and an unfaltering step, and meet his God as a father and friend without fear. . . . We have no craven fear of death; we are looking for life eternal, and an association with the Gods in celestial mansions. We are not ashamed of our religion, and we believe God is not ashamed of us. —*John Taylor* (GK, 20-21)

Since the organization of the world, myriads have come and have taken upon themselves bodies, and they have passed away, generation after generation, into another state of existence. And it is so today. And I suppose while we are mourning the loss of our friend, others are rejoicing to meet him behind the veil. —*John Taylor* (GK, 22)

Instead of crying to the people, prepare to die, our cry is, prepare to live forever. These mortal houses will drop off sometime, and when they are cleansed and purified, sanctified and glorified, we shall inherit them again forever and ever. Let all the Saints pursue a course to live. —*Brigham Young* (BY, 88)

We shall suffer no more in putting off this flesh and leaving the spirit houseless than the child, in its capacity, does in its first efforts to breathe the breath of this mortal life. —*Brigham Young* (BY, 368)

When you lay down this tabernacle, where are you going? Into the spiritual world. . . . Where is the spirit world? It is right here. —*Brigham Young* (BY, 376)

It is far better to die in a good cause than to live in a bad one; it is better to die doing good than to live doing evil. —*Brigham Young* (BY, 78)

[I]f we are striving with all the powers and faculties God has given us to improve upon our talents, to prepare ourselves to dwell in eternal life, and the grave receives our bodies while we are thus engaged, with what disposition will our spirits enter their next state? They will be still striving to do the things of God, only in a much greater degree—learning, increasing, growing in grace and in the knowledge of the truth. —*Brigham Young* (BY, 379)

We have more friends behind the veil than on this side, and they will hail us more joyfully than you were ever welcomed by your parents and friends in this world; and you will rejoice more when you meet them than you ever rejoiced to see a friend in this life. —*Brigham Young* (BY, 379-380)

How consoling to the mourners when they are called to part with a husband, wife, father, mother, child, or dear relative, to know that, although the earthly tabernacle is laid down and dissolved, they shall rise again to dwell in everlasting burnings in immortal glory, not to sorrow, suffer, or die any more; but they shall be heirs of God and joint heirs with Jesus Christ. —*Joseph Smith, Jr.* (STJS, 392)

The Lord takes many away even in infancy, that they may escape the envy of man, and the sorrows and evils of this present world; they were too pure, too lovely, to live on earth; therefore, if rightly considered, instead of mourning we have reason to rejoice as they are delivered from evil, and we shall soon have them again. —*Joseph Smith, Jr.* (STJS, 223)

I will tell you what I want. If tomorrow I shall be called to lie in yonder tomb, in the morning of the resurrection let me strike hands with my father, and cry, "My father," and he will say, "My son, my son."—*Joseph Smith, Jr.* (STJS, 328-329)

The only difference between the old and young dying is, one lives longer in heaven and eternal light and glory than the other, and is freed a little sooner from this miserable wicked world. Notwithstanding all this glory, we for a moment lose sight of it, and mourn the loss, but we do not mourn as those without hope. —*Joseph Smith, Jr.* (STJS, 224)

We have reason to have the greatest hope and consolations for our dead of any people on the earth; for we have seen them walk worthily in our midst, and seen them sink asleep in the arms of Jesus; and those who have died in the faith are now in the celestial kingdom of God. —*Joseph Smith, Jr.* (STJS, 403)

15. THE ATONEMENT

No member of the Church must ever forget the terrible price paid by our Redeemer who gave his life that all men might live—the agony of Gethsemane, the bitter mockery of his trial, the vicious crown of thorns tearing at his flesh, the blood cry of the mob before Pilate, the lonely burden of his heavy walk along the way to Calvary, the terrifying pain as great nails pierced his hands and feet, the fevered torture of his body as he hung that tragic day, the Son of God crying out, "Father, forgive them; for they know not what they do." (Luke 23:34) —*Gordon B. Hinckley* (BTE, 87-90)

Thanks be to God for the wonder and the majesty of His eternal plan. Thank and glorify His Beloved Son, who, with indescribable suffering, gave His life on Calvary's cross to pay the debt of mortal sin. He it was who, through His atoning sacrifice, broke the bonds of death and with Godly power rose triumphant from the tomb. He is our Redeemer, the Redeemer of all mankind. He is the Savior of the world. He is the Son of God, the Author of our Salvation. —*Gordon B. Hinckley* (Ensign, May 1985, 51)

Nothing is more important in the entire divine plan of salvation than the atoning sacrifice of Jesus Christ. We believe that salvation comes because of the atonement. In its absence the whole plan of creation would come to naught. —*Howard W. Hunter* (CR, Oct. 1968, 139)

The atonement that Christ wrought was in behalf of every individual. However, each must work out his or her own salvation, for we are not saved collectively. The worthiness of one's friends or family will not save him or her. There must be an individual effort. —*Howard W. Hunter* (WMJ, 53-54)

A study of the life of Christ and a testimony of His reality is something each of us should seek. As we come to understand His mission and the atonement which He wrought, we will desire to live more like Him. —*Howard W. Hunter* (CN, March 11, 1995, 7)

Because He [Jesus Christ] was God—even the son of God—He could carry the weight and burden of other men's sins on Himself. —*Ezra Taft Benson* (Ensign, Apr. 1991, 2)

No mortal being had the power or capability to redeem all other mortals from their lost and fallen condition, nor could any other voluntarily forfeit his life and thereby bring to pass a universal resurrection for all other mortals.

Only Jesus Christ was ably and willing to accomplish such a redeeming act of love. We may never understand nor comprehend in mortality how He accomplished what He did, but we must not fail to understand why He did what He did.

Everything He did was prompted by His unselfish, infinite love for us. —*Ezra Taft Benson* (Ensign, June 1990, 4)

Jesus perfected his life and became our Christ. Priceless blood of a god was shed, and he became our Savior; his perfected life was given, and he became our Redeemer; his atonement for us made possible our return to our Heavenly Father, and yet how thoughtless, how unappreciative are most beneficiaries! Ingratitude is a sin of the ages. —*Spencer W. Kimball* (Ensign, Feb. 1981, 5)

The Savior's blood, His atonement, will save us, but only after we have done all we can to save ourselves by keeping His commandments. All of the principles of the gospel are principles of promise by which the plans of the Almighty are unfolded to us. —*Harold B. Lee* (SHP, 246)

Jesus . . . atoned not only for Adam's transgressions but for the sins of all mankind. But redemption from individual sins depends upon individual effort, with each being judged according to his or her works.

The scriptures make it clear that while a resurrection will come to all, only those who obey the Christ will receive the expanded blessing of eternal salvation. —*Harold B. Lee* (Ensign, Apr. 1973, 5)

What did Christ do? He ransomed us. He restored us. He brought us back through his atonement, through the shedding of his blood. . . . He rescued us from captivity and bondage. That is what ransomed means. He liberated us from death. He paid the price that death required; and we, through his redemption, were recovered by the payment of the shedding of his blood. —*Joseph Fielding Smith* (CN, Mar. 9, 1935, 6)

The whole plan of redemption is based on vicarious sacrifice, One without sin standing for the whole human family, all of whom were under the curse. —*Joseph Fielding Smith* (DS1, 126)

A mortal man could not have stood it—that is, a man such as we are. I do not care what his fortitude what his power, there was no man ever born into this world that could have stood under the weight of the load that was upon the Son of God, when he was carrying my sins and yours and making it possible that we might escape from our sins. He carried that load for us if we will only accept him as our Redeemer and keep his commandments. —*Joseph Fielding Smith* (CN, Apr. 22, 1939)

[Jesus Christ] never paid any debt on the cross, or before he went on the cross, for the sins of any of us, if we will be rebellious. If we are rebellious, we will have to pay the price ourselves. —*Joseph Fielding Smith* (CN, Apr. 22, 1939)

Any man who believes that little children are born in sin and are tainted by original sin, or the sin of somebody else, has failed to comprehend the nature of the atonement of Jesus Christ. —*Joseph Fielding Smith* (DS2, 50)

The Church of Jesus Christ promulgates the doctrine that little children are redeemed and sanctified through the atonement of our Lord and Savior. If they die before reaching the age of accountability, they become heirs of the celestial kingdom of heaven. —*David O. McKay* (GI, 74-75)

This gospel will save the whole human family; the blood of Jesus will atone for our sins, if we accept the terms He has laid down; but we must accept those terms or else it will avail nothing in our behalf. —*Heber J. Grant* (LPS, 149)

By the atonement of Jesus Christ the sins of the repentant shall be washed away; though they be crimson they shall be made white as wool. —*Joseph F. Smith* (CR, Oct. 1899, 42)

Jesus, the Son of God, was sent into the world to make it possible for you and me to receive these extraordinary blessings. He had to make a great sacrifice. It required all the power that He had and all the faith that He could summon for Him to accomplish that which the Father required of Him. Had He fallen in the moment of temptation, what do you suppose would have become of us? Doubtless at some future period the plan would have been carried out by another person. But He did not fail, though the trial was so severe that He sweat great drops of blood. —*Lorenzo Snow* (LS, 98)

What is called the original sin was atoned for through the death of Christ irrespective of any action on the part of man; also man's individual sin was atoned for by the same sacrifice, but on condition of his obedience to the Gospel plan of salvation. —*Wilford Woodruff* (KRL, 61-62)

Jesus had to take away sin by the sacrifice of himself, the just for the unjust . . . And as he in his own person bore the sins of all, and atoned for them by the sacrifice of himself, so there came upon him the weight and agony of ages and generations, the indescribable agony consequent upon this great sacrificial atonement wherein he bore the sins of the world, and suffered in his own person the consequences of an eternal law of God broken by man. —*John Taylor* (GK, 116)

The death of Jesus Christ would not have taken place had it not been necessary. . . . But why this? Why should such a law exist? It is left with us as a matter of faith, that it was necessary he should come and, being necessary, he shrank not from the task, but came to take away sin by offering up himself. —*John Taylor* (GK, 109)

From the facts in the case and the testimony presented in the scriptures it becomes evident that through the great atonement, the expiatory sacrifice of the Son of God, it is made possible that man can be redeemed, restored, resurrected, and exalted to the elevated position designed for him in the creation as a Son of God. —*John Taylor* (GK, 114)

The suffering of the Son of God was not simply the suffering of personal death; for in assuming the position that he did in making an atonement for the sins of the world he bore the weight, the responsibility, and the burden of the sins of all men, which, to us, is incomprehensible. —*John Taylor* (GK, 116-117)

The moment the atonement of the Savior is done away, that moment, at one sweep, the hopes of salvation entertained by the Christian world are destroyed, the foundation of their faith is taken away, and there is nothing left for them to stand upon. When it is gone all the revelations God ever gave to the Jewish nation, to the Gentiles, and to us are rendered valueless, and all hope is taken from us at one sweep. —*Brigham Young* (BY, 27)

It requires all the atonement of Christ, the mercy of the Father, the pity of angels and the grace of the Lord Jesus Christ to be with us always, and then to do the very best we possibly can, to get rid of this sin within us, so that we may escape from this world into the celestial kingdom. —*Brigham Young* (BY, 60)

God . . . prepared a sacrifice in the gift of His own Son who should be sent in due time, to prepare a way, or open a door through which man might enter into the Lord's presence, whence he had been cast out for disobedience. . . . It must be shedding the blood of the Only Begotten to atone for man; for this was the plan of redemption; and without the shedding of blood was no remission. —*Joseph Smith, Jr.* (STJS, 71)

[W]henever the Lord revealed Himself to men in ancient days, and commanded them to offer sacrifice to Him, that it was done that they might look forward in faith to the time of His coming, and rely upon the power of that atonement for a remission of their sins. . . .

[A]ll things which God communicated to His people were calculated to draw their minds to the great object, and to teach them to rely upon God alone as the author it their salvation, as contained in His law. —*Joseph Smith, Jr.* (STJS, 74)

16. RESURRECTION

On Calvary he was the dying Jesus. From the tomb he emerged the living Christ. The cross had been the bitter fruit of Judas's betrayal, the summary of Peter's denial. The empty tomb now became the testimony of His divinity, the assurance of eternal life. —*Gordon B. Hinckley* (BTE, 87-90)

Of all the events of human history, none is so significant as the resurrection of the Son of God. . . .

Of all the victories in human history, none is so great, none so universal in its effect, none so everlasting in its consequences as the victory of the crucified Lord who came forth in the Resurrection that first Easter morning. —*Gordon B. Hinckley* (Ensign, May 1988, 65-66)

Can anyone believe that the Great Creator would provide for life and growth and achievement only to snuff it all into oblivion in the process of death? Reason says no. Justice demands better answer. The God of heaven has given one. The Lord Jesus Christ provided it.

His was the ultimate sacrifice, His sublime victory.

Doubters there may be. But is there a more fully attested experience in the history of humankind than the resurrection of Jesus that first Easter morn?—*Gordon B. Hinckley* (Ensign, May 1994,73)

Against the medals and monuments of centuries of men's fleeting victories stands the only monument necessary to mark the eternal triumph—an empty garden tomb. —*Howard W. Hunter* (Ensign, May 1986, 15)

Many questions come to men as they travel through this mortal realm, but the one of greatest concern to many is this: Is it true we will be resurrected and live in a future life? . . .

We can come to only one conclusion. The resurrection is a historical fact amply proved by authenticated documentary evidence and the testimony of competent witnesses. The man-made theories devised to discredit are without substantiation, and any discrepancies in the narrative are too slight to be given weight. —*Howard W. Hunter* (CR, Apr. 1963, 105-106)

There is a separation of the spirit and the body at the time of death. The resurrection will again unite the spirit with the body, and the body becomes a spiritual body, one of flesh and bones but quickened by the spirit instead of blood. Thus, our bodies after the resurrection, quickened by the spirit, shall become immortal and never die. —*Howard W. Hunter* (CR, Apr. 1969, 138)

The doctrine of the Resurrection is the single most fundamental and crucial doctrine in the Christian religion. It cannot be overemphasized, nor can it be disregarded. —*Howard W. Hunter* (Ensign, May 1986, 16)

Surely the resurrection is the center of every Christian's faith; it is the greatest of all of the miracles performed by the Savior of the world. Without it, we are indeed left hopeless. —*Howard W. Hunter* (CR, May 1988, 16)

Nothing matters if there is not a resurrection; everything would end in the darkness of death. . . . The reality of a resurrection gives hope; it is uplifting, joy to the righteous. —*Howard W. Hunter* (CN, March 11, 1995, 7)

Because Jesus Christ lives, resurrection will come to all mankind, good and evil. But individual salvation is predicated on more that just acknowledging His atoning sacrifice. Essentially, there must be effort of the part of the individual and compliance with ordinances prescribed by God Himself. —*Ezra Taft Benson* (CUC , 76)

There have been many in this dispensation who have seen Him. As one of those special witnesses so called in this day, I testify to you that He lives with a resurrected body. There is no truth or fact of which I am more confident than the truth of the literal resurrection of our Lord. —*Ezra Taft Benson* (Ensign, Apr. 1991, 2)

The greatest events of history are those which affect the greatest number for the longest periods. By this standard, no event could be more important to individuals or nations than the resurrection of the Master. . . . A glorious resurrection should be the goal of every man and woman, for it is a reality. Nothing is more absolutely universal than the resurrection. Every living being will be resurrected. —*Ezra Taft Benson* (Ensign, Apr. 1993, 4)

Only a God could bring about this miracle of resurrection. As a teacher of righteousness, Jesus could inspire souls to goodness; as a prophet, he could foreshadow the future; as an intelligent leader of men, he could organize a church; and as a possessor and magnifier of the priesthood, he could heal the sick, give sight to the blind, even raise other dead; but only as a God could he raise himself from the tomb, overcome death permanently, and bring incorruption in place of corruption, and replace mortality with immortality. —*Spencer W. Kimball* (SWK, 17)

This body will come forth in the resurrection. It will be free from all imperfections and scars and infirmities which came to it in mortality which were not self-inflicted. Would we have a right to expect a perfect body if we carelessly or intentionally damaged it?—*Spencer W. Kimball* (SWK, 37)

As to the resurrection of mankind taking place in an orderly manner, there can be no doubt, because of the revelations that have been given in this day. Those who are the more righteous will come forth in the morning of the first resurrection, coincident with the second coming of the Savior to this earth, and those less faithful at a time merited by the life each lived here in mortality. —*Harold B. Lee* (YLW, 241)

Heaven is not far removed from him who, in deep sorrow, looks confidently forward to a glorious day of resurrection. —*Harold B. Lee* (YLW, 246)

The only reason we don't have the same assurance about the resurrection as we have about birth is because we are not seeing that happen daily before our eyes as we see birth. Nobody questions the reality of birth, which is just as much a mystery to our understanding as the resurrection of a body that is dead. —*Harold B. Lee* (HBL, 62)

The resurrection is not a hard thing to believe. There are many things harder than that to believe. Life itself is a mystery. What do we know about it? Where does it come from? Is there anything more wonderful than the creation of the body? Why, bless your soul, that is more wonderful than to call together the elements that compose the body after death and cause life to come into them again. —*Joseph Fielding Smith* (CN, June 3, 1933, 5)

After the resurrection from the dead our bodies will be spiritual bodies, but they will be bodies that are tangible, bodies that have been purified, but they will nevertheless be bodies of flesh and bones. They will not be blood bodies. They will no longer be quickened by blood but quickened by the spirit which is eternal, and they shall become immortal and shall never die. —*Joseph Fielding Smith* (CR, Apr. 1917, 62)

Resurrected bodies have control over the elements, How do you think the bodies will get out of the graves at the resurrection? . . . Why should it appear any more impossible for a resurrected being to pass through solid objects than for a spirit, for a spirit is also matter?—*Joseph Fielding Smith* (DS2, 288)

Bodies will come up, of course, as they were laid down, but will be restored to their proper, perfect frame immediately. Old people will not look old when they come forth from the grave. Scars will be removed. No one will be bent or wrinkled. How foolish it would be for a man to come forth in the resurrection who had lost a leg and have to wait for it to grow again. Each body will come forth with its perfect frame. If there has been some deformity or physical impairment in this life, it will be removed. —*Joseph Fielding Smith* (DS2, 292)

To sincere believers in Christianity, to all who accept Christ as their Savior, his resurrection is not a symbolism, but a reality.

As Christ lived after death, so shall all men, each taking his place in the next world for which he has best fitted himself.

With this assurance, obedience to eternal law should be a joy, not a burden, for compliance with the principles of the gospel brings happiness and peace.

To this truth, may each recurring Easter morning give new emphasis and fill our souls with divine assurance that Christ is truly risen and through him man's immortality assured. —*David O. McKay* (GI, 64-65)

The resurrection is a miracle, however, only in the sense that it is beyond man's comprehension and understanding. To all who accept it as fact, it is but a manifestation of a uniform law of life. Because man does not understand the law, he calls it a miracle. There are many people who reject the reality of the resurrection of Jesus. They believe, or profess to believe, in the teachings of Christ, but do not believe in the virgin birth, nor in his literal resurrection from the grave; yet, this latter fact was the very foundation of the early Christian church. —*David O. McKay* (CR, Apr. 1966, 56)

It is nearly two thousand years since Jesus Christ our Lord came to earth and gave his life as a ransom for us that through him all might be resurrected from the dead. —*George Albert Smith* (CR, Apr. 1945, 139)

Not only do we believe that Jesus of Nazareth lived upon the earth, but we believe that he still lives, not as an essence, not as something incorporeal or intangible, but we believe in him as an exalted man; for he arose with the same body that was laid in the tomb of Arimathaea, the same body that was ministered to there by those who loved him. —*George Albert Smith* (GAS, 11)

We have assurance through the revelations that have been given by the Lord our God that the body and the spirit shall be eternally united and that there will come a time, through the blessing and mercy of God, when we will no more have sorrow but when we shall have conquered all of these things that are of a trying and distressing character, and shall stand up in the presence of the living God, filled with joy and peace and satisfaction. —*Heber J. Grant* (IE, 43:350)

A man will not awake on resurrection morning to find that all that he neglected to do in mortal life has been put to the credit side of his account and that the debit side of his ledger shows a clean page. . . . He whose every act has fitted him for the enjoyment of eternity will be far in advance of the man whose all has been centered on the things of this life. —*Heber J. Grant* (LPS, 19)

We are destined to come forth out of the grave as Jesus did, and to obtain immortal bodies as he did—that is, that our tabernacles are to become immortal as his became immortal, that the spirit and the body may be joined together and become one living being, indivisible, inseparable, eternal. —*Joseph F. Smith* (GD, 32-33)

I accept the doctrine of the resurrection with all my heart, and rejoice at its confirmation in nature with the awakening of each returning spring. The Spirit of God testifies to me, and has revealed to me, to my complete personal satisfaction, that there is life after death, and that the body which we lay down here will be reunited with our spirit, to become a perfect soul, capable of receiving a fulness of joy in the presence of God. —*Joseph F. Smith* (IE, 16:508-510)

Jesus, the Only Begotten of the Father . . . had power to lay down His life and take it up again, and if we keep inviolate the covenants of the gospel, remaining faithful and true to the end, we too, in His name and through His redeeming blood, will have power in due time to resurrect these our bodies after they shall have been committed to the earth. —*Joseph F. Smith* (JD, 18:227)

In the next life we will have our bodies glorified and free from sickness and death. Nothing is so beautiful as a person in a resurrected and glorified condition. There is nothing more lovely than to be in this condition and have our wives and children and friends with us. —*Lorenzo Snow* (CR, Oct. 1900, 63)

There is nothing more beautiful to look upon than a resurrected man or woman. There is nothing grander that I can imagine that a man can possess than a resurrected body. —*Lorenzo Snow* (CR, Oct. 1900, 4)

I believe in the resurrection of the dead, and I know it is a true principle. —*Wilford Woodruff* (WW, 285)

He had power, when all mankind had lost their life, to restore life to them again; and hence He is the Resurrection and the Life, which power no other man possesses. —*John Taylor* (LPS, 283)

Man is an eternal being; his body is eternal. It may die and slumber, but it will burst the barriers of the tomb and come forth in the resurrection of the just. —*John Taylor* (JD, 13:230)

The body is not perfect without the spirit, nor the spirit without the body; it takes the two to make a perfect man, for the spirit requires a tabernacle to give it power to develop itself and to exalt it in the scale of intelligence, both in time and eternity. —*John Taylor* (LPS, 41)

The only true riches in existence are for you and me to secure for ourselves a holy resurrection. —*Brigham Young* (BY, 372)

The resurrection from the dead may also, with propriety, be called a birth. —*Brigham Young* (BY, 374)

As concerning the resurrection, I will merely say that all men will come from the grave as they lie down, whether old or young; there will not be "added unto their stature one cubit," neither taken from it; all will be raised by the power of God, having spirit in their bodies, and not blood. —*Joseph Smith, Jr.* (STJS, 227)

All your losses will be made up to you in the resurrection, provided you continue faithful. . . .

The expectation of seeing my friends in the morning of the resurrection cheers my soul and makes me bear up against the evils of life. It is like their taking a long journey, and on their return we meet them with increased joy. —*Joseph Smith, Jr.* (STJS, 328-329)

17. THE JUDGMENT

The first principles alone are not sufficient; man is thereafter accountable in the eternal judgment for what he has done in life, whether good or evil. The atonement was for this very purpose, to bring about the resurrection and subsequent judgment of all men. —*Howard W. Hunter* (CR, Apr. 1973, 174)

God judges us not only by what we do, but by what we would do and desire to do if we had the opportunity. He will not withhold any blessing from us of which we are truly worthy. —*Ezra Taft Benson* (ETB, 362)

At the end of that millennial period we will all stand judgment. There is a partial judgment before, but the final judgment will be at the end. Then this earth will undergo a change and receive its paradisiacal glory and will be made a fit abode for the celestial beings. Those who live to inherit the celestial kingdom will live on this earth eternally. This is made very clear in the scriptures. —*Ezra Taft Benson* (ETB, 38)

In the judgment of God there will be no injustice and no soul will receive any blessing, reward, or glory which he has not earned, and no soul will be punished through deprivation or otherwise for anything of which he was not guilty. —*Spencer W. Kimball* (SWK, 47)

The Lord is merciful, but mercy cannot rob justice. His mercy extended to us when he died for us. His justice prevails when he judges us and give us the blessings which we have duly earned. —*Spencer W. Kimball* (Ensign, Aug. 1974, 2)

The judgment we shall face will be before the Righteous Judge who will take into account our capacities and our limitations, our opportunities and our handicaps. One who sins and repents and thereafter fills his life with purposeful effort may not lose as much in that day of righteous judgment as one who, though not committing serious sin, falls down miserably by omitting to do that which he had capacity and opportunity to do but would not. —*Harold B. Lee* (DSL, 100-101)

There are no successful sinners. All must one day stand before God and be judged, each according to the deeds done in the flesh. What do you think now? Is the burden of the sinner lighter than that of the saint?—*Harold B. Lee* (SHP, 221-222)

We are own judges of the place we shall have in the eternal world. Here and now in mortality, each one of us is having the opportunity of choosing the kind of laws we elect to obey. . . . The place we shall occupy in the eternal worlds will be determined by the obedience we yield to the laws of these various kingdoms during the time we have here in mortality upon this earth. —*Harold B. Lee* (HBL, 64)

The only measure by which you are going to be measured is, How will you compare with what you had the capacity to do? That is the measure the Lord's going to measure you by, to see whether or not you have done, to the best of your ability, whatever came within your hands this day. —*Harold B. Lee* (HBL, 64)

Suppose that when we meet the Master there is a frown, and he turned and shook His head and turned sadly away. Can you imagine anything that would be quite so discouraging or quite so heartbreaking? There will be nothing so terrifying to the human soul as to be told on resurrection morning that they will have to wait a thousand years before they shall come forth from the grave in resurrection. But imagine instead of that, He smiles, He opens his arms, and says "Come into my presence. You have been faithful in a few things, I will make you ruler over many things. —*Harold B. Lee* (HBL, 67)

That path which leads into the presence of God is straight, it is also strait, which means that those who enter into it will find it restricted; it is narrow; they cannot take with them that which does not apply, or which does not belong to the kingdom of God. All such things must be left behind when we enter into this narrow way which leads into the presence of God, where we can receive life eternal. —*Joseph Fielding Smith* (CN, Feb. 12, 1938, 3)

Every man will be judged according to his works, his opportunities for receiving the truth, and the intent of his heart. —*Joseph Fielding Smith* (IE, 20:360)

We have our agency and many, very, very many members of this Church, when they come to the judgment and are judged according to their works, are going to be consigned to the telestial kingdom; others to the terrestrial kingdom; because that is the law that they have willed to obey; and we are going to get our reward according to the law that we obey. —*Joseph Fielding Smith* (CN, Apr. 22, 623)

Who desires to enter the eternal world and be a servant, when the promise is held out that we may be sons and daughters of God? Yet there will be the vast majority who will enter into the eternal world as servants, and not as sons, and this simply because they think more of the world and its covenants, than they do of God and his covenants; simply because in their blindness of heart, they refuse to keep these sacred and holy commandments. Oh, what bitterness there will be in the day of judgment, when every man receives his reward according to his works!—*Joseph Fielding Smith* (IE, 34:706)

Salvation is an individual matter, and if a person who has been born under the covenant rebels and denies the Lord, he will lose the blessings of exaltation. Every soul will be judged according to his works and the wicked cannot inherit eternal life. We cannot force salvation upon those who do not want it. —*Joseph Fielding Smith* (DS2, 91)

Those who die without law will be redeemed, because they will be judged without law. But all who have received law and who have known the truth in a degree will be judged according to the truth that they have known, and if they have not lived up to that which they have known, or which they have been taught or had the privilege of receiving, then they cannot enter into the celestial kingdom. —*Joseph Fielding Smith* (CR, Oct. 1911, 120)

We are living eternal life, and our position hereafter will be the result of our lives here. Every man will be judged according to his works, and he will receive only that degree of glory that he has earned. —*George Albert Smith* (CR, Apr. 1945, 139)

We will not be judged as our brothers and sisters of the world are judged, but according to the greater opportunities placed in our keeping. We will be among those who have received the word of the Lord, who have heard His sayings, and if we do them it will be to us eternal life, but if we fail condemnation will result. —*George Albert Smith* (CR, Oct. 1906, 47)

If we only understood how near we are to the Judgment Day there are men and women in the various communities of this world who would now be on their knees in sack-cloth and ashes; but they think that time is so far off that they procrastinate the day of repentance. —*George Albert Smith* (CR, Oct. 1935, 121)

Every man will have to render an account of his stewardship, and every one will be held responsible for his own words, whether good or evil. . . . He knows our imperfections—all the causes, the "whys and wherefores" are made manifest unto Him. He judges us by our acts and the intents of our hearts. His judgments will be true, just and righteous; ours are obscured by the imperfections of man. —*Joseph F. Smith* (JD, 24:78)

Thank God for that noble, that just, that Godlike principle of the gospel of Jesus Christ, that every one of us will have to give an account for the deeds we do in the flesh, and that every man will be rewarded according to his works, whether they be good or evil. —*Joseph F. Smith* (LPS, 53)

We shall not be cast off, my brethren and sisters, for those sins which we ignorantly commit, which are the results of misunderstanding in all honesty before the Lord. The difficulty does not lie here; the danger lies in our failing to live up to that which we do know to be right and proper. For this we will be held responsible before the Lord; for this we will be judged and condemned unless we repent. —*Joseph F. Smith* (JD, 20:26)

We judge a man not always by his looks or appearance; not always by hearing him preach a sermon; but we judge him by what he has done or failed to do in the past. That is just the way the Lord intends to do with you or me exactly. We will be judged according to what we have done or what we have failed to [do] all along the line of our experiences. —*Lorenzo Snow* (CR, Oct. 1900, 3)

I expect that the Savior was about right when he said, in reference to the members of the Church, that five of them were wise and five were foolish; for when the Lord of heaven comes in power and great glory to reward every man according to the deeds done in the body, if he finds one half of those professing to be members of his Church prepared for salvation, it will be as many as can be expected, judging by the course that many are pursuing. —*Wilford Woodruff* (WW, 254)

[G]od has made each man a register within himself, and each man can read his own register, so far as he enjoys his perfect faculties. This can be easily comprehended. . . .

Now, if you are in possession of a spirit or intellectuality of that kind, whereby you are enabled to read your own acts, do you not think that that being who has placed that spirit and that intelligence within you holds the keys of that intelligence, and can read it whenever he pleases? Is not that philosophical, reasonable, and scriptural? I think it is. —*John Taylor* (GK, 25-26)

If I had time to enter into this subject alone, I could show you upon scientific principles that man himself is a self-registering machine, his eyes, his ears, his nose, the touch, the taste, and all the various senses of the body are so many media whereby man lays up for himself a record which perhaps nobody else is acquainted with but himself; and when the time comes for that record to be unfolded, all men that have eyes to see, and ears to hear, will be able to read all things as God himself reads them and comprehends them, and all things, we are told, are naked and open before him. —*John Taylor* (GK, 36)

It is not because somebody has seen things, or heard anything by which a man will be judged and condemned, but it is because that record that is written by the man himself in the tablets of his own mind—that record that cannot lie—will in that day be unfolded before God and angels, and those who shall sit as judges. —*John Taylor* (JD, 24:232)

We may succeed in hiding our affairs from men; but it is written that for every word and every secret thought we shall have to give an account in the day when accounts have to be rendered before God, when hypocrisy and fraud of any kind will not avail us; for by our works we shall be justified, or by them we shall be condemned. —*John Taylor* (JD, 24:232)

This is a subject I have reflected upon a great deal, and I have come to the conclusion that we shall be judged according to the deeds done in the body and according to the thoughts and intents of the heart. —*Brigham Young* (BY, 382)

I am far from believing that the children of men have been deprived of the privilege of receiving the Spirit of the Lord to teach them right from wrong. No matter what the traditions of their fathers were, those who were honest before the Lord, and acted uprightly, according to the best knowledge they had, will have an opportunity to go into the Kingdom of God. —*Brigham Young* (BY, 32)

Each and every intelligent being will be judged according to the deeds done in the body, according to his works, faith, desires, and honesty or dishonesty before God; every trait of his character will receive its just merit or demerit, and he will be judged according to the law of heaven. —*Brigham Young* (JD, 8:154)

If our souls and our bodies are not looking forth for the coming of the Son of Man; and after we are dead, if we are not looking forth, we shall be among those who are calling for the rocks to fall upon them. —*Joseph Smith, Jr.* (STJS, 182)

The great misery of departed spirits in the world of spirits, where they go after death, is to know that they come short of the glory that others enjoy and that they might have enjoyed themselves, and they are their own accusers. —*Joseph Smith, Jr.* (STJS, 347-348)

[T]here is to be a day when all will be judged of their works, and rewarded according to the same; that those who have kept the faith will be crowned with a crown of righteousness; be clothed in white raiment; be admitted to the marriage feast; be free from every affliction, and reign with Christ on the earth. —*Joseph Smith, Jr.* (STJS, 79-80)

A man is his own tormentor and his own condemner. Hence the saying, They shall go into the lake that burns with fire and brimstone. The torment of disappointment in the mind of man is as exquisite as a lake burning with fire and brimstone. I say, so is the torment of man. —*Joseph Smith, Jr.* (STJS, 401)

God judges men according to the use they make of the light which He gives them. —*Joseph Smith, Jr.* (STJS, 339)

18. Eternal Life—Kingdoms of Glory

Immortality is a free gift to all men because of the resurrection of Jesus Christ. Eternal life is the quality of life enjoyed by our Heavenly Father. Those who fully comply with His commandments believe the promise that they will have this quality of life. —*Ezra Taft Benson* (ETB, 26)

[N]ot all who claim to be Latter-day Saints will be exalted. —*Spencer W. Kimball* (MF, 7-9)

After a person has been assigned to his place in the kingdom, either in the telestial, the terrestrial, or the celestial, or to his exaltation, he will never advance from his assigned glory to another glory. That is eternal! That is why we must make our decisions early in life and why it is imperative that such decisions be right. —*Spencer W. Kimball* (MF , 243-244)

Some might say, "Well, I'd be satisfied to just become an angel," but you would not. One never would be satisfied just to be a ministering angel to wait upon other people when he could be the king himself. —*Spencer W. Kimball* (SWK, 51)

Exaltation requires diligence. Why will only a few reach exaltation in the celestial kingdom? Not because it was not available to them, not because they did not know of its availability, not because the testimony was not given to them, but because they would not put forth the effort to pattern their lives and make them like the Savior's life and establish them so well that there would be no deviation until the end. —*Spencer W. Kimball* (SWK, 52)

In order to gain entrance into the Kingdom of Heaven we must not only be good but we are required to do good and be good for something. —*Harold B. Lee* (DSL, 60)

Here upon this earth, when it is cleansed from unrighteousness, will be the eternal abode of you who are judged worthy of celestial glory. Here you may dwell without sin and without death with the redeemed of your Father's house and your posterity throughout eternity. —*Harold B. Lee* (DSL, 187)

One who lives . . . worthy of a testimony that God lives and that Jesus is the Christ, and who is willing to reach out to Him in constant inquiry to know if his course is approved, is the one who is living life to its full abundance here and is preparing for the celestial world, which is to live eternally with his Heavenly Father. —*Harold B. Lee* (SHP, 103)

Salvation means the attainment of the eternal right to live in the presence of God the Father and the Son as a reward for a good life in mortality. . . . In the choices of life—our friends, our education, our vocation, our companion in marriage—all these and more must be made with an eye single to eternal life. —*Harold B. Lee* (SHP, 334-335)

Immortality is a free gift to all mankind, but eternal life must be won by deeds done in the flesh. —*Harold B. Lee* (YLW, 254)

If you couldn't live the law of the gospel here, you wouldn't be very happy in the celestial kingdom where that is required over there, would you? You would have to be more comfortable in another place. —*Harold B. Lee* (HBL, 75-76)

Now, when we fail of that highest degree of glory and realize what we've lost, there will be a burning of the conscience that will be worse than any physical kind of fire that I assume one could suffer. —*Harold B. Lee* (HBL, 67)

No one can be deprived of exaltation who remains faithful. In other words, an undeserving husband cannot prevent a faithful wife from an exaltation and vice versa. In this case the faithful servant would be given to someone who is faithful. —*Joseph Fielding Smith* (DS2, 65)

This earth is a living body. It is true to the law given it. It was created to become a celestial body and the abode for celestial beings. —*Joseph Fielding Smith* (DS1, 72)

Very gladly would the Lord give to everyone eternal life, but since that blessing can come only on merit—through the faithful performance of duty—only those who are worthy shall receive it. . . . Such is the great mercy of the Lord. He will endeavor to save all his children and exalt as many as he possibly can. —*Joseph Fielding Smith* (DS2, 5-6)

Exaltation is to dwell in the presence of God and to be like him. —*Joseph Fielding Smith* (DS2, 13)

The time will come when "every knee shall bow, and every tongue shall confess," and yet the vast majority of mankind will go into the telestial kingdom eternally. —*Joseph Fielding Smith* (CN, Apr. 22, 1939, 7)

It has been asked if it is possible for one who inherits the telestial glory to advance in time to the celestial glory?
The answer to this question is, No! . . . .
The terrestrial and the telestial are limited in their powers of advancement, worlds without end. —*Joseph Fielding Smith* (DS2, 31-32)

What is damnation? It is being barred, or denied privileges of progression, because of failure to comply with law. All who fail to enter into the celestial kingdom are damned, or stopped in their progression, but they will enter into some other glory which they are entitled to receive. —*Joseph Fielding Smith* (IE, 19:427-428)

Eternal life is God's greatest gift to man, and the Lord in turn is glorified in man's immortality. Eternal life is the result of knowledge, and knowledge is obtained by doing the will of God. —*David O. McKay* (GI, 8)

In what, then, does true immortality consist? It consists in the persistence of personality after death. —*David O. McKay* (GI, 54)

God is our Father. He is the Father of our spirits and He has offered to His children in the world an inheritance if they will accept it, and that inheritance is eternal life in the celestial kingdom. Every one of His children has been or will be offered that opportunity. It doesn't make any difference what nationality we may belong to, if we keep the commandments of our Heavenly Father we will find eventually our place in the celestial kingdom. —*George Albert Smith* (SGO, 216)

It is not necessary for a man to be a president of a stake, or a member of the Quorum of the Twelve, in order to attain a high place in the celestial kingdom. The humblest member of the Church, if he keeps the commandments of God, will attain an exaltation just as much as any other man in the celestial kingdom. —*George Albert Smith* (CR, Oct. 1933, 25)

We will attain our exaltation in the Celestial Kingdom only on the condition that we share with our Father's other children the blessings of the Gospel of Jesus Christ and observe the commandments that will enrich our lives here and hereafter. —*George Albert Smith* (CR, Oct. 1938, 32)

This earth is the property of our Heavenly Father. Some day it will be cleansed and purified by fire. All disease and sorrow will be banished from it and it will become the celestial kingdom. —*George Albert Smith* (LPS, 268)

There are some people who have supposed that if we are quickened telestial bodies that eventually, throughout the ages of eternity, we will continue to progress until we will find our place in the celestial kingdom, but the scriptures and revelations of God have said that those who are quickened telestial bodies cannot come where God and Christ dwell, worlds without end. —*George Albert Smith* (CR, Oct. 1945, 172)

We as Latter-day Saints have all started out for the gift of salvation, and we should so order our lives that when we have finished our work we shall be worthy to go back into the presence of our Father and be worthy not only to receive an exaltation ourselves, but also to receive our wives and our children that have been sealed unto us that we shall possess them. —*Heber J. Grant* (CR, Oct. 1900, 59)

What are we working for? Wealth? Riches? If we have embraced the gospel of Jesus Christ, then we are working for eternal life. —*Heber J. Grant* (GS, 182)

I submit as a proposition that cannot be controverted, that no man can be exalted in the presence of God and attain to a fulness of glory and happiness in his kingdom and presence, save and except he will obey the plan that God has devised and revealed. —*Joseph F. Smith* (CR, Apr. 1902, 86)

We are immortal beings, and we are looking forward to the growth that is to be attained in an exalted life after we have proved ourselves faithful and true to the covenants that we have entered into here, and then we will receive a fulness of joy. —*Joseph F. Smith* (GD, 277-278)

We believe that we are on the road of advancement, of development in knowledge, in understanding, and in every good thing, and that we will continue to grow, advance, and develop throughout the eternities that are before us. That is what we believe. —*Joseph F. Smith* (CR, Apr. 1912, 8)

They are the offspring of the Almighty, He loves them all and His plans are for the salvation of the whole, and He will bring all up into that position in which they will be as happy and as comfortable as they are willing to be. —*Lorenzo Snow* (LS, 91)

The whole earth is the Lord's. The time will come when it will be translated and be filled with the Spirit and power of God. The atmosphere around it will be the Spirit of the Almighty. We will breathe that Spirit instead of the atmosphere that we now breathe. —*Lorenzo Snow* (LS, 191)

Godliness cannot be conferred, but must be acquired. —*Lorenzo Snow* (LPS, 79)

If you and I ever get into the celestial kingdom, we have got to keep the law of that kingdom. Show me the law that a man keeps and I will tell you where he is going. —*Wilford Woodruff* (LPS, 63)

No man, in time or in eternity, will ever be saved in the celestial kingdom of God without the gospel of Christ. —*Wilford Woodruff* (LPS, 87)

[N]o man will receive a celestial glory unless he abides a celestial law; no man will receive a terrestrial glory unless he abides a terrestrial law, and no man will receive a telestial glory unless he abides a telestial law. —*Wilford Woodruff* (WW, 111-112)

In the celestial kingdom of God there is oneness—there is union. —*Wilford Woodruff* (WW, 127)

How few there are on the earth today, or in any dispensation, who have been able to abide the celestial law of God. It brings down the hatred of the whole generation in which we live. No man can live the celestial law without bringing upon his head persecution. —*Wilford Woodruff* (JD, 22:209)

I marvel very much at the little interest manifested by the inhabitants of the earth generally in their future state. There is not a person here today but what is going to live on the other side of the veil as long as his Creator—to the endless ages of eternity, and the eternal destiny of every individual depends upon the manner in which the few short years of the life in the flesh are spent. I ask, in the name of the Lord, what is popularity to you or me? What is gold or silver, or this world's goods to any of us, any further than to enable us to obtain what we need to eat, drink, and wear, and to build up the kingdom of God? And for us to stop praying, and to become crazy after the riches of the world, is the very height of foolishness and folly. To see the way that some people act, you might suppose that they are going to live here eternally, and that their eternal destiny depends upon the number of dollars they have. —*Wilford Woodruff* (WW, 243)

I always have said and believed, and I believe today, that it will pay you and me and all the sons and all the daughters of Adam to abide the celestial law, for celestial glory is worth all we possess. If it calls for every dollar we own and our lives in the bargain, if we obtain an entrance into the celestial kingdom of God, it will amply repay us.

The Latter-day Saints have started out for celestial glory, and if we can only manage to be faithful enough to obtain an inheritance in the kingdom, where God and Christ dwell, we shall rejoice through the endless ages of eternity. —*Wilford Woodruff* (WW, 262)

We are placed here that it may be seen which law we will keep. Our Heavenly Father has placed before us the laws celestial, telestial, and terrestrial. If any man will obey the celestial law, he will be preserved by that law; all the glory, power and exaltation, belonging to that law, will be given to him. —*Wilford Woodruff* (WW, 268-269)

Is God merciful? Yes. Will he treat his children well? Yes. He will do the very best he can for all. But there are certain eternal laws by which the Gods in the eternal worlds are governed and which they cannot violate, and do not want to violate. These eternal principles must be kept, and one principle is that no unclean thing can enter into the kingdom of God. What, then, will be the result? Why, the people I have referred to—people who do not keep the celestial law—will have to go into a lesser kingdom, into a terrestrial, or perhaps a telestial, as the case may be. Is this according to the law of God? Yes, for if they are not prepared for the celestial kingdom, they must go to such a one as they are prepared to endure. —*John Taylor* (GK, 19)

We are told that if we cannot abide the law of the celestial kingdom we cannot inherit a celestial glory. Is not that doctrine? Yes. "But," says one, "are not we all going into the celestial kingdom?" I think not, unless we turn round and mend our ways very materially. It is only those who can abide a celestial glory and obey a celestial law that will be prepared to enter a celestial kingdom. —*John Taylor* (GK, 20)

It would be no blessing to you to be carried into the celestial kingdom, and obliged to stay therein, unless you were prepared to dwell there. —*Brigham Young* (BY, 95)

How many glories and kingdoms will there be in eternity? You will see the same variety in eternity as you see in the world. —*Brigham Young* (BY, 382)

A certain class of this people will go into the celestial kingdom, while others cannot enter there, because they cannot abide a celestial law; but they will attain to as good a kingdom as they desire and live for. —*Brigham Young* (BY, 383)

The men and women, who desire to obtain seats in the celestial kingdom, will find that they must battle every day. —*Brigham Young* (BY, 392)

God has in reserve a time, or period appointed in His own bosom, when He will bring all His subjects, who have obeyed His voice and kept His commandments, into His celestial rest. This rest is of such perfection and glory, that man has need of a preparation before he can, according to the laws of that kingdom, enter it and enjoy its blessings. —*Joseph Smith, Jr.* (STJS, 67)

Then I would exhort you to go on and continue to call upon God until you make your calling and election sure for yourselves, by obtaining this more sure word of prophecy, and wait patiently for the promise until you obtain it, etc. —*Joseph Smith, Jr.* (STJS, 333)

It is one thing to see the kingdom of God, and another thing to enter into it. We must have a change of heart to see the kingdom of God, and subscribe the articles of adoption to enter therein. —*Joseph Smith, Jr.* (STJS, 369)

Could you gaze into heaven five minutes, you would know more than you would by reading all that ever was written on the subject. —*Joseph Smith, Jr.* (STJS, 365)

When you climb up a ladder, you must begin at the bottom, and ascend step by step, until you arrive at the top; and so it is with the principles of the Gospel—you must begin with the first, and go on until you learn all the principles of exaltation. But it will be a great while after you have passed through the veil before you will have learned them. It is not all to be comprehended in this world; it will be a great work to learn our salvation and exaltation even beyond the grave. —*Joseph Smith, Jr.* (STJS, 392-393)

PRINCIPLES AND ORDINANCES

19. PRINCIPLES AND ORDINANCES

No force on earth can stop the Almighty from pouring down knowledge from heaven upon the heads of the Latter-day Saints if we will live in righteousness, obey the principles of the gospel, do what we ought to do as members of The Church of Jesus Christ of Latter-day Saints, and walk in obedience to the commandments of God. We will then receive enlightenment and knowledge and understanding and faith, and our lives will be enriched and be made more happy and more fruitful. —*Gordon B. Hinckley* (CN, Sept. 30, 1995, 2)

The pathway to exaltation is well defined. We are told to have faith—faith in the Lord Jesus Christ, and repent of those things which are not according to his teachings. After this change of mental attitude, and with firm resolution, we must declare ourselves by going into the waters of baptism, thereby making a covenant with the Lord to keep his commandments. Can we thereafter be a secret disciple? Can we stand on the sidelines and merely observe? This is a day for action. This is the time for decision, not tomorrow, not next week. This is the time to make our covenant with the Lord. Now is the time for those who have been noncommittal or who have had a halfhearted interest to come out boldly and declare belief in Christ and be willing to demonstrate faith by works. —*Howard W. Hunter* (CR, Oct. 1960, 109)

Truth is often on the scaffold—error on the throne. But time is on the side of truth, for truth is eternal. —*Ezra Taft Benson* (IE, Dec. 1965, 1151)

A man must not only stand for the right principles, but he must fight for them. Those who fight for principles can be proud of the friends they have gained and the enemies they have earned. —*Ezra Taft Benson* (ETB, 395)

The principles upon which the Church was established are divine and they have been clearly outlined, but the means of embracing and putting into operation those principles, the Lord has left very largely up to us to work out and plan. —*Ezra Taft Benson* (ETB, 148)

Man cannot be saved in ignorance of those saving principles of the gospel of Jesus Christ even if he were to have all the book learning in the world. —*Harold B. Lee* (SHP, 76)

A truth of the gospel is not a truth until you live it. You do not really believe in tithing and it is not a truth of the gospel to you until you pay it. The Word of Wisdom is not a truth of the gospel to you until you keep it. The Sabbath day is not a holy day unless you observe it. Fasting and paying fast offerings, consecrating your fast, are not truths of the gospel unless you live them. Temple marriage does not mean anything to you unless you have a temple marriage. A friend is not a friend unless you defend him. —*Harold B. Lee* (YLW, 37-38)

Every ordinance is sealed, with a promise of a reward based upon faithfulness. The Holy Spirit withdraws the stamp of approval where covenants are broken. —*Joseph Fielding Smith* (CN, Apr. 27, 1935, 7)

The gospel covenant is the promise of God to grant to man, through man's obedience and acceptance of the ordinances and principles of the gospel, the glory and exaltation of eternal life. It is the Father in Heaven who stipulates the terms of the covenant. Man has no say in the matter or right to alter or annul any provision of the covenant. His duty is to accept on the terms which are presented to him from the Almighty, in full faith and obedience, without complaint or desire because of personal weakness to alter or annul, what the Father offers for man's salvation. —*Joseph Fielding Smith* (CN, May 6, 1939, 3)

What is the new and everlasting covenant? I regret to say that there are some members of the Church who are misled and misinformed in regard to what the new and everlasting covenant really is. The new and everlasting covenant is the sum total of all gospel covenants and obligations. —*Joseph Fielding Smith* (CN, May 6, 1939, 5)

By fulness of the gospel is meant all the ordinances and principles that pertain to the exaltation in the celestial kingdom. —*Joseph Fielding Smith* (IE, 30:736)

There is no reason in the world why each member of the Church should not have a thorough understanding of the principles of the gospel, of the order of the Church, and the government of the Church, so that none need be led astray by any wind of doctrine, or notion that prevails among the children of men, which may come to his attention. —*Joseph Fielding Smith* (CR, Oct. 1918, 54)

Thousands upon thousands have died without repentance and remission of sins simply because they never heard the plan of salvation, and yet they were in all respects just as worthy as you and I. The justice of God will not bar them from his kingdom just because they never heard the gospel message; but the same conformance to the principles and obedience to law will be required of them as the Lord requires of the living. This is both just and reasonable; it is also scriptural. —*Joseph Fielding Smith* (DS2, 137)

This abundant life is obtained not only from spiritual exultation, but also by the application to daily life of the principles that Jesus taught. —*David O. McKay* (CR, Oct. 1937, 102)

There is no one great thing which we can do to obtain eternal life, and it seems to me that the great lesson to be learned in the world today is to apply in the little acts and duties of life the glorious principles of the gospel. —*David O. McKay* (CR, Oct. 1914, 88)

Faith, repentance, baptism by immersion, (for that was the form of baptism that our Master received) laying on of hands for the gift of the Holy Ghost, as taught by him, are the requirements in his Church that all men must subscribe to if they would obtain celestial glory. —*George Albert Smith* (CR, Oct. 1922, 99)

Every principle of the gospel has been revealed to us for our individual advancement and for our individual perfection. —*Heber J. Grant* (LPS, 87)

[T]hose who have not had the gospel preached to them in the flesh, will hear it in the spirit, for all must have the plan of salvation presented to them for their acceptance or rejection before they can become amenable to the law. —*Joseph F. Smith* (GD, 91)

It should be the desire of the Latter-day Saints to become as big and broad as the gospel which has been divinely revealed to them. They should, therefore, hold themselves open to the acceptance of all the truths of the gospel that have been revealed, that are now being revealed, and that will be revealed hereafter, and adopt them in the conduct of their daily lives. —*Joseph F. Smith* (IE, 15:845)

We should be men and women of faith and power as well as good works; and when we discover ourselves careless or indifferent in the least, it should be sufficient for us to know it in order to mend our ways and return to the path of duty. —*Lorenzo Snow* (LS, 48)

Establish the principles of Zion in your hearts, and then you will be worthy to receive Zion outside. —*Lorenzo Snow* (LS, 182)

I have heard many men say no ordinances are necessary, that belief only in the Lord Jesus Christ is necessary to be saved. I have not learned that myself from any revelation of God to man, either ancient or modern. But on the contrary, faith in Christ, repentance, and baptism for the remission of sins were taught by patriarchs and prophets and by Jesus Christ and His apostles. —*Wilford Woodruff* (WW, 19)

It is of the greatest importance that everything we do, that every ordinance we administer, that every principle we believe in, should be strictly in accordance with the mind and word, the will and law of God. —*John Taylor* (GK, 20)

There is not a principle associated with the gospel of the Son of God but what is eternal in its nature and consequences, and we cannot with impunity trample upon any principle that is correct without having to suffer the penalty thereof before God and the holy angels, and in many instances before men. —*John Taylor* (GK, 90)

We must carry out the word and will of God, for we cannot afford to ignore it nor any part of it. If faith, repentance, and baptism, and laying on of hands are right and true and demand our obedience, so do cooperation and the United Order. —*John Taylor* (GK, 250)

I do not think we can choose one principle and reject another to suit ourselves. I think that all of these things, as we have received them, one after another, are equally binding upon us. —*John Taylor* (GK, 251)

The principles of eternity and eternal exaltation are of no use to us, unless they are brought down to our capacities so that we practice them in our lives. —*Brigham Young* (BY, 14)

Show me one principle that has originated by the power of the Devil. You cannot do it. I call evil inverted good, or a correct principle made an evil use of. —*Brigham Young* (BY, 69)

The most effectual way to establish the religion of Heaven is to live it, rather than to die for it: I think I am safe in saying that there are many of the Latter-day Saints who are more willing to die for their religion than to live it faithfully. —*Brigham Young* (BY, 221)

True principles will abide, while all false principles will fall with those who choose and cleave to them. —*Brigham Young* (BY, 261)

All the ordinances, systems, and administrations on the earth are of no use to the children of men, unless they are ordained and authorized of God; for nothing will save a man but a legal administrator; for none others will be acknowledged either by God or angels. —*Joseph Smith, Jr.* (STJS, 305-310)

Repent of all your sins, and be baptized in water for the remission of them, in the name of the Father, and of the Son, and of the Holy Ghost, and receive the ordinance of the laying on of the hands of him who is ordained and sealed unto this power, that ye may receive the Holy Spirit of God. . . . These are the requirements of the new covenant, or first principles of the Gospel of Christ. —*Joseph Smith, Jr.* (STJS, 23)

Faith comes by hearing the word of god, through the testimony of the servants of God; that testimony is always attended by the Spirit of prophecy and revelation.

Repentance is a thing that cannot be trifled with every day. Daily transgression and daily repentance is not that which is pleasing in the sight of God.

Baptism is a holy ordinance preparatory to the reception of the Holy Ghost; it is the channel and key by which the Holy Ghost will be administered.

The Gift of the Holy Ghost by the laying on of hands, cannot be received through the medium of any other principle than the principle of righteousness, for if the proposals are not complied with, it is of no use, but withdraws. —*Joseph Smith, Jr.* (STJS, 169)

I preached to a large congregation at the stand, on the science and practice of medicine, desiring to persuade the Saints to trust in God when sick, and not in an arm of flesh, and live by faith and not by medicine, or poison; and when they were sick, and had called for the Elders to pray for them, and they were not healed, to use herbs and mild food. —*Joseph Smith, Jr.* (STJS, 216)

Now taking it for granted that the scriptures say what they mean, and mean what they say, we have sufficient grounds to go on and prove from the Bible that the gospel has always been the same; the ordinances to fulfill its requirements, the same, and the officers to officiate, the same; and the signs and fruits resulting from the promises, the same. —*Joseph Smith, Jr.* (STJS, 297)

The more sure word of prophecy means a man's knowing that he is sealed up unto eternal life by revelation and the spirit of prophecy, through the power of the holy priesthood. It is impossible for a man to be saved in ignorance. —*Joseph Smith, Jr.* (STJS, 336)

Ordinances instituted in the heavens before the foundation of the world, in the priesthood, for the salvation of men, are not to be altered or changed. All must be saved on the same principles. —*Joseph Smith, Jr.* (STJS, 344)

20. BAPTISM

Baptism is the primary ordinance of the gospel. It is the gate through which all come into the Church. It is so important that it is performed not only for the living but also for the dead, because those who are beyond the veil of death cannot move forward on the way to eternal life without this ordinance having been administered in their behalf. —*Gordon B. Hinckley* (Ensign, May 1988, 45-46)

May I suggest that in my judgment, no person who is a member of this church and has taken upon himself the covenants incident to membership can reasonably expect the blessings of the Lord upon his efforts unless being willing to bear his share of the burden of the Lord's kingdom. —*Gordon B. Hinckley* (Ensign, Jan. 1994, 6)

Before investigators are baptized they should commit themselves to each of the principles of the gospel. An investigator who will not commit to praying, going to Church, or living the Word of Wisdom is certainly not prepared for the serious baptismal covenant. —*Ezra Taft Benson* (ETB, 75)

Before being baptized the new convert should understand that this Church is like a bee-hive, and that activity earns the rewards of heaven, and that just believing will not take one far in his quest toward exaltation. —*Spencer W. Kimball* (SWK, 565)

Baptism is the door into the celestial kingdom. —*Joseph Fielding Smith* (DS2, 45)

The Lord has placed—and that in his own judgment—the age of accountability at eight years. After we get to be eight years of age, we are supposed to have understanding suffi-cient that we should be baptized. The Lord takes care of those who are under that age. —*Joseph Fielding Smith* (CN, Apr. 29, 1939, 7)

The mode of baptism is by immersion in water. . . . Baptism cannot be by any other means than immersion of the entire body in water, for the following reasons:
1. It is in the similitude of the death, burial, and resurrection of Jesus Christ, and of all others who have received the resurrection.
2. Baptism is also a birth and is performed in the similitude of the birth of a child into this world.
3. Baptism is not only a figure of the resurrection, but also is literally a transplanting or resurrection from one life to another—from the life of sin to the life of spiritual life. —*Joseph Fielding Smith* (DS2, 323-324)

Now a word as to the reason for the flood. It was the baptism of the earth, and that had to be by immersion. If the water did not cover the entire earth, then it was not baptized, for the baptism of the Lord is not pouring or sprinkling. These forms are strictly man made and not part of the gospel ordinances. —*Joseph Fielding Smith* (DS2, 320)

Membership is obtained by baptism, which is at once a burial and a birth—a burial of the old person, with all his frailties, faults, and sins, if any, and a coming forth to walk in a newness of life. Backbiting, faultfinding, slander, profanity, uncontrolled temper, avarice, jealousy, hatred, intemperance, fornication, lying, cheating, are all buried. That is part of what baptism by immersion signifies. . . . He comes forth to walk in a newness of life, sig-nifying that in the new life ahead there will be an effort to maintain honesty, loyalty, chasti-ty benevolence, and of doing good to men. —*David O. McKay* (CR, Oct. 1958, 90)

Make your baptism into this Church real by burying the old life, with all its vanity, indul-gence, jealousy, hatred, and rise from the waters of baptism in a newness of life, as Christ was raised from the grave. What a beautiful comparison!—*David O. McKay* (CR, Oct. 1961, 91)

There is no doubt in our minds that baptism is essential to salvation. Evidently the Redeemer of mankind believed it was. He in whose name we hope to gain eternal exalta-tion, and through whom we hope for a glorious resurrection, who came into the world and laid down his life that we might live again, thought it was important and necessary, and yet there are, many of our Father's children who do not understand and do not believe that the Lord requires it of all men. —*George Albert Smith* (CR, Oct. 1921, 40)

Is there any difference between the baptized and the unbaptized man? . . . Take two men, they may be equals in point of goodness, they may be equally moral, charitable, honest and just, but one is baptized and the other is not. There is a mighty difference between them, for one is the son of God redeemed by compliance with his laws, and the other remains in dark-ness. —*Joseph F. Smith* (GD, 97)

Baptism means immersion in water, and is to be administered by one having authority, in the name of the Father, and of the Son, and of the Holy Ghost. Baptism without divine authority is not valid. It is a symbol of the burial and resurrection of Jesus Christ, and must be done in the likeness thereof, by one commissioned of God, in the manner prescribed, otherwise it is illegal and will not be accepted by him, nor will it effect a remission of sins, the object for which it is designed. —*Joseph F. Smith* (GD, 99-100)

Faith and repentance go before baptism; and baptism before the remission of sins, and the reception of the Holy Ghost. Hence, we see the useless and unscriptural practice of baptizing infants. They cannot exercise faith and repentance, qualifications necessary previous to baptism; then, why require the outward work?—*Lorenzo Snow* (LPS, 110)

There is but one way in which men can receive salvation, exaltation, and glory, and that is through the order of baptism and the ordinances connected therewith. No mortal man or woman will ever receive celestial glory unless he or she has been baptized, receiving this ordinance personally or by proxy. That is the order that God has established. —*Lorenzo Snow* (LPS, 108)

Baptism for the remission of sins is an ordinance of the gospel. Says one, baptism is not essential to salvation. Jesus not only taught it, but rendered obedience himself to that requirement, not that he was baptized for the remission of sins—but, as he said, "to fulfil all righteousness," thus in this, as in all other respects giving the example for all who follow. —*Wilford Woodruff* (WW, 19)

Being baptized into this Church is only like learning the alphabet of our mother tongue—it is the very first step. But having received the first principles of the gospel of Christ, let us go on to perfection. —*Wilford Woodruff* (WW, 20)

Has water, in itself, any virtue to wash away sin? Certainly not; but the Lord says, "If the sinner will repent of his sins, and go down into the waters of baptism, and there be buried in the likeness of being put into the earth and buried, and again be delivered from the water, in the likeness of being born—if in the sincerity of his heart he will do this, his sins shall be washed away." Will the water of itself wash them away? No; but keeping the commandments of God will cleanse away the stain of sin. —*Brigham Young* (BY, 159)

A man may be saved, after the judgment, in the terrestrial kingdom, or in the telestial kingdom, but he can never see the celestial kingdom of God, without being born of water and the Spirit. —*Joseph Smith, Jr.* (STJS, 18)

We discover, in order to be benefited by the doctrine of repentance, we must believe in obtaining the remission of sins. And in order to obtain the remission of sins, we must believe in the doctrine of baptism in the name of the Lord Jesus Christ. And if we believe in baptism for the remission of sins, we may expect a fulfillment of the promise of the Holy Ghost, for the promise extends to all whom the Lord our God shall call. —*Joseph Smith, Jr.* (STJS, 98)

The doctrine of baptizing children, or sprinkling them, or they must welter in hell, is a doctrine not true, not supported in Holy Writ, and is not consistent with the character of God. All children are redeemed by the blood of Jesus Christ. —*Joseph Smith, Jr.* (STJS, 224)

Baptism is a sign to God, to angels, and to heaven that we do the will of God, and there is no other way beneath the heavens whereby God hath ordained for man to come to Him to be saved, and enter into the Kingdom of God, except faith in Jesus Christ, repentance, and baptism for the remission of sins, and any other course is in vain; then you have the promise of the gift of the Holy Ghost. —*Joseph Smith, Jr.* (STJS, 225)

[L]et us understand that the word baptize is derived from the Greek verb "*baptiso*," and means to immerse or overwhelm, and that sprinkle is from the Greek verb "*rantiso*," and means to scatter on by particles; then we can treat the subject as one inseparably connected with our eternal welfare; and always bear in mind that it is one of the only methods by which we can obtain a remission of sins in this world, and be prepared to enter into the joys of our Lord in the world to come. —*Joseph Smith, Jr.* (STJS, 295)

You might as well baptize a bag of sand as a man, if not done in view of the remission of sins and getting of the Holy Ghost. Baptism by water is but half a baptism, and is good for nothing without the other half—that is, the baptism of the Holy Ghost. —*Joseph Smith, Jr.* (STJS, 352)

Baptism itself without faith in God avails nothing. —*Joseph Smith, Jr.* (LPS, 105)

21. FAITH

When all is said and done, the only real wealth of the Church is the faith of the people. —*Gordon B. Hinckley* (Ensign, Nov. 1985, 50)

Of all our needs, I think the greatest is an increase in faith. —*Gordon B. Hinckley* (CR, Nov. 1987, 54)

Faith, which is of the very essence of personal conviction, has always been and always must be at the root of religious practice and endeavor. —*Gordon B. Hinckley* (FETR , 1)

Faith is not a theological platitude. It is a fact of life. Faith can become the very well-spring of purposeful living. —*Gordon B. Hinckley* (FETR , 79-84)

Shall any of us say that with faith we cannot do better than we are now doing?—*Gordon B. Hinckley* (Ensign, Nov. 1983, 53)

Let us strengthen our own faith and that of our children wile being gracious to those who are not of our faith. Love and respect will overcome every element of animosity. Our kindness may be the most persuasive argument for that which we believe. —*Gordon B. Hinckley* (Ensign, May 1998, 5)

Faith has always been a necessary condition of a righteous life. —*Howard W. Hunter* (CR, Oct. 1962, 22-23)

Those who lose or lack faith, live in the past—there is loss of hope for the future. What a great change comes into the life of one who finds an abiding faith to give assurance and confidence. —*Howard W. Hunter* (CR, Oct. 1962, 23)

There is no tangible, concrete evidence of the existence of God or the divinity of the Master in the legal sense, but not all inquiry for the truth results in proof by real or demonstrative evidence. It is fallacious to argue that because there is no demonstrative evidence of the existence of God he does not in fact exist. In the absence of evidence often thought necessary by the scientific world for positive proof, our search may take us into the realm of circumstantial evidence. We could spend hours describing the wonders of the universe, of the earth, of nature, of the human body, the exactness of the laws of physics, and a thousand things, all of which dictate to the conscience of a truth seeker that there is a creator and one who rules over the universe. —*Howard W. Hunter* (Ensign, May 1975, 37-39)

Faith is the element that builds the bridge in the absence of concrete evidence. —*Howard W. Hunter* (Ensign, May 1975, 37-39)

Our faith should remind us that he [Jesus Christ] can calm the troubled waters of our lives. —*Howard W. Hunter* (WMJ, 39-40)

I have sympathy for young men and women when honest doubts enter their minds and they engage in the great conflict of resolving doubts. These doubts can be resolved, if they have an honest desire to know the truth, by exercising moral, spiritual, and mental effort. They will emerge from the conflict into firmer, stronger, larger faith because of the struggle. They have gone from a simple, trusting faith, through doubt and conflict, into a solid, substantial faith that ripens into testimony. —*Howard W. Hunter* (WMJ, 64-65)

Disciples of Christ in every generation are invited, indeed commanded, to be filled with a perfect brightness of hope. —*Howard W. Hunter* (WMJ, 94-95)

Faith in Jesus Christ consists of complete reliance on Him. As God, He has infinite power, intelligence, and love. There is no human problem beyond His capacity to solve. Because He descended below all things, He knows how to help us rise above our daily difficulties.
Faith in Him means believing that even though we do not understand all things, He does. . . .
Faith in Him means trusting that He has all power over all men and all nations. There is no evil that He cannot arrest. All things are in His hands. This earth is His rightful dominion. Yet He permits evil so that we can make choices between good and evil. . . .
Unless we do His teachings, we do not demonstrate faith in Him. —*Ezra Taft Benson* (CUC, 132)

It is not blind obedience, even without total understanding, to follow a Father who has proved himself. —*Spencer W. Kimball* (SWK, 59)

If pain and sorrow and total punishment immediately followed the doing of evil, no soul would repeat a misdeed. If joy and peace and rewards were instantaneously given the doer of good, there could be no evil—all would do good and not because of the rightness of doing good. There would be no test of strength, no development of character, no growth of powers, no free agency. . . . There would also be an absence of joy, success, resurrection, eternal life, and godhood. —*Spencer W. Kimball* (IE, Mar. 1966, 178)

Far better to take from a man his flocks or herds, his lands or wealth, even his sight or limbs, than to be responsible for the loss of his faith. —*Spencer W. Kimball* (IE, May 48, 282)

It takes faith—unseeing faith—for young people to proceed immediately with their family responsibilities in the face of financial uncertainties. It takes faith for the young woman to bear her family instead of accepting employment, especially when schooling for the young husband is to be finished. It takes faith to observe the Sabbath when "time and a half" can be had working, when sales can be made, when merchandise can be sold. It takes a great faith to pay tithes when funds are scarce and demands are great. It takes faith to fast and have family prayers and to observe the Word of Wisdom. It takes faith to do home teaching, stake missionary work, and other service, when sacrifice is required. . . . But know this— that all these are of the planting, while faithful devout families, spiritual security, peace, and eternal life are the harvests. —*Spencer W. Kimball* (FPM, 11)

There will never be great happiness in the world any more, until men have faith in one higher than themselves. Without faith in God, men cannot have utter faith in themselves or in their work. —*Harold B. Lee* (DSL, 39)

The time is here when every one of you must stand on your own feet. The time is here when no man and woman will endure on borrowed light. Each will have to be guided by the light within himself. If you do not have it, you will not stand. —*Harold B. Lee* (DSL, 234)

With faith we become pioneers for the generations yet unborn and find ourselves becoming joyous in the contemplation of service we may render to our fellowmen even though the reward be but a martyr's crown. —*Harold B. Lee* (SHP, 337-338)

Learning by faith is no task for a lazy man. —*Harold B. Lee* (YLW, 119)

You must learn to walk to the edge of the light, and perhaps a few steps into the darkness, and you will find that the light will appear and move ahead of you. —*Harold B. Lee* (in The Holy Temple, by Boyd K. Packer, 184)

If we want to have a living, abiding faith, we must be active in the performance of every duty as members of this Church. —*Joseph Fielding Smith* (CN, Mar. 16, 1935, 7)

We, as Latter-day Saints, should walk in righteousness and in the spirit of faith. We should be willing and anxious to believe the words of the Lord and have more confidence in what has come from him than in what has come through the arm of flesh. Let us increase our faith and confidence in the Lord. —*Joseph Fielding Smith* (DS2, 314)

The great difficulty in the world today is unbelief, doubt, lack of faith. . . . The guidance of the Holy Ghost is offered to every member of the Church so that they may not walk in darkness but be protected from error and know the truth. If we live as we should, we will be entitled to this guidance so that we will not be deceived. The philosophies and doctrines of men today have a tendency to destroy faith in the Lord and cast doubt upon his revelations. —*Joseph Fielding Smith* (DS2, 322)

Faith in God cannot of course be other than personal. It must be yours; it must be mine; and, to be effective, must spring from the mind and heart. —*David O. McKay* (IE, 47:13)

The greatest need in the world today is faith in God and courage to do his will. —*David O. McKay* (CR, Apr. 1963, 95)

An unwavering faith in Christ is the most important need of the world today. It is more than a mere feeling. It is power that moves into action, and should be in human life the most basic of all motivating forces. —*David O. McKay* (CR, Apr. 1966, 58)

We know that faith is a gift of God; it is the fruitage of righteous living. It does not come to us by our command, but is the result of doing the will of our Heavenly Father. If we lack faith, let us examine ourselves to see if we have been keeping His commandments, and repent without delay if we have not. —*George Albert Smith* (SGO, 49)

From the beginning of time until now it has been the faithful man who has had the power of God. —*George Albert Smith* (SGO, 61)

If any lack faith it is because they have not kept the commandments of God. —*George Albert Smith* (CR, Apr. 1923, 77)

We are informed that without faith we cannot please God. It is the moving cause of all action, and Scripture is replete with evidences of the power of faith. —*George Albert Smith* (CR, Apr. 1923, 75)

Faith is a gift of God, and faith comes to all of us who serve God and supplicate Him for the guidance of His Spirit. There is no danger of any man or woman losing his or her faith in this Church if he or she is humble and prayerful and obedient to duty. I have never known of such an individual losing his faith. By doing our duty faith increases until it becomes perfect knowledge. —*Heber J. Grant* (CR, Apr. 1934, 131)

Get faith. If you haven't knowledge, have faith. Cultivate that faith and sooner or later knowledge will come. —*Heber J. Grant* (GS, 26)

My experience is that men who have sufficient faith to trust in God come out of difficulties, financial and otherwise, in a most miraculous and wonderful way. —*Heber J. Grant* (IE, 39:131-132)

If faith is dead without good works, then it follows that you can measure your faith by the good you accomplish. —*Heber J. Grant* (GS, 47)

I say to you that of all my acquaintances I have never known of one who, having fulfilled the law, kept the commandments of God and supplicated Him for His guidance, has ever lost the faith or the testimony of the divinity of this work in which we are engaged. —*Heber J. Grant* (LPS, 376)

The need of one's having a keen knowledge of the truth is paramount. So also is it that every latter-day Saint should have a deep-rooted conviction of the justice of God, and an implicit confidence and faith in his being and mercy. . . .
God is good; his promises never fail; to trust implicitly his goodness and mercy is a correct principle Let us, therefore, put our trust in him. —*Joseph F. Smith* (GD, 65-66)

A moral life is one of the means by which we cultivate faith, but it is not the only means. We may not see any moral virtue in the ordinance of baptism, in the laying on of hands, or in any other rite or ceremony of the Church, but our obedience to these rites and ordinances may be quite as helpful in developing our faith as any act of charity we may perform. Faith is always a gift of God to man, which is obtained by obedience, as all other blessings are. —*Joseph F. Smith* (GD, 212)

Those persons who received this work without religious motives, and without an honest conviction of its divine requirements, but solely for the "loaves and fishes," cannot possibly abide the test to which everyone's faith, sooner or later, must be brought; but will have his dishonesty and hypocrisy exposed, and will sooner or later apostatize. —*Lorenzo Snow* (LS, 52)

Revealed knowledge withstands all tests. Now you take a man, no matter from what country: if he be a man of integrity, when he receives a knowledge of the truth, he will stand to that knowledge? You cannot persecute it out of him by imprisoning him, or taking away his property, or by destroying every source of his happiness. Do what you can to annoy and oppress him, he will stand firm in his adherence to the principles which he knows are true. —*Lorenzo Snow* (LS, 53)

Now, if we really desire to draw near to God; if we wish to place ourselves in accord with the good spirits of the eternal worlds; if we wish to establish within ourselves that faith which we read about and by which ancient Saints performed such wonderful works, we must, after we obtain the Holy Spirit, hearken to its whisperings and conform to its suggestions, and by no act of our lives drive it from us. —*Lorenzo Snow* (LS, 109)

The first principle, then, ever taught to Father Adam was faith in the Messiah, who was to come in the meridian of time to lay down his life for the redemption of man. —*Wilford Woodruff* (WW, 18)

Put your trust in God and rely on his promises, living up to the light and knowledge you possess; and all will be well with you whether living or dying. —*Wilford Woodruff* (WW, 260)

I tell you trusting in the Lord in these days is an unpopular business with the world. But the Saints have to trust in the Lord, and we might as well begin and seek this kingdom and the interest of it, and the righteousness of it, and build it up first as last. —*Wilford Woodruff* (WW, 314)

We could progress a great deal faster, and could prosper a thousand times more than we do if we would be one in carrying out the counsels given us by the Lord through his servants. Remember the race is not to the swift, nor the battle to the strong; but to those who trust in the Lord. —*John Taylor* (GK, 180-181)

When men trust to themselves they trust in a broken reed, and when they trust in the Lord, they will never fail. —*John Taylor* (GK, 241)

I would rather trust in the living God than in any other power on earth. —*John Taylor* (GK, 343)

If the people will only be full of good works, I will insure that they will have faith in time of need. —*Brigham Young* (BY, 154)

I have faith in my God, and that faith corresponds with the works I produce. I have no confidence in faith without works. —*Brigham Young* (BY, 155)

My faith is, when we have done all we can, then the Lord is under obligation, and will not disappoint the faithful; he will perform the rest. —*Brigham Young* (BY, 155)

If the Latter-day Saints will walk up to their privileges, and exercise faith in the name of Jesus Christ, and live in the enjoyment of the fulness of the Holy Ghost constantly day by day, there is nothing on the face of the earth that they could ask for, that would not be given to them. —*Brigham Young* (BY, 156)

When faith springs up in the heart, good works will follow, and good works will increase that pure faith within them. —*Brigham Young* (BY, 156)

[N]o living, intelligent being, whether serving God or not, acts without belief. He might as well undertake to live without breathing as to live without the principle of belief. But he must believe the truth, obey the truth, and practice the truth, to obtain the power of God called faith. —*Brigham Young* (JD, 11:114)

Faith is the assurance which men have of the existence of things which they have not seen, and the principle of action in all intelligent beings. —*Joseph Smith, Jr.* (LF, 1)

In a word, is there anything that you would have done, either physical or mental, if you had not previously believed? Are not all your exertions of every kind, dependent on your faith?—*Joseph Smith, Jr.* (LF, 2)

Faith, then, is the first great governing principle which has power, dominion, and authority over all things; by it they exist, by it they are upheld, by it they are changed, or by it they remain, agreeable to the will of God. Without it there is no power, and without power there could be no creation nor existence!—*Joseph Smith, Jr.* (LF, 5)

[A]fter any portion of the human family are made acquainted with the important fact that there is a God, who has created and does uphold all things, the extent of their knowledge respecting his character and glory will depend upon their diligence and faithfulness in seeking after him, until, like Enoch, the brother of Jared, and Moses, they shall obtain faith in God, and power with him to behold him face to face. —*Joseph Smith, Jr.* (LF, 24)

Let us here observe, that three things are necessary in order that any rational and intelligent being may exercise faith in God unto life and salvation.

First, the idea that he actually exists.

Secondly, a correct idea of his character, perfections, and attributes.

Thirdly, an actual knowledge that the course of life which he is pursuing is according to his will. —*Joseph Smith, Jr.* (LF, 38)

[T]he real design which God of heaven had in view of making the human family acquainted with his attributes, was, that they, through the ideas of the existence of his attributes, might be enabled to exercise faith in him, and through the exercise of faith in him, might obtain eternal life. —*Joseph Smith, Jr.* (LF, 49)

For doubt and faith do not exist in the same person at the same time; so that persons whose minds are under doubts and fears cannot have unshaken confidence; and where unshaken confidence is not there faith is weak; and where faith is weak their persons will not be able to contend against all the opposition, tribulations, and afflictions which they will have to encounter in order to be heirs of God, and joint heirs with Christ Jesus; and they will grow weary in their minds, and the adversary will have power over them and destroy them. —*Joseph Smith, Jr.* (LF, 71)

[W]hen a man works by faith he works by mental exertion instead of physical force. —*Joseph Smith, Jr.* (LF, 72)

Because faith is wanting, the fruits are. No man since the world was had faith without having something along with it. The ancients quenched the violence of fire, escaped the edge of the sword, women received their dead, etc. By faith the worlds were made. A man who has none of the gifts has no faith; and he deceives himself, if he supposes he has. Faith has been wanting, not only among the heathen, but in professed Christendom also, so that tongues, healings, prophecy, and prophets and apostles, and all the gifts and blessings have been wanting. —*Joseph Smith, Jr.* (STJS, 304)

Faith comes by hearing the word of God. If a man has not faith enough to do one thing, he may have faith to do another: if he cannot remove a mountain, he may heal the sick. Where faith is there will be some of the fruits: all gifts and powers which were sent from heaven, were poured out on the heads of those who had faith. —*Joseph Smith, Jr.* (LPS, 98)

22. FORGIVENESS AND REPENTANCE

Is there a virtue more in need of application in our time than the virtue of forgiving and forgetting —*Gordon B. Hinckley* (BTE, 49)

God will forgive those who acknowledge the error of their ways and who demonstrate by the goodness of their lives the sincerity of their repentance. —*Gordon B. Hinckley* (Ensign, Nov. 1983, 82)

Here is a great lesson we all need to learn. There is no true forgiveness without forgetting. —*Gordon B. Hinckley* (Ensign, Jan. 1989, 5)

Eternal vigilance is the price of eternal development. Occasionally we may stumble. I thank the Lord for the great principle of repentance and forgiveness. When we drop the ball, when we make a mistake, there is held out to us the word of the Lord that he will forgive our sins and remember them no more against us. —*Gordon B. Hinckley* (Ensign, Nov. 1994, 48)

I invite all members of the Church to live with ever more attention to the life and example of the Lord Jesus Christ, especially the love and hope and compassion he displayed. I pray that we will treat each other with more kindness, more patience, more courtesy and forgiveness.

To those who have transgressed or been offended, we say, come back. The path of repentance, though hard at times, lifts one ever upward and leads to a perfect forgiveness.

To those who are hurt or are struggling and afraid, we say, let us stand with you and dry your tears. Come back. Stand with us in The Church of Jesus Christ of Latter-day Saints. —*Howard W. Hunter* (Ensign Nov. 1994, 8-9)

Rather than constantly dwelling on what we perceive as a mistake or a sin or a failure to the detriment of our progress in the gospel or our association with family and friends, it would be better for us to turn away from it. As with any mistake, we may repent by being sorrowful and by attempting to correct or rectify the consequences, to whatever extent possible. We should look forward with renewed faith. —*Howard W. Hunter* (WMJ, 113)

To dig a straight furrow, the plowman needs to keep his eyes on a fixed point ahead of him. That keeps him on a true course. If, however, he happens to look back to see where he has been, his chances of straying are increased. The results are crooked and irregular furrows. We invite those who are new members to fix their attention on their new goal and never look back on their earlier problems or transgressions except as a reminder of their growth and their worth and their blessings from God. If our energies are focused not behind us but ahead of us—on eternal life and the joy of salvation—we assuredly will obtain it. —*Howard W. Hunter* (WMJ, 150-151)

Godly sorrow is a gift of the Spirit. It is a deep realization that our actions have offended our Father and our God. It is the sharp and keen awareness that our behavior caused the Savior, He who knew no sin, even the greatest of all, to endure agony and suffering. Our sins caused Him to bleed at every pore. —*Ezra Taft Benson* (Ensign, Oct. 1989, 2)

Repentance means more than simply a reformation of behavior. Many men and women in the world demonstrate great will-power and self-discipline in overcoming bad habits and the weaknesses of the flesh. Yet at the same time they give no thought to the Master, sometimes even openly rejecting Him. Such changes of behavior, even if in a positive direction, do not constitute true repentance.

Faith in the Lord Jesus Christ is the foundation upon which sincere and meaningful repentance must be built. If we truly seek to put away sin, we must first look to Him who is the Author of our salvation. —*Ezra Taft Benson* (Ensign, Oct. 1989, 2)

Most repentance does not involve sensational or dramatic changes, but rather is a step by step, steady and consistent movement toward godliness. —*Ezra Taft Benson* (Ensign, Oct. 1989, 5)

Frequently people talk about time: How long before they can be forgiven? How soon may they go to the temple?

Repentance is timeless. The evidence of repentance is transformation. —*Spencer W. Kimball* (Ensign, May 1974, 4)

Repentance means suffering. If a person hasn't suffered, he hasn't repented. I don't care how many times he says he has. If he hasn't suffered, he hasn't repented. He has got to go through a change in his system whereby he suffers and then forgiveness is a possibility. Nobody can be forgiven unless there is adequate repentance. You bishops remember that, will you! The Savior can do almost anything in the world, but he can't forgive somebody who hasn't repented. —*Spencer W. Kimball* (SWK, 99)

No one can repent on the cross, nor in prison, nor in custody. One must have the opportunity of committing wrong in order to be really repentant. —*Spencer W. Kimball* (MF, 167)

Repentance is a lifelong task. Since all of us sin in greater or lesser degree, we are all in need of constant repentance, of continually raising our sights and our performance. One can hardly do the commandments of the Lord in a day, a week, a month, or a year. This is an effort which must be extended through the remainder of one's years. —*Spencer W. Kimball* (MF, 202)

Hope is indeed the great incentive to repentance, for without it no one would make the difficult, extended effort required—especially when the sin is a major one. —*Spencer W. Kimball* (Ensign, March, 1982, 2.)

To every forgiveness there is a condition. The plaster must be as wide as the sore. —*Spencer W. Kimball* (Ensign, March, 1982, 6.)

How grateful we should be that the Lord finished his preparation in our behalf! Now it is up to us to finish our preparations in our own behalf—by partaking of his loving forgiveness, which is the reward he eagerly desires to give all who truly repent. —*Spencer W. Kimball* (Ensign, Oct. 1982, 5)

In order for good to blossom it must be cultivated and exercised by constant practice, and to be truly righteous there is required a daily pruning of the evil growth of our characters by a daily repentance from sin. —*Harold B. Lee* (DSL, 93-94)

One may not wallow in the mire of filth and sin and conduct his life in a manner unlawful in the sight of God and then suppose that repentance will wipe out the effects of his sin and place him on the level he would have been on had he always lived a righteous and virtuous life. —*Harold B. Lee* (DSL, 99-100)

In one sentence, repentance means turning from that which we have done wrong in the sight of the Lord and never repeating that mistake again. . . .

When you have done all within your power to overcome your mistakes and have determined in your heart that you will never repeat them again, then to you can come that peace of conscience by which you will know that your sins have been forgiven. —*Harold B. Lee* (YLW, 321-322)

The Lord extends loving mercy and kindness in forgiving you of the sins you commit against Him or His work, but He can never remove the results of the sin you have committed against yourself in thus retarding your own advancement toward your eternal goal. —*Harold B. Lee* (SHP, 221)

Christ does not redeem any man from his individual sins who will not repent and who will not accept him. All those who refuse to accept him as the Redeemer and refuse to turn from their sins will have to pay the price of their own sinning. —*Joseph Fielding Smith* (CN, Apr. 22, 1939, 5)

It is possible for people to get so far in the dark through rebellion and wickedness that the spirit of repentance leaves them. It is a gift of God, and they get beyond the power of repentance. —*Joseph Fielding Smith* (DS2, 194)

How can a man obtain the remission of all his sins, if he has not repented of all his sins? The trouble with many of us is that we do not take the word of the Lord seriously; we do not think he means what he says. —*Joseph Fielding Smith* (DS2, 332)

Repentance is the turning away from that which is low and the striving for that which is higher. As a principle of salvation, it involves not only a desire for that which is better, but also a sorrow—not merely remorse—but true sorrow for having become contaminated in any degree with things sinful, vile, or contemptible. —*David O. McKay* (GI, 13)

Every principle and ordinance of the gospel of Jesus Christ is significant and important in contributing to the progress, happiness, and eternal life of man, but there is none more essential to the salvation of the human family than the divine and eternally operative principle, repentance. Without it, no one can be saved. Without it, no one can even progress. —*David O. McKay* (GI, 13)

Repentance means ever to change your thoughts and acts for the better. —*David O. McKay* (CR, Oct. 1953, 89)

As we analyze the situation we must come to the conclusion that there never was a time in the world's history when there was greater necessity everywhere for men to repent of their sins and seek the guidance of our Heavenly Father. There has never been a time since the Church was organized when there was greater need for us to humble ourselves before the Lord and seek his guidance. —*George Albert Smith* (CR, Oct. 1937, 47)

If there is any doubt in the mind of any man or woman in this Church who has been baptized and repented of their sins and who has had hands laid upon them for the gift of the Holy Ghost—if there is any doubt in their minds of the truth and divinity of this work it is because they have failed to measure up, it is because they have transgressed the laws of God, and because they have not kept the light of truth burning in their souls. We need repentance if that occurs to us; otherwise that assurance may depart from us to return again no more. —*George Albert Smith* (CR, Apr. 1939, 124)

Today I am thinking of the need not only of prayer, not only of faith—the world is teaching that, too—but I am thinking of the need, the sublime need, if I may use that term, of repentance from the things of the world and the turning away from the temptations that afflict mankind. —*George Albert Smith* (CR, Oct. 1944, 97)

There is nothing in the world that is more splendid than to have in our hearts a desire to forgive the sinner if he only repents. But I want to say, do not forgive the sinner if he does not repent. . . . [B]ut when they really and truly repent, it is one of the obligations that rest upon us to forgive those who have sinned. —*Heber J. Grant* (GS, 32)

Salvation will come only to those who repent and have their sins washed away by baptism, and who thereafter show by a godly life that their repentance is genuine. —*Heber J. Grant* (LPS, 139)

While there is life there is hope, and while there is repentance there is a chance for forgiveness; and if there is forgiveness, there is a chance for growth and development until we acquire the full knowledge of these principles that will exalt and save us and prepare us to enter into the presence of God the Father. —*Joseph F. Smith* (GD, 27-28)

[W]hen you seek to save either the living or the dead, bear it in mind that you can only do it on the principle of their repentance and acceptation of the plan of life. That is the only way in which you can succeed. —*Joseph F. Smith* (CR, Oct. 1907, 6-7)

If a person has determined that sin can easily be wiped out, and hence, that he will enjoy unlawful pleasures in youth, repenting in later life . . . time will wake him up to his serious and great mistake. He may and will be forgiven, if he repent . . . but all this will not return to him any loss sustained, nor place him on an equal footing with his neighbor who has kept the commandments of the better law. Nor will it place him in the position where he would have been, had he not committed wrong. —*Joseph F. Smith* (GD, 374)

I want to say to you that Latter-day Saints who harbor a feeling of unforgiveness in their souls are more guilty and more censurable than the one who has sinned against them. —*Joseph F. Smith* (CR, Oct. 1902, 86)

The Lord wishes to show leniency towards His children on earth, but He requires of them true repentance when they transgress or fail in any duty. —*Lorenzo Snow* (LS, 41)

If you see that you have weaknesses which have brought you into some trouble, do not be discouraged; but repent of that which you have done wrong, by which you have lost more or less of the Spirit of God, tell the Lord what you have done, and resolve in your hearts that you will do it no more. Then the Spirit of the Lord will be upon you. —*Lorenzo Snow* (CR, Oct. 1898, 56)

When men are called upon to repent of their sins, the call has reference to their own individual sins, not to Adam's transgressions. What is called the original sin was atoned for through the death of Christ irrespective of any action on the part of man; also man's individual sin was atoned for by the same sacrifice, but on condition of his obedience to the gospel plan of salvation when proclaimed in his hearing. —*Wilford Woodruff* (WW, 3)

And what is repentance? The forsaking of sin. The man who repents, if he be a swearer, swears no more; or a thief, steals no more; he turns away from all former sins and commits them no more. It is not repentance to say, I repent today, and then steal tomorrow; that is the repentance of the world, which is displeasing in the sight of God. —*Wilford Woodruff* (WW, 18)

Repentance must come, in order that the atonement may prove a benefit to us. Let all who are doing wrong cease doing wrong; live no longer in transgression, no matter of what kind; but live every day of your lives according to the revelations given, and so that your examples may be worthy of imitation. —*Brigham Young* (BY, 157)

But do not tell about your nonsensical conduct that nobody knows of but yourselves. Tell to the public that which belongs to the public. If you have sinned against the people, confess to them. . . . And if you have sinned against your God, or against yourselves, confess to God, and keep the matter to yourselves, for I do not want to know anything about it. —*Brigham Young* (BY, 158)

Ever keep in exercise the principles of mercy, and be ready to forgive our brother on the first intimations of repentance, and asking forgiveness; and should we even forgive our brother, or even our enemy, before he repent or ask forgiveness, our heavenly Father would be equally as merciful unto us. —*Joseph Smith, Jr.* (STJS, 175)

God did elect or predestinate, that all those who would be saved, should be saved in Christ Jesus, and through obedience to the Gospel; but He passes over no man's sins, but visits them with correction, and if His children will not repent of their sins He will discard them. —*Joseph Smith, Jr.* (STJS, 215)

We should take warning and not wait for the death-bed to repent, as we see the infant taken away by death, so may the youth and middle-aged, as well as the infant be suddenly called into eternity. Let this, then, prove as a warning to all not to procrastinate repentance, or wait till a death-bed, for it is the will of God that man should repent and serve Him in health, and in the strength and power of his mind, in order to secure his blessing, and not wait until he is called to die. —*Joseph Smith, Jr.* (STJS, 223-224)

All sins shall be forgiven, except the sin against the Holy Ghost; for Jesus will save all except the sons of perdition. What must a man do to commit the unpardonable sin? He must receive the Holy Ghost, have the heavens opened unto him, and know God, and then sin against Him. After a man has sinned against the Holy Ghost, there is no repentance for him. He has got to say that the sun does not shine while he sees it; he has got to deny Jesus Christ when the heavens have been opened unto him, and to deny the plan of salvation with his eyes open to the truth of it; and from that time he begins to be an enemy. —*Joseph Smith, Jr.* (STJS, 401-402)

23. MARRIAGE FOR ETERNITY

To think of eternal life without eternal love is to construct a paradox, a contradiction. —*Gordon B. Hinckley* (CR, Apr. 1972, 78)

Every man who truly loves a woman, and every woman who truly loves a man, hopes and dreams that their companionship will last forever. But marriage is a covenant sealed by authority. If that authority is of the state alone, it will endure only while the state has jurisdiction, and that jurisdiction ends with death. But add to the authority of the state the power of the endowment given by Him who overcame death, and that companionship will endure beyond life if the parties to the marriage live worthy of the promise. —*Gordon B. Hinckley* (BTE, 136-137)

Reason would deny that the Father who loves us all would tear asunder the most sacred relationship of all human experience and banish the companionship of marriage by those who love, honor, and respect one another. But there must be rules. There must be compliance. There must be obedience. The way is clear, made so through the exercise of the holy priesthood in these sacred temples. —*Gordon B. Hinckley* (Ensign, Nov. 1985, 60)

There is no more powerful principle of life to promote love, forbearance, and devotion in the home than that of eternal marriage. —*Howard W. Hunter* (CR, Oct. 1972, 67)

An eternal marriage is composed of a worthy man and a worthy woman, both of whom have been individually baptized with water and with the Spirit; who have individually gone to the temple to receive their own endowments; who have individually pledged their fidelity to God and to their partner in the marriage covenant; and who have individually kept their covenants, doing all that God expects of them. —*Howard W. Hunter* (WMJ, 53)

Let us plan for and teach and plead with our children to marry in the house of the Lord. Let us reaffirm more vigorously than we ever have in the past that it does matter where you marry and by what authority you are pronounced man and wife. —*Howard W. Hunter* (Ensign Nov. 1994, 88)

No sacrifice is too great to have the blessings of an eternal marriage. —*Ezra Taft Benson* (CR, Apr. 1979, 33-34)

When your children ask why we marry in the temple, you should teach them that temples are the only places on the earth where certain ordinances may be performed. You should also share with your children your personal feelings as you knelt together before the sacred altar and took upon yourselves covenants which made it possible for them to be sealed to you forever. —*Ezra Taft Benson* (ETB, 258)

Birth in the covenant entitles those children to a birthright blessing which guarantees them eternal parentage regardless of what happens to the parents, so long as the children remain worthy of the blessings. —*Ezra Taft Benson* (ETB, 259)

Any of you would go around the world for the sealing ordinance if you knew its importance, if you realized how great it is. No distance, no shortage of funds, no situation would ever keep you from being married in the holy temple of the Lord. —*Spencer W. Kimball* (SWK, 297)

You who are parties to a civil ceremony are to be married only during the period of your mortal lives. At death your marriage contract is to be dissolved and you are to be permanently separated or divorced from each other in the next life. Not only must this thought be a startling consideration, but if there be children and family life that too must end with death. —*Harold B. Lee* (DSL, 123)

Death and separation are not invited guests at the weddings of the righteous who marry according to the Lord's plan "for time and for all eternity. —*Harold B. Lee* (DSL, 131)

To help our youth abide by the principles involved in temple marriage, we must help them to understand that temple marriage is more than just a place where the ceremony occurs; it is a whole orientation to life and marriage and home. It is a culmination of building attitudes toward the Church, chastity, and about our personal relationship with God— and many other things. —*Harold B. Lee* (HBL, 244)

Nothing will prepare mankind for glory in the kingdom of God as readily as faithfulness to the marriage covenant. Through this covenant, perhaps more than any other, we accomplish the perfect decree of the Divine will, but this covenant is only one of many required of man who seeks to do the will of the Father. —*Joseph Fielding Smith* (IE, 34:643)

It fills my heart with sadness when I see in the paper the name of a daughter or a son of members of this Church, and discover that she or he is going to have a ceremony and be married outside of the temple of the Lord, because I realize what it means, that they are cutting themselves off from exaltation in the kingdom of God. —*Joseph Fielding Smith* (CR, Apr. 1941, 38)

Marriage in the temple is one of the most beautiful things in all the world. A couple is led there by love, the most divine attribute of the human soul. A young man looks, rightfully, upon that bride who will be the mother of his children as being as pure as a snowflake, as spotless as a sunbeam, as worthy of motherhood as any virgin. It is a glorious thing for a woman thus to wear the robes and be the pride of a young elder's heart, one who trusts her to be the head of his household.

She trusts him as being as worthy of fatherhood as she is of motherhood, and rightfully, too, because on his shoulders are the robes of the Holy Priesthood, testifying to his young bride, and to all, of his worthiness.

Together they stand in the house of the Lord to testify and covenant before him that they will be true to the covenants they make that day, each keeping himself or herself to the other and no one else. That is the highest ideal of marriage ever given to man. —*David O. McKay* (CR, Apr. 1969, 94)

The blessings and promises that come from beginning life together, for time and eternity, in a temple of the Lord cannot be obtained in any other way. Worthy young Latter-day Saint men and women who so begin life together find that their eternal partnership under the everlasting covenant becomes the foundation upon which are built peace, happiness, virtue, love, and all of the other eternal verities of life, here and hereafter. —*Heber J. Grant* (IE, 39:198-199)

I believe that no worthy young Latter-day Saint man or woman should spare any reasonable effort to come to the house of the Lord to begin life together. The marriage vows taken in these hallowed places and the sacred covenants entered into for time and all eternity are proof against many of the temptations of life that tend to break homes and destroy happiness. —*Heber J. Grant* (IE, 39:198)

There is no doubt in the mind of any true Latter-day Saint, man or woman, as to the fact of individual existence beyond the grave, as to the fact that we shall know each other, and as to the endless duration of the covenant of marriage that has been performed in the House of the Lord for time and eternity. —*Heber J. Grant* (LPS, 303)

[T]here is no principle of greater importance or more essential to the happiness of man— not only here, but especially hereafter, than that of marriage. —*Joseph F. Smith* (GD, 105)

We expect to have our wives and husbands in eternity. . . . I never could be happy again without the hope that I shall enjoy the society of my wives and children in eternity. If I had not this hope, I should be of all men most unhappy. —*Joseph F. Smith* (GD, 286)

When two Latter-day Saints are united together in marriage, promises are made to them concerning their offspring, that reach from eternity to eternity. They are promised that they shall have the power and the right to govern and control and administer salvation and exaltation and glory to their offspring worlds without end. . . . A man and a woman in the other life, having celestial bodies, free from sickness and disease, glorified and beautified beyond description, standing in the midst of their posterity, governing and controlling them, administering life, exaltation, and glory, worlds without end. —*Lorenzo Snow* (LPS, 304)

Why is a woman sealed to a man for time and all eternity? Because there is legitimate power on earth to do it. . . . When the books are opened, every one will find his proper mate, and have those that belong to him, and every one will be deprived of that which is surreptitiously obtained. —*John Taylor* (GK

There is not a young man in our community who would not be willing to travel from here to England to be married right, if he understood things as they are; there is not a young woman in our community, who loves the Gospel and wishes its blessings, that would be married in any other way. —*Brigham Young* (BY, 195)

Except a man and his wife enter into an everlasting covenant and be married for eternity, while in this probation, by the power and authority of the Holy Priesthood, they will cease to increase when they die; that is, they will not have any children after the resurrection. But those who are married by the power and authority of the priesthood in this life, and continue without committing the sin against the Holy Ghost, will continue to increase and have children in the celestial glory. —*Joseph Smith, Jr.* (STJS, 335-336)

In the celestial glory there are three heavens or degrees; and in order to obtain the highest, a man must enter into this order of the priesthood [meaning the new and everlasting covenant of marriage]; and if he does not, he cannot obtain it. He may enter into the other, but that is the end of his kingdom: he cannot have an increase. *—Joseph Smith, Jr.* (STJS, 336)

24. REVELATION

Revelation is fruitless unless it be listened to and obeyed. *—Gordon B. Hinckley* (BTE, 95-96)

Now, let me just say, categorically, that the things of God are understood by the Spirit of God, and one must have and seek and cultivate that Spirit, and there comes understanding and it is real. I can give testimony of that. *—Gordon B. Hinckley* (Ensign, Nov. 1996, 50-51)

Never again will the sun go down; never again will all men prove totally unworthy of communication with their Maker; never again will God be totally hidden from his children on earth. Revelation is here to remain. Prophets will follow each other in a never-ending succession, and the secrets of the Lord will be revealed without measure. *—Spencer W. Kimball* (SWK, 433)

For thousands of years there have been constant broadcasts from heaven of vital messages of guidance and timely warnings, and there has been a certain constancy in the broadcasts from the most powerful station. Throughout all those centuries there have been times when there were prophets who tuned in and rebroadcasted to the people. The messages have never ceased. *—Spencer W. Kimball* (IE, June 1970, 92)

When we understand with our hearts, then we know that the Spirit of the Lord is working upon us. *—Harold B. Lee* (SHP, 92)

We get our answers from the source of the power we list to obey. If we're following the ways of the devil, we'll get answers from the devil. If we're keeping the commandments of God, we'll get our answers from God. *—Harold B. Lee* (SHP, 138)

Every individual within his own station has the right to receive revelation by the Holy Ghost. . . .
Every man has the privilege to exercise these gifts and these privileges in the conduct of his own affairs; in bringing up his children in the way they should go; in the management of his business, or whatever he does. It is his right to enjoy the spirit of revelation and of inspiration to do the right thing, to be wise and prudent, just and good, in everything that he does. *—Harold B. Lee* (SHP, 141-142)

To say that the heavens are sealed and there is no revelation today is saying we do not believe in a living Christ today, or a living God today—we believe in one long since dead and gone. *—Harold B. Lee* (SHP, 150)

Testimony may be defined simply as divine revelation to the man of faith. *—Harold B. Lee* (SHP, 193)

It is contrary to the law of God for the heavens to be opened and messengers to come to do anything for man that man can do for himself. *—Joseph Fielding Smith* (CN, Apr. 1,1939, 7)

When a revelation comes for the guidance of this people, you may be sure that it will not be presented in some mysterious manner contrary to the order of the Church. It will go forth in such form that the people will understand that it comes from those who are in authority. —*Joseph Fielding Smith* (CR, Oct. 1918, 57)

If we love the truth, we never get tired of hearing it. No matter how many times we hear the truth expressed, if we love it, it is always new. —*Joseph Fielding Smith* (DS1, 294)

Man cannot determine, upon the strength of his own reason, unaided by the Spirit of God, the power and saving grace of the gospel principles and expect to find out God. He cannot do it!—*Joseph Fielding Smith* (CR, Apr. 1916, 7)

I want to say to the Latter-day Saints that it is our duty to put our faith in the revealed word of God, to accept that which has come through inspiration, through revelation unto his servants the prophets, both ancient and modern. And whenever you find any doctrine, any idea, any expression from any source whatsoever, that is in conflict with that which the Lord has revealed and which is found in the holy scriptures, you may be assured that it is false; and you should put it aside and stand firmly grounded in the truth in prayer and in faith, relying upon the Spirit of the Lord for knowledge, for wisdom, concerning these principles of truth. —*Joseph Fielding Smith* (CR, Apr. 1917, 65)

Revelation from the Lord is binding upon us whether we receive it or not; and if we reject it, we will be punished. —*Joseph Fielding Smith* (DS1, 280-281)

The Lord is withholding from us great and mighty truths because of the hardness of our hearts. Why should we clamor for more when we will not abide in what we already have? We are led by revelation today just as much as they were anciently. —*Joseph Fielding Smith* (DS3, 202)

If at this moment each one of you were asked to state in one sentence or phrase the most distinguishing feature of the Church of Jesus Christ of Latter-day Saints, what would be your answer? It occurs to me now that my answer would be this:
Divine authority by direct revelation. —*David O. McKay* (CR, Apr. 1937, 121)

One may so live that he may receive impressions and direct messages through the Holy Ghost. The veil is thin between those who hold the priesthood and those on the other side of the veil. —*David O. McKay* (CR, Oct. 1964, 92)

The distinction between this great Church and all other churches, from the beginning has been, that we believe in divine revelation; we believe that Our Father speaks to man today as he has done from the time of Adam. We believe and we know—which is more than mere belief—that Our Father has set his hand in this world for the salvation of the children of men. —*George Albert Smith* (CR, Apr. 1917, 37)

We do not believe that the heavens are sealed over our heads, but that the same father who loved and cherished the children of Israel, loves and cherishes us. We believe that we are as much in need of assistance of our Heavenly Father in the directing of our lives, as they were. We know that in the day and age in which we live the seal has been broken and God has again spoken from the Heavens. —*George Albert Smith* (GAS, 39)

The Lord gives to many of us the still, small voice of revelation. . . . It comes to each man, according to his needs and faithfulness, for guidance in matters that pertain to his own life. . . . This certain knowledge which we have that the guiding influence of the Lord may be felt in all the ways of life, according to our needs and faithfulness, is among the greatest blessings God grants unto men. With this blessing comes the responsibility to render obedience to the "still small voice."—*Heber J. Grant* (IE, 47:712)

We believe also in the principle of direct revelation from God to man. . . .

The moment this principle is cut off, that moment the Church is adrift, being severed from its ever-living head. In this condition it cannot continue, but must cease to be the Church of God and, like the ship at sea without captain, compass or rudder, is afloat at the mercy of the storms and the waves of ever contending human passions, and worldly interests, pride and folly, finally to be wrecked upon the strand of priestcraft and superstition. —*Joseph F. Smith* (GD, 104-105)

Every soul of us is entitled to inspiration from God to know what is our duty and how we are to do it. —*Joseph F. Smith* (CR, Oct. 1917, 5)

God has never revealed at any time that he would cease to speak forever to men. If we are permitted to believe that he has spoken, we must and do believe that he continues to speak, because he is unchangeable. —*Joseph F. Smith* (IE, 5:805)

Every man has the . . . right to enjoy the spirit of revelation and of inspiration to do the right thing, to be wise and prudent, just and good in everything that he does. I know that this is a true principle. —*Joseph F. Smith* (GD, 3)

To say that there is no need of new revelation, is equivalent to saying that we have no need of new truths—a ridiculous assertion. —*Joseph F. Smith* (LPS, 298)

On occasions of this kind, when we are assembled together to learn the will of God, it is of importance that we exercise faith, and have the spirit of prayer, that the Lord will cause something to be said that will instruct, and give us such information and knowledge as will be of use and service in our daily walk and under the circumstances that surround us. —*Lorenzo Snow* (LS, 90)

This gift of the Holy Ghost is a different principle from anything that we see manifested in the sectarian world. It is a principle of intelligence, and revelation. It is a principle that reveals things past, present, and to come, and these gifts of the Holy Ghost were to be received through obedience to the requirements of the gospel as proclaimed by the elders of the Church of Jesus Christ of Latter-day Saints in these days. —*Lorenzo Snow* (LS, 107)

We are entirely dependent upon the spirit of inspiration, and if there ever was a time, since Adam occupied the Garden of Eden, when the Spirit of God was more needed than at the present time, I am not aware of it. —*Lorenzo Snow* (LS, 109)

There is a way by which persons can keep their consciences clear before God and man, and that is to preserve within them the Spirit of God, which is the spirit of revelation to every man and woman. It will reveal to them, even in the simplest of matters, what they shall do, by making suggestions to them. We should try to learn the nature of this spirit, that we may understand its suggestions, and then we will always be able to do right. This is the grand privilege of every Latter-day Saint. We know that it is our right to have the manifestations of the Spirit every day of our lives. —*Lorenzo Snow* (CR, Apr. 1899, 52)

What is revelation? It is the inspiration of the Holy Ghost to man. This is the key, the foundation stone of all revelation. —*Wilford Woodruff* (LPS, 293)

I would to God that the inhabitants of the earth would get rid of the idea that revelation ceased when Christ was put to death. It is a false doctrine. Revelation belongs to the salvation of the children of men. —*Wilford Woodruff* (WW, 49)

Every man or woman that has ever entered into the church of God and been baptized for the remission of sins has a right to revelation, a right to the Spirit of God, to assist them in their labors, in their administrations to their children, in counseling their children and those over whom they are called upon to preside. The Holy Ghost is not restricted to men, nor to apostles or prophets; it belongs to every faithful man and woman, and to every child who is old enough to receive the gospel of Christ. —*Wilford Woodruff* (WW, 53)

Yes, we have revelation. The Church of God could not live twenty-four hours without revelation. —*Wilford Woodruff* (WW, 61)

With regard to our position before we came here, I will say that we dwelt with the Father and with the Son, as expressed in the hymn, "O My Father," that has been sung here. That hymn is a revelation, though it was given unto us by a woman—Sister Eliza R. Snow. There are a great many sisters who have the spirit of revelation. There is no reason why they should not be inspired as well as men. —*Wilford Woodruff* (WW, 61-62)

I wanted to say in regard to these matters is, that the Lord does communicate some things of importance to the children of men by means of visions and dreams as well as by the records of divine truth. And what is it all for? It is to teach us a principle. We may never see anything take place exactly as we see it in a dream or a vision, yet it is intended to teach us a principle. —*Wilford Woodruff* (WW, 286)

Every man should get the Spirit of God, and then follow its dictates. This is revelation. It doesn't make any difference what the spirit tells you to do; it will never tell you to do anything that is wrong. —*Wilford Woodruff* (WW, 294-294)

There are a great many things taught us in dreams that are true, and if a man has the spirit of God he can tell the difference between what is from the Lord and what is not. And I want to say to my brethren and sisters, that whenever you have a dream that you feel is from the Lord, pay attention to it. —*Wilford Woodruff* (JD, 22:333)

We believe that it is necessary for man to be placed in communication with God; that he should have revelation from him, and that unless he is placed under the influences of the inspiration of the Holy Spirit, he can know nothing about the things of God. —*John Taylor* (GK, 35)

Whoever heard of true religion without communication with God? To me the thing is the most absurd that the human mind could conceive. I do not wonder, when the people generally reject the principle of present revelation, that skepticism and infidelity prevail to such an alarming extent. I do not wonder that so many men treat religion with contempt, and regard it as something not worth the attention of intelligent beings, for without revelation religion is a mockery and a farce. If I can not have a religion that will lead me to God, and place me en rapport with him, and unfold to my mind the principles of immortality and eternal life, I want nothing to do with it.

The principle of present revelation, then, is the very foundation of our religion. —*John Taylor* (LPS, 289)

There is not a position that we can occupy in life, either as fathers, mothers, children, masters, servants, or as elders of Israel holding the holy priesthood in all its ramifications, but what we need continually is wisdom flowing from the Lord and intelligence communicated by him, that we may know how to perform correctly the various duties and avocations of life, and to fulfil the various responsibilities that rest upon us. —*John Taylor* (GK, 44-45)

A man may speak by the Spirit of God, but it requires a portion of that Spirit also in those who hear, to enable them to comprehend correctly the importance of the things that are delivered to them. —*John Taylor* (GK, 45-46)

There is no man living, and there never was a man living, who was capable of teaching the things of God only as he was taught, instructed and directed by the spirit of revelation proceeding from the Almighty. And then there are no people competent to receive true intelligence and to form a correct judgment in relation to the sacred principles of eternal life, unless they are under the influence of the same spirit, and hence speakers and hearers are all in the hands of the Almighty. —*John Taylor* (GK, 275)

Without revelation from God the world is but a wilderness. —*John Taylor* (GK, 32)

Every man and woman may be a revelator, and have the testimony of Jesus, which is the spirit of prophecy, and foresee the mind and will of God concerning them. —*Brigham Young* (BY, 91)

There are many spirits gone out into the world, and the false spirits are giving revelations as well as the Spirit of the Lord. —*Brigham Young* (BY, 72)

No person can receive a knowledge of this work, except by the power of revelation. —*Brigham Young* (BY, 35)

It is only where experience fails, that revelation is needed. —*Brigham Young* (BY, 416)

It has been observed that the people want revelation. . . . But before we desire more written revelation, let us fulfil the revelations that are already written, and which we have scarcely begun to fulfil. —*Brigham Young* (BY, 39)

The Lord has no confidence in those who reveal secrets, for he cannot safely reveal himself to such persons. —*Brigham Young* (BY, 40-41)

Such is the darkness and ignorance of this generation, that they look upon it as incredible that a man should have any intercourse with his Maker. —*Joseph Smith, Jr.* (STJS, 106)

[N]othing is a greater injury to the children of men than to be under the influence of a false spirit when they think they have the Spirit of God. —*Joseph Smith, Jr.* (STJS, 232-233)

And we shall at last have to come to this conclusion, whatever we may think of revelation, that without it we can neither know nor understand anything of God, or the devil; and however unwilling the world may be to acknowledge this principle, it is evident from the multifarious creeds and notions concerning this matter that they understand nothing of this principle, and it is equally as plain that without a divine communication they must remain in ignorance. —*Joseph Smith, Jr.* (STJS, 233)

[I]f we have direct revelations given us from heaven, surely those revelations were never given to be trifled with, without the trifler's incurring displeasure and vengeance upon his own head. —*Joseph Smith, Jr.* (STJS, 67)

Salvation cannot come without revelation; it is in vain for anyone to minister without it. No man is a minister of Jesus Christ without being a Prophet. No man can be a minister of Jesus Christ except he has the testimony of Jesus; and this is the spirit of prophecy. Whenever salvation has been administered, it has been by testimony. —*Joseph Smith, Jr.* (STJS, 182)

A person may profit by noticing the first intimation of the spirit of revelation; for instance, when you feel pure intelligence flowing into you, it may give you sudden strokes of ideas, so that by noticing it, you may find it fulfilled the same day or soon; (i.e.,) those things that were presented unto your minds by the Spirit of God, will come to pass; and thus by learning the Spirit of God and understanding it, you may grow into the principle of revelation, until you become perfect in Christ Jesus. —*Joseph Smith, Jr.* (STJS, 172-173)

When you see a vision, pray for the interpretation; if you get not this, shut it up; there must be certainty in this matter. An open vision will manifest that which is more important. Lying spirits are going forth in the earth. There will be great manifestations of spirits, both false and true. —*Joseph Smith, Jr.* (STJS, 184)

We never can comprehend the things of God and of heaven, but by revelation. We may spiritualize and express opinions to all eternity; but that is no authority. —*Joseph Smith, Jr.* (STJS, 325)

We can see that the doctrine of revelation far transcends the doctrine of no revelation; for one truth revealed from heaven is worth all the sectarian notions in existence. —*Joseph Smith, Jr.* (STJS, 381)

25. THE SACRAMENT

We recently stood in the Garden of Gethsemane in Jerusalem where in agony the Lord foresaw the terrible suffering he must endure, suffering so intense that it caused even the Son of God to bleed at every pore. There he was mocked and betrayed and delivered into the hands of wicked men.

My dear young friends, do we not mock him anew if we come to the sacrament table with unclean hands and impure hearts as we administer the emblems of his sacrifice?— *Gordon B. Hinckley* (CR, Oct. 1972, 107)

Every sacrament meeting ought to be a spiritual feast. It ought to be a time for meditation and introspection, a time for singing songs of praise to the Lord, a time of renewing one's covenants with him and our Eternal Father, and a time for hearing the word of the Lord with reverence and appreciation.

I plead with you who are responsible for these meetings that you strive a little more diligently to program them in such a manner that each sacrament meeting will become a time for spiritual refreshening. —*Gordon B. Hinckley* (Ensign, Nov. 1982, 47)

I asked myself this question: "Do I place God above all other things and keep all of His commandments?" Then came reflection and resolution. To make a covenant with the Lord to always keep his commandments is a serious obligation, and to renew that covenant by partaking of the sacrament is equally serious. The solemn moments of thought while the sacrament is being served have great significance. They are moments of self-examination, introspection, self-discernment—a time to reflect and to resolve. —*Howard W. Hunter* (Ensign, May 1977, 25)

It is vital that sacrament meetings be occasions when the gospel is taught by testimony. Too frequently they are not. Our primary responsibility is to be special witnesses of Him whom we represent. In all our assignments we must be certain to bear testimony of Jesus Christ and this grand and glorious work. —*Ezra Taft Benson* (ETB, 469)

That is the real purpose of the sacrament, to keep us from forgetting, to help us to remember. I suppose there would never be an apostate, there would never be a crime, if people remembered, really remembered, the things they had covenanted at the water's edge or at the sacrament table and in the temple. —*Spencer W. Kimball* (SWK, 112)

Every [sacrament] service should be carefully appraised and to it should be applied the yardstick: will it build spirituality?—*Spencer W. Kimball* (SWK, 515)

If the service is a failure to you, you have failed. No one can worship for you; you must do your own waiting upon the Lord. —*Spencer W. Kimball* (Ensign, Jan. 1978, 2)

The partaking of the sacrament is a renewal, a refreshing of our recollection of what it meant to be baptized as a member of the Church. We had the law of sacrifice before the coming of the Savior, and we have the sacrament administered since the Savior's death, repeatedly refreshing our minds of the covenant of the gospel of Jesus Christ which all of us have entered into. —*Harold B. Lee* (HBL, 208)

Personalize the sacramental prayers by repeating the words of the prayers in your mind, but substituting the pronoun I in the place of we or they.

If you will do this, it will do something to you. It will bring you close to God and help you understand more fully the meaning of the covenant. —*Harold B. Lee* (HBL, 209)

In my judgment the sacrament meeting is the most sacred, the most holy, of all the meetings of the Church. —*Joseph Fielding Smith* (CR, Oct. 1929, 60)

Amusement, laughter, light-mindedness, are all out of place in the sacrament meetings of the Latter-day Saints. We should assemble in the spirit of prayer, of meekness, with devotion in our hearts. I know of no other place where we can gather where we should be more reflective and solemn and where more of the spirit of worship should be maintained. —*Joseph Fielding Smith* (CR, Oct. 1929, 60)

Those members of the Church who habitually absent themselves from the sacrament meeting and who do not enter into the covenants which the sacrament requires of them, are guilty of grievous sin and are under grave condemnation. The Spirit of the Lord cannot dwell in them, and they deny to themselves the guidance of that Spirit. —*Joseph Fielding Smith* (DS2, 344)

The sacrament is a memorial of Christ's life and death. When we think of his life we think of sacrifice. Not a moment of his existence on earth did Christ think more of himself than he did of his brethren and the people whom he came to save, always losing himself for the good of others, and finally giving his life for the redemption of mankind. When we partake of the sacrament in his presence we remember him, his life of sacrifice, and service; and we are inspired by that thought and memory. There is nothing won in this life without sacrifice. —*David O. McKay* (CR, Oct. 1929, 11-13)

It is up to you bishops to see to it that the sacrament is administered only by boys and young men who are worthy to attend to this sacred ordinance, and that it is done reverently with a full understanding of its significance to them and to the audience. Let the sacrament hour be one experience of the day in which the worshiper tries at least to realize within himself that it is possible for him to commune with his God. —*David O. McKay* (CR, Apr. 1967, 86)

We believe that the sacrament is not the literal body and blood of our Lord; in other words, we do not believe in the doctrine of Transubstantiation. —*George Albert Smith* (CR, Apr. 1908, 36)

I say also to those who partake of the sacrament, we should consider seriously the covenants we make with our Father. Let us pay strict attention to those covenants, and let us see to it that we eat and drink worthy, for the blessings of our souls and for the increase of our spiritual strength. —*George Albert Smith* (CR, Apr. 1908, 37)

Before partaking of this sacrament, our hearts should be pure; our hands should be clean; we should be divested of all enmity toward our associates; we should be at peace with our fellow men; and we should have in our hearts a desire to do the will of our Father and to keep all of His commandments. If we do this, partaking of the sacrament will be a blessing to us and will renew our spiritual strength. —*George Albert Smith* (CR, Apr. 1908, 35)

We meet upon the Sabbath day for the purpose of partaking of the sacrament, the emblems of the Lord's body and blood which were broken and shed for us, and also to give and receive instruction as we may be led by the Spirit of God. —*Wilford Woodruff* (WW, 182)

We have met to partake of the sacrament of the Lord's supper, and we should endeavor to draw away our feelings and affections from things of time and sense. For in partaking of the sacrament we not only commemorate the death and sufferings of our Lord and Savior Jesus Christ, but we also shadow forth the time when he will come again and when we shall meet and eat bread with him in the kingdom of God. —*John Taylor* (GK, 227)

Whether we are poor or rich, if we neglect our prayers and our sacrament meetings, we neglect the Spirit of the Lord, and a spirit of darkness comes over us. —*Brigham Young* (BY, 170)

We are in the habit of partaking of the contents of the cup each Sabbath when we meet together, and I do pray you, my brethren and sisters, to contemplate this ordinance thoroughly, and seek unto the Lord with all your hearts that you may obtain the promised blessings by obedience to it. —*Brigham Young* (BY, 171-172)

It is one of the greatest blessings we could enjoy, to come before the Lord, and before the angels, and before each other, to witness that we remember that the Lord Jesus Christ has died for us. This proves to the Father that we remember our covenants, that we love his Gospel, that we love to keep his commandments, and to honor the name of the Lord Jesus upon the earth. —*Brigham Young* (BY, 172)

26. TEMPLE WORK

Reason demands that the family relationships shall continue after death. The human heart longs for it. The God of heaven has revealed a way whereby it may be secured. The sacred ordinances of the house of the Lord provide for it. —*Gordon B. Hinckley* (BTE, 131)

Many years ago the First Presidency determined that a convert to the Church should wait a year following baptism before going to the House of the Lord. It was the expectation that during that year, he or she would have grown in understanding, as well as in capacity to exercise that measure of self-discipline which would result in personal worthiness. —*Gordon B. Hinckley* (Ensign, May 1990, 50)

Everything that occurs in the temple is eternal in its consequences. We there deal with matters of immortality, with things of eternity, with things of man and his relationship to his Divine Parent and his Redeemer. Hands must be clean and hearts must be pure and thoughts concerned with the solemnities of eternity when in these sacred premises.

Here is taught the great plan of man's eternal journey. Here are solemnized covenants sacred and everlasting. Entering the temple is a privilege to be earned and not a right that automatically goes with Church membership. —*Gordon B. Hinckley* (Ensign, May 1990, 50-51)

Every temple, be it large or small, old or new, is an expression of our testimony that life beyond the grave is as real and certain as is mortality. —*Gordon B. Hinckley* (Ensign, May 1993, 74)

One of my concerns is that not enough of our people are making the efforts to get a temple recommend which becomes a symbol of their worthiness and the righteousness of their desires. —*Gordon B. Hinckley* (CN, Sept. 2, 1995, 2)

Genealogical research and temple ordinance work are required of every Latter-day Saint. —*Howard W. Hunter* (Ensign, Feb. 1971, 5)

Perhaps the greatest example of vicarious work for the dead is the Master himself. He gave his life as a vicarious atonement, that all who die shall live again and have life everlasting. He did for us what we could not do for ourselves. In a similar way we can perform ordinances for those who did not have the opportunity to do them in lifetime. —*Howard W. Hunter* (Ensign, Dec. 1971, 71)

Let us be a temple-attending and a temple-loving people. Let us hasten to the temple as frequently as time and means and personal circumstances allow. —*Howard W. Hunter* (Ensign, Oct. 1994, 5)

The temple is a place of beauty, it is a place of revelation, it is a place of peace. It is the house of the Lord. It is holy unto the Lord. It should be holy unto us. —*Howard W. Hunter* (Ensign, Oct. 1994, 5)

If we can pattern our life after the Master, and take His teaching and examples as the supreme pattern for our own, we will not find it difficult to be temple worthy, to be consistent and loyal in every walk of life, for we will be committed to a single, sacred standard of conduct and belief. —*Howard W. Hunter* (Ensign, Oct. 1994, 5)

I invite the Latter-day Saints to look to the temple of the Lord as the great symbol of your membership. It is the deepest desire of my heart to have every member of the Church worthy to enter the temple. It would please the Lord if every adult member would be worthy of—and carry—a current temple recommend. The things that we must do and not do to be worthy of a temple recommend are the very things that ensure we will be happy as individuals and as families. —*Howard W. Hunter* (Ensign, Nov. 1994, 9)

Keep a picture of a temple in your home that your children may see it. Teach them about the purposes of the house of the Lord. Have them plan from their earliest years to go there and to remain worthy of that blessing. —*Howard W. Hunter* (Ensign, Nov. 1994, 9)

If proximity to a temple does not allow frequent attendance, gather in the history of your family and prepare the names for the sacred ordinances performed only in the temple. This family research is essential to the work of the temples, and blessings surely will come to those who do that work. —*Howard W. Hunter* (Ensign, Nov. 1994, 9)

Let us make the temple, with temple worship and temple covenants and temple marriage, our ultimate earthly goal and the supreme mortal experience. —*Howard W. Hunter* (Ensign , Nov. 1994, 88)

Let us prepare every missionary to go to the temple worthily and to make that experience an even greater highlight than receiving the mission call. —*Howard W. Hunter* (Ensign, Nov. 1994, 88)

Temple ordinances are absolutely crucial; we cannot return to God's presence without them. I encourage everyone to worthily attend the temple or to work toward the day when you can enter that holy house to receive your ordinances and covenants. —*Howard W. Hunter* (Ensign, Nov. 1994, 88)

Temples are really the gateways to heaven. —*Ezra Taft Benson* (ETB, 255)

I love the temples of God. This is the closest place to heaven on earth—the house of the Lord. —*Ezra Taft Benson* (ETB, 253)

Now let me say something to all who can worthily go to the house of the Lord. When you attend the temple and perform the ordinances that pertain to the house of the Lord, certain blessings will come to you: You will receive the spirit of Elijah, which will turn your hearts to your spouse, to your children, and to your forebears. You will love your family with a deeper love than you have loved before. You will be endowed with power from on high as the Lord has promised. —*Ezra Taft Benson* (Ensign, Aug. 1985, 10)

Much more must be done in our personal genealogical research. We have an obligation to do temple work for our kindred dead. This means that we will do the necessary research in order for the names of our progenitors to be sent to the temples. We have an individual responsibility to see that we are linked to our progenitors. —*Ezra Taft Benson* (ETB, 161)

Every time a temple is dedicated to the Lord the darkness pushes farther back, prison doors are opened, and light comes into the world. —*Spencer W. Kimball* (SWK, 534)

I am looking forward to the day when a temple will not close. They won't have any holidays, ever, and there won't be any night or day. The temple will have its lights on all night long and will be going night and day and full all the time. When vacation times comes, they let people go on vacations but they don't let the temple go on vacation. —*Spencer W. Kimball* (SWK, 539)

I hope to see us dissolve the artificial boundary line we so often place between missionary work and temple and genealogical work, because it is the same great redemptive work!—*Spencer W. Kimball* (Ensign, Jan. 1977, 3)

The requirements for entry into the temple are that a newly baptized member should not be given a temple recommend for even his own temple ordinances until he has been a member of the Church at least one year. Any flexibility in this requirement would be out of order in the Lord's church. It is analogous to making sure that before one is ready to eat meat, he is taught to drink milk; and one year is the length of time prescribed for this learning process. —*Harold B. Lee* (YLW, 215-217)

As the Savior was empowered to perform a vicarious work for all mankind by his atonement, so a merciful and just God has made it possible that faithful members of the Church might become "saviors on Mt. Zion" by doing work for their kindred dead, by which the doors to eternal salvation might be opened to them that thereby they might receive the same privileges as though they had been given the opportunity to receive the gospel while they lived as mortal beings. —*Harold B. Lee* (DSL, 138)

The only place on earth where we can receive the fullness of the blessings of the priesthood is in the holy temple. That is the only place where, through holy ordinances, we can receive that which will qualify us for exaltation in the celestial kingdom. —*Harold B. Lee* (SHP, 117)

Members of the Church who have been admitted to the temple do not discuss even among themselves outside the temple these temple ceremonies because of their sacred character. —*Harold B. Lee* (DSL, 137)

The Lord did a great vicarious work for all men, and he has delegated power to us in a lesser degree to perform a vicarious work for the dead. So we, too, may become saviors to our fellow men in this manner, performing work for them that they cannot perform for themselves. —*Joseph Fielding Smith* (DS2, 162)

Some people think we have got to do the work in the temple for everybody. Temple work belongs to the celestial kingdom, not to the other kingdoms. There will be millions of people, countless as the sands upon the seashore, who will not enter into the celestial kingdom. . . . There will be no need to do temple work for them. —*Joseph Fielding Smith* (CN, Jan. 5, 1935, 7)

The work for the dead is not intended for those who had every opportunity to receive it, who had it taught to them, and who then refused to receive it, or had not interest enough to attend to these ordinances when they were living. —*Joseph Fielding Smith* (CN, Feb. 12, 1938, 7)

They who go into the spirit world, who hold the priesthood of God, teach the dead the everlasting gospel in that spirit world; and when the dead are willing to repent and receive those teachings, and the work is done for them here vicariously, they shall have the privilege of coming out of the prison house to find their place in the kingdom of God. —*Joseph Fielding Smith* (CN, Feb. 12, 1938, 7)

There is no work connected with the gospel that is of a more unselfish nature than the work in the house of the Lord for our dead. Those who work for the dead do not expect to receive any earthly remuneration or reward. It is, above all, a work of love, which is begotten in the heart of man through faithful and constant labor in these saving ordinances. There are no financial returns, but there shall be great joy in heaven with those souls whom we have helped to their salvation. —*Joseph Fielding Smith* (IE, 20:362)

It matters not even if we have been baptized and have had hands laid on our heads for the reception of the Holy Ghost, if we willfully neglect the salvation of our dead, then we shall stand rejected of the Lord, because we have rejected our dead. —*Joseph Fielding Smith* (DS2, 145)

The greatest and grandest duty of all is to labor for the dead. —*Joseph Fielding Smith* (DS2, 148-149)

We have been so busy in other pursuits, principally in the accumulation of worldly goods that we cannot carry with us, that we have had no time or inclination to do the work for our dead. If one hundredth part of the energy expended by the members of the Church in other ways were directed in the channels of temple work where it properly belongs, we could accomplish a great deal more work than we are now doing for the salvation of the dead. —*Joseph Fielding Smith* (DS2, 151)

All nations and races have a just claim upon God's mercies. Since there is only one plan of salvation, surely there must be some provision made whereby the "uncounted dead" may hear of it and have the privilege of either accepting or rejecting it. Such a plan is given in the principle of salvation for the dead. —*David O. McKay* (GI, 17)

Think of the devotion and the faithfulness of those who day after day go into these temples and officiate for those who have passed to the other side, and know this that those who are on the other side are just as anxious about us. They are praying for us and for our success. They are pleading, in their own way, for their descendants. —*George Albert Smith* (CR, Apr. 1937, 35)

The Lord is helping us; it is marvelous how the way is opened and how other people frequently are prompted to prepare their genealogies. But sometimes we fail to take advantage of our opportunities to prepare our genealogies, notwithstanding the Lord has very pointedly said that unless we take care of our temple work we will be rejected with our dead. This is a very serious thing. This is something that we cannot change, if we have wasted our opportunities until life passes. . . .

If we do our part, our genealogies will be unfolded to us—sometimes in one way, sometimes in another. So I want to suggest to you, my brethren and sisters: let us do our part. —*George Albert Smith* (SGO, 178)

We can generally do that which we wish to do. A young man can find an immense amount of time to spend with his sweetheart. He can arrange affairs to do that. We can arrange our affairs to get exercise in the shape of golf and otherwise. We can arrange our affairs to have amusements. And if we make up our minds to do so we can arrange our affairs to do temple work. —*Heber J. Grant* (CR, Apr. 1928, 8-9)

One of the great works in this gospel of salvation, devolving upon us as Saints, is to labor in the temples of God for the salvation of our dead. —*Heber J. Grant* (CR, Oct. 1913, 87)

You cannot take a murderer, a suicide, an adulterer, a liar, or one who was or is thoroughly abominable in his life, here, and simply by the performance of an ordinance of the gospel, cleanse him from sin and usher him into the presence of God. God has not instituted a plan of that kind, and it cannot be done. —*Joseph F. Smith* (GD, 477)

There is, no doubt, great leniency given to people who are anxious to do the work for their dead, and in some instances, very unworthy people may have the work done for them; it does not follow, however, that they will receive any benefit therefrom, and the correct thing is to do the work only for those of whom we have the testimony that they will receive it. However, we are disposed to give the benefit of the doubt to the dead, as it is better to do the work for many who are unworthy than to neglect one who is worthy. —*Joseph F. Smith* (GD, 438-439)

Missionary work is more successful in spirit prison than on earth. A wonderful work is being accomplished in our temples in favor of the spirits in prison. I believe, strongly too, that when the gospel is preached to the spirits in prison, the success attending that preaching will be far greater than that attending the preaching of our elders in this life. —*Lorenzo Snow* (LS, 98)

Do you know what will be the main labor during the thousand years of rest? It will be that which we are trying to urge the Latter-day Saints to perform at the present time. Temples will be built all over this land, and the brethren and sisters will go into them and perhaps work day and night in order to hasten the work and accomplish the labors necessary before the Son of Man can present His kingdom to His Father. —*Lorenzo Snow* (LS, 97)

There is hardly any principle the Lord has revealed that I have rejoiced more in than in the redemption of our dead; that we will have our fathers, our mothers, our wives and our children with us in the family organization, in the morning of the first resurrection and in the celestial kingdom. These are grand principles. They are worth every sacrifice. —*Wilford Woodruff* (WW, 147)

We have a great work before us in the redemption of our dead. The course that we are pursuing is being watched with interest by all heaven. . . . It takes as much to save a dead-man as a living one. The eyes of these millions of people are watching over these Latter-day Saints. Have we any time to spend in trying to get rich and in neglecting our dead? I tell you no. —*Wilford Woodruff* (WW, 148)

God is no respecter of persons; he will not give privileges to one generation and with-hold them from another; and the whole human family, from father Adam down to our day, have got to have the privilege, somewhere, of hearing the gospel of Christ; and the genera-tions that have passed and gone without hearing that gospel in its fulness, power and glory, will never be held responsible by God for not obeying it. Neither will he bring them under condemnation for rejecting a law they never saw or understood; and if they live up to the light they had they are justified so far, and they have to be preached to in the spirit world. But nobody will baptize them there, and somebody has got to administer for them by proxy here in the flesh, that they may be judged according to men in the flesh and have part in the first resurrection. —*Wilford Woodruff* (WW, 149)

Oh, I wish many times that the veil were lifted off the face of the Latter-day Saints. I wish we could see and know the things of God as they do who are laboring for the salva-tion of the human family who are in the spirit world; for if this were so, this whole people, with very few, if any, exceptions, would lose all interest in the riches of the world, and instead thereof their whole desires and labors would be directed to redeem their dead, to per-form faithfully the work and mission given us on earth. —*Wilford Woodruff* (WW, 152)

We want the Latter-day Saints from this time to trace their genealogies as far as they can, and to be sealed to their fathers and mothers. Have children sealed to their parents, and run this chain through as far as you can get it. —*Wilford Woodruff* (WW, 157)

I will here say that two weeks before I left St. George, the spirits of the dead gathered around me, wanting to know why we did not redeem them. Said they, "You have had the use of the Endowment House for a number of years, and yet nothing has ever been done for us. We laid the foundation of the government you now enjoy, and we never apostatized from it, but we remained true to it and were faithful to God."

These were the signers of the Declaration of Independence, and they waited on me for two days and two nights. I thought it very singular, that notwithstanding so much work had been done, and yet nothing had been done for them. The thought never entered my heart, from the fact, I suppose, that heretofore our minds were reaching after our more immediate friends and relatives.

I straightway went into the baptismal font and called upon Brother McAllister to baptize me for the signers of the Declaration of Independence, and fifty other eminent men, mak-ing one hundred in all, including John Wesley, Columbus, and others. —*Wilford Woodruff* (WW, 160-161)

We read sometimes about the millennium, But what do we know about it? It is a time when this work will be going on, and temples, thousands of them, will be reared for the accomplishment of the objects designed, in which communications from the heavens will be received in regard to our labors, how we may perform them, and for whom. —*John Taylor* (GK, 287)

Now, I will ask, whoever thought of building temples until God revealed it? Did you? If you did, I wish you would tell us of it. And did you know how to build them? No. And did you know how to administer in them after they were built? No, you did not. We are indebted to the Lord for these things. —*John Taylor* (GK, 288)

Giving endowments to a great many proves their overthrow, through revealing things to them which they cannot keep. They are not worthy to receive them. —*Brigham Young* (BY, 397)

This doctrine of baptism for the dead is a great doctrine, one of the most glorious doctrines that was revealed to the human family; and there are light, power, glory, honor and immortality in it. —*Brigham Young* (BY, 399)

Let me give you a definition in brief. Your endowment is, to receive all those ordinances in the house of the Lord, which are necessary for you, after you have departed this life, to enable you to walk back to the presence of the Father, passing the angels who stand as sentinels, being enabled to give them the key words, the signs and tokens, pertaining to the holy Priesthood, and gain your eternal exaltation in spite of earth and hell. —*Brigham Young* (JD, 2:31)

The greatest responsibility in this world that God has laid upon us is to seek after our dead. —*Joseph Smith, Jr.* (LPS, 120)

The Saints have the privilege of being baptized for those of their relatives who are dead, whom they believe would have embraced the Gospel, if they had been privileged with hearing it, and who have received the Gospel in the spirit, through the instrumentality of those who have been commissioned to preach to them while in prison. —*Joseph Smith, Jr.* (STJS, 204)

There is a way to release the spirits of the dead; that is by the power and authority of the Priesthood—by binding and loosing on earth. This doctrine appears glorious, inasmuch as it exhibits the greatness of divine compassion and benevolence in the extent of the plan of human salvation.

This glorious truth is well calculated to enlarge the understanding, and to sustain the soul under troubles, difficulties and distresses. For illustration, suppose the case of two men, brothers, equally intelligent, learned, virtuous and lovely, walking in uprightness and in all good conscience, so far as they have been able to discern duty from the muddy stream of tradition, or from the blotted page of the book of nature.

One dies and is buried, having never heard the Gospel of reconciliation; to the other the message of salvation is sent, he hears and embraces it, and is made the heir of eternal life. Shall the one become the partaker of glory and the other be consigned to hopeless perdition? Is there no chance for his escape? Sectarianism answers "none." Such an idea is worse than atheism. —*Joseph Smith, Jr.* (STJS, 218)

If there is one word of the Lord that supports the doctrine of baptism for the dead, it is enough to establish it as a true doctrine. Again; if we can, by the authority of the Priesthood of the Son of God, baptize a man in the name of the Father, of the Son, and of the Holy Ghost, for the remission of sins, it is just as much our privilege to act as an agent, and be baptized for the remission of sins for and in behalf of our dead kindred, who have not heard the Gospel, or the fullness of it. —*Joseph Smith, Jr.* (STJS, 228)

It is not only necessary that you should be baptized for your dead, but you will have to go through all the ordinances for them, the same as you have gone through to save yourselves. —*Joseph Smith, Jr.* (STJS, 413)

THE COMMANDMENTS

27. THE COMMANDMENTS

To love the Lord is not just counsel, it is not just well-wishing, it is a commandment. It is the first and great commandment incumbent upon each of us because love of God is the root from which springs all other types of love; love of God is the root of all virtue, of all goodness, of all strength of character, of all fidelity to do right. —*Gordon B. Hinckley* (CN, March 2, 1996, 2)

He loves the Lord with all his heart who loves nothing in comparison of him, and nothing but in reference to him, who is ready to give up, do, or suffer anything in order to please and glorify him. He loves God with all his soul, or rather with all his life, who is ready to give up life for his sake and to be deprived of the comforts of the world to glorify him. He loves God with all his strength who exerts all the powers of his body and soul in the service of God. He loves God with all his mind who applies himself only to know God and his will, who sees God in all things and acknowledges him in all ways. —*Howard W. Hunter* (CR, Apr. 1965, 58)

One of Satan's most frequently used deceptions is the notion that the commandments of God are meant to restrict freedom and limit happiness. Young people especially sometimes feel that the standards of the Lord are like fences and chains, blocking them from those activities that seem most enjoyable in life. But exactly the opposite is true. The gospel plan is the plan by which men are brought to a fullness of joy. —*Ezra Taft Benson* (Ensign, Oct. 1989, 2)

There are Church members who are steeped in lethargy. They neither drink nor commit the sexual sins. They do not gamble nor rob nor kill. They are good citizens and splendid neighbors, but spiritually speaking they seem to be in a long, deep sleep. They are doing nothing seriously wrong except in their failures to do the right things to earn their exaltation. —*Spencer W. Kimball* (MF, 211-212)

Whoever said that sin was not fun? Whoever claimed that Lucifer was not handsome, persuasive, easy, friendly? Whoever said that sin was unattractive, undesirable, or nauseating in its acceptance?

Transgression wears elegant gowns and sparkling apparel. It is highly perfumed, has attractive features, a soft voice. It is found in educated circles and sophisticated groups. It provides sweet and comfortable luxuries. Sin is easy and has a big company of bedfellows. It promises immunity from restrictions, temporary freedoms. It can momentarily satisfy hunger, thirst, desire, urges, passions, wants, without immediately paying the price. But, it begins tiny and grows to monumental proportions. It grows drop by drop, inch by inch. —*Spencer W. Kimball* (Ensign, June 1976, 3)

Conscience tells the individual when he is entering forbidden worlds, and it continues to prick until silenced by the will or by sin's repetition. —*Spencer W. Kimball* (Ensign, Nov. 1980, 94)

We do not kill. We are even careful about killing animals, unless we need them for food. When I was a little boy. . . I would see boys there with a flipper flipping the birds up in the trees. . . . Isn't that a terrible thing, to take life just for the fun of it?—*Spencer W. Kimball* (SWK, 191)

We learn from the scriptures that because the exercise of faith has always appeared to be more difficult than relying on things more immediately at hand, carnal man has tended to transfer his trust in God to material things. . . . Whatever thing a man sets his heart and his trust in most is his god; and if his god doesn't also happen to be the true and living God of Israel, that man is laboring in idolatry. —*Spencer W. Kimball* (Ensign, June 1976, 3)

As one studies the commandments of God, it seems crystal clear that the all-important thing is not where we live, but whether or not our hearts are pure. —*Harold B. Lee* (SHP, 24)

If I were to ask you what is the heaviest burden one may have to bear in this life, what would you answer? The heaviest burden that one has to bear in this life is the burden of sin. —*Harold B. Lee* (SHP, 184)

The most important of all the commandments of God is that one that you are having the most difficulty keeping today. —*Harold B. Lee* (HBL, 82)

Any conduct on the part of an individual that does not advance him toward the goal of eternal life is not only wasted energy but actually becomes the basis of sin. —*Harold B. Lee* (DSL, 8)

The man who has received the truth and yet will not walk in it deserves the greater condemnation. —*Joseph Fielding Smith* (CR, Oct. 1926, 120)

Every member of this Church who violates the Sabbath day, who is not honest in the paying of his tithing, who will not keep the Word of Wisdom, who wilfully violates any of the other commandments the Lord has given us, is ungrateful to the Son of God, and when ungrateful to the Son of God is ungrateful to the Father who sent him. —*Joseph Fielding Smith* (CR, Oct. 5, 1947, 149)

Our Father in Heaven does not give us commandments or advice that are not of importance. —*George Albert Smith* (CR, Apr. 1908, 35)

The laws of the Lord, so-called, the counsels contained in the Holy Scriptures, the revelations of the Lord to us in this day and age of the world, are but the sweet music of the voice of our Father in Heaven, in His mercy to us. They are but the advice and counsel of a loving parent, who is more concerned in our welfare than earthly parents can be, and consequently that which at one time seemed to bear the harsh name of law, to me is now the loving and tender advice of an all-wise Heavenly Father. And so I say that it is not hard for me to believe that it is best to keep the commandments of God. —*George Albert Smith* (CR, Oct. 1911, 43-44)

It doesn't make any difference how unreasonable it may appear to the human family; if the Lord makes a promise to his people, that promise will be fulfilled. —*George Albert Smith* (GAS, 6)

We must save ourselves and stand for our own sins. We cannot blame our negligence upon somebody else. —*Heber J. Grant* (GS, 5)

By the assistance of our Heavenly Father there is no obligation and no law in the Church that we cannot fulfill. —*Heber J. Grant* (CR, Oct. 1900, 33)

We rejoice in knowing that no man or woman who keeps the commandments of God ever loses the testimony of the divinity of this work in which we are engaged. —*Heber J. Grant* (CR, Apr. 1912, 106)

There is no power given to the adversary of men's souls to destroy us if we are doing our duty. If we are not absolutely honest with God, then we let the bars down, then we have destroyed part of the fortifications by which we are protected, and the devil may come in. But no man has ever lost the testimony of the gospel, no man has ever turned to the right or to the left, who had the knowledge of the truth, who was attending to his duties, who was keeping the Word of Wisdom, who was paying his tithing, who was responding to the calls and duties of his office and calling in the Church. —*Heber J. Grant* (CR, Oct. 1900, 60)

There are no people that make the sacrifices that we do, but for us it is not a sacrifice but a privilege—the privilege of obedience, the privilege of entering into a working partnership with our Father in Heaven and earning the choice blessings promised to those who love Him and keep His commandments. —*Heber J. Grant* (IE, 42:457)

I desire to seek first the Kingdom of God. I do know and bear witness to you that if I do it, all other things for my good will be added unto me. And what I bear witness to pertaining to myself, I bear witness to for all the Latter-day Saints. . . .
We have started out for life eternal, the greatest of all gifts of God to man, and keeping the commandments of God will bring it to us. —*Heber J. Grant* (CR, Oct. 1899, 19-20)

The Lord, you know, does not send collectors around once a month to collect bills. He does not send us our account once a month. We are trusted by the Lord. We are agents. We have our free will. And when the battle of life is over, we have had the ability and the power and the capacity to have done those things which the Lord required us to do and we cannot blame anybody else. —*Heber J. Grant* (LPS, 326)

There is no liberty that men enjoy or pretend to enjoy in the world that is not founded in the will and in the law of God. —*Joseph F. Smith* (GD, 53)

Until we do our duty, however, in that which we have received, until we are faithful over the things that are now committed into our hands, until we live our religion as we have it now, as the Lord has given it to us, to add commandments, to add light and intelligence to us over that which we have already received, which we have not yet fully obeyed, would be to add condemnation upon our heads. —*Joseph F. Smith* (CR, Oct. 1917, 5)

It is perfectly natural that the children should inherit from their fathers, and if they sow the seeds of corruption, crime and loathsome disease, their children will reap the fruits thereof. Not in accordance with God's wishes, for his wish is that men will not sin and therefore will not transmit the consequences of their sin to their children. —*Joseph F. Smith* (CR, Oct. 1912, 9)

I do not believe any man should kill animals or birds unless he needs them for food, and then he should not kill innocent little birds that are not intended for food for man. I think it is wicked for men to thirst in their soul to kill almost everything which possesses animal life. —*Joseph F. Smith* (GD, 266)

The Lord never has, nor will He require things of His children which it is impossible for them to perform. —*Lorenzo Snow* (LS, 37)

We believe that God is no respecter of persons, but that He confers blessings upon all His children in proportion to the light they have, or in proportion as they proceed according to the light and knowledge they possess in the different circumstances of life that may surround them. —*Lorenzo Snow* (LS, 107)

[I]n obeying every law that is given to exalt us and to do us good, it is all for our individual benefit and the benefit of our children, and it is not of any particular benefit of the Lord, only as he is pleased in the faithfulness of his children and desires to see them walk in the path which leads to salvation and eternal life. —*Wilford Woodruff* (WW, 179)

I have never committed a sin in this church and kingdom, but what it has cost me a thousand times more than it was worth. —*Wilford Woodruff* (WW, 278)

With regard to the law of God, it is all right. We can well afford to keep it and trust in him. —*Wilford Woodruff* (WW, 263)

God is unchangeable, so are also his laws, in all their forms, and in all their applications, and being himself the essence of law, the giver of law, the sustainer of law, all of those laws are eternal in all their operations, in all bodies and matter, and throughout all space. It would be impossible for him to violate law, because in so doing he would strike at his own dignity, power, principles, glory, exaltation and existence. —*John Taylor* (GK, 69)

There is not a man of us but what is willing to acknowledge at once that God demands strict obedience to his requirements. But in rendering that strict obedience, are we made slaves? No, it is the only way on the face of the earth for you and me to become free, and we shall become slaves of our own passions, and of the wicked one, and servants to the Devil, if we take any other course. —*Brigham Young* (BY, 225)

Love the Lord thy God with all thy heart, and then speak evil of thy neighbor? No! No! Love the Lord thy God with all thy heart, and speak that which is not true? No, oh, no! Love the Lord thy God with all thy heart, and take that which is not thy own? No, no, no! Love the Lord thy God with all thy heart, and seek after riches of the world and forsake your religion? No! Love the Lord thy God with all thy heart and take his name in vain, curse and swear? No, never! If the love of God was really in the hearts of all who call themselves Latter-day Saints, there would be no more swearing, no more lying, no more deceiving, no more speaking evil of one another . . . —*Brigham Young* (BY, 21)

I do not hate any man on earth or in hell. The worst wish I have for the wicked is that they may be obliged to live according to good and wholesome laws. —*Brigham Young* (BY, 456)

God has given certain laws to the human family, which, if observed, are sufficient to prepare them to inherit this [celestial] rest. This, then, we conclude, was the purpose of God in giving His laws to us: If not, why, or for what were they given? If the whole family of man were as well off without them as they might be with them, for what purpose or intent were they ever given? Was it that God wanted to merely show that He could talk? It would be nonsense to suppose that He would condescend to talk in vain: for it would be in vain, and to no purpose whatever (if the law of God were of no benefit to man). —*Joseph Smith, Jr.* (STJS, 67-68)

[N]o murderer hath eternal life. . . . The prayers of all the ministers in the world can never close the gates of hell against a murderer. —*Joseph Smith, Jr.* (STJS, 213-214)

Whatever God requires is right, no matter what it is, although we may not see the reason thereof till long after the events transpire. —*Joseph Smith, Jr.* (STJS, 287)

[A]s God has designed our happiness—and the happiness of all His creatures, he never has—He never will institute an ordinance or give a commandment to His people that is not calculated in its nature to promote that happiness which He has designed, and which will not end in the greatest amount of good and glory to those who become the recipients of his law and ordinances. —*Joseph Smith, Jr.* (STJS, 288)

I made this my rule: When the Lord commands, do it. —*Joseph Smith, Jr.* (HC 2, 170)

28. OBEDIENCE

We are a people who have taken upon us a solemn covenant and the name of the Lord Jesus Christ. Let us strive a little harder to keep the commandments, to live as the Lord has asked us to live. We are his children. He delights in our good behavior and I think He grieves when we misbehave. —*Gordon B. Hinckley* (CN, Apr. 6, 1996, 14)

Our world cries out for more disciplined living of the commandments of God. —*Howard W. Hunter* (Ensign , Sept. 1994, 2)

Are we prepared to surrender to God's commandments? Are we prepared to achieve victory over our appetites? Are we prepared to obey righteous law?—*Howard W. Hunter* (WMJ, 96)

Surely the Lord loves, more than anything else, an unwavering determination to obey his counsel. —*Howard W. Hunter* (WMJ, 156)

We need to keep the commandments of God, and we need to encourage all to do so. Obedience is the most genuine way to show our love for God. —*Howard W. Hunter* (CN, March 11, 1995 7)

The great task of life is to learn the will of the Lord and then do it. —*Ezra Taft Benson* (Ensign, May 1988, 6)

Why did God put the first commandment first? Because He knew that if we truly loved Him we would want to keep all of His other commandments. . . .
When we put God first, all other things fall into their proper place or drop out of our lives. Our love of the Lord will govern the claims of our affection, the demands on our time, the interests we pursue, and the order of our priorities. —*Ezra Taft Benson* (Ensign, May 1988, 4)

The Lord expects of us righteousness and obedience to His commandments in return for the bounties of life He has so richly bestowed upon us. —*Spencer W. Kimball* (CR, Nov. 1982, 4)

[S]in may be either the willful breaking of divine law or you may sin by your failure and neglect in thought, word or deed to keep the commandments of the Lord. —*Harold B. Lee* (DSL, 82)

Build a bonfire sometime and watch the beautiful moths and insects come wheeling in because of the enticement of the bright lights. Round and round, closer and closer they whirl until their daring prompts a fatal mistake and they fall with singed wings to their doom in the burning furnace of tempting fascination. I've seen beautiful young human butterflies playing with the tempting fires of sin. . . .

Many of these beautiful human butterflies winged for heavenly flight have fallen with wings singed and badly seared because of their curiosity about the forbidden. The more I see of life, the more I am convinced that we must impress you young people with the awfulness of sin rather than to content ourselves with merely teaching the way of repentance. —*Harold B. Lee* (DSL, 87-88)

As one keeps the commandments of God, he is not only persuaded as to the righteousness of the course that is being followed under the leadership of the Church, but he also will have the Spirit of the Lord to guide him in his individual activities. —*Harold B. Lee* (YLW, 146)

Never at any time has the Lord given to man a commandment which was not intended to exalt him and bring him nearer to eternal companionship with the Father and the Son. Too many of us receive the commandments of the Lord in the spirit of indifference or with the attitude of mind toward them that they have been given for the sole purpose of depriving us of some comfort or pleasure without any real profit to be derived in the observance of them. —*Joseph Fielding Smith* (CN, May 6, 1939, 3)

The man who is guided by the Holy Spirit and who keeps the commandments of God, who abides in God, will have the clearest understanding and the better judgment always, because he is directed by the Spirit of truth. And the man who relies upon himself, or the knowledge of other men, will not have as clear a vision as will the man who abides in the truth and is directed by the Holy Spirit. —*Joseph Fielding Smith* (CN, Mar. 30, 1940, 1)

Of course, the Lord is no respecter of persons, and all souls are precious in his sight, but he no doubt loves those who obey his voice and who are willing to walk in his truth, more than he does those who fail to do so. —*Joseph Fielding Smith* (CR, Apr. 1928, 66)

Men are rebellious; they are not willing to live in that law and profit thereby; they are not willing to receive the good things of the earth as the Lord would give to them in abundance; but in their narrow-mindedness, shortsightedness, and in their greed and selfishness, they think they know better than the Lord does. And so, they pursue another course, and the result is that the blessings of the Lord are withdrawn, and in the place thereof come calamity, destruction, plagues, and violence. Men have themselves to blame. —*Joseph Fielding Smith* (CN, May 4, 1935, 3)

We are covenant-breakers; we violate the Sabbath day, we will not keep it holy; we do not keep our bodies clean; I do not believe we pray—a large part of us, I mean. As far as the fast day is concerned, we have forgotten it. We are not half as good as we think we are. We need repentance, and we need to be told to repent. We need to have our attention called to these conditions that we might repent and turn to the Lord with full purpose of heart. —*Joseph Fielding Smith* (CN, May 4, 1935, 6)

We obey law from a sense of right.
We honor law because of its necessity and strength to society.
We sustain law by keeping it in good repute. —*David O. McKay* (CR, Apr. 1937, 28)

We cannot live the commandments without first knowing them, and we cannot expect to know all or more than we now know unless we comply with or keep those we have already received. —*David O. McKay* (CR, Apr. 1936, 45)

There is only one way that we can enjoy our lives, and that is by being obedient to the teachings of an all-wise Father who knows the end from the beginning. —*George Albert Smith* (CR, Apr. 1932, 44)

My understanding is that the most important mission that I have in this life is: first to keep the commandments of God, as they have been taught to me; and next, to teach them to my Father's children who do not understand them. —*George Albert Smith* (CR, Oct. 1916, 50)

There is no gain in this world or in the world to come but by obedience to the law of our Heavenly Father. —*George Albert Smith* (CR, Apr. 1918, 41)

If we will honor God and keep his commandments and live as we should, no matter where the storms may strike, the winds may blow, and the lightnings may flash, we will be as the children of God always have been when they have kept his commandments: we will be under the protecting hand of him who is all-powerful. —*George Albert Smith* (CR, Apr. 1949, 171)

Every blessing we enjoy is the result of keeping the commandments of God. Every blessing we desire we must obtain on those same terms. —*George Albert Smith* (CR, Apr. 1947, 166)

The beauty of the gospel of Jesus Christ is that it makes us all equal in as far as we keep the commandments of the Lord. In as far as we observe to keep the laws of the church we have equal opportunities for exaltation. As we develop faith and righteousness, our light is made to shine as a guide and blessing to those with whom we mingle. —*George Albert Smith* (SGO, 113)

Throughout the world, those who have not faith in God, have not complied with his teachings, have not listened to the whisperings of the still small voice, have not done their best, else the Lord would not have forsaken them. The spirit of God continues to strive with men everywhere, as long as they make the effort to keep his commandments. When men abandon the truth, refuse to do the right, the Lord of necessity withdraws his spirit and men are left to the buffetings of the adversary. —*George Albert Smith* (CR, Oct. 1916, 48)

Why was it necessary for the flood to come? Why did the Lord permit the cities of the plains to be destroyed by fire? It was because the people would not take advantage of their opportunities. They were not only wasting their lives here upon the earth but were also bringing into the world another generation which would follow their bad example. In both cases, it seems to me, our Heavenly Father in his wisdom and mercy cleansed the earth by the flood and cleared the way for a righteous people to dwell here if they would. —*George Albert Smith* (CR, Oct. 1936, 71-72)

Unhappiness has always followed violating the advice of our Heavenly Father. —*George Albert Smith* (CR, Apr. 1944, 31)

A man once said to me—or remarked in a place where I happened to be—"Why, these people here seem to think I am full of the devil, but I am not." And I said to him, "My brother, did you ever know anybody that was full of the devil and knew it?" That is one of the tricks of the devil: To get possession of you and keep you from knowing it. And that is one of our difficulties. —*George Albert Smith* (CR, Apr. 1948, 180)

There is but one path of safety to the Latter-day Saints, and that is the path of duty. It is not a testimony, it is not marvelous manifestation, it is not knowing that the gospel of Jesus Christ is true, that it is the plan of salvation—it is not actually knowing that the Savior is the Redeemer, and that Joseph Smith was His prophet that will save you and me; but it is the keeping of the commandments of God, living the life of a Latter-day Saint. —*Heber J. Grant* (CR, Apr. 1915, 82)

Of what good are our faith, our repentance, our baptism, and all the sacred ordinances of the gospel by which we have been made ready to receive the blessings of the Lord, if we fail, on our part, to keep the commandments? All that we expect, or all that we are promised, is predicated on our own actions, and if we fail to act, or to do the work which God has required of us, we are little better than those who have not received the principles and ordinances of the gospel. —*Heber J. Grant* (IE, 24:259)

It has ever been my desire, in laboring among the Latter-day Saints, to inspire them with a desire to obey the commandments of God. —*Heber J. Grant* (GS, xx)

I say to all Latter-day Saints: Keep the commandments of God. That is my keynote speech, just those few words: Keep the commandments of God. —*Heber J. Grant* (CR, Oct. 1920, 10)

Now may the Lord help you and me, and every soul that has a knowledge of this gospel, to realize that the first and foremost thing of our lives is to serve God and keep His commandments, and that we do not propose to let anybody do it any better than we will. That is the ambition we should have. —*Heber J. Grant* (IE, 44:713)

The one thing that you and I need to worry about, and the only thing, is with regard to keeping the commandments of the Lord, living our religion as Latter-day Saints. —*Heber J. Grant* (CR, Oct. 1931, 4-5)

When I realize how many of those who have been wonderfully blessed of the Lord have fallen by the wayside, it fills me with humility. It fills me with the spirit of meekness and with an earnest desire that I may ever seek to know the mind and the will of God and to keep His commandments rather than to follow out my own desires. —*Heber J. Grant* (CR, Apr. 1899, 26)

We are not ready and willing to keep the commandments of God, but we are ready and willing to carry out our own wishes. We do not ask what it is desired that we should do, but generally suit ourselves as to what we would like to do. Is this right? No, it is not. I feel that there is plenty of room for improvement, and we should improve. —*Heber J. Grant* (CR, Apr. 1898, 15)

I am sorry to say that there are many professed Latter-day Saints who are spiritually dead.

We many times ask ourselves the question, why does this man progress in the plan of life and salvation, while his neighbor, of equal intelligence and ability, of apparently the same testimony and power, and perchance greater power, stands still?

I will tell you why. One keeps the commandments of our Heavenly Father, and the other fails to keep them. —*Heber J. Grant* (CR, Apr. 1900, 21-22)

There are a great many people who are very active in preaching this gospel who fail to obey it themselves. Let us obey, and then we shall find that there is no power on earth or beneath the earth that can stop us in good works. —*Heber J. Grant* (CR, Apr. 1931, 130)

No man need fear in his heart when he is conscious of having lived up to the principles of truth and righteousness as God has required it at his hands, according to his best knowledge and understanding. —*Joseph F. Smith* (CR, Apr. 1904, 2)

Obedience is one of the first principles or laws of heaven. Without obedience, there can be no order, no government, no union, no plan or purpose carried out. And that obedience must be voluntary; it must not be forced, there must be no coercion. Men must not be constrained against their will to obey the will of God; they must obey it because they know it to be right, because they desire to do it, and because it is their pleasure to do it. God delights in the willing heart. —*Joseph F. Smith* (GD, 64-65)

We shall never see the day in time nor in eternity, when it will not be obligatory, and when it will not be a pleasure as well as a duty for us, as his children, to obey all the commandments of the Lord throughout the endless ages of eternity. —*Joseph F. Smith* (CR, Apr. 1898, 68)

Whoso will keep the commandments of God, no matter whether it be you or any other people, they will rise and not fall, they will lead and not follow, they will go upward and not downward. God will exalt them and magnify them before the nations of the earth, and he will set the seal of his approval upon them, will name them as his own. This is my testimony to you. —*Joseph F. Smith* (IE, 6:501)

We should enjoy our religion. No religion has in it such prospects as has the religion of the Latter-day Saints. . . . Nothing is so beautiful as a person in a resurrected and glorified condition. There is nothing more lovely than to be in this condition and have our wives and children and friends with us. So long as we are faithful, nothing can prevent us from getting all the enjoyment that can be secured through prospects of this kind. . . . Now, brethren and sisters, be faithful, keep the commandments of God. —*Lorenzo Snow* (LS, 62)

It is not in the economy of the Almighty to permit His people to be destroyed. If we will do right and keep His commandments, He will surely deliver us from every difficulty. —*Lorenzo Snow* (LS, 172)

Make this a land of Zion in very deed by keeping the commandments of God thereon; and strive to teach your children in such a way, both by example and precept, that they will unhesitatingly follow in your footsteps and become as valiant for the truth as you have been. —*Lorenzo Snow* (LS, 181)

Let us be obedient to the voice of truth, and ever be found in the path of duty; and there let us continue. Let a man do this, and he continues to advance; he will grow in the knowledge of God, and in influence, and in everything that is good. —*Lorenzo Snow* (LS, 28)

[W]e must seek the ability to . . . sanctify our motives, desires, feelings, and affections, that they may be pure and holy, and our will in all things be subservient to the will of God, and have no will of our own except to do the will of our Father. —*Lorenzo Snow* (JD, 20:189)

If I ever obtain a full salvation it will be by my keeping the laws of God. —*Wilford Woodruff* (WW, 23)

I realize that the salvation of this people does not depend upon the great amount of teaching, instruction, or revelation that is given unto them, but their salvation depends more upon their obeying the commandments of God which are given unto them, their becoming a doer of the word, and following the counsel of those who are set to lead them. —*Wilford Woodruff* (WW, 24)

[W]e can, as individuals and as a people, afford to maintain our integrity in this our day and generation, regardless of consequences. We can afford to be true and faithful to God; we can afford to carry our every principle and commandment which God had given us; we can afford to do this. —*Wilford Woodruff* (WW, 83)

I know that I cannot afford to disobey any commandment which God has given to me, because there is no man who holds the priesthood, and possessing the inspiration and the gifts of God and the light of truth, but would be ashamed both in the flesh and in the spirit world to meet his God, and to be obliged to acknowledge that he did not obey his commandments. —*Wilford Woodruff* (WW, 84)

I feel that of all people under heaven we ought to be the most grateful to our God; and that we ought to remember to keep our covenants, and humble ourselves before him, and labor with all our hearts to discharge faithfully the responsibilities which devolve upon us, and the duties which are required at our hands. For we can afford to do anything which God requires of us; but none of us can afford to do wrong. It would cost far more than this world with all its wealth is worth for the Latter-day Saints to do wrong and come under the disfavor of Almighty God. —*Wilford Woodruff* (WW, 122-123)

We have learned this, that God lives; we have learned that when we call upon him he hears our prayers; we have learned that it is the height of human happiness to fear God and observe his laws and keep his commandments; we have learned that it is a duty devolving upon us to try and make all men happy and intelligent, which happiness and intelligence can only be obtained through obedience to the laws of God. —*John Taylor* (GK, 30)

You will be damned if you do act as you please unless you please to do and to keep the laws of God. We cannot violate his laws with impunity nor trample under foot these eternal principles which exist in all Nature. If all Nature is compelled to be governed by law or suffer loss, why not man?—*John Taylor* (GK, 79)

Our safety and happiness and our wealth depend upon our obedience to God and his laws, and our exaltation in time and eternity depends upon the same thing. —*John Taylor* (GK, 248)

As Latter-day Saints we believe this gospel has been restored, and further, we know that we are in possession of it. . . . Through obedience to its principles, and the reception of the Holy Ghost, you Latter-day Saints do know that this is the work of God; and if you don't know it, it is because you are not living your religion, and keeping the commandments of God. —*John Taylor* (GK, 15)

Let us then seek to be one, honor our God, honor our religion, and keep the commandments of God, and seek to know his will, and then to do it. —*John Taylor* (GK, 143)

We are here to serve God and keep his commandments; and if we will purge ourselves from our iniquities, live our religion, and keep the commandments of God, there is no power on this side of hell, nor on the other, that can harm us, for God will be on our side to protect us in the position we occupy. —*John Taylor* (GK, 226)

We cannot run our own way and have the blessing of God. Every one who attempts it will find he is mistaken. God will withdraw his Spirit from such, and they will be left to themselves to wander in the dark, and go down to perdition. . . . He expects us to live our religion, to obey his laws and keep his commandments. —*John Taylor* (GK, 230)

It is for us to keep the commandments, to train up our children in the fear of God, to live unto God, and I will risk the balance. —*John Taylor* (GK, 276)

Every son and daughter of God is expected to obey with a willing heart every word which the Lord has spoken, and which he will in the future speak to us. . . . [A]ny thing short of this clips the salvation and the glory of the Saints. —*Brigham Young* (BY, 220)

I cannot save you. I can tell you how to save yourselves, but you must do the will of God. —*Brigham Young* (BY, 220)

Wherever the wisdom of God directs, let our affections and the labour of our lives be centered to that point, and not set our hearts on going east or west, north or south, on living here or there, on possessing this or that; but let our will be swallowed up in the will of God, allowing him to rule supremely within us until the spirit overcomes the flesh. —*Brigham Young* (JD, 9:106)

The same principle will embrace what is called sanctification. When the will, passions, and feelings of a person are perfectly submissive to God and His requirements, that person is sanctified. It is for my will to be swallowed up in the will of God, that will lead me into all good, and crown me ultimately with immortality and eternal lives. —*Brigham Young* (JD, 2:123)

I am responsible for the doctrine I teach; but I am not responsible for the obedience of the people to that doctrine. —*Brigham Young* (BY, 168)

If you wish to receive and enjoy the favor of our Heavenly Father, do his will. —*Brigham Young* (BY, 223)

Do you think that people will obey the truth because it is true, unless they love it? No, they will not. Truth is obeyed when it is loved. —*Brigham Young* (BY, 220)

The devil has no power over us only as we permit him. The moment we revolt at anything which comes from God, the devil takes power. —*Joseph Smith, Jr.* (STJS, 206)

Be virtuous and pure; be men of integrity and truth; keep the commandments of God; and then you will be able more perfectly to understand the difference between right and wrong—between the things of God and the things of men; and your path will be like that of the just, which shineth brighter and brighter unto the perfect day. —*Joseph Smith, Jr.* (STJS, 277)

If a man gets a fullness of the priesthood of God he has to get it in the same way that Jesus Christ obtained it, and that was by keeping all the commandments and obeying all the ordinances of the house of the Lord. —*Joseph Smith, Jr.* (STJS, 345)

Certainly, if the law of man is binding upon man when acknowledged, how much more must the law of heaven be! And as much as the law of heaven is more perfect than the law of man, so much greater must be the reward if obeyed. The law of man promises safety in temporal life; but the law of God promises that life which is eternal, even an inheritance at God's own right hand, secure from all the powers of the wicked one. —*Joseph Smith, Jr.* (STJS, 63)

Happiness is the object and design of our existence; and will be the end thereof, if we pursue the path that leads to it; and this path is virtue, uprightness, faithfulness, holiness, and keeping all the commandments of God. But we cannot keep all the commandments without first knowing them, and we cannot expect to know all, or more than we now know unless we comply with or keep those we have already received. —*Joseph Smith, Jr.* (STJS, 287)

Any man may believe that Jesus Christ is the Son of God, and be happy in that belief, and yet not obey his commandments, and at last be cut down for disobedience to the Lord's righteous requirements. —*Joseph Smith, Jr.* (STJS, 348)

The object with me is to obey and teach others to obey God in just what He tells us to do. It mattereth not whether the principle is popular or unpopular, I will always maintain a true principle, even if I stand alone in it. —*Joseph Smith, Jr.* (STJS, 375)

To get salvation we must not only do some things, but everything which God has commanded. —*Joseph Smith, Jr.* (LPS, 139)

29. CHASTITY AND VIRTUE

Was there ever adultery without dishonesty? In the vernacular, the evil is described as "cheating." And cheating it is, for it robs virtue, it robs loyalty, it robs sacred promises, it robs self-respect, it robs truth. —*Gordon B. Hinckley* (BTE, 44)

For your own sake, for your happiness now and in all the years to come, and for the happiness of the generations who come after you avoid sexual transgression as you would a plague. —*Gordon B. Hinckley* (CR, May 1987, 47-48)

To hope for peace and love and gladness out of promiscuity is to hope for that which will never come. To wish for freedom out of immorality is to wish for something that cannot be. —*Gordon B. Hinckley* (Ensign, Aug. 1989, 5-6)

I believe in the beauty of personal virtue. There is so much of ugliness in the world in which we live. It is expressed in coarse language, in sloppy dress and manners, in immoral behavior which mocks the beauty of virtue and always leaves a scar. Each of us can and must stand above this sordid and destructive evil, this ugly stain of immorality. —*Gordon B. Hinckley* (Ensign, Aug. 1992, 2-7)

Let me say that any young man who asks for sexual favors from a young woman whom he may be dating on the basis that he loves her, is saying in the strongest terms that he does not love her. Such an expression is one of lust and not of love. —*Gordon B. Hinckley* (CN, May 4, 1996, 2)

We believe in chastity before marriage and total fidelity after marriage. That sums it up. That is the way to happiness in living. That is the way to satisfaction. It brings peace to the heart and peace to the home. —*Gordon B. Hinckley* (Ensign, Nov. 1996, 49)

Stay away from those things which will tear you down and destroy you spiritually. Stay away from television shows which lead to unclean thoughts and unclean language. Stay away from videos which will lead to evil thoughts. They won't help you. They will hurt you. Stay away from books and magazines which are sleazy and filthy in what they say and portray. Keep thyself pure. —*Gordon B. Hinckley* (CR, May 1997, 49)

Pornography, with its sleazy filth, sweeps over the earth like a horrible, engulfing tide. It is poison. Do not watch it or read it. It will destroy you if you do. It will take from you your self-respect. It will rob you of a sense of the beauties of life. It will tear you down and pull you into a slough of evil thoughts and possibly evil actions. Stay away from it. Shun it as you would a foul disease, for it is just as deadly. Be virtuous in thought and deed. —*Gordon B. Hinckley* (Ensign, Nov. 1997, 51)

One of the standards on which your happiness is based, now and in your future, is moral purity. The world would tell you that this standard is old-fashioned and out of date. The world would have you accept a so-called new morality, which is nothing more than immorality. —*Ezra Taft Benson* (NE, June 1986, 5)

When it comes to the law of chastity, it is better to prepare and prevent than it is to repair and repent. —*Ezra Taft Benson* (ETB, 284)

Be careful in the selection of your friends. If in the presence of certain persons you are lifted to nobler heights, you are in good company. But if your friends or associates encourage base thoughts, then you had best leave them. —*Ezra Taft Benson* (ETB, 562)

If you are engaged in things where you do not feel you can pray and ask the Lord's blessings on what you are doing, you are engaged in the wrong kind of activity. —*Ezra Taft Benson* (ETB, 562)

Old values are upheld by the Church not because they are old, but rather because through the ages they have proved right. It will always be the rule. —*Spencer W. Kimball* (Ensign, Nov. 1980 3)

Once the carnal in man is no longer checked by the restraints of family life and by real religion, there comes an avalanche of appetites which gathers momentum that is truly frightening. As one jars loose and begins to roll downhill, still another breaks loose, whether it is an increase in homosexuality, corruption, drugs, or abortion. Each began as an appetite that needed to be checked but which went unchecked. Thus misery achieves a ghastly momentum. —*Spencer W. Kimball* (CR, May 1978, 76)

Sex involvement outside of marriage locks the doors to temples, and thus bars the way to eternal life. —*Spencer W. Kimball* (SWK, 272)

Homosexuality is an ugly sin.
There is today a strong clamor to make such practices legal by passing legislation. Some would also legislate to legalize prostitution. They have legalized abortion, seeking to remove from this heinous crime the stigma of sin.
We do not hesitate to tell the world that the cure for these evils is not in surrender. —*Spencer W. Kimball* (CR, Nov. 1977, 73)

Holding hands would generally not be immoral, but it would depend on whether or not one's mind ran rampant. . . . Two people could embrace, kiss, dance, look, and I can conceive of one of them being immoral and the other innocent of sin. —*Spencer W. Kimball* (SWK, 282)

Pornographic and erotic stories and pictures are worse than polluted food. Shun them. The body has power to rid itself of sickening food. The person who entertains filthy stories or pornographic pictures and literature record them in his marvelous human computer, the brain, which can't forget such filth. Once recorded, it will always remain there, subject to recall. —*Spencer W. Kimball* (Ensign, Oct. 1985, 6)

To have strength to overcome temptation is Godlike. The strong, the virtuous and the true of every generation have lived pure, clean lives, not because their emotions were less impelling nor because their temptations were fewer but because their will to do was greater and their faith in divine guidance won them strength through prayer that proved their kinship with the great Exemplar who gave us the pattern for the perfect life. —*Harold B. Lee* (DSL, 43)

As we see the hideous dress standards among the men and women, as we learn of the terrifying portrayal of filth and rot in entertainment places, we say . . . never go to any place that you wouldn't take your priesthood with you. —*Harold B. Lee* (Ensign, Nov. 1971, 14)

We have been taught that adultery is a crime second only to the shedding of innocent blood. We cannot treat it lightly. For a man to destroy another man's home is too serious an offense to be readily forgiven. Such a man should not be permitted to come back in the Church, under any circumstances, at least until years have elapsed. He should be placed on probation for that length of time to see if he can, or will, remain clean. Even then I confess I do not know what disposition the Lord will make of him. To permit him to come back within a short time has a very evil effect upon other members of the Church who begin to think that this enormous crime is not so serious after all. —*Joseph Fielding Smith* (DS2, 94)

Our passions are virtues to perpetuate life. Prostitute them, and you have the vilest of sins!—*David O. McKay* (GI, 356)

Chastity is a virtue to be prized as one of life's noblest achievements. It contributes to the virility of manhood. It is the crowning virtue of womanhood . . . It is a chief contributing factor to a happy home; it is the source of strength and perpetuity of the nation. —*David O. McKay* (IE, 52:560)

Chastity is the crown of beautiful womanhood, and self-control is the source of true manhood, if you will know it, not indulgence. —*David O. McKay* (CR, Apr. 1952, 86)

In the Church there is but one standard of morality. No young man has any more right to sow his wild oats in youth than has a young girl; she is taught that second only to the crime of taking human life is that of losing her virtue, and that should be also the ideal among young men. —*David O. McKay* (CR, Apr. 1966, 107)

A chaste, not a profligate, life is the source of virile manhood. The test of true womanhood comes when the woman stands innocent at the court of chastity. All qualities are crowned by this most precious virtue of beautiful womanhood. It is the most vital part of the foundation of a happy married life and is the source of strength and perpetuity of the race. —*David O. McKay* (CR, Apr. 1967, p.8)

We choose carefully the atmosphere that we breathe, that we may live in health. But sometimes, in our carelessness, we place ourselves in subjection to immoral influences that destroy our resistance of evil, and we are led to do things that we ought not to do and would not do if under the influence of the Lord. —*George Albert Smith* (CR, Oct. 1929, 23)

When you are finished with your earth life, you will be the sum of your thoughts. Don't spend time with unworthy thoughts. Be satisfied with the good you see around you—then increase it. Examine your thinking, find out to what direction it is leading you, and try to make certain that you choose the way which places great value on eternal life. That is of prime importance. —*George Albert Smith* (GAS, 28)

There is no true Latter-day Saint who would not rather bury a son or a daughter than to have him or her lose his or her virtue—realizing that virtue is of more value than anything else in the wide world. —*Heber J. Grant* (IE, 44:73)

There are at least three dangers that threaten the Church within, and the authorities need to awaken to the fact that the people should be warned unceasingly against them. As I see these, they are flattery of prominent men in the world, false educational ideas, and sexual impurity.

But the third subject mentioned—personal purity, is perhaps of greater importance than either of the other two. We believe in one standard of morality for men and women. If purity of life is neglected, all other dangers set in upon us like the rivers of waters when the flood gates are opened. —*Joseph F. Smith* (IE, 17:476)

And now we desire with holy zeal to emphasize the enormity of sexual sins. Though often regarded as insignificant by those not knowing the will of God, they are, in his eyes an abomination, and if we are to remain his favored people they must be shunned as the gates of hell. —*Joseph F. Smith* (GD, 275)

Sexual union is lawful in wedlock, and if participated in with right intent is honorable and sanctifying. But without the bonds of marriage, sexual indulgence is a debasing sin, abominable in the sight of Deity. . . . It is a deplorable fact that society persists in holding women to stricter account than men in the matter of sexual offense. What shadow of excuse, not to speak of justification, can be found for this outrageous and cowardly discrimination? Can moral defilement be any the less filthy and pestilential in man than in woman?—*Joseph F. Smith* (GD, 309)

[I]t has always been considered, among all intelligent and right thinking people in the nations, both in a social and political capacity, that it is in the interests of humanity that the marital relations should be sustained, that virtue and chastity should be preserved, and that in proportion as these principles are disregarded has the elevation or degradation of the race been manifested. —*John Taylor* (GK, 279)

God . . . has planted . . . a natural desire in woman towards man, and in man towards woman and a feeling of affection, regard, and sympathy exists between the sexes. We bring it into the world with us, but that, like everything else, has to be sanctified. An unlawful gratification of these feelings and sympathies is wrong in the sight of God, and leads down to death, while a proper exercise of our functions leads to life, happiness, and exaltation in this world and the world to come. And so it is in regard to a thousand other things. —*John Taylor* (GK, 61)

[W]hile a flood of corruption, destructive of all true morality and virtue, is sweeping over the land, we must erect barriers to stop its contaminating influence. You have the young in your charge. Teach and impress them by every means in your power how dreadful a sin is unchastity. They are taught to shrink in horror from murder; and they should be taught to shrink with abhorrence from the next great sin to shedding blood, and that is unchastity. —*John Taylor* (GK, 283)

The principle of pure affection is the gift of God, and it is for us to learn to control it and exercise proper dominion over it. —*Brigham Young* (BY, 194)

Learn the will of God, keep his commandments and do his will, and you will be a virtuous person. —*Brigham Young* (BY, 194)

Any man who humbles a daughter of Eve to rob her of her virtue, and cast her off dishonored and defiled, is her destroyer, and is responsible to God for the deed. If the refined Christian society of the nineteenth century will tolerate such a crime, God will not; but he will call the perpetrator to an account. He will be damned; in hell he will lift up his eyes, being in torment, until he has paid the uttermost farthing, and made a full atonement for his sins. —*Brigham Young* (BY, 194)

30. HONESTY

How rare a gem, how precious a jewel is the man or woman in whom there is neither guile nor deception nor falsehood!—*Gordon B. Hinckley* (BTE, 45-46)

Where there is honesty, other virtues will follow. —*Gordon B. Hinckley* (BTE, 46)

Well has the Lord said, "Thou shalt not covet," Let not selfishness canker our relationships. Let not covetousness destroy our happiness. Let not greed for that which we do not need and cannot get with honesty and integrity bring us down to ruin and despair. —*Gordon B. Hinckley* (Ensign, March 1990, 6)

It is the love of money and the love of those things which money can buy which destroys us. We all need money to supply our needs. But it is the love of it which hurts us, which warps our values, which leads us away from spiritual things and fosters selfishness and greed. —*Gordon B. Hinckley* (CR, May 1997, 49)

Most individuals do not intend to be dishonest, dishonorable, or immoral. They seem to allow their characters to erode by a series of rationalizations, lies, and compromises. Then when grave temptation presents itself, they haven't the strength of character to do what they know to be right. —*Ezra Taft Benson* (ETB, 367)

Honor is like the precious stone, the price of which is greatly depressed by a single flaw. —*Spencer W. Kimball* (SWK, 192)

Another area in which numerous people show a lack of total honesty and integrity is on the highway. Is it dishonest to break speed limits? . . .
Why should we need inspectors, policemen, game wardens? Should it not be enough that the rules be published? Why must grown men be watched and checked?—*Spencer W. Kimball* (SWK, 197)

It is the first, the worst and the most insidious and damaging form of cheating—to cheat oneself. —*Spencer W. Kimball* (SWK, 198)

One might be smart and clever; one might be full of wit and humor; one might be dexterous in performance, but if he has not honor and integrity, he has little or nothing. —*Spencer W. Kimball* (SWK, 388)

You young men must realize that no reputable business executive or banker would care to take a chance on an employee who gambles. Lessons learned from such games make you less dependable in places where honesty and integrity are requisite. —*Harold B. Lee* (DSL, 159)

He indeed is a superior person whose thoughts smell of the sunshine, whose passions are honest and pure, and whose association is inspiring and uplifting. —*Harold B. Lee* (YLW, 71)

Whenever you find a man who spends his time abusing his neighbors, trying to tear down other people, you put it down that that man is not possessed of the Spirit of the Lord. But when a man tries to build up, when he tries to show you a better way, even though he be deceived, you may know that he is honest; but never the man who tries to tear you to pieces, who tries to destroy, without offering you something better in return. Never is such a man honest. —*Joseph Fielding Smith* (CR, Oct. 1910, 41)

We should put forth every effort to supplant the aristocracy of wealth with the aristocracy of character and to awaken in the minds of the youth a realization that to be honest, to be dependable, to be a loyal citizen of the country, to be true to the standards of the gospel are the noblest ideals of life. —*David O. McKay* (GI, 265)

The foundation of a noble character is integrity. —*David O. McKay* (CR, Apr. 1964, 6)

Let us live honest, sincere lives. Let us be honest with ourselves, honest with our brethren, honest with our families, honest with men with whom we deal—always honest; for eyes are upon us, and the foundation of all character rests upon the principles of honesty and sincerity. —*David O. McKay* (CR, Apr. 1968, 97)

To be just, one must of necessity be honest, fair, and impartial. He will be respectful and reverential. . . . True manhood possesses justice and is an attribute of the divine nature. —*David O. McKay* (CR, Apr. 1968, 7)

I want to say to you that the punishment that is meted out to those who are dishonest, when they are apprehended and hailed before the courts of the land, is insignificant when compared with the spiritual punishment that befalls us when we transgress the law of honesty and violate the commandments of God. —*George Albert Smith* (SGO, 52)

You put me in jail and I would always look for an opportunity to escape. But if you put me in a room with doors and windows, unbarred and unguarded, and you draw a line and ask for my promise that I will never try to escape, I'll never step across that line. —*George Albert Smith* (CP, 23)

The fundamental thing for a Latter-day Saint is to be honest. The fundamental thing for a Latter-day Saint is to value his word as faithfully as his bond; to make up his mind that under no circumstances, no matter how hard it may be, by and with the help of the Lord, he will dedicate his life and his best energies to making good his promise. —*Heber J. Grant* (IE, 41:712)

If there be anything despicable, if there be anything that can never, no, never, enter into the kingdom of God, it is a wilful liar. —*Joseph F. Smith* (GD, 409)

To me the principle of integrity is one of the greatest blessings we can possibly possess. He who proves true to himself or his brethren, to his friends and his God, will have the evidence within him that he is accepted; he will have the confidence of his God and of his friends. —*Wilford Woodruff* (WW, 260-261)

It is proper that men should be honest with themselves, that they should be honest with each other in all their words, dealings, intercourse, intercommunication business arrangements, and everything else. They ought to be governed by truthfulness, honesty, and integrity, and that man is very foolish indeed who would not be true to himself, true to his convictions and feelings in regard to religious matters. —*John Taylor* (GK, 231)

We should be strictly honest, one with another, and with all men; let our word always be as good as our bond; avoid all ostentation of pride and vanity; and be meek, lowly, and humble; be full of integrity and honor; and deal justly and righteously with all men; and have the fear and love of God continually before us, and seek for the comforting influence of the Holy Ghost to dwell with us. —*John Taylor* (GK, 343)

If you love the truth you can remember it. —*Brigham Young* (BY, 10)

Honest hearts produce honest actions—holy desires produce corresponding outward works.
Fulfil your contracts and sacredly keep your word. —*Brigham Young* (BY, 232)

Simple truth, simplicity, honesty, uprightness, justice, mercy, love, kindness, do good to all and evil to none, how easy it is to live by such principles! A thousand times easier than to practice deception!—*Brigham Young* (BY, 232)

A parent may whip a child, and justly, too, because he stole an apple; whereas if the child had asked for the apple, and the parent had given it, the child would have eaten it with a better appetite; there would have been no stripes; all the pleasure of the apple would have been secured, all the misery of stealing lost. —*Joseph Smith, Jr.* (STJS, 287-288)

31. PROFANITY

It is a tragic and unnecessary thing that boys and girls use foul language. It is inexcusable for a girl so to speak. It is likewise serious for the boy who holds the priesthood. This practices is totally unacceptable for one authorized to speak in the name of God. To blaspheme His holy name or to speak in language that is debauched is offensive to God and man.

The man or the boy who must resort to such language immediately says that he is poverty-ridden in his vocabulary. He does not enjoy sufficient richness of expression to be able to speak effectively without swearing or using foul words. —*Gordon B. Hinckley* (CR, Nov. 1987, 48)

I plead with you young women never to indulge in dirty, sleazy talk of any kind. There is so much of it and it is so common. There is no need to use such language. It only advertises to others that your vocabulary is so deficient that you cannot express yourself without picking words up out of the gutter. Do not do it. Please do not do it. Do not use such filthy language, and do not profane the name of the Lord. —*Gordon B. Hinckley* (Ensign, May 1996, 94)

Swearing or cursing is usually the result of an effort of one who is inarticulate to impress others. Blasphemy is a disgusting habit which commands no respect. —*Howard W. Hunter* (CR, Apr. 1965, 56)

Even as we should think of the name of Christ more often, and use it more wisely and well, how tragic it is, and how deeply we are pained, that the name of the Savior of mankind has become one of the most common and most ill-used of profanities. . . . May we all do more to respect and revere his holy name and gently, courteously encourage others to do the same. —*Howard W. Hunter* (WMJ, 8)

Do not make your mind a dumping ground for other people's garbage. —*Ezra Taft Benson* (ETB, 304-305)

Modesty in dress and language and deportment is a true mark of refinement and a hallmark of a virtuous Latter-day Saint woman. Shun the low and the vulgar and the suggestive. —*Ezra Taft Benson* (CLP , 20)

Profanity insults God. In the hospital one day I was wheeled out of the operating room by an attendant who stumbled, and there issued from his angry lips vicious cursing with a combination of the names of the Savior. Even half-conscious, I recoiled and implored: "Please! Please! That is my Lord whose names you revile." There was a deathly silence, then a subdued voice whispered: "I am sorry."—*Spencer W. Kimball* (IE, May 1953, 320)

Language is like music; we rejoice in beauty, range, and quality in both, and we are demeaned by the repetition of a few sour notes. —*Spencer W. Kimball* (Ensign, Feb. 1981, 4)

It is a terrible thing for any human being to use the name of Deity in disrespect. —*Spencer W. Kimball* (Ensign, Feb. 1981, 4-5)

We should hold the name of Deity in the most sacred and solemn respect. Few things are so distressing or shock the feelings of a refined person more than to hear some uncouth, ignorant, or filthy creature bandy around the name of Deity. —*Joseph Fielding Smith* (DS1, 12-13)

The great lesson for us to learn, in all our preaching, writing, and conversations, is to use the titles of Deity sparingly, not with familiarity, or with lack of reverence. —*Joseph Fielding Smith* (DS1, 16)

Vulgarity is often the first step down the road to indulgence. To be vulgar is to give offense to good taste or refined feelings. A young man who would tell a vulgar joke in the presence of ladies discloses a nature leaning towards that which is low and coarse. A girl who would encourage it and laugh at it is taking a step toward that which is crude and unrefined. —*David O. McKay* (CR, Apr. 1949, 14)

Reverence for God's name should be dominant in every home. Profanity should never be expressed in a home in this Church. It is wrong; it is irreverent to take God's name in vain. There is no provocation that will justify it. Let us apply that quality and that virtue of reverence at all times. —*David O. McKay* (CR, Apr. 1967, 87)

We should stamp out profanity, and vulgarity, and everything of that character that exists among us; for all such things are incompatible with the gospel and inconsistent with the people of God. —*Joseph F. Smith* (CR, Oct. 1901, 2)

It is a disgrace for men of education and intelligence to be unable to utter five words without an oath. Every child ought to point the finger of scorn at any man that will come down to such a mean standard. —*John Taylor* (GK, 273)

Who is your enemy and mine? He that teaches language that is unbecoming, that presents falsehood for truth, that furnishes false premises to build upon instead of true, or that is full of anger and mischief to his fellow beings. I call no others enemies. —*Brigham Young* (BY, 71)

I would not associate with those who blaspheme the name of God, nor would I let my family associate with them. By this you may know whether you are in the path that leads to life and salvation. If you can bear the name of the Deity lightly spoken of and blasphemed, and not be shocked at it, you may know that you are not in the path. —*Brigham Young* (BY, 78)

32. THE SABBATH DAY

Now, I make a plea to our people to refrain form shopping on Sunday. You may say, "The little bit that I do doesn't make a bit of difference." It makes all the difference in the word to you and to your children who will see your example. —*Gordon B. Hinckley* (CN, June 1, 1996, 14)

The Sabbath of the Lord is becoming the play day of the people. It is a day of golf and football on television, of buying and selling in our stores and markets. Are we moving to mainstream America as some observers believe? In this I fear we are. What a telling truth it is to see the parking lots of the markets filled on Sunday in communities that are predominately LDS. —*Gordon B. Hinckley* (Ensign, Nov. 1997, 69)

There is no way we can separate the activities of worship on the Sabbath day from the many pursuits of the weekday by calling one religious and the other temporal. Both are spiritual. God has ordained them thus, for they consist of our thoughts and actions as we wend our way through this part of eternity. Thus our business transactions, our daily labors, our trade or profession, or whatever we do become part of living the gospel. —*Howard W. Hunter* (CR, Oct. 1961, 109)

Remember, Sunday is the Lord's day—a day to do His work. —*Ezra Taft Benson* (ETB, 440)

I am grateful for the Sabbath day. I sometimes wonder what I would do without it. I mean that literally. A day of rest, but more than a day of rest—a day of prayer, a day of worship, a day of devotion, a day to be spiritually fed, a day to reflect on the purpose of life and the privileges, opportunities, and obligations which are ours as members of the Church. —*Ezra Taft Benson* (ETB, 440)

It would appear that the reason the Sabbath day is so hard to live for so many people is that it is still written on tablets of stone rather than being written in their hearts. —*Spencer W. Kimball* (SWK, 218)

[I]f one can measure each Sabbath activity by the yardstick of worshipfulness; if one is honest with his Lord and with himself . . . it is quite unlikely that there will be Sabbath breaking in that person's life. —*Spencer W. Kimball* (SWK, 219)

Let us not be like the Church member who partakes of the sacrament in the morning, then defiles the Sabbath that afternoon by cleaning the house or by watching television or by choosing an afternoon of sleep over an afternoon of service. —*Spencer W. Kimball* (Ensign, June 1975, 3)

The Savior knew that the ox gets in the mire on the Sabbath, but he knew also that no ox deliberately goes into the mire every week. —*Spencer W. Kimball* (IE, Dec. 1953, 948)

You who make the violation of the Sabbath a habit, by your failure to "keep it holy," are losing a soul full of joy in return for a thimble full of pleasure. —*Harold B. Lee* (DSL, 148)

Do not suppose that strict observance of the law of the Sabbath is alone sufficient to keep your spiritual bodies in good health. Every day of the week must give nourishment to your spiritual selves. Family and secret prayers, the reading of the scriptures, love in your homes and unselfish daily service to others are manna from heaven to feed your souls. —*Harold B. Lee* (DSL, 149)

Again, I have wondered how members of the Church can go to the sacrament service and partake of these emblems, and make these solemn covenants, and then immediately after the close of the meeting go out to some place of amusement, to attend a picture show, a baseball game, or some resort, or to gather at some home to play cards. . . . The fact remains, however, that when we indulge in habits of this kind we are covenant breakers guilty of offenses. —*Joseph Fielding Smith* (DS2, 345)

The Sabbath day has become a day of pleasure, a day of boisterous conduct, a day in which the worship of God has departed, and the worship of pleasure has taken its place.

I am sorry to say that many of the Latter-day Saints are guilty of this. We should repent. —*Joseph Fielding Smith* (CR, Oct. 1932, 89)

Our children will have to be taught to discern between good and evil, otherwise in many respects they will not be able to understand why they are not permitted to indulge in practices that are common with their neighbors. Unless they are instructed in the doctrines of the Church, they will not, perhaps, understand why there is any harm in the Sunday concert, a Sunday theatre, picture show, ball game, or something of that kind, when their playmates, without restraint and with encouragement, indulge in these things forbidden of the Lord on his holy day. —*Joseph Fielding Smith* (CR, Oct. 1916, 72)

Let us not make Sunday a holiday. It is a holy day, and on that day we should go to the house of worship and seek our God. If we seek him on the Sabbath day, get into his presence on that day, we shall find it less difficult to be in his presence the following days of the week. —*David O. McKay* (GI, 413)

True religion cannot be worn only on Sundays, laid aside as you put aside your Sunday clothes, and left to lie in mothballs during the week. True spirituality should be expressed in daily activity. —*David O. McKay* (CR, Apr. 1958, 130)

Churches are dedicated and set apart as houses of worship. This means that all who enter do so, or at least pretend to do so, with an intent to get nearer the presence of the Lord than they can on the street or amidst the worries of a workaday life. In other words, we go to the Lord's house to meet him and to commune with him in spirit. —*David O. McKay* (CR, Apr. 1967, 87)

"Remember the Sabbath Day to keep it holy." That seems such a little thing for us to do, in return for the blessings we enjoy. But to forget that it is the Lord's Day, as some of us appear to do, is ungrateful. He has set apart one day in seven, not to make a burden, but to bring joy into our lives, and cause that our homes may be the gathering place of the family, that parents and children may assemble around the family hearth, increasing our love for one another. —*George Albert Smith* (CR, Oct. 1932, 23)

This very day upon which we meet here to worship, *viz.*, the Sabbath, has become the play-day of this great nation—the day set apart by thousands to violate the commandment that God gave long, long ago, and I am persuaded that much of the sorrow and distress that is afflicting and will continue to afflict mankind is traceable to the fact that they have ignored his admonition to keep the Sabbath day holy. —*George Albert Smith* (CR, Oct. 1935, 120)

I want to say that you lose every time you violate the Sabbath day, you lose more than you can gain, no matter what you may think you are going to gain, but your boys and girls sometimes do not understand that. Teach it to them. —*George Albert Smith* (CR, Oct. 1948, 187-188)

A sacred Sabbath is not automobile riding to the canyons on Sunday. A sacred Sabbath is not going out on excursions on Sunday. A sacred Sabbath is to attend our meetings and to read the Scriptures, to supplicate God, and to have our minds set upon the things that are calculated to save us in this life and in the life to come. —*Heber J. Grant* (LPS, 363)

My belief is that it is the duty of Latter-day Saints to honor the Sabbath day and keep it holy, just as the Lord has commanded us to do. Go to the house of prayer. Listen to instructions. Bear your testimony to the truth. . . . When we go home, get the family together. Let us sing a few songs. Let us read a chapter or two in the Bible, or in the Book of Mormon, or in the book of Doctrine and Covenants. Let us discuss the principles of the gospel which pertain to advancement in the school of divine knowledge, and in this way occupy one day in seven. I think it would be profitable for us to do this. *—Joseph F. Smith* (GD, 242-243)

[L]ike faithful Saints demand that the Sabbath day, as far as you and yours are concerned, shall be devoted to the Lord our God. *—Joseph F. Smith* (IE, 13:1910)

We have no right to break the Sabbath. We have no right to neglect our meetings to attend to our labors. I do not believe that any man, who has ever belonged to this Church and kingdom, since its organization, has made anything by attending to his farm on the Sabbath: but if your ox falls into a pit, get him out; to work in that way is all just and right, but for us to go farming to the neglect of our meetings and other duties devolving upon us, is something we have no right to do. The Spirit of God does not like it, it withdraws itself from us, and we make no money by it. We should keep the Sabbath holy. We should attend our meetings. *—Wilford Woodruff* (JD, 21:191)

I call upon you, ye Latter-day Saints, to repent of your iniquities, and keep the Sabbath day holy, set it aside as a day of rest, a day of meeting together to perform your sacraments and listen to the words of life, and thus be found keeping the commandments, and setting a good example before your children. *—John Taylor* (GK, 339)

To serve the Lord is one of the great objects of our existence; and I appreciate as a great privilege the opportunity we enjoy of worshiping God on the Sabbath day. And when we do meet to worship God, I like to see us worship him with all our hearts. I think it altogether out of place on such occasions to hear people talk about secular things; these are times, above all others perhaps, when our feelings and affections should be drawn out towards God. *—John Taylor* (GK, 228)

Now, remember, my brethren, those who go skating, buggy riding or on excursions on the Sabbath day—and there is a great deal of this practiced—are weak in the faith. Gradually, little by little, little by little, the spirit of their religion leaks out of their hearts and their affections. *—Brigham Young* (BY, 165)

We are under the necessity of assembling here from Sabbath to Sabbath . . . What for? To keep us in remembrance of our God and our holy religion. Is this custom necessary? Yes; because we are so liable to forget—so prone to wander, that we need to have the Gospel sounded in our ears as much as once, twice, or thrice a week, or, behold, we will turn again to our idols. *—Brigham Young* (BY, 165)

Monday, Tuesday, Wednesday, Thursday, Friday, and Saturday must be spent to the glory of God, as much as Sunday, or we shall come short of the object of our pursuit. *—Brigham Young* (BY, 166)

When people assemble to worship they should leave their worldly cares where they belong, then their minds are in a proper condition to worship the Lord, to call upon him in the name of Jesus, and to get his Holy Spirit, that they may hear and understand things as they are in eternity, and know how to comprehend the providences of our God. This is the time for their minds to be open, to behold the invisible things of God, that he reveals by his Spirit. *—Brigham Young* (BY, 167)

33. THE LAW OF THE FAST

It is not a burden to refrain from two meals a month and give the value thereof to assist in caring for the poor. It is, rather, a blessing. Not only will physical benefits flow from the observance of this principle, but spiritual values also. Our program of the fast day and the fast offering is so simple and so beautiful that I cannot understand why people everywhere do not take it up. —*Gordon B. Hinckley* (Ensign, Nov. 1985, 85)

Think, my brethren, of what would happen if the principles of fast day and the fast offering were observed throughout the world. The hungry would be fed, the naked clothed, the homeless sheltered. Our burden of taxes would be lightened. The giver would not suffer, but would be blessed by his small abstinence. A new measure of concern and unselfishness would grow in the hearts of people everywhere. Can anyone doubt the divine wisdom that created this program which has blessed the people of this Church as well as many who are not members of the Church?—*Gordon B. Hinckley* (Ensign, May 1991, 52-53)

To discipline ourselves through fasting brings us in tune with God, and fast day provides an occasion to set aside the temporal so that we might enjoy the higher qualities of the spiritual. As we fast on that day we learn and better understand the needs of those who are less fortunate. —*Howard W. Hunter* (Ensign, Nov. 1985, 74)

To make a fast most fruitful, it should be coupled with prayer and meditation; physical work should be held to a minimum, and it is a blessing if one can ponder on the scriptures and the reason for the fast. —*Ezra Taft Benson* (CR, Nov. 1974, 66-67)

Sometimes we have been a bit penurious and figured that we had for breakfast one egg and that cost so many cents and then we give that to the Lord. I think that when we are affluent, as many of us are, that we ought to be very, very generous. . . .

I think we should . . . give, instead of the amount saved by our two meals of fasting, perhaps much, much more—ten times more when we are in a position to do it. —*Spencer W. Kimball* (CR, Apr. 1974, 184)

Fast offerings have long constituted the means from which the needs of the Lord's poor have been provided. It has been, and now is, the desire and objective of the Church to obtain from fast offerings the necessary funds to meet the cash needs of the welfare program, and to obtain from welfare production projects the commodity needs. If we give a generous fast offering, we shall increase our own prosperity both spiritually and temporally. —*Spencer W. Kimball* (Ensign, Aug. 1984, 6)

If we were united in paying our fast offerings and observing the law of the fast as fully as the Lord has taught it, and if we were united in carrying out the principles of the welfare program as they have been given to us by our leaders today, we would be free from want and distress and would be fully able to care for our own. Our failure to be united would be to allow our needy to become the pawns of politicians in the public mart. —*Harold B. Lee* (YLW, 45)

If there were no other virtue in fasting but gaining strength of character, that alone would be sufficient justification for its universal acceptance. —*David O. McKay* (GI, 210)

The regularly constituted fast consists of abstinence from food once each month, from the evening meal of Saturday to the evening meal on the following Sunday; that is, it means missing two meals on the first Sunday of each month. The value of those two meals given as a voluntary donation for the relief of those who are hungry or otherwise in distress constitutes the fast offering. Think what the sincere observance of this rule would mean spiritually if every man, woman, and child were to observe the fast and contribute the resultant offering, with the sincere desire of blessing the less fortunate brother or sister or sorrowing child!—*David O. McKay* (GI, 210)

If we inspire in the hearts of the people a desire to do their duty, it will be the easiest thing in the world to take care of all those who are in distress among this people. The fast day donation alone, if we were absolutely honest with the Lord, would take care of the poor among us. —*Heber J. Grant* (GS, 122)

Every living soul among the Latter-day Saints that fasts two meals once a month will be benefited spiritually and be built up in the faith of the gospel of the Lord Jesus Christ—benefited spiritually in a wonderful way—and sufficient means will be in the hands of the bishops to take care of all the poor. —*Heber J. Grant* (GS, 123)

It would be a simple matter for people to comply with this requirement to abstain from food and drink one day each month, and to dedicate what would be consumed during that day to the poor, and as much more as they pleased. The Lord has instituted this law; it is simple and perfect, based on reason and intelligence, and would not only prove a solution to the question of providing for the poor, but it would result in good to those who observe the law. It would call attention to the sin of over-eating, place the body in subjection to the spirit, and so promote communion with the Holy Ghost, and insure a spiritual strength and power which the people of the nation so greatly need. As fasting should always be accompanied by prayer, this law would bring the people nearer to God, and divert their minds once a month at least, from the mad rush of worldly affairs and cause them to be brought into immediate contact with practical, pure and undefiled religion. —*Joseph F. Smith* (GD, 132)

A man may fast and pray till he kills himself, and there isn't any necessity for it; nor wisdom in it. I say to my brethren, when they are fasting, and praying for the sick, and for those who need faith and prayer, do not go beyond what is wise and prudent in fasting and prayer. The Lord can hear a simple prayer offered in faith, in half a dozen words, and he will recognize fasting that may not continue more than twenty-four hours, just as readily and as effectually as he will answer a prayer of a thousand words and fasting for a month. Now, remember it. —*Joseph F. Smith* (GD, 368)

It was remarked this morning that some people said they could not fast because it made their head ache. Well, I can fast, and so can any other man; and if it makes my head ache by keeping the commandments of God, let it ache. —*Wilford Woodruff* (WW, 180)

34. THE LAW OF TITHING

As you discipline yourselves in the expenditure of your means, beginning with your obligations to your Father in heaven, the cankering selfishness that leads to so much strain in domestic affairs will go out of your lives, for if you will share with the Lord whom you do not see, you will deal more graciously, more honestly, and more generously with those whom you do see. As you live honestly with God, you will be inclined to live honestly with one another. —*Gordon B. Hinckley* (Ensign, June 1971, 72)

The Lord will open the windows of heaven according to our need, and not according to our greed. If we are paying tithing to get rich, we are doing it for the wrong reason. The basic purpose for tithing is to provide the Church with the means needed to carry on His work.

The blessing to the giver is an ancillary return, and that blessing may not be always in the form of financial or material benefit. —*Gordon B. Hinckley* (Ensign, May 1982, 40)

We can pay our tithing. This is not so much a matter of money as it is a matter of faith. —*Gordon B. Hinckley* (Ensign, Nov. 1985, 85)

The Lord has established the law of tithing, and because it is his law, it becomes our obligation to observe it if we love him and have a desire to keep his commandments and receive his blessings. In this way it becomes a debt. The man who doesn't pay his tithing because he is in debt should ask himself if he is not also in debt to the Lord. —*Howard W. Hunter* (CR, Apr. 1964, 36)

A testimony of the law of tithing comes from living it. Like all other of God's laws, when we live them we receive the blessings. —*Howard W. Hunter* (CR, Apr. 1964, 35-36)

It may be that we make a gift and also pay an obligation with our tithes. The payment of the obligation is to the Lord. The gift is to our fellow men for the upbuilding of God's kingdom. If one thoughtfully observes the proselyting done by the missionaries, the teaching program of the Church, the great educational system, and the building program to erect houses of worship, there will come a realization that it is not a burden to pay tithing, but a great privilege. —*Howard W. Hunter* (CN, March 11, 1995, 7)

The law of consecration is a celestial law, not an economic experiment. —*Ezra Taft Benson* (ETB, 121)

The law of consecration is a law for an inheritance in the celestial kingdom. God, the Eternal Father, His Son Jesus Christ, and all holy beings abide by this law. It is an eternal law. It is a revelation by God to His Church in this dispensation. Though not in full operation today, it will be mandatory for all Saints to live the law in its fullness to receive celestial inheritance. —*Ezra Taft Benson* (ETB, 123)

No one is ever too poor to pay tithing, and the Lord has promised that he will open the windows of heaven when we are obedient to his law. He can give us better salaries, he can give us more judgment in the spending of our money. He can give us better health, he can give us greater understanding so that we can get better positions. He can help us so that we can do the things we want to do. However, if we like luxuries or even necessities more than we like obedience, we will miss the blessings which he would like to give us. —*Spencer W. Kimball* (SWK, 212)

The Lord is not looking at the amount; all he is looking at is the percentage. —*Spencer W. Kimball* (SWK, 213)

You are not generous or liberal but merely honest when you pay your tithes. —*Spencer W. Kimball* (FPM, 289)

I have had difficulty understanding how a people who are not able to sacrifice to a point where they can pay a tenth of their interest annually and abstain from two meals on the first Sunday of the month and pay that as an offering for the care of the needy can believe that we are more than ten percent ready for the United Order. —*Harold B. Lee* (SHP, 280)

To members of the Church of Jesus Christ, therefore, tithing is as much a law of God as is baptism. —*David O. McKay* (CR, Apr. 1929, 100)

I suppose people think when they pay their tithing that they are making a sacrifice, but they are not; they are making a real investment that will return an eternal dividend. Our Heavenly Father gives us all that we have. He places all in our hands, authorizing us to retain for our own use nine-tenths of it, and then He asks that we put His tenth where He directs, where He knows it will accomplish the most good in developing His Church. —*George Albert Smith* (CR, Apr. 1941, 28)

Prosperity comes to those who observe the law of tithing. When I say prosperity I am not thinking of it in terms of dollars and cents alone, although as a rule the Latter-day Saints who are the best tithe payers are the most prosperous men, financially. But what I count as real prosperity, as the one thing of all others that is of great value to every man and woman living, is the growth in a knowledge of God, and in a testimony, and in the power to live the gospel and to inspire our families to do the same. That is prosperity of the truest kind. —*Heber J. Grant* (CR, Apr. 1925, 10)

Tithing is a law of God and the payment of tithes brings peace and joy to the Latter-day Saint who does it. There is a satisfaction that comes into the heart of the man who is absolutely honest with the Lord, in contributing of his means to the building up of the Church of Christ, and into the heart of every true, full tithe payer. —*Heber J. Grant* (CR, Oct. 1929, 4-5)

Some people have found it very hard to pay their tithing. The harder it is for an individual to comply with requirements of the Lord in the payment of his tithing, the greater the benefit when he finally does pay it. The Lord loves a generous giver. No man living upon the earth can pay donations for the poor . . . without removing selfishness from his soul, no matter how selfish he was when he started in. That is one of the finest things in all the world for men—to get to that point where the selfishness in their natures is cured. When it is eradicated from their dispositions, they are glad and anxious and willing and seeking the opportunity to do good with the means that the Lord places in their hands, instead of trying to get more of it. —*Heber J. Grant* (IE, 43:713)

I believe that when a man is in financial difficulty, the best way to get out of that difficulty (and I speak from personal experience, because I believe that more than once in my life I have been in the financial mud as deep as almost anybody) is to be absolutely honest with the Lord, and never to allow a dollar to come into our hands without the Lord receiving ten per cent of it. —*Heber J. Grant* (CR, Oct. 1921, 6-7)

By this principle (tithing) the loyalty of the people of this Church shall be put to the test. By this principle it shall be known who is for the kingdom of God and who is against it. —*Joseph F. Smith* (CR, Apr. 1900, 47)

When one comes to a bishop and asks for assistance because of his or her straitened circumstances, the first thing the bishop should do is to inquire if he or she is a tithe-payer. He should know whether the name is on the book of the law of the Lord, and if not on the book, if he or she has been derelict and negligent in relation to this principle of tithing, he or she has no claim upon the bishop, neither have their children; and if, under those circumstances, the bishop assists him, it will simply be out of pure charity and not because such have any claim upon the Church. —*Joseph F. Smith* (GD, 231)

If we could live up to the law of consecration, then there would be no necessity for the law of tithing, because it would be swallowed up in the greater law. The law of consecration requires all; the law of tithing only requires one-tenth of your increase annually. —*Joseph F. Smith* (LPS, 335)

The time has now come for every Latter-day Saint, who calculates to be prepared for the future and to hold his feet strong upon a proper foundation, to do the will of the Lord and to pay his tithing in full. That is the word of the Lord to you, and it will be the word of the Lord to every settlement throughout the land of Zion. . . . There is no man or woman that now hears what I am saying who will feel satisfied if he or she fails to pay a full tithing. —*Lorenzo Snow* (LS, 155)

[A] part of a tithing is no tithing at all, no more than immersing only half a person's body is baptism. —*Lorenzo Snow* (LS, 155-156)

One of the best things to do under such a temptation as that is to give, so as to be sure, a trifle more than is required. —*Lorenzo Snow* (CR, Apr. 1899, 51)

There is a widow, whose income is ten dollars; she pays one for tithing, and then has to appeal to the bishop for support. Here is a rich man who has an income of one hundred thousand dollars, and pays ten thousand for his tithing. There remains ninety thousand, and he does not need it, but the poor widow requires much more than she had before complying with the law of tithing.

Now what would be the operation of the celestial law? The widow has not enough for her support, therefore nothing is required of her by the celestial law, or the law of the united order. This rich man with his ninety thousand dollars, continues to increase his riches, pays his tithing fully, and yet wholly disregards the law of stewardship, or the law of temporal union. I cannot believe that a Latter-day Saint is justified in ignoring the higher law. —*Lorenzo Snow* (LS, 166)

The purpose of the [united] order is to make the members of the Church equal and united in all things, spiritual and temporal; to banish pride, poverty, and iniquity; and introduce a condition of things that will prepare the pure in heart for the advent of the world's Redeemer. —*Lorenzo Snow* (LS, 167)

The law of tithing is a test by which the people as individuals shall be proved. Any man who fails to observe this principle shall be known as a man who is indifferent to the welfare of Zion, who neglects his duty as a member of the Church, and who does nothing toward the accomplishment of the temporal advancement of the kingdom of God. He contributes nothing, either, toward spreading the gospel to the nations of the earth, and he neglects to do that which would entitle him to receive the blessings and ordinances of the gospel. —*Lorenzo Snow* (CR, Apr. 1900, 47)

Tithing is a commandment of God to the people, and should be observed. —*Wilford Woodruff* (WW, 177)

Of course, we are required to practice what we preach. I believe in that doctrine. . . . I would not preach tithing if I did not pay it. I consider it my duty to pay my tithing. I consider it is a law of God to me, and I am no poorer for obeying it. —*Wilford Woodruff* (WW, 179-180)

It is the principle and not the tithing we pay that is esteemed of the Lord; he cares not for our tithing, but he cares about our doing right. If we cannot be faithful in a few things, we cannot expect to be made rulers over many things. —*John Taylor* (GK, 265)

We have been taught to pay our tithing, that we might acknowledge to God that we are his people, and that if he gave us all we ask, we might give one-tenth back to him, and by that act acknowledge his hand. Does the Lord care about these things? . . .

No. He does not care about them, so far as they benefit him, but he does so far as they develop perfection in the saints of God, and show that they acknowledge his hand as the author and the giver of every blessing they enjoy. —*John Taylor* (GK, 265)

I do not suppose for a moment, that there is a person in this Church, who is unacquainted with the duty of paying tithing, neither is it necessary to have revelation every year upon the subject. There is the Law—pay one-tenth. —*Brigham Young* (BY, 174)

[I]f we neglect our tithes and offerings we will receive the chastening hand of the Lord. We may just as well count on this first as last. If we neglect to pay our tithes and offerings we will neglect other things and this will grow upon us until the spirit of the Gospel is entirely gone from us, and we are in the dark, and know not whither we are going. —*Brigham Young* (BY, 174)

If we live our religion we will be willing to pay tithing. —*Brigham Young* (BY, 176)

Here is a character—a man—that God has created, organized, fashioned and made,—every part and particle of my system from the top of my head to the soles of my feet, has been produced by my Father in Heaven; and he requires one-tenth part of my brain, heart, nerve, muscle, sinew, flesh, bone, and of my whole system. —*Brigham Young* (BY, 176)

We are not our own, we are bought with a price, we are the Lord's; our time, our talents, our gold and silver, our wheat and fine flour, our wine and our oil, our cattle, and all there is on this earth that we have in our possession is the Lord's, and he requires one-tenth of this for the building up of his Kingdom. Whether we have much or little, one-tenth should be paid in for tithing. —*Brigham Young* (BY, 176)

It is for my own benefit, it is for your benefit; it is for my own wealth and happiness, and for your wealth and happiness that we pay tithing and render obedience to any requirement of Heaven. . . . We are doing this for our own happiness, welfare and exaltation, and for nobody else's. —*Brigham Young* (BY, 176-177)

We do not ask anybody to pay tithing, unless they are disposed to do so; but if you pretend to pay tithing, pay it like honest men. —*Brigham Young* (BY, 177)

The matter of consecration must be done by the mutual consent of both parties; for to give the Bishop power to say how much every man shall have, and he be obliged to comply with the Bishop's judgment, is giving to the Bishop more power than a king has; and, upon the other hand, to let every man say how much he needs, and the Bishop be obliged to comply with his judgment, is to throw Zion into confusion, and make a slave of the Bishop. The fact is, there must be a balance or equilibrium of power, between the Bishop and the people; and thus harmony and good-will may be preserved among you. —*Joseph Smith, Jr.* (STJS, 32)

When we consecrate our property to the Lord it is to administer to the wants of the poor and needy, for this is the law of God; it is not for the benefit of the rich, those who have no need . . . Now for a man to consecrate his property, wife and children, to the Lord, is nothing more nor less than to feed the hungry, clothe the naked, visit the widow and fatherless, the sick and afflicted, and do all he can to administer to their relief in their afflictions, and for him and his house to serve the Lord. In order to do this, he and all his house must be virtuous, and must shun the very appearance of evil. —*Joseph Smith, Jr.* (STJS, 145-146)

35. THE WORD OF WISDOM

Our bodies are sacred. They were created in the image of God. They are marvelous, the crowning creation of Deity. No camera has ever matched the wonder of the human eye. No pump was ever built that could run so long and carry such heavy duty as the human heart. The ear and the brain constitute a miracle. The capacity to pick up sound waves and convert them into language is almost beyond imagination. Look at your finger and contemplate the wonder of it. Clever men have tried to match it, but have never fully succeeded. These, with other of our parts and organs, represent the divine, omnipotent genius of God, who is our Eternal Father. I cannot understand why anyone would knowingly wish to injure his body. And yet it happens around us every day as men and boys drink alcoholic beverages and use illegal drugs. What a scourge these are. For a little temporary lift they take into their systems that which robs them of self-control, becomes habit-forming, is terribly expensive, enslaves, and yields no good. —*Gordon B. Hinckley* (Ensign, May 1996, 48)

We can be grateful for the Word of Wisdom. Healthful foods, proper rest, adequate exercise, and a clear conscience can prepare us to tackle the trials that lie ahead. —*Ezra Taft Benson* (ETB, 476)

In all love, we give you warning that Satan and his emissaries will strive to entice you to use harmful substances, because they well know if you partake, your spiritual powers will be inhibited and you will be in their evil power. —*Ezra Taft Benson* (CR, May 1983, 54-55)

To a great extent we are physically what we eat. Most of us are acquainted with some of the prohibitions of the Word of Wisdom, such as no tea, coffee, tobacco, or alcohol. But what needs additional emphasis are the positive aspects—the need for vegetables, fruits, and grains, particularly wheat. We need a generation of people who eat in a healthier manner. —*Ezra Taft Benson* (Ensign, Sept. 1988, 5)

This temple of God is the body that the Lord has given us. It has been given to us to last a long time. It is a terrible criminal act for a person to go out and shorten his life by suicide or by any other method if it is intentional, by shortening it with the things that will create an early death. That isn't the way the Lord arranged it. —*Spencer W. Kimball* (SWK, 187)

People need help who feel that a party cannot be held, a celebration enjoyed, without liquor. What a sad admission that a party must have liquor for people to have a good time. How barren must some guests be if they must be inebriated!—*Spencer W. Kimball* (IE, Dec. 1967, 52)

Any defilement of these bodies of ours, then, by the taking of substances into our bodies expressly counseled against, will result, not only in a certain bodily harm, but in a loss of the spiritual companionship promised by obedience, for in truth, the body is the temple of the Holy Ghost. —*Harold B. Lee* (HBL, 204)

The healthy man, who takes care of his physical being, has strength and vitality; his temple, if you please, is a fit place for his spirit to reside in. —*David O. McKay* (CR, Oct. 1907, 61)

To our boys I would say that if they want to live physically; if they want to be men strong in body, vigorous in mind; if they want to be good in sports, enter the basketball game, enter the football game, enter the contest in running and jumping; if they want to be good Scouts; if they want to be good citizens, in business, anywhere, avoid tobacco and live strictly the religious life. —*David O. McKay* (CR, Apr. 1965, 79)

I am fully convinced that the Lord in His mercy, when He gave us the Word of Wisdom, gave it to us, not alone that we might have health while we live in the world, but that our faith might be strengthened, that our testimony of the divinity of the mission of our Lord and Master might be increased, that thereby we might be better prepared to return to His presence when our labor here is complete. —*George Albert Smith* (CR, Apr. 1907, 29)

It is regrettable that in the world today in many cases men do not appreciate that this temple of the body is sacred and should be so held, that this body of ours was given to us as a tabernacle for the spirit while we are here in mortality, but that the spirit that is in this tabernacle came from God. He is the Father of it. If men realized that, how much more careful they would be to protect this tabernacle and keep it wholesome and delightful. —*George Albert Smith* (CR, Oct. 1944, 97)

All who hope to be called Saints should certainly be observers of the Word of Wisdom. —*George Albert Smith* (CR, Oct. 1923, 72)

As I read the Word of Wisdom, I learn that it is adapted to the weakest of all the weak who are or can be called Saints. And I believe that it would be a wonderful aid in the advancement of the kingdom of God if all the Latter-day Saints would obey this simple commandment of the Lord. —*Heber J. Grant* (CR, Oct. 1907, 22)

It is a disgrace for a man blessed with the Priesthood of God and with a testimony that God lives burning in his heart, to be so weak that a little insignificant cup of coffee is his master. How he must swell up in vanity when he thinks what a wonderful man he is that a cup of coffee is his master. The example is pernicious. —*Heber J. Grant* (CR, Oct. 1900, 34-35)

I would like it known that if we as a people never used a particle of tea or coffee or of tobacco or of liquor, we would become one of the most wealthy people in the world. Why? Because we would have increased vigor of body, increased vigor of mind; we would grow spiritually; we would have a more direct line of communication with God, our Heavenly Father. —*Heber J. Grant* (IE, 44:73)

Drink brings cruelty into the home; it walks arm in arm with poverty; its companions are disease and plague; it puts chastity to flight; it knows neither honesty nor fair dealing; it is a total stranger to truth; it drowns conscience; it is the bodyguard of evil; it curses all who touch it.

Drink has brought more woe and misery, broken more hearts, wrecked more homes, committed more crimes, filled more coffins, than all the wars the world has suffered. —*Heber J. Grant* (CR, Oct. 1942, 8)

Nothing is more detrimental to the physical and moral growth of a boy than the use of the cigarette. —*Heber J. Grant* (LPS, 313)

Many people are inconsistent in that they study concerning the needs of the body, and observe strictly the laws of health, yet they disregard the equally urgent needs of the spirit. For the spirit, as well as the body, needs food. Some people are either ignorant or thoughtless concerning the great blessings promised to those who observe the Word of Wisdom. —*Joseph F. Smith* (IE, 21:103)

We have been called upon by the Lord and his servants to keep the Word of Wisdom; it is time we did it. —*Wilford Woodruff* (WW, 176)

The Word of Wisdom applies to Wilford Woodruff, the President of the Church, and it applies to all the leaders of Israel as well as to the members of the Church; and if there are any of these leading men who cannot refrain from using tobacco or liquor in violation of the Word of Wisdom, let them resign and others take their places. As leaders of Israel, we have no business to indulge in these things. —*Wilford Woodruff* (WW, 176)

There is a tendency, almost amounting to an epidemic in some places, among the young people to indulge in cigaret smoking. The habit is filthy, and pernicious generally. God has spoken so plainly on this subject that there is no room to question the impropriety of this practice. The teachers should make it their especial business in all kindness and in a mild instructive spirit to reason and remonstrate with young people upon this habit. Every effort should be made to check its growth among us. —*John Taylor* (GK, 340)

Now, Elders of Israel, if you have a right to chew tobacco, you have a privilege I have not; if you have a right to drink whiskey, you have a right that I have not; if you have a right to transgress the Word of Wisdom, you have a right that I have not. —*Brigham Young* (BY, 183)

The blessings of food, sleep, and social enjoyment are ordained of God for his glory and our benefit, and it is for us to learn to use them and not abuse them, that his Kingdom may advance on the earth, and we advance in it. —*Brigham Young* (BY, 182)

I know that some say the revelations upon these points are not given by way of commandment. Very well, but we are commanded to observe every word that proceeds from the mouth of God. —*Brigham Young* (BY, 182-183)

[L]et us seek to extend the present life to the uttermost, by observing every law of health, and by properly balancing labor, study, rest, and recreation, and thus prepare for a better life. —*Brigham Young* (BY, 186)

My mind becomes tired, and perhaps some of yours do. If so, go and exercise your bodies. —*Brigham Young* (BY, 190)

I understand that some of the people are excusing themselves in using tea and coffee, because the Lord only said "hot drinks" in the revelation of the Word of Wisdom. Tea and coffee are what the Lord meant when he said "hot drinks."—*Joseph Smith, Jr.* (LPS, 317)

No official member in this Church is worthy to hold an office after having the word of wisdom properly taught him; and he, the official member, neglecting to comply with and obey it. —*Joseph Smith, Jr.* (LPS, 318)

RIGHTEOUS LIVING

36. RIGHTEOUS LIVING

Let the light of the gospel shine in your faces wherever you go and in whatever you do. —*Gordon B. Hinckley* (Ensign, Nov. 1984, 86)

Each time we planned a program, each time we became involved in an activity, each time we mapped a course in our lives, if we applied the gauge, "Will this please my Heavenly Father?" we would be spared so much of pain and regret and enjoy so much of success and achievement that it would be wonderful. —*Gordon B. Hinckley* (Ensign, May 1985, 48)

The goodness of the world in which we live is the accumulated goodness of many small and seemingly inconsequential acts. —*Gordon B. Hinckley* (Ensign, Aug. 1992, 7)

Now, my brethren and sisters, the time has come for us to stand a little taller, to lift our eyes and stretch our minds to a greater comprehension and understanding of the grand millennial mission of this The Church of Jesus Christ of Latter-day Saints. This is a season to be strong. It is a time to move forward without hesitation, knowing well the meaning, the breadth, and the importance of our mission. It is a time to do what is right regardless of the consequences that might follow. It is a time to be found keeping the commandments. It is a season to reach out with kindness and love to those in distress and to those who are wandering in darkness and pain. It is a time to be considerate and good, decent and courteous toward one another in all of our relationships. In other words, to become more Christlike. —*Gordon B. Hinckley* (Ensign, May 1995, 71)

To be true to ourselves means being an example of righteous living in all situations and circumstances. —*Gordon B. Hinckley* (Ensign, May 1996, 92)

In order to be effective in one's life, religion must be a vibrant influence. It must be an influence that becomes a part of one's thinking and conduct. —*Howard W. Hunter* (CR, Oct. 1969, 112)

Christ's supreme sacrifice can find full fruition in our lives only as we accept the invitation to follow him. This call is not irrelevant, unrealistic, or impossible. To follow an individual means to watch him or listen to him closely; to accept his authority, to take him as a leader, and to obey him; to support and advocate his ideas; and to take him as a model. Each of us can accept this challenge. —*Howard W. Hunter* (Ensign, Jan. 1984, 71)

Let us study the Master's every teaching and devote ourselves more fully to his example. —*Howard W. Hunter* (Ensign , Nov. 1994, 8-9)

What a marvelous example for us to follow! Even in the midst of great personal sorrow and pain, our Exemplar reached out to bless others. . . . His was not a life focused on the things he did not have. It was a life of reaching out in service to others. *—Howard W. Hunter* (WMJ, 55)

Perhaps no promise in life is more reassuring than that promise of divine assistance and spiritual guidance in times of need. It is a gift freely given from heaven, a gift that we need from our earliest youth through the very latest days of our lives. *—Howard W. Hunter* (WMJ, 116)

The gospel of Jesus Christ must become the motivating influence in all that we do. There must be more striving within in order to follow the great example set by the Savior if we are to become more like him. This becomes our great challenge. *—Howard W. Hunter* (Ensign, Sept. 1994, 2-3)

Theology is a science—religion is an art. The sciences stress the acquisition of knowledge while the concern of the arts is mainly the development of specific skills. . . . Theology represents what we know and say regarding God—our beliefs. Religion is what we do about it—the way we live our beliefs. *—Ezra Taft Benson* (ETB, 337-338)

We live in a world where the philosophies and practices of man surround us. The only way one can keep a spiritual outlook is to invest time to determine the Lord's mind and will for us. *—Ezra Taft Benson* (CUC, 35)

"What would Jesus do?" or "What would He have me do?" are the paramount personal questions of this life. Walking in His way is the greatest achievement of life. That man or woman is most truly successful whose life most closely parallels that of the Master. *—Ezra Taft Benson* (CUC , 46-47)

In all my sermons, my objective is to get people to doing things, the good things, the right things. Knowledge is of no value unless used. When I know the requirements of the Lord and see how far that we his people come from fully meeting those requirements, it gives me a great urge to do all in my power to help the people of his Church to measure up to all the requirements. *—Spencer W. Kimball* (SWK, xix)

Now, in addition to the ordinances there must be righteousness. Neither will exalt alone. *—Spencer W. Kimball* (SWK, 147)

Live in such a way that if the enemies of the Church choose to speak critically of you, they must do so falsely. Never be a cause of any embarrassment to the Church. *—Spencer W. Kimball* (Ensign, Aug. 1980, 2)

Unless the good and the truth are taught just as effectively and as militantly from home and pulpit, by the radio and television, the billboards and the moving pictures as are things that tempt us to do evil, we are giving Satan and his hosts great odds in this contest for eternal life. *—Harold B. Lee* (DSL, 87)

Your spiritual body needs nourishment at frequent intervals in order to assure its health and vigor. Earthly food does not satisfy this need. Food to satisfy your spiritual needs must come from spiritual sources. Principles of eternal truth, as contained in the gospel and the proper exercise by engaging in spiritual activities are essential to the satisfying of your spiritual selves. *—Harold B. Lee* (DSL, 145)

Beautiful, luscious fruit does not grow unless the roots of the parent tree have been planted in rich, fertile soil and unless due care is given to proper pruning, cultivation, and irrigation. So likewise the luscious fruits of virtue and chastity, honesty, temperance, integrity, and fidelity are not to be found growing in that individual whose life is not founded on a firm testimony of the truths of the gospel and of the life and the mission of the Lord Jesus Christ. To be truly righteous, there is required a daily pruning of the evil growth of our characters by daily repentance from sin. —*Harold B. Lee* (SHP, 218-219)

How many thousands are there among us today who are living such lives that would make them, unless they repent, afraid to die, and that in their dying they might be afraid to live hereafter?—*Harold B. Lee* (YLW, 220)

✴ Today, we are faced with probably the most dangerous of all the tests of time, and that is the test of gold, affluence, and ease. —*Harold B. Lee* (YLW, 343)

Our religion is an everyday religion. We are expected to live in accordance with the principles of truth every day of our lives, for these principles are just as true in the middle of the week as they are on the Sabbath day. —*Joseph Fielding Smith* (CR, Oct. 1913, 71)

There is no valid excuse on the part of any member of the Church for a display of ignorance of the fundamental principles of the gospel as they are now revealed and published for the benefit of the world, for our attention has been forcibly called to them, and we have been commanded to make ourselves familiar with them by study and also by faith. They are accessible and within the reach of all. —*Joseph Fielding Smith* (DS1, 302)

If we accept the spirit entity of man as real and eternal, how utterly foolish to ignore or to neglect its development by giving most, if not all, of our attention to physical needs, pleasures, and passions!—*David O. McKay* (GI, 389)

There is not a principle which is taught by the Savior of men but is applicable to the growth, development, and happiness of mankind. Every one of his teachings seems to touch the true philosophy of living. I accept them wholeheartedly. I like to study them. I like to teach them. It is a job to try to live them. —*David O. McKay* (CR, Apr. 1963, 98)

Wisdom comes through effort. All good things require effort. That which is worth having will cost part of your physical being, your intellectual power and your soul power. —*David O. McKay* (CR, Oct. 1965, 144)

Let me emphasize that the noblest aim in life is to strive to live to make other lives better and happier. —*David O. McKay* (CR, Apr. 1961, 131)

If the gospel of Jesus Christ does not make me a better man, then I have not developed as I should, and if our neighbors, not in this church, can live among us from year to year and see no evidence of the benefits that come from keeping the commandments of God in our lives, then there is need for reform in Israel. —*George Albert Smith* (CR, Oct. 1916, 49)

Are we doing our duty, are we performing the labor that the Lord has entrusted in our care, or are we idly floating down stream, going with the tide, taking it for granted that in the last day we will be redeemed?—*George Albert Smith* (CR, Oct. 1916, 49)

There is only one aristocracy that God recognizes, and that is the aristocracy of righteousness. —*George Albert Smith* (SGO, 216)

For those who have been made partakers of the gospel of Jesus Christ in these latter days there is no excuse if we are not living a righteous life. —*George Albert Smith* (CR, Oct. 1926, 103)

Happiness may only be enjoyed when the Spirit of the Lord is with us. When the spirit of the adversary is with us it keeps us away from that joy and comfort and satisfaction that are the result of righteousness. —*George Albert Smith* (GAS, 90)

We can legislate until doomsday but that will not make men righteous. It will be necessary for people who are in the dark to repent of their sins, correct their lives, and live in such a righteous way that they can enjoy the spirit of our Heavenly Father. —*George Albert Smith* (CR, Oct. 1949, 6)

Someone has said of the people of the world that they would rather believe a lie and be damned than accept the truth. That is rather a severe statement, but I think perhaps it will bear acceptance as fact. —*George Albert Smith* (CR, Oct. 1949, 5)

Everyone should possess the spirit of the work, a spirit of love, a spirit of kindness, a spirit of charity for the weaknesses and frailties of mankind. —*George Albert Smith* (CR, Oct. 1927, 46)

⸙   The Gospel of Jesus Christ is a gospel of blessing, not a gospel of boasting, not a gospel of fault-finding and criticism, but a gospel of industry, purity, obedience, peace, love, charity, kindness, faith and patience. Therefore, as members of his great Church we ought to be exemplars in this regard to all the world. —*George Albert Smith* (CR, Apr. 1935, 44)

⸙   Live in such a way that if people could read your thoughts they would be able to see in you one worthy to be called a son or daughter of our Heavenly Father. —*George Albert Smith* (GAS, 130)

What kind of men and women should we be, as Latter-day Saints, in view of this wonderful knowledge that we possess, that God lives, that Jesus is the Christ, that Joseph Smith is a prophet of God? We should be the most honest, the most virtuous, the most charitable-minded, the best people upon the face of the earth. —*Heber J. Grant* (CR, Oct. 1925, 9-10)

No man can teach the gospel of Jesus Christ under the inspiration of the living God and with power from on high unless he is living it.

Preaching and talking mean but very little unless our lives are lived in perfect harmony with our teachings. —*Heber J. Grant* (GS, 79)

If we are loyal, if we are true, if we are worthy of this gospel, of which God has given us a testimony, there is no danger that the world can ever injure us. We can never be injured, my brethren and sisters, by any mortals, except ourselves. If we fail to serve God, if we fail to do right, then we rob ourselves of the ability and power to grow, to increase in faith and knowledge, to have power with God, and with the righteous. —*Heber J. Grant* (CR, Apr. 1931, 130)

There is nothing in all the world that is of more value than so to order our lives that those who know us best shall love us; and, above all, the one thing that is of greater value than life itself is to so live that God loves us. And I can say to you that every man, woman, and child that has lived the gospel of Jesus Christ and continues to do so has the love of God Almighty, our Father in Heaven and of His Son Jesus Christ, our Redeemer. —*Heber J. Grant* (GS, 102)

No people upon the face of the earth have ever been blessed as have been the Latter-day Saints; no people have ever had the many manifestations of the kindness and mercy and long-suffering of God that have been bestowed upon us, and I say we, above all men and women upon the earth should live Godlike and upright lives. —*Heber J. Grant* (GS, 374)

There are two spirits striving with us always, one telling us to continue our labor for good, and one telling us that with the faults and failings of our nature we are unworthy. —*Heber J. Grant* (IE, 44:267)

There are two spirits striving with all men—one telling them what to do that is right, and one telling them what to do that will please themselves, that will gratify their own pride and ambition. If we live as we ought to live, we will always follow that spirit that teaches us to do that which is right. —*Heber J. Grant* (CR, Apr., 1938, 12)

Are we so living that the good deeds we perform bring credit to the work of God? Are our examples worthy of the imitation of all men? Do we by our examples show that we have faith in the Gospel? We are told that faith without works is dead; that as the body without the spirit is dead, so also is faith without works dead, and I am sorry to say that there are many professed Latter-day Saints who are spiritually dead. —*Heber J. Grant* (CR, Apr. 1900, 21)

Pure intelligence comprises not only knowledge, but also the power to properly apply that knowledge. —*Joseph F. Smith* (GD, 58)

We should seek to do good in the world. This is our duty. —*Joseph F. Smith* (CR, Oct. 1899, 69)

[W]e must practice as well as profess. We must be what God requires us to be, or else we are not his people. —*Joseph F. Smith* (GD, 3)

It requires no especial bravery on the part of men to swim with the currents of the world. When a man makes up his mind to forsake the world and its follies and sins, and identify himself with God's people, who are everywhere spoken evil of, it takes courage, manhood, independence of character, superior intelligence and a determination that is not common among men; for men shrink from that which is unpopular, from that which will not bring them praise and adulation, from that which will in any degree tarnish that which they call honor or a good name. —*Joseph F. Smith* (CR, Oct. 1903, 1-2)

We do not believe in worshiping God or being religious on the Sabbath day only; but we believe it is as necessary to be religious on Monday, Tuesday and every day in the week, as it is on the Sabbath day. . . . In short, we believe it is necessary to live our religion every day in the week, every hour in the day, and every moment. —*Joseph F. Smith* (GD, 82)

It is remarkable how easy it is to learn sin and how hard it is to forget it. —*Joseph F. Smith* (GD, 325)

The idea is not to do good because of the praise of men, but to do good because in doing good we develop godliness within us; and this being the case, we shall become allied to godliness, which will in time become part and portion of our being. —*Lorenzo Snow* (LS, 7)

And now all the Latter-day Saints have to do, all that is required of us to make us perfectly safe under all circumstances of trouble or persecution, is to do the will of God: to be honest, faithful, and to keep ourselves devoted to the principles that we have received; do right one by another; trespass upon no man's rights; live by every word that proceedeth from the mouth of God, and His Holy Spirit will aid and assist us under all circumstances, and we will come out of the midst of it all abundantly blessed in our houses, in our families, in our flocks, in our fields—and in every way God will bless us. —*Lorenzo Snow* (LS, 12)

One of the chief difficulties that many suffer from is, that we are too apt to forget the great object of life, the motive of our Heavenly Father in sending us here to put on mortality, as well as the holy calling with which we have been called; and hence, instead of rising above the little transitory things of time, we too often allow ourselves to come down to the level of the world without availing ourselves of the divine help which God has instituted, which alone can enable us to overcome them. —*Lorenzo Snow* (LS, 36)

The god of the world is the gold and the silver. The world worships this god. It is all-powerful to them, though they might not be willing to acknowledge it. Now it is designed, in the providence of God, that the Latter-day Saints should show whether they have so far advanced in the knowledge, in the wisdom and in the power of God that they cannot be overcome by the god of the world. —*Lorenzo Snow* (LS , 62)

The heavens are full of blessings, and the Lord is willing to bestow them upon us. —*Wilford Woodruff* (WW, 221)

We should seek to do all the good we can, so that we may feel justified when we get through. —*Wilford Woodruff* (WW, 180)

It is the privilege of every man and woman in this kingdom to enjoy the spirit of prophecy, which is the Spirit of God; and to the faithful it reveals such things as are necessary for their comfort and consolation, and to guide them in their daily duties. —*Wilford Woodruff* (WW, 61)

You will find, my brethren and sisters, there are but a very few comparatively, either male or female, who have had independence of mind enough, as well as honesty of heart sufficient to receive the gospel of Christ. It takes independence of mind, honesty of heart, faith in God, and firmness of character to live the life of a Latter-day Saint. —*Wilford Woodruff* (WW, 261)

I feel to say to the Latter-day Saints everywhere, brethren and sisters, do good and you will reap good; what you sow you will also reap. —*Wilford Woodruff* (WW, 262)

Union, virtue, and perseverance, will prepare the way for the millennium. —*John Taylor* (GK, 341)

I have a desire, when anything comes along, to learn the will of God, and then to do it, and to teach my brethren to do it, that we may all grow up unto Christ our living head, that we may be acquainted with correct principles and govern ourselves accordingly. —*John Taylor* (GK, 44)

What is the reason we do not always comprehend things right? Because, in many instances, we give way to temptation. We let our old prepossessions, feelings, and influences, by which we have been governed heretofore, predominate over the Spirit of God, and we fall into error and darkness. . . It is not enough, then, that we are baptized and have hands laid upon us for the gift of the Holy Ghost. It is not enough even that we go further than this, and receive our washing and our anointings, but that we daily and hourly and all the time live up to our religion, cultivate the Spirit of God, and have it continually within us. —*John Taylor* (GK, 85)

There is an inexorable law of God that requires from his professed followers the principles of virtue, honor, truth, integrity, righteousness, justice, judgment, and mercy. —*John Taylor* (GK, 225)

Are we not the framers of our own destiny? Are we not the arbitrators of our fate? This is another part of my text, and I argue from it that it is our privilege to determine our own exaltation or degradation. It is our privilege to determine our own happiness or misery in the world to come. . . .

If I am doing right, I am preparing for thrones, principalities, and dominions, resolved by the help of God that no man shall rob me of my crown. —*John Taylor* (GK, 341)

I never ask the Lord to do a thing I could do for myself. —*John Taylor* (GK, 78)

All that the Lord requires of us is a perfect submission in our hearts to his will. —*Brigham Young* (BY, 20)

The first great principle that ought to occupy the attention of mankind, that should be understood by the child and the adult . . . is the principle of improvement. The principle of increase, of exaltation, of adding to that we already possess, is the grand moving principle and cause of the actions of the children of men. —*Brigham Young* (BY, 87)

If there be any who think they can gain the presence of the Father and the Son by fighting for, instead of living, their religion, they will be mistaken, consequently the quicker we make up our minds to live our religion the better it will be for us. —*Brigham Young* (BY, 392)

Sin consists in doing wrong when we know and can do better. —*Brigham Young* (JD, 2:133)

We know enough to damn us; and when we know enough for that, we know enough to save us, if that knowledge is improved upon. —*Brigham Young* (BY, 4)

Can you not live it for one hour? Begin at a small point; can you not live to the Lord for one minute? Yes. Then can we not multiply that by sixty and make an hour, and live that hour to the Lord? Yes; and then for a day, a week, a month, and a year? Then, when the year is past, it has been spent most satisfactorily. —*Brigham Young* (BY, 94)

Strive to be righteous, not for any speculation, but because righteousness is lovely, pure, holy, beautiful, and exalting; it is designed to make the soul happy and full of joy, to the extent of the whole capacity of man, filling him with light, glory, and intelligence. —*Brigham Young* (BY, 428)

Now, in this world, mankind are naturally selfish, ambitious and striving to excel one above another; yet some are willing to build up others as well as themselves. —*Joseph Smith, Jr.* (STJS, 331)

An actual knowledge to any person, that the course of life which he pursues is according to the will of God, is essentially necessary to enable him to have that confidence in God without which no person can obtain eternal life. —*Joseph Smith, Jr.* (LF, 67)

Unless they have an actual knowledge that the course they are pursuing is according to the will of God they will grow weary in their minds, and faint. . . . nothing short of an actual knowledge of their being the favorites of heaven, and of their having embraced the order of things which God has established for the redemption of man, will enable them to exercise that confidence in Him necessary for them to overcome the world, and obtain that crown of glory which is laid up for them that fear God. —*Joseph Smith, Jr.* (LF, 67-68)

In pitching my tent we found three massasaugas or prairie rattlesnakes, which the brethren were about to kill, but I said, "Let them alone—don't hurt them! How will the serpent ever lose its venom, while the servants of God possess the same disposition, and continue to make war upon it? Men must become harmless before the brute creation, and when men lose their viscious dispositions and cease to destroy the animal race, the lion and the lamb can dwell together, and the sucking child can play with the serpent in safety." The brethren took the serpents carefully on sticks and carried them across the creek. I exhorted the brethren not to kill a serpent, bird, or an animal of any kind during our journey unless it became necessary in order to preserve ourselves from hunger. —*Joseph Smith, Jr.* (STJS, 86)

When God offers a blessing or knowledge to a man, and he refuses to receive it, he will be damned. —*Joseph Smith, Jr.* (STJS, 362)

37. CHARITY

I am one who believes that love, like faith, is a gift of God. —*Gordon B. Hinckley* (FETR , 44)

Brutality reigns where Christ is banished. Kindness and forbearance govern where Christ is recognized and his teachings are followed. —*Gordon B. Hinckley* (Ensign, Dec. 1983, 2)

As his followers, we cannot do a mean or shoddy or ungracious thing without tarnishing his [the Mercy is the very essence of the gospel of Jesus Christ. The degree to which each of us is able to extend it becomes an expression of the reality of our discipleship under Him who is our Lord and Master. —*Gordon B. Hinckley* (Ensign, May 1990, 69)

Selfishness is the antithesis of love. It is a cankering expression of greed. It destroys self-discipline. It obliterates loyalty. It tears up sacred covenants. It afflicts both men and women. —*Gordon B. Hinckley* (Ensign, May 1991, 73)

Love the Lord your God, and love His Son, and be ever grateful for their love for us. Whenever other love fades, there will be that shining, transcendent, everlasting love of God for each of us and the love of His Son, who gave His life for us. —*Gordon B. Hinckley* (CN, March 2, 1996, 2)

The greatest motivating influence for righteousness and for service to one's fellowmen is the divine principle of love. —*Howard W. Hunter* (CR, Apr. 1966, 49)

I suggest to you that the Lord has prepared a touchstone for you and me, an outward measurement of inward discipleship that marks our faithfulness. . . . [Jesus Christ] will measure our devotion to him by how we love and serve our fellowmen. What kind of mark are we leaving on the Lord's touchstone? Are we truly good neighbors? Does the test show us to be twenty-four-karat gold, or can the trace of fool's gold be detected?—*Howard W. Hunter* (WMJ, 143-144)

We need to remember that though we make our friends, God has made our neighbors—everywhere. Love should have no boundary; we should have no narrow loyalties. —*Howard W. Hunter* (WMJ, 145)

Poor, indeed, and destitute are those who disclaim being religious because they do not have sufficient love for their fellowmen to be concerned and have compassion. —*Howard W. Hunter* (WMJ, 162)

We need to be kinder with one another, more gentle and forgiving. We need to be slower to anger and more prompt to help. We need to extend the hand of friendship and resist the hand of retribution. In short, we need to love one another with the pure love of Christ, with genuine charity and compassion and, if necessary, shared suffering, for that is the way God loved us. —*Howard W. Hunter* (WMJ, 169)

When all else fails, charity—Christ's love—will not fail. It is the greatest of all divine attributes. —*Howard W. Hunter* (WMJ, 171)

The pure love of Christ seeks only the eternal growth and joy of others. —*Ezra Taft Benson* (CR, Nov. 1986, 47)

Charity, that greatest of godly virtues, would never be possible without property rights, for one cannot give what one does not own. —*Ezra Taft Benson* (ETB, 608)

[Profit] provides man with moral choices. With profit, man can choose to be greedy and selfish; he can invest and expand, thereby providing others with jobs; and he can be charitable. Charity is not charity unless it is voluntary. It cannot be voluntary if there is nothing to give. —*Ezra Taft Benson* (ETB, 630)

Tolerance is ability to see another's viewpoint. The most lovable quality any human being can possess is tolerance. It is the vision that enables one to see things from another's viewpoint. It is the generosity that concedes to others the right to their own opinions and peculiarities. It is the bigness that enables us to let people be happy in their own way instead of our way. —*Spencer W. Kimball* (SWK, 235)

Racial prejudice is of the devil. Racial prejudice is of ignorance. There is no place for it in the gospel of Jesus Christ. —*Spencer W. Kimball* (SWK, 237)

[L]ove without discipline, love without deep conviction of right and wrong, without courage to fight the wrong, such love becomes sentimentalism. Conversely, the virtues of righteous indignation without love can be harsh and cruel. —*Spencer W. Kimball* (SWK, 245)

How does true love express itself into action? Perhaps the truest human expression of love in the world today is the love of a mother for her child, or the love of a father for his son. —*Harold B. Lee* (HBL, 296)

I am sure that I can say with you that the great power that will save us is the power of love. —*Harold B. Lee* (HBL, 297)

Our success [in priesthood programs] will be measured in part by our capacity to love those whom we seek to lead and to serve. . . . When we truly love others we will act in their eternal interests and not to meet our own ego needs. —*Harold B. Lee* (HBL, 481)

Love is the divinest attribute of the human soul. I am not so sure but sympathy is next to it—sympathy for the afflicted, for suffering animals, for our brethren and sisters. That is a Godlike virtue. —*David O. McKay* (CR, Sept.-Oct. 1950, 163)

Benevolence in its fullest sense is the sum of moral excellence, and comprehends every other virtue. It is the motive that prompts us to do good to others and leads us to live our life for Christ's sake. All acts of kindness, of self-denial, of self-devotion, of forgiveness, of charity, of love, spring from this divine attribute. —*David O. McKay* (CR, Apr. 1968, 8)

True Christianity is love in action. There is no better way to manifest love for God than to show an unselfish love for one's fellowmen. —*David O. McKay* (CR, Oct. 1969, 88)

I want every one of you to know that I do not have an enemy, that is, there is no one in the world that I have any enmity towards. All men and all women are my Father's children, and I have sought during my life to observe the wise direction of the Redeemer of Mankind, to love my neighbor as myself. —*George Albert Smith* (CR, Apr. 1949, 87)

But do not forget no matter how much you may give in money, no matter how you may desire the things of this world to make yourselves happy, your happiness will be in proportion to your charity and to your kindness and to your love of those with whom you associate here on earth. —*George Albert Smith* (PCM, 199)

I haven't any animosity in my heart toward any living human being. I know some that I wish would behave themselves a little better than they do, but that is their loss, not mine. —*George Albert Smith* (CR, Apr. 1946, 185)

Let us evidence by our conduct, by our gentleness, by our love, by our faith, that we do keep that great commandment that the Savior said was like unto the first great commandment, "Thou shalt love thy neighbor as thyself."—*George Albert Smith* (CR, Apr. 1949, 10)

Now I want to make all mistakes on the side of mercy. But once in a while I want to see justice get just a little bit of a chance among the people. —*Heber J. Grant* (GS, 201)

[I]t is by love, genuine love of our fellows, that we accomplish the most. —*Heber J. Grant* (GS, 152)

Charity, or love, is the greatest principle in existence. If we can lend a helping hand to the oppressed, if we can aid those who are despondent and in sorrow, if we can uplift and ameliorate the condition of mankind, it is our mission to do it, it is an essential part of our religion to do it. —*Joseph F. Smith* (GD, 254)

We are governed by law, because we love one another, and are actuated by long-suffering and charity, and good will. . . . Ours is a Church where law is dominant, but the law is the law of love. —*Joseph F. Smith* (GD, 144)

✻ Be upright, just, and merciful, exercising a spirit of nobility and godliness in all your intentions and resolutions—in all your acts and dealings. Cultivate a spirit of charity, be ready to do for others more than you would expect from them if circumstances were reversed. Be ambitious to be great, not in the estimation of the worldly minded, but in the eyes of God. —*Lorenzo Snow* (LS, 10)

There is something grand in the consideration of the fact that the Lord loves us with a most ardent love. . . . He never leaves us. He is always before us, and upon our right hand and our left hand. Continually He watches over us. —*Lorenzo Snow* (CR Oct. 1898, 2)

[L]ove one another, and work the works of righteousness, and look after the welfare of all, and seek to promote the happiness of all. —*John Taylor* (GK, 341)

We should commence our labors of love and kindness with the family to which we belong; and then extend them to others. —*Brigham Young* (BY, 271)

The Latter-day Saints have got to learn that the interest of their brethren is their own interest, or they never can be saved in the celestial kingdom of God. —*Brigham Young* (BY, 271)

✻ Envy not those who do better than you do; do not pursue them with malice, but try to shape and frame your life by theirs. —*Brigham Young* (BY, 272)

The genius of our religion is to have mercy upon all, do good to all, as far as they will let us do good to them. —*Brigham Young* (BY, 272)

Dear Brethren:—It is a duty which every Saint ought to render to his brethren freely— to always love them, and ever succor them. To be justified before God we must love one another. —*Joseph Smith, Jr.* (HC 2, 229)

Until we have perfect love we are liable to fall and when we have a testimony that our names are sealed in the Lamb's book of life we have perfect love and then it is impossible for false Christ's to deceive us. —*Joseph Smith, Jr.* (STJS, 15)

The man who willeth to do well, we should extol his virtues, and speak not of his faults behind his back. . . . The kindness of a man should never be forgotten. That person who never forsaketh his trust, should ever have the highest place of regard in our hearts, and our love should never fail, but increase more and more, and this is my disposition and these my sentiments. —*Joseph Smith, Jr.* (STJS, 41)

Nothing is so much calculated to lead people to forsake sin as to take them by the hand, and watch over them with tenderness. When persons manifest the least kindness and love to me, O what power it has over my mind, while the opposite course has a tendency to harrow up all the harsh feelings and depress the human mind. . . .

The nearer we get to our heavenly Father, the more we are disposed to look with compassion on perishing souls; we feel that we want to take them upon our shoulders, and cast their sins behind our backs. . . . [I]f you would have God have mercy on you, have mercy on one another. —*Joseph Smith, Jr.* (STJS, 269-270)

If we would secure and cultivate the love of others, we must love others, even our enemies as well as friends. —*Joseph Smith, Jr.* (STJS, 350)

38. COMMITMENT

Lord s] image. Nor can we do a good and gracious and generous act without burnishing more brightly the symbol of him whose name we have taken upon ourselves. —*Gordon B. Hinckley* (BTE, 90)

✳ In this work there must be commitment. There must be devotion. We are engaged in a great eternal struggle that concerns the very soul of the sons and daughters of God. We are not losing. We are winning. We will continue to win if we will be faithful and true. We can do it. We must do it. We will do it. There is nothing the Lord has asked of us that in faith we cannot accomplish. —*Gordon B. Hinckley* (CR, Nov. 1986, 44)

The strength of the Church lies in the conviction carried in the hearts of its members, by the individual members of the Church. It is the privilege, it is the opportunity, it is the obligation of every Latter-day Saint to gain for himself or herself a certain knowledge that this is the work of the Almighty, that God our Eternal Father lives and watches over His children when they look to Him in faith; that Jesus is the Christ, the Son of God, the Redeemer of all mankind, who rose from the dead to become the firstfruits of them that slept. That testimony . . . is the most precious possession that any of us can hold—*Gordon B. Hinckley* (CN, Apr. 22, 1995, 3)

✳ The religion of which you are a part is seven days a week, it isn't just Sunday; it isn't the block plan, it isn't just three hours in Church; it isn't just the time you spend in seminary, it's all the time—24 hours a day, seven days a week, 365 days a year. —*Gordon B. Hinckley* (CN, Apr. 6, 1996, 14)

The ability to stand by one's principles, to live with integrity and faith according to one's belief—that is what matters. That devotion to true principle—in our individual lives, in our homes and families, and in all places that we meet and influence other people—that devotion is what God is ultimately requesting of us. It requires commitment—wholesouled, deeply held, eternally cherished commitment to the principles we know to be true. —*Howard W. Hunter* (Ensign, Oct. 1994, 5)

Men who only carry out that which is within their duty and go no further have no claim to any reward beyond the scope of that duty and are unprofitable servants. —*Howard W. Hunter* (CR, Apr. 1966, 48)

Whatever the past may have been in our individual lives, it is gone. The future lies ahead, and we must face it with resolution. —*Howard W. Hunter* (CR, Apr. 1961, 18)

As plowing requires an eye intent on the furrow to be made and is marred when one looks backward, so will they come short of exaltation who prosecute the work of God with a distracted attention or a divided heart. We may not see clearly the end of the furrow, but we dare not look back. Eternity stretches on ahead, challenging us to be faithful. —*Howard W. Hunter* (CR, Apr. 1961, 18)

How much of a normal day, a working week, or a fleeting month is devoted to "Jesus, the very thought of thee"? Perhaps for some of us, not enough.

Surely life would be more peaceful, surely marriages and families would be stronger, certainly neighborhoods and nations would be safer and kinder and more constructive if more of the gospel of Jesus Christ "with sweetness" could fill our breasts. —*Howard W. Hunter* (WMJ, 7-8)

The world needs individuals who are willing to step forward and declare themselves. The world needs individuals who will lift the load of responsibility to their shoulders and carry it high under the banner of Jesus Christ—individuals who are willing to defend the right openly. —*Howard W. Hunter* (WMJ, 65)

If we are "too busy" to hold a Church calling, we had better look at our priorities. *Ezra Taft Benson* (ETB, 452)

We must be devoted to sound principles in word and deed: principle above party, principle above pocketbook, principle above popularity. —*Ezra Taft Benson* (ETB, 688)

We have an increasing number who have been convinced, through the Book of Mormon, that Jesus is the Christ. Now we need an increasing number who will use the Book of Mormon to become committed to Christ. We need to be convinced and committed. —*Ezra Taft Benson* (AWW, 56-57)

The "lengthening of our stride" suggests urgency instead of hesitancy, "now," instead of tomorrow; it suggests not only an acceleration, but efficiency. It suggests, too, that the whole body of the Church move forward in unison with a quickened pace and pulse, doing our duty with all our heart, instead of halfheartedly. It means, therefore, mobilizing and stretching all our muscles and drawing on all our resources. —*Spencer W. Kimball* (SWK, 174-175)

One of the most serious human defects in all ages is procrastination, an unwillingness to accept personal responsibilities now. —*Spencer W. Kimball* (MF, 7-9)

The Master's plan is a program of doing, of living, not merely knowing. Knowledge itself is not the end. It is how we righteously live and apply that knowledge in our own lives and how we apply it to help others that describes our character. —*Spencer W. Kimball* (Ensign, Sept. 1983, 6)

Conversion must mean more than just being a "card carrying" member of the Church with a tithing receipt, a membership card, a temple recommend, etc. It means to overcome the tendencies to criticize and to strive continually to improve inward weaknesses and not merely the outward appearances. —*Harold B. Lee* (SHP, 354-355)

✣ Do all that you can do and leave the rest to God, the Father of us all. It is not enough to say I will do my best, but rather, I will do everything that is within my power; I will do all that is necessary. —*Harold B. Lee* (SHP, 239)

Brothers and sisters, if we will just resolve here and now that we are going forward whether it is a big task or small task, whether it is going to take great effort or whether it is not, whatever it is, we are going to do it, and the Lord is going to stand by our side. When we get up against closed doors, if we have done all we know how to do, then the Lord will open the doors and we will move forward. —*Harold B. Lee* (HBL, 1)

Does anybody consider that giving up the things that pertain to this world is a sacrifice? Some people would look upon it that way, but it isn't. You cannot sacrifice anything for the gospel of Jesus Christ. It would be just as consistent if a man gave me a dollar and I gave him ten cents, and then I would go out and say that was a great sacrifice I made. —*Joseph Fielding Smith* (CN, May 6, 1939, 7)

I wish we all loved the gospel to the extent that we would be willing to do anything the Lord asks of us irrespective of what the world thinks or does. Why can not the Latter-day Saints uphold the standards and the regulations of the Church with united effort notwithstanding what the world might do or think?—*Joseph Fielding Smith* (DS3, 294-295)

There has been, and is today, too much discrepancy between belief and practice, between the proclamation of high ideals and the application of these ideals to daily life and living. —*David O. McKay* (CR, Oct. 1937, 100)

In the soil of self-satisfaction, true growth has poor nourishment. —*David O. McKay* (GI, 12)

In this old world, the easiest way seems to be the indulgent way. . . . One never develops character by yielding to wrong. —*David O. McKay* (GI, 377-378)

If you have something that the Lord asks or expects you to do and you don't know just how to proceed, do your best. Move in the direction that you ought to go; trust the Lord, give him a chance, and he will never fail you. —*George Albert Smith* (SGO, 16)

Brethren and sisters, let us go to our homes. If our houses are not in order, let us set them in order. Let us renew our determination to honor God and keep his commandments, to love one another, to make our homes the abiding place of peace. Each of us can contribute to that in the homes in which we live. —*George Albert Smith* (SGO, 197-198)

I say there is need in all Israel today—there is need for this man addressing you to examine himself—there is need for everyone of us to look about ourselves and see wherein we are neglecting our privileges and our duty, for tomorrow it may be too late. Today is the acceptable time of the Lord. Let us set our houses in order. . . . Let us love one another that our Heavenly Father may be able to bless us, and he will bless us if we love one another and do good to all his children. —*George Albert Smith* (CR, Oct. 1930, 69)

I have often said in my remarks to the Saints, that each and every one of us are the architects of our own lives; that God will bless us in proportion to our faithfulness and diligence. —*Heber J. Grant* (CR, Apr. 1902, 94)

✣ I realize that it requires a constant effort on the part of each and every one of us to make a success of our lives. It requires no effort at all to roll down the hill, but it does require an effort to climb the hill to the summit. It needs no effort to walk in the broad way that leads to destruction; but it needs an effort to keep in the straight and narrow path that leads to life eternal. —*Heber J. Grant* (CR, Oct. 1900, 33)

I wish in my heart that all the members of the Church would have the loyalty in their souls, not only to believe the word of the Lord, but to put it into practice.

Let our actions count. That is the thing of real value. —*Heber J. Grant* (GS, 39)

Never be found among the number that try to see how little they can do; but always be found among the number that try to see how much they can do. —*Heber J. Grant* (GS, 97)

The gospel teaches us to do here just what we would be required to do in the heavens, with God and the angels, if we would listen to its teachings, and obey it, and put it into practice. —*Joseph F. Smith* (GD, 213)

[S]o far as I am concerned, I am so selfish that I am seeking after my salvation, and I know that I can find it only in obedience to the laws of God, in keeping the commandments, in performing works of righteousness, following in the footsteps of our file leader, Jesus the Exemplar and the Head of all. He is the Way of life, he is the Light of the world, he is the Door by which we must enter, in order that we may have a place with him in the celestial kingdom of God. —*Joseph F. Smith* (GD, 261-262)

The Lord hates a quitter, and there should be no such thing as quitting when we put our hands to the plow to save men. —*Joseph F. Smith* (LPS, 384)

How can a Latter-day Saint feel justified in himself unless he is seeking to purify himself even as God is pure—unless he is seeking to keep his conscience void of offense before God and man every day of his life? . . . [T]here may be a certain time or times in our life, when we are greatly tried and perhaps overcome; even if this be so, that is no reason why we should not try again, and that, too, with redoubled energy and determination to accomplish our object. —*Lorenzo Snow* (LS, 33-34)

Try, keep trying daily and hourly in all your avocations, in all your walks of life, in all your associations, to be perfect, even as our Father in Heaven is perfect. —*Lorenzo Snow* (LS, 38)

There are many important things required at our hands, and many things which we can do, when assisted by the Spirit of the Lord, which may at times seem almost impossible to accomplish. —*Lorenzo Snow* (CR, Apr. 1898, 12)

Nothing can be more foolish than the idea of a man laying off his religion like a cloak or garment. There is no such thing as a man laying off his religion unless he lays off himself. Our religion should be incorporated within ourselves, a part of our being that cannot be laid off. If there can be such a thing as a man laying off his religion, the moment he does so he gets onto ground he knows nothing about, he gives himself over to the powers of darkness. —*Lorenzo Snow* (LS, 23)

Nothing should deter us from the exercise of every power that God has bestowed upon us, to make our salvation and exaltation sure. —*Lorenzo Snow* (CR, Oct. 1899, 2)

I feel and see the importance of this work, and I see the necessity of our walking up to the line of our duty, that we may live and walk daily in the light of the Lord. —*Wilford Woodruff* (WW, 58)

Truth is what we are after, and we are not afraid of the doctrines of any man; we are willing to stand by the revelations of God. —*Wilford Woodruff* (WW, 63)

Brethren and sisters, it is our duty to be true to God and to be faithful. . . .

The Lord has given us commandments concerning many things, and we have carried them out as far as we could; but when we cannot do it, we are justified. The Lord does not require at our hands things that we cannot do. —*Wilford Woodruff* (WW, 210-211)

I sincerely desire, in the remaining days I have to spend here, that I may do what little good I can. I wish to magnify my calling; I wish to do my duty; I wish to know the mind and will of God, and try to do it. I pray not only that these blessings may be given to me, but to all the elders of Israel and the Latter-day Saints, which may God grant, for Christ's sake. —*Wilford Woodruff* (WW, 274)

It is our business to be saints. And to be worthy of that character it is our duty to live by the principles of virtue, truth, integrity, holiness, purity, and honor, that we may at all times secure the favor of Almighty God; that his blessings may be with us and dwell in our bosoms; that the peace of God may abide in our habitations; that our fields, our flocks, and our herds may be blessed of the Lord; and that we, as a people, may be under his divine protection. —*John Taylor* (GK, 40-41)

We frequently think a little more of a nice span of horses, or a nice wagon, or a favorite cow, and such things, than we do of God's work as our boys sometimes get attached to a few marbles thinking that they are everything. They do not like to leave their marbles to obey father or mother, and God finds us about the same. We get a few dollars, or a farm, and a little stock, and a few other things, and we cannot afford to neglect these. We cannot afford to take time to pray, nor to listen to the voice of Father, we are so busy playing marbles. And occasionally when we play marbles among the dollars, we try to cheat one another, as boys sometimes do at marbles, and try to take advantage one of another. I never like to see boys cheat and never like to see men cheat at their kind of marbles. Our feelings and affections get placed on wrong things.

We are here to build up Zion, and to establish the kingdom of God. —*John Taylor* (GK, 48)

I will tell you the only thing I am afraid of about the saints is that they will forget their God and that they will not live their religion. —*John Taylor* (GK, 232-233)

Let us take a course to be saved today, and, when evening comes, review the acts of the day, repent of our sins, if we have any to repent of, and say our prayers; then we can lie down and sleep in peace until the morning, arise with gratitude to God, commence the labors of another day, and strive to live the whole day to God and nobody else. —*Brigham Young* (BY, 16)

Persons must so live that they can enjoy the light of the Holy Spirit, or they will have no confidence in themselves, in their religion, or in their God, and will sooner or later turn from the faith. —*Brigham Young* (BY, 33)

When the people do all they can, the Lord is bound to do the rest. —*Brigham Young* (BY, 65)

If we will only practice what we profess, I tell you we are at the defiance of hell. —*Brigham Young* (BY, 227)

It is the privilege of every Elder to speak of the things of God; and could we all come together with one heart and one mind in perfect faith the veil might as well be rent today as next week, or any other time, and if we will but cleanse ourselves and covenant before God, to serve Him, it is our privilege to have an assurance that God will protect us at all times. —*Joseph Smith, Jr.* (STJS, 14-15)

If a man stands and opposes the world of sin, he may expect to have all wicked and corrupt spirits arrayed against him. —*Joseph Smith, Jr.* (STJS, 292)

✟ I am like a huge, rough stone rolling down from a high mountain; and the only polishing I get is when some corner gets rubbed off by coming in contact with something else, striking with accelerated force against religious bigotry, priest-craft, lawyer-craft, doctor-craft, lying editors, suborned judges and jurors, and the authority of perjured executives, backed by mobs, blasphemers, licentious and corrupt men and women—all hell knocking off a corner here and a corner there. Thus I will become a smooth and polished shaft in the quiver of the Almighty. —*Joseph Smith, Jr.* (HC, 5:401)

39. COURAGE AND FEAR

Yes, this work requires sacrifice, it requires effort, it means courage to speak out and faith to try. This cause does not need critics; it does not need doubters. It needs men and women of solemn purpose—*Gordon B. Hinckley* (CR, Oct. 1969, 115-116)

✗ Let us recognize that fear comes not of God, but rather that this gnawing, destructive element comes from the adversary of truth and righteousness. Fear is the antithesis of faith. It is corrosive in its effects, even deadly. —*Gordon B. Hinckley* (FETR , 13-14)

Brethren and sisters, we have nothing to fear if we stay on the Lord's side. If we will be prayerful, seeking wisdom from God, who is the source of all true wisdom; if we will cultivate a spirit of love and peace and harmony in our homes; if we will fulfill our assigned responsibilities in the Church with enthusiasm and faithfulness; if we will reach out to our neighbors and others in a spirit of Christian love and appreciation, helping those in distress wherever we may find them; if we will be honest with the Lord in the payment of our tithes and offerings, we shall be blessed as God has promised. Our Father has made explicit covenants with his people. He is in a position to keep those covenants. It is my testimony that he does so. —*Gordon B. Hinckley* (Ensign, May 1983, 80)

Indifference to the Savior or failure to keep the commandments of God brings about insecurity, inner turmoil, and contention. —*Howard W. Hunter* (WMJ, 30-31)

One may live in beautiful and peaceful surrounding, yet, because of inner dissension and discord, be in a state of constant turmoil. On the other hand, one may be in the midst of utter destruction and the bloodshed of war, yet have the serenity of unspeakable peace. If we look to the ways of the world, we will find turmoil and confusion. If we will but turn to God, we will find peace for the restless soul. —*Howard W. Hunter* (WMJ, 30-31)

Knowing what we know, and living as we are supposed to live, there really is no place, no excuse, for pessimism and despair. —*Howard W. Hunter* (WMJ, 91)

Every individual person has a particular set of challenges that sometimes seem to be earmarked for us personally. We understood that in our premortal existence.
. . . When these experiences humble us and refine us and teach us and bless us, they can be powerful instruments in the hands of God to make us better people, to make us more grateful, more loving and more considerate of other people in their own times of difficulty. —*Howard W. Hunter* (WMJ, 91)

We must believe that God has all power, that he loves us, and that his work will not be stopped or frustrated in our individual lives or in the world generally. He will bless us as a people because he always has blessed us as a people. He will bless us as individuals because he always has blessed us as individuals. —*Howard W. Hunter* (WMJ, 92-93)

He who fears loses strength for the combat of life in the fight against evil. —*Howard W. Hunter* (WMJ, 95)

A timid, fearing people cannot do their work well, and they cannot do God's work at all. The Latter-day Saints have a divinely assigned mission to fulfill that simply must not be dissipated in fear and anxiety. —*Howard W. Hunter* (WMJ, 95)

We must remember that the same forces of resistance that prevent our progress also afford us opportunities to overcome. God will have a tried people!—*Howard W. Hunter* (WMJ, 102)

Courage—and this is as true of spiritual courage as it is of physical courage—is not acting in the absence of fear. Courage is acting in spite of fear. If we stood tall in the gospel, we would soon find that it is easier to act than it is to remain idle or to cower in a corner. —*Howard W. Hunter* (WMJ, 135)

Life has a fair number of challenges in it, and that's true of life in the 1990s. Despair, Doom and Discouragement are not acceptable views of life for a Latter-day Saint. However high on the charts they are on the hit parade of contemporary news, we must not walk on our lower lip every time a few difficult moments happen to confront us.

We need to have faith and hope, two of the great fundamental virtues of any discipleship of Christ. —*Howard W. Hunter* (CN, March 11, 1995, 7)

Remember, it is truth that makes men courageous enough to become Christlike. It is the truth that makes men and nations free. —*Ezra Taft Benson* (NE, Sept. 1979, 42)

There is no security in unrighteousness. The sinful always live in despair. —*Ezra Taft Benson* (ETB, 338)

Great battles can make great heroes and heroines. . . . Some of the greatest battles we will face will be fought within the silent chambers of our own souls. —*Ezra Taft Benson* (KRL, 214)

Being human, we would expel from our lives, sorrow, distress, physical pain, and mental anguish and assure ourselves of continual ease and comfort. But if we closed the doors upon such, we might be evicting our greatest friends and benefactors. Suffering can make saints of people as they learn patience, long-suffering, and self-mastery. The sufferings of our Savior were part of his education. —*Spencer W. Kimball* (IE, Mar. 1966, 178)

The Lord has not promised us freedom from adversity and affliction. Instead, he has given us the avenue of communication known as prayer, whereby we might humble ourselves and seek His help and divine guidance. I have previously said that "they who reach down into the depths of life where, in the stillness, the voice of God is heard, have the stabilizing power which carries them poised and serene through the hurricane of difficulties. —*Spencer W. Kimball* (Ensign, May 1982, 5)

One who has a testimony of the purpose of life sees the obstacles and trials of life as opportunities for gaining the experience necessary for the work of eternity. —*Harold B. Lee* (YLW, 196)

Whatever may be necessary that I might be more refined to purge out all that which may be in me or which I have done that has not pleased the Lord, I would hope that

I would stand ready to receive. Please God that I will not fail or flinch in the time of trial or testing. —*Harold B. Lee* (YLW, 353)

True heroism defends the right and faces disaster without cringing. In this regard the Savior was the personification of true courage and heroism. —*David O. McKay* (CR, Apr. 1936, 58)

It is easy enough to do right when in good company, but it is not easy to defend the right when the majority of the crowd are opposing it; and yet, that is the time to show true courage. —*David O. McKay* (GI, 356-357)

Truth is loyalty to the right as we see it; it is courageous living of our lives in harmony with our ideals; it is always power. —*David O. McKay* (CR, Apr. 1959, 73)

The greatest comfort in this life is the assurance of having a close relationship with God, and I believe in the statement that "the greatest battle of life is fought within the silent chambers of your own soul." . . . It is a good thing to sit down and commune with yourself, to come to an understanding with yourself and decide in that silent moment what your duty is to your family, to your Church, to your country, and what you owe to your fellowmen. —*David O. McKay* (CR, Apr. 1967, 84-85)

The companionship of the spirit of the Lord is an antidote for weariness, for fear and all those things that sometimes overtake us in life. —*George Albert Smith* (CR, Oct. 1945, 115)

I am not afraid of any individual ever injuring me, but I am afraid that perchance I may fail to be as faithful and diligent as I ought to be; I am afraid I may fail to use all the talents God has given me, in the way I ought to use them. —*Heber J. Grant* (CR, Apr. 1909, 111)

It is braver and more honorable to promptly disavow and fly from error, no matter what the present seeming cost, or to frankly acknowledge a mistake, and apologize for it, and thus get rid of it, than to crouch beneath the burden, which is moral cowardice. —*Joseph F. Smith* (GD, 267)

We should never be discouraged in those daily tasks which God has ordained to the common lot of man. Each day's labor should be undertaken in a joyous spirit and with the thought and conviction that our happiness and eternal welfare depend upon doing well that which we ought to do, that which God has made it our duty to do. —*Joseph F. Smith* (GD, 285)

They the Saints may be afflicted and pass through numerous trials of a severe character, but these will prove blessings in disguise and bring them out brighter and better than they were before. The people of God are precious in His sight; His love for them will always endure, and in His might and strength and affection, they will triumph and be brought off more than conquerer. —*Lorenzo Snow* (LS, 121)

You and I cannot be made perfect except through suffering; Jesus could not. In His prayer and agony in the Garden of Gethsemane, He foreshadowed the purifying process necessary in the lives of those whose ambition prompts them to secure the glory of a celestial kingdom. None should try to escape by resorting to any compromising measures. "All who journey soon or late, Must come within the garden gate, And kneel alone in darkness there, And battle hard, yet not despair."—*Lorenzo Snow* (LS, 118)

And if we could read in detail the life of Abraham, or the lives of other great and holy men, we would doubtless find that their efforts to be righteous were not always crowned with success. Hence we should not be discouraged if we should be overcome in a weak moment; but, on the contrary, straightway repent of the error or the wrong we may have committed, and as far as possible repair it, and then seek to God for renewed strength to go on and do better. —*Lorenzo Snow* (LS, 34)

We must not allow ourselves to be discouraged whenever we discover our weakness. We can scarcely find an instance in all the glorious examples set us by the prophets, ancient or modern, wherein they permitted the evil one to discourage them; but on the other hand they constantly sought to overcome, to win the prize, and thus prepare themselves for a fulness of glory. —*Lorenzo Snow* (LS, 35-36)

I would say, let the motto be to every elder in Israel, and to every person worthy to be called a Saint: "Fear not, and never stand still, but move on."—*Lorenzo Snow* (LS, 46)

You may surround any man or woman with all the wealth and glory that the imagination of man can grasp, and are they satisfied? No. There is still an aching void. On the other hand, show me a beggar upon the streets, who has the Holy Ghost, whose mind is filled with that spirit and power, and I will show you a person who has peace of mind, who possesses true riches, and those enjoyments that no man can obtain from any other source. The servants of God, in every age of the world, have been sustained and nerved up to do their duty by this power; and I will say to the Latter-day Saints, if they will be faithful, and do what they should do, and listen to the counsel given to them, they need not have any fears about anything, for the whole work is in the hands of God. —*Wilford Woodruff* (WW, 5-6)

The Lord has been watching over us from the hour of our birth. —*Wilford Woodruff* (WW, 263)

It is better for us to fall in defense of truth, than to deny the words of God, and go to hell. It is better to suffer stripes for the testimony of Christ, than to suffer and fall by our sins and transgressions, and then to have to suffer afterwards. I would rather seal my testimony with my blood, and lay my body to rest in the grave, and have my spirit go to the other side of the veil, to enjoy a long eternity of light, truth, blessings, and knowledge which the Lord will bestow upon every man who keeps his law, than to spend a few short years of earthly pleasure, and he deprived of those blessings, and the society of my friends and brethren behind the veil. —*Wilford Woodruff* (WW, 278-279)

And I will also say we cannot be fruitful in the things of the kingdom of God, except we are diligent in searching for the things of God. It is our duty to do so. —*Wilford Woodruff* (WW, 140)

Though all the powers of darkness may war against us, the Lord is our friend, and He will sustain us and give us power to build up Zion and to carry out this work until the coming of the Son of Man. Therefore let your hearts be comforted. —*Wilford Woodruff* (WW, 219)

We have been called to pass through trials many times, and I do not think we should complain, because if we had no trials we should hardly feel at home in the other world in the company of the prophets and apostles who were sawn asunder, crucified, etc., for the word of God and testimony of Jesus Christ. —*Wilford Woodruff* (JD, 23:328)

In the economy of God, it was not only necessary that man, but the Savior also should be perfected by suffering. —*John Taylor* (GK, 94)

I used to think, if I were the Lord, I would not suffer people to be tried as they are. But I have changed my mind on that subject. Now I think I would, if I were the Lord, because it purges out the meanness and corruption that stick around the Saints, like flies around molasses. —*John Taylor* (GK, 333)

I have seen men tempted so sorely that finally they would say, "I'll be damned if I'll stand it any longer." Well, you will be damned if you do not. So you had better bear it and go to the Lord and say, O God, I am sorely tempted; Satan is trying to destroy me, and things seem to be combined against me. O Lord, help me! Deliver me from the power and grasp of the devil. Let thy Spirit descend upon me that I may be enabled to surmount this temptation and to ride above the vanities of this world. This would be far better than giving way to sin, and proving yourself unworthy of the association of the good and pure. —*John Taylor* (GK, 333-334)

We have learned many things through suffering. We call it suffering. I call it a school of experience. I never did bother my head much about these things. . . . I have never looked at these things in any other light than trials for the purpose of purifying the Saints of God, that they may be, as the scriptures say, as gold that has been seven times purified by the fire. —*John Taylor* (GK, 334)

We complain sometimes about our trials. We need not do that. These are things that are necessary for our perfection. —*John Taylor* (GK, 335)

When the Lord fights the battles of the Saints, he does it so effectually that nobody gets nervous but the enemy. —*Brigham Young* (BY, 20)

So far as suffering goes I have compared it a great many times, in my feelings and before congregations, to a man wearing an old, worn-out, tattered and dirty coat, and somebody comes along and gives him one that is new, whole and beautiful. This is the comparison I draw when I think of what I have suffered for the Gospel's sake—I have thrown away an old coat and have put on a new one. No man or woman ever heard me tell about suffering. "Did you not leave a handsome property in Ohio, Missouri, and Illinois?" Yes. "And have you not suffered through that?" No, I have been growing better and better all the time, and so have this people. —*Brigham Young* (BY, 348)

Every trial and experience you have passed through is necessary for your salvation. —*Brigham Young* (BY, 345)

If the Saints could realize things as they are when they are called to pass through trials, and to suffer what they call sacrifices, they would acknowledge them to be the greatest blessings that could be bestowed upon them. —*Brigham Young* (BY, 345)

We are the happiest people when we have what are called trials; for then the Spirit of God is more abundantly bestowed upon the faithful. —*Brigham Young* (BY, 347)

I do not regard my own life. I am ready to be offered a sacrifice for this people; for what can our enemies do? Only kill the body, and their power is then at an end. Stand firm, my friends; never flinch. Do not seek to save your lives, for he that is afraid to die for the truth will lose eternal life. Hold out to the end, and we shall be resurrected and become like Gods, and reign in celestial kingdoms, principalities, and eternal dominions. —*Joseph Smith, Jr.* (LPS, 37)

40. CRITICISM AND COURTESY

It is so easy to find fault. It is so much nobler to speak constructively. —*Gordon B. Hinckley* (Ensign, Nov. 1981, 96)

I am suggesting that as we go through life we "accentuate the positive." I am asking that we look a little deeper for the good, that we still voices of insult and sarcasm, that we more generously compliment virtue and effort. I am not asking that all criticism be silenced. Growth comes of correction. Strength comes of repentance. Wise are those who can acknowledge mistakes pointed out by others and change their course. —*Gordon B. Hinckley* (FETR , 74)

Any man who tries to find humor at the expense of that which is sacred to another is deeply flawed in character. Shame on those who stoop to such actions in the name of fun and on those who witness and laugh. Simple courtesy would dictate a decent respect for that which is sacred to neighbors and associates in one's society. —*Gordon B. Hinckley* (Ensign, Nov. 1983, 74)

Be friendly. Be understanding. Be tolerant. Be considerate. Be respectful of the opinions and feelings of other people. Recognize their virtues, don't look for their faults. Look for their strengths and their virtues and you will find strength and virtues which will be helpful in your own life. —*Gordon B. Hinckley* (CN, Dec. 2, 1995, 2)

We need more understanding in our relationships with one another, in business and in industry, between management and labor, between government and the governed. We need understanding in that most important of all social units, the family; understanding between children and parents and between husband and wife. Marriage would bring happiness, and divorce would be unknown if there were understanding hearts. Hatred tears down, but understanding builds up. —*Howard W. Hunter* (WMJ, 190)

This is the usual course of a man's life as he turns toward evil. First, he is a silent observer, then he becomes a consenting spectator, and finally he is an active participant. —*Howard W. Hunter* (CR, Oct. 1964, 107)

Brethren, if you can receive counsel, and will seek it, you will prosper in the work; if you cannot, you will not be magnified. I have seen a few over the years who were determined to pursue their own course, their own program. I have come to see that receiving counsel is a test of obedience by which the Lord magnifies His servants. —*Ezra Taft Benson* (ETB, 333)

The critical and complaining adult will be less effective than the interested and understanding. Love and understanding are only effective when they are genuine. We must love our young people, whether they are in righteousness or in error. In this way we can give them a chance to discern and to learn. But we must also give them a fair choice. —*Ezra Taft Benson* (ETB, 494)

Now is the time for all who claim membership in The Church of Jesus Christ of Latter-day Saints to stand firm and demonstrate their allegiance to the kingdom of God. It cannot be done as a critic or an idle spectator on the sidelines. —*Ezra Taft Benson* (CUC , 84-85)

I bear you my testimony that the experiences I have had have taught me that those who criticize the leaders of this church are showing signs of spiritual sickness which, unless curbed, will bring about eventual spiritual death. —*Harold B. Lee* (YLW, 224)

When all you can see in persons is the evil, there's something wrong with you, there's something wrong with me. But if we'll see the God or the good in men, and not the evil, then we're on the Lord's side. —*Harold B. Lee* (HBL, 199)

Therein lies one of the greatest problems among those who are criticizing and finding fault and wanting exceptions, because they don't trust the Lord. —*Harold B. Lee* (HBL, 516)

Let us look around us and see how quickly men who attempt unauthoritatively to steady the ark die spiritually. Their souls become embittered, their minds distorted, their judgments faulty, and their spirits depressed. Such is the pitiable condition of men who, neglecting their own responsibilities spend their time in finding fault with others. —*David O. McKay* (CR, Apr. 1936, 60)

Let us, as we seek first the kingdom of God, avoid backbiting and evil speaking. Gossip bespeaks either a vacant mind or one that entertains jealousy or envy. Let us avoid self-righteousness. —*David O. McKay* (CR, Oct. 1954, 133)

There is a difference in criticism. If we can criticize constructively under the influence of the spirit of the Lord, we may change beneficially and properly some of the things that are being done. But if we have the spirit of fault-finding, of pointing out the weaknesses and failings of others in a destructive manner, that never comes as a result of the companionship of the Spirit of our Heavenly Father and is always harmful. —*George Albert Smith* (CR, Oct. 1934, 50)

There are two influences in the world today, and have been from the beginning. One is an influence that is constructive, that radiates happiness and builds character. The other influence is one that destroys, turns men into demons, tears down and discourages. We are all susceptible to both. The one comes from our Heavenly Father, and the other comes from the source of evil that has been in the world from the beginning, seeking to bring about the destruction of the human family. —*George Albert Smith* (SGO, 42)

I stand here to plead with you not to permit words of criticism or unkindness to pass your lips about those whom the Lord has called to lead us. Do not be found in the companionship of those who would belittle them or weaken their influence among the children of men. If you do, I can say to you that you will find yourselves in the power of the adversary. —*George Albert Smith* (SGO, 48)

Unkind things are not usually said under the inspiration of the Lord. The Spirit of the Lord is a spirit of kindness; it is a spirit of patience; it is a spirit of charity and love and forbearance and long suffering; and there are none of us who do not need all these virtues that are the result of the possession of the Spirit of our Heavenly Father. —*George Albert Smith* (CR, Apr. 1937, 34)

I have given much advice to the Latter-day Saints in my time, and one of the principal items was never to criticize anyone but ourselves. I believe in fault-finding for breakfast, dinner and supper but only with our own dear selves. —*Heber J. Grant* (CR, Apr. 1902, 60)

The meddler, the gossip, the fault-finder . . . soon ruin their own capacity for observing the better side of human nature; and, not finding it in others, search in vain for its influence in their own souls. —*Joseph F. Smith* (GD, 111-113)

As a rule, it is not necessary to be constantly offering advice to those who in our judgment are possessed of some fault. In the first place, our judgments may be in error, and in the second place, we may be dealing with a man who is strongly imbued with the spirit of repentance, and who, conscious of his weakness, is constantly struggling to overcome it. The utmost care, therefore, should be observed in all our language that implies a reproach of others. —*Joseph F. Smith* (GD, 263-264)

Do I blame President Young because he chastises us? No. Would he be a father to us, a prophet, and a high priest of God, if he saw his brethren going wrong, and would not warn and chastise them? The chastisement of a friend is far better than the kisses of an enemy. —*Wilford Woodruff* (WW, 84)

Still there is a lesson that we have been learning that none of us is perfect in. Our judgment is not perfect and as we are not perfect in our sphere, we need not expect to find others perfect in theirs. And as we are not perfect ourselves, we may have need to come to the throne of mercy and ask for wisdom and support, and we can come to the Lord with faith and full assurance. —*John Taylor* (GK, 169)

When you feel like talking about your rights, let me advise you to go into your closet, forget your imaginary rights, and ask the Lord to give you wisdom to guide you aright, that you may act before him as children of the light, and not be the means of throwing a stumbling block in the way of others. By pursuing this course, you will get along much easier, and there will not be nearly so much of that spirit of grumbling and complaining. —*John Taylor* (GK, 342)

When you see people, professing to be Latter-day Saints, examining the faults of others, you may know that they are not walking in the path of obedience as strictly as they should. —*Brigham Young* (BY, 269)

I can merely say that if persons only understand the path of duty and walk therein, attaining strictly to whatever is required of them, they will have plenty to do to examine themselves and to purify their own hearts; and if they look at their neighbors and examine their conduct, they will look for good and not for evil. —*Brigham Young* (BY, 270)

If you are ever called upon to chasten a person, never chasten beyond the balm you have within you to bind up. —*Brigham Young* (BY, 278)

I will give you one of the Keys of the mysteries of the Kingdom. It is an eternal principle, that has existed with God from all eternity: That man who rises up to condemn others, finding fault with the Church, saying that they are out of the way, while he himself is righteous, then know assuredly, that man is in the high road to apostasy; and if he does not repent, will apostatize, as God lives. —*Joseph Smith, Jr.* (STJS, 177-178)

I have one request to make of the President and members of the society, that you search yourselves—the tongue is an unruly member—hold your tongues about things of no moment—a little tale will set the world on fire. —*Joseph Smith, Jr.* (STJS, 268)

If you have evil feelings, and speak of them to one another, it has a tendency to do mischief. . . .
I now counsel you, that if you know anything calculated to disturb the peace or injure the feelings of your brother or sister, hold your tongues and the least harm will be done. —*Joseph Smith, Jr.* (STJS, 291)

I told them I was but a man, and they must not expect me to be perfect; if they expected perfection from me, I should expect it from them; but if they would bear with my infirmities and the infirmities of the brethren, I would likewise bear with their infirmities. —*Joseph Smith, Jr.* (STJS, 302)

It is an insult to a meeting for persons to leave just before its close. If they must go out, let them go half an hour before. No gentlemen will go out of a meeting just at closing. —*Joseph Smith, Jr.* (STJS, 320)

Flattery is also a deadly poison. A frank and open rebuke provoketh a good man to emulation; and in the hour of trouble he will be your best friend. —*Joseph Smith, Jr.* (STJS, 156)

How vain and trifling have been our spirits, our conferences, our councils, our meetings, our private as well as public conversations—too low, too mean, too vulgar, too condescending for the dignified characters of the called and chosen of God, according to the purposes of His will, from before the foundation of the world!—*Joseph Smith, Jr.* (STJS, 157)

41. DECISION MAKING

The course of our lives is not determined by great, awesome decisions. Our direction is set by the little day-to-day choices which chart the track on which we run. —*Gordon B. Hinckley* (CR, Oct. 1972, 106-107)

The Lord is forgiving, but sometimes life is not forgiving.
In the world in which we walk we must be careful. The temptations are tremendous. We all know about them. The little decisions can be so crucial and so everlastingly important in their consequences. —*Gordon B. Hinckley* (Ensign, Nov. 1994, 49)

The decisions we make, individually and personally, become the fabric of our lives. That fabric will be beautiful or ugly according to the threads of which it is woven. I wish to say particularly to the young men who are here that you cannot indulge in any unbecoming behavior without injury to the beauty of the fabric of your lives. Immoral acts of any kind will introduce an ugly thread. Dishonesty of any kind will create a blemish. Foul and profane language will rob the pattern of its beauty. —*Gordon B. Hinckley* (Ensign, May 1995, 53)

Please remember this one thing. If our lives and our faith are centered upon Jesus Christ and his restored gospel, nothing can ever go permanently wrong. On the other hand, if our lives are not centered on the Savior and his teachings, no other success can ever be permanently right. —*Howard W. Hunter* (1988-89 Devotional and Fireside Speeches, 1989, 112)

Let us be conscious of the fact that our future is being fashioned by the decisions we make. May we exercise our faith and our agency in choosing the blessings God has set before us in the great gospel plan of our Savior. —*Howard W. Hunter* (WMJ, 79-80)

The friends we choose, the choices we make, and what we do about these choices are the determining guidelines that form and mold our lives, but choices alone are not enough. The best goals, the best of friends, and the best of opportunities are all meaningless unless they are translated into reality through our daily actions.
Belief must be realized in personal achievement. Real Christians must understand that the gospel of Jesus Christ is not just a gospel of belief; it is a plan of action. —*Howard W. Hunter* (WMJ, 131)

Because the gospel is a long-range—even an eternal—goal, it must be broken up into short-range, immediate objectives that can be achieved today and tomorrow and the next day. —*Howard W. Hunter* (WMJ, 132)

There is good reason to make our decision now to serve the Lord. . . when the complications and temptations of life are somewhat removed, and when we have the time and more of an inclination to take an eternal perspective, we can more clearly evaluate what will bring us the greatest happiness in life. We should decide now, in the light of the morning, how we will act when the darkness of night and when the storms of temptation arrive. —*Howard W. Hunter* (WMJ, 157)

Wise decisions are the stepping-stones of progress. They are the building blocks of life. Decisions are the ingredients of success. —*Ezra Taft Benson* (ETB, 387)

Our decisions have made us what we are. Our eternal destiny will be determined by the decisions we yet will make. —*Ezra Taft Benson* (ETB, 389)

Get the facts—then decide promptly. As an excuse for postponing decisions, do not rely on the old clichés some people use, such as "I want to sleep on it." We don't make decision in our sleep. However, don't jump to conclusions or make snap judgments. Get the facts, be sure of the base principles, and weigh the consequences. Then decide! —*Ezra Taft Benson* (ETB, 389)

Sometimes the Lord hopefully waits on His children to act on their own, and when they do not, they lose the greater prize, and the Lord will either drop the entire matter and let them suffer the consequences or else He will have to spell it out in greater detail. Usually, I fear, the more He has to spell it out, the smaller is our reward. —*Ezra Taft Benson* (ETB, 530)

Thoughts lead to acts, acts lead to habits, habits lead to character—and our character will determine our eternal destiny. —*Ezra Taft Benson* (CUC , 39)

Each day we personally make many decisions showing the cause we support. The final outcome is certain—the forces of righteousness will win. But what remains to be seen is where each of us personally, now and in the future, will stand in this battle—and how tall we will stand. —*Ezra Taft Benson* (Ensign, Sept. 1988, 2)

Are you going to yield to the easy urge to follow the crowd, or are you going to raise your head above the crowd and let them follow you? Are you going to slip off into mediocrity, or are you going to rise to the heights which your Heavenly Father set for you? . . . The decision is yours and yours only. —*Spencer W. Kimball* (SWK, 147)

It is a tenet of my faith that every normal person has the capacity, with God's help, to meet the challenge of whatever circumstances may confront him. —*Spencer W. Kimball* (NE, Apr. 1971, 2)

It is better for something to be underway than under advisement. —*Spencer W. Kimball* (Ensign, July 1979, 2)

Right decisions are easiest to make when we make them well in advance, having ultimate objectives in mind; this saves a lot of anguish at the fork, when we're tired and sorely tempted. —*Spencer W. Kimball* (NE, Apr. 1971, 2)

Luxuries do make comfort. They do not make character. —*Spencer W. Kimball* (SWK, 354)

I often pray that the Lord will bless the people with prosperity, but not too much, so that we will need to sacrifice and to find priorities. —*Spencer W. Kimball* (SWK, 354)

As I study the story of the Redeemer and his temptations, I am certain he spent his energies fortifying himself against temptation rather than battling with it to conquer it. —*Spencer W. Kimball* (KRL, 192.)

God has given laws with penalties affixed so that man might be made afraid of sin and guided into paths of truth and duty. —*Harold B. Lee* (DSL, 95)

Don't trade a soul full of spiritual strength which might be yours to help you resist temptations with which you may be daily confronted for a thimbleful of worldly pleasure in which you might other wise indulge. —*Harold B. Lee* (YLW, 73)

As with every day of your life, you can never relive any part of it except in memory; and if any day be wasted or misspent, that day becomes only one of regret and remorse. To live one's life to the fullest, then, becomes a daily responsibility for which you need the constant guidance of divine powers to avoid the pitfalls that make for long detours back onto the path of safety and truth. —*Harold B. Lee* (YLW, 339)

Every thought we think and every act we do is making an impression on our characters and is determining what our characters shall be. We are the product of what we think and how we act. —*Harold B. Lee* (HBL, 605)

Good reputations iron out difficulties; bad reputations multiply them. —*Harold B. Lee* (HBL, 605)

There exists an eternal law that each human soul shall shape its own destiny. —*David O. McKay* (GI, 300)

I am trying to emphasize that each one is the architect of his own fate, and he is unfortunate, indeed, who will try to build himself without the inspiration of God, without realizing that he grows from within, not from without. —*David O. McKay* (CR, Oct. 1951, 7)

One who persistently bids for popularity at the expense of health and character is a foolish man. —*David O. McKay* (GI, 411)

So live, then, that each day will find you conscious of having wilfully made no person unhappy. No one who has lived a well-spent day will have a sleepless night because of a stricken conscience. —*David O. McKay* (CR, Apr. 1958, 8)

Why of course you will be held accountable for your thoughts, because when your life is completed in mortality, it will be the sum of your thoughts. That one suggestion has been a great blessing to me all my life, and it has enabled me upon many occasions to avoid thinking improperly, because I realize that I will be, when my life's labor is complete, the product of my thoughts. —*George Albert Smith* (SGO, 63)

The Lord, all down through the ages, has spoken to his leaders and teachers who are inspired, but when the world refuses to heed after it has been properly taught, it places itself in a position of saying to our Heavenly Father who owns this world—he is our landlord—"We do not need you. We will do just as we please."

Unfortunately, people who think that way do not realize how they are shortening their own experiences in life, and setting the stage for the sorrows that may follow. —*George Albert Smith* (CR, Oct. 1949, 167)

We should have the ambition, we should have the desire, we should make up our minds that, so far as the Lord Almighty has given to us talent, we will do our full share in the battle of life. It should be a matter of pride that no man shall do more than you will do, in proportion to your ability, in forwarding the work of God here upon the earth. That has been my ambition all my life—to do my full share. —*Heber J. Grant* (IE, 42:585)

There is nothing like example. I like to encourage people to do their duty and to have a mind to do something, and if they have the mind and the desire, I am convinced they can do almost anything they want to within the bounds of reason. —*Heber J. Grant* (IE, 44:459)

The policy of living for today is not only destructive of our material interests, but it begets a selfishness harmful to religion and discreditable to patriotism. —*Joseph F. Smith* (GD, 351)

Beware of the lazy and the proud; their infection in each case is contagious. —*Joseph F. Smith* (GD, 373)

[T]here must be an inward feeling of the mind that is conscious of the responsibility that we are under, that recognizes the fact that the eye of God is upon us and that our every act and the motives that prompt it must be accounted for; and we must be constantly en rapport with the Spirit of the Lord. —*Lorenzo Snow* (LS, 38)

There is no necessity for Latter-day Saints to worry over the things of this world. They will all pass away. Our hearts should be set on things above; to strive after that perfection which was in Christ Jesus, who was perfectly obedient in all things unto the Father, and so obtained His great exaltation and became a pattern unto His brethren. Why should we fret and worry over these temporal things when our destiny is so grand and glorious?—*Lorenzo Snow* (LS, 38)

You must learn to govern yourself, or you never will be saved in the kingdom of God. —*Lorenzo Snow* (LS, 119)

In all your acts and conduct, ever have the consciousness that you are now preparing and making yourselves a life to be continued through eternities. Act upon no principle that you would be ashamed or unwilling to act upon in heaven—employ no means in the attainment of an object that an enlightened conscience disapproves. When feelings and passions excite you to action, let principles pure, honorable, and virtuous govern you. —*Lorenzo Snow* (LS, 101)

I shall be held accountable before the God of heaven—and so will all men—for the course I pursue in this life. —*Wilford Woodruff* (WW, 192)

I do not feel that I am justified in setting my heart upon the things of this world to the neglect of any duty that God requires at my hands. —*Wilford Woodruff* (WW, 277)

We are now laying a foundation for ourselves and our posterity; and what is it that will flash upon our minds if we turn away from the truth? We shall think of the time when we thought we were the Saints of God. We shall think of our associations with this people, and these reflections will greatly increase our misery. —*John Taylor* (GK, 232)

There is nothing that makes things go so well among the saints of God as living their religion and keeping the commandments of God, and when they don't do that, then things go awkward and cross and every other way but the right way. —*John Taylor* (GK, 233)

So live that when you wake in the spirit-world you can truthfully say, "I could not better my mortal life, were I to live it over again." . . . Live godly lives, which you cannot do without living moral lives. —*Brigham Young* (BY, 370)

Every person who will examine his own experience—who will watch closely the leading of his own desires—will learn that the very great majority prefer to do good rather than to do evil, and would pursue a correct course, were it not for the evil power that subjects them to its sway. In wrong doing, their own consciences condemn them. —*Brigham Young* (BY, 67)

It is as manly and as praiseworthy for an individual to make the choice to do good, work righteousness and love and serve God—it is more noble, than to choose the downward road.

One or the other will be the choice of every individual. Do not trifle with evil, or you will be overcome by it before you know. *—Brigham Young* (BY, 77)

[T]ime is all the capital stock there is on the earth; and you should consider your time golden, it is actually wealth, and, if properly used, it brings that which will add to your comfort, convenience, and satisfaction. *—Brigham Young* (BY, 214)

No consideration whatever ought to deter us from showing ourselves approved in the sight of God, according to His divine requirement. *—Joseph Smith, Jr.* (STJS, 82)

[N]o man is capable of judging a matter, in council, unless his own heart is pure; and that we frequently are so filled with prejudice, or have a beam in our own eye, that we are not capable of passing right decisions. *—Joseph Smith, Jr.* (STJS, 83-84)

42. DISCIPLINE

Integrity, loyalty, and strength are virtues whose sinews are developed through the struggles that go on within a man as he practices self-discipline under the demands of divinely spoken truth. *—Gordon B. Hinckley* (BTE, 4-5)

One of the great tragedies we witness almost daily is the tragedy of men of high aim and low achievement. Their motives are noble. Their proclaimed ambition is praiseworthy. Their capacity is great. But their discipline is weak. They succumb to indolence. Appetite robs them of will. *—Gordon B. Hinckley* (BTE, 60)

When temptation comes your way, name that boastful, deceitful giant "Goliath!" and do with him as David did to the Philistine of Gath. *—Gordon B. Hinckley* (Ensign, May 1983, 46-51)

The only conquest that brings satisfaction is the conquest of self. *—Gordon B. Hinckley* (Ensign, Aug. 1989, 5)

Anger is not an expression of strength. It is an indication of one's inability to control his thoughts, his words, his emotions. Of course it is easy to get angry. When the weakness of anger takes over, the strength of reason leaves. Cultivate within yourselves the mighty power of self-discipline. *—Gordon B. Hinckley* (Ensign, Nov. 1991, 51)

Developing spirituality and attuning ourselves to the highest influences of Godliness is not an easy matter. It takes time and frequently involves a struggle. It will not happen by chance, but is accomplished only through deliberate effort and by calling upon God and keeping his commandments. *—Howard W. Hunter* (WMJ, 182)

None of us has attained perfection of the zenith of spiritual growth that is possible in mortality. Every person can and must make spiritual progress. . . . With faith in the Lord Jesus Christ and obedience to his gospel, a step at a time improving as we go, pleading for strength, improving our attitudes and our ambitions, we will find ourselves successfully in the fold of the Good Shepherd. That will require discipline and training and exertion and strength. *—Howard W. Hunter* (WMJ, 184-185)

The greatest work in all the world is the building of men and women of character. Without character there is not much that is worthwhile. *—Ezra Taft Benson* (ETB, 274)

Character is the one thing we make is this world and take with us into the next. *—Ezra Taft Benson* (ETB, 373)

There is something higher than intellect. There is something higher than excellence. It is dedication to principle. It is self-mastery, self-control. It is living what one really believes in his heart. —*Ezra Taft Benson* (ETB, 445)

You will never wish or dream yourself into heaven. You must pay the price in toil, in sacrifice, and righteous living. —*Ezra Taft Benson* (NE, Sept. 1979, 44)

He truly is free who is master of situations, habits, passions, urges, and desires. If one must yield to appetite or passion and follow its demands, he is truly the servant of a dictator. —*Spencer W. Kimball* (SWK, 153)

Mastery of life is achieved by the ceaseless practice of mechanics which make up the art of living. Daily unselfish service to others is one of the rudimentary mechanics of the successful life. —*Spencer W. Kimball* (SWK, 250)

If we dress in a shabby or sloppy manner, we tend to think and act the same way. I am positive that personal grooming and cleanliness, as well as the clothes we wear, can be tremendous factors in the standards we set and follow on the pathway to immortality and eternal life. —*Spencer W. Kimball* (Ensign, Apr. 1979, 2)

One of the numerous rewards in girding ourselves to do hard things is in the creation of a capacity for doing of the still harder things. —*Spencer W. Kimball* (SWK, 362)

The overcoming of obstacles and the solution of problems involve the expenditure of energy that builds character, that increases the capacity of the individual. . . . Remember it is the pursuit of easy things that makes men weak. —*Harold B. Lee* (DSL, 14-15)

"To follow the course of least resistance makes men and rivers crooked." The darkest day in the life of a youth is that day when he sits down to contemplate how he can get something for nothing. —*Harold B. Lee* (DSL, 15)

Learning is the beginning of action; nothing is really learned until it is applied. May you learn to know the truth by living it. —*Harold B. Lee* (DSL, 34)

Resist the devil, and he will flee from you. Court him, and you will soon have shackles, not on your wrists, but on your soul. —*David O. McKay* (GI, 352)

A man who cannot control his temper is not very likely to control his passion, and no matter what his pretensions in religion, he moves in daily life very close to the animal plane. —*David O. McKay* (CR, Apr. 1958, 5)

One never develops character by yielding to wrong. —*David O. McKay* (CR, Apr. 1959, 74)

Man's chief concern in life should not be the acquiring of gold or of fame or of material possessions. It should not be the development of physical prowess, nor of intellectual strength, but his aim, the highest in life, should be the development of a Christlike character. —*David O. McKay* (CR, Apr. 1965, 79)

A man's reaction to his appetites and impulses when they are aroused gives the measure of that man's character. In these reactions are revealed the man's power to govern or his forced servility to yield. —*David O. McKay* (CR, Apr. 1967, 8)

A man is not at his best when he is a slave to some habit. —*David O. McKay* (CR, Oct. 1969, 7)

The world needs more godliness and less godlessness; more self-discipline, less self-indulgence; more power to say with Christ, "Father . . . not my will, but thine, be done." (Luke 22:42)—*David O. McKay* (CR, Apr. 1969, 5)

One of our difficulties in this world today is that too many of our Father's children do not believe in God. They have an idea that they can do just as they please and they throw their lives away. . . . The [pathway] of righteousness is the highway to happiness. —*George Albert Smith* (CP, 25)

I do not believe we accomplish very much in life unless we are enthusiastic, unless we are in earnest, and unless we practice what we preach. —*Heber J. Grant* (CR, Apr. 1910, 40)

I believe that we can accomplish any object that we make up our minds to, and no boy or girl ought to sit down and say, because she cannot do as well as somebody else, that she will not do anything. God has given to some people ten talents. To others, He has given one. But they who improve the one talent will live to see the day when they will far outshine those who have ten talents but fail to improve them. —*Heber J. Grant* (IE, 4:684-685)

The man that grows each day of his life is the man that fills the plain, simple, everyday duties which devolve upon him. —*Heber J. Grant* (GS, 184)

I have found nothing in the battle of life that has been of more value to me than to perform the duty of today to the best of my ability. I know that where young men do this, they will be better prepared for the labors of tomorrow. —*Heber J. Grant* (IE, 3:82)

Every individual should have a desire to grow and increase in capacity and in ability to do things. Certainly by mere exertion of the will, by mere desire, we accomplish nothing. We must put with that desire the labor to accomplish the things we desire. —*Heber J. Grant* (IE, 41:391)

No man is safe unless he is master of himself; and there is no tyrant more merciless or more to be dreaded than an uncontrollable appetite or passion. —*Joseph F. Smith* (GD, 247)

Let us conquer ourselves, and then go to and conquer all the evil that we see around us, as far as we possibly can. And we will do it without using violence; we will do it without interfering with the agency of men or of women. We will do it by persuasion, by long-suffering, by patience, and by forgiveness and love unfeigned. —*Joseph F. Smith* (CR, Oct. 1906, 129)

The labor that is upon us is to subdue our passions, conquer our inward foes, and see that our hearts are right in the sight of the Lord. —*Joseph F. Smith* (GD, 341)

Our first enemy we will find within ourselves. It is a good thing to overcome that enemy first and bring ourselves into subjection to the will of the Father, and into strict obedience to the principles of life and salvation which he has given to the world for the salvation of men. —*Joseph F. Smith* (CR, Oct. 1914, 128)

We ought to improve ourselves and move faster toward the point of perfection. . . . It is our duty to try to be perfect, and it is our duty to improve each day, and look upon our course last week and do things better this week; do things better today than we did them yesterday, and go on and on from one degree of righteousness to another. —*Lorenzo Snow* (LS, 154)

We should labor for perfection so far as possible, and seek to go onward. There is no man or woman who can stand still any great length of time. In this path over which we are moving we are very likely to go backward if we undertake to stand still or act indifferently. —*Lorenzo Snow* (LS, 95)

It is impossible to advance in the principles of truth, to increase in heavenly knowledge, except we exercise our reasoning faculties and exert ourselves in a proper manner. —*Lorenzo Snow* (LS, 29)

If we expect to improve, to advance in the work immediately before us, and finally to obtain possession of those gifts and glories, coming up to that condition of exaltation we anticipate, we must take thought and reflect, we must exert ourselves, and that too to the utmost of our ability. —*Lorenzo Snow* (LS, 29)

Character approved of God is worth securing, even at the expense of a lifetime of constant self-denial. —*Lorenzo Snow* (LS, 101)

I consider that it is one of the greatest victories for a man to gain, to learn how to control himself. Show me a man who does control himself and I will show you a safe man. . . . The moment a man or a woman becomes angry he or she shows a great weakness, and so it is with any of us when we do anything wrong. —*Wilford Woodruff* (WW, 260)

Any man who undertakes to serve God has to round up his shoulders and meet it, and any man who will not trust in God and abide in his cause even unto death is not worthy of a place in the celestial kingdom. —*Wilford Woodruff* (WW, 263)

If there are any, however, who think themselves men, let them show it, not by vain glory or empty boast, but by virtue, meekness, purity, faith, wisdom, intelligence, and knowledge, both of earthly and heavenly things. —*John Taylor* (GK, 35)

If we understand ourselves and our position, it ought to be with us, the kingdom of God first and ourselves afterwards. If we can learn to accomplish a little thing, the Lord will probably tell us to do a greater, because we are prepared to do it. . . . If we are the people of God, and he is trusting to us to accomplish these great purposes, we have got to do a little more than we have done, and we have got to be willing and obedient to the dictation of the Spirit of the Lord and his servants whom he had placed over us. If we do this, every labor we engage in will be joyous and pleasant to us, peace will reign in our bosoms and the peace of God will abide in our habitations. —*John Taylor* (GK, 131-132)

Anybody can preach. He is a poor simpleton that cannot. It is the easiest thing in the world. But, as President Young says, it takes a man to practice. —*John Taylor* (GK, 213)

A man may learn letters and study all the various branches of scholastic education to the day of his death; but if he does not attain to strict self-discipline, his learning will not amount to much. The catalogue of man's discipline he must compile himself. —*Brigham Young* (Apr. 7, 1852—address given in the Tabernacle on Temple Square)

When you are tempted to do wrong, do not stop one moment to argue, but tell Mr. Devil to walk out of your barn. —*Brigham Young* (BY, 81)

Now I charge you again, and I charge myself not to get angry. Never let anger arise in your hearts. No, Brigham, never let anger arise in your heart, never, never! Although you may be called upon to chastise and to speak to the people sharply, do not let anger arise in you, no, never!—*Brigham Young* (BY, 265)

No man can ever become a ruler in the Kingdom of God, until he can perfectly rule himself; then is he capable of raising a family of children who will rise up and call him blessed. —*Brigham Young* (BY, 265)

If you first gain power to check your words, you will then begin to have power to check your judgment, and at length actually gain power to check your thoughts and reflections. —*Brigham Young* (BY, 267-268)

To conquer and subdue, and school ourselves until we bring everything into subjection to the law of Christ, is our work. —*Brigham Young* (BY, 267)

43. EDUCATION

I am aware of the "publish or perish" pressure under which teachers work in some of our universities, but I should like to say to these teachers that your learned monographs will yield little satisfaction as the years pass if you discover that while you published, your students perished. . . .

Your students deserve more than your knowledge. They deserve and hunger for your inspiration. They want the warm glow of personal relationships. This always has been the hallmark of a great teacher "who is the student's accomplice in learning rather than his adversary." This is the education worth striving for and the education worth providing. —*Gordon B. Hinckley* (CR, Oct. 1965, 52)

I have concluded that the work of the world is not done by intellectual geniuses. It is done by men of ordinary capacity who use their abilities in an extraordinary manner. As a member of this church you have the obligation to seek learning and to improve your skills. —*Gordon B. Hinckley* (CR, Oct. 1972, 107)

Education is a shortcut to proficiency. It makes it possible to leapfrog over the mistakes of the past. Regardless of the vocation you choose, you can speed your journey in getting there through education—*Gordon B. Hinckley* (Ensign, Nov. 1981, 40-41)

What a charge has been laid upon us to grow constantly toward eternity! None of us can assume that we have learned enough. As the door closes on one phase of life, it opens on another, where we must continue to pursue knowledge. Ours ought to be a ceaseless quest for truth. That truth must include spiritual and religious truth as well as secular. As we go forward with our lives and our search for the truth, let us look for the good, the beautiful, the positive. —*Gordon B. Hinckley* (FETR , 73)

There is need for another education, without which the substance of our secular learning may lead only to our destruction. I refer to the education of the heart, of the conscience, of the character, of the spirit—these indefinable aspects of our personalities which determine so certainly what we are and what we do in our relationships one with another. —*Gordon B. Hinckley* (FETR , 81)

Do we encourage education? By all means. Every young woman ought to be encouraged to refine her skills and increase her abilities, to broaden her knowledge and strengthen her capacity. —*Gordon B. Hinckley* (Ensign, Sept. 1988, 10)

Brothers and Sisters, we need to do everything necessary to adequately prepare ourselves for employment or careers. We owe it to ourselves to do our best, and we owe our best in providing for our families. —*Howard W. Hunter* (Ensign, Nov. 1975, 124)

Chance always favors the prepared life. . . .

May I say once more to the youth of the Church—prepare, believe, be ready, have faith. Do not say or do or be that which would limit your service or render you ineffective in the kingdom of God. Be ready when your call comes, for surely it will come. —*Howard W. Hunter* (Ensign, May 1978, 34-35)

While waiting for promised blessings, one should not mark time, for failure to move forward is to some degree retrogression. Each of us must be anxiously engaged in good causes, including our own development. The personal pursuit of hobbies or crafts, the seeking of knowledge and wisdom, particularly of the things of God, and the development and honing of skills are all things that could productively occupy our time. —*Howard W. Hunter* (WMJ, 55-56)

It is essential to remember that it is more important to be able to think and hence to act in terms of gospel principles and teachings than it is to merely memorize gospel facts. —*Howard W. Hunter* (WMJ, 135)

Bad experiences are an expensive school that only fools keep going to. —*Ezra Taft Benson* (NE, May 1975, 16-17)

Our lives, to be successful, must constitute a constant pursuit of truth—all truth. —*Ezra Taft Benson* (ETB, 116)

True religion accepts and embraces all truth; science is slowly expanding her arms and reaching into the invisible domain, in search of truth. The two are meeting daily; science as a child; true religion as the mother. Truth is truth, whether labeled science or religion. —*Ezra Taft Benson* (ETB, 118)

We encourage earthly knowledge in many areas, but remember, if there is ever a conflict between earthly knowledge and the words of the prophet, you stand with the prophet, and you will be blessed and time will vindicate you. —*Ezra Taft Benson* (ETB, 137)

Wisdom comes with experience and struggle, not just with going through a university matriculation. —*Ezra Taft Benson* (ETB, 295)

In gearing the curricula to the middle of the class, our system too often has not provided sufficient challenge for the better student. Champions seldom become champions by competing only against mediocrity. —*Ezra Taft Benson* (ETB, 298-299)

It is not the search for knowledge—or knowledge itself—that costs a man his faith. It is rather the conceit of small minds proving anew that a little knowledge can be a dangerous thing. —*Ezra Taft Benson* (ETB, 304)

One must select wisely a source of news; otherwise it would be better to be uninformed than misinformed. —*Ezra Taft Benson* (ETB, 322)

It seems to me that the best way to get ready for tomorrow is by being sure that we are living up to the opportunities of today. —*Ezra Taft Benson* (ETB, 552)

If men are really humble, they will realize that they discover, but do not create, truth. —*Spencer W. Kimball* (Ensign, Sept. 1978, 3)

It is highly significant to realize that the greatest intellect in human history—the most talented individual ever to grace this globe—chose to be a teacher!—*Spencer W. Kimball* (SWK, 523)

True education prepares one for "making a life," not merely the "making of a living."—*Spencer W. Kimball* (SWK, 388)

The things of God—and often the things of his earth—cannot be understood by the spirit of man, but are understood only through the Spirit of God. —*Spencer W. Kimball* (Ensign, Sept. 1983, 6.)

Did you ever think that scientists have discovered anything that God didn't already know?—*Harold B. Lee* (CR, Oct. 1972, 131)

Measure every teaching to be found in the world of book-learning by the teachings of revealed truth as contained in the Gospel of Jesus Christ. —*Harold B. Lee* (DSL, 192)

Keep yourself growing in the faith as you seek secular learning. You show me one who has grown so sophisticated as to want to reform the church of its practices or its standards or who declares revelations of the Lord as merely "church policy," and I will show you one who is wavering in the faith or one who has lost it. —*Harold B. Lee* (YLW, 22-23)

We charge our teachers to give constant stimulation to budding young scientists and scholars in all fields and to urge them to push further and further into the realms of the unknown. —*Harold B. Lee* (YLW, 117)

One is too small for a grand eternity when he, because of a little learning, closes against himself the doors of the greatest of all institutions of learning, the "University of Spirituality." . . . may I enjoin you, with all the power at my command, to be true to your ideals. —*Harold B. Lee* (YLW, 270)

Now I understand that knowledge is very important, but there is a great fund of knowledge in the possession of men that will not save them in the kingdom of God. What they have got to learn are the fundamental things of the gospel of Jesus Christ. They have got to learn to have faith in God. They must learn to obey him. They have got to learn his commandments, his ordinances, and keep them, and unless they do, all their learning and all their knowledge will be of little benefit to them. —*Joseph Fielding Smith* (DS1, 291)

Christ did not study chemistry, or physics or sociology in the colleges of his day. Indeed, as we know them, these subjects were neither devised nor taught in his day.

But he did so live as to receive knowledge by revelation from the Holy Ghost, thus setting the pattern for all of us. We are commanded to seek learning, even by study and also by faith. I think we should do all we can during our student years to learn those things which will benefit us during our mortal probations and enable us to have the means and talents to further the Lord's work on earth. —*Joseph Fielding Smith* (KRL, 163)

I wish to say that education is an investment, not an expense. —*David O. McKay* (GI, 434)

Teaching is the noblest profession in the world. —*David O. McKay* (GI, 436)

A man may possess a profound knowledge of history and of mathematics; he may be authority in psychology, biology, or astronomy; he may know all the discovered truths pertaining to geology and natural science; but if he has not with this knowledge that nobility of soul which prompts him to deal justly with his fellow men, to practice virtue and holiness in personal life, he is not a truly educated man. —*David O. McKay* (IE, 45:12)

True education is awakening a love for truth, a just sense of duty, opening the eyes of the soul to the great purpose and end of life. It is not to teach the individual to love the good for personal sake; it is to teach him to love the good for the sake of the good itself; to be virtuous in action because he is so in heart; to love God and serve him supremely, not from fear, but from delight in his perfect character. —*David O. McKay* (CR, Apr. 1965, 8)

Any education is undoubtedly better than none, but a free people, to remain free, must ever strive for the highest and best. —*David O. McKay* (CR, Apr. 1968, 93)

Gaining knowledge is one thing, and applying it, quite another. Wisdom is the right application of knowledge, and true education—the education for which the Church stands—is the application of knowledge to the development of a noble and God-like character. —*David O. McKay* (CR, Apr. 1968, 93-94)

You may go through all the universities throughout the land, gain all the knowledge they have to give you, and yet you will be far short, if you do not have the knowledge that Jesus is the Christ and that God lives and is indeed our Eternal Father. —*George Albert Smith* (SGO, 54)

If we will live the teachings of Jesus of Nazareth, if we will observe the advice and counsel of the prophets of God, if we will carry out the program that the Lord has given to the Church with which we are identified, we will lead all the world in knowledge and intelligence and in power, because we may have all that the world has, plus the inspiration of the Almighty. —*George Albert Smith* (CR, Apr. 1946, 124)

There is no conflict between true science and true religion; that the truth, no matter from what source we derive it, all originates with our Heavenly Father. . . . Instead of trying to find a conflict between science and religion we do well to understand them both, to the end that we will be able to harmonize them. —*George Albert Smith* (CR, Apr. 1928, 45)

Let us seek to better our condition—intellectually, physically, morally, and above all let us seek for the inspiration of Almighty God to guide us in all the walks of life. —*Heber J. Grant* (CR, Apr. 1911, 25)

I have seen nothing and read nothing but what has confirmed me in the conviction that the mere development and improvement of the body and the intellect by education, without developing the spirit, does not accomplish what education ought to do for a person. —*Heber J. Grant* (IE, 26:1091)

I rejoice to know that whatever degree of intelligence we attain unto in this life shall rise with us in the life to come, and we shall have just that much the advantage of those who have not gained intelligence, because of their failure to study diligently. —*Heber J. Grant* (CR Oct. 1907, 24)

I remember speaking, upon one occasion, in one of our great Church schools. I said that I hoped it would never be forgotten that the one and only reason why there was any necessity for a Church school was to make Latter-day Saints. —*Heber J. Grant* (LPS, 405)

It is not what you eat that benefits you, but what you digest. What you hear today is of no use to you unless you put it into practice. —*Heber J. Grant* (LPS, 403)

Truth and error can never agree; but truth, no matter where it is found is consistent and will always harmonize with every other truth. . . . [T]he time will come when all theories, ideas and opinions which are not in harmony with that which the Lord has declared, must come to an end; for that which remains and will endure and abide forever, will be the truth. —*Joseph F. Smith* (GD, 86-87)

Our young people are diligent students. They reach out after truth and knowledge with commendable zeal and in so doing they must necessarily adopt for temporary use many theories of men. As long, however, as they recognize them as scaffolding, useful for research purposes, there can be no special harm in them. It is when these theories are settled upon as basic truth that trouble appears and the searcher then stands in grave danger of being led hopelessly from the right way. Philosophic theories of life have their place and use, but they are out of their place in church schools or anywhere else when they seek to supplant the revelations of God. —*Joseph F. Smith* (SHP, 143)

The greatest achievement mankind can make in this world is to familiarize themselves with divine truth, so thoroughly, so perfectly, that the example or conduct of no creature living in the world can ever turn them away from the knowledge that they have obtained. —*Joseph F. Smith* (GD, 3-4)

It is no discredit to our intelligence or to our integrity to say frankly in the face of a hundred speculative questions, "I do not know."—*Joseph F. Smith* (GD, 9)

The whole idea of Mormonism is improvement—mentally, physically, morally, and spiritually. No half-way education suffices for the Latter-day Saint. He holds with Herbert Spencer that the function of education is to "prepare man for complete living," but he also maintains that "complete living" should be interpreted "life here and hereafter."—*Lorenzo Snow* (LS, 27)

Some things we have to learn by that which we suffer, and knowledge secured in that way, though the process may be painful, will be of great value to us in the other life. —*Lorenzo Snow* (LS, 30)

We learn by sharing our knowledge with others. —*Lorenzo Snow* (LS, 30)

Do not be discouraged because you cannot learn all at once; learn one thing at a time, learn it well, and treasure it up, then learn another truth and treasure that up, and in a few years you will have a great store of useful knowledge which will not only be a great blessing to yourselves and your children, but to your fellow men. —*Wilford Woodruff* (WW, 269)

We are after the truth. We commenced searching for it, and we are constantly in search of it, and so fast as we find any true principle revealed by any man, by God, or by holy angels, we embrace it and make it part of our religious creed. —*John Taylor* (GK, 47)

We are open for the reception of all truth, of whatever nature it may be, and are desirous to obtain and possess it, to search after it as we would for hidden treasures; and to use all the knowledge God gives to us to possess ourselves of all the intelligence that he has given to others; and to ask at his hands to reveal unto us his will, in regard to things that are the best calculated to promote the happiness and well-being of human society. —*John Taylor* (GK, 48)

You will see the day that Zion will be as far ahead of the outside world in everything pertaining to learning of every kind as we are today in regard to religious matters. You mark my words, and write them down, and see if they do not come to pass. —*John Taylor* (GK, 275)

All the intelligence which men possess on the earth, whether religious, scientific, or political—proceeds from God. Every good and perfect gift proceeds from him, the fountain of light and truth, wherein there is no variableness nor shadow of turning. —*John Taylor* (GK, 271)

In relation to the education of the world generally, a great amount of it is of very little value, consisting more of words than ideas; and whilst men are verbose in their speaking or writing, you have to hunt for ideas or truth like hunting, for a grain of wheat among piles of chaff or rubbish. It is true that a great amount of it is really valuable, and it is for us to select the good from the bad. —*John Taylor* (GK, 269)

Whom does their learning benefit? Certainly not the multitude. I will tell you my idea of true intelligence and true eloquence. It is not as some people do—to take a very small idea and use a great many grandiloquent words without meaning—something to befog and mystify it with—something to tickle the ear and please the imagination only. That is not true intelligence. But it is true intelligence for a man to take a subject that is mysterious and great in itself, and to unfold and simplify it so that a child can understand it. I do not care what words you make use of, if you have the principles and are enabled to convey those principles to the understandings of men. —*John Taylor* (GK, 270)

Intelligence is given unto us to improve upon. —*Brigham Young* (BY, 52)

I will not say, as do many, that the more I learn the more I am satisfied that I know nothing; for the more I learn the more I discern an eternity of knowledge to improve upon. —*Brigham Young* (BY, 250)

No matter what your circumstances are, whether you are in prosperity or in adversity, you can learn from every person, transaction, and circumstance around you. —*Brigham Young* (BY, 250)

Our education should be such as to improve our minds and fit us for increased usefulness; to make us of greater service to the human family; to enable us to stop our rude methods of living, speaking, and thinking. —*Brigham Young* (BY, 255)

We want every branch of science taught in this place that is taught in the world. But our favorite study is that branch which particularly belongs to the Elders of Israel—namely, theology. Every Elder should become a profound theologian—should understand this branch better than all the world. —*Brigham Young* (BY, 258)

I shall not cease learning while I live, nor when I arrive in the spirit-world; but shall there learn with greater facility; and when I again receive my body, I shall learn a thousand times more in a thousand times less time; and then I do not mean to cease learning, but shall still continue my researches. —*Brigham Young* (JD, 8:10)

The best way to obtain truth and wisdom is not to ask it from books, but to go to God in prayer, and obtain divine teaching. —*Joseph Smith, Jr.* (STJS, 217)

In knowledge there is power. God has more power than all other beings, because he has greater knowledge; and hence he knows how to subject all other beings to Him. He has power over all. —*Joseph Smith, Jr.* (STJS, 321)

A fanciful and flowery and heated imagination beware of; because the things of God are of deep import; and time, and experience, and careful and ponderous and solemn thoughts can only find them out. Thy mind, O man! if thou wilt lead a soul unto salvation, must stretch as high as the utmost heavens, and search into and contemplate the darkest abyss, and the broad expanse of eternity—thou must commune with God. How much more dignified and noble are the thoughts of God, than the vain imaginations of the human heart! None but fools will trifle with the souls of men. —*Joseph Smith, Jr.* (STJS, 156-157)

Add to your faith knowledge, etc. The principle of knowledge is the principle of salvation. This principle can be comprehended by the faithful and diligent; and every one that does not obtain knowledge sufficient to be saved will be condemned. The principle of salvation is given us through the knowledge of Jesus Christ. —*Joseph Smith, Jr.* (LPS, 400)

A man is saved no faster than he gets knowledge. —*Joseph Smith, Jr.* (LPS, 400)

44. ENTERTAINMENT

Let there be music in the home. If you have teenagers who have their own recordings, you will be prone to describe the sound as something other than music. Let them occasionally hear something better. Expose them to it. It will speak for itself. More of appreciation will come than you may think. It may not be spoken, but it will be felt, and its influence will become increasingly manifest as the years pass—*Gordon B. Hinckley* (BTE, 56)

No good will come of going to movies that are designed to take from you your money and give you in exchange only weakened wills and base desires—*Gordon B. Hinckley* (Ensign, Nov. 1981, 40-41)

Time is always precious to busy people, and we are robbed of its worth when hours are wasted in reading or viewing that which is frivolous and of little value. —*Howard W. Hunter* (CR, Nov. 1979, 64)

Don't see R-rated movies or vulgar videos or participate in any entertainment that is immoral, suggestive, or pornographic. Don't listen to music that is degrading. —*Ezra Taft Benson* (CR, May 1986, 45)

With the abundance of books available today, it is a mark of a truly educated person to know what not to read. —*Ezra Taft Benson* (CUC , 33)

Successful parents have found that it is not easy to rear children in an environment polluted with evil. Therefore, they take deliberate steps to provide the best of wholesome influences. Moral principles are taught. Good books are made available and read. Television watching is controlled. Good and uplifting music is provided. But most importantly, the scriptures are read and discussed as a means to help develop spiritual-mindedness. —*Ezra Taft Benson* (Ensign, Aug. 1993, 2-4)

Be concerned about the types of programs your family is watching on television or hearing on radio. There is so much today that is unsavory and degrading, so much that gives the impression that the old sins of Sodom and Gomorrah are the "in thing" to do today. —*Spencer W. Kimball* (Ensign, May 1978, 45)

Too many of us spend far too much time watching the television or in habits and activities that do not enlarge ourselves or bless others. Would that we might lift ourselves to higher visions of what we could do with our lives! There should be no people who have a higher desire to obtain truth, revealed and secular, than Latter-day Saints. —*Spencer W. Kimball* (Ensign, Sept. 1983, 6.)

Leisure-time activities that promote idleness should be shunned. For this reason principally card playing is discountenanced by the Church. There seems to be something so all-absorbing in this type of game that those who indulge make of it almost their ruling passion in life, with certainly little compensation in mental development in comparison with the time spent. —*Harold B. Lee* (DSL, 158)

In your laughter, may I suggest that you beware of the boisterous laugh that reveals the vacant mind. —*Harold B. Lee* (DSL, 154)

The home that fosters entertainments for its youth within its walls and that church which provides socials commenced and ended with prayer, will have their reward in happy homes of the parents of tomorrow. —*Harold B. Lee* (DSL, 158)

The reading habit, like charity, should begin at home. It is the duty of every parent to provide in his home a library of suitable books to be at the service of the family. The library need not be large, nor the books of the most expensive binding, but there should be a well chosen variety of the most select that can be obtained. —*Joseph Fielding Smith* (DS3, 204)

I believe in physical sport, I believe in recreation and amusement of the kind that is beneficial to the body and the mind of man, and that play of the proper kind is good and ought to be indulged in at times, especially by those whose work is such that they do not get the necessary physical exercise required by their bodies. —*Joseph Fielding Smith* (CR, Oct. 1916, 73)

Our people are encouraged, not curtailed, in every kind of needful recreation and amusement; but all things which the world seeks, leading to evil, such as card playing, raffling, and indulging in playing machines of chance, are frowned upon as destructive of morals and abiding faith in that which is just and true. —*Joseph Fielding Smith* (IE, 58:303)

I doubt whether it is possible to dance most of the prevalent fad dances in a manner to meet LDS standards. —*David O. McKay* (IE, 72:46-47)

Music is truly the universal language, and when it is excellently expressed, how deeply it moves our souls!—*David O. McKay* (IE, 43:309)

I would like to call attention to the fact that in our day our Heavenly Father has given a revelation, teaching us that it is our privilege, yea, our blessing, to sing, and that our songs should be sung in righteousness. —*George Albert Smith* (SGO, 159)

There is a growing tendency in this age to live much more rapidly. Instead of thinking seriously of the purposes of life, many of our young people are devoted to light amusements. "What shall we do tomorrow for fun?" "What shall we do next day for pleasure?" "Let's go to the show tonight." "Let's go to the dance tomorrow night." . . .
Those who pursue pleasure in this life to excess are likely to forsake the ways of the Lord. —*George Albert Smith* (CR, Apr. 1915, 95)

We do have excellent hymns in this Church. Even our Primary children, beginning in their tender years, are taught not only to sing the songs of the world, but they are taught to sing the praises of our Heavenly Father and to give thanksgiving in the music that is prepared. What a comforting, uplifting influence there is in music. —*George Albert Smith* (CR, Apr. 1935, 47)

Many of our picture shows, radio programs, magazines, books, etc., are unfit for respectable communities, and unless we neutralize the influence of these things by wholesome teaching and environment, . . . some of those whom we love may slip away from us, and when it is too late we will realize that we have been sleeping on our privileges. —*George Albert Smith* (CR, Oct. 1932, 25)

I have read nothing except condemnation of card-playing and the wasting of your time in doing something that brings no good, bodily, intellectually, or in any way, and sometimes leads your children to become gamblers, because they become expert card-players. The Church as a Church requests its members not to play cards. I hope you understand me, and I want you to know that I am speaking for the Church when I ask the people to let cards alone. —*Heber J. Grant* (CR, Apr. 1926, 10)

The more beautiful the music by which false doctrine is sung, the more dangerous it becomes. I appeal to all Latter-day Saints, and especially to our choirs, never to sing the words of a song, no matter how beautiful and inspiring the music may be, where the teachings are not in perfect accord with the truths of the gospel. —*Heber J. Grant* (IE, 15:786)

To my mind the musician who pays little or no attention to the words of a song destroys half the value and charm of his or her singing. —*Heber J. Grant* (IE, 15:784)

[I]nstead of wasting the time in senseless practices that lead only to mischief and sometimes to serious evil and wrongdoing; instead of doing this, seek out of the best books knowledge and understanding. Read history. Read philosophy, if you wish. Read anything that is good, that will elevate the mind and will add to your stock of knowledge. —*Joseph F. Smith* (CR, Oct. 1903, 98)

Good music is gracious praise of God. It is delightsome to the ear, and it is one of our most acceptable methods of worshiping God. —*Joseph F. Smith* (CR, Oct. 1899, 69)

Again, all amusements become pernicious when pursued excessively. —*Joseph F. Smith* (GD, 332)

The desire to get something of value for little or nothing is pernicious; and any proceeding that strengthens that desire is an effective aid to the gambling spirit, which has proved a veritable demon of destruction to thousands. —*Joseph F. Smith* (GD, 327)

Why, there are some people who think that the fiddle, for instance, is an instrument of the devil and it is quite wrong to use it. I do not think so, I think it is a splendid thing to dance by. But some folks think that we should not dance. Yes, we should enjoy life in any way we can. Some people object to music. Why, music prevails in the heavens and among the birds! God has filled them with it. . . . We have no idea of the excellency, beauty, harmony and symphony of the music in the heavens. —*John Taylor* (GK, 62)

Recreation and diversion are as necessary to our well-being as the more serious pursuits of life. —*Brigham Young* (BY, 238)

There is no music in hell, for all good music belongs to heaven. Sweet harmonious sounds give exquisite joy to human beings capable of appreciating music. —*Brigham Young* (BY, 242-243)

Those who cannot serve God with a pure heart in the dance should not dance. —*Brigham Young* (BY, 243)

If you wish to dance, dance; and you are just as much prepared for a prayer meeting after dancing as ever you were, if you are Saints. If you desire to ask God for anything, you are as well prepared to do so in the dance as in any other place, if you are Saints. —*Brigham Young* (BY, 243)

45. Gratitude and Humility

Our society is afflicted by a spirit of thoughtless arrogance unbecoming those who have been so magnificently blessed. How grateful we ought to be for the bounties we enjoy. Absence of gratitude is the mark of the narrow, uneducated mind. It bespeaks a lack of knowledge and the ignorance of self-sufficiency. It expresses itself in ugly egotism and frequently in wanton mischief—*Gordon B. Hinckley* (FETR , 81-82)

Where there is gratitude, there is humility, as opposed to pride—*Gordon B. Hinckley* (FETR , 82)

I urge you to lift your heads and walk in gratitude. Spare yourselves from the indulgence of self-pity. It is always self-defeating. Subdue the negative and emphasize the positive. Count your blessings and not your problems. —*Gordon B. Hinckley* (Ensign, Nov. 1985, 86)

As a result of the many miracles in our lives, we should be more humble and more grateful, more kind and more believing. —*Howard W. Hunter* (Ensign, May 1989, 17)

Contrition is costly: it costs us our pride and our insensitivity, but it especially costs us our sins. —*Howard W. Hunter* (WMJ, 9)

Surely the lessons of history ought to teach us that pride, haughtiness, self-adulation, conceit, and vanity contain all of the seeds of self-destruction for individuals, cities, or nations. —*Howard W. Hunter* (WMJ, 14)

Humility is an attribute of Godliness possessed by true saints. It is easy to understand why a proud man fails. He is content to rely upon himself only. . . . Our genuine concern should be for the success of others. The proud man shuts himself off from God, and when he does so, he no longer lives in the light. —*Howard W. Hunter* (WMJ, 142)

The two groups who have the greatest difficulty in following the prophet are the proud who are leaned and the proud who are rich. The learned may feel the prophet is only inspired when he agrees with them; otherwise, the prophet is just giving his opinion—speaking as a man. The rich may feel they have no need to take counsel of a lowly prophet. —*Ezra Taft Benson* (ETB, 138)

Acquire humility. There is no true success without it. —*Ezra Taft Benson* (ETB, 370)

Pride does not look up to God and care about what is right. It looks sideways to man and argues who is right. —*Ezra Taft Benson* (AWW, 78)

Pride is characterized by "What do I want out of life?" rather than by "What would God have me do with my life?" It is a self-will as opposed to God's will. It is the fear of man over the fear of God. —*Ezra Taft Benson* (AWW, 78)

In the scriptures there is no such thing as righteous pride. It is always considered as a sin. —*Ezra Taft Benson* (Ensign, May 1989, 4)

Pride is essentially competitive in nature. . . .
The proud make every man their adversary by pitting their intellects, opinions, works, wealth, talents, or any other worldly measuring device against others. —*Ezra Taft Benson* (Ensign, May 1989, 4)

When pride has a hold on our hearts, we lose our independence of the world and deliver our freedoms to the bondage of men's judgment. The world shouts louder than the whisperings of the Holy Ghost. The reasoning of men overrides the revelations of God. —*Ezra Taft Benson* (Ensign, May 1989, 5)

Humility does not mean weakness. It does not mean timidity; it does not mean fear. A man can be humble and fearless. A man can be humble and courageous. Humility is the recognition of our dependence upon a higher power, a constant need for the Lord's support in His work. —*Ezra Taft Benson* (Ensign, Sept. 1990, 5)

Ingratitude, thou sinful habit! . . .we live in liberty and privilege. Do we appreciate that and do we express our gratitude in solemn thanksgiving?—*Spencer W. Kimball* (SWK, 120)

When one becomes conscious of his great humility, he has already lost it. When one begins boasting of his humility, it has already become pride—the antithesis of humility. —*Spencer W. Kimball* (IE, Aug. 1963, 656)

A person with great spirituality shows appreciation to God. —*Harold B. Lee* (YLW, 197)

A man who delivers a good sermon that some people have been impressed with, if he understands anything, he will wisely get down on his knees that night when he gets home and thank God that somehow the Lord blessed him that he was able to say something to impress someone. You give thanks to the Lord. —*Harold B. Lee* (HBL, 195)

When men become humble they soon become proud they're humble. I think there's a lot of that. Humility is one or the rarest qualities in all the world. —*Harold B. Lee* (HBL, 617-618)

The crime of ingratitude is one of the most prevalent and I might say at the same time one of the greatest with which mankind is afflicted. The more the Lord blesses us the less we love him. —*Joseph Fielding Smith* (DS1, 132-133)

Ingratitude is, I think, the most prevalent of all sins, and one of the greatest, because every soul who refuses to abide in the truth, who will not walk in the light and understanding of the commandments which Jesus Christ has given, is ungrateful. —*Joseph Fielding Smith* (CR, Apr. 1944, 50)

The pure in heart are those who are sincere. Inward purity stands in contrast with painted hypocrisy. One who cherishes his virtue is always in the best of company. He lives nearest the Eternal. Surely it is he who will see God. —*David O. McKay* (IE, 48:104)

Let us not put away from us the things of God. Let us retain in our homes the influence of prayer and of thanksgiving, and let gratitude rise to him who is the Author of our being and the Giver of all good. Let us appreciate all these blessings, yes, but not forget the Giver. Let him know by the conduct of our lives that we appreciate him and all that we enjoy. —*George Albert Smith* (SGO, 109-110)

It is not what we receive that enriches our lives, it is what we give. —*George Albert Smith* (CR, Apr. 1935, 46)

Everything that you can think of in the way of comfort and information has been presented to this dispensation. Unfortunately, notwithstanding these blessings, there is a tendency to worship the gift and to forget the Giver. —*George Albert Smith* (CR, Apr. 1926, 143-144)

It seems to be the hardest thing in the world for people to grow in wealth and keep the spirit of the gospel. —*Heber J. Grant* (GS, 31)

The grateful man sees so much in the world to be thankful for, and with him the good outweighs the evil. Love overpowers jealousy, and light drives darkness out of his life. Pride destroys our gratitude and sets up selfishness in its place. How much happier we are in the presence of a grateful and loving soul, and how careful we should be to cultivate, through the medium of a prayerful life, a thankful attitude toward God and man!—*Joseph F. Smith* (GD, 263)

And I believe that one of the greatest sins of which the inhabitants of the earth are guilty today is the sin of ingratitude, the want of acknowledgment, on their part, of God and his right to govern and control. We see a man raised up with extraordinary gifts, or with great intelligence, and he is instrumental in developing some great principle. He and the world ascribe his great genius and wisdom to himself. He attributes his success to his own energies, labor and mental capacity. He does not acknowledge the hand of God in anything connected with his success, but ignores him altogether and takes the honor to himself. —*Joseph F. Smith* (GD, 270)

I have thought sometimes that one of the greatest virtues the Latter-day Saints could possess is gratitude to our Heavenly Father for that which He has bestowed upon us and the path over which He has led us. It may be that walking along in that path has not always been of the most pleasant character; but we have afterwards discovered that those circumstances which have been very unpleasant have often proved of the highest advantage to us. We should always be pleased with the circumstances that surround us and that which the Lord requires at our hands. —*Lorenzo Snow* (CR, Apr. 1899, 2)

Always cultivate a spirit of gratitude. It is actually the duty of every Latter-day Saint to cultivate a spirit of gratitude. —*Lorenzo Snow* (LS, 62)

I feel to say that there is no people under heaven who have so much cause to rejoice and to be grateful as the Latter-day Saints. —*Wilford Woodruff* (WW, 131)

The gold and the silver are God's, and the cattle upon a thousand hills. All that we possess is the gift of God. We should acknowledge him in all things. We sometimes talk about men having this right and the other right. We have no rights, only such as God gives us. —*John Taylor* (GK, 248)

I rejoice in afflictions, for they are necessary to humble and prove us, that we may comprehend ourselves, become acquainted with our weakness and infirmities; and I rejoice when I triumph over them, because God answers my prayers; therefore I feel to rejoice all the day long. —*John Taylor* (GK, 234)

Unless God blesses our exertions we shall have nothing. It is the Lord that gives the increase. —*Brigham Young* (BY, 22)

I do not know of any, excepting the unpardonable sin, that is greater than the sin of ingratitude. —*Brigham Young* (BY, 229)

There are a great many wise men and women too in our midst who are too wise to be taught; therefore they must die in their ignorance, and in the resurrection they will find their mistake. —*Joseph Smith, Jr.* (STJS, 346)

46. HAPPINESS

Life in the service of the Lord is good. It is beautiful. It is rewarding. —*Gordon B. Hinckley* (Ensign, Nov. 1984, 86)

You will never be happy if you go through life thinking only of yourself. Get lost in the best cause in the world—the cause of the Lord. The work of the quorums, and of the auxiliary organizations, temple work, welfare service work, missionary work. You will bless your own life as you bless the lives of others. —*Gordon B. Hinckley* (Ensign, Jan. 1994, 7)

If we will live the gospel, if we will put our trust in God, our Eternal Father, if we will do what we are asked to do as members of The Church of Jesus Christ of Latter-day Saints, we will be the happiest and most blessed people on the face of the earth, my brothers and sisters. —*Gordon B. Hinckley* (CN, Nov. 4, 1995, 2)

We have a lot of gloomy people in the Church because they do not understand, I guess, that this is the gospel of happiness. It is something to be happy about, to get excited about. —*Gordon B. Hinckley* (CN, Feb. 13, 1996, 2)

We need to have a little humor in our lives. We better take seriously that which should be taken seriously, but at the same time we can bring in a touch of humor now and again. If the time ever comes when we can't smile at ourselves, it will be a sad time. —*Gordon B. Hinckley* (CN, Feb. 13, 1996, 2)

Life is to be enjoyed, not just endured. —*Gordon B. Hinckley* (Ensign, May 1996, 94)

In a world too preoccupied with winning through intimidation and seeking to be number one, no large crowd is standing in line to buy books that call for mere meekness. But the meek shall inherit the earth, a pretty impressive corporate takeover—and done without intimidation! Sooner or later, and we pray sooner than later, everyone will acknowledge that Christ's way is not only the right way, but ultimately the only way to hope and joy. —*Howard W. Hunter* (WMJ, 9)

There are those who declare it is old-fashioned to believe in the Bible. Is it old-fashioned to believe in Jesus Christ, the Son of the Living God? Is it old-fashioned to believe in his atoning sacrifice and the resurrection? If it is, I declare myself to be old-fashioned and the Church to be old-fashioned. In great simplicity, the Master taught the principles of life eternal and lessons that bring happiness to those with the faith to believe. —*Howard W. Hunter* (WMJ, 23)

Whenever we tackle a gospel imperative, immediate goals will help us master it. Our decision to read scripture becomes quite practical when we decide to read a chapter at night before we go to sleep. We should set up long-range and eternal goals, to be sure—they will be the guides and inspiration of a lifetime; but we should not forget the countless little immediate objectives to be won tomorrow and tomorrow and tomorrow. To win and pass these objectives marks our progress toward the greater goals and ensures happiness and the feelings of success along the way. —*Howard W. Hunter* (WMJ, 134-136)

An honorable man or woman is one who learns early that one cannot do wrong and feel right. —*Ezra Taft Benson* (NE, July 1984, 4)

To be different may be embarrassing if one is wrong—but it is an enviable distinction to be different if one is right. —*Ezra Taft Benson* (ETB, 455)

Remember this: There is no one great thing that you can do which will determine your happiness or success in life. Life is a series of little things—how you do your work from day to day, personal honesty in your everyday contacts, a smile and a handshake, courtesy and kindness—these are the "little things" that become the sum of your character. —*Ezra Taft Benson* (ETB, 462)

Be right and then be easy to live with, if possible—but in that order. —*Ezra Taft Benson* (BYU, 1979)

That man is greatest and most blessed and joyful whose life most closely approaches the pattern of the Christ. This has nothing to do with earthly wealth, power, or prestige. The only true test of greatness, blessedness, joyfulness is how close a life can come to being like the Master, Jesus Christ. —*Ezra Taft Benson* (Ensign, Dec. 1988, 2)

And when we are asked why we are such a happy people, our answer is: "Because we have everything—life with all its opportunities, death without fear, eternal life with endless growth and development."—*Spencer W. Kimball* (Ensign, Nov. 1974, 110)

One of the differences between true joy and mere pleasure is that certain pleasures are realized only at the cost of someone else's pain. Joy, on the other hand, springs out of self-lessness and service, and it benefits rather than hurts others. —*Spencer W. Kimball* (Ensign, Oct. 1985, 4)

If we would truly reform mankind, we must first reform ourselves. . . . The abundant life begins from within and then moves outward to other individuals. If there is richness and righteousness in us, then we can make a difference in the lives of others. —*Spencer W. Kimball* (Ensign, Oct. 1985, 4)

I think I would be safe in saying, and I believe you would agree with me, that perhaps never before in the history of the world has so much been said about the abundant life and so little effort expended in obtaining the essentials that make for an abundant life. —*Harold B. Lee* (SHP, 97-98)

If one feels strong surges of happiness and desire from the quiet of a happy home, from the unfolding of a beautiful life, from the revelation of divine wisdom, or from a love for the beautiful, the true and good, he is having a taste of the fullness of the joy that the living of a rich, full life only can bring. —*Harold B. Lee* (SHP, 342)

There never will be a time of peace, happiness, justice tempered by mercy, when all men will receive that which is their right and privilege to receive, until they get in their hearts the love of God. —*Joseph Fielding Smith* (CN, Feb. 6, 1932, 5)

Man is a social being. God designed him to be such. From infancy to old age, he is dependent upon others for his development, education, and happiness. In the right kind of social groups, the more a man gives, the more he receives; the more he teaches, the more he learns; the more happiness he bestows, the happier he becomes. —*David O. McKay* (GI, 197)

Joy is sweeter than pleasure. Joy is an emotion excited with the acquisition or expectation of good. Pleasure is a state of gratification of the senses or mind and may be sensuous. It may be self-indulgence. It is nearly always transitory. Joy and happiness are permanent. —*David O. McKay* (GI, 219)

We live our lives most completely when we strive to make the world better and happier. The law of pure nature, survival of the fittest, is self-preservation at the sacrifice of all else; the law of true spiritual life is deny self for the good of others. —*David O. McKay* (GI, 352-353)

Happiness is not an external condition, it is a state of the spirit and an attitude of the mind. —*David O. McKay* (CR, Oct. 1934, 93-94)

True happiness is found in living the Christ's life—on Monday as well as on Sunday. He who is virtuous only at intervals proves that his pretended virtue is but a sham. Such a person lacks sincerity, the foundation of a true character, without which happiness is impossible. He who seeks for happiness alone seldom finds it, but he who lives, that is, who loses himself to give happiness to others, finds that a double portion has come to himself. —*David O. McKay* (GI, 502-503)

This Church of Jesus Christ commonly known as "Mormonism," is in the world to make people happy. Happiness is the end, really, of our existence. That happiness comes most effectively through service to our fellow men, and the Church is the most effective means in the world through which that service may be rendered. —*David O. McKay* (CR, Oct. 1953, 132)

Too many are vainly seeking shortcuts to happiness. It should always be kept in mind that that which is most worthwhile in life requires strenuous effort. When a man seeks something for nothing and shuns effort, he is in no position to resist temptation. —*David O. McKay* (CR, Apr. 1967, 7)

Do we want to be happy? Do we want our homes to be happy? If we do, let them be the abiding place of prayer, thanksgiving and gratitude. —*George Albert Smith* (CR, Apr. 1944, 32)

The world tonight needs what we are here for—the inspiration of the Almighty. The trouble in the world is that the majority of our Father's children do not have that inspiration. . . . That is why there is so much sorrow in the world, because people do not live for that inspiration. —*George Albert Smith* (SGO, 212)

It isn't only what we receive that makes us happy; it is what we give, and the more we give of that which is uplifting and enriching to our Father's children, the more we have to give. It grows like a great fountain of life and bubbles up to eternal happiness. —*George Albert Smith* (SGO, 231-234)

I can say to you that if we have the spirit of the Lord burning in our souls we cannot be unhappy. —*George Albert Smith* (CR, Apr. 1944, 31)

The Lord wants us to be happy. That is why he gave us the gospel of Jesus Christ. —*George Albert Smith* (CR, Apr. 1949, 192)

I want to say that the happiest people in all the world are those who obey the counsel of our Heavenly Father. —*George Albert Smith* (CR, Oct. 1948, 8)

Though the world may be filled with distress, and the heavens gather blackness, and the vivid lightnings flash, and the earth quake from center to circumference, if we know that God lives, and our lives are righteous, we will be happy, there will be peace unspeakable because we know our Father approves our lives. —*George Albert Smith* (CR, Oct. 1915, 28)

It is not what we have that makes us happy; it is not the material things of life that enrich our lives; but it is what we are. The nearer we are like our Heavenly Father and his beloved Son Jesus Christ, the happier we are. —*George Albert Smith* (CR, Apr. 1946, 184-185)

I want to say that the only way of happiness is the pathway of righteousness. There is no other way. We refer to them as commandments, though I have always looked upon them as the loving advice of a kind Heavenly Father who, knowing all things, has pointed the way that his children might be happy. —*George Albert Smith* (CR, Apr. 1944, 28)

There is a peace and a contentment which comes into the heart when we live within our means. There is no question about it.
If there is any one thing that will bring peace and contentment into the human heart, and into the family, it is to live within our means. And if there is any one thing that is grinding and discouraging and disheartening, it is to have debts and obligations that one cannot meet. —*Heber J. Grant* (GS, 111)

The real secret of happiness in life and the way in which to prepare ourselves for the hereafter is service, and it is because we give service more than any other people in the world that we are happy. —*Heber J. Grant* (GS, 187)

I am converted to the thought that the way to peace and happiness in life is by giving service. Service is the true key, I believe, to happiness . . . When we perform any acts of kindness, they bring a feeling of satisfaction and pleasure into our hearts, while ordinary amusements pass away. —*Heber J. Grant* (GS, 187)

Time will vindicate the laws of God and the truth that individual human happiness is found in duty and not in pleasure and freedom from care. —*Joseph F. Smith* (GD, 281)

The education then of our desires is one of far-reaching importance to our happiness in life. —*Joseph F. Smith* (GD, 297)

It is a matter of the greatest importance that the people be educated to appreciate and cultivate the bright side of life rather than to permit its darkness and shadows to hover over them. —*Joseph F. Smith* (GD, 155)

[M]any of the people lose that portion of happiness that they might enjoy because of not reflecting seriously upon their duties and acting wisely and prudently. —*Lorenzo Snow* (LS, 95)

Only knowledge brings permanent happiness. . . . We have got to obtain knowledge before we obtain permanent happiness; we have got to be wide awake to the things of God.
Though we may now neglect to improve our time, to brighten up our intellectual faculties, we shall be obliged to improve them sometime. We have got so much ground to walk over; and if we fail to travel today, we shall have so much more to travel tomorrow. —*Lorenzo Snow* (LS, 28)

Make others happy, and you will be happy yourselves. —*Lorenzo Snow* (LS, 63)

Men may be very good, and yet they may not be very wise, nor so useful as they might be; but the gospel is given to make us wise, and to enable us to get those things in our minds that are calculated to make us happy. —*Lorenzo Snow* (LS, 19)

Take the greatest portion of mankind as an example, and how are they seeking for happiness? By serving the devil as fast as they can. —*Wilford Woodruff* (WW, 259)

If we really understood that we could not obtain happiness by walking in the paths of sin and breaking the laws of God, we should then see the folly of it, every man and every woman would see that to obtain happiness we should go to work and perform the works of righteousness, and do the will of our Father in heaven, for we shall receive at his hand all the happiness, blessing, glory, salvation, exaltation, and eternal lives, that we ever do receive either in time or eternity. —*Wilford Woodruff* (WW, 259-260)

A great many people have tried to seek for happiness independent of first seeking the kingdom of heaven, but they have always found it an uphill business, and so shall we if we try it. —*Wilford Woodruff* (WW, 173)

So far as I am personally concerned, I am here as a candidate for eternity—for heaven and for happiness. I want to secure by my acts a peace in another world that will impart that happiness and bliss for which I am seeking. —*John Taylor* (GK, 9)

If any man wishes to introduce peace into his family or among his friends, let him cultivate it in his own bosom; for sterling peace can only be had according to the legitimate rule and authority of heaven, and obedience to its laws. —*John Taylor* (GK, 319)

We look upon it that the greatest happiness that we can attain to is in securing the approbation of our Heavenly Father, in fearing God, in being made acquainted with his laws—with the principles of eternal truth and with those things that we consider will best promote not only our temporal, but our eternal happiness. —*John Taylor* (GK, 342)

We want to see beautiful cities, beautiful houses, and pleasant homes, and everything around you calculated to promote your happiness and well being. —*John Taylor* (GK, 268)

Beautify your private squares at your own homes. Let every man make his own grounds pleasant and agreeable. —*John Taylor* (GK, 268)

Without the light of the Spirit of Christ, no person can truly enjoy life. —*Brigham Young* (BY, 34)

The wicked do not know how to enjoy life, but the closer we live to God the better we know and understand how to enjoy it. Live so that you can enjoy the Spirit of the Lord continually. —*Brigham Young* (BY, 80)

O, consistency, thou art one of the fairest jewels in the life of a Saint. —*Brigham Young* (BY, 233)

The whole world are after happiness. It is not found in gold and silver, but it is in peace and love. —*Brigham Young* (BY, 235)

When man is industrious and righteous, then is he happy. —*Brigham Young* (BY, 235)

Happiness consists not of having, but of being—not of possessing, but of enjoying. It is a warm glow of the heart at peace with itself. A martyr at the stake may have happiness that a king on his throne might envy. Man is the creator of his own happiness. It is the aroma of life lived in harmony with high ideals. For what a man has he may be dependent upon others; what he is rests with him alone. What he obtains in life is but acquisition; what he attains is true growth. —*Joseph Smith, Jr.* (STJS, 255—256)

47. PERSONAL RESPONSIBILITY

We can improve today without waiting for tomorrow. We can alter circumstances ourselves, without waiting for others. We can hold back the forces that would debilitate and weaken us. We can strengthen the forces that will improve the world. —*Gordon B. Hinckley* (BTE, 16)

I wish with all my heart we would spend less time talking about rights and more time about responsibilities. —*Gordon B. Hinckley* (Ensign, Nov. 1983, 84)

Can anything be more false or dishonest than gratification of passion without acceptance of responsibility?—*Gordon B. Hinckley* (Ensign, Aug. 1989, 5)

This witness, this testimony, can be the most precious of all gifts of God. It is a heavenly bestowal when there is the right effort. It is the opportunity, it is the responsibility of every man and woman in this Church to obtain within himself or herself a conviction of the truth of this great latter-day work and of those who stand at its head, even the living God and the Lord Jesus Christ. —*Gordon B. Hinckley* (Ensign, May, 1998, 70)

Why face life's burdens alone, Christ asks, or why face them with temporal support that will quickly falter? to the heavy laden, Christ's yoke gives the power and peace of standing side by side with a God who will provide the support, balance, and the strength to meet our challenges and endure our tasks here in the hardpan field of mortality. —*Howard W. Hunter* (WMJ, 13-14)

We should at every opportunity ask ourselves, "What would Jesus do?" and then act more courageously upon the answer. —*Howard W. Hunter* (Ensign , Nov. 1994, 87)

To the extent that our mortal powers permit, we should make every effort to become like Christ—the one perfect and sinless example this world has ever seen. . . .

We must know Christ better than we know him; we must remember him more often than we remember him; we must serve him more valiantly than we serve him. Then we will drink water springing up unto eternal life and will eat the bread of life.

What manner of men and women ought we to be? Even as he is. —*Howard W. Hunter* (Ensign, May 1994, 64)

Total cleanliness in thought and action is required if one is to be Christlike. —*Spencer W. Kimball* (SWK, 13)

The cultivation of Christlike qualities is a demanding and relentless task—it is not for the seasonal worker or for those who will not stretch themselves, again, and again. —*Spencer W. Kimball* (Ensign, Nov. 1978, 102)

To compare your opinion with the Lord's proven truths might be like a grain of sand compared to the bulk and height of Mount Everest. —*Spencer W. Kimball* (SWK, 392)

Remember:
If there be eyes to see, there will be visions to inspire.
If there be ears to hear, there will be revelations to experience.
If there be hearts which can understand, know this: that the exalting truths of Christ's gospel will no longer be hidden and mysterious, and all earnest seekers may know God and his program. —*Spencer W. Kimball* (SWK, 454)

Perhaps even more important than trying to speculate as to what Jesus would do in a given situation is to endeavor to determine what Jesus would have us do. Of course, in order to give intelligent answers to such questions, one must have intimate acquaintance with the life of the Master and the account of His ministry. —*Harold B. Lee* (SHP, 26-27)

Beautiful roses don't grow in a garden unless the rosebush has been planted in fertile soil, cultivated, watered, and fertilized by someone who loves roses. Just so, beautiful flowers of honesty, integrity, virtue, and loyalty do not blossom in an individual unless his feet have been planted in a firm, sure testimony of the Lord Jesus Christ. —*Harold B. Lee* (SHP, 111)

How are we going to prove the spirits and understand which are right and which are wrong unless we ourselves are walking in the light?—*Joseph Fielding Smith* (CR, Oct. 1931, 15)

It should not be necessary that we be continually taught and admonished in these simple truths in the gospel of Jesus Christ. We ought so to prepare ourselves through study and through faith, through observance of the law of the gospel, through attendance at meetings and the magnifying of our callings generally, to know what the Lord expects at our hands without the necessity of someone telling us. —*Joseph Fielding Smith* (CR, Apr. 1914, 91-92)

It is not easy, I know, but the true Christian is he who exemplifies in his "acts," his "walks" and his "talks" that which his tongue says he believes. —*David O. McKay* (GI, 541)

There is one responsibility that no man can evade. That is the responsibility of personal influence. The effect of your words and acts is tremendous in this world. Every moment of life you are changing to a degree the life of the whole world. Every man has an atmosphere or a radiation that is affecting every person in the world. You cannot escape it. Into the hands of every individual is given a marvelous power for good or for evil. It is simply the constant radiation of what a man really is. Every man by his mere living is radiating positive or negative qualities. Life is a state of radiation. To exist is to be the radiation of our feelings, natures, doubts, schemes, or to be the recipient of those things from somebody else. You cannot escape it. Man cannot escape for one moment the radiation of his character. You will select the qualities that you will permit to be radiated. —*David O. McKay* (CR, Oct. 1969, 87)

The all-important thing for you and me is to discover whether we are walking in the straight and narrow path that leads to life eternal, and if we are not, wherein have we allowed the adversary to blind our minds and to cause us to depart from that path which will lead us back into the presence of God? Each one should search his own heart to find out wherein he has failed, and then he should diligently seek our Heavenly Father for the assistance of His Holy Spirit, that he may come back into the straight path. —*Heber J. Grant* (IE, 15:786)

From my boyhood I have desired to learn the principles of the gospel in such a way and to such an extent that it would matter not to me who might fall from the truth, who might make a mistake, who might fail to continue to follow the example of the Master, my foundation would be sure and certain in the truths that I have learned, though all men else go astray and fail of obedience to them. —*Joseph F. Smith* (GD, 3)

One fault to be avoided by the Saints, young and old, is the tendency to live on borrowed light, with their own hidden under a bushel; to permit the savor of their salt of knowledge to be lost; and the light within them to be reflected, rather than original. . . . Men and women should become settled in the truth, and founded in the knowledge of the gospel, depending upon no person for borrowed or reflected light, but trusting only upon the Holy Spirit. —*Joseph F. Smith* (IE, 8:61)

We do not look for absolute perfection in man. Mortal man is not capable of being absolutely perfect. Nevertheless, it is given to us to be as perfect in the sphere in which we are called to be and to act, as it is for the Father in heaven to be pure and righteous in the more exalted sphere in which he acts. —*Joseph F. Smith* (GD, 132)

To walk safely and steadfastly without leaning upon the arm of flesh is the individual duty of every Latter-day Saint. Such a duty becomes a responsibility which men owe to themselves and to their God. —*Joseph F. Smith* (GD, 253)

All the trouble is our eyes have been closed, we have been in a deep sleep; let us wake up and attend to our duty, and make it the first business we do.

Go to, and if you have not the Spirit of God, make it your first business to get it, that your minds may be opened to see the things of God as they are; it is your privilege and mine, that we may be prepared for what is to come. —*Wilford Woodruff* (WW, 181)

It will do me no good if I apostatize because somebody's family follows the fashions of Babylon, or because some man or woman or some set of men and women do wrong. Let us cease this kind of work, and all of us look to ourselves. It will do me no good if I apostatize because I think someone else does not do right. We should lay this aside. There is too much of it in the Zion of God today, and has been a good while, finding fault with this, that, and the other, instead of looking at home. —*Wilford Woodruff* (WW, 264)

There are more people attending to the eleventh commandment in the city of Nauvoo than in any other place of the same size on the globe—that is they mind their own business in Nauvoo, without interfering with others. —*John Taylor* (GK, 337)

There are those in this Church who calculate to be saved by the righteousness of others. They will miss their mark. . . . I forewarn you therefore to cultivate righteousness and faithfulness in yourselves, which is the only passport into celestial happiness. —*Brigham Young* (BY, 390)

Salvation is an individual operation. I am the only person that can possibly save myself. When salvation is sent to me, I can reject or receive it. In receiving it, I yield implicit obedience and submission to its great Author throughout my life, and to those whom he shall appoint to instruct me; in rejecting it, I follow the dictates of my own will in preference to the will of my Creator. —*Brigham Young* (BY, 390)

Take care of yourselves, and live as long as you can, and do all the good you can. —*Brigham Young* (BY, 186)

I repeat that it is as much as any one can well do to take care of himself by performing every duty that pertains to his temporal and eternal welfare. —*Brigham Young* (BY, 83)

Let the Saints remember that great things depend on their individual exertion, and that they are called to be co-workers with us and the Holy Spirit in accomplishing the great work of the last days; and in consideration of the extent, the blessings and glories of the same, let every selfish feeling be not only buried, but annihilated; and let love to God and man predominate, and reign triumphant in every mind. —*Joseph Smith, Jr.* (STJS, 203)

48. PRAYER

A generation or two ago family prayer in the homes of Christian people throughout the world was as much a part of the day's activity as was eating. As that practice has diminished, our moral decay has ensued. —*Gordon B. Hinckley* (BTE, 31)

I feel satisfied that there is no adequate substitute for the morning and evening practice of kneeling together—father, mother, and children. This, more than heavy carpets more than lovely draperies, more than cleverly balanced color schemes, is the thing that will make for better and more beautiful homes. —*Gordon B. Hinckley* (BTE, 31)

As we go forward in our lives, let us never forget to pray. God lives. He is near. He is real. He is our Father. He is accessible to us. He is the author of eternal truth, the Master of the universe. The handle is ready, and the door can be opened to His abundance. —*Gordon B. Hinckley* (Ensign, Jan. 1994, 2)

If prayer is only a spasmodic cry at the time of crisis, then it is utterly selfish, and we come to think of God as a repairman or a service agency to help us only in our emergencies. We should remember the Most High day and night—always—not only at times when all other assistance has failed and we desperately need help. If there is any element in human life on which we have a record of miraculous success and inestimable worth to the human soul, it is prayerful, reverential, devout communication with our Heavenly Father. —*Howard W. Hunter* (Ensign, Nov. 1977, 52)

Jesus was careful to place the petition "Hallowed be thy name" at the very forefront of his prayer. Unless that reverent, prayerful, honorable attitude toward God is uppermost in our hearts, we are not fully prepared to pray. If our first thought is of ourselves and not of God, we are not praying as Jesus taught. It was his supreme hope that our Father's name and station would be kept beautiful and holy. —*Howard W. Hunter* (Ensign, Nov. 1977, 52)

Prayer, reverence, worship, devotion, respect for the holy—these are basic exercises of our spirit and must be actively practiced in our lives or they will be lost. —*Howard W. Hunter* (Ensign, Nov. 1977, 54)

We believe, and testify to the world, that communication with our Father in Heaven and direction from the Lord are available today. —*Howard W. Hunter* (Ensign, Nov. 1981, 13)

The value of a man is evidenced in part by the dust on his knees. —*Ezra Taft Benson* (ETB, 422)

A great panacea for all problems and personal doubts is prayer—private and family prayer, night and morning. —*Ezra Taft Benson* (ETB, 494)

Our public prayers need not be everlasting to be immortal. . . . An invocation should set the spiritual tone of the meeting, and the benediction should leave the people on a high spiritual plane, because they have been present when one has talked with God. It is the feeling rather than the length which determines a good public prayer. —*Ezra Taft Benson* (ETB, 427)

After making a request through prayer, we have a responsibility to assist in its being granted. We should listen. Maybe while we are on our knees, the Lord wants to counsel us. In addition to asking and thanking the Lord for things, we might well stay on our knees long enough to report for duty and ask Him if He has any marching orders for us. —*Ezra Taft Benson* (ETB, 427)

Answers to prayer come most often by a still voice and are discerned by our deepest, innermost feelings. I tell you that you can know the will of God concerning yourselves if you will take the time to pray and to listen. —*Ezra Taft Benson* (NE, June 1986, 8)

I don't believe it is possible for a man to be happy who doesn't pray every day—and not just once. I think you need the strength that comes from prayer. —*Ezra Taft Benson* (ETB, 428)

Prayer is the passport to spiritual power. —*Spencer W. Kimball* (SWK, 115)

Prayer is an armor of protection against temptation and I promise you that if you will teach your children to pray, fervently and full of faith, many of your problems are solved before they begin. —*Spencer W. Kimball* (SWK, 117)

I sometimes wonder if perhaps the dial of the heavenly radio is not turned off when long and wordy prayers are sent heavenward. I feel sure that there is too much to do in heaven for the Lord and his servants to sit indefinitely listening to verbose praises and requests, for as we are told in Matthew, he knows, before we ask, our needs and desires. (See Matthew 6:8)—*Spencer W. Kimball* (SWK, 120)

None of us should get so busy that we crowd out contemplation and praying. —*Spencer W. Kimball* (SWK, 136)

Learning the language of prayer is a joyous, lifetime experience. Sometimes ideas flood our mind as we listen after our prayers. Sometimes feelings press upon us. A spirit of calmness assures us that all will be well. But always, if we have been honest and earnest, we will experience a good feeling—a feeling of warmth for our Father in Heaven and a sense of his love for us. —*Spencer W. Kimball* (Ensign, Oct. 1981, 4)

We must never forget that we are to live the gospel as honestly and earnestly as we pray. —*Spencer W. Kimball* (Ensign, Oct. 1981, 4)

The thing that all of us should strive for is to so live, keeping the commandments of the Lord, that He can answer our prayers, the prayers of our loved ones, the prayers of the General Authorities, for us. —*Harold B. Lee* (SHP, 144)

If you want the blessing, don't just kneel down and pray about it. Prepare yourselves in every conceivable way you can in order to make yourselves worthy to receive the blessing you seek. —*Harold B. Lee* (SHP, 244)

We have the right to call upon the Lord in prayer and in faith for help, for guidance, for the assistance of his Holy Spirit, and we will receive it. —*Joseph Fielding Smith* (DS1, 245)

As surely as you can tune in on the radio and hear voices from afar, so sure am I that God our Father lives, and the soul of man can commune with him through the Holy Spirit. I give you that as my testimony; I know it. —*David O. McKay* (CR, Sept.-Oct. 1950, 112)

Sincere praying implies that when we ask for any virtue or blessing, we should work for the blessing and cultivate the virtue. —*David O. McKay* (TF, 208)

God is not merely a force though he is that. He is not merely something away out of our touch, but he is as near as your father is to you and my father to me. I like to think when I have a task to perform that in secret I can say, "Father, guide me today," and feel that I shall have added strength to do that task. I may not succeed always. My own inhibitions and weaknesses may prevent my doing so, but there is strength in the assurance that I can go to him and ask him for help and guidance. That is what you can do. —*David O. McKay* (CR, Apr. 1967, 134)

Children who are reared in homes where they do not have family prayers and secret prayers lose a great deal, and I fear that, in the midst of the world's confusion, of hurry and bustle, many times homes are left without prayer and without the blessings of the Lord; these homes cannot continue to be happy. —*George Albert Smith* (SGO, 207)

If we have sought the Lord we shall be strengthened, our faith will be increased, our power to direct will be increased and we will not feel the weakness that possesses men when they are left alone. Rather, we will feel the strength and power of our Heavenly Father, for He helps us. —*George Albert Smith* (CR, Apr. 1942, 14)

I have always felt that if we are doing the Lord's work and ask him for his help and protection, he will guide and take care of us. —*George Albert Smith* (GAS, 195)

We should know that our prayers will not avail us much unless we repent of our sins. —*George Albert Smith* (CR, Oct. 1944, 95)

Now, the one thing above all others, that I want impressed on the heart and soul of the young people, is to pray to the Lord. . . . I have little or no fear for the boy or the girl, the young man or the young woman, who honestly and conscientiously supplicate God twice a day for the guidance of His Spirit. I am sure that when temptation comes they will have the strength to overcome it by the inspiration that shall be given to them. Supplicating the Lord for the guidance of His Spirit places around us a safeguard, and if we earnestly and honestly seek the guidance of the Spirit of the Lord, I can assure you that we will receive it. —*Heber J. Grant* (GS, 26)

Next to the committing of sin there is no more fruitful cause of apostasy among the Latter-day Saints than when we put our trust in the arm of flesh. I firmly believe that no man who honestly bows down every day of his life and supplicates God in sincerity for the light of His Holy Spirit to guide him will ever become proud and haughty. On the contrary, his heart will become filled with meekness, humility, and childlike simplicity. —*Heber J. Grant* (GS, 31)

When men stop praying for God's Spirit, they place confidence in their own unaided reason and they gradually lose the Spirit of God, just as near and dear friends, by never writing to or visiting with each other, will become perfect strangers, so to speak. The minute a man stops supplicating God for His Spirit and direction, just so soon he begins to become a stranger to Him and His works. —*Heber J. Grant* (GS, 254)

I have had my prayers answered time and time again, and not only have I had my prayers answered but I know as I know that I live that God hears and answers the prayers of honest people. —*Heber J. Grant* (CR, Oct. 1941, 12)

The Lord will hear and answer the prayers we offer to Him and give us success if it is for our best good. He never will and never has forsaken those who serve Him with full purpose of heart; and the temptations that come from below, although strong, never are successful if we are faithful. But we must always be prepared to say "Father, thy will be done," and leave the time and the manner and the nature of our blessings to God in His wisdom. —*Heber J. Grant* (LPS, 380)

The prayerful and humble man will always realize and feel that he is dependent upon God for every blessing that he enjoys, and in praying to God he will not only pray for the light and the inspiration of His Holy Spirit to guide him, but he will feel to thank God for the blessings he receives, realizing that life, that health, that strength, and that all the intelligence which he possesses comes from God, who is the Author of his existence. —*Heber J. Grant* (LPS, 374)

It is our privilege to ask God to bless the elements that surround us and to temper them for our good, and we know he will hear and answer the prayers of his people, according to their faith. —*Joseph F. Smith* (CR, Apr. 1898, 10)

My brethren and sisters, do not learn to pray with your lips only. Do not learn a prayer by heart, and say it every morning and evening. That is something I dislike very much. It is true that a great many people fall into the rut of saying over a ceremonious prayer. They begin at a certain point, and they touch at all the points along the road until they get to the winding up scene; and when they have done, I do not know whether the prayer has ascended beyond the ceiling of the room or not. —*Joseph F. Smith* (CR, Oct. 1899, 71-72)

If I have any forte it is prayer to God. —*Wilford Woodruff* (WW, 221)

There is one admonition of our Savior that all the Saints of God should observe, but which, I fear, we do not as we should, and that is, to pray always and faint not. I fear, as a people, we do not pray enough in faith. We should call upon the Lord in mighty prayer, and make all our wants known unto him. For if he does not protect and deliver us and save us, no other power will. Therefore our trust is entirely in him. Therefore our prayers should ascend into the ears of our Heavenly Father day and night. —*Wilford Woodruff* (WW, 221)

I have more faith in prayer before the Lord than almost any other principle on earth. If we have no faith in prayer to God, we have not much in either Him or the gospel. —*Wilford Woodruff* (JD, 17:249)

If you have a farm, dedicate it to God, and pray that his blessing may be upon it. If you build a house, dedicate it to God; also your garden, your cattle and sheep, and all that you possess, and pray that his blessing may rest upon you and upon everything that pertains to you. —*John Taylor* (GK, 248)

If men would be as valiant in trying to pray to God to give them wisdom and power to control themselves and their thoughts and passions . . . They would then feel ten thousand times more interest in the kingdom and to work for the spread of true and holy principles. —*John Taylor* (GK, 331)

Although the Christian religion, under whatever form it may be practised, teaches mankind to pray unto God in the name of the Lord Jesus Christ, yet it is very few who suppose that their prayers amount to anything, that God will listen to their supplications, or that they will prove of any special benefit. A feeling of this kind tends more or less to unbelief instead of faith in God, and hence we find very few men in our day who act as men of God did in former days, that is, seek unto him for guidance and direction in the affairs of life. —*John Taylor* (JD, 14:357)

Practice your religion today, and say your prayers faithfully. —*Brigham Young* (BY, 42)

You know that it is one peculiarity of our faith and religion never to ask the Lord to do a thing without being willing to help him all that we are able; and then the Lord will do the rest. —*Brigham Young* (BY, 43)

I shall not ask the Lord to do what I am not willing to do. —*Brigham Young* (BY, 43)

It matters not whether you or I feel like praying, when the time comes to pray, pray. If we do not feel like it, we should pray till we do. . . . You will find that those who wait till the Spirit bids them pray, will never pray much on this earth. —*Brigham Young* (BY, 44)

If the Devil says you cannot pray when you are angry, tell him it is none of his business, and pray until that species of insanity is dispelled and serenity is restored to the mind. —*Brigham Young* (BY, 45)

It is a great thing to inquire at the hands of God, or to come into His presence; and we feel fearful to approach Him on subjects that are of little or no consequence, to satisfy the queries of individuals, especially about things the knowledge of which men ought to obtain in all sincerity, before God, for themselves, in humility by the prayer of faith. —*Joseph Smith, Jr.* (STJS, 31)

49. REVERENCE

In the process of moral decline, reverence is one of the first virtues to disappear, and there should be serious concern about that loss in our times. —*Howard W. Hunter* (Ensign, Nov. 1977, 52)

Occasionally we visit too loudly, enter and leave meetings too disrespectfully in what should be an hour of prayer and purifying worship. Reverence is the atmosphere of heaven. Prayer is the utterance of the soul to God the Father. We do well to become more like our Father by looking up to him, by remembering him always, and by caring greatly about his world and his work. —*Howard W. Hunter* (Ensign, Nov. 1977, 52)

True reverence is a vital quality, but one that is fast disappearing in the world as the forces of evil broaden their influences. We cannot fully comprehend the power for good we can wield if the millions of members of Christ's true church will serve as models of reverent behavior. We cannot imagine the additional numbers of lives we could touch. Perhaps even more important, we cannot foresee the great spiritual impact on our own families if we become the reverent people we know we should be. —*Spencer W. Kimball* (SWK, 224-225)

Reverence indicates high culture and true faith in Deity and in his righteousness. —*David O. McKay* (CR, Oct. 1951, 180)

A great man is reverent. —*David O. McKay* (GI, 226)

Reverence embraces regard, deference, honor, and esteem. Without some degree of it there would be no courtesy, no gentility, no consideration of other's feelings or of other's rights. It is the fundamental virtue in religion. Reverence is one of the signs of strength, irreverence one of the surest indications of weakness. No man will rise high who jeers at sacred things. The fine loyalties of life must be reverenced, or they will be foresworn in the day of trial. —*David O. McKay* (CR, Oct. 1955, 91)

If there were more reverence in human hearts there would be less room for sin and sorrow, and there would be increased capacity for joy and gladness. —*David O. McKay* (CR, Apr. 1967, 87)

It is the height of rudeness, except in an emergency, to leave a worshiping assembly before dismissal. —*David O. McKay* (CR, Apr. 1967, 87)

In all the work that we do let us not lose sight of the spiritual part of it. —*Heber J. Grant* (GS, 79)

No self-respecting person will go to a house devoted to the service of God to whisper, gossip and visit; rather, it is one's duty to put on self-restraint, to give one's undivided attention to the speaker, and concentrate the mind upon his words that his thoughts may be grasped to one's benefit and profit. —*Joseph F. Smith* (GD, 334)

Self-respect, deference for sacred things, and personal purity are the beginnings and the essence of wisdom. . . . Such a seeming simple thing, then, as proper conduct in a house of worship leads to good results in many respects. Good conduct leads to self-respect, which creates purity of thought and action. Pure thought and noble action lead to a desire to serve God in the strength of manhood. —*Joseph F. Smith* (IE, 9:338-339)

Now, in this fast age we are passing from a polite age to a vary rude one in many respects. When I was a boy sixty-five years ago, and went to school, I never thought of passing a man whom I knew in the street, or a woman, without taking off my hat and making a bow. I never thought of saying "yes" or "no" to those that were placed over me. I was taught to say "yes, sir," and "no, sir"; but today it is "yes" and "no," "I will," "I won't," "I shall" and "I shan't." Now, when I see this rudeness amongst us, I sometimes wish that the spirit of the New England fathers was more among the people. But I do hope, brethren, sisters and friends, when a man stops talking and the choir rises to sing, that you will keep your seats. You can afford to do this as well as the President of the Church, the Twelve Apostles, or others who are sitting on this stand. You don't see us jump and run for the door the moment a speaker is done. The Lord is displeased with any such thing. —*Wilford Woodruff* (WW, 183)

I will say, on the other hand, that the Presidency, the Twelve, and the elders who preach in this house expect that the people will have the Spirit of the Lord, that they may come to understanding; and this is just as much required that they may comprehend what is said unto them as it is required of the brethren who speak, to teach doctrine, principle, truth, and the revelations of Jesus Christ. —*Wilford Woodruff* (WW, 182)

And I will here say, as I have often said, that all men, and all women, regardless of the position they occupy, or the office they hold, are dependent upon the Lord for his Spirit to assist them in their labors. —*Wilford Woodruff* (WW, 183)

50. SERVICE

To all I say, Serve with faith. —*Gordon B. Hinckley* (CR, Apr. 1967, 53)

I might continue telling you of those who begin with noble objectives but then slow down, or of those who are strong starters and weak finishers. So many in the game of life get to first base, or second, or even third, but then fail to score. They are inclined to live unto themselves, denying their generous instincts, grasping for possessions, and, in their self-centered, uninspired living, sharing neither talent nor faith with others. —*Gordon B. Hinckley* (BTE, 61-62)

The most effective medicine for the sickness of self-pity is to lose ourselves in the service of others. —*Gordon B. Hinckley* (FETR , 39-40)

Passive acceptance is not enough. Vibrant testimony comes of anxious seeking. Strength comes of active service in the Master's cause. —*Gordon B. Hinckley* (FETR , 85)

Christmas means giving—and "the gift without the giver is bare." Giving of self; giving of substance; giving of heart and mind and strength in assisting those in need and in spreading the cause of His eternal truth—these are of the very essence of the true spirit of Christmas. —*Gordon B. Hinckley* (Ensign, Dec. 1983, 2)

Our imperative need is to be found doing our duty individually in the callings which have come to us. —*Gordon B. Hinckley* (Ensign, May 1983, 6)

No man can live fully and happily who lives only unto himself. —*Gordon B. Hinckley* (Ensign, Aug. 1992, 2-7)

Most of us will be quiet, relatively unknown folks who come and go and do our work without fanfare. To those of you who may find that lonely or frightening or just unspectacular, I say, you are "no less serviceable" than the most spectacular or your associates. You, too, are part of God's army. —*Howard W. Hunter* (Ensign, Apr. 1992, 64)

If you feel that much of what you do does not make you very famous, take heart. Most of the best people who ever lived weren't very famous, either. Serve and grow, faithfully and quietly. —*Howard W. Hunter* (Ensign, Apr. 1992, 67)

We must not allow ourselves to focus on the fleeting light of popularity or substitute that attractive glow for the substance of true but often anonymous labor that brings the attention of God, even if it does not get coverage on the six o' clock news. In fact, applause and attention can become the spiritual Achilles' hill of even the most gifted among us. —*Howard W. Hunter* (Ensign, Apr. 1992, 66)

It is important to be appreciated. But our focus should be on righteousness, not recognition; on service, not status. The faithful visiting teacher, who quietly goes about her work month after month is just as important to the work of the Lord as those who occupy what some see as more prominent positions in the Church. Visibility does not equate to value. —*Howard W. Hunter* (Ensign, Nov. 1992, 96-97)

It is the thousands of little deeds and tasks of service and sacrifice that constitute the giving, or losing, of one's life for others and for the Lord. —*Howard W. Hunter* (WMJ, 105)

True religion consists not only in refraining from evil (that is, remaining unspotted), but in deliberately and purposefully doing acts of kindness and service to others. —*Howard W. Hunter* (WMJ, 160-161)

I believe a man should prepare for the worst while working for the best. Some people prepare and don't work, while others work but don't prepare. Both are needed if we would be of maximum service to our God, our family, and our country. —*Ezra Taft Benson* (ETB, 264)

Try as you may, you cannot put the Lord in your debt. For every time you try to do His will, He simply pours out more blessing upon you. Sometimes the blessings may seem to you to be a little slow in coming—perhaps this tests your faith—but come they will and abundantly. —*Ezra Taft Benson* (ETB, 359)

If you would find yourself, learn to deny yourself for the blessing of others. Forget yourself and find someone who needs your service, and you will discover the secret to the happy, fulfilled life. —*Ezra Taft Benson* (CR, May 1979, 34)

Only when you lift a burden, God will lift your burden. Divine paradox this! The man who staggers and falls because his burden is too great can lighten that burden by taking on the weight of another's burden. You get by giving, but your part of giving must be given first. —*Spencer W. Kimball* (SWK, 251)

God does notice us, and he watches over us. But it is usually through another mortal that he meets our needs. Therefore, it is vital that we serve each other in the kingdom. —*Spencer W. Kimball* (Ensign, Dec. 1974, 2)

So often, our acts of service consist of simple encouragement or of giving mundane help with mundane tasks—but what glorious consequences can flow from mundane acts and from small but deliberate deeds!—*Spencer W. Kimball* (Ensign, Dec. 1974, 2)

None of us should become so busy in our formal Church assignments that there is no room left for quiet Christian service to our neighbors. —*Spencer W. Kimball* (SWK, 256)

We become more substantive as we serve others—indeed, it is easier to "find" ourselves because there is so much more of us to find!?—*Spencer W. Kimball* (Ensign, Oct. 1985, 3)

Let us ponder prayerfully how we may effectively and lovingly give service to our families, neighbors, and fellow Saints. And let us know that when we learn to do this we have learned one of the great truths of eternity. —*Spencer W. Kimball* (Ensign, Sept. 1983, 6.)

When you begin to make service to meet others needs your constant practice, you are beginning a program that will make you successful in your chosen field and your own needs will begin automatically to take care of themselves. —*Harold B. Lee* (DSL, 200)

Service and obedience are the keys that unlock the door to the celestial glory. Now you remember that and write it on the tablets of your heart, and remember that is the sure way to safety in this church. —*Harold B. Lee* (HBL, 179)

There is only one way to thank your Heavenly Father, and that is by faithfulness in what he has given you in the way of time, means, and talent in service to those less fortunate than you. —*Harold B. Lee* (HBL, 194-195)

If you would be happy, render a kind service, make somebody else happy. —*David O. McKay* (CR, Oct. 1936, 105)

Character and the service you have rendered will determine your position and place in the next world. —*David O. McKay* (GI, 501)

That which we do for God and our fellow men lives forever; that which we do just for ourselves cannot endure. —*David O. McKay* (GI, 507)

❂ Spirituality results in the greatest good when expressed in acts, not merely in day dreams. —*David O. McKay* (CR, Oct. 1954, 8)

If you are true followers of the Savior, you are striving to serve your fellowmen in love. —*David O. McKay* (CR, Apr. 1966, 107)

The Gospel of Jesus Christ is a gospel of giving, not only of our substance but of ourselves, and I thank my Heavenly Father that I belong to such an organization that has been so instructed. —*George Albert Smith* (CR, Oct. 1934, 52)

Make a motto in life: always try to assist someone else to carry his burden. The true key to happiness in life is to labor for the happiness of others. —*Heber J. Grant* (IE, 5:288)

Some people think they are not appreciated and are not allowed sufficient scope for usefulness. There is but one person who can curtail an individual's usefulness, and that is himself. —*Heber J. Grant* (GS, 183)

I have been impressed with the fact that there is a spirit growing in the world today to avoid giving service, an unwillingness to give value received, to try to see how little we can do and how much we can get for doing it. This is all wrong. Our spirit and aim should be to do all we possibly can, in a given length of time, for the benefit of those who employ us and for the benefit of those with whom we are associated. —*Heber J. Grant* (IE, 43:137)

One can never tell what will be the result of faithful service rendered, nor do we know when it will come back to us or to those with whom we are associated. The reward may not come at the time, but in dividends later. I believe we will never lose anything in life by giving service, by making sacrifices, and doing the right thing. —*Heber J. Grant* (IE, 43:137)

The wise man is, therefore, going to steer his course away from the living death of pleasure-seeking. He is not going into bondage or debt to buy automobiles and other costly equipages to keep pace with the rush of fashionable pleasure-seeking . . . [S]hall we not call a halt in this pleasure craze, and go about the legitimate business of true Latter-day Saints, which is to desire and strive to be of some use in the world? Shall we not instead do something to increase the genuine joy and welfare and virtue of mankind as well as our own by helping to bear the burdens under which the toilers are groaning, by rendering loving, devoted and unselfish service to our fellow men?—*Joseph F. Smith* (IE, 12:744)

We have just got to feel, brethren, that there are other people besides ourselves; we have got to look into the hearts and feelings of others, and become more godly than what we are now. —*Lorenzo Snow* (LS, 145)

We should be ready at all times to exercise all the power, means, and influence we possess in the service of our God. —*Lorenzo Snow* (LS, 28)

Serve faithfully and be cheerful. Brethren and sisters, the thing you should have in your mind, and which you should make a motto in your life, is this: Serve God faithfully, and be cheerful. —*Lorenzo Snow* (LS, 61)

There is always opportunity to do good to one another. When you find yourselves a little gloomy, look around you and find somebody that is in a worse plight than yourself; go to him and find out what the trouble is, then try to remove it with the wisdom which the Lord bestows upon you; and the first thing you know, your gloom is gone, you feel light, the Spirit of the Lord is upon you, and everything seems illuminated. —*Lorenzo Snow* (CR, Apr. 1899, 2-3)

Because one man is more talented than another, he should not use that talent to take advantage of his brother and then expect that God will approve of his actions, for he will not do it. He never did, nor ever will. We should operate for one another's interest, having sympathetic feelings for each other. —*John Taylor* (GK, 63-64)

It is lawful to do good always, and anyone who seeks to promote the welfare of the human family is a benefactor of mankind and ought to be sustained. —*John Taylor* (GK, 43)

The best of us are not too good; we all of us might be better, and do better, and enjoy life better, having more of the Spirit of the Lord in our own homes and in our own hearts, and do more to promote the welfare of all who come within our reach and influence. —*John Taylor* (GK, 228)

To be gentle and kind, modest and truthful, to be full of faith and integrity, doing no wrong is of God; goodness sheds a halo of loveliness around every person who possesses it, making their countenances beam with light, and their society desirable because of its excellency. —*Brigham Young* (BY, 280)

Every moment of human life should be devoted to doing good somewhere and in some way. —*Brigham Young* (BY, 280)

A man who wishes to receive light and knowledge, to increase in the faith of the Holy Gospel, and to grow in the knowledge of the truth as it is in Jesus Christ, will find that when he imparts knowledge to others he will also grow and increase. . . . Wherever you see an opportunity to do good, do it, for that is the way to increase and grow in the knowledge of the truth. —*Brigham Young* (BY, 335)

Let us realize that we are not to live to ourselves, but to God; by so doing the greatest blessings will rest upon us both in time and in eternity. —*Joseph Smith, Jr.* (STJS, 203)

God Almighty is my shield; and what can man do if God is my friend? . . . I have no desire but to do all men good. I feel to pray for all men. We don't ask any people to throw away any good they have got; we only ask them to come and get more. —*Joseph Smith, Jr.* (STJS, 310)

51. SUCCESS

The truest mark of your success in life will be the quality of your marriage. —*Gordon B. Hinckley* (Ensign, May 1998], 51)

Because we are being constantly exposed to the world's definition of greatness, it is understandable that we might make comparisons between what we are and what others are—or seem to be—and also between what we have and what others have. Although it is true that making comparisons can be beneficial and may motivate us to accomplish much good and to improve our lives, we often allow unfair and improper comparisons to destroy our happiness when they cause us to feel unfulfilled or inadequate or unsuccessful. Sometimes, because of these feelings, we are led into error and dwell on our failures while ignoring aspects of our lives that may contain elements of true greatness. —*Howard W. Hunter* (WMJ, 103-104)

To do one's best in the face of the commonplace struggles of life, and possibly in the face of failure, and to continue to endure and to persevere in the ongoing difficulties of life when those struggles and tasks contribute to others' progress and happiness and one's own eternal salvation—this is true greatness. —*Howard W. Hunter* (WMJ, 107)

True greatness is never a result of a chance occurrence or a one-time effort or achievement. Greatness requires the development of character. It requires a multitude of correct decisions in the everyday choices between good and evil. —*Howard W. Hunter* (WMJ, 108)

As we evaluate our lives, it is important that we look not only at our accomplishments but also at the conditions under which we have labored. We are each unique; we have each had different starting points in the race of life; we each have a unique mixture of talents and skills; we each have our own set of challenges and constraints with which to contend. Therefore, our judgment of ourselves and our achievements should not merely include the size, the magnitude, and the number of our accomplishments; it should also include the conditions that have existed and the effects that our efforts have had on others. —*Howard W. Hunter* (WMJ, 108-109)

Remember that our attitudes are most important tools to success. Knowledge is power only when it is used constructively. —*Howard W. Hunter* (WMJ, 135)

Be assured that one kind of ability we must have is "stick-ability." No matter how good the beginning, success comes only to those who "endure to the end."—*Howard W. Hunter* (WMJ, 135)

The greatest yardstick of success is to see how closely we can walk each moment in His [Jesus Christ's] steps. —*Ezra Taft Benson* (Ensign, Sept. 1988, 6)

Success is many things to many people, but to every child of God it ultimately will be to inherit his presence and there be comfortable with him. —*Harold B. Lee* (DSL, 2)

Successful living is born of gospel living. Keep the commandments taught herein, search the scriptures, pray always and be obedient, and eternal success will be yours. —*Harold B. Lee* (DSL, 2)

God's measure of our worth in His kingdom will not be the high positions we have held here among man, nor in His church, nor the honors we have won, but rather the lives we have led and the good we have done. —*Harold B. Lee* (SHP, 348)

I think the finest recipe that I could give, to obtain happiness, would be: Keep the commandments of the Lord. That is easy to remember, and if we will do that we may be sure of success. —*George Albert Smith* (CR, Oct. 1934, 47-48)

Every Latter-day Saint who is loyal to the principles of the gospel is not seeking wealth; he is not asking himself the question, "What have I?" and "What can I gain?" The true Latter-day Saint is asking, "What can I do to better myself, to encourage those with whom I am associated, and to uplift the children of God?" That is the inspiration that comes to every Latter-day Saint who realizes the force of this gospel that we have espoused. —*Heber J. Grant* (CR, Oct. 1909, 30)

The great trouble is that there are many people who, as they grow and increase in the things of this world, set their hearts upon them and lose the Spirit of the Lord. Therefore, that which is counted by the world as success is failure. —*Heber J. Grant* (CR, Oct. 1911, 23-24)

I assert with confidence that the law of success, here and hereafter, is to have a humble and a prayerful heart, and to work, work, WORK.

The Lord is no respecter of persons, and will give success to all who work for it. If I can only impress upon the minds of the youth of Zion the eloquence, the inexpressible eloquence of work, I shall feel fully repaid. —*Heber J. Grant* (IE, 3:195)

We are the architects and builders of our lives, and if we fail to put our knowledge into actual practice and do the duties that devolve upon us we are making a failure of life. —*Heber J. Grant* (GS, 182)

The trouble with a great many people is, they are not willing to pay the price; they are not willing to make the fight for success in the battle of life. —*Heber J. Grant* (CR, Oct. 1910, 5)

He who so lives that those who know him best shall love him most; and that God, who knows not only his deeds, but also the inmost sentiments of his heart, shall love him; of such and one, only—notwithstanding he may die in poverty—can it be said indeed and of a truth, "he should be crowned with the wealth of success"—*Heber J. Grant* (CR, Oct. 1911, 24)

If you fail, never mind. Go right on; try it again; try it somewhere else. Never say quit. Do not say it cannot be done. Failure is a word that should be unknown . . . in all the organizations of the Church everywhere. The word "fail" ought to be expunged from our language and our thoughts. . . .

If we continue to try, failing, as it were, or missing one mark, should not discourage us; but we should fly to another, keep on in the work, keep on doing, patiently, determinedly doing our duty, seeking to accomplish the purpose we have in view. —*Joseph F. Smith* (GD, 133)

The standard of success as declared by the word of God, is the salvation of the soul. The greatest gift of God is eternal life. —*Joseph F. Smith* (GD, 125)

If we are poor, and have not as much as our neighbor possesses, do not envy him, and do not worry about it. As I said in the beginning of my remarks, there is an eternity before us, and we shall always be ourselves, and nobody else, and what we do not gain today we will gain tomorrow, or some other time. —*Lorenzo Snow* (LS, 131)

Now an individual, in order to secure the highest and greatest blessings to himself, in order to secure the approbation of the Almighty, and in order to continually improve in the things pertaining to righteousness, he must do all things to the best advantage. Let him go to work and be willing to sacrifice for the benefit of his friends. If he wants to build himself up, the best principle he can do it upon is to build up his friends. —*Lorenzo Snow* (LS, 148)

Take the man who has a large share of this world's goods, and examine what kind of a man he is; try his spirit, and you will generally find that it is often one of the greatest trials that can come upon him, to be called upon to part with any of his property. —*Lorenzo Snow* (LS, 163)

It is better for a people to be wise, to get righteousness, to be the friends of God, than to occupy any other positions in life. . —*Wilford Woodruff* (WW, 6)

All the knowledge that we can accumulate from experience and observation, and from the revelations of God to man, goes to show that the riches of this world are fleeting and transitory, while he that has eternal life abiding in him is rich indeed. —*Wilford Woodruff* (WW, 279)

The Lord has blessed us. He has blessed the earth for our use; and we ought to dedicate our families, our fields, our crops, our herds, to God. —*Wilford Woodruff* (WW, 174)

I will tell you a secret. If we could only prepare ourselves to do the will of God and keep his commandments and live our religion so that God could trust us with more means than we have, he would so order things, and that too by natural ways, that our desires in that direction would be fully gratified. But we are not prepared for it. It would only destroy us and lead us to the devil and the Lord knows it. —*John Taylor* (GK, 248)

Wisdom is better than wealth. To be great, be good; to be rich, be contented; and to be respected, respect yourself. —*John Taylor* (GK, 342)

[I]t is necessary that we should all the time be under the guidance and direction of the Almighty, for without him we can do nothing. —*John Taylor* (GK, 200)

To be great is to be good before the Heavens and before all good men. —*Brigham Young* (BY, 231)

It is the duty of a Saint of God to gain all the influence he can on this earth, and to use every particle of that influence to do good. If this is not his duty, I do not understand what the duty of man is. —*Brigham Young* (BY, 285)

Few men know what to do with riches when they possess them. —*Brigham Young* (BY, 312)

If, by industrious habits and honorable dealings, you obtain thousands or millions, little or much, it is your duty to use all that is put in your possession, as judiciously as you have knowledge, to build up the Kingdom of God on the earth. —*Brigham Young* (BY, 313-314)

The more we are blessed with means, the more we are blessed with responsibility; the more we are blessed with wisdom and ability, the more we are placed under the necessity of using that wisdom and ability in the spread of righteousness, the subjugation of sin and misery, and the amelioration of the condition of mankind. The man that has only one talent and the man that has five talents have responsibility accordingly. If we have a world of means, we have a world of responsibility. —*Brigham Young* (BY, 315)

The question will not arise with the Lord, nor with the messengers of the Almighty, how much wealth a man has got, but how has he come by this wealth and what will he do with it?—*Brigham Young* (BY, 315)

And if there are any among you who aspire after their own aggrandizement, and seek their own opulence, while their brethren are groaning in poverty, and are under sore trials and temptations, they cannot be benefited by the intercession of the Holy Spirit, which maketh intercession for us day and night with groanings that cannot be uttered.

We ought at all times to be very careful that such highmindedness shall never have place in our hearts; but condescend to men of low estate, and with all long-suffering bear the infirmities of the weak. —*Joseph Smith, Jr.* (STJS, 148-168)

52. WORK

The best antidote I know for worry is work. The best medicine for despair is service. the best cure for weariness is the challenge of helping someone who is even more tired. —*Gordon B. Hinckley* (Ensign, June 1989, 73-74)

Industry, enthusiasm, and hard work lead to enlightened progress. You have to stay on your feet and keep moving if you are going to have light in your life. . . .

I have learned that when people of goodwill labor cooperatively in an honest and dedicated way, there is no end to what they can accomplish. —*Gordon B. Hinckley* (Ensign, May 1993, 53-54)

There is no substitute under the heavens for productive labor. It is the process by which dreams become realities. It is the process by which idle visions become dynamic achievements.

Most of us are inherently lazy. We would rather play than work. We would rather loaf than work. A little play and a little loafing are good. But it is work that spells the difference in the life of a man or woman. —*Gordon B. Hinckley* (Ensign, Aug. 1992, 2-7)

We will learn more, grow more, achieve more, serve more, and benefit more from a life of industry than from a life of ease. —*Howard W. Hunter* (Ensign, Nov. 1975, 122)

We work so that we may have the necessities of life, conserving time and energy left over for service in the Lord's work. Sometimes it seems that the men who work the hardest at their occupations are the men most willing to devote time to church service. —*Howard W. Hunter* (Ensign, Nov. 1975, 122)

Honorable employment is honest employment. Fair value is given and there is no defrauding, cheating, or deceit. Its product or service is of high quality, and the employer, customer, client, or patient receives more than he or she expected. Honorable employment is moral. It involves nothing that would undermine public good or morality. For example, it does not involve traffic in liquor, illicit narcotics, or gambling. Honorable employment is useful. It provides goods or services which make the world a better place in which to live. Honorable employment is also remunerative. It provides enough income so that we may be self-sufficient and able to support our families, while leaving us enough time free to be good fathers and church workers. —*Howard W. Hunter* (Ensign, Nov. 1975, 122-123)

Work is our blessing, not our doom. God has a work to do, and so should we. Retirement from work has depressed many a man and hastened his death. —*Ezra Taft Benson* (CR, Nov. 1974, 66)

Every young person requires the spur of economic insecurity to force him to do his best. We must have the courage to stand against undue governmental paternalism and the cowardly cry that "the world owes me a living." Nobody owes us anything for goods we do not produce, or work we do not do!—*Ezra Taft Benson* (ETB, 482)

Children must be taught to work at home. They should learn there that honest labor develops dignity and self-respect. They should learn the pleasure of work, of doing a job well. —*Ezra Taft Benson* (Ensign, July 1992, 2)

Waste is unjustified, and especially the waste of time—limited as that commodity is in our days of probation. One must live, not only exist; he must do, not merely be; he must grow, not just vegetate. —*Spencer W. Kimball* (MF, 92)

Those of us in the Lord's work must recognize that work is a spiritual necessity as well as an economic necessity. Our pioneer forebears understood this. —*Spencer W. Kimball* (Ensign, May 1981, 79-80.)

No true Latter-day saint, while physically or emotionally able, will voluntarily shift the burden of his own or his family's well being to someone else. So long as he can, under the inspiration of the Lord and with his own labors, he will supply himself and his family with the spiritual and temporal necessities of life. —*Spencer W. Kimball* (Ensign, Aug. 1984, 4)

Recreation, as a diversion, is as necessary to our temporal welfare as are the more serious activities of life. One who keeps continually at a single pursuit of business or study will become as a machine, and other traits or talents of his nature may not receive proper development. You remember the old saying, "All work and no play makes Jack a dull boy," but likewise don't forget either the wise counsel of one of our leaders today that "all play and no work is likely to make Jack a worthless boy."—*Harold B. Lee* (DSL, 2)

Work brings happiness, and that happiness is doubled to him who initiates the work. —*David O. McKay* (CR, Oct. 1909, 90)

In our physical being there is no development; there is no growth without activity; in the intellectual world there is no advancement without effort, work; and in the spiritual world, in the development of our spirits, there is no growth without effort. There is no salvation without work. —*David O. McKay* (CR, Oct. 1909, 90)

Too much leisure is dangerous. Work is a divine gift. —*David O. McKay* (GI, 497)

I wish to impress upon the Latter-day Saints that we get in this life what we work for, and I want to urge every Latter-day Saint to be a worker.

Men should have a pride in doing their full share and never want to be paid for that which they have not earned. Men should be rewarded for doing the best that they can. —*Heber J. Grant* (IE, 42:585)

We are attempting to get our people not to be satisfied to take charity, if it is possible for them to earn their own living, and even to be ready and willing to make some sacrifice, even though they might be offered a little more in charity than they could earn themselves; we do want them to earn what they receive. —*Heber J. Grant* (GS, 124)

I do not know of anything that destroys a person's health more quickly than not working. It seems to me that lazy people die young while those who are ready and willing to labor and who ask the Lord day by day to help them to do more in the future than they have ever done in the past, are the people whom the Lord loves, and who live to a good old age. —*Heber J. Grant* (IE, 39:131)

It is by exercise and by practice that we become proficient in any of the vocations or avocations of life, whether it be of a religious or of a secular character. —*Heber J. Grant* (GS, 184)

Nothing destroys the individuality of a man, a woman, or a child so much as the failure to be self-reliant. —*Heber J. Grant* (GS, 184)

The aim of the Church is to help the people to help themselves. Work is to be re-enthroned as the ruling principle of the lives of our Church membership. —*Heber J. Grant* (CR, Oct. 1936, 3)

Let every man feel that he is the architect and builder of his own life, and that he proposes to make a success of it by working. —*Heber J. Grant* (CR, Oct., 1936, 13)

It is a bad thing for men to think the world owes them a living, and all they have to do is to beg or steal to get it. —*Joseph F. Smith* (CR, Apr. 1898, 48)

Labor is the key to the true happiness of the physical and spiritual being. If a man possesses millions, his children should still be taught how to labor with their hands. —*Joseph F. Smith* (GD, 527)

The wise steward who is willing and industrious should not be made to sacrifice his time and substance to support the idle and shiftless. —*Joseph F. Smith* (LPS, 342)

The spirit of genius is the spirit of hard work, plodding toil, whole-souled devotion to the labor of the day. —*Joseph F. Smith* (LPS, 397)

Labor is the manufacturer of wealth. It was ordained of God as the medium to be used by man to obtain his living. —*John Taylor* (GK, 266)

I used to think, if I were the Lord, I would give the people everything they wanted—all the money, all the honor, all the riches, and all the splendor their hearts could desire. But experience and observation have caused me to change my mind, for I know that such policy would not be good for the human family. —*John Taylor* (GK, 341)

My experience has taught me, and it has become a principle with me, that it is never any benefit to give, out and out, to man or woman, money, food, clothing, or anything else, if they are able-bodied, and can work and earn what they need, when there is anything on the earth, for them to do. This is my principle, and I try to act upon it. To pursue a contrary course would ruin any community in the world and make them idlers. People trained in this way have no interest in working; "but," say they, "we can beg, or we can get this, that, or the other." No, my plan and counsel would be, let every person, able to work, work and earn what he needs. —*Brigham Young* (BY, 274)

After suitable rest and relaxation there is not a day, hour or minute that we should spend in idleness. —*Brigham Young* (BY, 290)

Have I any good reason to say to my Father in Heaven, "Fight my battles," when he has given me the sword to wield, the arm and the brain that I can fight for myself? Can I ask him to fight my battles and sit quietly down waiting for him to do so? I cannot. I can pray the people to hearken to wisdom, to listen to counsel; but to ask God to do for me that which I can do for myself is preposterous to my mind. —*Brigham Young* (BY, 426)

If we all labor a few hours a day, we could then spend the remainder of our time in rest and the improvement of our minds. This would give an opportunity to the children to be educated in the learning of the day, and to possess all the wisdom of man. —*Brigham Young* (BY, 302)

53. FAMILY

The family . . . is a divine institution, the most important both in mortality and in eternity. —*Gordon B. Hinckley* (BTE, 130)

The strength of any community lies in the strength of its families. The strength of any nation lies in the strength of its families. —*Gordon B. Hinckley* (Ensign, Nov. 1990, 53-56)

I believe in the family where there is a husband who regards his companion as his greatest asset and treats her accordingly; where there is a wife who looks upon her husband as her anchor and strength, her comfort and security; where there are parents who look upon those children as blessings and find a great and serious and wonderful challenge in their nurture and rearing. The cultivation of such a home requires effort and energy, forgiveness and patience, love and endurance and sacrifice; but it is worth all of these and more. —*Gordon B. Hinckley* (Ensign, Aug. 1992, 2-7)

I want to emphasize that which is already familiar to you, and that is the importance of binding our families together with love and kindness, with appreciation and respect, and with teaching the ways of the Lord so that children will grow in righteousness and avoid the tragedies which are overcoming so many families across the world. —*Gordon B. Hinckley* (CN, May 4, 1996, 2)

Perhaps our greatest concern is with families. The family is falling apart all over the world. The old ties that bound together father and mother and children are breaking everywhere. . . . There are too many broken homes among our own. The love that led to marriage somehow evaporates, and hatred fills its place. Hearts are broken, children weep Can we not do better? Of course, we can. It is selfishness that brings about most of these tragedies. If there is forbearance, if there is forgiveness, if there is anxious looking after the happiness of one s companion, then love will flourish and blossom. . . .

This is a malady with a cure. The prescription is simple and wonderfully effective. It is love. It is plain, simple, everyday love and respect. It is a tender plant that needs nurturing. But it is worth all of the effort we can put into it. —*Gordon B. Hinckley* (Ensign, Nov., 1997, 69)

The Church has the responsibility—and the authority—to preserve and protect the family as the foundation of society. The pattern for family life, instituted from before the foundation of the world, provides for children to be born and to be nurtured by a father and mother who are husband and wife, lawfully married. Parenthood is a sacred obligation and privilege, with children welcomed as a "heritage of the Lord" (Ps. 127:3). (Isa. 2:3). —*Howard W. Hunter* (Ensign Nov. 1994, 8-9)

The Church will never be stronger than its families, and this nation will never rise above its homes and its families. —*Ezra Taft Benson* (ETB, 493)

There is no theme I would rather speak to than home and family, for they are at the very heart of the gospel of Jesus Christ. The Church, in large part, exists for the salvation and exaltation of the family. —*Ezra Taft Benson*(CLP , 25)

Successful families do things together: family projects, work, vacations, recreation, and reunions. —*Ezra Taft Benson* (Ensign, Aug. 1993, 2)

To any thoughtful person it must be obvious that intimate association without marriage is sin; that children without parenthood and family life is tragedy; that society without basic family life is without foundation and will disintegrate into nothingness and oblivion. —*Spencer W. Kimball* (CR, July 1973, 15)

Our success, individually and as a church, will largely be determined by how faithfully we focus on living the gospel in the home. . . . Church programs should always support and never detract from gospel-centered family activities. —*Spencer W. Kimball* (Ensign, May 1978, 100)

Youth are the children of yesterday, and the parents of the children of tomorrow. What a youth is today depends largely upon what he learned as a child, and the lessons of today become the deeds of tomorrow. —*Harold B. Lee* (DSL, 20)

As important as our many programs and organizational efforts are, these should not supplant the home; they should support the home. —*Harold B. Lee* (YLW, 66)

I pray that our families in the Church can have many opportunities together so that strong bonds will be formed. Then, if the children should stray away temporarily from the path of truth and duty, the strongest bond that can be forged in their minds will be their fear of losing their place in the eternal family circle. —*Harold B. Lee* (YLW, 80)

The thought of a nation without the family unit as its fundamental foundation; where all the citizens are, comparatively, strangers to each other, and where natural affection is not found; where no family ties bind the groups together, is one of horror. Such a condition could lead to but one end—anarchy and dissolution. —*Joseph Fielding Smith* (CN, Apr. 2, 1932, 6)

Eventually, when this work is perfected, and Christ delivers up to his Father the keys and makes his report, and death is destroyed, then that great family from the days of Adam down, of all the righteous, those who have kept the commandments of God, will find that they are one family, the family of God, entitled to all the blessings that pertain to the exaltation. —*Joseph Fielding Smith* (CR, Oct. 1948, 154)

Next to eternal life, the most precious gift that our Father in heaven can bestow upon man is his children. —*David O. McKay* (IE, 52:804)

Our country's most precious possession is not our vast acres of range land supporting flocks and herds; not productive farms; not our forests; not our mines nor oil wells producing fabulous wealth. Our country's greatest resource is our children. —*David O. McKay* (CR, Oct. 1951, 5-6)

A man succeeds and reaps the honors of public applause, when in truth, a steadfast and courageous woman has in large measure made it all possible—has by her tact and encouragement held him to his best, has had faith in him when his own faith has languished, has cheered him with the unfailing assurance, "You can, you must, you will."—*David O. McKay* (TL, 53-54)

One of the greatest evidences to me of the divinity of this work is that it teaches there is eternal life on the other side, and that there will be a reunion there of the loved ones who have known each other here. Consequently, as parents, we may well be patient and loving toward our children, for they will eternally abide with us on the other side, if we and they are faithful. —*George Albert Smith* (CR, Oct. 1905, 29)

Children are the offspring of God, their spirits were begotten in the holy heavens of our Father, and they are given to us for our blessing. —*George Albert Smith* (CR, Oct. 1907 p. 36)

I would rather take one of my children to the grave than I would see him turn away from this Gospel. I would rather take my children to the cemetery, and see them buried in innocence, than I would see them corrupted by the ways of the world. —*Joseph F. Smith* (GD, 279)

The riches of all my earthly joys is my precious children. —*Joseph F. Smith* (PCM, 149)

Let families put themselves in possession of all the good they can—be in a position to do right, and be continually in the path to exaltation and glory. —*Lorenzo Snow* (LS, 138)

If a child or relative of mine forsakes the Gospel, the holy Priesthood, his God, and the Kingdom of God, farewell to that child or relative, whether near or distant. I own none as relatives, only those who love and serve our Lord and Savior, Jesus Christ. —*Brigham Young* (BY, 204)

54. ABUSE IN THE HOME

I do not hesitate to say that no one who is a professed follower of Christ, and no one who is a professed member of Christ's Church, can engage in the abuse of children without offending God, who is their Father, and repudiating the teachings of the Savior and his prophets. —*Gordon B. Hinckley* (FETR , 70)

Any man involved in an incestuous relationship is unworthy to hold the priesthood. He is unworthy to hold membership in the Church and should be dealt with accordingly. . . . If there be any within the sound of my voice who are guilty of such practices, let them repent forthwith, make amends where possible, develop within themselves that discipline which can curb such evil practices, plead with the Lord for forgiveness, and resolve within their hearts henceforth to walk with clean hands. —*Gordon B. Hinckley* (Ensign, May 1985, 50)

No man who has been ordained to the priesthood of God can with impunity indulge in either spouse or child abuse. Such activity becomes an immediate repudiation of his right to hold and exercise the priesthood and to retain membership in the Church. —*Gordon B. Hinckley* (Ensign, Nov. 1985, 51)

I am satisfied that the more unkindly a wife is treated the less attractive she becomes. She loses pride in herself. She develops a feeling of worthlessness. Of course it shows.

A husband who domineers his wife, who demeans and humiliates her, and who makes officious demands upon her not only injures her, but he also belittles himself. . . .

My brethren, you who have had conferred upon you the priesthood of God, you know, as I know, that there is no enduring happiness, that there is no lasting peace in the heart, no tranquillity in the home, without the companionship of a good woman. —*Gordon B. Hinckley* (Ensign, Nov. 1991, 51)

The law of procreation has never been rescinded. —*Ezra Taft Benson* (ETB, 539)

I would beseech our young people to reserve for the marriage relationship those sweet and lovely and intimate associations. Not only that, but when those associations come, let them be primarily for the purpose of procreation, for the having of a family, because it is not pleasing in the sight of God to enjoy the pleasures of those associations and refuse to accept the responsibility of parenthood. —*Ezra Taft Benson* (ETB, 539)

Let me warn the sisters in all seriousness that you who submit yourselves to an abortion or to an operation that precludes you from safely having additional healthy children are jeopardizing your exaltation and your future membership in the kingdom of God. —*Ezra Taft Benson* (ETB, 541)

Do not curtail the number of your children for personal or selfish reasons. Material possessions, social convenience, and so-called professional advantages are nothing compared to a righteous posterity. In the eternal perspective, children—not possessions, not position, not prestige—are our greatest jewels. —*Ezra Taft Benson* (CLP , 28)

Perhaps there are women in the world who exasperate their husbands, but no man is justified in resorting to physical force or in exploding his feelings in profanity. There are men, undoubtedly, in the world who are thus beastly, but no man who holds the priesthood of God should so debase himself. —*David O. McKay* (CR, Oct. 1951, 181)

He is a weak man who will curse or condemn some loved one because of a little accident. What good does it do him? He would be a man if he would develop his spirit and control that anger, control his tongue. A little thing? Trace it, and you will find that not yielding and not controlling it bring many an unhappy hour in your home. —*David O. McKay* (GI, 490)

Let us instruct young people who come to us, to know that a woman should be queen of her own body. The marriage covenant does not give the man the right to enslave her or to abuse her or to use her merely for the gratification of his passion. Your marriage ceremony does not give you that right. —*David O. McKay* (CR, Apr. 1952, 86-87)

I want to say that the priesthood does not give any man a right to abuse his wife. The priesthood does give him a right to be kind, to be faithful, to be honorable, to teach the truth and to teach his children the truth, and when he does that he will not fall away into sin. —*George Albert Smith* (CR, Apr. 1949, 189)

I can not understand how a man can be unkind to any woman, much less to the wife of his bosom, and the mother of his children, and I am told that there are those who are absolutely brutal, but they are unworthy the name of men. —*Joseph F. Smith* (GD, 352)

55. ADOPTION AND ABORTION

I realize that notwithstanding all of the teaching that can be done, there will be those who will not heed and will go their willful way only to discover to their shock and dismay that they are to become parents, while they are scarcely older than children themselves.

Abortion is not the answer. This only compounds the problem. It is an evil and repulsive escape that will someday bring regret and remorse.

Marriage is the more honorable thing. This means facing up to responsibility. It means giving the child a name, with parents who together can nurture, protect, and love.

When marriage is not possible, experience has shown that adoption, difficult though this may be for the young mother, may afford a greater opportunity for the child to live a life of happiness. —*Gordon B. Hinckley* (Ensign, Nov. 1994, 53)

Let me warn the sisters in all seriousness that you who submit yourselves to an abortion or to an operation that precludes you from safely having additional healthy children are jeopardizing your exaltation and your future membership in the kingdom of God. —*Ezra Taft Benson* (ETB, 541)

We realize that some women, through no fault of their own, are not able to bear children. To these lovely sisters, every prophet of God has promised that they will be blessed with children in the eternities and that posterity will not be denied them. Through pure faith, pleading prayers, fasting, and special priesthood blessings, many of these same lovely sisters, with their noble companions at their sides, have had miracles take place in their lives and have been blessed with children. Others have prayerfully chosen to adopt children, and to these wonderful couples we salute you for the sacrifices and love you have given to those children you have chosen to be your own. —*Ezra Taft Benson* (ETB, 541)

Abortion is a calamity, and if the gospel came into play in the lives of men and women, an abortion would be rare indeed, if at all. . . .

Abortion must be considered one of the most revolting and sinful practices in this day, when we are witnessing a frightening evidence of permissiveness leading to sexual immorality. We take the solemn view that any tampering with the fountains of life is serious, morally, mentally, psychologically, physically. —*Spencer W. Kimball* (CR, May 1975, 107)

In America and elsewhere in the world, the family limitation program is gaining much strength. Latter-day Saints do not believe in this. We believe in following the admonition of the Lord in having large families and rearing them righteously. We hope that our Latter-day Saints will not trade children for accommodation and luxury. —*Spencer W. Kimball* (SWK, 325)

May I say here that we in the Church are unalterably opposed to abortion. The only exception would be in cases where doctors find it necessary to perform an abortion to save the life of the mother. We reaffirm that the first purpose of marriage is to bring children in the world and they ought to be welcomed. —*Harold B. Lee* (DSL, 246-247)

Some say that with an abortion during the first few months of pregnancy there is nothing wrong. That is one of the most hellish things that has ever been said to try to destroy the fountains of life. —*Harold B. Lee* (HBL, 197)

The time of quickening is when the mother feels the life of her unborn infant. —*Joseph Fielding Smith* (DS2, 280)

There should be no orphan child depending upon charity in this land. If you have no children of your own, if you realize the admonition of the Savior, then some of you who desire this blessing should reach out your arms and adopt some of these homeless children. . . . I do not hesitate to say that the blessing that will return to the one whose home is opened to a child without parents will not only be that they will rejoice in the growth and development of that child but that other blessings of our Father will be added to them in proportion to their good works. —*George Albert Smith* (CR, Oct. 1907, 38-39)

56. BIRTH CONTROL

The law of procreation has never been rescinded. —*Ezra Taft Benson* (ETB, 539)

I would beseech our young people to reserve for the marriage relationship those sweet and lovely and intimate associations. Not only that, but when those associations come, let them be primarily for the purpose of procreation, for the having of a family, because it is not pleasing in the sight of God to enjoy the pleasures of those associations and refuse to accept the responsibility of parenthood. —*Ezra Taft Benson* (ETB, 539)

Do not curtail the number of your children for personal or selfish reasons. Material possessions, social convenience, and so-called professional advantages are nothing compared to a righteous posterity. In the eternal perspective, children—not possessions, not position, not prestige—are our greatest jewels. —*Ezra Taft Benson* (CLP , 28)

How do you think that the Lord looks upon those who use the contraceptives because in their selfish life it is not the convenient moment to bear children? . . . How do you think the Lord feels about women who forego the pleasures and glories of motherhood that they might retain their figures, that their social life might not be affected, that they might avoid the deprivations, pains, and agonies of childbearing and birthing? How do you think the Lord feels as he views healthy parents who could have children but who deliberately close the doors by operation or by contraceptives, close the doors upon spirits eager to enter into mortal bodies?—*Spencer W. Kimball* (SWK, 329)

Young married couples who postpone parenthood until their degrees are attained might be shocked if their expressed preference were labeled idolatry. —*Spencer W. Kimball* (MF, 40)

When a man and a woman are married and they agree, or covenant, to limit their offspring to two or three, and practice devices to accomplish this purpose, they are guilty of iniquity which eventually must be punished. —*Joseph Fielding Smith* (DS2, 87)

If the responsibilities of parenthood are wilfully avoided here, then how can the Lord bestow upon the guilty the blessings of eternal increase? It cannot be, and they shall be denied such blessings. —*Joseph Fielding Smith* (IE, 34:644)

Some young couples enter into marriage and procrastinate the bringing of children into their homes. They are running a great risk. Marriage is for the purpose of rearing a family, and youth is the time to do it. I admire these young mothers with four or five children around them now, still young, happy. —*David O. McKay* (GI, 466)

Seeking the pleasures of conjugality without a willingness to assume the responsibilities of rearing a family is one of the onslaughts that now batter at the structure of the American home. Intelligence and mutual consideration should be ever-present factors in determining the coming of children to the household. When the husband and wife are healthy and free from inherited weaknesses and diseases that might be transmitted with injury to their offspring, the use of contraceptives is to be condemned. —*David O. McKay* (IE, 51:618)

Marriage is ordained of God that children might be so trained that they may eventually be worthy of Christ's presence; and that home is happiest in which they are welcomed, as God and nature intended they should be. —*David O. McKay* (GI, 469)

The most important treasures that we have are the sons and daughters that God sends to our homes. I want to say to the Latter-day Saints one of the responsibilities of every married couple is to rear a family to the honor and glory of God. Those who follow the customs and habits of the world in preference to that blessing will some day find that all the things they have struggled for are wasted away like ashes, while those who have reared their families to honor God and keep his commandments will find their treasures not altogether here upon earth in mortality, but they will have their treasures when the celestial kingdom shall be organized on this earth, and those treasures will be their sons and daughters and descendants to the latest generation. —*George Albert Smith* (CR, Apr. 1947, 164)

No Latter-day Saint woman, understanding or comprehending the Gospel of Jesus Christ, will refuse the legitimate opportunity to bear sons and daughters in the image of God. No man properly realizing his privileges and opportunities, would do anything to prevent himself being a father in Israel, and having the privilege of rearing and educating children created in the likeness of our Father whom we worship. —*George Albert Smith* (CR, Oct. 1907, 36)

I raise my voice among the sons and daughters of Zion, and warn you that if you dry up the springs of life and abuse the power that God has blessed you with, there will come a time of chastening to you, that all the tears you may shed will never remove. Remember the first great commandment; fulfill that obligation. —*George Albert Smith* (CR, Oct. 1907, 38)

I believe that where people undertake to curtail or prevent the birth of their children that they are going to reap disappointment by and by. I have no hesitancy in saying that I believe this is one of the greatest crimes of the world today, this evil practice. —*Joseph F. Smith* (GD, 278-279)

There are multitudes of pure and holy spirits waiting to take tabernacles, now what is our duty?—to prepare tabernacles for them; to take a course that will not tend to drive those spirits into the families of the wicked, where they will be trained in wickedness, debauchery, and every species of crime. It is the duty of every righteous man and woman to prepare tabernacles for all the spirits they can. —*Brigham Young* (BY, 197)

57. DIVORCE

The remedy for most marriage stress is not in divorce. It is in repentance. It is not in separation. It is in simple integrity that leads a man to square up his shoulders and meet his obligations. It is found in the Golden Rule. —*Gordon B. Hinckley* (Ensign, May 1991, 74)

There may be now and again a legitimate cause for divorce. I am not one to say that it is never justified. But I say without hesitation that this plague among us, which seems to be growing everywhere, is not of God, but rather is the work of the adversary of righteousness and peace and truth. —*Gordon B. Hinckley* (Ensign, May 1991, 74)

To those who have experienced divorce: Don't let disappointment or a sense of failure color your perception of marriage or of life. Do not lose faith in marriage or allow bitterness to canker your soul and destroy you or those you love or have loved. —*Howard W. Hunter* (WMJ, 56)

Every divorce is the result of selfishness on the part of one or the other or both parties to a marriage contract. Someone is thinking of self-comforts, conveniences, freedoms, luxuries, or ease. —*Spencer W. Kimball* (SWK, 313)

Divorce is not a cure for difficulty, but is merely an escape, and a weak one. The divorce itself does not constitute the entire evil, but the very acceptance of divorce as a cure is also a serious sin of this generation. . . . Marriage never was easy. It may never be. It brings with it sacrifice, sharing and a demand for great selflessness. —*Spencer W. Kimball* (SWK, 314)

Bishops, never encourage your members to get a divorce. Encourage them to be reconciled, to adjust their lives, their own personal lives generally. —*Spencer W. Kimball* (SWK, 314)

Sometimes, as we travel throughout the Church, a husband and wife will come to us and ask if, because they are not compatible in their marriage—they having had a temple marriage—it wouldn't be better if they were to free themselves from each other and then seek more congenial partners. To all such we say, whenever a couple who have been married in the temple say they are tiring of each other, it is an evidence that either one or both are not true to their temple covenants. Any couple married in the temple who are true to their covenants will grow dearer to each other, and love will find a deeper meaning on their golden wedding anniversary than on the day they were married in the house of the Lord. Don't you mistake that. —*Harold B. Lee* (YLW, 313)

When divorce comes to those who are married in the temple, it has come because they have violated the covenants and the obligations they have taken upon themselves to be true to each other, true to God, true to the Church. —*Joseph Fielding Smith* (CR, Oct. 1951, 121)

When a man and a woman are married in the temple for time and all eternity and then separate, the children will go with the parent who is justified and who has kept the covenants. If neither of them has kept his covenants, the children may be taken away from both of them and given to somebody else, and that would be by virtue of being born under the covenant. —*Joseph Fielding Smith* (DS2, 91-92)

Except in cases of infidelity or other extreme conditions, the Church frowns upon divorce, and authorities look with apprehension upon the increasing number of divorces among members of the Church. —*David O. McKay* (IE, 46:657)

As teachers, we are to let the people know, and warn these men—and this is not imagination—who, after having lived with their wives and brought into this world four and five and six children, get tired of them and seek a divorce, that they are on the road to hell. —*David O. McKay* (CR, Apr. 1949, 183)

The number of broken marriages can be reduced if couples realize even before they approach the altar that marriage is a state of mutual service, a state of giving as well as of receiving, and that each must give of himself or herself to the utmost. —*David O. McKay* (CR, Apr. 1964, 6)

To look upon marriage as a mere contract that may be entered into at pleasure in response to a romantic whim, or for selfish purposes, and severed at the first difficulty or misunderstanding that may arise, is an evil meriting severe condemnation. —*David O. McKay* (CR, Apr. 1969, 8-9)

One of the serious evils of our day is divorce, the breaking up of families, the infidelity of husband and wife. There are fewer divorces among the Latter-day Saints than among other people. In our own communities the divorce rate is lower among members of our Church who have been properly married in the temple, as compared with those married by civil ceremony, showing that the teachings of the gospel of Jesus Christ, when observed, tend to make the marriage covenant sacred. Thereby the evil of divorce is greatly lessened. —*Heber J. Grant* (IE, 44:329)

It is saddening to note the frequency of divorces in the land, and the growing inclination to look upon children as an encumbrance instead of as a precious heritage from the Lord. These evils should not gain a foothold among the people of God. —*Lorenzo Snow* (LS, 141)

I never counselled a woman to follow her husband to the Devil. If a man is determined to expose the lives of his friends, let that man go to the Devil and to destruction alone. —*Brigham Young* (BY, 201)

58. HOME LIFE

The home is the cradle of virtue, the place where character is formed and habits are established. The home evening is the opportunity to teach the ways of the Lord. —*Gordon B. Hinckley* (BTE, 55-58)

Discipline with severity or with cruelty inevitably leads not to correction but to resentment and bitterness. It cures nothing; it only aggravates the problem. It is self-defeating. . . . There is no discipline in all the world like the discipline of love. It has a magic all its own. —*Gordon B. Hinckley* (FETR , 70-71)

As children grow through the years, their lives, in large measure, become an extension and a reflection of family teaching. —*Gordon B. Hinckley* (Ensign, May 1990, 70)

We have many failures in the world, but the greatest of these, in my judgment, is that failure which is found in broken homes. Immeasurable is the heartache.

The root of most of this lies in selfishness. The cure for most of it can be found in repentance on the part of the offender and forgiveness of the part of the offended. —*Gordon B. Hinckley* (Ensign, Aug. 1992, 5)

There is too much selfishness. There is too much of worldliness in our homes. We need to get back to the basics of respect one for another and concern one for another, love and appreciation for another, working together, worshipping together and living together as families who love the Lord and look to Him for light and strength and comfort. —*Gordon B. Hinckley* (CN, Nov. 4, 1995, 2)

The basic failure is in our homes. Parents haven't measured up to their responsibilities. It is evident. A nation will rise no higher than the strength of its homes. If you want to reform a nation, you begin with families, with parents who teach their children principles and values that are positive and affirmative and will lead them to worthwhile endeavors. . . . Parents have no greater responsibility in this world than the bringing up of their children in the right way, and they will have no greater satisfaction as the years pass than to see those children grow in integrity and honesty and make something of their lives. —*Gordon B. Hinckley* (Ensign, Nov., 1996, 48-49)

The principle of eternal marriage is a most powerful stabilizing influence in promoting the kind of home needed to rear children who are happy and well adjusted. —*Howard W. Hunter* (CR, Oct. 1972, 67)

Monday night has been set aside as an evening for the family together. No Church activity or social appointments may be sponsored on this night. —*Ezra Taft Benson* (ETB, 529)

May I heartily commend to all—whether or not you are a Latter-day Saint—to gather your family about you on a once-a-week basis for a family home evening night. Such evenings where scriptures are read, skits acted out, songs sung around the piano, games played, special refreshments enjoyed, and family prayers offered, like links in an iron chain, bind a family together with love, tradition, strength, and loyalty to each other. —*Ezra Taft Benson* (ETB, 531)

Some spiritually alert parents hold early-morning devotional with their families in their homes. They have a hymn, prayer, and then read and discuss the Book of Mormon. —*Ezra Taft Benson* (AWW, 11)

I like to compare the home evening, family prayer, and other associated activities of the Church for the saving of the family, when they are conscientiously carried out, with an umbrella. If the umbrella is not opened up, it is little more than a cane and can give little protection from the storms of nature. Likewise, God-given plans are of little value unless they are used. —*Spencer W. Kimball* (SWK, 334)

The home should be a place where reliance on the Lord is a matter of common experience, not reserved for special occasions. —*Spencer W. Kimball* (Ensign, Jan. 1984, 5.)

We could refer to all the components of personal and family preparedness, not in relation to holocaust of disaster, but in cultivating a life-style that is on a day-to-day basis its own reward. —*Spencer W. Kimball* (Ensign, Aug. 1984, 5)

A true Latter-day Saint home is a haven against the storms and struggles of life. Spirituality is born and nurtured by daily prayer, scripture study, home gospel discussions and related activities, home evenings, family councils, working and playing together, serving each other, and sharing the gospel with those around us. Spirituality is also nurtured in our actions of patience, kindness, and forgiveness toward each other and in our applying gospel principles in family circle. Home is where we become experts and scholars in gospel righteousness, learning and living gospel truths together. —*Spencer W. Kimball* (Ensign, Jan. 1982, 3)

So I beg of you to lay the foundations of the home on a solid, firm foundation of love, trust, and faith. Start the day with family prayer. Kneel together before you retire. There may have been some rough edges through the day and a good way to smooth them out is by kneeling together in prayer. See to it. —*Harold B. Lee* (DSL, 149)

Remember always that the most important of the Lord's work you and I will ever do will be within the walls of our own homes. —*Harold B. Lee* (SHP, 255)

Much of what we do organizationally, then, is scaffolding, as we seek to build the individual, and we must not mistake the scaffolding for the soul. —*Harold B. Lee* (SHP, 309)

We must remember that in some of our young, the offense over adult hypocrisy is not always their desire to "get something on us," but a deep sense of disappointment. They truly want us to be what we pretend to be, because when we are, it is a testimony to them that we really believe. —*Harold B. Lee* (YLW, 65)

Family life is God's own method of training the young, and homes are largely what mothers make them. —*Harold B. Lee* (YLW, 295-296)

Happiness comes from unselfish service. And happy homes are only those where there is a daily striving to make sacrifices for each other's happiness. —*Harold B. Lee* (HBL, 296)

There is no substitute for a righteous home. That may not be so considered in the world, but it is and ought to be in the Church of Jesus Christ of Latter-day Saints. The family is the unit in the kingdom of God. —*Joseph Fielding Smith* (CR, Oct. 1948, 152-153)

You cannot teach one thing and do another. Example is the way we teach the gospel. —*Joseph Fielding Smith* (DS3, 298)

Home is the center from which woman rules the world. It is there she teaches her child self-restraint, develops in him the confidence and strength that spring from self-control. It is there the child learns respect for the rights of others. It is in a well-directed home that men and women first develop a consciousness that true happiness lies in conforming one's life to the laws of nature and to the rules of social conduct. —*David O. McKay* (IE, 50:641)

Make home your hobby, for, if anyone makes a loving home with all his heart, he can never miss heaven. —*David O. McKay* (CR Apr. 1935, 116)

The home is the place to teach the virtues of society. —*David O. McKay* (CR, Oct. 1955, 129)

God help us to defend the truth—better than that, to live it, to exemplify it in our homes. —*David O. McKay* (CR, Oct. 1964 92)

Unity, harmony, goodwill are virtues to be fostered and cherished in every home. —*David O. McKay* (CR, Apr. 1967, 5)

In the well-ordered home we may experience on earth a taste of heaven. —*David O. McKay* (CR Apr. 1969, 5)

Let our homes be sanctuaries of peace and hope and love. Wherever we go let us radiate sunshine that will attract others and will make them desire to know what the Gospel of Jesus Christ really is. —*George Albert Smith* (CR, Oct. 1941, 101)

That prophet of the Lord gave to us this advice: That we should so arrange our time that one evening each week would find the Latter-day Saints in their own homes, associated with their own children, and there teach them the things that the Lord has decreed that they should know. It is not sufficient that my children are taught faith, repentance and baptism, and the laying on of hands for the gift of the holy Ghost in the auxiliary organizations. My Father in heaven has commanded that I should do that myself. —*George Albert Smith* (CR, Apr. 1926, 145-146)

I pray that the love of the gospel of our Lord will burn in our souls and enrich our lives, that it will cause husbands to be kinder to wives, and wives to be kinder to husbands, parents to children, and children to parents. —*George Albert Smith* (CR, Oct. 1948, 167-168)

In our homes, brethren and sisters, it is our privilege, nay, it is our duty, to call our families together to be taught the truths of the Holy Scriptures. —*George Albert Smith* (CR, Apr. 1914, 12)

I am convinced that one of the greatest things that can come into any home to cause the boys and girls in that home to grow up in a love of God, and in a love of the gospel of Jesus Christ, is to have family prayer. . . . I believe that there are very few who go astray, that very few lose their faith, who have once had a knowledge of the gospel, and who never neglect their prayers in their families, and their secret supplications to God. —*Heber J. Grant* (CR, Oct. 1923, 7-8)

The Lord has called upon us to pray with our families and in secret, that we may not forget God. If we neglect this, we lose the inspiration and power from heaven; we become indifferent, lose our testimony, and go down into darkness. —*Heber J. Grant* (GS, 156)

The husband should treat his wife with the utmost courtesy and respect. The husband should never insult her; he should never speak slightly of her, but should always hold her in the highest esteem in the home, in the presence of their children. . . . The wife, also should treat the husband with the greatest respect and courtesy. Her words to him should not be keen and cutting and sarcastic. She should not pass slurs or insinuations at him. She should not nag him. She should not try to arouse his anger or make things unpleasant about the home. The wife should be a joy to her husband, and she should live and conduct herself at home so the home will be the most joyous, the most blessed place on earth to her husband. —*Joseph F. Smith* (CR, Apr. 1905, 84-85)

But what are we doing in our homes to train our children; what to enlighten them? What to encourage them to make home their place of amusement, and a place where they may invite their friends for study or entertainment?—*Joseph F. Smith* (IE, 11:301-303)

What then is an ideal home-model home, such as it should be the ambition of the Latter-day Saints to build; such as a young man starting out in life should wish to erect for himself? And the answer came to me: It is one in which all worldly considerations are secondary. —*Joseph F. Smith* (IE, 8:385)

Home is the center from which woman rules the world. It is there she teaches her child self-restraint, develops in him the confidence and strength that spring from self-control. It is there the child learns respect for the rights of others. It is in a well-directed home that men and women first develop a consciousness that true happiness lies in conforming one's life to the laws of nature and to the rules of social conduct. —*David O. McKay* (IE, 50:641)

The loss of fortune is nothing compared with the loss of home. When the club becomes more attractive to any man than his home, it is time for him to confess in bitter shame that he has failed to measure up to the supreme opportunity of his life and has flunked in the final test of true manhood. No other success can compensate for failure in the home. This is the one thing of limitless potentialities on earth. The poorest shack of a home in which love prevails over a united family is of greater value to God and future humanity than the richest bank on earth. In such a home God can work miracles and will work miracles. —*David O. McKay* (CR Apr. 1935, 116)

Make home your hobby, for, if anyone makes a loving home with all his heart, he can never miss heaven. —*David O. McKay* (CR Apr. 1935, 116)

The home is the place to teach the virtues of society. —*David O. McKay* (CR, Oct. 1955, 129)

God help us to defend the truth—better than that, to live it, to exemplify it in our homes. —*David O. McKay* (CR, Oct. 1964 92)

Unity, harmony, goodwill are virtues to be fostered and cherished in every home. —*David O. McKay* (CR, Apr. 1967, 5)

In the well-ordered home we may experience on earth a taste of heaven. —*David O. McKay* (CR Apr. 1969, 5)

The wife should never in the presence of her children speak disrespectfully of her husband. If she thinks her husband has done wrong (he might have done), she should never speak of it in the presence of her children. She should take him out of the presence of her children and there tell him of his faults, in a pleasant way, but never in the presence of the children speak disrespectfully of the father. And the father the same. He has no right to speak disrespectfully of his wife in the presence of her children. And I pray God to give the husband and wife the spirit and the understanding to correct themselves in such matters. —*Lorenzo Snow* (CR, Oct. 1897, 32-33)

In some quarters there has been ruinous neglect on the part of parents in making their homes attractive to their children. A well-ordered, lovely home, in which peace and goodwill prevail is a place of perpetual delight to those who reside there, whether old or young. Where such homes exist the young who live there are not found loafing at street corners or stores, nor spending their time in gadding about from house to house and in improper company at late hours. . . . In after years those children will think of that home as the brightest and dearest spot in their memories; in their minds it will always be surrounded by a heavenly halo. —*John Taylor* (GK, 284)

In our daily pursuits in life, of whatever nature and kind, Latter-day Saints . . . should maintain a uniform and even temper, both when at home and when abroad. They should not suffer reverses and unpleasant circumstances to sour their natures and render them fretful and unsocial at home, speaking words full of bitterness and biting acrimony to their wives and children, creating gloom and sorrow in their habitations, making themselves feared rather than loved by their families. —*Brigham Young* (BY, 203-204)

59. THE MARRIAGE RELATIONSHIP

True love is not so much a matter of romance as it is a matter of anxious concern for the well being of one's companion. —*Gordon B. Hinckley* (Ensign, June 1971, 71-72)

We seldom get into trouble when we speak softly. It is only when we raise our voices that the sparks fly and tiny molehills become great mountains of contention. . . . The voice of heaven is a still small voice; likewise, the voice of domestic peace is a quiet voice.

There is need for a vast amount of discipline in marriage, not of one's companion, but of one's self. —*Gordon B. Hinckley* (Ensign, June 1971, 72)

I know of no single practice that will have a more salutary effect upon your lives than the practice of kneeling together as you begin and close each day. Somehow the little storms that seem to afflict every marriage are dissipated when, kneeling before the Lord, you thank him for one another, in the presence of one another, and then together invoke his blessings upon your lives, your home, your loved ones, and your dreams. —*Gordon B. Hinckley* (Ensign, June 1971, 72)

Let virtue garnish your courtship, and absolute fidelity be the crown jewel of your marriage. —*Gordon B. Hinckley* (Ensign, June 1989, 72)

To our young adults of marriageable circumstances, I hope you will not put off marriage too long. I do not speak so much to the young women as to the young men whose prerogative and responsibility it is to take the lead in this matter. Don't go on endlessly in a frivolous dating game. Look for a choice companion, one you can love, honor, and respect, and make a decision. —*Gordon B. Hinckley* (Ensign, March 1990, 6)

Too many who come to marriage have been coddled and spoiled and somehow led to feel that everything must be precisely right at all times, that life is a series of entertainments, that appetites are to be satisfied without regard to principle. How tragic the consequences of such hollow and unreasonable thinking!—*Gordon B. Hinckley* (Ensign, May 1991, 73)

As a matter of priesthood responsibility, a man, under normal circumstances, should not unduly postpone marriage. Brethren, the Lord has spoken plainly on this matter. It is your sacred and solemn responsibility to follow his counsel and the words of his prophets. —*Howard W. Hunter* (Ensign, Nov. 1994, 49)

Honor your wife's unique and divinely appointed role as a mother in Israel and her special capacity to bear and nurture children. . . . You share, as a loving partner, the care of the children. Help her to manage and keep up your home. Help teach, train, and discipline your children.

You should express regularly to your wife and children your reverence and respect for her. Indeed, one of the greatest things a father can do for his children is to love their mother. —*Howard W. Hunter* (Ensign, Nov. 1994, 50)

The Lord intended that the wife be a helpmeet for man (meet means equal)—that is, a companion equal and necessary in full partnership. Presiding in righteousness necessitates a shared responsibility between husband and wife; together you act with knowledge and participation in all family matters. For a man to operate independent of or without regard to the feeling and counsel of his wife in governing the family is to exercise unrighteous dominion. —*Howard W. Hunter* (Ensign, Nov. 1994, 50-51)

Tenderness and respect—never selfishness—must be the guiding principles in the intimate relationship between husband and wife. Each partner must be considerate and sensitive to the other's needs and desires. Any domineering, indecent, or uncontrolled behavior in the intimate relationship between husband and wife is condemned by the Lord.

Any man who abuses or demeans his wife physically or spiritually is guilty of grievous sin and in need of sincere and serious repentance. Differences should be worked out in love and kindness and with a spirit of mutual reconciliation. A man should always speak to his wife lovingly and kindly, treating her with the utmost respect. Marriage is like a tender flower, brethren, and must be nourished constantly with expressions of love and affection. —*Howard W. Hunter* (Ensign, Nov. 1994, 51)

Our wives are our most precious eternal helpmates, our companions. They are to be cherished and loved. —*Ezra Taft Benson* (CUC , 52-53)

Honorable marriage is more important than wealth, position, and status. As husband and wife, sacrifice for each other and your children, the Lord will bless you, and your commitment to the Lord and your service in His kingdom will be enhanced. —*Ezra Taft Benson* (CLP, 54)

One good yardstick as to whether a person might be the right one for you is this: in her presence, do you think your noblest thoughts, do you aspire to your finest deeds, do you wish you were better than you are?—*Ezra Taft Benson* (CLP, 54)

Restraint and self-control must be ruling principles in the marriage relationship. Couples must learn to bridle their tongues as well as their passions. —*Ezra Taft Benson* (Ensign, July 1992, 2)

Marriage is ordained of God. It is not merely a social custom. Without proper and successful marriage, one will never be exalted. —*Spencer W. Kimball* (SWK, 291)

"Soulmates" are fiction and an illusion; and while every young man and young woman will seek with all diligence and prayerfulness to find a mate with whom life can be most compatible and beautiful, yet it is certain that almost any good man and any good woman can have happiness and a successful marriage if both are willing to pay the price. —*Spencer W. Kimball* (Ensign, Mar. 1977, 3)

Sweethearts should realize before they take the vows that each must accept literally and fully that the good of the little new family must always be superior to the good of either spouse. Each party must eliminate the "I" and the "my" and substitute therefore "we" and "our."—*Spencer W. Kimball* (Ensign, Mar. 1977, 3)

I want to tell you that there are no marriages that can ever be happy ones unless two people work at it. —*Spencer W. Kimball* (SWK, 307)

When problems affect a couple the easy thing is to stand on one's pride and quarrel . . . The hard thing, when problems arise, is to swallow pride, eat humble pie, analyze the situation, accept the blame that is properly due and then grit one's teeth, clench one's fists, and develop the courage to say, "I'm sorry."—*Spencer W. Kimball* (SWK, 307)

When we speak of marriage as a partnership, let us speak of marriage as a full partnership. We do not want our LDS women to be silent partners or limited partners in that eternal assignment! Please be a contributing and full partner. —*Spencer W. Kimball* (Ensign, Nov. 1978, 102)

Those who allow the marriage ceremony to terminate the days of "courtship" are making a well-nigh fatal mistake. If the new bride were to discover that her husband was just an actor before their marriage and now his quest is ended he stands revealed as a cheap counterfeit of his former self either in appearance or conduct, that would indeed be a shocking experience. Evidences and tokens of your love and a daily proof of your unselfishness toward her and your family will make love's flame burn more brightly with the years. Do you girls suppose that the same attention to personal details is less important after marriage? Surely the same qualities and traits in you that first attracted him are just as important in married life in keeping alive the flame of his affection and romantic desire. —*Harold B. Lee* (DSL, 173-174)

You must remember that the prime purpose of your marriage under God's command is to build the bridge from the eternity of spirits to mortality, over which God's spirit children might come into mortal bodies. Your failure to remember that revealed truth will be your failure to attain the highest bliss in married life. —*Harold B. Lee* (DSL, 174)

You, too, may live in the enchantment of your happy homes long after the bloom of youth has faded if you but seek to find the pure diamond quality in each other that needs but the polishing of success and failure, adversity and happiness to bring luster and sparkle that will shine with brilliance even through the darkest night. —*Harold B. Lee* (DSL, 178)

Husband and wife must feel equal responsibilities and obligations to teach each other. Two of the things that today strike at the security of modern homes is that young husbands have never sensed their full obligation in supporting a family, and young wives have sidestepped the responsibility of settling down to the serious business of raising a family and making a home. —*Harold B. Lee* (YLW, 339)

When a man marries a woman who was married previously to her husband in the temple but who has now died, he does so, or should, with his eyes open. If the children are born to this woman and her "time" husband, he has no claim upon those children. They go with the mother. This is the law. Certainly a man cannot in reason expect to take another man's wife, after that man is dead, and rear a family by her and then claim the children. —*Joseph Fielding Smith* (DS2, 78-79)

Rome, Greece, Babylon, Egypt, and many other nations owe their downfall to the breaking of the sacred covenant of marriage. The anger of a just God was kindled against them for their immorality. The bones of dead civilizations on this American continent bear silent but convincing evidence that it was unchastity and the disregard of this sacred covenant which brought them to their final judgment. —*Joseph Fielding Smith* (IE, 34:643)

Marriage in the light of revelation is an institution with the stamp of divinity upon it, and no person and no state can deprecate that institution with impunity. —*David O. McKay* (GI, 466)

Appreciation is a great virtue, and if husbands and wives expressed it more frequently in our homes, wives would be happier, and husbands would probably be more kind. —*David O. McKay* (GI, 475)

Marriage is the preserver of the human race. Without it, the purposes of God would be frustrated; virtue would be destroyed to give place to vice and corruption, and the earth would be void and empty. —*Joseph F. Smith* (GD, 272)

We hold that no man who is marriageable is fully living his religion who remains unmarried. He is doing a wrong to himself by retarding his progress, by narrowing his experiences, and to society by the undesirable example that he sets to others, as well as he, himself, being a dangerous factor in the community. —*Joseph F. Smith* (GD, 275)

The believer and unbeliever should not be yoked together, for sooner or later, in time or in eternity, they must be divided again. —*Joseph F. Smith* (GD, 275)

I think that young men and young women, too, should be willing, even at this day, and in the present condition of things, to enter the sacred bonds of marriage together and fight their way together to success, meet their obstacles and their difficulties, and cleave together to success, and cooperate in their temporal affairs, so that they shall succeed. Then they will learn to love one another better, and will be more united throughout their lives, and the Lord will bless them more abundantly. —*Joseph F. Smith* (GD, 278)

There is nothing that I can think of, in a religious way, that would grieve me more intensely than to see one of my boys marry an unbelieving girl, or one of my girls marry an unbelieving man. —*Joseph F. Smith* (CR, Oct. 1909, 5-6)

Marriage constitutes the most sacred relationship existing between man and woman. It is of heavenly origin, and is founded upon eternal principles. —*Joseph F. Smith* (LTT, 46)

Another word of the Lord to me is that, it is the duty of these young men here in the land of Zion to take the daughters of Zion to wife, and prepare tabernacles for the spirits of men, which are the children of our father in heaven. They are waiting for tabernacles, they are ordained to come here, and they ought to be born in the land of Zion instead of Babylon. This is the duty of the young men in Zion; and when the daughters of Zion are asked by the young men to join with them in marriage, instead of asking "Has this man a fine brick house, a span of fine horses and a fine carriage?" they should ask "Is he a man of God? Has he the Spirit of God with him? Is he a Latter-day Saint? Does he pray? Has he got the Spirit upon him to qualify him to build up the kingdom?" If he has that, never mind the carriage and brick house, take hold and unite yourselves together according to the law of God. —*Wilford Woodruff* (WW, 271)

It is our duty to get married at the proper time. It is the law of God. Therefore I would like to see you young men take these daughters of Zion to wife. —*Wilford Woodruff* (WW, 272)

You husbands now and then quarrel with your wives, and you wives quarrel with your husbands. . . . I will say, cease such folly, and have another kind of feeling; and treat everybody not as he always treats us, for that would not always be right; but let us do unto all men as we would have them do unto us. —*John Taylor* (GK, 228)

Husbands, do you love your wives and treat them right, or do you think that you yourselves are some great moguls who have a right to crowd upon them? They are given to you as a part of yourself, and you ought to treat them with all kindness, with mercy and long suffering, and not be harsh and bitter, or in any way desirous to display your authority. Then, you wives, treat your husbands right, and try to make them happy and comfortable. Endeavor to make your homes a little heaven, and try to cherish the good Spirit of God. —*John Taylor* (GK, 284)

I will give each of the young men in Israel, who have arrived at an age to marry, a mission to go straightway and get married to a good sister, fence a city lot, lay out garden and orchard and make a home. This is the mission that I give to all young men in Israel. —*Brigham Young* (BY, 196)

I say so to every man upon the face of the earth; if he wishes to be saved he cannot be saved without a woman by his side. —*Brigham Young* (LPS, 301)

When a seal is put upon the father and mother, it secures their posterity, so that they cannot be lost, but will be saved by virtue of the covenant of their father and mother. —*Joseph Smith, Jr.* (STJS, 360)

60. PARENTAL RESPONSIBILITIES

It is so obvious that the great good and the terrible evil in the world today are the sweet and the bitter fruits of the rearing of yesterday's children. As we train a new generation, so will the world be in a few years. If you are worried about the future, then look to the upbringing of your children. —*Gordon B. Hinckley* (BTE, 35)

I have seen conscientious men and women, people who are faithful and true, people who try to observe the teachings of the Church, who still experience broken hearts over the conduct of their children. . . . To any who may have such sons or daughters, may I suggest that you never quit trying. They are never lost until you have given up. Remember that it is love, more than any other thing, that will bring them back. Punishment is not likely to do it. Reprimands without love will not accomplish it. Patience, expressions of appreciation, and that strange and remarkable power which comes with prayer will eventually win through. —*Gordon B. Hinckley* (FETR , 65-67)

Inherent in the very act of creation is responsibility for the child who is created. None can with impunity run from that responsibility.

It is not enough simply to provide food and shelter for the physical being. There is an equal responsibility to provide nourishment and direction to the spirit and the mind and the heart. —*Gordon B. Hinckley* (Ensign, Nov. 1993, 59)

My plea—and I wish I were more eloquent in voicing it—is a plea to save the children. Too many of them walk with pain and fear, in loneliness and despair. Children need sunlight. They need happiness. They need kindness and refreshment and affection. Every home, regardless of the cost of the house, can provide an environment of love which will be an environment of salvation. —*Gordon B. Hinckley* (Ensign, Nov. 1994, 54)

You parents, love your children. Cherish them. They are so precious. They are so very, very important. They are the future. You need more than your own wisdom in rearing them. You need the help of the Lord. Pray for that help and follow the inspiration which you receive. —*Gordon B. Hinckley* (Ensign, Nov. 1995, 89)

Let us not misunderstand. The responsibilities of parenthood are of the greatest importance. The results of our efforts will have eternal consequences for us and the boys and girls we raise. Anyone who becomes a parent is under strict obligation to protect and love his children and assist them to return to their Heavenly Father. —*Howard W. Hunter* (CR, Oct. 1983, 16)

A successful parent is one who has loved, one who has sacrificed, and one who has cared for, taught, and ministered to the needs of a child. If you have done all of these and your child is still wayward or troublesome or worldly, it could well be that you are, nevertheless, a successful parent. Perhaps there are children who have come into the world that would challenge any set of parents under any set of circumstances. Likewise, perhaps there are others who would bless the lives of, and be a joy to, almost any father or mother. —*Howard W. Hunter* (CR, Oct. 1983)

There are many in the Church and in the world who are living with feelings of guilt and unworthiness because some of their sons and daughters have wandered or strayed from the fold. We understand that conscientious parents try their best, yet nearly all make mistakes. One does not launch into such a project as parenthood without soon realizing that there will be many errors along the way. Surely our Heavenly Father knows, when he entrusts his spirit children into the care of young and inexperienced parents, that there will be mistakes and errors in judgment. —*Howard W. Hunter* (WMJ, 111-112)

We must not give up hope for a child who has strayed. Many who have appeared to be completely lost have returned. We must be prayerful and, if possible, let our children know or our love and concern. —*Howard W. Hunter* (WMJ, 113)

Each of us is unique. Just as each of us starts at a different point in the race of life, and just as each of us had different strengths and weaknesses and talents, so each child is blessed with his own special set of characteristics. We must not assume that the Lord will judge the successes of one in precisely the same way as another. As parents we often assume that, if our children do not become overachievers in every way, we have failed. We should be careful in our judgments. —*Howard W. Hunter* (WMJ, 114)

We plead with parents to spend time with their children, both in teaching them and in building positive relationships. These are the things that create and foster strong family units and a stable society. —*Ezra Taft Benson* (ETB, 497)

Praise your children more than you correct them. Praise them for even their smallest achievement. Encourage your children to come to you for counsel with their problems and questions by listening to them every day. Discuss with them such important matters as dating, sex, and other matters affecting their growth and development, and do it early enough so they will not obtain information from questionable sources. —*Ezra Taft Benson* (CR, Nov. 81, 107)

May we always keep in mind that these spirits that have entered our homes are choice spirits. Many of them have been born under the covenant. As we look into their faces and contemplate their needs, we might well consider that some of them were probably choicer spirits up there than we were. It is a grave responsibility. May we not shirk it. —*Ezra Taft Benson* (ETB, 502)

It seems to me it would be a fine thing if every set of parents would have in every bedroom in their house a picture of the temple so the boy or girl from the time he is an infant could look at the picture every day and it becomes a part of his life. —*Spencer W. Kimball* (Ensign, Oct. 1979, 3)

Wise parents will see to it that their teaching is orthodox, character-building, and faith-promoting. —*Spencer W. Kimball* (SWK, 332)

Setting limits to what a child can do means to that child that you love him and respect him. If you permit the child to do all the things he would like to do without any limits, that means to him that you do not care much about him. —*Spencer W. Kimball* (SWK, 340-341)

We want you parents to create work for your children. Insist on them learning their lessons in school. Do not let them play all the time. There is a time for play, there is a time to work, and there is a time to study. —*Spencer W. Kimball* (SWK, 360)

What we do know is that righteous parents who strive to develop wholesome influences for their children will be held blameless at the last day, that they will succeed in saving most of their children, if not all. —*Spencer W. Kimball* (Ensign, Jan. 1984, 3-4.)

Teach your little children while they are at your knee and they will grow up to be stalwart. They may start away, but your love and your faith will bring them back. —*Harold B. Lee* (YLW, 292)

The time for a mother or father to teach a child is when the child has a question that needs to be answered. —*Harold B. Lee* (YLW, 76)

[A] more perfect combination of parents might be found in a mother who was firm beneath her gentleness and a father who was gentle beneath his firmness, which is a good formula for all parents to follow. —*Harold B. Lee* (YLW, 78)

Those who refuse as husbands and wives to have children are proving themselves already too small for the infinitude of God's creative powers. —*Harold B. Lee* (YLW, 267)

I say to you Latter-day Saint mothers and fathers, if you will rise to the responsibility of teaching your children at home . . . the day will soon be dawning when the whole world will come to our doors and will say 'Show us your way that we may walk in your path.'—*Harold B. Lee* (IE, Dec. 1964, 1081)

Parents will be responsible for the actions of their children, if they have failed to teach their children by example and by precept. —*Joseph Fielding Smith* (DS1, 316)

You are to teach by example as well as precept. You are to kneel with your children in prayer. You are to teach them in all humility of the mission of our Savior, Jesus Christ. You have to show them the way, and the father who shows his son the way will not say to him: "Son, go to Sunday School, or go to Mutual, or go to the priesthood meeting," but he will say: "Come and go with me." He will teach by example. —*Joseph Fielding Smith* (CR, Oct. 1948, 153-154)

One of the paramount duties, I might say the paramount duty, of parents is to win and merit the confidence and respect of their children. . . . Too few parents have the confidence of their children. —*David O. McKay* (CR, Apr. 1944, 107)

Example is more potent than precept. Parents have the duty to be what they would have their children become in regard to courtesy, sincerity, temperance, and courage to do right at all times. —*David O. McKay* (CR, Apr. 1935, 114)

There is something in the depths of the human soul which revolts against neglectful parenthood. —*David O. McKay* (CR, Apr. 1935, 112-113)

The most effective way to teach is by example. . . . Parents should ever keep in mind that admonition is of much more avail when example conforms to the admonition given. —*David O. McKay* (CR, Oct. 1954, 9-11)

The best time to teach the child obedience is between the ages of two to four. It is then that the child should learn that there are limits to his actions, that there are certain bounds beyond which he cannot pass with impunity. This conformity to some conditions can be easily obtained with kindness, but with firmness. —*David O. McKay* (CR, Apr. 1955, 27)

Children are more influenced by sermons you act than by sermons you preach. It is the consistent parent who gains the trust of his child. When children feel that you reciprocate their trust, they will not violate your confidence nor bring dishonor to your name. —*David O. McKay* (CR, Apr. 1955, 26—27)

The greatest duty that fathers and mothers have to perform is the religious training and development of their child's character. —*David O. McKay* (CR, Apr. 1968, 146)

Children are the jewels that will enrich the crowns of parents in the hereafter, if they take advantage of the opportunity given them. —*George Albert Smith* (SGO, 148)

Our children are the most precious gifts that our Father in Heaven bestows upon us. If we can guide their feet in the pathway of salvation, there will be joy eternal for us and for them. —*George Albert Smith* (CR, Apr. 1915, 95)

It is the duty of fathers and mothers to call their families together and instruct them. —*George Albert Smith* (CR, Apr. 1929, 32)

Nobody else can perform the part that God has assigned to us as parents. We have assumed an obligation when we have been the means of bringing children into the world. We can't place that responsibility upon any organization. It is ours. —*George Albert Smith* (CR, Apr. 1933, 72)

If we as parents will so order our lives that our children will know and realize in their hearts that we are in very deed Latter-day Saints, that we actually know what we are talking about, they, by seeking after the Lord, will get that same testimony. —*Heber J. Grant* (GS, 154)

I have heard men and women say that they were going to let their sons and daughters grow to maturity before they sought to teach them the principles of the gospel, that they were not going to cram the gospel down them in their childhood, before they were able to comprehend it. When I hear men and women say this, I think they are lacking faith in the principles of the gospel and do not comprehend it as they should. The Lord has said it is our duty to teach our children in their youth, and I prefer to take His word for it rather than the words of those who are not obeying His commandments. It is folly to imagine that our children will grow up with a knowledge of the gospel without teaching. —*Heber J. Grant* (CR, Apr. 1902, 79-80)

I pray that your example may be such that your children will live the gospel of Jesus Christ, because that is of more value than anything else in the world. —*Heber J. Grant* (GS, 156)

The Lord has given us a commandment that we shall teach our children the principles of the gospel and have them baptized when they are eight years of age. If we fail to keep this commandment, the blessings that are promised to us by the Lord will be revoked, and we will have mourning and sorrow in seeing our children grow up without a desire to serve God. —*Heber J. Grant* (GS, 164)

A man and woman who have embraced the gospel of Jesus Christ and who have begun life together, should be able by their power, example and influence to cause their children to emulate them in lives of virtue, honor, and in integrity to the kingdom of God which will redound to their own interest and salvation. No one can advise my children with greater earnestness and solicitude for their happiness and salvation than I can myself. Nobody has more interest in the welfare of my own children than I have. —*Joseph F. Smith* (GD, 278)

Teach your children so that they cannot commit sin without violating their conscience, teach them the truth, that they may not depart from it. . . . [I]f you will make them to feel that you love them, that you are their parents, that they are your children, and keep them near to you, they will not go very far from you, and they will not commit any very great sin. —*Joseph F. Smith* (CR, Apr. 1902, 87)

Those things which we call extraordinary, remarkable, or unusual may make history, but they do not make real life. After all, to do well those things which God ordained to be the common lot of all man-kind, is the truest greatness. To be a successful father or a successful mother is greater than to be a successful general or a successful statesman. One is universal and eternal greatness, the other is ephemeral. —*Joseph F. Smith* (JI, Dec. 15, 1905, 752)

The parents in Zion will be held responsible for the acts of their children, not only until they become eight years old, but, perhaps, throughout all the lives of their children, provided they have neglected their duty to their children while they were under their care and guidance and the parents were responsible for them. —*Joseph F. Smith* (CR, Apr. 1910, 6)

God forbid that there should be any of us so unwisely indulgent, so thoughtless and so shallow in our affection for our children that we dare not check them in a wayward course, in wrong-doing and in their foolish love for the things of the world more than for the things of righteousness, for fear of offending them. —*Joseph F. Smith* (GD, 286)

We have our little follies and our weaknesses; we should try to overcome them as fast as possible, and we should inculcate this feeling in the hearts of our children, that the fear of God may grow up with them from their very youth, and that they may learn to comport themselves properly before Him under all circumstances. —*Lorenzo Snow* (LS, 35)

None of us know what course our children will take. We set good examples before them, and we strive to teach them righteous principles. But when they come to years of accountability they have their agency and they act for themselves. —*Wilford Woodruff* (WW, 249)

Let us all look at home, and each one try to govern his own family and set his own house in order, and do that which is required of us, realizing that each one is held responsible before the Lord for his or her individual actions only. —*Wilford Woodruff* (WW, 264)

Our children should not be neglected; they should receive a proper education in both spiritual and temporal things. That is the best legacy any parents can leave to their children. We should teach them to pray, and instil into their minds while young every correct principle. Ninety-nine out of every hundred children who are taught by their parents the principles of honesty and integrity, truth and virtue, will observe them through life. Such principles will exalt any people or nation who make them the rule of their conduct. Show me a mother who prays, who has passed through the trials of life by prayer, who has trusted in the Lord God of Israel in her trials and difficulties, and her children will follow in the same path. —*Wilford Woodruff* (WW, 267-268)

Train your children to be intelligent and industrious. First teach them the value of healthful bodies, and how to preserve them in soundness and vigor; teach them to entertain the highest regard for virtue and chastity, and likewise encourage them to develop the intellectual faculties with which they are endowed. —*John Taylor* (JD, 14:357)

Parents, are you full of fidelity yourselves to every principle of godliness, and do you surround your sons and daughters with every safeguard to shield them from the arts of the vile? Do you teach them that chastity in both man and woman should be more highly esteemed than life itself? Or do you leave them in their ignorance and inexperience to mix with any society they may choose, at any hour that may be convenient to them, and to be exposed to the wiles of the seducer and the corrupt? These are questions you will all have to answer either to your shame and condemnation or to your joy and eternal happiness. —*John Taylor* (GK, 283)

We are commanded of the Lord to obtain knowledge, both by study and by faith, seeking it out of the best books. And it becomes us to teach our children, and afford them instructions in every branch of education calculated to promote their welfare, leaving those false acquirements which tend to infidelity, and to lead away the mind and affection from the things of God. —*John Taylor* (GK, 268)

Teach your children from their youth, never to set their hearts immoderately upon an object of this world. —*Brigham Young* (BY, 207)

Bring up your children in the love and fear of the Lord; study their dispositions and their temperaments, and deal with them accordingly, never allowing yourself to correct them in the heat of passion; teach them to love you rather than to fear you. —*Brigham Young* (BY, 207)

We should never permit ourselves to do anything that we are not willing to see our children do. We should set them an example that we wish them to imitate. Do we realize this?—*Brigham Young* (BY, 208)

Parents should never drive their children, but lead them along, giving them knowledge as their minds are prepared to receive it. Chastening may be necessary betimes, but parents should govern their children by faith rather than by the rod, leading them kindly by good example into all truth and holiness. —*Brigham Young* (BY, 208)

Children need directing and teaching what is right in a kind, affectionate manner. —*Brigham Young* (BY, 209)

61. FATHERS—ROLES AND RESPONSIBILITIES

How much more beautiful would be the world and the society in which we live if every father looked upon his children as the most precious of his assets, if he led them by the power of example in kindness and love, and if in times of stress he blessed them by the authority of the holy priesthood. —*Gordon B. Hinckley* (BTE, 40)

Any man who will make his wife's' comfort his first concern, will stay in love with her throughout their lives and through the eternity yet to come. —*Gordon B. Hinckley* (CN, Dec. 2, 1995, 2)

My brethren, you will never have in all your lives a greater asset than the woman into whose eyes you looked as you joined hands over the altar in the House of the Lord. She will be your most precious possession in time or eternity. Respect her as your companion. Respect her and live with honor together and there will be happiness in your lives. —*Gordon B. Hinckley* (CN, May 4, 1996, 2)

I regret that there are some men undeserving of the love of their wives and children. There are children who fear their fathers, and wives who fear their husbands. If there be any such men within the hearing of my voice, as a servant of the Lord I rebuke you and call you to repentance. Discipline yourselves. Master your temper. Most of the things that make you angry are of very small consequence. And what a terrible price you are paying for your anger. Ask the Lord to forgive you. Ask your wife to forgive you. Apologize to your children. —*Gordon B. Hinckley* (Ensign, Nov. 1996, 68)

Effective family leadership, brethren, requires both quantity and quality time. —*Howard W. Hunter* (Ensign, Nov. 1994, 50-51)

We encourage you, brethren, to remember that priesthood is a righteous authority only. Earn the respect and confidence of your children through your loving relationship with them. A righteous father protects his children with his time and presence in their social, educational, and spiritual activities and responsibilities. Tender expressions of love and affection toward children are as much the responsibility of the father as the mother. Tell your children you love them. —*Howard W. Hunter* (Ensign, Nov. 1994, 51)

We urge you to do all in your power to allow your wife to remain in the home, caring for the children while you provide for the family the best you can. We further emphasize that men who abandon their family and fail to meet their responsibility to care for those they have fathered may find their eligibility for a temple recommend and their standing in the Church in jeopardy. In cases of divorce or separation, men must demonstrate that they are meeting family support payments mandated by law and obligated by the principles of the Church in order to qualify for the blessings of the Lord. —*Howard W. Hunter* (Ensign, Nov. 1994, 51)

First and foremost, nothing except God Himself takes priority over your wife in your life—not work, not recreation, not hobbies. Your wife is your most precious eternal helpmate—your companion. —*Ezra Taft Benson* (CR , Nov. 87, 48)

Once you determine that a high priority in your life is to see that your wife and your children are happy, you will do all in your power to do so. I am not just speaking of satisfying material desires, but of filling other vital needs such as appreciation, compliments, comforting, encouraging, listening, and giving love and affection. —*Ezra Taft Benson* (CR, May 81, 34)

A man may succeed in business or his Church calling, but if he fails in his home he will face eternity in disappointment. —*Ezra Taft Benson* (ETB, 509)

Fatherhood is not a matter of station or wealth; it is a matter of desire, diligence, and determination to see one's family exalted in the celestial kingdom. If that prize is lost, nothing else really matters. —*Ezra Taft Benson* (CUC , 62)

A good model is the best teacher. Therefore, a father's first responsibility is to set the proper example. —*Ezra Taft Benson* (AWW, 67)

We have heard of men who have said to their wives, "I hold the priesthood and you've got to do what I say." Such a man should be tried for his membership. —*Spencer W. Kimball* (SWK, 316)

In family life, men must and should be considerate of their wives, not only in the bearing of children, but in caring for them through childhood. The mother's health must be conserved, and the husband's consideration for his wife is his first duty, and self-control a dominant factor in all their relationships. —*Spencer W. Kimball* (CR, Nov. 1976, 127)

Don't neglect your wives, you brethren. Don't neglect your children. Take time for family home evening. Draw your children around about you. Teach them, guide them, and guard them. There was never a time when we needed so much the strength and the solidarity of the home. —*Harold B. Lee* (Ensign, July 1973, 98-99)

We must impress upon every father that he will be held responsible for the eternal welfare of his family: that means coming into the Church with his family; that means going to sacrament meeting with his family; that means holding family home evenings to keep his family intact; it means preparing himself to take them to the temple, so that there can be prepared thereby the steps that will make for an eternal family home. —*Harold B. Lee* (Ensign, July 1972, 2)

Any young man who carelessly neglects this great commandment to marry, or who does not marry because of a selfish desire to avoid the responsibilities which married life will bring, is taking a course which is displeasing in the sight of God. Exaltation means responsibility. There can be no exaltation without it. —*Joseph Fielding Smith* (DS2, 74)

The father, particularly, if he be a member of the Church and holds the priesthood, who fails to set a proper example before his children is a delinquent and is a contributor to child delinquency. —*David O. McKay* (CR, Oct. 1948, 118)

Fathers may and should exercise a helpful, restraining influence, where a mother's tenderness and love might lead to indulgence on the part of the children. In this respect, however, every father should ever keep in mind that he was once a mischievous youngster himself and deal with his boy sympathetically. —*David O. McKay* (IE, 49:691)

I ask today that every father in the Church see to it that, in all sincerity, he impress his children with the reality of the existence of God, and with the reality that God will guide and protect his children. You carry that responsibility. —*David O. McKay* (CR, Oct. 1922, 78)

Say nothing that will hurt your wife, that will cause her tears, even though she might cause you provocation. . . . He is a weak man who flies into a passion, whether he is working a machine or plowing or writing or whatever he may be doing in the home. A man of the priesthood should not fly into a passion. Learn to be dignified. —*David O. McKay* (CR, Oct. 1954, 85)

Fathers, I do not care how much property you have, what honor you may attain to—it is immaterial to me whether your names are written in the records of history because of your accomplishments, or of mere monetary things. The greatest blessings are your boys and your girls. I fear that we may neglect our opportunities with these young people and spend more time with material things than we should, and I repeat, so that not any of us will forget it, that the most precious gifts given to us are our husbands, our wives and our children, with whom we may have companionship throughout eternity. —*George Albert Smith* (SGO, 152)

Live in such a way, in love and kindness, that peace and prayer and thanksgiving will be in your homes together. Do not let your homes just be a place to hang your hats at night and get your meals and then run off some place else but let your homes be the abiding place of the Spirit of the Lord. —*George Albert Smith* (CR, Apr. 1948, 183-184)

I am asking myself the question, "How many of you who are here tonight, before you came here to wait upon the Lord, put your arms around the woman who stood by your side, the mother of your children, and told her that you were grateful that she would keep the home-fires burning when you couldn't be there?" I wonder if we appreciate the daughters of God as He appreciates them. Do we treasure their virtues and their faith and their devotion and their motherhood as our Heavenly Father does?—*George Albert Smith* (CR, Apr. 1943, 90-91)

Don't do anything yourselves that you would have to say to your boy, "Don't do it." Live so that you can say, "My son, do as I do, follow me, emulate my example." That is the way fathers should live, every one of us; and it is a shame, a weakening, shameful thing for any member of the Church to pursue a course that he knows is not right, and that he would rather his children should not follow. —*Joseph F. Smith* (CR, Apr. 1915, 7)

The man that will be angry at his boy, and try to correct him while he is in anger, is in the greatest fault; he is more to be pitied and more to be condemned than the child who has done wrong. You can only correct your children by love, in kindness, by love unfeigned, by persuasion, and reason. —*Joseph F. Smith* (GD, 317)

It becomes the duties of fathers in Israel to wake up and become saviors of men, that they may walk before the Lord in that strength of faith, and that determined energy, that will insure them the inspiration of the Almighty to teach the words of life to their families. —*Lorenzo Snow* (LS, 135)

A husband should value his wife. To the husbands I say: Many of you do not value your wives as you should. —*Lorenzo Snow* (LS, 135)

I wish to say a few words to the elders. I suppose we are all elders. Do you teach your families the way of life and salvation? Do you teach your wives and children the counsel of God? We should impress upon the minds of our children the evil consequences of committing sin or breaking any of the laws of God, they should be made to understand that by doing wrong they will inherit sorrow and tribulation which they can easily escape by doing right, and they should learn this principle by precept without learning sorrow and affliction by experience from doing wrong. —*Wilford Woodruff* (WW, 104-105)

Every father, after he has received his patriarchal blessing, is a patriarch to his own family, and has the right to confer patriarchal blessings upon his family; which blessings will be just as legal as those conferred by any patriarch of the church: in fact it is his right; and a patriarch in blessing his children, can only bless as his mouthpiece. —*John Taylor* (GK, 146)

Let the husband and father learn to bend his will to the will of his God, and then instruct his wives and children in this lesson of self-government by his example as well as by precept. —*Brigham Young* (BY, 198)

It is for the husband to learn how to gather around his family the comforts of life, how to control his passions and temper, and how to command the respect, not only of his family but of all his brethren, sisters, and friends. —*Brigham Young* (BY, 198)

I can pick out scores of men in this congregation who have driven their children from them by using the wooden rod. Where there is severity there is no affection or filial feeling in the hearts of either party; the children would rather be away from father than be with him. —*Brigham Young* (BY, 203)

62. MOTHERS—ROLES AND RESPONSIBILITIES

In this age when more and more women are turning to daily work, how tremendous it is once in a while to stop and recognize that the greatest job that any woman will ever do will be in nurturing and teaching and lifting and encouraging and rearing her children in righteousness and truth. —*Gordon B. Hinckley* (Ensign, June 1971, 72)

Yours, my sisters, is the privilege to teach, yours the responsibility, yours the opportunity. —*Gordon B. Hinckley* (Ensign, Nov. 1985, 87)

Let every mother realize that she has no greater blessing than the children which have come to her as a gift from the Almighty; that she has no greater mission than to rear them in light and truth, and understanding and love; that she will have no greater happiness than to see them grow into young men and women who respect principles of virtue, who walk free from the stain of immorality and from the shame of delinquency. —*Gordon B. Hinckley* (CR, Nov. 1993, 60)

Begin early to expose children to books. The mother who fails to read to her small children does a disservice to them and a disservice to herself. It takes time, yes, much of it. It takes self-discipline. It takes organizing and budgeting the minutes and hours of the day. But it will never be a bore as you watch young minds come to know characters, expressions, and ideas. Good reading can become a love affair, far more fruitful in long-term effects than many other activities in which children use their time. —*Gordon B. Hinckley* (FETR , 69)

If the purpose of your daily employment is simply to get money for a boat or a fancy automobile or some other desirable but unnecessary thing, and in the process you lose the companionship of your children and the opportunity to rear them, you may find that you have lost the substance while grasping at the shadow. —*Gordon B. Hinckley* (Ensign, Nov. 1983, 83)

I recognize . . . that there are some women (it has become very many in fact) who have to work to provide for the needs of their families. To you I say, do the very best you can. I hope that if you are employed full-time you are doing it to ensure that basic needs are met and not simply to indulge a taste for an elaborate home, fancy cars, and other luxuries. The greatest job that any mother will ever do will be in nurturing, teaching, lifting, encouraging, and rearing her children in righteousness and truth. None other can adequately take her place. —*Gordon B. Hinckley* (Ensign, Nov. 1996, 69)

Our wives deserve great credit for the heavy work load they carry day in and day out within our homes. No one expends more energy than a devoted mother and wife. —*Howard W. Hunter* (Ensign, Nov. 1975, 124)

It seems to me that there is a great need to rally the women of the Church to stand with and for the Brethren in stemming the tide of evil that surrounds us and in moving forward the work of our Savior. —*Howard W. Hunter* (Ensign, Nov. 1992, 96)

As you are anxiously engaged in good causes, you can show others that by taking Christ into their lives and accepting his gospel, with its saving ordinances and covenants, they can reach their true potential in this life and in the hereafter. —*Howard W. Hunter* (Ensign, Nov. 1994, 97)

Working mothers should remember that their children usually need more of mother than of money. —*Ezra Taft Benson* (ETB, 526)

Our young people need love and attention, not indulgence. They need empathy and understanding, not indifference from mothers and fathers. They need the parents' time. A mother's kindly teachings and her love for and confidence in a teenage son or daughter can literally save them from a wicked world. —*Ezra Taft Benson* (CLP , 36)

Do you know one reason why righteous mothers love their children so much? It is because they sacrifice so much for them. We love what we sacrifice for and we sacrifice for what we love. —*Ezra Taft Benson* (Ensign, Dec. 1988, 6)

No woman has ever been asked by the Church authorities to follow her husband into an evil pit. She is to follow him as he follows and obeys the Savior of the world, but in deciding this, she should always be sure she is fair. —*Spencer W. Kimball* (Ensign, Mar. 1976, 70)

Let every working mother honestly weigh the matter and be sure the Lord approves before she rushes her babies off to the nursery, her children off to school, her husband off to work, and herself off to her employment. Let her be certain that she is not rationalizing herself away from her children merely to provide for them greater material things. Let her analyze well before she permits her precious ones to come home to an empty house where their plaintive cry, "Mother," finds no loving answer. —*Spencer W. Kimball* (IE, Dec. 1963, 1071)

We want our women to be well educated, for children may not recover from the ignorance of their mothers. —*Spencer W. Kimball* (SWK, 320)

When you have fully complemented your husband in home life and borne the children, growing up full of faith, integrity, responsibility, and goodness, then you have achieved, your accomplishments supreme, without peer, and you will be the envy through time and eternity of your sisters who have spent themselves in selfish pursuits. —*Spencer W. Kimball* (SWK, 327)

A child needs a mother available more than all the things which money can buy. —*Spencer W. Kimball* (IE, June 1963, 490)

You are bound to the law of your husband only so far as he keeps the law of God and no further. —*Harold B. Lee* (YLW, 33)

She must, if she would support her husband, be an honest, loving critic, and must not constantly say, "You are absolutely perfect, darling; I worship at your shrine—you can do no wrong." Rather, she should tactfully comment and point out ways and means to improve. Yes, each mother will live again in the lives of her children, but her greatest success will be her husband's success. Her greatest reward will be when she can say, when her husband succeeds or when she has a child who excels, "I helped him along the way."—*Harold B. Lee* (YLW, 77)

Don't give up on the boy or girl in that insufferable state of superegoism through which some teenagers go. I plead with you for those boys and those girls. Don't give up on the boy or girl in that impossible stage of independence and disregard of family discipline. —*Harold B. Lee* (YLW, 275)

Now, you sisters, polish your husbands as best you can while you have them here, and then hope that the Lord will continue the process beyond the veil. —*Harold B. Lee* (YLW, 277)

If you would reform the world from error and vice, begin by enlisting the mothers. The future of society is in the hands of mothers. If the world were in danger, only the mothers could save it. —*Harold B. Lee* (YLW, 294)

There is nothing in the teachings of the gospel which declares that men are superior to women. The Lord has given unto men the power of priesthood and sent them forth to labor in his service. A woman's calling is in a different direction. The most noble, exalting calling of all is that which has been given to women as the mothers of men. Women do not hold the priesthood, but if they are faithful and true, they will become priestesses and queens in the kingdom of God, and that implies that they will be given authority. —*Joseph Fielding Smith* (DS3, 178)

The more woman becomes like man, the less he will respect her; civilization weakens as man's estimate of woman lessens. —*David O. McKay* (GI, 378)

A beautiful, modest, gracious woman is creation's masterpiece. When to these virtues a woman possesses as guiding stars in her life righteousness and godliness and an irresistible impulse and desire to make others happy, no one will question if she be classed among those who are the truly great. —*David O. McKay* (GI, 449)

Motherhood is just another name for sacrifice. —*David O. McKay* (GI, 456)

Mothers, do not forget that you owe something to your children and to your husband. You, too, can keep yourself attractive. You, too, can refrain from finding fault. You, too, can contribute to the happiness and contentment of the home, the sweetest place on earth. That is about as near heaven as you will get here. Do not make it a hell. Some do. —*David O. McKay* (CR, Oct. 1955, 130)

A growing desire for economic independence or a too eager willingness to improve financial circumstances has influenced too many of our mothers to neglect the greatest of all responsibilities—the rearing of a family. —*David O. McKay* (CR, Apr. 1965, 6)

It is a mother's duty so to live that her children will associate with her everything that is beautiful, sweet, and pure. —*David O. McKay* (CR, Apr. 1965, 7)

If I have done anything that I should not have done in my life, it would be something that I could not have learned in my mother's home. —*George Albert Smith* (SGO, 194)

Look over the world and study the characters who have carved out of the conditions that surrounded them, the fame that has attached to great names, and I think you will agree with me that seldom may be found in this world a great man who did not have a great mother. —*George Albert Smith* (SGO, 140)

I am grateful that I had a mother who devoted herself to her children. Whatever I may have accomplished in life, or may still accomplish, will be due in a large measure to my mother. God bless the name and memory of mother. —*George Albert Smith* (SGO, 146)

Without the wonderful work of the women I realize that the Church would have been a failure. The mother in the family far more than the father, is the one who instills in the hearts of the children, a testimony and a love for the gospel of Jesus Christ. . . . [W]herever you find a woman who is devoted to this work, almost without exception you will find that her children are devoted to it. —*Heber J. Grant* (GS, 150)

It is more blessed to give than to receive, and the women are always ready and willing to give, more than the men are. There is a willingness to sacrifice on the part of our dear sisters, and of women generally, all over the world, that we do not find in men. They are leaders in all things that make for spiritual uplift. —*Heber J. Grant* (GS, 151)

A mother's love seems to be the most perfect and the most sincere, the strongest of any love we know anything about. I, for one, rejoice in it because of its wonderful example to me. —*Heber J. Grant* (GS, 152)

I have often said, and will repeat it, that the love of a true mother comes nearer being like the love of God than any other kind of love. —*Joseph F. Smith* (GD, 315)

There are people fond of saying that women are the weaker vessels. I don't believe it. Physically, they may be; but spiritually, morally, religiously and in faith, what man can match a woman who is really convinced? . . . They are always more willing to make sacrifices, and are the peers of men in stability, Godliness, morality and faith. —*Joseph F. Smith* (GD, 352)

You mothers, teach your children that when they get any money they should pay one-tenth of it to the Lord, however little it may be. Educate them to pay their tithing in full. —*Lorenzo Snow* (LS, 157)

The thought has impressed itself upon me that the brethren of this Church, myself included, have been wonderfully favored of the Lord in having the companionship and assistance of such faithful, loyal wives and mothers as He has blessed us with. It is difficult to imagine what we should have done or what progress the work of the Lord would have made without them. When we have been absent on foreign missions, their missions at home have generally been no less arduous than ours abroad; and in the midst of trial and privation they have exhibited a patience, a fortitude, and a self-help that has been truly inspiring. Thank God for the women of this Church. —*Lorenzo Snow* (LS, 139)

No mother in Israel should let a day pass over her head without teaching her children to pray. You should pray yourselves, and teach your children to do the same, and you should bring them up in this way, that when you have passed away and they take your places in bearing off the great work of God, they may have principles instilled into their minds that will sustain them in time and in eternity. I have often said it is the mother who forms the mind of the child. —*Wilford Woodruff* (WW, 222)

I consider that the mother has a greater influence over her posterity than any other person can have. And the question has arisen some time: "When does this education begin?" Our prophets have said, "When the spirit life from God enters into the tabernacle." The condition of the mother at that time will have its effect upon the fruit of her womb; and from the birth of the child, and all through life, the teachings and the example of the mother govern and control, in a great measure, that child, and her influence is felt by it through time and eternity. —*Wilford Woodruff* (WW, 269)

Sisters, put away from you the vanities and frivolities of the world, administer to the poor and the afflicted. The sisters know how to sympathize with and administer to those who are poor, afflicted, and downcast; and let the brethren help them in their kindly ministrations. —*John Taylor* (GK, 177)

Let the sisters take care of themselves, and make themselves beautiful . . . Make yourselves like angels in goodness and beauty. —*Brigham Young* (BY, 215)

We believe that women are useful, not only to sweep houses, wash dishes, make beds, and raise babies, but that they should stand behind the counter, study law or physic, or become good bookkeepers and be able to do the business in any counting house, and all this to enlarge their sphere of usefulness for the benefit of society at large. In following these things they but answer the design of their creation. —*Brigham Young* (BY, 216-217)

It is the calling of the wife and mother to know what to do with everything that is brought into the house, laboring to make her home desirable to her husband and children, making herself an Eve in the midst of a little paradise of her own creating, securing her husband's love and confidence, and tying her offspring to herself, with a love that is stronger than death, for an everlasting inheritance. —*Brigham Young* (BY, 198)

Now, I say the women have great influence. Look at the nations of the earth. Any nation you like, no matter which, and you enlist the sympathies of the female portion of it and what is there you cannot perform?—*Brigham Young* (BY, 199)

[I]f you promise a chastisement, keep your word, but be cautious!—*Brigham Young* (BY, 210)

Mothers, will you be missionaries? We will appoint you a mission to teach your children their duty, and instead of ruffles and fine dresses to adorn the body, teach them that which will adorn their minds. —*Brigham Young* (BY, 210)

When I go into a house, I can soon know whether the woman is an economical housekeeper or not; and if I stay a few days, I can tell whether a husband can get rich or not. If she is determined on her own course, and will waste and spoil the food entrusted to her, that man will always be poor. —*Brigham Young* (BY, 213)

63. YOUTH—ROLES AND RESPONSIBILITIES

"What are little girls made of? Sugar and spice, and everything nice." So goes the old nursery rhyme. But more importantly, they are the promise of the future. Through them, eventually, must filter the qualities of all of the earlier generations, which will become the bone and the tissue, the minds and the spirits, of the generations yet to be.

To you young girls I say with all of the strength and conviction I can muster, be sweet, be good, be strong and virtuous and wonderful. —*Gordon B. Hinckley* (Ensign, Nov. 1983, 81)

The Lord expects each of us to live productive and useful lives. Youth is the season of preparation, and we will please him if we apply ourselves to train our minds and hands that we may make a more substantial contribution to he society of which we are a part. —*Gordon B. Hinckley* (Ensign, May 1985, 49)

When we save a girl, we save generations. No one can foretell the consequences of faithfulness in the life of a young woman. —*Gordon B. Hinckley* (Ensign, Sept. 1988, 10)

My dear young friends, I repeat that the most important decision of life is the decision concerning your companion. Choose prayerfully, and when you are married, be fiercely loyal one to another. Selfishness is the great destroyer of happy family life. If you will make your first concern the comfort, the well-being, and the happiness of your companion, sublimating any personal concern to that loftier goal, you will be happy, and your marriage will go on throughout eternity. —*Gordon B. Hinckley* (CN, Sept. 2 1995, 2)

Children ought to respect their parents. . . . Children need to overcome their selfishness and look to their parents for love and understanding and training and wisdom. —*Gordon B. Hinckley* (CN, Nov. 4, 1995, 2)

Young women, guard and protect your virtue as you would your very life. We want you to live the morally clean life all of your life. We want the morally clean life to be your way of life. —*Ezra Taft Benson* (CLP , 18)

Now, there are some things that come only with age, and one of those is wisdom. Father and mother may be bent over, in part because of the responsibility of bearing you and caring for you. Just remember you need them, you need their counsel. —*Ezra Taft Benson* (ETB, 520-521)

Youth have a duty to themselves. They need to develop in themselves the finest characteristics of mankind: Inward peace, faith, humility, integrity, charity, courage, thrift, cooperation, and an ability for good hard work—all ingredients for a good character. —*Ezra Taft Benson* (ETB, 552)

Your most important friendships should be with your own brothers and sisters and with your father and mother. —*Ezra Taft Benson* (CLP , 14)

There will be a new spirit in Zion when the young women will say to their boyfriends, "If you cannot get a temple recommend, then I am not about to tie my life to you, even for mortality!" And the young returned missionary will say to his girlfriend, "I am sorry, but as much as I love you, I will not marry out of the holy temple."—*Ezra Taft Benson* (CLP , 22)

Wanted! Youth who will maturely carve their own destinies from the hard marble of life with the chisels of courage and mallets of determination and undeviating purpose. —*Spencer W. Kimball* (SWK, 161)

Do not take the chance of dating nonmembers, or members who are untrained and faithless. A girl may say, "Oh, I do not intend to marry this person. It is just a `fun' date." But one cannot afford to take a chance on falling in love with someone who may never accept the gospel. —*Spencer W. Kimball* (MF, 241-242)

Get a notebook, my young folks, a journal that will last through all time, and maybe the angels may quote from it for eternity. —*Spencer W. Kimball* (NE, Oct. 1975, 4)

I remind you young men that regardless of your present age, you are building your life; it will be cheap and shoddy or it will be valuable and beautiful; it will be full of constructive activities or it can be destructive; it can be full of joy and happiness, or it can be full of misery. It all depends upon you and your attitudes, for your altitude, or the height you climb, is dependent upon your attitude or your response to situations. —*Spencer W. Kimball* (CR, May 1985, 47)

You are building today the castles you will live in throughout eternity and deciding the place you will occupy in your Father's business hereafter. There is joy in heaven when you who are failing reform your ways and return to a standard of activity that assures your success. There will be mourning in heaven if you fail in life's education, but there is nothing your Heavenly Father can do about it unless you open the door by prayer and the living of a good life and invite him to counsel with you. —*Harold B. Lee* (DSL, 86)

The youth who seeks constantly for a thrill in his pleasures is following a dangerous road. He is hunting for the "rapture of the moment" and in so doing he may "lose the peace of years." Tell me what you do when you don't have to do anything and I'll tell you what you are. —*Harold B. Lee* (DSL, 159)

You sons and daughters, pray before you go out on a date—pray that you may have a good time and conduct yourselves according to Church standards that the Lord will help you to come home safely. —*Harold B. Lee* (DSL, 223)

Youth, if you want to be guided by wisdom, stay close to your parents. Listen to the counsel of your father and your mother and lean heavily upon the experience of their lives, because they are entitled to inspiration in the rearing of their family. —*Harold B. Lee* (SHP, 376)

I wish this could be driven into the hearts of all our youth today. There never was a truly great man who was not at the same time truly virtuous. —*Harold B. Lee* (HBL, 605)

Young people: Is it the body you are going to serve and be a slave to or is it the spirit you are going to develop, and live happily in this life and in the world to come?—*David O. McKay* (IE, 52:602)

To be the worthy son or the worthy daughter of noble parents is one of the greatest responsibilities of youth, one of the important duties of life. Disloyalty to righteous parents is as reprehensible as disloyalty to God. There is a sacred trust in sonship which should never be violated. —*David O. McKay* (IE, 43:395)

We are living in an age of gadgetry which threatens to produce a future generation of softness. Flabbiness of character more than flabbiness of muscles lies at the root of most of the problems facing American youth. —*David O. McKay* (CR, Apr. 1959, 72)

He is recreant, indeed, who for selfish indulgence would bring disgrace upon his parents, and upon the good name he bears. —*David O. McKay* (CR, Apr. 1959, 73)

Girls, follow that sweet mother and her teachings. Boys, be true to your fathers who try to live the gospel; then strangers, seeing such homes, will say, "Well, if that is the result of Mormonism, I think it is good." You will show your faith by your works in everyday life. —*David O. McKay* (CR, Oct. 1961, 124-125)

A girl who sacrifices self-respect for social popularity debases true womanhood. A spotless character, founded upon the ability to say "no" in the presence of those who mock and jeer, wins the respect and love of men and women whose opinion is most worthwhile. —*David O. McKay* (CR, Apr. 1967, 7)

I want to say to the boys and girls, to the young men and women, to the youth of the Church and of all the world: Honor your fathers and your mothers. Honor the names that you bear, because some day you will have the privilege and the obligation of reporting to them (and to your Father in heaven) what you have done with their name. —*George Albert Smith* (SGO, 112)

Our Latter-day Saint youth today have a glorious heritage, rich blessings and abundant opportunity to achieve success, if they will but retain the ideals that drove their forefathers on to many remarkable accomplishments. —*George Albert Smith* (SGO, 154)

If our youth today are to enjoy the same faith, integrity, modesty, humility and kindness of their forebears, and avail themselves of the developments that are yet to come, they may, if they will, be among the most intelligent and happiest youth of the world. —*George Albert Smith* (SGO, 156)

And I say to all of you, honor your fathers and mothers. Let them know you appreciate them by what you do for them. One of the commandments of God is to love and honor thy father and mother. And we may best honor them and honor our Father in Heaven by doing the things we know we should do. —*George Albert Smith* (GAS, 131)

Isn't it strange that one mother can take care of ten children but ten children can't take care of one mother?—*George Albert Smith* (CP, 34)

So far as the youth of Zion are concerned, I have no fear, because those who are keeping the commandments of the Lord are progressing and growing in strength and in power and in influence. Those who are drifting away from the principles of the gospel are losing in influence and power and prestige. —*Heber J. Grant* (IE, 39:471)

I sympathize with our young people because of the temptations that beset them. I urge them as I always have to live the gospel of Jesus Christ fully. In that way they will have health and happiness and will meet with success in this life and will have an eternity of joy in store for them in the life to come. I bless them with courage to meet the problems that lie ahead. —*Heber J. Grant* (IE, 43:267)

So children, remember your parents. After they have nurtured you through the tender years of your infancy and childhood, after they have fed and clothed and educated you, after having given you a bed to rest upon and done all in their power for your good, don't you neglect them when they become feeble and are bowed down with the weight of their years. Don't you leave them, but settle down near them, and do all in your power to minister to their comfort and well-being. —*Joseph F. Smith* (GD, 314)

Our youth should . . . be given to understand that what are generally considered as the pleasures of youth are on the wing, and will soon pass, leaving in their rear only sad remembrances of wasted opportunities that cannot be recalled. They should not be permitted to waste their time and their parents' substance in frivolous pastime and riotous living, which can only result in vicious or evil habits being formed. —*Joseph F. Smith* (GD, 320)

I would plead with you, my young brethren and sisters, to honor your fathers and your mothers, that your days may be long in the land which the Lord hath given to them and to you. Be obedient and loving to them; and after they have climbed to the summit of the hill of life, perhaps through many a hard-fought struggle, and begin to descend, try to do all in your power to make the road smooth and pleasant for them. By their devotion to you and to your welfare they have proved themselves worthy of your affection, and God expects you to be loyal to them. —*Lorenzo Snow* (LS, 137)

You are now laying a foundation in the bloom and beauty of youth and in the morning of your days to step forth upon the stage of life to act a conspicuous part in the midst of the most important dispensation and generation in which man has ever lived. And I can say in truth and safety that the result of your future lives, the influence which you will exert among man, and finally your eternal destiny for time and eternity, will in a great measure depend upon the foundation which you lay in the days of your youth, the manner in which you store your mind and cultivate while young. —*Wilford Woodruff* (WW, 265-266)

It is one of the greatest blessings that God ever bestowed upon children that they have had parents who were in possession of true principles in relation to their Heavenly Father, salvation, eternal life, and were qualified and capable of teaching and traditionating their children in the same that they may be qualified to fulfil the object of their creation; while on the other hand, it is one of the greatest calamities that can befall a nation or people to be overwhelmed with false views in relation to themselves. —*Wilford Woodruff* (WW, 266)

Love your fathers and mothers, appreciate and enjoy their society while you are with them, for you will soon enough be called to part with them, and if you live to see that day you will see the time when you will fully appreciate their society and know the worth of their counsel. —*Wilford Woodruff* (WW, 266-267)

Be kind to your brothers and sisters and all with whom you associate; kind words and good manners will cost you nothing and will add greatly to the happiness of those around you. Be true to yourselves by doing right in all things, by improving well your time and talents, by being wise, virtuous, and good. Be true to your God by keeping his commandments and doing his will, for he holds your destiny and the destiny of your parents and of all men in his own hands and he will reward all according to their works, whether they be good or evil, and all will be amply paid for doing well. —*Wilford Woodruff* (WW, 267)

You may say to yourselves, "If I can do as well as my parents, I think I shall do well, and be as good as I want to be, and I should not strive to excel them." But if you do your duty you will far excel them in everything that is good—in holiness, in physical and intellectual strength, for this is your privilege, and it becomes your duty. —*Brigham Young* (BY, 202-203)

Let me say to the boys sixteen years old and even younger, make up your minds to mark out the path of rectitude for yourselves, and when evil is presented, let it pass by unnoticed by you, and preserve yourselves in truth, in righteousness, virtue and holiness before the Lord. —*Brigham Young* (BY, 205)

64. SINGLE LIFE

There are some young women, and even some young men, who worry themselves almost sick over the question of whether they will have opportunity for marriage. Of course marriage is desirable; of course it is to be hoped for and worked for and sought after. Buy worrying about it will never bring it. In fact, it may have the opposite effect, for there is nothing that dulls a personality so much as a negative outlook. Some of our people may not marry in this life, but they should not forget that life can still be as rich and productive and joyful as anything they can possible imagine. And the key to that joy will be in giving service to others. —*Gordon B. Hinckley* (FETR, 40)

I recognize that there are many unmarried women who long to have a child. Some think of bringing this about by artificial impregnation. This the Church strongly discourages. Those who do so may expect to be disciplined by the Church. A child so conceived and born cannot be sealed to one parent. This procedure frustrates the eternal family plan. —*Gordon B. Hinckley* (Ensign, Nov. 1985, 89)

Keep marriage and motherhood in their true perspective. A happy marriage is the aim of every young woman. I know that some will be denied this opportunity. I urge you not to spend your time in self-pity. Rather, keep yourselves alive and vivacious in those activities which will bring satisfaction into your lives while associating with others who are vigorously pursuing lofty objectives. Remember always that you are not alone. There are thousands like you. And you are not helpless, a victim of fate. You can in large measure master your fate and strengthen your self-worth in reaching out to those who need and will appreciate your talents, your contributions, your help. —*Gordon B. Hinckley* (Ensign, Nov. 1989, 96-98)

The Church is for all members. In acknowledging the single or married state of individual Church members, we hope we are not misunderstood, for our intent is not to stereotype them. All of us, single or married, have individual identities and needs, among which is the desire to be seen as a worthwhile individual child of God. —*Howard W. Hunter* (WMJ, 52-53)

To those who are unmarried women: The promises of the prophets of God have always been that the Lord is mindful of you; if you are faithful, all blessings will be yours. To be without marriage and a family in this life is but a temporary condition; and eternity is a long time. . . . Fill your lives with worthwhile, meaningful activities. —*Howard W. Hunter* (WMJ, 56)

Just as those who do not hear the gospel in this life, but who would have received it with all their hearts had they heard it, will be given the fullness of the gospel blessings in the next world—so, too, the women of the Church who do not in this life have the privileges and blessings of a temple marriage, through no fault of their own, who would have responded if they had an appropriate opportunity—will receive all those blessings in the world to come. We desire all you sisters to know how much we love and appreciate you. We respect you for your valiant and devoted service! —*Spencer W. Kimball* (Ensign, Nov. 1978, 74)

You young women advancing in years who have not yet accepted a proposal of marriage, if you make yourselves worthy and ready to go to the house of the Lord and have faith in this sacred principle, even though the privilege of marriage does not come to you now, the Lord will reward you in due time and no blessing will be denied you. You are not under obligation to accept a proposal from someone unworthy of you for fear you will fail of your blessings. —*Harold B. Lee* (DSL, 129)

Some of you do not now have a companion in your home. Some of you have lost your wife or husband or you may not yet have found a companion. In your ranks are some of the noblest members of the Church—faithful, valiant, striving to live the Lord's commandments, to help build the kingdom on earth, and to serve your fellow men. —*Harold B. Lee* (DSL, 249)

Brethren, we are not doing our duty as holders of the priesthood when we go beyond the marriageable age and withhold ourselves from an honorable marriage to these lovely women, who are seeking the fulfillment of a woman's greatest desire to have a husband, a family, and a home. —*Harold B. Lee* (Ensign, Jan. 1974, 99-100)

My advice is to our girls, if you cannot find a husband who would be true to his religion and have faith in the gospel of our Lord, it is better to abide in "single blessedness." It is better to suffer some denial in mortal life and receive life everlasting than to lose your salvation in the kingdom of God. Remember the Lord will make up to you in joy and eternal union more than you have temporarily lost if you will be true and faithful. —*Joseph Fielding Smith* (DS2, 78)

I desire to give a little explanation for the comfort and consolation of parties in this condition. There is no Latter-day Saint who dies after having lived a faithful life who will lose anything because of having failed to do certain things when opportunities were not furnished him or her. In other words, if a young man or a young woman has no opportunity of getting married, and they live faithful lives up to the time of their death, they will have all the blessings, exaltation, and glory that any man or woman will have who had this opportunity and improved it. That is sure and positive. —*Lorenzo Snow* (LS, 138)

THE PRIESTHOOD

65. THE PRIESTHOOD

We of the priesthood are all part of the army of the Lord. We must be united. An army that is disorganized will not be victorious. It is imperative that we close ranks, that we march together as one. We cannot have division among us and expect victory. We cannot have disloyalty and expect unity. We cannot be unclean and expect the help of the Almighty. —*Gordon B. Hinckley* (CR, Nov. 1986, 43-45)

Many men seem to think that because they have been ordained, the priesthood is theirs in perpetuity to exercise as they choose. They feel they can break a covenant and a commandment here and there, and sin in this way or that, and yet still have within themselves the power of the priesthood and that God will ratify that which they speak in His holy name and in the name of the Redeemer. This becomes mockery, and I believe that in such an exercise, they take the name of God in vain. They profane the name of His Beloved Son. They desecrate the sacred gift which came through ordination, and the authority which they have lost because of transgression. —*Gordon B. Hinckley* (Ensign, Sept. 1992, 70)

Every bearer of the priesthood within his sphere of influence and responsibility is to teach the gospel through precept and example. That is, he should be teaching by example of living the gospel; also through words, learning experiences, and instructional materials.

Every bearer of the priesthood is to prepare himself to be an effective teacher by study, prayer, and faith.

Every bearer of the priesthood should seek the direction of the Spirit to guide him in his own life and to inspire him in his teaching efforts.

Every bearer of the priesthood has a sacred stewardship in the kingdom of God. Our time, our talents, our property, our priesthood callings are part of this stewardship. —*Howard W. Hunter* (Ensign, June 1971, 51)

I am confident in my own mind that there is no greater position that could come to any man than to receive the priesthood of God, coupled with the testimony of the divinity of this work; and those two should always go together. In other words, a man who does not have a testimony of the gospel should never be ordained to the Melchizedek Priesthood. The honors of men, the wealth of the world, are as nothing by comparison to the honor and the blessing which come to us when we were ordained to the priesthood. —*Ezra Taft Benson* (ETB, 215)

This is not a plaything. The priesthood of God is the most serious thing in the world. It was by the priesthood the world was created. And it is by the priesthood that your world will be created; and if you ever become a god in a world of your own, with your wife, your family, it will be through the magnifying of this priesthood which you hold. —*Spencer W. Kimball* (SWK, 496)

I have frequently said in blessings that I have given, "According to thy faith, be it unto you." If they have not any faith, then they have no right to demand a blessing. —*Spencer W. Kimball* (SWK, 511)

[P]riesthood is the power by which God works through man. —*Harold B. Lee* (SHP, 251-252)

The holders of the priesthood must say to themselves: "We can't be holders of the priesthood and be like other men. We must be different, because priesthood means a fellowship in the royal household of the kingdom of God. —*Harold B. Lee* (Ensign , Jan. 1974, 97)

After it is all said and done, brethren, our greatest responsibility is to teach the gospel of Jesus Christ and to teach the doctrines of the kingdom. If we fail in that, we have failed in the most important thing all of us should be doing. —*Harold B. Lee* (HBL, 481)

Brethren of the priesthood, in your own circle, in your own home, in your own lives, you must do all you can of your own free will, and bring to pass much righteousness. Our job and your job, my job, is to look after the man behind the one in front of you. That is a little difficult for some people to figure out. And when you find out that one, and put him in line, then you are prepared to go out and search for the other ones. —*Harold B. Lee* (Ensign, June 1971, 62)

Priesthood is divine authority which is conferred upon men that they may officiate in the ordinances of the gospel. In other words, priesthood is a part of God's own power, which he bestows upon his chosen servants that they may act in his name in proclaiming the gospel and officiating in all the ordinances thereof. —*Joseph Fielding Smith* (DS3, 80)

In regard to the holding of the priesthood in pre-existence, I will say that there was an organization there just as well as an organization here, and men there held authority. Men chosen to positions of trust in the spirit world held priesthood. —*Joseph Fielding Smith* (DS3, 81)

I plead with the members of the Priesthood throughout the Church to practice self-mastery. . . . Be master of yourselves, master of your appetites, master of your passions. —*David O. McKay* (CR, Oct. 1958, 89)

[E]very man who holds the priesthood, if he lives properly, soberly, industriously, humbly, and prayerfully, is entitled to the inspiration and guidance of the Holy Spirit. I know that it is true!—*David O. McKay* (CR, Oct. 1964, 92)

People should be made to understand that just to bow before the Lord in prayer does not give them divine authority. To live up to the requirements that are made of honesty, virtue, truth, etc., does not give them divine authority. Our Heavenly Father has made it plain to the children of men that only under the hands of those who possess divine authority may we obtain the power to become members of the Celestial kingdom. —*George Albert Smith* (CR, Apr., 1934, 28)

The priesthood that you hold is the power of God, conferred upon you from on high. Holy beings had to be sent to earth a little over a hundred years ago in order to restore that glorious blessing that had been lost to the earth for hundreds of years. Surely we ought to be grateful for our blessings. —*George Albert Smith* (CR, Oct. 1945, 118)

The fact that they hold the priesthood will be to many men a condemnation, because of the manner in which they have treated it, regarding it as though it were something ordinary. —*George Albert Smith* (CR, Apr. 1948, 184)

I say to you that it is not an insignificant thing to hold the Priesthood of God—to have the right to influence the powers of the heavens for good; and it is not a slight thing for us to neglect to honor the Priesthood of God in those who preside over us. —*Heber J. Grant* (GS, 8)

The Priesthood in general is the authority given to man to act for God. Every man ordained to any degree of the Priesthood, has this authority delegated to him.

But it is necessary that every act performed under this authority shall be done at the proper time and place, in the proper way, and after the proper order. The power of directing these labors constitutes the keys of the Priesthood. —*Joseph F. Smith* (GD, 136)

What Is The Priesthood? It is nothing more nor less than the power of God delegated to man by which man can act in the earth for the salvation of the human family, in the name of the Father and the Son and the Holy Ghost, and act legitimately; not assuming that authority, nor borrowing it from generations that are dead and gone. —*Joseph F. Smith* (CR, Oct. 1904, 5)

Where the Melchizedek or Holy Priesthood does not exist, there can be no true Church of Christ in its fullness. —*Joseph F. Smith* (LPS, 181)

The object of the priesthood is to make all men happy, to diffuse information, to make all partakers of the same blessings in their turn. —*Lorenzo Snow* (LS, 60)

The priesthood or authority in which we stand is the medium or channel through which our Heavenly Father has purposed to communicate light, intelligence, gifts, powers, and spiritual and temporal salvation unto the present generation. —*Lorenzo Snow* (LPS, 183)

The Lord would not permit me to occupy this position one day of my life, unless I was susceptible to the Holy Spirit and to the revelations of God. It is too late in the day for this Church to stand without revelation. The spirit of revelation belongs to the priesthood. —*Wilford Woodruff* (WW, 57)

[E]verything that God has caused to be done for the salvation of man, from the coming of man upon the earth to the redemption of the world, has been and will be by virtue of the everlasting priesthood. —*Wilford Woodruff* (WW, 64)

My views are that whenever the inhabitants of the earth were prepared for the gospel of Jesus Christ and the power of the priesthood, it has been bestowed upon them. —*Wilford Woodruff* (WW, 65)

If we have the Holy Priesthood upon our heads and do not live our religion, of all men we are under the greatest condemnation. —*Wilford Woodruff* (JD, 21:125)

To define all the laws of the priesthood would be impossible, for it is living power, not a dead letter, and although these instructions may be of general use, the living priesthood must regulate its own affairs. —*John Taylor* (GK, 127)

The priesthood is placed in the church for this purpose, to dig, to plant, to nourish, to teach correct principles, and to develop the order of the kingdom of God. —*John Taylor* (GK, 129)

The power manifested by the priesthood is simply the power of God, for he is the head of the priesthood, with Jesus as our President and great High Priest; and it is upon this principle that all the works of God have been accomplished, whether on the earth or in the heavens. —*John Taylor* (GK, 2)

Our Heavenly Father is desirous to promote the happiness and welfare of the whole of the human family; and if we, any of us, hold any priesthood, it is simply for that same purpose, and not for our personal aggrandizement, or for our own honor, or pomp, or position; but we hold it in the interest of God and for the salvation of the people, that through it we may promote their happiness, blessing, and prosperity, temporal and spiritual, both here and in the world to come. That is why the priesthood is conferred upon us, and if we do not use it in this way, then there is a malfeasance in office; then we violate our obligations before God, and render ourselves unworthy of the high calling that the Lord has conferred upon us. The priesthood always was given for the blessing of the human family. People talk about it as though it was for the special benefit of individuals. —*John Taylor* (GK, 199-200)

The question, "What is priesthood?" has often been asked me. I answer, it is the rule and government of God, whether on earth, or in the heavens; and it is the only legitimate power, the only authority that is acknowledged by him to rule and regulate the affairs of his kingdom. —*John Taylor* (GK, 314-315)

The power of all truth dwells in the bosom of our Father and God, which he dispenses to his children as he will, by the means of his eternal Priesthood. He is enthroned in the light, glory and power of truth. He has abided the truth, and is thereby exalted, and his power, light and glory are eternal. The Gospel and the Priesthood are the means he employs to save and exalt his obedient children to the possession with him of the same glory and power to be crowned with crowns of glory, immortality and eternal lives. —*Brigham Young* (BY, 5)

When the faithful Elders, holding this Priesthood, go into the spirit world they carry with them the same power and Priesthood that they had while in the mortal tabernacle. —*Brigham Young* (BY, 132)

[W]hen they ordain a man to the holy ministry, let him be a faithful man, who is able to teach others also; that the cause of Christ suffer not. It is not the multitude of preachers that is to bring about the glorious millennium! but it is those who are "called, and chosen, and faithful. —*Joseph Smith, Jr.* (STJS, 56-57)

Wherever the ordinances of the Gospel are administered, there is the Priesthood. —*Joseph Smith, Jr.* (STJS, 180)

Although there are two Priesthoods, yet the Melchizedek Priesthood comprehends the Aaronic or Levitical Priesthood, and is the grand head, and holds the highest authority which pertains to the priesthood . . .

It is the channel through which the Almighty commenced revealing His glory at the beginning of the creation of the earth, and through which He has continued to reveal Himself to the children of men to the present time, and through which He will make known his purposes to the end of time. —*Joseph Smith, Jr.* (STJS, 190-191)

All Priesthood is Melchizedek, but there are different portions or degrees of it. That portion which brought Moses to speak with God face to face was taken away; but that which brought the ministry of angels remained. All the prophets had the Melchizedek Priesthood and were ordained by God himself. —*Joseph Smith, Jr.* (STJS, 205)

66. AARONIC PRIESTHOOD
—KEYS, RIGHTS, AND PRIVILEGES

This Aaronic Priesthood, bestowed by John the Baptist, also includes the keys of baptism by immersion for the remission of sins. It is one thing to repent. it is another to have our sins remitted or forgiven. The power to bring this about is found in the Aaronic Priesthood. —*Gordon B. Hinckley* (Ensign, May 1988, 45-46)

I want to emphasize, boys, that the holding of the Aaronic Priesthood, and the exercise of its power, is not a small or unimportant thing. The bestowal of these keys in this dispensation was one of the greatest and most significant things incident to the entire Restoration. It was the first bestowal of divine authority in this, the dispensation of the fullness of times. It is the priesthood of God, with authority to act in the name of the Savior of mankind. —*Gordon B. Hinckley* (Ensign, May 1988, 45-46)

The holy priesthood includes the power to bless. For those of the Aaronic Priesthood, it carries with it the authority to administer to the congregation the emblems of the flesh and blood of the Lord who gave His life as a sacrifice for all. The sacrament and the partaking of these emblems is the very heart of our Sabbath worship. It includes a renewal of covenants with God. It carries with it a promise of His Holy Spirit to be with us. It is a blessing without peer to be enjoyed by all and made possible by the authority given to worthy young men. Boys, treasure it. Be worthy of it. —*Gordon B. Hinckley* (Ensign, Oct. 1988, 72)

Priesthood is the power by which our Heavenly Father works through men, through deacons, through teachers, through priest, and I have a feeling that we are not impressing that upon our young men. They are not taking the understanding of their priesthood as seriously as they might. —*Harold B. Lee* (Ensign, July 1973, 98)

The Aaronic Priesthood embraces the offices that have to do with the temporal matters of the Church, the crying of repentance and baptism for the remission of sins. —*Joseph Fielding Smith* (DS3, 103)

The most important thing that may be accomplished by the Aaronic Priesthood is to prepare boys to be worthy of promotion to the Melchizedek Priesthood. The most important thing the Melchizedek Priesthood can do for the men is to prepare them for eternal life in the celestial kingdom. —*George Albert Smith* (GAS, 28)

I hold to the doctrine that the duty of a teacher is as sacred as the duty of an apostle, in the sphere in which he is called to act, and that every member of the Church is as much in duty bound to honor the teacher who visits him in his home, as he is to honor the office and counsel of the presiding quorum of the Church. They all have the Priesthood; they are all acting in their callings, and they are all essential in their places, because the Lord has appointed them and set them in his Church. —*Joseph F. Smith* (CR, Apr. 1904, 2)

I desire to impress upon you the fact that it does not make any difference whether a man is a priest or an apostle, if he magnifies his calling. A priest holds the key of the ministering of angels. Never in my life, as an apostle, as a seventy, or as an elder, have I ever had more of the protection of the Lord than while holding the office as a priest. The Lord revealed to me by visions, by revelations, and by the Holy Spirit, many things that lay before me. —*Wilford Woodruff* (WW, 300)

That the lesser priesthood is a part of, or an appendage to the greater, or the Melchizedek priesthood, and has power in administering outward ordinances. The lesser, or Aaronic priesthood can make appointments for the greater in preaching; can baptize, administer the sacrament, attend to the tithing, buy lands, settle people on possessions, divide inheritances, look after the poor, take care of the properties of the church, attend generally to temporal affairs; act as common Judges in Israel, and assist in ordinances of the temple, under the direction of the greater or Melchizedek Priesthood: They hold the keys of the ministering of angels and administer in outward ordinances, the letter of the gospel, and the baptism of repentance for the remission of sins. —*John Taylor* (GK, 155-157)

[I]f a Priest understands his duty, his calling, and ministry, and preaches by the Holy Ghost, his enjoyment is as great as if he were one of the Presidency; and his services are necessary in the body, as are also those of Teachers and Deacons. —*Joseph Smith, Jr.* (STJS, 132-133)

67. MELCHIZEDEK PRIESTHOOD —KEYS, RIGHTS, AND PRIVILEGES

We in the Church recognize that the fulfillment of all blessings given under authority of the priesthood is conditioned upon two things: one, the worthiness and faithfulness of the recipient, and, two, the overriding will and wisdom of God. —*Gordon B. Hinckley* (Ensign, May 1981, 20)

[The priesthood] is veritably the power of the Almighty given to man to act in His name and in His stead. It is a delegation of divine authority, different from all other powers and authorities on the face of the earth. Small wonder that it was restored to a man by resurrected beings who held it anciently, that there might be no question concerning its authority and validity. Without it there could be a church in name only, lacking authority to administer in the things of God. With it, nothing is impossible in carrying forward the work of the kingdom of God. It is divine in its nature. It is both temporal and eternal in its authority. —*Gordon B. Hinckley* (Ensign, Oct. 1988, 71)

In its ultimate expression the holy priesthood carries with it the authority to seal on the earth and have that sealing effective in the heavens. It is unique and wonderful. It is the authority exercised in the temples of God. It condemns both the living and the dead. It is of the very essence of eternity. It is divine power bestowed by the Almighty as a part of His great plan for the immortality and eternal life of man. —*Gordon B. Hinckley* (Ensign, Oct. 1988, 72)

You have a lot of brethren, your brethren, who are not active in the Church. And who do you suppose the Lord expects to go out and bring them in? He is not going to send angels from heaven to bring them in, when He has a whole group of men here who bear His priesthood, every one who has the authority to act in His name. He expects you to go out, and in a spirit of love and understanding and fellowship to put your arms around those brethren and to win them into activity. And I say to you that if you do your part, the Lord won't permit you to fail. —*Ezra Taft Benson* (ETB, 231)

To be like the Savior—what a challenge for any person! He is a member of the Godhead. He is the Savior and Redeemer. He was perfect in every aspect of His life. There was no flaw or failing in Him. Is it possible for us as priesthood holders to be even as He is? The answer is yes. Not only can we, but that is our charge. (3 Nephi 27:27) He would not give us that commandment if He did not mean for us to do it. —*Ezra Taft Benson* (Ensign, Nov. 1986, 45)

The wreck of a plane, killing a hundred people; the sinking of a vessel, drowning a thousand; the killing of a million in a great world war would be nothing compared to your losing your membership, your priesthood, your blessings. They might never be restored to you. Men who die may live again, but when the spiritual death is total, it were better that a man were never born. —*Spencer W. Kimball* (SWK, 502-503)

A child leaving to go away to school or on a mission, a wife suffering stress, a family member being married or desiring guidance in making an important decision—all these are situations in which the father, in exercise of his patriarchal responsibility, can bless his family. —*Spencer W. Kimball* (Ensign, Nov. 1974, 110)

All elders of the Church, meaning all who hold the Melchizedek Priesthood, have all the priesthood necessary to preside in any calling in the Church, if they are called by those in authority, sustained by a vote of the people, and then ordained to the office and given the keys of that office by those in authority. —*Harold B. Lee* (SHP, 251)

When one becomes a holder of the priesthood, he becomes an agent of the Lord. He should think of his calling as though he were on the Lord's errand. That is what it means to magnify the priesthood. . . . Whatever you do according to the will of the Lord is the Lord's business. —*Harold B. Lee* (SHP, 255)

When a person holds the Melchizedek Priesthood as an elder, seventy or high priest, he holds the Aaronic Priesthood. When a person is ordained to an office in the Aaronic Priesthood, and then receives an office in the Melchizedek Priesthood, none of the former authority is taken away. The Melchizedek has authority to officiate in the Aaronic. —*Joseph Fielding Smith* (DS3, 103-104)

Some members of the Church have been confused in thinking that Elijah came with the keys of baptism for the dead or of salvation for the dead. Elijah's keys were greater than that. They were the keys of sealing, and those keys of sealing pertain to the living and embrace the dead who are willing to repent. —*Joseph Fielding Smith* (DS3, 130)

It is the privilege and duty of the elders to bless the sick by the laying on of hands. If they have pure olive oil which has been consecrated for this purpose, one of them should use it in anointing the sick, and then they should by the laying on of hands seal the anointing. If no oil is to be had, then they should administer by the laying on of hands in the power of the priesthood and in the prayer of faith, that the blessing sought may come through the power of the Spirit of the Lord. This is in accordance with the divine plan inaugurated in the beginning. —*Joseph Fielding Smith* (CN, Sept. 1, 1934)

A faithful father who holds the Melchizedek Priesthood may bless his own children, and that would be a patriarchal (father's) blessing. Such a blessing could be recorded in the family records, but it would not be preserved in the archives of the Church. —*Joseph Fielding Smith* (DS3, 172)

To hold the priesthood is an individual blessing but it requires, it demands, righteous living. —*David O. McKay* (CR, Apr. 1962, 95)

Let us realize that we are members of the greatest fraternity, the greatest brotherhood—the brotherhood of Christ—in all the world, and do our best each day, all day, to maintain the standards of the priesthood. —*David O. McKay* (CR, Oct. 1964, 92)

Brethren, it is a favor from the Lord to receive the priesthood; it is a great privilege to represent our Heavenly Father. It is a blessing that, if we are faithful, will open the doors of the celestial kingdom and give us a place there to live throughout the ages of eternity. Do not trifle with this priceless blessing. —*George Albert Smith* (CR, Apr. 1949, 191-192)

Think of what it means to be a royal priesthood, not a make-believe, but a royal priesthood, everyone having contact, if we will, with the power of our Heavenly Father, the great King of kings and Lord of lords. —*George Albert Smith* (CR, Oct. 1948, 190)

In the matter of administering to the sick, according to the order and practice established in the Church, care should be taken to avoid unwarranted repetitions. When an administration is made, and when the blessing pronounced upon the afflicted one has been received, the ordinance should not be repeated, rather let the time be given to prayer and thanksgiving for the manifestation of divine power already granted and realized. —*Joseph F. Smith* (GD, 205)

It is the priesthood that will give you character, renown, wisdom, power, and authority, and build you up here below among the children of men; and above, exalt you to peace and happiness, to glory, to thrones and dominions, even through countless eternities. —*Lorenzo Snow* (LPS, 203)

And now, where is the man among you [who], having once burst the veil and gazed upon this purity, the glory, the might, majesty and dominion of a perfected man, in celestial glory, in eternity, will not cheerfully resign mortal life—suffer most excruciating tortures—let limb be torn from limb, sooner than dishonor or resign his priesthood. —*Lorenzo Snow* (LPS, 203)

We have the same priesthood that Jesus had, and we have got to do as He did, to make sacrifice of our own desires and feelings as He did; perhaps not to die martyrs as He did, but we have got to make sacrifices in order to carry out the purposes of God, or we shall not be worthy of this holy priesthood, and be saviors of the world. —*Lorenzo Snow* (JD, 23:341-342)

Can you tell me where the people are who will be shielded and protected form these great calamities and judgments which are even now at our doors? I'll tell you. The priesthood of God who honor their priesthood and who are worthy of their blessings are the only ones who shall have this safety and protection. —*Wilford Woodruff* (WW, 230)

The highest calling the Lord ever called any human being to, in any age of the world, has been to receive the Holy Priesthood, with its keys and powers, and to be called to go forth to the inhabitants of the earth and teach them the principles of the gospel of Jesus Christ, and to qualify and prepare them for a part in the first resurrection and to go back into the presence of God, their Creator, to dwell in glory worlds without end. —*Wilford Woodruff* (WW, 64)

The same priesthood exists on the other side of the veil. . . . [E]very apostle, every seventy, every elder, etc., who has died in the faith, as soon as he passes to the other side of the veil, enters into the work of the ministry, and there is a thousand times more to preach there than there is here. —*Wilford Woodruff* (WW, 77)

Do we comprehend these things? Do we comprehend that if we abide the laws of the priesthood we shall become heirs of God and joint-heirs with Jesus Christ? I realize that our eyes have not seen, our ears have not heard, neither hath it entered into our hearts to conceive the glory that is in store for the faithful. —*Wilford Woodruff* (WW, 80)

The Melchizedek priesthood holds the mysteries of the revelations of God. Wherever that priesthood exists, there also exists a knowledge of the laws of God; and wherever the gospel has existed, there has always been revelation; and where there has been no revelation, there never has been the true gospel. —*John Taylor* (GK, 139)

[T]he Melchizedek priesthood holds the right of presidency, and has power and authority over all the offices in the church, in all ages of the world, to administer in spiritual things. —*John Taylor* (GK, 155-157)

[O]ne great privilege of the Priesthood is to obtain revelations of the mind and will of God. —*Joseph Smith, Jr.* (STJS, 131-132)

The power of the Melchizedek Priesthood is to have the power of "endless lives"; for the everlasting covenant cannot be broken. —*Joseph Smith, Jr.* (STJS, 361)

68. AARONIC PRIESTHOOD RESPONSIBILITIES

This is the gospel of repentance, and yours is the responsibility and the authority under the priesthood which you hold to teach this gospel of repentance. You recognize, or course, that if you are to do so effectively, your own life must be an example. —*Gordon B. Hinckley* (Ensign, Nov. 1982, 46)

It is totally wrong for you to take the name of the Lord in vain and indulge in filthy and unseemly talk at school or at work, and then kneel at the sacrament table on Sunday. You cannot drink beer or partake of illegal drugs and be worthy of the ministering of angels. You cannot be immoral in talk or in practice and expect the Lord to honor your service in teaching repentance or baptizing for the remission of sins. As those holding His holy priesthood, you must be worthy fellow servants. —*Gordon B. Hinckley* (Ensign, May 1988, 46)

There is so much of distress in this world. There are those, so many of them, who cry out in loneliness and fear with a desperate need for listening ears and understanding hearts. There are single parents struggling to rear families. There are houses that need painting, yards that need cleaning, whose owners have neither the strength nor the means to get it done. There are strong young men among us. There are thousands of you in these congregations tonight, young men of the Aaronic Priesthood, who can bless others and be blessed while giving such service. —*Gordon B. Hinckley* (Ensign, May 1989, 49)

We are concerned, brethren, with our need to provide continually significant opportunities for our young men to stretch their souls in service. Young men do not usually become inactive in the Church because they are given too many significant things to do. No young man who has really witnessed for himself that the gospel works in the lives of the people will walk away from his duties in the kingdom and leave them undone. —*Spencer W. Kimball* (Ensign, May 1985, 46)

It is the duty of the teacher to visit the homes of the people, to teach them, to see that there is no iniquity in the Church; that there is no fault-finding one with another, no backbiting, no false speaking one against another, and, more than that, to see that the members of the Church perform their duty. That great responsibility rests upon the teacher. He is to see that the members pray, that they fast upon the fast day, that they are paying their tithing, in the season thereof, that they are attending their fast meetings in the wards, week by week; and all these things are required of the teacher as he visits in the homes of the people. And if the teacher does not see to these things, then the sin lieth at his door. —*Joseph Fielding Smith* (CR, Oct. 1919, 114)

The Lord says: "The teacher's duty is to watch over the church always, . . ." (D. & C. 20:53) Not just once a month but always a teacher; no hour in the day when you are free from that responsibility! There is no day in the week when you are free and when you should not feel it your duty to do something . . . O teachers, yours is an important calling! God help you to be true to it, to feel that part of the responsibility of carrying on God's work, in this the last dispensation, rests upon you. —*David O. McKay* (CR, Oct. 1916, 59-60)

When priests and teachers understand their duties and seek to enjoy the spirit of their offices, they can do an immense amount of good; for they are brought directly into contact with the people. They learn their wants, are made familiar with their weaknesses, and are in a position to check the growth of evil tendencies in parents and in children. —*John Taylor* (GK, 158-159)

We start in with the teacher and with the priest, whose duty it is to know the position of all the members in their several districts, if they do their duty they will know really and truly the position of all those who come under their charge. —*John Taylor* (GK, 159-160)

What is the duty of the priests? Only to hold office? No; it is to visit the members of the various wards, and to see that there are no hard feelings, troubles, or difficulty among the people, to anticipate the occurrence of anything of that sort, put things right, and see that the ordinances of the church are carried out. —*John Taylor* (GK, 160)

69. MELCHIZEDEK PRIESTHOOD RESPONSIBILITIES

All of you, of course, are familiar with binoculars. When you put the lenses to your eyes and focus them, you magnify and in effect bring closer all within your field of vision. But if you turn them around and look through the other end, you diminish and make more distant that which you see.

So it is with our actions as holders of the priesthood. When we live up to our high and holy calling, when we show love for God through service to fellowmen, when we use our strength and talents to build faith and spread truth, we magnify our priesthood. When, on the other hand, we live lives of selfishness, when we indulge in sin, when we set our sights only on the things of the world rather than on the things of God, we diminish our priesthood. —*Gordon B. Hinckley* (Ensign, May 1989, 47)

As holders of the priesthood, we must live by a greater loyalty than other men. We must live with loyalty to God, in whose name we are authorized to speak and act. —*Gordon B. Hinckley* (Ensign, Nov. 1994, 49)

If every man in this church who has been ordained to the Melchizedek Priesthood were to qualify himself to hold a temple recommend, and then were to go to the house of the Lord and renew his covenants in solemnity before God and witnesses, we would be a better people. There would be little or no infidelity among us. Divorce would almost entirely disappear. So much of heartache and heartbreak would be avoided. There would be a greater measure of peace and love and happiness in our homes. There would be fewer weeping wives and weeping children. There would be a greater measure of appreciation and of mutual respect among us. And I am confident the Lord would smile with greater favor upon us. —*Gordon B. Hinckley* (Ensign, Nov. 1995, 53)

The bishop, and others in comparable positions, can forgive in the sense of waiving the penalties. In our loose connotation we sometimes call this forgiveness, but it is not forgiveness in the sense of "wiping out" or absolution. —*Spencer W. Kimball* (MF, 332-333)

One breaks the priesthood covenant by transgressing commandments—but also by leaving undone his duties. Accordingly, to break this covenant one needs only to do nothing. —*Spencer W. Kimball* (MF, 96)

As we magnify our priesthood callings, I hope we will always remember that the Church is a support to the family. The Church does not and must not seek to displace the family, but is organized to help create and nurture righteous families as well as righteous individuals. —*Spencer W. Kimball* (Ensign, May 1981, 45.)

In all our priesthood callings we must never forget that the business of the church and kingdom of God is to save souls, and that all over whom we preside are our Father's children, and He will aid us in our endeavors to save every one. —*Harold B. Lee* (SHP, 254-255)

I wonder if we realize the greatness of our callings—yes, all the elders in this Church—do they realize that they hold the Melchizedek Priesthood? Do they know that through their faithfulness and their obedience, according to the revelations of the Lord, they are entitled to receive all that the Father has—to become the sons of God, joint-heirs with our Elder Brother, Jesus Christ, entitled to the exaltations in the celestial kingdom? Do we realize that? We, too, if we do realize it, should be like those of former days, and every man that hath this hope in him, will purify himself even as Christ is pure. —*Joseph Fielding Smith* (CR, Oct. 1942, 18)

We have these two great responsibilities—every man holding the priesthood—first, to seek our own salvation; and, second, our duty to our fellow men. Now I take it that my first duty is, so far as I am individually concerned, to seek my own salvation. That is your individual duty first, and so with every member of the Church.

Our duty to our fellow men in the world is a responsibility resting especially on the shoulders of the men holding the priesthood. Our duty is to preach the gospel, to teach the nations of the earth, to go out and bring people in the Church. That duty is upon the Church. —*Joseph Fielding Smith* (DS2, 145)

The apostle is under no greater commandment to be true to his covenant and membership in the Church than is the ordinary elder, or seventy, or any other individual holding the priesthood. It is true the apostle has a greater responsibility, or calling, in the priesthood, but no greater responsibility to be true to gospel principles and commandments. Especially is this so, if the elder has received the ordinances of the house of the Lord. —*Joseph Fielding Smith* (IE, 41:653)

All men may, by virtue of the priesthood and the gift of the Holy Ghost, become witnesses for Christ. In fact that is just what every elder in the Church should be. —*Joseph Fielding Smith* (DS3, 146)

Our lives are wrapped up with the lives of others. We are happiest as we contribute to the lives of others. I say that because the priesthood you hold means that you are to serve others. —*David O. McKay* (CR, Sept.-Oct. 1950, 112)

It is our obligation when we accept the priesthood to set an example worthy of imitation by our fellow men. It is not what we say that will influence them. It is what we do. It is what we are. —*David O. McKay* (CR, Oct. 1948, 174)

There are two conditions which should always be considered when the priesthood is conferred. The first of these is the individual's worthiness to receive it. The second is the service which he can render to the Church and to his fellowmen. —*David O. McKay* (CR, Oct. 1965, 104)

It is your duty and mine, as bearers of the priesthood, by tact and brotherly love and faith, to overcome the prejudice that the adversary has sown in the hearts of our Father's children against us, to break down the animosity that exists in some cases, even in the minds of good men and good women, and teach them the gospel of our Lord, that it is the power of God unto salvation unto all those who believe and obey it. —*George Albert Smith* (CR, Apr. 1917, 36)

To be ordained to the Priesthood may not prove a blessing. We should not at any time feel that it will be a blessing to us, unless we honor it, unless we magnify it, and have in our hearts the desire that the Lord intended we should have, when He bestowed that gift upon us, and we should always desire to do good. —*George Albert Smith* (CR, Apr. 1941, 27)

I know that the authority of our Heavenly Father is upon the earth for the blessing of mankind, not to make those who receive that authority arrogant, but to make them humble; not to make those who have received special privileges feel that they are greater than others, but to make us humble in our souls, prayerful in our hearts, and considerate of all men in all that we do, and thus exemplify by upright lives that which our Heavenly Father desires us to teach. —*George Albert Smith* (CR, Oct. 1928, 94)

The one thing now that I desire to impress upon the minds of my brethren bearing the Holy Priesthood is that we should live so near to the Lord, be so humble in our spirits, so tractable and pliable, under the influence of the Holy Spirit, that we will be able to know the mind and will of the Father . . . under all circumstances. —*Joseph F. Smith* (CR, Oct. 1903, 86)

It is the duty of this vast body of men holding the holy Priesthood, which is after the order of the Son of God, to exert their influence and exercise their power for good among the people of Israel and the people of the world. It is their bounden duty to preach and to work righteousness, both at home and abroad. —*Joseph F. Smith* (GD, 157)

Every man who holds the office of high priest in the Church, or has been ordained a high priest, whether he is called to active position in the Church or not—inasmuch as he has been ordained a high priest, should feel that he is obliged—that it is his bounden duty, to set an example before the old and young worthy of emulation, and to place himself in a position to be a teacher of righteousness, not only by precept but more particularly by example. —*Joseph F. Smith* (GD, 182)

Our lives are wrapped up with the lives of others. We are happiest as we contribute to the lives of others. I say that because the priesthood you hold means that you are to serve others. —*David O. McKay* (CR, Sept.-Oct. 1950, 112)

It is our obligation when we accept the priesthood to set an example worthy of imitation by our fellow men. It is not what we say that will influence them. It is what we do. It is what we are. —*David O. McKay* (CR, Oct. 1948, 174)

There are two conditions which should always be considered when the priesthood is conferred. The first of these is the individual's worthiness to receive it. The second is the service which he can render to the Church and to his fellowmen. —*David O. McKay* (CR, Oct. 1965, 104)

If we as elders fail to keep the covenants we have made, namely, to use our time, talents, and ability for the upbuilding of the kingdom of God upon the earth, how can we reasonably expect to come forth in the morning of the First Resurrection, identified with the great work of redemption? If we in our manner, habits and dealings, imitate the Gentile world, thereby identifying ourselves with the world, do you think, my brethren, that God will bestow upon us the blessings we desire to inherit? I tell you no, He will not!—*Lorenzo Snow* (LS, 44)

Much difficulty would be avoided, and our condition and situation would be much more encouraging if we all honored the office in which we are called to act. —*Lorenzo Snow* (LS, 76)

Very few indeed have enough moral courage to be strictly honest, faithful, virtuous, and honorable in all positions—these few will hold the priesthood and receive its fulness, but no others.

Purity, virtue, fidelity, and godliness must be sought ambitiously, or the crown cannot be won. Those principles must be incorporated with [in] ourselves—woven into our constitutions—becoming a part of us, making us a center, a fountain of truth, of equity, justice, and mercy, of all that is good and great. —*Lorenzo Snow* (LS, 79)

And now I call upon all who hold this priesthood, the presiding officers of this stake, and the bishops, and the high council, to go forth and feed the flock. Take an interest in them. . . . Work for them, and do not confine your thoughts and feelings to your personal aggrandizement. Then God will give you revelation, inspiration upon inspiration, and teach you how to secure the interests of the Saints in matters pertaining to their temporal and spiritual welfare. —*Lorenzo Snow* (LS, 82)

[E]very seventy, and every high priest, and every man bearing the Holy Priesthood should live in that way to get revelation to guide and direct him in his labors. —*Wilford Woodruff* (WW, 52)

Let all Israel remember that the eternal and everlasting priesthood is bestowed upon us for the purpose alone of administering in the ordinances of life and salvation, both for the living and the dead, and no man on earth can use that priesthood for any other purpose than for the work of the ministry, the perfecting of the Saints, edifying the body of Christ, establishing the kingdom of heaven, and redeeming Zion. If we attempt to use it for unrighteous purposes, like lightning from heaven, our power, sooner or later, falls, and we fail to accomplish the designs of God. —*Wilford Woodruff* (WW, 69-70)

God has no respect for persons in this priesthood any further than as they magnify their callings and do their duty. —*Wilford Woodruff* (WW, 298)

It has been justly remarked here that we have got to labor ourselves until we get the Spirit of God, and then we can walk out among the people and correct them; but if we as seventies, as high priests, and apostles, and elders bearing the priesthood, if we are resolved to set our hearts upon things of this earth, without being engaged in the interest of the kingdom of God, what can we expect of the people? Not anything. —*Wilford Woodruff* (WW, 328)

As elders of Israel, very few of us fully comprehend our position, our calling, or relationship to God, our responsibility, or work the Lord requires at our hands. The Lord has given unto us the priesthood. This is conferred upon us that we may administer in the ordinances of life and salvation. But to enable us to perform our duties acceptably, there is one thing we need, one and all of us, and that is the Holy Spirit. —*Wilford Woodruff* (WW, 124)

O ye Elders of Israel who have received the Holy Priesthood, we have this work laid upon our shoulders, we have to take hold and build up this kingdom or be damned. . . . We cannot afford to treat lightly this work. We cannot undertake to serve God and mammon. . . . We have got to take one side or the other. —*Wilford Woodruff* (LPS, 199-200)

The order of the church is for us to fulfil and magnify the calling to which we are called, and do it with an eye single to the glory of God, each man fulfilling the various duties and responsibilities of his office. —*John Taylor* (GK, 151)

Now, the idea is not that one or a dozen men have to bear off this kingdom. For what is the priesthood conferred upon you? Is it to follow the "devices and desires of your own hearts," as I used to hear them say in the Church of England when I was a boy? Is it to do that? I think not. Or were we enlisted to God, for time and eternity? I think we were; and we want to wake up to the responsibilities which devolve upon us, and honor our calling and magnify our priesthood. —*John Taylor* (GK, 199)

Until a selfish individual interest is banished from our minds, and we become interested in the general welfare, we shall never be able to magnify our holy Priesthood as we should. —*Brigham Young* (BY, 133)

Whoever is ordained to the office of an Elder to a certain degree possesses the keys of the Melchizedek Priesthood; and suppose only one Elder should be left on the earth, could he go and set in order the Kingdom of God? Yes, by revelation. —*Brigham Young* (BY, 139)

I advise all to go on to perfection, and search deeper and deeper into the mysteries of Godliness. A man can do nothing for himself unless God direct him in the right way; and the Priesthood is for that purpose. —*Joseph Smith, Jr.* (STJS, 409)

70. QUORUM RESPONSIBILITIES

I am satisfied, my brethren, that there is enough of expertise, of knowledge, of strength, of concern in every priesthood quorum to assist the troubled members of that quorum if these resources are properly administered. —*Gordon B. Hinckley* (Ensign , Nov. 1977, 86)

It is the obligation of the priesthood quorum to set in motion those forces and facilities which will equip the needy member to provide on a continuing basis for himself and his family. —*Gordon B. Hinckley* (Ensign Nov. 1977, 86)

Each quorum has direct access to the home teachers. These brethren of the priesthood have not only the responsibility to teach, but also to inquire, to learn, and even by the power of the Holy spirit to discern the needs of those for whom they are given responsibility. —*Gordon B. Hinckley* (Ensign, Nov. 1977, 86)

Home teaching is not to be undertaken casually. A home teaching call is to be accepted as if extended to you personally by the Lord Jesus Christ. —*Ezra Taft Benson* (Ensign, May 1987, 48)

There is no greater Church calling than that of home teacher. There is no greater Church service rendered to our Father in Heaven's children than the service rendered by a humble, dedicated, committed home teacher. —*Ezra Taft Benson* (Ensign, May 1987, 49-50)

Fundamental to effective home teaching is to know well your message, teach it by the Spirit, and make praying and reading the scriptures an integral part of that message. —*Ezra Taft Benson* (Ensign, May 1987, 50-51)

Remember, both quality and quantity home teaching are essential in being an effective home teacher. You should have quality visits, but you should also make contact with each of your families each month. As shepherds to all of your families, both active and less active, you should not be content with only reaching the ninety and nine. Your goal should be 100 percent home teaching every month. —*Ezra Taft Benson* (Ensign, May 1987, 50-51)

The priesthood home teaching program can become a huge umbrella under which all the people of the Church may huddle for protection from the storms of adversity, sin, crime, delinquency, carelessness in activity, and immorality; but, of course, like an ordinary umbrella, if it is leaky and is not whole, stretched silk will be little protection. —*Spencer W. Kimball* (SWK, 524)

Quorum leaders were given the responsibility of selecting, training, and supervising quorum members in visiting with and teaching assigned families of their own quorum members. —*Harold B. Lee* (SHP, 298)

The priesthood quorums and the auxiliary organizations are the carefully guarded channels provided within the Church through which precious truths are to be disseminated. —*Harold B. Lee* (YLW, 56)

The key to effective home teaching lies in the ability of the home teachers and the family to build a relationship in which all are comfortable enough that practical things can be done to help, and significant and specific inquiries can be made about conditions in the home without giving offense or being ritualistic. This relationship can be built on love and trust, but love and trust require a concern that goes beyond the giving of a lesson; they involve having home teachers who know their families and their needs and respond to these needs specifically and appropriately. —*Harold B. Lee* (HBL, 497)

Every person holding an office in the priesthood should be enrolled and receive membership in the proper quorum where his membership is recorded. One of the main purposes of a quorum of priesthood is to help every individual member of that quorum in all things pertaining to the quorum—in his spirituality, in his temporal salvation, in all his needs. —*Joseph Fielding Smith* (IE, 41:680)

Where a quorum of priesthood has failed to function, and has been indifferent to the responsibilities assigned to it, the presidency of the stake will be held responsible first, and then officers of the quorum next. If officers refuse to work, or are incapable, then they should be released, and faithful and willing men called to act in their stead. —*Joseph Fielding Smith* (IE, 41:653)

The Lord has placed the responsibility for the training and the conduct of the members of the quorum upon the shoulders of the president of the quorum. He has given him two counselors to assist him in that work, This direction and care of the quorum may not be transferred to the shoulders of some other. Men who are the most capable for these positions of presidency should be sought. —*Joseph Fielding Smith* (CR, Oct. 1945, 95)

There is opportunity in these quorum groups for fellowship, brotherhood, and organized service. No man who is worthy of that fellowship can be kept out from it—not one!—*David O. McKay* (CR, Apr. 1963, 97)

If priesthood meant only personal honor, blessing, or individual elevation, there would be no need of groups or quorums. The very existence of such groups established by divine authorization proclaims our dependence upon one another, the indispensable need of mutual help and assistance. We are, by divine right, social beings. —*David O. McKay* (CR, Oct. 1968, 84-85)

Today the perfunctory obligations of the ward teachers are fairly well performed, but the looking after of individuals is woefully neglected. —*David O. McKay* (IE, 49:470)

These representatives of the bishop—the ward teachers—are the men who reach the individual, the men upon whom the responsibility rests to convert, to comfort, and to teach. Ward teachers are on the firing line. —*David O. McKay* (IE, 41:200)

To give help, encouragement, and inspiration to every individual is the great responsibility and privilege of ward teachers. —*David O. McKay* (IE, 41:201)

Why are you organized as a high priesthood? . . . It is a kind of normal school, where they may be taught lessons in the presidency, and be prepared to judge and act in the various places which they may be called to. —*John Taylor* (GK, 198)

71. PRIESTHOOD OFFICES

Under the revelations of the Lord, the Church is to be presided over by three presiding high priests. They are to be assisted by a council of Twelve apostles, who in turn are to be assisted by those of the First Quorum of the Seventy. A Presiding Bishopric of the three are responsible for temporal affairs under the direction of the Presidency. All of these are priesthood officers. That power divinely given is the authority by which they govern. It is so in the stakes and the wards with presidencies and bishoprics. It is so in the quorums. The auxiliary officers carry forth their work under direction and delegation from the priesthood. Without the priesthood there might be the form of a church, but not the true substance. —*Gordon B. Hinckley* (Ensign, Oct. 1988, 72)

We are calling a group of wise and mature men with long experience in the Church and with freedom to go wherever circumstances dictates as members of the Second Quorum of the Seventy. . . . As Seventies they are called to preach the gospel and to be especial witnesses of the Lord Jesus Christ as set forth in the revelations. —*Gordon B. Hinckley* (CR, May 1997, 5-6)

Patriarchal blessings are revelations to the recipients—a white line down the middle of the road to protect, inspire, motivate toward activity and righteousness.

An inspired patriarchal blessing could light the way and lead the recipient on a path to fulfillment. It could lead him to become a new man and to have in his body a new heart. —*Spencer W. Kimball* (SWK, 505)

Extreme care should be taken in the giving of patriarchal blessings. They should be given only in the spirit of prayer and humility. Patriarchs should sit down with the candidates for blessings and question them in relation to their lives, what they have done in the Church and otherwise. They should feel of their spirits, discover if they have been active or inactive in the Church, learn all about them that they can; then, relying on the Spirit of the Lord, patriarchs should give them conservative blessings. —*Joseph Fielding Smith* (DS3, 171)

Elders and high priests are appointed to officiate in the ministry in spiritual things in the stakes of Zion, and from among the high priests come the presiding officers of the Church and in the stakes and wards of the Church. —*Joseph Fielding Smith* (CN, Sept. 9, 1933, 4)

Every member of the Council of the Twelve Apostles should have, and I feel sure have had, the knowledge of the resurrection of Jesus Christ. This does not have to come by direct visitation of the Savior, but it does come from the testimony of the Holy Ghost. . . . The testimony of the Holy Ghost is the strongest testimony that can be given. It is better than a personal visit. It is for this reason that the Savior said that all manner of sin and blasphemy against the Holy Ghost could not be forgiven. —*Joseph Fielding Smith* (DS3, 153-154)

The bishop may be a humble man. Some of you may think you are superior to him, and you may be, but he is given authority direct from our Father in heaven. You recognize it. Seek his advice, the advice of your stake president. If they cannot answer your difficulties or your problems, they will write to the General Authorities and get the advice needed. Recognition of authority is an important principle. —*David O. McKay* (CR, Oct. 1965, 105)

If it were necessary, though I do not expect the necessity will ever arise, and there was no man left on earth holding the Melchizedek Priesthood, except an elder—that elder, by the inspiration of the Spirit of God and by the direction of the Almighty, could proceed and should proceed, to organize the Church of Jesus Christ in all its perfection, because he holds the Melchizedek Priesthood. But the house of God is a house of order, and while the other officers remain in the Church, we must observe the order of the priesthood. —*Joseph F. Smith* (GD, 148)

The Lord never did intend that one man should have all power, and for that reason he has placed in his Church, presidents, apostles, high priests, seventies, elders and the various officers of the lesser Priesthood, all of which are essential in their order and place according to the authority bestowed on them. —*Joseph F. Smith* (CR, Oct. 1901, 82)

I have had men frequently come to me and want to pass by the presidents of stakes. I pass them back again! I tell them to go to their presidents. Again I have men come to me who wish to pass by their bishops; I send them back to their bishops, as I wish to honor all men in their place. I have enough to do without interfering with the little details of others: and so on from them to the elders, priests, teachers and deacons, every man in his place. —*John Taylor* (GK, 134)

The duty of a High Priest is to administer in spiritual and holy things, and to hold communion with God. . . . And again, it is the High Priests' duty to be better qualified to teach principles and doctrines, than the Elders. —*Joseph Smith, Jr.* (STJS, 30)

An Evangelist is a Patriarch . . . Wherever the Church of Christ is established in the earth, there should be a Patriarch for the benefit of the posterity of the Saints. —*Joseph Smith, Jr.* (STJS, 173)

LEADERSHIP

72. LEADERSHIP

The yoke of Church responsibility, the burden of Church leadership become opportunities rather than problems to him who wears the mantle of dedicated membership in the Church of Jesus Christ. —*Gordon B. Hinckley* (BTE, 6)

Loyalty to leadership is a cardinal requirement of all who serve in the army of the Lord. —*Gordon B. Hinckley* (Ensign, May 1990, 51)

May our vision not be so narrow that we would relegate revelation to only the ancients. God is merciful and loves his children in all ages and has revealed himself to this time in history. —*Howard W. Hunter* (Ensign, May 1981, 65)

One who rationalizes that he or she has a testimony of Jesus Christ but cannot accept direction and counsel from the leadership of His church is in a fundamentally unsound position and is in jeopardy of losing exaltation. —*Ezra Taft Benson* (CUC , 15)

Leadership is the ability to encourage the best efforts of others in working toward a desirable goal. —*Spencer W. Kimball* (Ensign, Mar. 1976, 2)

You have no right to resign any more than you have to call yourself to the work. —*Spencer W. Kimball* (SWK, 479)

When we cannot accept those who represent Him [Jesus Christ] here, it would not be a bit easier to accept the Master Himself, were He to appear. —*Harold B. Lee* (YLW, 31)

The wisest statement we can make is, "I don't know," to the many questions youth may ask on matters about which the Lord has not spoken. We must never presume to elucidate upon a matter on which the Lord has revealed but a little. —*Harold B. Lee* (YLW, 109)

No man who ever followed the teachings or took advice or counsel from one who stands as the representative of the Lord ever went astray; but men who refused to accept counsel have gone astray and into forbidden paths, and in some instances have even denied the faith. —*Joseph Fielding Smith* (CR, Oct. 1912, 124)

I have no right to raise my hand in opposition to a man who is appointed to any position in this Church, simply because I may not like him, or because of some personal disagreement or feeling I may have, but only on the grounds that he is guilty of wrong doing, of transgression of the laws of the Church which would disqualify him for the position which he is called to hold. —*Joseph Fielding Smith* (CR, June 1919, 92)

Paramount in the life of a bishopric of a ward is to win and merit the confidence of the people of their ward. . . . There are too few officers in the Church who have the confidence of the members, particularly of the young people of wards and stakes. —*David O. McKay* (CR, Apr. 1944, 107)

To be trusted is a greater compliment than to be loved. —*David O. McKay* (CR, Apr. 1928, 104-105)

You will find that those who do not do their duty, are always complaining about somebody that does, and making excuses for themselves. I have never found a man who was keeping the commandments of God that had any criticism to offer concerning any administration of the affairs of the Church. —*Heber J. Grant* (CR, Apr. 1900, 22)

The moment a spirit enters the heart of a member to refrain from sustaining the constituted authorities of the Church, that moment he becomes possessed of a spirit which inclines to rebellion or dissension; and if he permits that spirit to take a firm root in his mind, it will eventually lead him into darkness and apostasy. —*Joseph F. Smith* (GD, 224)

I want to say to you that there never was a time since the organization of the Church of Jesus Christ of Latter-day Saints, when a man led the Church, not for one moment. It was not so in the days of Joseph; it was not so in the days of Brigham Young; it has not been so since; it never will be so. The direction of this work among the people of the world will never be left to men. It is God's work, let me tell you. —*Joseph F. Smith* (GD, 76)

No man can be more happy than by obeying the living prophet's counsel. You may go from east to west, from north to south, and tread this footstool of the Lord all over, and you cannot find a man that can make himself happy in this Church, only by applying the counsel of the living prophet in this life; it is a matter of impossibility for a man to receive a fulness who is not susceptible of receiving and carrying out the living prophet's counsel. —*Lorenzo Snow* (LS, 86)

The very moment that men in this kingdom attempt to run ahead or cross the path of their leaders, no matter in what respect, the moment they do this they are in danger of being injured by wolves. —*Wilford Woodruff* (JD 5:83)

There is an appointed way, however, in which revelation from the Lord for the government of his church is received. There is but one man on the earth, at a time, who holds this power. But every individual member has the privilege of receiving revelation from the Lord for his guidance in his own affairs, and to testify to him concerning the correctness of public teachings and movements. —*Wilford Woodruff* (WW, 54)

Then I hope my brethren and sisters will feel in their hearts to sustain the Presidency of the Church, by their faith, works, and prayers, and not suffer them to carry all the load, while we hide ourselves in the rear. If we should do this we are not worthy, we are not worthy of our position as elders in Israel, and fathers and mothers in Israel. Let each one bear their share; and if we will correct our own follies, and set in order our own houses, and do that which is right, we shall then do some good, and help to lift the load that rests upon those that lead. —*Wilford Woodruff* (WW, 88)

The only marvel I have had all my life has been that the Lord ever chose me for anything, especially as an apostle and as president. But that is his own business; it was not mine. —*Wilford Woodruff* (WW, 274)

If anything under the heavens should humble men before the Lord and before one another, it should be the fact that we have been called of God. —*Wilford Woodruff* (JD, 21:317)

Now we are sometimes fond, that is, some of us are, of talking about our authority. It is a thing I care very little about. I tell you what I want to do if I can: I want to know the will of God so that I may do it; and I do not want to dictate or domineer or exercise arbitrary control. Then again, all men ought to be under proper control to the presidency and priesthood presiding over them. If I were a bishop, I should want to know what the president of my stake desired, and I should confer with him. —*John Taylor* (GK, 170)

If I violate any law of the Church, bring me up for it. If any one else does, bring him up for it. But don't go sneaking around back-biting and misrepresenting. Let us act as men, at least, if we won't be saints. But we should be true to our calling and profession and honor our God. —*John Taylor* (GK, 174)

When I hear persons say that they ought to occupy a station more exalted than they do, and hide the talents they are in possession of, they have not the true wisdom they ought to have. There is a lack in them, or they would improve upon the talents given. —*Brigham Young* (BY, 135)

I am more afraid that this people have so much confidence in their leaders that they will not inquire for themselves of God whether they are led by him. . . . Let every man and woman know, by the whispering of the Spirit of God to themselves, whether their leaders are walking in the path the Lord dictates, or not. —*Brigham Young* (BY, 135)

I will inform you that it is contrary to the economy of God for any member of the Church, or any one, to receive instruction for those in authority, higher than themselves. —*Joseph Smith, Jr.* (STJS, 29)

I saw the Twelve Apostles of the Lamb, who are now upon the earth, who hold the keys of this last ministry, in foreign lands, standing together in a circle, much fatigued, with their clothes tattered and feet swollen, with their eyes cast downward, and Jesus standing in their midst, and they did not behold Him. The Savior looked upon them and wept. —*Joseph Smith, Jr.* (STJS, 127)

It is also the privilege of any officer in this Church to obtain revelations, so far as relates to his particular calling and duty in the Church. —*Joseph Smith, Jr.* (STJS, 131-132)

If any person should ask me if I were a prophet, I should not deny it, as that would give me the lie; for, according to John, the testimony of Jesus is the spirit of prophecy; therefore, if I profess to be a witness or teacher, and have not the spirit of prophecy, which is the testimony of Jesus, I must be a false witness; but if I be a true teacher and witness, I must possess the spirit of prophecy, and that constitutes a prophet; and any man who says he is a teacher or a preacher of righteousness, and denies the spirit of prophecy, is a liar, and the truth is not in him; and by this key false teachers and impostors may be detected. —*Joseph Smith, Jr.* (STJS, 303)

73. EFFECTIVE LEADERSHIP

It is imperative that the president himself select his counselors because theirs must be a compatible relationship. He must have absolute confidence in them. They must have confidence in him. They must work together in a spirit of mutual trust and respect. —*Gordon B. Hinckley* (Ensign, Nov. 1990, 49)

It is the prerogative of the president to make the decision, and it is the duty of the counselors to back him in that decision. His decision then becomes their decision, regardless of their previous ideas. —*Gordon B. Hinckley* (Ensign, Nov. 1990, 49)

No president in any organization in the Church is likely to go ahead without the assurance that his counselors feel good about the proposed program. A man or woman thinking alone, working alone, arriving at his or her own conclusions, can take action which might prove to be wrong. But when three kneel together in prayer, discuss every aspect of the problem which is before them, and under the impressions of the Spirit reach a united conclusion, then we may have the assurance that the decision is in harmony with the will of the Lord. —*Gordon B. Hinckley* (Nov. 1990, 49)

In the Church today a leader generally gets in performance what he truly expects. He needs to think tall. —*Ezra Taft Benson* (ETB, 372)

Whenever I have been inclined to think the honors were coming to me as I go about the Church, then I remember that it is not to me, but to the position I hold that honors come. I am but a symbol. —*Spencer W. Kimball* (IE, Nov. 1958, 940)

Evidence of improved leadership will bring more consistent study of the scriptures, greater concern of the holders of the priesthood in watching over the Church, more devotion to family duties, more of our young people married worthily in the temple, greater faith and righteous exercise of the priesthood, and so on. —*Harold B. Lee* (SHP, 310)

The only true record that will ever be made of my service in my new calling will be the record that I may have written in the hearts and lives of those with whom I have served and labored, within and without the Church. —*Harold B. Lee* (SHP, 169)

The most potent influence in training our youth to cherish life, to keep their word of honor, to have increased respect for human kind and love of justice, is the life and personality of the teacher. —*David O. McKay* (GI, 431)

No bishop, no counselor, no stake president, no man holding a responsible position in this Church can afford to sidestep to the slightest degree his great responsibility of living the gospel as he preaches it and of being an example to the flock. —*David O. McKay* (CR, Oct. 1968, 84)

You cannot neglect the business of the Church, as the presiding officers of the stakes of Zion, and expect the Lord to carry on. He desires to do it through you. You have been given divine authority. It comes through only one source and that is our Heavenly Father. He will expect each of us, wherever we go, when this conference is completed, to hold the banner of righteousness aloft and teach by example as well as precept, those to whom we minister the gospel of Jesus Christ our Lord. —*George Albert Smith* (CR, Apr. 1942, 14)

Love the people into living righteously. —*George Albert Smith* (PCE, 267)

This Church, that bears the name of Jesus Christ, is directed by him, and he will permit no man or group of men to destroy it. He will not permit the men who preside over his Church to lead the people into error, but he will sustain them with his almighty power. He will magnify them in the eyes of good and great men and women. He will bless their ministry and it will be fraught with success. Those who oppose and find fault will not find joy in their opposition. Those who criticize and seek to destroy the influence of the leaders of the Church will suffer the result of their wrong-doing. —*George Albert Smith* (CR, Apr. 1934, 29)

We feel that in all the stakes of Zion, every stake president, every counselor to a stake president, every stake clerk, and every high councilor, standing at the head of the people in the stake we ask them to kindly step aside unless they are living up to these laws. They are given the responsibility of presiding, and every officer who is a presiding officer should say from today: "I am going to serve the Lord, so that my example will be worthy of imitation." . . . I pray from the bottom of my heart that God will give each and every man and woman who holds an office in any stake or ward the spirit and the feeling and the determination from this day, to renew his covenants with God, to live his religion; and if we are too weak to do these things, we should step aside and let somebody else take our place. —*Heber J. Grant* (CR, Oct., 1937, 129-130)

I will ask no man to be more liberal with his means than I am with mine, in proportion to what he possesses, for the advancement of God's kingdom. I will ask no man to observe the Word of Wisdom any more closely than I will observe it. I will ask no man to be more conscientious and prompt in the payment of his tithes and his offerings than I will be. I will ask no man to be more ready and willing to come early and to go late, and to labor with full power of mind and body, than I will labor always in humility. —*Heber J. Grant* (CR, June 1919, 2-3)

Teaching by precept without example is mighty poor teaching. —*Heber J. Grant* (CR, Apr. 1911, 24)

The moment a man in a subordinate position begins to usurp the authority of his leader, that moment he is out of his place, and proves by his conduct that he does not comprehend his duty, that he is not acting in the line of his calling, and is a dangerous character. He will set bad examples, he will mislead, he will lead others into error, having fallen into error himself; indeed, he is in error the moment he acts contrary to and independent of the direction of his presiding officer; and if he continues in that course he will go astray entirely. —*Joseph F. Smith* (GD, 185)

Though one teach with the eloquence of an angel, yet one's good practices, good examples, one's acts, constantly manifesting whole-heartedness for the interests of the people, teach much more eloquently, much more effectually. —*Lorenzo Snow* (LS, 191)

My faith is that no man, in this or any other generation, is able to teach and edify the inhabitants of the earth without the inspiration of the Spirit of God. —*Wilford Woodruff* (WW, 57)

"If a thing is well done no one will ask how long it took to do it, but who did it." There is no room for shoddy performance in the Church. An able leader will expect quality, and he will let those whom he assigns know that he expects quality. —*John Taylor* (GFC, 139)

It was asked me by a gentleman how I guided the people by revelation. I teach them to live so that the Spirit of revelation may make plain to them their duty day by day that they are able to guide themselves. —*Brigham Young* (BY, 41)

We shall never have the keys of authority committed to us to be rulers until we will rule just as God would rule if he were here himself. —*Brigham Young* (BY, 146)

I wish you to build up every man who is in the faith of the Gospel who is in the faith of God, angels, and good men; and if you strive to pull down good men who are around you, you are sure to fall yourselves. —*Brigham Young* (BY, 147)

You must not chasten them severely; you must chasten according to the spirit that is in the person. . . . There is a great variety. Treat people as they are. —*Brigham Young* (BY, 150)

I have had some people ask me how I manage and control the people. I do it by telling them the truth and letting them do just as they have a mind to. —*Brigham Young* (BY, 355)

When the Twelve or any other witnesses stand before the congregations of the earth, and they preach in the power and demonstration of the Spirit of God, and the people are astonished and confounded at the doctrine, and say, "That man has preached a powerful discourse, a great sermon," then let that man or those men take care that they do not ascribe the glory unto themselves, but be careful that they are humble, and ascribe the praise and glory to God and the Lamb; for it is by the power of the Holy Priesthood and the Holy Ghost that they have power thus to speak. —*Joseph Smith, Jr.* (STJS, 175-176)

The Saints need not think because I am familiar with them and am playful and cheerful, that I am ignorant of what is going on. Iniquity of any kind cannot be sustained in the Church, and it will not fare well where I am; for I am determined while I do lead the Church, to lead it right. —*Joseph Smith, Jr.* (STJS, 343)

I have no enmity against any man. I love you all; but I hate some of your deeds. I am your best friend, and if persons miss their mark it is their own fault. If I reprove a man, and he hates me, he is a fool; for I love all men, especially these my brethren and sisters. —*Joseph Smith, Jr.* (STJS, 406)

I have sometimes spoken too harshly from the impulse of the moment, and inasmuch as I have wounded your feelings, brethren, I ask your forgiveness, for I love you and will hold you up with all my heart in all righteousness, before the Lord, and before all men . . . And I will now covenant with you before God, that I will not listen to or credit any derogatory report against any of you, nor condemn you upon any testimony beneath the heavens, short of that testimony which is infallible, until I can see you face to face, and know of a surety; and I do place unremitted confidence in your word, for I believe you to be men of truth. And I ask the same of you, when I tell you anything, that you place equal confidence in my word, for I will not tell you I know anything that I do not know. —*Joseph Smith, Jr.* (STJS, 125)

The way to get along in any important matter is to gather unto yourselves wise men, experienced and aged men, to assist in council in all times of trouble. —*Joseph Smith, Jr.* (STJS, 334)

74. LATTER-DAY PROPHETS

We either have a prophet or we have nothing; and having a prophet, we have everything. —*Gordon B. Hinckley* (BTE, 123)

I am satisfied that the peace and the progress and the prosperity of this people lie in doing the will of the Lord as that will is articulated by him who presides over this church. If we fail to observe his counsel, we repudiate his sacred calling. If we abide his counsel, we shall be blessed of God. —*Gordon B. Hinckley* (BTE, 126)

The First Presidency and the Council of the Twelve Apostles, called and ordained to hold the keys of the priesthood, have the authority and responsibility to govern the church, to administer its ordinances, to expound its doctrine, and to establish and maintain its practices. Each man who is ordained an Apostle and sustained a member of the Council of the Twelve is sustained as a prophet, seer, and revelator. —*Gordon B. Hinckley* (Ensign, May 1994, 54)

Let me give you a crucial key to help you avoid being deceived. It is this—learn to keep your eye on the prophet. He is the Lord's mouthpiece and the only man who can speak for the Lord today. Let his inspired counsel take precedence. Let his inspired words be a basis for evaluating the counsel of all lesser authorities. Then live close to the Spirit so you may know the truth of all things. —*Ezra Taft Benson* (ETB, 134)

The world prefers that prophets either be dead or minded their own business. Some so-called experts of political science want the prophet to keep still on politics. Some would-be authorities on evolution want the prophet to keep still on evolution. And so the list goes on and on.

How we respond to the words of a living prophet when he tells us what we need to know, but would rather not hear, is a test of our faithfulness. —*Ezra Taft Benson* (ETB, 139-140)

The President of the Church alone may declare the mind and will of God to His people. No officer nor any other church in the world has this high and lofty prerogative. When the President proclaims any such new doctrine, he will declare it to be a revelation from the Lord. —*Harold B. Lee* (SHP, 109-110)

Do you suppose that when the Lord has a prophet on the earth, He is going to take some round-about means of revealing things to His children? That is what He has a prophet for. —*Harold B. Lee* (SHP, 159)

Yes, we believe in a living prophet, seer, and revelator, and I bear you my solemn witness that we have a living prophet, seer, and revelator. We are not dependent only upon the revelations given in the past as contained in our standard works—as wonderful as they are—but we have a mouthpiece to whom God does reveal and is revealing His mind and will. God will never permit him to lead us astray. —*Harold B. Lee* (SHP, 164)

A prophet is one who teaches by the voice of inspiration the words of eternal life, and who officiates in the saving ordinances of the gospel, predicting is only one qualification of a prophet. —*Joseph Fielding Smith* (DS1, 185)

Every man who can say knowingly that the Lord Jesus Christ is the Redeemer of the world and the Only Begotten Son of God, is a prophet. Every man that holds the priesthood, and magnifies his calling, is a prophet; and he has a right to the inspiration of the Holy Spirit, so far as he is concerned—but not to receive revelation for the Church. There is only one who is appointed to that office. —*Joseph Fielding Smith* (DS1, 185)

Now the reason for prophets in this day is that we might be guided in all truth, that we might draw near unto God, that we might know his ways and walk in his paths in righteousness. —*Joseph Fielding Smith* (DS1, 186)

An Apostle's duty as commissioned is to be a special witness of the Lord Jesus Christ, to bear witness to his doctrine, of its effect upon mankind. —*David O. McKay* (GI, 251)

When we are instructed by the President of the Church, we believe he tells us what the Lord would have us do. To us it is just something more than the advice of man. We believe this and it searches our souls and we are prompted to renew our determination to be what God would have us be. —*George Albert Smith* (CR, Apr. 1930, 66)

Wherever the people have listened to the prophets they have had success and happiness and they have been making preparation for eternal joy. —*George Albert Smith* (CR, Oct. 1936, 71)

I know of nothing that I feel is of so great value in life as to be obedient to the counsel and advice of the Lord, and of His servants in this our day. —*Heber J. Grant* (GS, 69-70)

I know that the path of safety for the Latter-day Saints is not only to sing, "We thank Thee, O God, for a Prophet, to guide us in these latter days," but to be ready and willing and anxious to be guided. —*Heber J. Grant* (CR, Oct. 1913, 88)

Life eternal is what we are working for. Do not allow the wisdom, the riches or the education of the world, or anything else, to blind our eyes to the fact that this is God's work, and that the mouthpiece of God is on the earth. When he speaks, let us be ready and willing, with our time, our talents and all that has been given us to labor to fulfill what God desires. —*Heber J. Grant* (CR, Oct. 1903, 9-10)

I testify in the name of Israel's God that he will not suffer the head of the Church, whom he has chosen to stand at the head, to transgress his laws and apostatize; the moment he should take a course that would in time lead to it, God would take him away. Why? Because to suffer a wicked man to occupy that position would be to allow, as it were, the fountain to become corrupted, which is something he will never permit. —*Joseph F. Smith* (JD, 24:192)

Whatever counsel the Presidency of this Church have been led to give unto this people, it has been dictated by the Spirit and power of God, and our safety and salvation lies in obeying that counsel and putting it into practice. We should learn to listen to the operation and manifestation of the Spirit of Truth.

Pray for the Presidency of this Church—pray for them to have the spirit of revelation. —*Wilford Woodruff* (WW, 87-88)

I say to Israel, the Lord will never permit me or any other man who stands as president of this Church to lead you astray. It is not in the program. It is not in the mind of God. If I were to attempt that the Lord would remove me out of my place. —*Wilford Woodruff* (WW, 212-213)

I clearly saw and understood, by the spirit of revelation manifested to me, that if I was to harbor a thought in my heart that Joseph could be wrong in anything, I would begin to lose confidence in him, and that feeling would grow from step to step, and from one degree to another, until at last I would have the same lack of confidence in his being the mouthpiece of the Almighty. —*Brigham Young* (JD, 4:297)

The Lord Almighty leads this Church, and he will never suffer you to be led astray if you are found doing your duty. You may go home and sleep as sweetly as a babe in its mother's arms, as to any danger of your leaders leading you astray, for if they should try to do so the Lord would quickly sweep them from the earth. —*Brigham Young* (BY, 137)

This morning I read German and visited with a brother and sister from Michigan, who thought that "a prophet is always a prophet;" but I told them that a prophet was a prophet only when he was acting as such. —*Joseph Smith, Jr.* (STJS, 313)

75. CHURCH LEADERS

A prophet is one who has been called and raised up by the Lord to further God's purposes among his children. He is one who has received the priesthood and speaks with authority. Prophets are teachers and defenders of the gospel. They bear witness of the divinity of the Lord Jesus Christ. Prophets have foretold future happenings, but this is not the most important of their responsibilities, although it may be some evidence of prophetic power. —*Howard W. Hunter* (CR, Oct. 1963, 101)

I have a personal conviction that after the long period of spiritual darkness in the world, the gospel has been restored in its fullness through divine revelation, and the Church of Christ has again been established on earth—that this restored Church has the same organization that existed in the original Church, including those of apostolic calling who do bear witness of the divinity of Christ, his death, and resurrection, and that he is the Son of God. —*Howard W. Hunter* (CR, Oct. 1965, 115)

I have witnessed the refining processes through which the Lord chips, buffs, and polishes those whom He selected to hold keys of His kingdom, that they become polished shafts in His hand. —*Ezra Taft Benson* (ETB, 145)

The bishop's first and foremost responsibility is the Aaronic Priesthood and the young women of his ward. Bishops, stay close to both your young men and young women. Give as much attention to the young women's program in your ward as you do the young men's programs. Be as concerned about the young women's activities and classes, their camp-outs and socials, their firesides and conferences as you are the young men's. —*Ezra Taft Benson* (Ensign, Nov. 1986, 85)

An ideal stake will have a president who loves the word of God and is a student of the scriptures, who will know that true conversion comes first by knowing the will of God and, secondly, by living its principles carefully. He will be an unbiased judge, who will be governed by justice and never by any personal reasons. In his role as judge he will conduct interviews with stake leaders and members who will be placed in positions of trust and responsibility. He will want to be in tune with the Holy Spirit in order to best serve these people and to guide them and redirect them where necessary. —*Spencer W. Kimball* (SWK, 473)

A bishop is ordained with an everlasting endowment, and it is lost only through unworthiness which brings Church discipline, even to excommunication. He is set apart as bishop of a ward to provide it leadership. He becomes the judge, spiritual adviser, inspirer, counselor, discipliner. He becomes by ordination and setting apart the father of his people and should know them individually by name and nature and weakness and strength. He should foresee and forestall possible problems and, if some develop, be able and ready to help in their solution. His ward family should be his enlarged family and receive the same general interest as his own flesh and blood children. —*Spencer W. Kimball* (SWK, 474)

Had Oliver Cowdery remained true, had he been faithful to his testimony and his calling as the "Second Elder" and Assistant President of the Church, I am just as satisfied as I am that I am here that Oliver Cowdery would have gone to Carthage with the Prophet Joseph Smith and laid down his life instead of Hyrum Smith. That would have been his right. Maybe it sounds a little strange to speak of martyrdom as being a right, but it was a right. Oliver Cowdery lost it and Hyrum Smith received it. According to the law of witnesses—and this is a divine law—it had to be. —*Joseph Fielding Smith* (CN, Apr. 8, 1939, 8)

I rejoice that in all my associations with the General Authorities of the Church since I was six years of age I have never heard one word, in public or in private, fall from the lips of these men, but what would be for the benefit, for the uplift, for the improvement morally and intellectually, physically, and spiritually of the Latter-day Saints. —*Heber J. Grant* (CR, Apr. 1917, 24)

It is expected of a bishop to know all the people in his ward, not only those who are faithful members of the Church, diligent in the performance of their duties and prominent by their good acts, but to know those who are cold and indifferent, those who are lukewarm, those who are inclined to err and to make mistakes; and not only these, but it is expected that the bishops, through their aides in their wards, will become acquainted, not only with their members, male and female, but that they will know also the stranger that is within their gates and be prepared to minister solace, comfort, good counsel, wisdom and every other aid possible to be rendered to those who are in need, whether they are of the household of faith or are strangers to the truth. —*Joseph F. Smith* (CR, Apr. 1913, 4)

[A]n Apostle must possess a divine knowledge, by revelation from God, that Jesus lives—that He is the Son of the living God. —*Lorenzo Snow* (LS, 84)

The Bishops should be a Perfect example to their Wards in all things. —*Brigham Young* (BY, 144)

76. DEVELOPING LEADERSHIP CAPACITY

It is an axiom as true as life itself that we grow as we serve. The Church of Jesus Christ of Latter-day Saints is, among other things, a great school for the development of leadership. I have told the groups of our missionaries, as I have met with them in various parts of the world, "You're not much to look at, but you're all the Lord has." And the miracle is that as they serve the Lord, they become giants in capacity and in achievement. —*Gordon B. Hinckley* (CR, Apr. 1972, 76)

Growth comes as we constantly seek to achieve that which is just beyond our immediate capacity. One of the noteworthy aspects of the Church program is that it constantly motivates men to stretch themselves, to reach a little higher. —*Gordon B. Hinckley* (CR, Apr. 1972, 77)

There is no small or unimportant duty in the kingdom of God. And out of the fulfillment of each responsibility comes the strength to undertake something new and more demanding. The men who sit tonight on the stand in this Tabernacle and the priesthood leaders across the world are for the most part the lengthened shadow of boys who tried earnestly to do what they were asked to do. —*Gordon B. Hinckley* (CR, Oct. 1972, 108)

The important thing, the wonderful thing that I see in this Church everywhere I go all over the world, is men and women who are very ordinary, really, by the standards of the world, who are doing marvelous and wonderful things as leaders in this Church. Not of their own strength and capacity, but because the Spirit of the Lord comes into their lives and the Holy Ghost teaches through them. And the Holy Ghost can teach us things that we cannot teach one another. Never forget that. —*Gordon B. Hinckley* (CN, Dec. 2, 1995, 2)

One who is hungering and thirsting after knowledge will not fail to gain a preeminent place of leadership among his fellowmen. —*Ezra Taft Benson* (ETB, 239)

Shrink not from duty as it is made known. Accept responsibility. Be grateful for work. Hesitate not to do your full share of it. —*Ezra Taft Benson* (CN, June 4, 1947, 5)

I am confident that as leaders we do not do enough fasting and praying. . . . It will do more to give you the real spirit of your office and calling and permit the Spirit to operate through you than anything I know. —*Ezra Taft Benson* (ETB, 331-332)

Effective management is the art of multiplying yourself through others. . . . Authority and responsibility may be delegated. Accountability may not be delegated. The most eligible candidate for a bigger job is the man who has already trained his own replacement. —*Ezra Taft Benson* (ETB, 379)

I believe that to tell a man what is expected of him is more important than to prescribe exactly how he is to get the job done. —*Ezra Taft Benson* (CR, May 1981, 34)

When we try to do another individual's work for him or her, we are really saying, "I have no need of you." Even when we might do something better than the individual who stands in his place, we must not seek to supplant lest no growth occur in that individual. —*Harold B. Lee* (Ensign Jan. 1974, 99-100)

It would be well that when you have noticed a splendid piece of work or an excellent sermon, you don't merely say, "That was wonderful, that was a fine talk," but if you could point out the specific things in that talk or in that performance which needed to be particularly commended. Such commendation would be much more appreciated than merely a generalized "That was fine" or "That was good."—*Harold B. Lee* (HBL, 199)

It is natural for followers to tire, at times, of too much rhetoric and oratory. Given a choice between exhortation and example, most of us prefer example. —*Harold B. Lee* (HBL, 508)

It is a wise leader who does not make his flock depend upon him for too much or too much of the time. —*Harold B. Lee* (HBL, 514-515)

What do we accomplish if we spend our time and means preaching in the world to make converts to the gospel, if we place instructors before the youth in the stakes and wards who destroy the faith in the hearts of the young people in the divine message entrusted to our care?—*Joseph Fielding Smith* (CR, Apr. 1928, 66)

77. THE OBLIGATION OF LEADERSHIP

Here is a great key to reactivation of many of those who have fallen by the wayside. Each has a talent that can be employed. It is the task of leaders to match those talents with needs, and then to offer a challenge. —*Gordon B. Hinckley* (Ensign, Nov. 1982, 8)

Each of our temples has on its face the statement "Holiness to the Lord," to which I should like to add the injunction "Keep His House holy!"

I submit that every man who holds the Melchizedek Priesthood has an obligation to see that the House of the Lord is kept sacred and free of any defilement. This obligation rests primarily and inescapably upon the shoulders of bishops and stake presidents. They become the judges of worthiness concerning those eligible to enter the temple. Additionally, each of us has an obligation—first, as to his own personal worthiness, and secondly, as to the worthiness of those whom he may encourage or assist in going to the House of the Lord. —*Gordon B. Hinckley* (Ensign, May 1990, 50)

We are becoming a great global society. But our interest and concern must always be with the individual. Every member of this church is an individual man or woman, boy or girl. Our great responsibility is to see that each is "remembered and nourished by the good word of God" (Moro. 6:4), that each has opportunity for growth and expression and training in the work and say of the Lord, that none lacks the necessities of life, that the needs of the poor are met, that each member shall have encouragement, training, and opportunity to move forward on the road of immortality and eternal life. This, I submit, is the inspired genius of this the Lord's work. —*Gordon B. Hinckley* (Ensign, May 1995, 52-53)

We know, for example, that the time a leader spends in personal contact with members is more productive than time spent in meetings and administrative duties. Personal contact is the key to converting the inactive member. —*Ezra Taft Benson* (ETB, 147)

While I do not believe in stepping out of the path of duty to pick up a cross I don't need, a man is a coward who refuses to pick up a cross that clearly lies within his path. No cross, no crown. No gall, no glory. No thorns, no throne. —*Ezra Taft Benson* (ETB, 394)

Righteous concern about conditions is commendable when it leads to constructive action. But undo worry is debilitating. When we have done what we can do, then let us leave the rest to God. —*Ezra Taft Benson* (IE, June 1967, 59)

Give a pig and a boy everything each wants, and you will get a good pig and a bad boy. —*Ezra Taft Benson* (ETB, 564)

When you are tempted to reprimand a fellow worker, don't. Try an interesting challenge and a pat on the back instead. Our Father's children throughout the world are essentially good. He loves them. We should also. —*Ezra Taft Benson* (ETB, 377)

Remember that you are the coach, not the quarterback on this great team. When you get a man to assume his duties, you have not only blessed his family and done the world a favor. But you have helped him to develop and grow. —*Ezra Taft Benson* (ETB, 380)

When known transgressions have been duly reported to the proper ecclesiastical officers of the Church, the individual may rest the case and leave the responsibility with the Church officers. If those officers tolerate sin in the ranks, it is an awesome responsibility for them and they will be held accountable. —*Spencer W. Kimball* (MF, p. 262)

I fear at times that all too often many of our members come to church, set through a class or meeting, and then return home having been largely uninformed. It is especially unfortunate if this happens at a time when they may be entering a period of stress, temptation, or personal or family crisis. We all need to be touched and nurtured by the Spirit, and effective teaching is one of the most important ways this can happen. We regularly do vigorous enlistment and reactivation work to get members to come to church, but often do not watch over what they receive when they do attend. —*Spencer W. Kimball* (Ensign, May 1981, 45.)

Never must we allow supposed mercy to the unrepentant sinner to rob the justice by which true repentance from sinful practices is predicated. —*Harold B. Lee* (DSL, 246)

The Savior's disciples are the salt of society in every dispensation. Salt preserves food from corruption and seasons it, making it wholesome and acceptable; in like manner the Master's disciples are to purify the society in which they move, setting a good example and counteracting every corrupt tendency. —*Harold B. Lee* (YLW, 11)

I find some of our brethren who are engaged in leadership positions justifying their neglect of their families because they say that they are engaged in the Lord's work. I say to them, "My dear brother, do you realize that the most important part of the Lord's work that you will do is the work that you do within the walls of your own home? That is the most important work of the Lord. Don't get your sense of values mixed up. —*Harold B. Lee* (YLW, 33)

You who come to be leaders must be prepared to tell those you call that you prayed about this, and you have the inspiration or the gift of prophecy to know that they were the ones the Lord wanted in this position. And until you are prepared to say that, you are not prepared to call that person by the gift of prophecy. When you are prepared to say that, then you will have one who will respond with all the dedication in the world. —*Harold B. Lee* (HBL, 552)

How careful our instructors in our schools, institutes, seminaries, priesthood classes and auxiliaries should be to guard the revealed truth from heaven! How fearful we should be lest we teach that which is false and thereby lead souls astray, in paths that lead to death and away from the exaltation in the kingdom of God. There is no greater crime in all the world than to teach false doctrines and lead the unsuspecting astray, away from the eternal truths of the gospel. —*Joseph Fielding Smith* (CN, June 12, 1949, 21-22)

Good order in the classroom is essential to instil into the hearts and lives of young men and young women the principle of self-control. They want to talk, and they want to whisper, but they cannot do it, because it will disturb somebody else. Learn the power and lesson of self-mastery. —*David O. McKay* (CR, Sept.-Oct. 1950, 166)

Our most precious possession is the youth of the land, and to instruct them to walk uprightly and to become worthy citizens in the kingdom of God is our greatest obligation. —*David O. McKay* (CR, Apr. 1953, 15)

No true leader of the Church will ever profane the name of God or his Beloved Son, especially in the presence of his sons, or in the presence of any other young people. Profanity is a vice. We can set a proper example also by speaking well of others. The Lord has admonished us not to engage in backbiting. Another worthy example is exercising self-control, controlling our temper by not speaking angrily in the home. Let calmness be characteristic of our home life. —*David O. McKay* (CR, Apr. 1959, 75)

I should like to emphasize the need for more spirituality, for more meditation and communion with our Father in heaven. I ask that you men of the priesthood—you stake presidents, you bishops, and other leaders in stakes and wards—see to it that a spirit of reverence is maintained in our homes and houses of worship. —*David O. McKay* (CR, Apr. 1967, 85)

There is no question but that impressions made upon the minds of little innocent children and young boys and girls have a more lasting effect upon their future lives than impressions made at any other time. It is like writing, figuratively speaking, upon a white piece of paper, with nothing on it to obscure or confuse what you may write. —*Heber J. Grant* (IE, 42:135)

There is no dividend that any human being can draw from bonds or stocks, or anything in the wealth of the world, that compares with the knowledge in one's heart that he or she has been an instrument in the hands of God of shaping some life for good. —*Heber J. Grant* (IE, 42:135)

Criticism does not have any effect upon a man who is doing his duty. A man who does his duty has the approval of his own conscience and that is the finest pay in all the world. —*Heber J. Grant* (IE, 42:585)

Each and every one of our teachers has the opportunity and the power under the inspiration of the Spirit of God, to make an impression upon the hearts and souls of little innocent children and young boys and girls who are starting out in the battle of life. . . . The important thing for you is to have a love of your work and to do your work under the inspiration of the Spirit of the living God. —*Heber J. Grant* (IE, 42:135)

Those who have authority should not be rulers, nor dictators; they should not be arbitrary; they should gain the hearts, the confidence and love of those over whom they preside, by kindness and love unfeigned, by gentleness of spirit, by persuasion, by an example that is above reproach and above the reach of unjust criticism. In this way, in the kindness of their hearts, in their love for their people, they lead them in the path of righteousness, and teach them the way of salvation, by saying to them, both by precept and example: Follow me, as I follow our head. This is the duty of those who preside. —*Joseph F. Smith* (CR, Apr. 1915, 5)

I know, as the God of Israel lives, that I have no power, nor have I had, in this Church, to perform any work pertaining to this kingdom, until it has been given unto me by the God of heaven. . . . And the moment that I attempt to become lifted up in the pride of my heart, because of any position that I hold, that moment I become a very unwise man. So with anyone else. The higher our position the more our responsibility. —*Wilford Woodruff* (WW, 88)

If anybody supposes that the Presidency and apostles here are never tempted of the devil, they are mistaken. We are tempted all the time, more or less, and we have to war against these things in order to stand and maintain our position. —*Wilford Woodruff* (WW, 90)

If our eyes were opened, if the veil were lifted, and we could see our condition, our responsibility, and could comprehend the feelings of God our heavenly Father, and the heavenly hosts, and the justified spirits made perfect, in their watch-care over us, in their anxiety about us in our labors here in the flesh; we would all feel that we have no time to waste in folly or anything else which brings to pass no good. —*Wilford Woodruff* (WW, 102-103)

The Lord holds each man responsible for that portion of his flock which is placed in his care. —*John Taylor* (GK, 170)

If the time was that the Elders of Israel could not be chastened and corrected for their wrongs, and be set right, you may know that they have proved recreant to the faith. And if those who are appointed to lead this people dare not rise up and tell them of their iniquity and chastise them therefor, and teach them the way of life and salvation, you may know that your leaders have fallen from their station. —*Brigham Young* (BY, 148)

Every man, before he makes an objection to any item that is brought before a council for consideration, should be sure that he can throw light upon the subject rather than spread darkness, and that his objection be founded in righteousness, which may be done by men applying themselves closely to study the mind and will of the Lord, whose spirit always makes manifest and demonstrates the truth to the understanding of all who are in possession of the Spirit. —*Joseph Smith, Jr.* (STJS, 112)

78. QUALIFICATIONS FOR LEADERSHIP

The stake president of course must be the spiritual anchor. He also must be able to manage the complex affairs of the stake, and therefore he must have administrative ability or at least the capacity to learn. On occasion, he stands as a judge of the people and must be a man of wisdom and discernment. But wealth and financial success are not criteria for Church service. I think I speak for all of my brethren when I say that in selecting a man to preside over a stake of Zion there is much of prayer with much of seeking the will of the Lord, and only when that will is recognized is action taken. —*Gordon B. Hinckley* (Ensign, May 1982, 41-42)

Personal worthiness is the key to fitness for the office in the kingdom of God. —*Gordon B. Hinckley* (Ensign, May 1982, 41-42)

Some express concern that the President of the Church is likely always to be a rather elderly man, to which my response is, "What a blessing!" . . .

To my mind there is something tremendously reassuring in knowing that for the foreseeable future we shall have a President who has been disciplined and schooled, tried and tested, whose fidelity to the work and whose integrity in the cause have been tempered in the forge of service, whose faith has matured, and whose nearness to God has been cultivated over a period of many years. —*Gordon B. Hinckley* (Ensign, May 1983, 6-7)

Let me now speak directly to the thousands of bishops who are in attendance tonight. Let me say first that I love you for your integrity and goodness. You must be men of integrity. You must stand as examples to the congregations over which you preside. —*Gordon B. Hinckley* (Ensign, Nov. 1988, 48-50)

Jesus taught his disciples to watch and pray; however, he taught them that prayerful watching does not require sleepless anxiety and preoccupation with the future, but rather the quiet, steady attention to present duties. —*Howard W. Hunter* (Ensign, May 1974, 18)

I believe that all the truly great men of the earth have been men who trusted in god and who have striven to do that which is right as they understood the right. —*Ezra Taft Benson* (IE, June 1954, 406)

Any leader who, without reservation, cannot declare his testimony that God and Jesus Christ appeared to Joseph Smith can never be a true leader, a true shepherd. —*Ezra Taft Benson* (ETB, 101)

First, let us do our homework, because action without proper education can lead to fanaticism. But after we have done our homework, let us take action, because education without action can only lead to frustration and failure. —*Ezra Taft Benson* (ETB, 301)

What good is a sleepy, neutralized, lukewarm giant as a leader? We have too many potential spiritual giants who should be more vigorously lifting their homes, the kingdom, and the country. We have many who feel they are good men, but they need to be good for something—stronger patriarchs, courageous missionaries, valiant genealogists and temple workers, dedicated patriots, devoted quorum members. In short, we must be shakened and awakened from a spiritual snooze. —*Ezra Taft Benson* (ETB, 403-404)

Sometimes in the Church we have people who lose their faith because a bishop or a high councilor or a stake president goes astray. They fail to realize that all these people also are human, and while they have weaknesses they are striving to live better, but sometimes they succumb to the whirlpool of temptations about them. . . . They fail to realize that if we waited until we could find absolutely perfect people to man the organizations in the Church, we would never have an organization. —*Spencer W. Kimball* (SWK, 459-460)

The setting apart may be taken literally; it is a setting apart from sin, apart from the carnal; apart from everything which is crude, low, vicious, cheap, or vulgar; set apart from the world to a higher plane of thought and activity. —*Spencer W. Kimball* (SWK, 478)

We are not yet perfect as Jesus was, but unless those about us can see us striving and improving, they will not be able to look to us for example, and they will see us as less than fully serious about the things to be done. —*Spencer W. Kimball* (Ensign, Aug. 1985, 5)

When a member releases the keys that he formerly held, the keys do not belong to him anymore. They belong to somebody else, and he doesn't have the authority he once had because there is order in the Church. —*Harold B. Lee* (YLW, 215-217)

One of the marks of true leadership in yourself is the ability to generously approve the good and to constructively criticize the bad in those whom you expect to follow your leadership. —*Harold B. Lee* (DSL, 27)

Not only must we avoid sin but we must avoid the very appearance of evil. No person of high station ever fell in sin or into disrepute without shattering the ideals or dream castles of some youth who had faith in him. —*Harold B. Lee* (DSL, 37)

You cannot lift another soul until you are standing on higher ground than he is. You must be sure, if you would rescue the man, that you yourself are setting the example of what you would have him be. You cannot light a fire in another soul unless it is burning in your own soul. You teachers, the testimony that you bear, the spirit with which you teach and with which you lead, is one of the most important assets that you can have, as you help to strengthen those who need so much, wherein you have so much to give. Who of us, in whatever station we may have been in, have not needed strengthening?—*Harold B. Lee* (SHP, 187)

A person cannot teach something that he does not himself observe. We are all expected to keep the commandments of the Lord, and it is our privilege and blessing as teachers, if we do keep the commandments, to receive thereby the qualifications of a teacher. —*Harold B. Lee* (YLW, 96)

Someone has said that not all teaching is done in the classroom. How true this is! A true teacher is always in character. Her students' eyes are always upon her. She is their teacher wherever they see her. —*Harold B. Lee* (YLW, 133)

It matters not what a man's training or what his schooling may be—how many degrees he holds—if he has not faith in the gospel of Jesus Christ and has no testimony received from the Spirit of the Lord of the divine truth which has been revealed he is not qualified to teach in any organization within the Church. —*Joseph Fielding Smith* (CR, Apr. 1928, 65)

The first thing to do, my brethren, is to look to yourselves, to see whether or not you are prepared to teach. No man can teach that which he himself does not know. —*David O. McKay* (CR, Oct. 1916, 59)

It is ridiculous to attempt to lead a young man or a young woman to obtain a testimony of the work of God, if the man or woman who is attempting to lead does not have that testimony himself or herself. —*David O. McKay* (IE, 22:900)

No man can teach the gospel of Jesus Christ under the inspiration of the living God and with power from on high unless he is living it. He can go on as a member and we will pray for him, no matter how many years it may require, and we will never put a block in his way, because the gospel is one of love and of forgiveness, but we want true men and women as our officers in the Priesthood and in the Relief Society. —*Heber J. Grant* (IE, 44:267)

There has never been a time in the Church when its leaders were not required to be courageous men; not alone courageous in the sense that they were able to meet physical dangers, but also in the sense that they were steadfast and true to a clear and upright conviction. —*Joseph F. Smith* (GD, 155)

In leaders undue impatience and a gloomy mind are almost unpardonable, and it sometimes takes almost as much courage to wait as to act. It is to be hoped, then, that the leaders of God's people, and the people themselves, will not feel that they must have at once a solution of every question that arises to disturb the even tenor of their way. —*Joseph F. Smith* (GD, 156)

Every man should be willing to be presided over; and he is not fit to preside over others until he can submit sufficiently to the presidency of his brethren. —*Joseph F. Smith* (IE, 21:105)

Above all things let me say to the presidents of stakes and counselors and presidents of missions, and to the bishops and their counselors—let me say to you all, live exemplary lives, so that you can each say to the people: "Come and follow me, follow my example, obey my precepts; be in union with me, and follow Christ."—*Joseph F. Smith* (CR, Oct. 1906, 8)

Under the celestial law of the kingdom of God men must unite together; men must love one another; men must stand by this Holy Priesthood and maintain the powers of it while they dwell in the flesh, in order to honor God and to be prepared to receive their inheritance in the world to come. —*Wilford Woodruff* (WW, 97)

I was once preaching to a large assembly in Collinsville, Connecticut; when I got through, a young clergyman came forward, and asked me if I had received any diploma from college. I answered him, "No."
"Do you know," said he, "that a man who has not received a college diploma has no right to preach?"
"No, sir," I said, "I do not know it."
"Well, sir," he said, "that is the case."
I then asked him to inform me how it was that Jesus preached, without receiving a college diploma?"—*Wilford Woodruff* (WW, 308)

Of all lessons, the living lesson is the best. Children are surprisingly shrewd in detecting inconsistencies between the instructions and habits of their instructors. Besides, the teacher who seeks to live up to his own advice not only benefits his scholars, but his teachings exert a salutary influence upon himself, and he profits by his own lessons. —*John Taylor* (GK, 276)

79. SUCCESSION

This transition of authority, in which I have participated a number of times, is beautiful in its simplicity. It is indicative of the way the Lord does things. Under His procedure a man is selected by the prophet to become a member of the Council of the Twelve Apostles. He does not choose this as a career. . . . The years pass. He is schooled and disciplined in the duties of his office. He travels over the earth in fulfilling his apostolic calling. It is a long course of preparation, in which he comes to know the Latter-day Saints wherever they may be and they come to know him. The Lord tests his heart and his substance. In the natural course of events, vacancies occur in that council and new appointments are made. Under this process a particular man becomes the senior Apostle. Residing latent in him . . . are all of the keys of the priesthood. But authority to exercise those keys is restricted to the President of the Church. At his passing, that authority becomes operative in the senior Apostle, who is then named, set apart, and ordained a prophet and President by his associates of the Council of the Twelve.

There is no electioneering. There is no campaigning. There is only the quiet and simple operation of a divine plan which provides inspired and tested leadership. —*Gordon B. Hinckley* (Ensign, May 1986, 46-47)

God knows all things, the end from the beginning, and no man becomes President of the Church of Jesus Christ by accident, or remains there by chance, or is called home by happenstance. —*Ezra Taft Benson* (NE, May 1975, 16-17)

Since the death of his servants is in the power and control of the Lord, he permits to come to the first place only the one who is destined to take that leadership. Death and life become the controlling factors. Each new apostle in turn is chosen by the Lord and revealed to the then living prophet who ordains him.

The matter of seniority is basic in the first quorums of the Church. All the apostles understand this perfectly, and all well-trained members of the Church are conversant with this perfect succession program. —*Spencer W. Kimball* (Ensign, Jan. 1973, 33)

No man comes to the demanding position of the Presidency of the Church except his heart and mind are constantly open to the impressions, insights, and revelations of God. —*Spencer W. Kimball* (SWK, 466)

Occasionally the question is asked as to whether or not one other than the senior member of the Twelve could become President. Some thought on this matter would suggest that any other than the senior member could become President of the Church only if the Lord reveals to that President of the Twelve that someone other than himself could be selected. —*Harold B. Lee* (HBL, 535)

There is no mystery about the choosing of the successor to the President of the Church. The Lord settled this a long time ago, and the senior apostle automatically becomes the presiding officer of the Church, and he is so sustained by the Council of the Twelve which becomes the presiding body of the Church when there is no First Presidency. The president is not elected, but he has to be sustained both by his brethren of the Council and by the members of the Church. —*Joseph Fielding Smith* (DS3, 156)

You need have no fear, my dear brothers and sisters, that any man will ever stand at the head of the Church of Jesus Christ unless our Heavenly Father wants him to be there. —*Heber J. Grant* (IE, 40:735)

At the death of the President of the Church, the Twelve Apostles become the presiding authority of the Church, and the president of the Twelve is really the President of the Church by virtue of his office as much while presiding over the Twelve Apostles as while presiding over his two counselors. —*Wilford Woodruff* (WW, 91-92)

CHURCH HISTORY AND MISSION

80. CHURCH HISTORY AND MISSION

The gospel is not a philosophy of repression, as so many regard it. It is a plan of freedom that gives discipline to appetite and direction to behavior. —*Gordon B. Hinckley* (CR, Apr. 1965, 78)

We have a challenge to meet, a work to do beyond the comprehension of any of us—that is, to assist our Heavenly Father to save His sons and daughters of all generations, both the living and the dead, to work for the salvation not only of those in the Church, but for those presently outside, wherever they may be. No body of people on the face of the earth has received a stronger mandate from the God of heaven than have we of this Church. —*Gordon B. Hinckley* (Ensign, May 1990, 97)

As we are spoken of as Mormons, we must so live that our example will enhance the perception that Mormon can mean in a very real way, "more good."—*Gordon B. Hinckley* (Ensign, Nov. 1990, 52-53)

I submit that the Church of Jesus Christ is as necessary in the lives of men and women today as it was when established by him, not by passive interest or a profession of faith, but by an assumption of active responsibility. In this way the Church brings us out of the darkness of an isolated life into the light of the gospel, where belief is turned into doing according to the admonitions of scripture. —*Howard W. Hunter* (CR, Oct. 1967, 13-14)

Faith in the existence of a divine and real and living personal God . . . is the everlasting foundation upon which The Church of Jesus Christ of Latter-day Saints is built today. —*Howard W. Hunter* (Ensign, May 1991, 64)

It is unity that has thus far enabled the Church, its ward and stakes, branches and districts, and members, to construct temples and chapels, seek after the dead, watch over the Church, and build faith. More must be done. These great purposes of the Lord could not have been achieved with dissension, jealousy or selfishness. —*Howard W. Hunter* (CN, March 11, 1995, 7)

Church history provides us with a lesson that when resistance and opposition are greatest, our faith, commitment, and growth have the greatest opportunity for advancement; when opposition is least, the tendency is to be complacent and lose faith. —*Howard W. Hunter* (WMJ, 99)

The Church will continue its opposition to error, falsehood, and immorality. The mission of the Church is to herald the message of salvation and make unmistakably clear the pathway to exaltation. Our mission is to prepare a people for the coming of the Lord. The power of God and the righteousness of the Saints will be the means by which the Church will be spared. —*Ezra Taft Benson* (CR, May 1980, 33-34)

Any church that you know of may possibly be able to take you for a long ride, and bring you some degree of peace and happiness and blessing, and they can carry you to the veil, and there they drop you. The Church of Jesus Christ picks you up on this side of the veil and, if you live its commandments, carries you right through the veil as though it weren't there and on through the eternities to exaltation. —*Spencer W. Kimball* (SWK, 422)

The strength of this church is not in organization, not in strong authority, but in the individual testimony that burns in the breast of every member in it. —*Harold B. Lee* (YLW, 113)

If this were the work of man, it would fail, but it is the work of the Lord, and he does not fail. And we have the assurance that if we keep the commandments and are valiant in the testimony of Jesus and are true to every trust, the Lord will guide and direct us and his church in the paths of righteousness, for the accomplishment of all his purposes. —*Joseph Fielding Smith* (CR, Apr. 1970, 113)

The responsibility resting upon the members of the Church in this dispensation is far greater than that given to any other dispensation. This being the last dispensation, it is our responsibility to labor, not only for ourselves, but also for all the righteous dead of all other dispensations for whom the work has to be done. —*Joseph Fielding Smith* (DS2, 244)

At one time it grieved me to know that this Church was not numbered among Protestant churches. But now I realize that the Church of Jesus Christ is more than a protest against the errors and evils of Catholicism. This Church was established in the only way in which the Church of Jesus Christ can be established—by direct authority from God. —*David O. McKay* (CR, Apr. 1927, 105)

Without his divine guidance and constant inspiration, we [the Church] cannot succeed. With his guidance, with his inspiration, we cannot fail. —*David O. McKay* (CR, Apr. 1951, 157)

That is the mission of the gospel of Jesus Christ—to make evil-minded men and women good, and to make good men and women better; in other words, to change men's lives, to change human nature. —*David O. McKay* (CR, Oct. 1958, 94)

I have had men ask me: "Of what benefit is your church more than any other church?" I have tried, in a tactful way to explain to them the difference. Any organization may band together for worship, but that does not give them divine authority. Any group of churches may mass together and organize community churches; that does not give them divine authority. Men may unite for good purposes, but authority from our Heavenly Father is only obtained in his way, and his way in former days was by calling and ordaining men and setting them apart for the work. The same thing is true in our day. —*George Albert Smith* (CR, Apr. 1934, 28)

Do not make any mistake in these days of uncertainty. This is God's work. This is his Church. It is the way that our Heavenly Father has provided to prepare us for eternal happiness. I pray that when the time comes for us to go hence we shall be entitled to a place in the celestial kingdom in the companionship of our loved ones and of the best people who have lived upon the earth. —*George Albert Smith* (SGO, 195-196)

We do not amount to very much in point of numbers when compared with the multitude of our Father's children, but we are intended to be the leaven of the religious world. —*George Albert Smith* (CR, Oct. 1938, 32)

I say to you Latter-day Saints, there are no other people in all the world who have all the information that we have with reference to the divinity of the Savior; and if we did not believe in Him we would be under greater condemnation than the others that have never had that information. —*George Albert Smith* (SGO, 229)

The gospel of Jesus Christ will solve the problem and be a panacea for the ills that afflict mankind. —*George Albert Smith* (CR, Apr. 1925, 68-69)

If we do our part, if we will keep the commandments of God, if we will love one another and observe the commandment of the Savior that we love our neighbor as ourself, then will we have strength, and power, and wisdom, and might, among the children of men, and the people of the world will love us, and they will not hate us because they will see in us the riches of righteousness and the blessings which come from the power of our Heavenly Father. —*George Albert Smith* (CR, Apr. 1942, 16)

The destiny of the Latter-day Saints is very great. I realize that the prophecies that have been made with reference to this people will all have to be fulfilled. . . . That the Saints will fulfill their destiny, that they will accomplish all that God desires them to accomplish, I have no doubt. Whether we, as individuals, shall do all that is possible for us to do is a personal matter. —*Heber J. Grant* (CR, Apr. 1902, 92-94)

There is no question in my mind but what the Lord is going to multiply the Latter-day Saints and bless them more abundantly in the future than He has ever done in the past, provided of course we are humble and diligent; provided we seek for the advancement of God's kingdom, and not to do our own mind and will. —*Heber J. Grant* (CR, Apr. 1899, 28)

Unless we as a people are united in our faith and in our labors, we cannot be acceptable in the sight of our Heavenly Father. —*Heber J. Grant* (GS, 97)

Any Latter-day Saint that thinks for one minute that this Church is going to fail is not a really converted Latter-day Saint. There will be no failure in this Church. It has been established for the last time, never to be given to another people and never to be thrown down. —*Heber J. Grant* (LPS, 168)

There is no fundamental principle, or truth, anywhere in the universe, that is not embraced in the gospel of Jesus Christ. —*Joseph F. Smith* (LPS, 84)

If we will only continue to build upon the principles of righteousness, of truth, of justice, and of honor, I say to you there is no power beneath the celestial kingdom that can stay the progress of this work. And as this work shall progress, and shall gain power and influence among men, so the powers of the adversary and of darkness will diminish before the advancement and growth of this kingdom, until the kingdom of God, and not of men, will triumph. —*Joseph F. Smith* (CR, Apr. 1914, 4)

[A]s soon as we convert our religion into a system of philosophy, none but philosophers can understand, appreciate, or enjoy it. God, in his revelation to man, has made his word so simple that the humblest of men, without special training, may enjoy great faith, comprehend the teachings of the gospel, and enjoy undisturbed their religious convictions. —*Joseph F. Smith* (GD, 8-9)

I desire to say that "Mormonism," as it is called, is still, as always, nothing more and nothing less than the power of God unto salvation, unto every soul that will receive it honestly and will obey it. —*Joseph F. Smith* (CR, Apr. 1910, 5)

Yet here in this region of salt, alkali, and sagebrush, all but treeless and waterless, a region condemned by Webster, decried by Bridger, and shunned by the overland emigrant as a valley of desolation and death, Mormonism set up its standard and proceeded to work out its destiny. Beneath its touch—the touch of untiring industry, divinely blessed and direct-ed—the desert blossomed, the wilderness became a fruitful field, and cities and towns sprang up by hundreds in the midst of the once barren waste. —*Lorenzo Snow* (LS, 152)

A religious system is of but little account when it possesses no virtue nor power to bet-ter the condition of people spiritually, intellectually, morally, and physically. —*Lorenzo Snow* (LS, 18)

The gospel binds together the hearts of all its adherents; it makes no difference, it knows no difference between the rich and the poor; we are all bound as one individual to perform the duties which devolve upon us. —*Lorenzo Snow* (LS, 22)

Am I prepared to make any sacrifice that He may require at my hands? I would not give the ashes of a rye straw for any religion that was not worth living for and that was not worth dying for; and I would not give much for the man that was not willing to sacrifice his all for the sake of his religion. —*Lorenzo Snow* (LS, 116)

This Church will stand, because it is upon a firm basis. It is not from man; it is not from the study of the New Testament or the Old Testament; it is not the result of the learning that we received in colleges nor seminaries, but it has come directly from the Lord. The Lord has shown it to us by the revealing principle of the Holy Spirit of light and every man can receive this same spirit. —*Lorenzo Snow* (CR, Apr. 1900, 3)

Mormonism, a nickname for the real religion of the Latter-day Saints, does not profess to be a new thing, except to this generation. It proclaims itself as the original plan of salva-tion, instituted in the heavens before the world was, and revealed from God to man in dif-ferent ages. . . . Mormonism, in short, is the primitive Christian faith restored, the ancient gospel brought back again—this time to usher in the last dispensation, introduce the Millennium, and wind up the work of redemption as pertaining to this planet. —*Lorenzo Snow* (LPS, 91)

If any man has a truth that we have not, we say, "Let us have it." I am willing to exchange all the errors and false notions I have for one truth, and should consider that I had made a good bargain. We are not afraid of light and truth. Our religion embraces every truth in heav-en, earth or hell; it embraces all truth, the whole gospel and plan of salvation, and the ful-filment of the whole volume of revelation that God has ever given. —*Wilford Woodruff* (WW, 17)

Mormonism is . . . the living, breathing, energetic, intelligent power; instead of the dead, withered, lifeless, inanimate body or form. It introduces man to a knowledge of himself, shows him his relationship to his fellow man, to the world, to saints, angels, spirits, and to God. It unfolds his origin and destiny, and unlocks the dark impenetrable future; the heav-ens are unveiled, and eternity is laid open. —*John Taylor* (GK, 1-3)

It shall be "The kingdom of God or nothing" with us. That is my text, I believe; and we shall stick to it—we will maintain it; and, in the name of Israel's God, the kingdom of God shall roll on, and all the powers of earth and hell cannot stop its progress. It is onward, onward, ONWARD, from this time henceforth, to all eternity. —*John Taylor* (JD, 6:26-27)

We know that we have embraced the principles of eternal truth, and we also know that we cannot get rid of them. I tested them thoroughly at the commencement. If I could have overthrown them by truth, I would; but I could not. I had either to embrace Mormonism or acknowledge myself dishonest. I believed, obeyed, and rejoiced in the gospel. Since

I received and obeyed the truth, I have never seen anything to cause me to waver. I have examined our religion closely and have found nothing to doubt. —*John Taylor* (GK, 8)

When Mormonism was presented to me, my first inquiry was, "Is it scriptural? Is it reasonable and philosophical?" This is the principle I would act upon today. No matter how popular the theories or dogmas preached might be, I would not accept them unless they were strictly in accordance with the scriptures, reason, and common sense. . . . In every principle presented to us, our first inquiry should be, "Is it true? Does it emanate from God?" If he is its author it can be sustained just as much as any other truth in natural philosophy; if false, it should be opposed and exposed just as much as any other error. —*John Taylor* (GK, 236)

Truth commends itself to every honest person, it matters not how simply it is told, and when it is received it seems as though we had been acquainted with it all our lives. It is the testimony of the majority of the Latter-day Saints that when they first heard the Gospel preached, as contained in the Bible and Doctrine and Covenants, although entirely new to them, it seemed as though they already understood it, and that they must have been "Mormons" from the beginning. —*Brigham Young* (BY, 432)

We wish the brethren to understand the facts just as they are; that is, there is neither man or woman in this Church who is not on a mission. That mission will last al long as they live, and it is to do good, to promote righteousness, to teach the principles of truth, and to prevail upon themselves and everybody around them to live those principles that they may obtain eternal live. This is the mission of every Latter-day Saint. —*Brigham Young* (JD, 12:19)

I want to say to my friends that we believe in all good. If you can find a truth in heaven, earth or hell, it belongs to our doctrine. We believe it; it is ours; we claim it. —*Brigham Young* (BY, 2)

We have the Gospel of life and salvation, to make bad men good and good men better. We are to preach, exhort, expound, continue in our duty, be fervent in spirit, bearing and forbearing with our brethren, being filled with love and kindness. —*Brigham Young* (BY, 6)

My religion is to know the will of God and do it. —*Brigham Young* (BY, 8)

The error I speak of, is the definition of the word "Mormon." It has been stated that this word was derived from the Greek word "*mormo*." This is not the case. There was no Greek or Latin upon the plates from which I, through the grace of God, translated the Book of Mormon. . . . We say from the Saxon, "good"; the Dane, "god"; the Goth, "goda"; the German, "gut"; the Dutch, "goed"; the Latin, "bonus"; the Greek, "kalos"; the Hebrew, "tob"; and the "Egyptian, "mon." Hence, with the addition of "more," or the contraction, "mor," we have the word "mormon"; which means, literally, "more good."—*Joseph Smith, Jr.* (STJS, 334-335)

And if we go to hell, we will turn the devils out of doors and make a heaven of it. Where this people are, there is good society. What do we care where we are, if the society be good? I don't care what a man's character is; if he's my friend—a true friend, I will be a friend to him, and preach the Gospel of salvation to him, and give him good counsel, helping him out of his difficulties. —*Joseph Smith, Jr.* (STJS, 354)

One of the grand fundamental principles of "Mormonism" is to receive truth, let it come from whence it may. —*Joseph Smith, Jr.* (STJS, 351)

[A] religion that does not require the sacrifice of all things never has power sufficient to produce the faith necessary unto life and salvation. —*Joseph Smith, Jr.* (LF, 69)

If it has been demonstrated that I have been willing to die for a "Mormon," I am bold to declare before Heaven that I am just as ready to die in defending the rights of a Presbyterian, a Baptist, or a good man of any other denomination; for the same principle which would trample upon the rights of the Latter-day Saints would trample upon the rights of the Roman Catholics, or of any other denominations who may be unpopular and too weak to defend themselves. —*Joseph Smith, Jr.* (STJS, 351)

Have the Presbyterians any truth? Yes. Have the Baptists, Methodists, etc., any truth? Yes. They all have a little truth mixed with error. We should gather all the good and true principles in the world and treasure them up, or we shall not come out true "Mormons."—*Joseph Smith, Jr.* (STJS, 355)

No unhallowed hand can stop the work from progressing; persecutions may rage, mobs may combine, armies may assemble, calumny may defame, but the truth of God will go forth boldly, noble, and independent, till it has penetrated every continent, visited every clime, swept every country, and sounded in every ear, till the purposes of God shall be accomplished, and the Great Jehovah shall say the work is done. —*Joseph Smith, Jr.* (HC 4:540)

The fundamental principles of our religion are the testimony of the Apostles and Prophets, concerning Jesus Christ, that He died, was buried, and rose again the third day, and ascended into heaven; and all other things which pertain to our religion are only appendages to it. But in connection with these, we believe in the gift of the Holy Ghost, the power of faith, the enjoyment of the spiritual gifts according to the will of God, the restoration of the house of Israel, and the final triumph of truth. —*Joseph Smith, Jr.* (STJS, 139)

I told Stephen Markham that if I and Hyrum were ever taken again we should be massacred, or I was not a prophet of God. —*Joseph Smith, Jr.* (STJS, 425)

I am going like a lamb to the slaughter, but I am calm as a summer's morning. I have a conscience void of offense toward God and toward all men. If they take my life I shall die an innocent man, and my blood shall cry from the ground for vengeance, and it shall be said of me, 'He was murdered in cold blood!'"—*Joseph Smith, Jr.* (STJS, 28)

81. BUILDING THE KINGDOM

The work of the Lord will continue to move forward. No power under the heavens can deflect it from its course. We may expect that there will be some who will try. Their efforts will be like chipping away at a granite block with a chisel of wood. The stone will not be damaged, but the chisel will be broken. —*Gordon B. Hinckley* (Ensign, May 1986, 47)

This Church does not belong to its President. Its head is the Lord Jesus Christ, whose name each of us has taken upon ourselves. We are all in this great endeavor together. We are here to assist our Father in His work and His glory, "to bring to pass the immortality and eternal life of man" (Moses 1:39). Your obligation is as serious in your sphere of responsibility as is my obligation in my sphere. No calling in this church is small or of little consequence. All of us in the pursuit of our duty touch the lives of others. To each of us in our respective responsibilities the Lord has said: "Wherefore, be faithful; stand in the office which I have appointed unto you; succor the weak, lift up the hands which hang down, and strengthen the feeble knees" (D&C 81:5). —*Gordon B. Hinckley* (Ensign, May 1995, 71)

You can't stop the work of the Lord from going forward. You can stop yourself from enjoying its blessings, but you cannot stop the work of the Lord from going forward. This is His work and regardless of what we do individually, He will find a way to accomplish His eternal purpose. —*Gordon B. Hinckley* (CN, Sept. 30, 1995, 2)

With so great an inheritance, we can do no less than our very best. Those who have gone before expect this of us. We have a mandate from the Lord. —*Gordon B. Hinckley* (CR, May 1997, 67)

This is a season of a thousand opportunities. It is ours to grasp and move forward. What a wonderful time it is for each of us to do his or her small part in moving the work of the Lord on to its magnificent destiny. —*Gordon B. Hinckley* (Ensign, Nov. 1997, 67)

Joseph Smith was not only a great man, but he was an inspired servant of the Lord, a prophet of God. His greatness consists in one thing—the truthfulness of his declaration that he saw the Father and the Son and that he responded to the reality of that divine revelation. —*Howard W. Hunter* (Ensign, May 1991, 64)

The clarion call of the Church is for all to come unto Christ, regardless of their particular circumstances. —*Howard W. Hunter* (WMJ, 53)

This is the church of Jesus Christ, not the church of marrieds or singles or any other group or individual. The gospel we preach is the gospel of Jesus Christ, which encompasses all the saving ordinances and covenants necessary to save and exalt every individual who is willing to accept Christ and keep the commandments that he and our Father in Heaven have given.
Each commandment given is for our benefit and happiness. To love and serve God and to love and serve his Son, our Savior Jesus Christ, should be our goal. —*Howard W. Hunter* (WMJ, 53)

We should have the ambition, we should have the desire, we should make up our minds that, so far as the Lord Almighty has given to us talent, we will do our full share in the battle of life. It should be a matter of pride that no man shall do more than you will do, in proportion to your ability, in forwarding the work of God here upon the earth. —*Howard W. Hunter* (WMJ, 152)

The gospel provides the only way the world will ever know peace. We need to be kinder with one another, more gentle and forgiving. We need to be slower to anger and more prompt to help. We need to extend the hand of friendship and resist the hand of retribution. In short we need to love one another with the pure love of Christ, with genuine charity and compassion and if necessary, shared suffering for that is the way God loves us. —*Howard W. Hunter* (CN, March 11, 1995, 7)

Remember that rational problem-solving procedures, though helpful, will not be solely sufficient in the work of the kingdom. God's work must be done by faith, prayer, and by the Spirit. —*Ezra Taft Benson* (ETB, 373)

It is time for us, as members of the Church, to walk in all the ways of the Lord, to use our influence to make popular that which is sound and to make unpopular that which is unsound. We have the scriptures, the prophets, and the gift of the Holy Ghost. Now we need eyes that will see, ears that will hear, and hearts that will hearken to God's direction. —*Ezra Taft Benson* (Ensign, Nov. 1988, 87)

We should be willing to generously give of our time, talents, and means to the Church. No matter what happens to the world, the Church will grow in strength and will be intact when the Lord comes again. —*Ezra Taft Benson* (Ensign, Dec. 1988, 2)

We must begin to think about our obligation rather than our convenience. The time, I think, has come when sacrifice must be an important element again in the Church. —*Spencer W. Kimball* (SWK, 572)

Defining and describing Zion will not bring it about. That can only be done through consistent and concerted daily effort by every single member of the Church. No matter what the cost in toil or sacrifice, we must "do it." That is one of my favorite phrases: "Do It."—*Spencer W. Kimball* (Ensign, March 1985, 3)

This people must increase in beauty before the world and have an inward loveliness that may be observed by mankind as a reflection in holiness and in those inherent qualities of sanctity. The borders of Zion, where the righteous and pure in heart may dwell, must now begin to be enlarged; the stakes of Zion must be strengthened—all this so that Zion may arise and shine by becoming increasingly diligent in carrying out the plan of salvation throughout the world. —*Harold B. Lee* (YLW, 138)

I bear witness that until a person has been willing to sacrifice all he possesses in the world, not even withholding his own life if it were necessary for the upbuilding of the kingdom, then only can he claim kinship to Him who gave His life that men might be. —*Harold B. Lee* (HBL, 178)

Nothing gives our efforts in building the kingdom more power than an exemplary life. —*Harold B. Lee* (HBL, 507)

Every individual radiates some influence. Our influence should be for good, for the building up of the kingdom of God. We should have no other purpose, only to bring to pass this great work and see it established in the earth as the Lord would have it. —*Joseph Fielding Smith* (CR, Apr. 1951, 153)

We are advancing, we are gaining in knowledge, in wisdom, and in power. This is as it should be, and as it will always be in the Church and kingdom of our Father; for there must be progression, there must be advancement. Knowledge will be poured down upon this people, and the Lord will make known unto us from time to time, through revelation, and the Spirit of inspiration, many things that are for our good, when we are prepared and ready to receive them. —*Joseph Fielding Smith* (DS1, 244)

Now, my brethren and sisters, as in the world so in the Church, we have two classes; we have the builders, and we have the murmurers. Let each ask himself in which class shall I be placed?—*David O. McKay* (CR, Apr. 1909, 66)

In the Church of Jesus Christ, there are no masters and no servants, but all working for everyone and each one for all. —*David O. McKay* (GI, 144)

Organizations as individuals are either progressing or retrogressing; they seldom if ever stand still. To progress is to obey the law of life. If the Church or any part of it were not improving, you may rest assured that it would be deteriorating. No ward, stake, or branch of the Church can long remain stationary. It is a source of satisfaction to all of us to realize that we belong to a Church that is moving forward. —*David O. McKay* (CR, Oct. 1938, 131)

The Church is little, if at all, injured by persecution and calumnies from ignorant, misinformed, or malicious enemies. A greater hindrance to its progress comes from faultfinders, shirkers, commandment-breakers, and apostate cliques within its own ecclesiastical and quorum groups. —*David O. McKay* (CR, Apr. 1967, 9)

Brethren, there is nothing that can stop the progress of truth excepting only our weaknesses or failure to do our duty. —*David O. McKay* (CR, Oct. 1969, 89)

Are we performing the labor that the Lord has entrusted to our care? do we sense the responsibility that is upon us? or are we idly floating down stream, going with the tide taking it for granted that in the last day, we will be redeemed?—*George Albert Smith* (CR, Oct. 1916, 49)

If there has been burned into our souls a desire to serve God and keep his commandments by living our religion and teaching it to his children, then we are laying up for ourselves eternal riches of which no one can rob us. —*George Albert Smith* (CR, Oct. 1926, 106)

Good men, and truly great men, possess the Spirit of our Father wherever they may be in the world. They are desirous to build up, and not to tear down, and that would be our mission and labor while we remain upon the earth. —*George Albert Smith* (CR, Oct. 1906, 47)

The saving of souls, including our own soul, is the one great labor of all others that is most valuable and important, and that will bring to us the blessings of our Father and the good will of our Lord and Master, Jesus Christ. —*Heber J. Grant* (IE, 24:259)

I say, what doth it profit to go to the ends of the earth and proclaim the gospel of Jesus Christ, and yet fail to do your duty here in laboring for the advancement of God's kingdom? I say to the Latter-day Saints, be honest with God, pay your tithes and your offerings, support every institution of Zion, build up the Church of Christ, pray for the authorities of the Church, and then sustain them in every labor and in all that they undertake to do. —*Heber J. Grant* (CR, Apr. 1900, 24)

If any man lacks the Spirit of God, let him go to work and labor for the advancement of the kingdom of God, and he will have the Spirit of God. —*Heber J. Grant* (GS, 182)

Every man among us carries on his shoulders the reputation of his Church, and as you and I live the gospel of Jesus Christ, we bring credit to the work of the Lord that has been established again upon the earth in this dispensation. —*Heber J. Grant* (IE, 41:327)

[T]here is a greater desire in my heart to labor for the spread of truth and the building up of the Church of Christ here upon the earth today than there has been ever before, and I believe that ought to be the ambition of each and every one of us. —*Heber J. Grant* (IE, 41:391)

So far as our property is concerned it is of no actual value to us, only as we are ready and willing to use it for the advancement of God's Kingdom. It is our duty to provide for our families; but it is not our duty to live in extravagance. It is not our duty to labor to gain wealth for the adornment of our persons. . . . Whenever we learn to be willing to use the means that God gives us for the onward advancement of His Kingdom, Latter-day Saints will not have any particular financial trouble; the Lord will bless them with an abundance. —*Heber J. Grant* (PC, 232-233)

As we grow and increase in knowledge and in the testimony of the Spirit of God, we must also grow and increase in labor and effort for the advancement of the work of God or we will lose the Spirit of God. —*Heber J. Grant* (LPS, 401)

It is very essential to our individual welfare that every man and every woman who has entered into the covenants of the gospel, through repentance and baptism, should feel that as individuals it is their bounden duty to use their intelligence, and the agency which the Lord has given them, for the promotion of the interests of Zion and the establishment of her cause in the earth. —*Joseph F. Smith* (GD, 90)

The genius of the gospel is not that of negative goodness—mere absence of what is bad; it stands for aggressive energy well directed, for positive goodness—in short, for work. —*Joseph F. Smith* (GD, 369)

We should try to ascertain how we should spend the money and the information that God has given us. The answer is simple—for the glory of God. —*Lorenzo Snow* (LS, 107)

This is what I ask my Father in yonder worlds, that my circumstances ever may be such that I can perform His work and labor as an active agent in His hands to accomplish His purposes on the earth. —*Lorenzo Snow* (LS, 47)

Although the Lord will work and accomplish wonders in regard to the deliverance of His people, when impediments arise in the path of their progress and no human power or ability can remove them, then God by His power will do so; but it is the business of those who profess to be engaged in His work to move on, to go forward, and that too without murmuring or having to be urged. So long as there remains a step forward to be taken, that step should be taken. —*Lorenzo Snow* (LS, 171)

Here is the great trouble with men of the world, and too much so with the Elders of Israel: we forget that we are working for God; we forget that we are here in order to carry out certain purposes that we have promised the Lord that we would carry out. It is a glorious work that we are engaged in. It is the work of the Almighty, and He has selected the men and the women whom He knows from past experience will carry out His purposes, as a general thing. —*Lorenzo Snow* (LPS, 151)

I want the Latter-day Saints to stop murmuring and complaining at the providence of God. Trust in God. Do your duty. Remember your prayers. Get faith in the Lord, and take hold and build up Zion. All will be right. —*Wilford Woodruff* (WW, 252)

The Lord is preparing a people to receive his kingdom and his church, and to build up his work. That, brethren and sisters, is our labor. —*Wilford Woodruff* (WW, 210)

We must roundup our shoulders, and bear off this kingdom. —*Wilford Woodruff* (WW, 84-85)

I say to all men—Jew and Gentile, great and small, rich and poor—that the Lord Almighty has power within himself, and is not dependent upon any man, to carry on his work; but when he does call men to do his work they have to trust in him. —*Wilford Woodruff* (WW, 123-124)

We have nothing else to do but to build up the kingdom of God. —*Wilford Woodruff* (WW, 124)

There is no time to throw away, and I would to God that the elders of Israel could fully realize and comprehend the great work that God has put upon their shoulders—the building up of his kingdom. —*Wilford Woodruff* (WW, 146)

Remember that it is a great deal better to suffer wrong than to do wrong. We have enlisted in this kingdom for the purpose of working righteousness, growing up in righteousness and in purity that we might have a heaven in our families, in our city and neighborhoods, a Zion right in our midst, live in it ourselves, and persuade everybody else to abide its holy laws. —*John Taylor* (GK, 331)

The Lord has given us a certain work to accomplish; and the feelings or ideas of men in the world in relation to this work have but little to do with us. We are gathered here for the express purpose of building up the church and kingdom of God upon the earth. —*John Taylor* (GK, 162)

We must be philosophers too, and make it appear that our philosophy is better than theirs and then show them that religion is at the bottom of it. —*John Taylor* (GK, xxxv)

We are here to do the will of God, to build up the kingdom of God, and to establish the Zion of God. —*John Taylor* (GK, 124)

What is the first thing necessary to the establishment of his kingdom? It is to raise up a prophet and have him declare the will of God; the next is to have people yield obedience to the word of the Lord through that prophet. If you cannot have these, you never can establish the kingdom of God upon the earth. —*John Taylor* (GK, 214)

We are here to cooperate with God in the salvation of the living, in the redemption of the dead, in the blessings of our ancestors, in the pouring out of blessings upon our children; we are here for the purpose of redeeming and regenerating the earth on which we live, and God has placed his authority and his counsels here upon the earth for that purpose, that men may learn to do the will of God on the earth as it is done in heaven. This is the object of our existence; and it is for us to comprehend the position. —*John Taylor* (GK, 286)

The time will yet come when he that will not take up his sword to fight against his neighbor, must needs flee to Zion for safety. All those who are not fond of blood and carnage and desolation, if they want to be preserved will flee to Zion. Have we not got to have a Zion for them to flee to? Yes. And what is Zion? The pure in heart. We want to organize in such a way, and advocate and maintain such correct principles, that they will become the admiration of all honest men, who will flee that they can be protected and find safety and an asylum in Zion. —*John Taylor* (JD, 20:266)

The only business that we have on hand is to build up the Kingdom of God and prepare the way of the Son of Man. —*Brigham Young* (BY, 88)

Do we realize that if we enjoy a Zion in time or in eternity we must make it for ourselves?—*Brigham Young* (BY, 118)

If we wish this Church and Kingdom of God upon earth, to be like a fine, healthy, growing tree, we should be careful not to let the dead branches remain too long. —*Brigham Young* (BY, 440)

We ought to have the building up of Zion as our greatest object. —*Joseph Smith, Jr.* (STJS, 183)

The advancement of the cause of God and the building up of Zion is as much one man's business as another's. The only difference is, that one is called to fulfill one duty, and another duty . . . [P]arty feelings, separate interests, exclusive designs should be lost sight of in the one common cause, in the interest of the whole. —*Joseph Smith, Jr.* (STJS, 261)

I had a conversation with a number of brethren in the shade of the building on the subject of our persecutions in Missouri and the constant annoyance which has followed us since we were driven from that state. I prophesied that the Saints would continue to suffer much affliction and would be driven to the Rocky Mountains, many would apostatize, others would be put to death by our persecutors or lose their lives in consequence of exposure of disease, and some of you will live to go and assist in making settlements and build cities and see the Saints become a mighty people in the midst of the Rocky Mountains. —*Joseph Smith, Jr.* (STJS, 286)

[W]e have the revelation of Jesus, and the knowledge within us is sufficient to organize a righteous government upon the earth, and to give universal peace to all mankind, if they would receive it, but we lack the physical strength, as did our Savior when a child, to defend our principles, and we have a necessity to be afflicted, persecuted and smitten, and to bear it patiently until Jacob is of age, then he will take care of himself. —*Joseph Smith, Jr.* (STJS, 439-440)

82. PERFECTING THE SAINTS

The lives of our people must become the only meaningful expression of our faith and, in fact, therefore, the symbol of our worship. —*Gordon B. Hinckley* (Ensign, May 1975, 92)

We must continue even with greater effectiveness to strengthen and sustain one another. . . . We must close ranks and march shoulder to shoulder, the weak helping the strong, those with much assisting those with little. No power on earth can stop this work if we shall so conduct ourselves. —*Gordon B. Hinckley* (Ensign, May 1982, 44-46)

In times of disciplinary councils the three brethren of the bishopric, or the three brethren of the stake presidency, or the three brethren of the presidency of the Church, sit together, discuss matters together, pray together, in the process of reaching a decision. I wish to assure you, my brethren, that I think there is never a judgment rendered until after prayer has been had. Action against a member is too serious a matter to result from the judgment of men alone, and particularly of one man alone. There must be the guidance of the Spirit, earnestly sought for and then followed, if there is to be justice. —*Gordon B. Hinckley* (Ensign, Nov. 1990, 49)

My brethren and sisters, I would hope, I would pray, that each of us would resolve to seek those who need help, who are in desperate and difficult circumstance, and lift them in the spirit of love into the embrace of the Church, where strong hands and loving hearts will warm them, comfort them, sustain them, and put them on the way of happy and productive lives. —*Gordon B. Hinckley* (Ensign, Nov. 1996, 86)

It is not an easy thing to become a member of this Church. In most cases it involves setting aside old habits, leaving old friends and associations, and stepping into a new society which is different and somewhat demanding. With the ever-increasing number of converts, we must make an increasingly substantial effort to assist them as they find their way. Every one of them needs three things: a friend, a responsibility, and nurturing with "the good word of God" (Moro. 6:4). It is our duty and opportunity to provide these things. —*Gordon B. Hinckley* (CR, May 1997, 47)

I am hopeful that a great effort will go forward throughout the Church, throughout the world, to retain every convert who comes into the Church.

This is serious business. There is no point in doing missionary work unless we hold to the fruits of that effort. The two must be inseparable. —*Gordon B. Hinckley* (Ensign, Nov. 1997, 50)

I know of no stronger weapons in the hands of the adversary against any group of men or women in this church than the weapons of divisiveness, faultfinding, and antagonism. —*Howard W. Hunter* (CR, May 1976, 106)

The Lord, our Good Shepherd, expects us to be his under shepherds and recover those who are struggling or are lost. We can't tell you how to do it, but as you become involved and seek inspiration, success will result from efforts in your areas, regions, stakes, and wards. —*Howard W. Hunter* (WMJ, 85-86)

There is a real sifting going on in the Church, and it is going to become more pronounced with the passing of time. It will sift the wheat from the tares, because we face some difficult days, the like of which we have never experienced in our lives. And those days are going to require faith and testimony and family unity, the like of which we have never had. —*Ezra Taft Benson* (ETB, 107)

If you don't have a ward choir, you are not organized fully, any more than if you do not have a Relief Society. —*Spencer W. Kimball* (SWK, 518)

The Sunday School must remember that it is not enough to teach ethics and good practices and common courtesies. It must teach exaltation through live faith in God. —*Spencer W. Kimball* (SWK, 531)

Our responsibility as brothers and sisters in the Church is to help those who may be lost to find their way, and to help those who have lost that which is precious to find their treasure again. . . . Every member has the obligation to strengthen his fellow members. —*Spencer W. Kimball* (Ensign, June 1983, 3)

We build character as we encourage people to care for their own needs. . . . Welfare Services is not a program, but the essence of the gospel. It is the gospel in action. —*Spencer W. Kimball* (Ensign, Aug. 1984, 4)

When we baptize somebody it is a crime to let them just slide slowly back out of the Church and out of the gospel because of a lack of fellowship. —*Spencer W. Kimball* (SWK, 258)

I believe there is none who cannot be converted—or I might say reactivated—if the right person makes the right approach at the right time in the right way with the right spirit. —*Spencer W. Kimball* (Ensign, June 1983, 5)

The greatest responsibility that a member of Christ's church has ever had is to become truly converted—and it is just as important to stay converted. —*Harold B. Lee* (SHP, 90-92)

The real strength of the Church is to be measured by the increase in the hearts of the Latter-day Saints by which loyalty, faith, knowledge, patience, virtue, sobriety, integrity, and willingness to sacrifice are the outward evidences; by the way in which the opposition of worldly things is broken down; and by the way the Church moves on to its glorious destiny for which our Lord and Master gave his life that the world might be saved and the powers of evil be overthrown. —*Harold B. Lee* (Ensign, Nov. 1971, 17)

We ask the Church members to strive to emulate the example of our Lord and Master Jesus Christ, who gave us the new commandment that we should love one another. I wish we could remember that. —*Harold B. Lee* (Ensign, July 1972, 103)

We must, as a Church and as individuals, keep ourselves clean, our minds pure, our souls clean, uncontaminated by the sins of the world. It is the duty of each one of us individually to keep the good name of this Church unsullied. —*Joseph Fielding Smith* (CR, Apr. 1944, 51-52)

Build up and strengthen the members of the Church in faith in God; goodness knows we need it. There are so many influences at work to divide us asunder, right among the members of the Church, and there is going to come, one of these days in the near future, a separation of the wheat from the tares, and we are either wheat or tares. We are going to be on one side or the other. —*Joseph Fielding Smith* (DS3, 16)

The great majority of those who become members of the Church are literal descendants of Abraham through Ephraim, son of Joseph, Those who are not literal descendants of Abraham and Israel must become such, and when they are baptized and confirmed they are grafted into the tree and are entitled to all the rights and privileges as heirs. —*Joseph Fielding Smith* (DS3, 246)

No matter what doubters and scoffers say, the mission of the Church of Jesus Christ is to eliminate sin and wickedness from the hearts of men, and so to transform society that peace and good will prevail on this earth. —*David O. McKay* (CR, Apr. 1941, 109)

One thing though is clearly defined in my mind, and that is this: That we have greater responsibility than ever to learn and to live the gospel of Jesus Christ. —*David O. McKay* (CR, Apr. 1936, 58)

The real test of any church or religion is the kind of men it makes. —*David O. McKay* (GI, 335)

The Church, with its complete organization, offers service and inspiration to all. It is "pre-eminently a social religion." In quorums and auxiliaries it "aims by training the individual conscience and will to establish a closely knit, world-wide fraternity." It is in no sense ascetic. Instead of taking men out of the world, it seeks to develop perfect, Godlike men in the midst of society, and through them to solve the problems of society. —*David O. McKay* (CR, Apr. 1963, 98)

Members of The Church of Jesus Christ of Latter-day Saints are under obligation to make the sinless Son of Man their ideal—the One Perfect Being who ever walked the earth. —*David O. McKay* (CR, Apr. 1968, 10)

With all my soul, I plead with members of the Church, and with people everywhere, to think more about the gospel; more about the developing of the spirit within; to devote more time to the real things in life, and less time to those things which will perish. —*David O. McKay* (CR, Apr. 1968, 144)

Now, my brethren and sisters, the hour is drawing to a close, wherein our great conference gathering will soon have become an event of the past. The sessions themselves will be mere history, but the messages, we hope, will ever remain on the tablets of our memories and will become moving factors in our daily lives. —*David O. McKay* (CR, Apr. 1954, 140)

What I am saying is, we leave this conference today with greater responsibility than ever before, as men of the priesthood, as women of the Church, to make our homes such as will radiate to our neighbors harmony, love, community duties, loyalty. Let our neighbors see it and hear it. Never must there be expressed in a Latter-day Saint home an oath, a condemnatory term, an expression of anger or jealousy or hatred. Control it! Do not express it! You do what you can to produce peace and harmony, no matter what you may suffer. —*David O. McKay* (CR, Apr. 1963, 129-131)

We cannot be indifferent to the teachings of the gospel; we must not drift down the stream of life without an effort. Every day we should do something worth while. —*George Albert Smith* (CR, Oct. 1921, 43)

The promise of the Lord that we may enjoy eternal life is conditional. That is, we must serve the Lord our God with all our hearts; we must serve him by caring for his children, by blessing mankind wherever our influence can be exerted. —*George Albert Smith* (CR, Oct. 1921, 42)

Today when I think of this marvelous land in which we live, our world-famed Temple Square, our homes and farms, and our buildings that have been dedicated to the worship of our Father in heaven, it seems to me that we ought to examine ourselves and check on our lives to see whether or not we are living up to our privileges and are worthy of that which the Lord has given us. —*George Albert Smith* (SGO, 122)

I feel that the hymns that have been taught the sons and daughters of the Latter-day Saints in the Sunday School are a continuous sermon of righteousness. I am sure that they have inspired many of us to do the things that the Lord would like us to do. —*George Albert Smith* (SGO, 164)

It is not my privilege to judge some of these that have made mistakes and are still making mistakes. . . . But it is my privilege, if I see them doing the wrong thing, to in some way, if possible, turn them back into the pathway that leads to eternal life in the Celestial kingdom. —*George Albert Smith* (CR, Apr. 1937, 34)

If we conclude that the instruction is meant only for somebody else, we are liable to continue in the same old way to the end of our days, and discover when it is too late that the advice was for us as well as for the other person. —*George Albert Smith* (CR, Apr. 1906, 52)

The patient, untiring, prayerful labors we devote to our young people who need help, and to those generally who for some cause or another have withdrawn themselves from us, often return to reward us in unspeakable joy and satisfaction in the years to come.

May we labor long and unceasingly, with patience, and forgiveness, and prayerful determination among all such who need our help!—*Heber J. Grant* (IE, 43:205)

We find recorded in the Doctrine and Covenants that if we labor all the days of our life and save but one person, great shall be our joy with that person in the life to come. And if that one person is only our dear self, that is the thing that counts. —*Heber J. Grant* (IE, 39:396)

We should go to meeting to learn. We should ask God to strengthen us to overcome evil. —*Heber J. Grant* (GS, 98)

The gospel . . . takes the selfish, sordid man and makes of him a generous, noble, freehearted individual—one that we can love, one that God can love. —*Heber J. Grant* (GS, 24)

I maintain that it is the absolute duty of each and every member of the Church of Jesus Christ of Latter-day Saints to so order his life that his example will be worthy of the imitation of all men, thus bringing credit and blessings to himself and his posterity and also making friends for the work of the Lord. This should be the loftiest ambition of every Latter-day Saint. —*Heber J. Grant* (IE, 3:192)

[If] we kept in our minds the one central thing, namely, the making of Latter-day Saints in our schools, then they would be fulfilling the object of their existence. —*Heber J. Grant* (IE, 26:866)

I cannot save you; you cannot save me; we cannot save each other, only so far as we can persuade each other to receive the truth, by teaching it. When a man receives the truth he will be saved by it. He will not be saved merely because some one talks to him, but because he received and acted upon it. —*Joseph F. Smith* (CR, Apr. 1902, 86)

If "Mormonism" is anything at all more than other religions, it is that it is practical, that the results of obedience to it are practical, that it makes good men better men, and that it takes even bad men and makes good ones of them. That is what "Mormonism" will do, if we will only permit it to do it, if we will bow to its mandates and adopt its precepts in our lives, it will make us the sons and the daughters of God, worthy eventually to dwell in the presence of the Almighty in the heavens. —*Joseph F. Smith* (CR, Apr. 1905, 86)

The difficulty is not in getting the Latter-day Saints to do right, but in getting them to comprehend what is right. —*Joseph F. Smith* (GD, 81)

In Christ's Church we cannot be neutral or inert. We must either progress or retrograde. It is necessary for the Latter-day Saints to keep pushing on in order that they may keep their faith alive and their spirits quickened to the performance of their duties. . . . Every man should be laboring for his own good and as far as possible for the good of others. —*Joseph F. Smith* (GD, 115-116)

Our being edified at conference depends on us. It becomes necessary that we prepare our hearts to receive and profit by the suggestions that may be made by the speakers during the progress of the conference, which may be prompted by the Spirit of the Lord. I have thought, and still think, that our being edified does not so much depend upon the speaker as upon ourselves. —*Lorenzo Snow* (CR, Oct. 1898, 1)

We ought to understand that we have espoused a system of religion that is calculated in its nature to increase within us wisdom and knowledge; that we have entered upon a path that is progressive, that will increase our spiritual, intellectual, and physical advantages, and everything pertaining to our own happiness and the well-being of the world at large. —*Lorenzo Snow* (LS, 26)

Knowing our religion to be true, we ought to be the most devoted people on the face of the earth to the cause we have embraced. . . . We ought not to be lukewarm, or negligent in attending to our duties, but with all our might, strength, and souls we should try to understand the spirit of our calling and nature of the work in which we are engaged. —*Lorenzo Snow* (LS, 43)

The Church, no doubt, needs purifying. We have hypocrites among us, milk-and-water Saints, those professing to be Saints, but doing nothing to render themselves worthy of membership; and too many of us have been pursuing worldly gains, rather than spiritual improvements, have not sought the things of God with that earnestness which becomes our profession. —*Lorenzo Snow* (LS, 149-150)

Let us decree in our hearts, let us inwardly testify to the Lord, that we will be a better people, a more united people at our next conference than we are today. This should be the feeling and determination of every man and woman present in this solemn assembly. I feel in my heart that I will try to be more devoted than I have been in the past to the interests of the kingdom of God and the carrying out of His purposes. —*Lorenzo Snow* (LS, 193)

There is this privilege that every Latter-day Saint should seek to enjoy, to know positively that his work is accepted of God. I am afraid Latter-day Saints are not much better and perhaps they are worse than other people if they do not have this knowledge and seek to do right. —*Lorenzo Snow* (CR, Apr. 1898, 13)

I cannot imagine anything that is so vastly important as to work for and obtain one's own individual exaltation and glory. That undoubtedly is one great purpose for which we came into the world. . . . We should labor for perfection so far as possible. —*Lorenzo Snow* (CR, Apr. 1898, 12)

It is the privilege of Latter-day Saints, when they get into difficulties, to have supernatural power of God, and in faith, day by day, to secure from the circumstances which may surround us that which will be beneficial and advance us in the principles of holiness and sanctification, that we may as far as possible be like our Father. —*Lorenzo Snow* (CR, Oct. 1898, 2)

The whole Church and kingdom of God, men and women, should have, each for himself and herself, the testimony of Jesus Christ which is the spirit of prophecy. This should be in the possession of every man and woman in the Church, for their own government and guidance. —*Wilford Woodruff* (WW, 17)

Why did God choose Joseph Smith, why did he choose that boy to open up this dispensation and lay the foundation of this church? Why didn't he choose some great man, such as Henry Ward Beecher? I have had but one answer in my life to give to such a question, namely, that the Lord Almighty could not do anything with them, he could not humble them. —*Wilford Woodruff* (WW, 44)

I feel that we as a people have got to rise up and clothe ourselves with the power of God. There must be a reformation, or a change, in our midst. There is too much evil among us. The devil has got too much power over us. A good many that bear the name of Christ and the Holy Priesthood, are getting cold in the things of God. We must wake up; we must trim our lamps, and be prepared for the coming of the Son of Man. —*Wilford Woodruff* (WW, 81)

We are called upon to work with the Lord just as fast as we are prepared to receive the things of his kingdom. But I am satisfied there has got to be a great change with us in many respects before we are prepared for the redemption of Zion and the building up of the New Jerusalem. I believe the only way for us is to get enough of the Spirit of God that we may see and understand our duties and comprehend the will of the Lord. —*Wilford Woodruff* (WW, 111)

One of the proverbs common among the Saints of God in the dispensation in which we live—the dispensation of the fulness of times, is, "The kingdom of God or nothing.". . . This kingdom has been given into the hands of the Latter-day Saints to establish on the earth, and unless we labor for its advancement we shall certainly fall short of salvation. —*Wilford Woodruff* (WW, 142-143)

We are the only people under heaven who are one, and we are not half as much one as we ought to be; we have to improve. We are the only people in the whole Christian world who make any pretensions to oneness in building up the Zion of God on the earth. We profess to be one in the gospel, and we have to become so in temporal matters. We have to become of one heart and mind in giving attention and obedience to the counsel of God in all things, both spiritual and temporal. —*Wilford Woodruff* (WW, 166)

There has been something said about men turning away from the Church of Christ. If a man has not the witness in himself, he is not governed by the principles of eternal truth, and the sooner such people leave this Church the better. —*John Taylor* (GK, 230)

We ought to have a heaven upon earth—to be really the Zion of our God the pure in heart each one seeking another's welfare. —*John Taylor* (GK, 72)

If we are provided for, we have not obtained it from anybody else, but from the Lord God of Israel, who has watched over and protected his people just as he said he would do. He said it was his business to take care of his saints, but, then, it is our business to be saints. —*John Taylor* (GK, 232)

I will tell you another thing: A great many of the Latter-day Saints will fail, a great many of them are not now and never have been living up to their privileges, and magnifying their callings and their priesthood, and God will have a reckoning with such people, unless they speedily repent.

There is a carelessness, a deadness, an apathy, a listlessness that exists to a great, extent among the Latter-day Saints. —*John Taylor* (GK, 137)

God expects to have a people who will be men of clean hands and pure hearts . . [H]e expects us to be Saints, not in name, not in theory, but in reality. —*John Taylor* (GK, 123)

It is in vain for the elders of Israel to teach the principles of truth unless the people are prepared to receive them; and it is vain for the Lord to communicate his will unto the people unless the people possess a portion of his Spirit, to comprehend something of that will and the designs of God towards them, and towards the earth upon which they dwell. Nor can the Lord work with them unless they are prepared to cooperate with him in the establishment of his kingdom upon the earth. —*John Taylor* (GK, 211)

We have a great mission to perform—we have to try to govern ourselves according to the laws of the kingdom of God, and we find it one of the most difficult tasks we ever undertook, to learn to govern ourselves, our appetites, our dispositions, our habits, our feelings, our lives, our spirits, our judgment, and to bring all our desires into subjection to the law of the kingdom of God and to the spirit of truth. —*John Taylor* (GK, 214)

Are we Scandinavians; are we English; are we Scotch, Swiss or Dutch, as the case may be? No; the Spirit of God, which we obtained through obedience to the requirements of the gospel, having been born again, of the water and of the Spirit, has made us of one heart, one faith, one baptism; we have no national or class divisions of that kind among us. —*John Taylor* (GK, 247)

The great thing that we, as a people, have to do is to seek after and cleave unto our God, to be in close affinity with him, and to seek for his guidance, and his blessing and Holy Spirit to lead and guide us in the right path. —*John Taylor* (JD, 18:281)

Human beings are expected by their Creator to be actively employed in doing good every day of their lives, either in improving their own mental and physical condition or that of their neighbors. —*Brigham Young* (BY, 88)

The sin that will cleave to all the posterity of Adam and Eve is, that they have not done as well as they knew how. —*Brigham Young* (BY, 89)

This people must go forward, or they will go backward. —*Brigham Young* (BY, 90)

You will be no more perfect in your sphere, when you are exalted to thrones, principalities, and powers, than you are required to be and are capable of being in your sphere today. —*Brigham Young* (BY, 389)

I care little for a man's language, if his spirit proves to me that he has the love of God within him. —*Brigham Young* (BY, 333)

When a person opens his mouth, no matter what he talks about, to a person of quick discernment he will disclose more or less of his true sentiments. You cannot hide the heart, when the mouth is open. If you want to keep your heart secret, keep your mouth shut. —*Brigham Young* (BY, 334)

If a congregation wish to be instructed so as to understand alike and alike receive an increase of wisdom and knowledge, their minds must be intent on the subject before them. They must not suffer their thoughts to be roaming over the earth; they must not permit their minds to be scanning and traversing their every-day duties and avocations. —*Brigham Young* (BY, 335)

If I attain to the knowledge of all true principles that have ever existed, and do not govern myself by them, they will damn me deeper in hell than if I had never known anything about them. —*Brigham Young* (BY, 429)

"Will everybody be damned, but Mormons?"
Yes, and a great portion of them, unless they repent, and work righteousness. —*Joseph Smith, Jr.* (STJS, 137)

And now dear and well beloved brethren—and when we say brethren, we mean those who have continued faithful in Christ, men, women and children—we feel to exhort you in the name of the Lord Jesus, to be strong in the faith in the new and everlasting covenant, and nothing frightened at your enemies. . . . Therefore hold on even unto death . . . Brethren, from henceforth, let truth and righteousness prevail and abound in you; and in all things be temperate; abstain from drunkenness, and from swearing, and from all profane language, and from everything which is unrighteous or unholy; also from enmity, and hatred, and covetousness, and from every unholy desire. —*Joseph Smith, Jr.* (STJS, 147-148)

Friendship is one of the grand fundamental principles of "Mormonism"; [it is designed] to revolutionize and civilize the world, and cause wars and contentions to cease and men to become friends and brothers. —*Joseph Smith, Jr.* (STJS, 354)

If the whole Church should go to with all their might to save their dead, seal their posterity, and gather their living friends, and spend none of their time in behalf of the world, they would hardly get through before night would come, when no man can work. —*Joseph Smith, Jr.* (STJS, 373)

Any person who is exalted to the highest mansion has to abide a celestial law, and the whole law too.
But there has been a great difficulty in getting anything into the heads of this generation. It has been like splitting hemlock knots with a corn-dodger for a wedge, and a pumpkin for a beetle. Even the Saints are slow to understand. —*Joseph Smith, Jr.* (STJS, 373)

As a Church and a people it behooves us to be wise, and to seek to know the will of God, and then be willing to do it. —*Joseph Smith, Jr.* (STJS, 284)

83. PIONEER HERITAGE

In our times of abundance, it is good occasionally to be taken back to earlier days, to have our minds refocused on the struggles of the early Latter-day Saints, to remind us of the necessity for labor if the earth is to be made to yield, of the importance of faith in God if there is to be lasting achievement, and of the need to recognize that many of the so-called old values are worthy of present application. —*Gordon B. Hinckley* (FETR , 102-103)

One hundred and fifty years ago our people were leaving Nauvoo and threading their way across the prairies of Iowa. None of us, I am confident, can appreciate the measure of sacrifice which they made in leaving their comfortable homes to brave the tempests of the wilderness on a journey that would not end until they reached this valley of the Great Salt Lake. Their suffering was immeasurable. They died by the hundreds for this cause of which each one of us is a part. . . . Ours is the blessing to live in a better season. The terrible persecutions of the past are behind us. Today we are looked upon with respect by people across the world. We must always be worthy of that respect. We must earn it, or we will not have it. —*Gordon B. Hinckley* (Ensign, Nov. 1996, 5)

A noble heritage has always been regarded as one of life's greatest treasures. —*Ezra Taft Benson* (ETB, 161)

In the early frontier days of this country, a special breed of men and women came here from all over the world, seeking not only opportunity, but freedom. They were strong, proud, and fiercely independent. They believed that the surest helping hand was at the end of their own sleeves. They shared one thing in common—and unshakable faith in God and in themselves. And that, without doubt, is the secret of success as viable today as it was yesterday. —*Ezra Taft Benson* (ETB, 570)

Our pioneer ancestors did not look to government to care for their families. They knew that their families were their treasure and their own responsibility. —*Spencer W. Kimball* (Ensign, May 1981, 79-80.)

The only true inheritance we have from our pioneer heritage is the knowledge and understanding that the basic principles of courage, honesty, integrity, virtue, and charity are the verities that have made men free. In our veins runs the blood of a virile ancestry, and in our sinews their strength that gives to us, as their descendants, the will to do and the capacity to achieve, even as they have achieved. —*Harold B. Lee* (YLW, 180)

If you would be a builder in that world of tomorrow, you must . . . meet the problems of today with the faith, courage and determination of the pioneers of 1847. —*Harold B. Lee* (DSL, 210)

The opinion of the world at that time was that the exodus meant the end of Mormonism, and that the Latter-day Saints had gone to their destruction; for without the necessary means to support life, and isolated as they were from the rest of civilization, they must surely perish in the barren and distant West. Such, too, would doubtless have been the case had not the protecting hand of Jehovah guided them. Is it any wonder under such trying conditions that the hearts of those weak in the faith should fail them. —*Joseph Fielding Smith* (DS1, 251)

We came into these valleys for one purpose. What was it? The primary purpose was to serve the Lord, to keep his commandments, to worship him in spirit and truth without interference, according to the dictates of our conscience. —*Joseph Fielding Smith* (DS3, 349)

If we want to honor our Heavenly Father today and please him, there is no better way than for us to live up to the ideals and standards of those who came here one hundred years ago. Their determination to serve God and keep his commandments brought them success and happiness. . . . They believed in the promises of the Lord, that if they would be blessed and prospered they must seek first, not last, the Kingdom of God and His righteousness. —*George Albert Smith* (SGO, 41-42)

I want to see the temple built in a manner that it will endure through the Millennium. This is not the only temple we shall build; there will be hundreds of them built and dedicated to the Lord. . . . And when the Millennium is over . . . I want that temple still to stand as a proud monument of the faith, perseverance and industry of the Saints of God in the mountains, in the nineteenth century. —*Brigham Young* (BY, 395)

84. PROCLAIMING THE GOSPEL

The most persuasive gospel tract is the exemplary life of a faithful Latter-day Saint. —*Gordon B. Hinckley* (Ensign, May 1982, 44-46)

We all need to be reminded to share the gospel with our associates. I emphasize the word share. I like it. I deprecate the use of what might be perceived as force and pressure upon those who live among us. I think it unnecessary. Neighborliness and exemplary living of the gospel of Jesus Christ, with an awareness of opportunity to quietly and graciously lead them in the direction of the Church, will accomplish much more, and will be resisted less and appreciated more by those we seek to help. —*Gordon B. Hinckley* (Ensign, May 1984, 46)

Along with the need for young elders and sisters, there is a growing need for couples in the mission field. Older married couples are doing a wonderful work in the missions. Many more are needed. —*Gordon B. Hinckley* (Ensign, Oct. 1987, 4)

There should be a stake mission in every stake, unless there is a rather rare situation where there are few, if any, nonmembers and where all members are active. . . . After a convert's baptism, stake missionaries are responsible for teaching the fellowshipping lessons to assist converts in making the tremendous adjustment that usually comes with baptism into the Church. . . . If we lose only one new convert, it is too great a loss. That loss can be avoided with well-organized stake missions whose missionaries and members work with the converts to assist them in becoming well grounded in the faith. —*Gordon B. Hinckley* (Ensign, Oct. 1987, 4)

Prepare now to go on a mission. It will not be a burden. It will not be a waste of time. It will be a great opportunity and a great challenge. It will do something for you that nothing else will do for you. It will sharpen your skills. It will train you in leadership. It will bring testimony and conviction into your heart. You will bless the lives of others as you bless your own. It will bring you nearer to God and to His Divine Son as you bear witness and testimony of Him. Your knowledge of the gospel will strengthen and deepen. Your love for your fellowman will increase. Your fears will fade as you stand boldly in testimony of the truth. —*Gordon B. Hinckley* (CR, May 1997, 50)

[M]issionaries must be sure that conversion is real, that it is life-changing, that it is something that is to last forever and go on through generations.

Nobody gains when there is baptism without retention. The missionary loses, and while the Church gains statistically, the membership suffers, really, and the enthusiasm of the convert turns to ashes. —*Gordon B. Hinckley* (CN, July 4, 1998, 4)

We are committed to declare to all the world that Jesus of Nazareth is the Savior of mankind, that he has paid for our sins by his atoning sacrifice, that he has risen from the dead, and that he lives today. Our responsibility is to help the people of the world understand the true nature of our Father in Heaven: that he is a personal God, a loving father, and one to whom each of us may go with our problems and concerns. —*Howard W. Hunter* (Ensign, Nov. 1981, 12)

As we try to understand the spirit of reconciliation sweeping the globe and to give it meaning within the gospel context, we have to ask ourselves: Could this not be the hand of the Lord removing political barriers and opening breaches in heretofore unassailable walls for the teaching of the gospel, all in accord with a divine plan and a divine timetable? Surely taking the gospel to every kindred, tongue, and people is the single greatest responsibility we have in mortality. —*Howard W. Hunter* (Ensign, Sept. 1990, 9-10)

To satisfy the new demands being made upon us in this great missionary work of the last days, perhaps some of us (particularly the older generation whose families are raised) need to take stock to determine whether "walls" that we have built in our own minds need to come down.

For example, how about the "comfort wall" that seems to prevent many couples and singles form going on a mission? How about the financial wall" of debt that interferes with some members' ability to go, or the "grandchildren wall," or the "health wall," or the "lack of self-confidence wall," or the "self-satisfied wall," or the "transgression wall," or the walls of fear, doubt, or complacency? Does anyone really doubt for a minute that with the help of the Lord he or she could bring those walls crashing down?

We have been privileged to be born in these last days, as opposed to some earlier dispensation, to help take the gospel to all the earth. There is no greater calling in this life. If we are content to hide behind self-made walls, we willingly forgo the blessings that are otherwise ours. —*Howard W. Hunter* (Ensign, Sept. 1990, 9-10)

A great indicator of your personal conversion to the gospel of Jesus Christ is the desire to share it with others. For this reason the Lord gave a charge to every member of the Church to be a missionary. —*Howard W. Hunter* (CN, March 11, 1995, 7)

Missionary work is not easy. It is the most demanding, the most compelling, the most exhausting, and yet, with it all, the most happy and most joyful work in all the world. —*Ezra Taft Benson* (ETB, 201)

Missionaries should be taught that it doesn't matter where they serve, but how. Position doesn't save anyone, but faithfulness does. Aspiring to positions of responsibility can destroy the spirit of the mission as well as the spirit of a missionary. —*Ezra Taft Benson* (ETB, 202)

The Lord needs every member of the Church having the faith and the courage to set a date to have someone prepared to be taught by the missionaries. Would each member of the Church prayerfully consider this sacred challenge?—*Ezra Taft Benson* (Ensign, May 1988, 84)

One of the greatest secrets of missionary work is work. If a missionary works, he will get the Spirit; if he gets the Spirit, he will teach by the Spirit; if the teaches by the Spirit, he will touch the hearts of the people, and he will be happy. Then there will be no homesickness nor worrying about families, for all time and talents and interests are centered on the work of the ministry. Work, work, work—there is no satisfactory substitute, especially in the missionary work. —*Ezra Taft Benson* (Ensign, Sept. 1990, 6)

We could use hundreds of couples. You just go and talk to your bishop—that is all you need to do. Tell him, "We are ready to go, if you can use us." I think you will probably get a call. —*Spencer W. Kimball* (SWK, 551)

We believe that there are many good men and women . . . who are kept from the truth by just not knowing where it is found. —*Spencer W. Kimball* (SWK, 552)

We should not worry because someone chides us a little for directing the missionaries to them. What a small price to pay for such a glorious blessing!

Sometimes we forget that it is better to risk a little ruffling in the relationship of a friend than it is to deprive them of eternal life by leaving them silent. —*Spencer W. Kimball* (SWK, 554)

No greater service can be given to the missionary calling of this Church than to be exemplary in positive Christian virtues in our lives. —*Spencer W. Kimball* (SWK, 555)

To convince people of the divinity of the work one must of necessity be humble. To be arrogant or "cocky" is to threaten to drive away the Holy Ghost who alone can convince and bring testimonies. —*Spencer W. Kimball* (SWK, 569)

We have already asked you, and we now repeat that request, that every family, every night and every morning, in family prayer and in secret prayers, too, pray to the Lord to open the doors of other nations so that their people, too, may have the gospel of Jesus Christ. —*Spencer W. Kimball* (SWK, 586)

Every member has the obligation and the calling to take the gospel to those around him. We want every man, woman, and child to assume his rightful responsibility. —*Spencer W. Kimball* (Ensign, Feb. 1983, 3)

I feel the Lord has placed, in a very natural way within our circles of friends and acquaintances, many persons who are ready to enter into his Church. We ask that you prayerfully identify those persons and then ask the Lord's assistance in helping you introduce them to the gospel. And in your conversation telling how you acquired such knowledge and what it means to you and what it might mean to someone else is a powerful witness for the Lord. —*Spencer W. Kimball* (Ensign, Feb. 1983, 4)

I wonder if we are doing all we can. Are we complacent in our assignment to teach the gospel to others? Are we prepared to lengthen our stride? To enlarge our vision?

Remember, our ally is our God. He is our commander. He made the plans. He gave the commandment. —*Spencer W. Kimball* (Ensign, Apr. 1984, 4)

I am asking for missionaries who have been carefully trained through the family and the organizations of the Church, and who come to the mission with a great desire. I am asking that we train prospective missionaries much better, much earlier, much longer, so that each anticipates his mission with great joy.

The question is frequently asked: "Should every able young man fill a mission?" And the answer has been given by the Lord. It is "Yes." Every able young man should fill a mission. —*Spencer W. Kimball* (Ensign, Apr. 1984, 5)

The most important responsibility that we, as members of the Church of Jesus Christ, have is to see that we are converted to the truthfulness of the gospel. Then we must share this truth with others. —*Harold B. Lee* (SHP, 90-92)

May we sense the fact that true love for our neighbor consists not in descending to his level but rather in so living that we aid him in an upward climb. —*Harold B. Lee* (SHP, 228-229)

No one can be saved who doesn't want to be saved. There must be a desire before we can extend the saving graces of the gospel of Jesus Christ to those who are round about us. —*Harold B. Lee* (HBL, 14)

If the worth of souls is great and our joy shall be great in heaven with those we may be able to bring unto the strait and narrow way, what will be our feelings if, through any teachings of ours, one soul is barred from the celestial kingdom? If that which we have taught and practiced shall destroy the faith of one individual so that he does not accept the truth, and that fact is made known unto us when we stand before the judgment seat, then, let me ask, how great will be our sorrow? How great will be the condemnation which we will merit in that we have barred, through our influence and through our teachings, one of the children of our Father from entering into eternal exaltation?—*Joseph Fielding Smith* (CR, Apr. 1923, 138-139)

I am willing to defend any man in the privilege which is his by his agency. If he wants to worship a cat or a dog; the sun or the moon; a crocodile or a bull—and men have done all these things—that is his privilege. But it is also my privilege and right to try to teach him to do better and to accept a better worship. I will defend him in his rights, and at the same time endeavor to teach him that he may see more clearly and walk in the light of truth. —*Joseph Fielding Smith* (CR, Oct. 1936, 60-61)

It is our individual duty to preach the gospel by precept and by example among our neighbors. —*Joseph Fielding Smith* (DS1, 307)

We should warn all men and give them the opportunity of repentance, of serving the Lord and keeping his commandments if they will. If they will not, yet we have saved our souls. We are clear from the blood of this generation. That is our duty. —*Joseph Fielding Smith* (DS1, 309-310)

There are certain standards by which we should be guided in calling our missionaries: First, call no young man or young woman for the purpose of saving him or her. The young man is getting wayward, and you think a mission would do him good. It would. But that is not why you are sending him out. Choose the young men and young women who are worthy to represent the Church, see that they are sufficiently mature, and, above all, that they have good character. —*David O. McKay* (CR, Apr. 1950, 176)

Man radiates what he is, and that radiation affects to a greater or lesser degree every person who comes within that radiation. —*David O. McKay* (CR, Apr. 1950, 34)

Let me urge more diligence in living the principles of the Gospel. We may preach, we may write, and publish books, but the most effective way of preaching the Gospel to the nations of the world, is by example. —*David O. McKay* (CR, Apr. 1953, 48)

Every member a missionary!—*David O. McKay* (CR, Apr. 1959, 122)

There's one responsibility which no man can evade, and that's the responsibility of personal influence. What you are thunders so loud in my ears, I cannot hear what you say. And what you are is the result of a silent, subtle radiation of your personality. The effect of your words and acts is tremendous in this world. —*David O. McKay* (Address to the North British Mission, 1961)

There is no teaching of morality without personality, and the best means of preaching the gospel is by your personal contact. Personal contact is what will influence those investigators. That personal contact—the nature of it, its effect—depends upon you. That is the thing I wish to emphasize. Each one should remember that somewhere there is an honest soul waiting to hear the truth, and it may be that you are the only one who can reach that inquiring soul. —*David O. McKay* (CR, Oct. 1969, 86)

As we go forward, each of us, each having an influence with our neighbors and our friends, let us not be too timid. We do not need to annoy people, but let us make them feel and understand that we are interested, not in making them members of the Church for membership, but in bringing them into the Church that they may enjoy the same blessings that we enjoy. —*George Albert Smith* (SGO, 115)

Let us set the world an example of righteousness, which will preach the gospel as it has never been preached in all the years that have passed. This is our mission and it is indeed a privilege that we should prize. —*George Albert Smith* (CR, Apr. 1923, 78)

One man said to me, "Would you have us give up all that we have had, all these blessings that we have enjoyed, to join your church?" I replied, "Not a blessing, not one good thing would we ask you to give up. But we do say to you, we will be glad to share with you, if you will permit us to do so, without cost to you, some of the blessings of our Heavenly Father that you have not received in the past and which are now at your very door."—*George Albert Smith* (CR, Oct. 1931, 120)

Today as I stand here, I realize that in this city, in the Catholic Church, the Presbyterian Church, the Methodist, the Baptist, the Episcopalian, and the other churches, I have brothers and sisters that I love. They are all my Father's children, He loves them and he expects me and he expects you, to let our lights so shine that these other sons and daughters of his, seeing our good works, will be constrained to accept all the truth of the Gospel of Jesus Christ our Lord. —*George Albert Smith* (CR, Oct. 1945, 174)

We have received a wonderful gift, but with that gift comes a great responsibility. We have been blessed of the Lord with a knowledge beyond our fellows, and with that knowledge comes the requirement that we share it with his children, wherever they may be. —*George Albert Smith* (CR, Apr. 1922, 53)

Surely we would stand condemned, if one of our associates in life should stand in the presence of the Great Judge and say of us that we could have made an effort, but that because of our neglect he would be deprived of a place in the celestial kingdom. Let none of us, my brethren and sisters, be justly accused in that way. —*George Albert Smith* (CR, Oct. 1921, 42-43)

Men cannot teach what they do not themselves know. —*George Albert Smith* (CR, Oct. 1921, 38)

To some it may sound selfish to hear us say, "This is the only true Church." But we are only repeating what the Savior said, and he knows. It is the Church that he recognizes, and it bears his name. We do not say that in unkindness to our brothers and sisters, and they are our brothers and sisters, in other churches, or in no church, but we say it with the hope that they may feel the love that is in our hearts when we reach out to them with the desire that the happiness that has been ours may be theirs and may continue, not only now, but throughout the ages of eternity. —*George Albert Smith* (SGO, 199)

How happy it will make you, if when that time comes, when you stand in the presence of the great Judge to give an account of the few years of life that have been spent in mortality, if these our Father's children that He loves as much as He loves us, standing by us, say, "Heavenly Father, it was this man, it was this woman who first brought to me the information of Thy glorious truth that provoked in me a desire to seek after Thee more fervently than I had done before. It was this man or this woman who did this blessed thing for me."—*George Albert Smith* (SGO, 233)

It is not necessary for you to be called to go into the mission field in order to proclaim the truth. Begin on the man who lives next door by inspiring confidence in him, by inspiring love in him for you because of your righteousness, and your missionary work has already begun. —*George Albert Smith* (CR, Oct. 1916, 51)

It is my firm conviction, my brethren and sisters, that unless we stir ourselves more than we are doing, that when we go to the other side of the veil, we will meet there men and women who have been our neighbors, and associates, and lived among us, that will condemn us because we have been so inconsiderate of them in not telling them of the truth of the gospel of our Lord. —*George Albert Smith* (CR, Oct. 1916, 49)

We spend most of our time, many of us, seeking the things of this life that we will be compelled to leave when we go from here, yet there are the immortal souls all around us whom, if we would, we could teach and inspire to investigate the truth, and implant in their hearts a knowledge that God lives. What treasure in all the world could be so precious to us, for, we would have their gratitude here and their everlasting and eternal appreciation in the world to come. —*George Albert Smith* (CR, Oct. 1916, 49-50)

I feel that some of us are selfish. We are so glad to enjoy our blessings, we are so happy to be surrounded by the comforts of life and to have the association of the best men and women that can be found in the world, that we forget our duty to others. How happy we could be if we would strive to be more potent for good in the world by ministering to those who have not yet understood the Gospel of our Lord. —*George Albert Smith* (CR, Oct. 1933, 27)

A dozen men qualified for the work are worth more in the mission field than a hundred who are ignorant of the truth and who themselves have to be taught before they are capable of explaining it to others. —*George Albert Smith* (CR, Oct. 1916, 48)

May God help each and every one of us who has a knowledge of the gospel, to live it, that our lives may preach its truth. —*Heber J. Grant* (IE, 42:585)

I would rather die in poverty knowing that my family could testify that, to the best of my ability with which God had endowed me, I had observed His laws and kept His commandments, and by my example, had proclaimed the gospel, than to have all the wealth of the world. —*Heber J. Grant* (CR, Apr. 1925, 10)

The greatest and the most wonderful preacher among the Latter-day Saints is the man or the woman who lives the gospel of the Lord Jesus Christ. . . . It is by our works, our diligence, our faithfulness, our energy, that we can preach this gospel. The people of the world are beginning to recognize, to know and to comprehend the fact that the fruits of the gospel of Jesus Christ, as taught by the Latter-day Saints, are good fruits. —*Heber J. Grant* (CR, Oct. 1922, 185-186)

The missionary work of the Latter-day Saints is the greatest of all the great works in all the world. —*Heber J. Grant* (CR, Oct. 1921, 5-6)

There is also more blessing comes to us in going forth to proclaim the gospel of Jesus Christ, and laboring for the salvation of the souls of men, than can possibly come to us by merely having a knowledge of the truth of our religion, and then remaining at home to mingle and labor in the ordinary affairs of life, and accumulate the wealth of this world that perishes with the using. One great trouble is that we ofttimes lose sight of what is the most valuable labor for us to perform, the labor that will be most pleasing in the sight of our Heavenly Father. —*Heber J. Grant* (CR, Oct. 1907, 23-24)

I want to emphasize that we as a people have one supreme thing to do, and that is to call upon the world to repent of sin, to come to God. And it is our duty above all others to go forth and proclaim the gospel of the Lord Jesus Christ, the restoration again to the earth of the plan of life and salvation. —*Heber J. Grant* (CR, Apr. 1927, 175)

Every Latter-day Saint should have a desire, above all other things, that his life should proclaim the truth, and that his life should be a teacher of the truth, not only to the world, but especially to his own family. —*Heber J. Grant* (CR, Apr. 1923, 9)

[W]e have a mission in the world: each man, each woman, each child who has grown to understanding or to the years of accountability, ought to be an example to the world. They ought not only to be qualified to preach the truth, to bear testimony of the truth, but ought to live so that the very life they live, the very words they speak, their every action in life will be a sermon to the unwary and to the ignorant, teaching them goodness, purity, uprightness, faith in God and love for the human family. —*Joseph F. Smith* (CR, Apr. 1916, 6-7)

[O]ne of the indispensable qualifications of the elders who go out into the world to preach is humility, meekness and love unfeigned, for the well-being and the salvation of the human family, and the desire to establish peace and righteousness in the earth among men. . . . You may learn all the wisdom of men, but that will not qualify you to do these things like the humble, guiding influence of the Spirit of God will. —*Joseph F. Smith* (CR, Apr. 1915, 138)

Men are not converted by eloquence or oratory: they are convinced when they are satisfied that you have the truth and the Spirit of God. —*Joseph F. Smith* (GD, 357)

There is a way to reach every human heart, and it is your business to find the way to the hearts of those to whom you are called on this mission. —*Lorenzo Snow* (LS, 68)

This, then, should be our aim and object: to learn to make ourselves useful—to be saviours to our fellowmen, to learn how to save them, to communicate to them a knowledge of the principles that are necessary to raise them to the same degree of intelligence that we have ourselves. —*Lorenzo Snow* (LS, 60)

"O Lord, may it be so; may I have power through thy Spirit to touch the hearts of these thy people." That very short prayer is all that an elder needs to make. It is all you need to make. "May I say something to save these souls."—*Lorenzo Snow* (LS, 67)

There is no mortal man that is so much interested in the success of an elder when he is preaching the gospel as the Lord that sent him to preach to the people who are the Lord's children. —*Lorenzo Snow* (LPS, 304)

It does not make any difference what age a man is in preaching the gospel, whether he is twenty-five, ninety, or five hundred years of age, if he is only inspired by the spirit and power of God. —*Wilford Woodruff* (WW, 275)

Certainly there has been nothing in this work that I have had greater consolation in, than in preaching the gospel to my fellow men and in administering unto them the ordinances of the house of God, both for the living and the dead. —*Wilford Woodruff* (WW, 133-134)

I wish to say a few words to the missionaries—to those who are going abroad to preach the gospel of Christ. I want to give you a word of exhortation and counsel, brethren: that is, whenever you are in doubt about any duty or work which you have to perform, never proceed to do anything until you go and labor in prayer and get the Holy Spirit. Wherever the Spirit dictates you to go or to do, that will be right; and, by following its dictates, you will come out right. —*Wilford Woodruff* (WW, 134)

There is no elder who has gone out to preach and who has baptized anybody but knows that he has had to have revelation to enable him to magnify his calling. He could not live without this and do his duty. —*Wilford Woodruff* (WW, 135)

The whole secret of our success as far as making converts is concerned is, that we preach the same gospel in all its simplicity and plainness that Jesus preached, and that the Holy Ghost rests upon those who receive it, filling their hearts with joy and gladness unspeakable, and making them as one; and they then know of the doctrine for themselves whether it be of God or man. —*Wilford Woodruff* (WW, 136)

I would rather have a son in the vineyard, saving the souls of men, than to have him heaping up gold at home and becoming a millionaire. —*Wilford Woodruff* (LPS, 383)

There never was a set of men since God made the world under a stronger responsibility to warn this generation, to lift up our voices long and loud, day and night so far as we have the opportunity and declare the words of God unto this generation. We are required to do this. This is our calling. It is our duty. It is our business. —*Wilford Woodruff* (JD, 21:122)

What is it we have to do? We must spread forth the light of the gospel. Why? Because God has communicated a system of religion which is calculated to ennoble and exalt the human family. —*John Taylor* (GK, 50)

But Jesus said, My sheep hear my voice, and they know me, and a stranger they will not follow, because they know not the voice of a stranger. And why do not the millions of the inhabitants of the earth embrace the gospel? Because they are not sheep; that is all. And if the goats kick up and cut a few antics, you need not be astonished. It is the nature of goats, is it not?—*John Taylor* (GK, 105)

We are sending the gospel to the nations of the earth. Why? Because God has commanded it. —*John Taylor* (GK, 235)

We want men to preach the gospel who are honorable and upright men, and full of the Holy Ghost. And when such men go, they go with our faith, carrying with them our esteem and love and affection. —*John Taylor* (GK, 239)

[I]f you do not magnify your callings, God will hold you responsible for those whom you might have saved had you done your duty. —*John Taylor* (JD, 20:22-23)

The Gospel must be preached to the world, that the wicked may be left without excuse. —*Brigham Young* (BY, 319)

When I came into this Church, I started right out as a missionary, and took a text, and began to travel on a circuit. Truth is my text, the Gospel of salvation my subject, and the world my circuit. —*Brigham Young* (BY, 322)

We do not wish a man to enter on a mission, unless his soul is in it. —*Brigham Young* (BY, 322)

If you go on a mission to preach the Gospel with lightness and frivolity in your hearts, looking for this and that, and to learn what is in the world, and not having your minds riveted—yes, I may say riveted—on the cross of Christ, you will go and return in vain. —*Brigham Young* (BY, 325)

You know that I have said that, if it were now my calling to go and preach the Gospel, I could make as many converts as I ever did; for I would go in such a manner that the bitterly prejudiced would have to labor hard to find out that I was a "Mormon" until I had induced them to love the truth. Then they would say, "If that is `Mormonism' I want it."—*Brigham Young* (BY, 326)

I had only traveled a short time to testify to the people, before I learned this one fact, that you might prove doctrine from the Bible till doomsday, and it would merely convince a people, but would not convert them. . . . Nothing short of a testimony by the power of the Holy Ghost would bring light and knowledge to them—bring them in their hearts to repentance. Nothing short of that would ever do. —*Brigham Young* (BY, 330)

No man ever preached a Gospel sermon, except by the gift and power of the Holy Ghost sent down from heaven. Without this power, there is no light in the preaching. —*Brigham Young* (BY, 333)

A few words now, with regard to preaching. The greatest and loudest sermon that can be preached, or that ever was preached on the face of the earth, is practice. No other is equal to it. —*Brigham Young* (BY, 336)

Love is one of the chief characteristics of Deity, and ought to be manifested by those who aspire to be the sons of God. A man filled with the love of God, is not content with blessing his family alone, but ranges through the whole world, anxious to bless the whole human race. —*Joseph Smith, Jr.* (HC 4:227)

If you do your duty, it will be just as well with you, as though all men embraced the Gospel. —*Joseph Smith, Jr.* (STJS, 57)

All are to preach the Gospel, by the power and influence of the Holy Ghost; and no man can preach the Gospel without the Holy Ghost. —*Joseph Smith, Jr.* (STJS, 132)

Souls are as precious in the sight of God as they ever were; and the Elders were never called to drive any down to hell, but to persuade and invite all men every where to repent, that they may become the hears of salvation. —*Joseph Smith, Jr.* (STJS, 92-93)

After all that has been said, [our] greatest and most important duty is to preach the Gospel. —*Joseph Smith, Jr.* (HC 2:478)

Oh, ye elders of Israel, hearken to my voice; and when you are sent into the world to preach, tell those things you are sent to tell . . . Declare the first principles, and let mysteries alone, lest ye be overthrown. —*Joseph Smith, Jr.* (STJS, 325-326)

If I esteem mankind to be in error, shall I bear them down? No. I will lift them up, and in their own way too, if I cannot persuade them my way is better; and I will not seek to compel any man to believe as I do, only by the force of reasoning, for truth will cut its own way. —*Joseph Smith, Jr.* (STJS, 351)

85. TRUTHFULNESS OF THE RESTORED GOSPEL

These are the questions I should like to leave with you: "It's true isn't it? Then what else matters?" —*Gordon B. Hinckley* (BTE, 3-4)

I wish to say that none of us ever need hesitate to speak up for this Church, for its doctrine, for its people, for its divine organization and divinely given responsibility. It is true. It is the work of God. The only things that can ever embarrass this work are acts of disobedience to its doctrine and standards by those of its membership. That places upon each of us a tremendous responsibility. This work will be judged by what the world sees of our behavior. God give us the will to walk with faith, the discipline to do what is right at all times and in all circumstances, the resolution to make of our lives a declaration of this cause before all who see us. —*Gordon B. Hinckley* (Ensign, Nov. 1996, 51)

I give you my solemn testimony that this Church will never be led astray. It is in the hands of God, and should any of its leaders ever attempt to lead it astray, His is the power to remove them. —*Gordon B. Hinckley* (Ensign, May 1996, 93)

You have been given a great and precious gift. You can speak truth. You must speak truth. You can bear testimony of the great and good things of the gospel. This is your gift. Neglect it not!—*Gordon B. Hinckley* (CR, May 1997, 49)

Joseph Smith's greatness consists in one thing—the truthfulness of his declaration that he saw the Father and the son and that he responded to the reality of that divine revelation. He was directed to reestablish the true and living Church, restored in these modern times as it existed in the day of the Savior's own mortal ministry. The Prophet Joseph Smith was fearless in pursuing this divine mission. —*Howard W. Hunter* (CN, March 11, 1995, 7)

Nothing short of this total vision to Joseph could have served the purpose to clear away the mists of the centuries. Merely an impression, a hidden voice, a dream could [not] have dispelled the old vagaries and misconceptions. —*Spencer W. Kimball* (SWK, 430)

I bear you my solemn testimony—to you who may be wavering and who haven't yet developed a testimony—that this is the Lord's work. I know Jesus Christ lives, and that He is closer to this church and appears more often in holy places than any of us realize. The time is hastening when He shall come again to reign as the Lord of Lords and King of Kings. —*Harold B. Lee* (YLW, 9-10)

How I wish I could impress you who must daily walk out on the swaying bridge of worldliness and sin which flows as a turbulent stream below you, how I wish that when you have twinges of doubt and fear that cause you to lose the rhythm of prayer and faith and love, may you hear my voice as one calling to you from further along on life's bridge, "have faith—this is the way—for I can see further ahead than you." I would fervently pray that you could feel the love flowing from my soul to yours, and know of my deep compassion toward each of you as you face your problems of the day. —*Harold B. Lee* (DSL, 234)

Mormonism, as it is called, must stand or fall on the story of Joseph Smith. He was either a prophet of God, divinely called, properly appointed and commissioned, or he was one of the biggest frauds this world has ever seen. There is no middle ground. —*Joseph Fielding Smith* (CN, Apr. 1, 1939.1)

As I stand now, in what I might call the twilight of life, with the realization that in a not-far-distant day I shall be called upon to give an account of my mortal stewardship, I bear testimony again of the truth and divinity of this great work.

I know that God lives and that he sent his beloved Son into the world to atone for our sins.

I know that the Father and the Son appeared to the Prophet Joseph Smith to usher in this final gospel dispensation.

I know that Joseph Smith was and is a prophet; moreover, that this is the Lord's church, and the gospel cause shall roll forward until the knowledge of the Lord covers the earth as the waters cover the sea. —*Joseph Fielding Smith* (CR, Oct. 1971, 165)

The gospel of Jesus Christ, as revealed to the Prophet Joseph Smith, is in very deed in every way the power of God unto salvation. It gives to every man the perfect life here, and through obedience to gospel principles it gives us eternal life. —*David O. McKay* (CR, Oct. 1966, 136)

Of all the blessings that have come to me in life the most precious is the knowledge that God lives and that this is his work, because that comprehends all other blessings that I may hope to enjoy in this life or in the life that is to come. —*George Albert Smith* (CR, Apr. 1927, 82)

Our Father in his mercy, has led this people over the many snares and pitfalls that the adversary has prepared. The world have seen the development of the Church and they have marveled, and people have said, "What has made its people what they are?" The answer comes ringing true, because it is our Father's work, and no power on the earth can stay its progress. —*George Albert Smith* (CR, Oct. 1921, 161)

Either Joseph Smith did see God and did converse with Him, and God Himself did introduce Jesus Christ to the boy Joseph Smith, and Jesus Christ did tell Joseph Smith that he would be the instrument in the hands of God of establishing again upon the earth the true gospel of Jesus Christ—or Mormonism, so-called, is a myth. And Mormonism is not a myth! It is the power of God unto salvation. It is the Church of Jesus Christ, established under His direction, and all the disbelief of the world cannot change the fundamental facts connected with the Church of Jesus Christ of Latter-day Saints. —*Heber J. Grant* (IE, 41:519)

I want to bear my testimony to you and tell you that every drop of blood in my body, every ounce of wisdom in my brain, testifies to you, that beyond the shadow of doubt, I am converted to my religion. We have the gospel! We have the plan of life and salvation, and I know it. . . . I know that Joseph Smith is a prophet of God, and may God help us to live, that others, seeing our good deeds, will investigate the plan of life and salvation, I ask, in the name of Jesus Christ, Amen. —*Heber J. Grant* (PC, 257)

My religion is the religion of God. It is the religion of Jesus Christ, otherwise it would be absolutely worthless to me, and it would be worthless to all other men, so far as religion is concerned. —*Joseph F. Smith* (GD, 394)

But notwithstanding the unbelief so prevalent throughout Christendom, God restored his ancient gospel to Joseph Smith, giving him revelation, opening the heavens to him, and making him acquainted with the plan of salvation and exaltation of the children of men. I was well acquainted with him, and have carefully examined the revelations given through him, and notwithstanding all the aspersions that have been cast upon him, I believe that, with the exception of Jesus Christ, there never was a greater prophet upon this wide earth than he. —*John Taylor* (GK, 33)

I have traveled hundreds and thousands of miles to preach this gospel among all grades and conditions of men, and there is one thing that always gave me satisfaction—I never yet found a man in any part of the world who could overturn one principle that has been communicated to us; they will attempt it, but error is a very singular weapon with which to combat truth; it never can vanquish it. —*John Taylor* (GK, 242)

I feel like shouting Hallelujah, all the time, when I think that I ever knew Joseph Smith, the Prophet whom the Lord raised up and ordained, and to whom he gave keys and power to build up the Kingdom of God on earth and sustain it. These keys are committed to this people, and we have power to continue the work that Joseph commenced, until everything is prepared for the coming of the Son of Man. This is the business of the Latter-day Saints, and it is all the business we have on hand. —*Brigham Young* (BY, 458)

I rejoice in hearing the testimony of my aged friends. You don't know me; you never knew my heart. No man knows my history. I cannot tell it: I shall never undertake it. I don't blame any one for not believing my history. If I had not experienced what I have, I could not have believed it myself. I never did harm any man since I was born in the world. My voice is always for peace.

I cannot lie down until all my work is finished. I never think any evil, nor do anything to the harm of my fellowman. When I am called by the trump of the archangel and weighed in the balance, you will all know me then. I add no more. God bless you all. —*Joseph Smith, Jr.* (STJS, 406-407)

86. THE STATE OF THE CHURCH

This work stands as an anchor of stability, an anchor of values, in a world whose values are shifting. We stand for something. Our values find their roots in the teachings of the gospel of Jesus Christ. These are unchanging. They are today as they were when Jesus walked the roads of Palestine. They are as applicable now as they were then. They have been tested in the cauldron of human history, and they have not been found wanting. We expect great things of our people. This religion is demanding. It requires self-discipline. It requires study and courage and faith. People are responding to this as they feel the ground under them shake with uncertainties in a world of crumbling values. —*Gordon B. Hinckley* (CN, Apr. 6, 1996, 14)

Mormonism, so-called, is a world religion, not simply because its members are now found throughout the world, but chiefly because it has a comprehensive and inclusive message based upon the acceptance of all truth, restored to meet the needs of all mankind. —*Howard W. Hunter* (WMJ, 60)

Imagine a father with many sons, each having different temperaments, aptitudes and spiritual traits. Does he love one son less than another? Perhaps the son who is least spiritually inclined has the father's attention, prayers, and pleadings more than the others. Does that mean he loves the others less? Do you imagine our Heavenly Father loving one nationality of his offspring more exclusively than others? . . . As our Father loves all his children, we must love all people—of every race, culture, nationality—and teach them the principles of the gospel so that they might embrace it and come to a knowledge of the divinity of the Savior. Only they are favored who keep his commandments. —*Howard W. Hunter* (WMJ, 74-75)

The gospel net draws in the good and the bad, the best and the worst. The worst because the devil, before the final cleansing, will put some of his followers within the kingdom in order to try and destroy it. We have some of them within the kingdom today, and in due course their number shall be known. Time has a way of taking care of all things, of elevating the good and bringing down the bad. —*Ezra Taft Benson* (NE, May 1975, 18)

While our generation will be comparable in wickedness to the days of Noah, when the Lord cleansed the earth by flood, there is a major difference this time. It is that God has saved for the final inning some of His strongest children, who will help bear off the kingdom triumphantly. That is where you come in, for you are the generation that must be prepared to meet your God. —*Ezra Taft Benson* (ETB, 105)

And so the gathering is taking place. Korea is the gathering place for Koreans, Australia for Australians, Brazil for Brazilians, England for the English. And so we move forward toward the confirmation of this great program the Lord has established for us. —*Spencer W. Kimball* (SWK, 440)

In answer to questions as to whether or not there may have been any dropouts or members who have fallen away, our answer has always been to recall the Master's parable of the sower. When the sower went out to sow, some of the seeds fell on fertile ground, but among the seeds that fell on fertile ground, some produced thirtyfold, some sixtyfold, and some ninetyfold. So today, in about that same ratio, we have some who are partially active, some who are more so, and some who are thoroughly active in the Church; but we are always reaching out to the ones who have strayed away, and we are constantly trying to bring them back into full activity. —*Harold B. Lee* (YLW, 145)

When we examine ourselves . . . we discover that we are still not doing exactly as we ought to do, notwithstanding all our experience. We discern that there are things which we fail to do that the Lord expects us to perform . . . But we feel thankful and grateful that we are enabled now, through our past experience, to accomplish many things that we could not do in former times and that we are able to escape individual sins that have brought trouble upon us in times past. While we congratulate ourselves in this direction, we certainly ought to feel that we have not yet arrived at perfection. There are many things for us to do yet. —*Lorenzo Snow* (CR, Apr. 1900, 1-2)

There is hardly a tithe of the people who have been baptized in water for the remission of sins that have died in the faith. . . . Many a time in my reflections I have wished I could fully comprehend the responsibility I have to God, and the responsibility every man is under who bears the priesthood in this generation. But I tell you, brethren, I think our hearts are set too much upon the things of this world. We do not appreciate, as men bearing the Holy Priesthood in this generation should, the mighty responsibility we are under to God and high heaven, as well as to the earth. I think we are too far from the Lord. —*Wilford Woodruff* (WW, 102)

Thousands of temptations assail, and you make a miss here and a slip there, and say that you have not lived up to all the knowledge you have. True; but often it is a marvel to me that you have lived up to so much as you have, considering the power of the enemy upon the earth. Few that have ever lived have fully understood that power. I do not fully comprehend the awful power and influence Satan has upon the earth, but I understand enough to know that it is a marvel that the Latter-day Saints are as good as they are. —*Brigham Young* (BY, 80)

THE CHURCH AND THE WORLD

87. THE CHURCH AND THE WORLD

Religion, to be effective, must be a vital and timely force in the lives of men. —*Gordon B. Hinckley* (BTE, 93)

All of us are the products of the elements to which we are exposed. We can give direction to those elements and thereby improve the result. I pray that we shall make an effort to improve the environment in which we and our children live. —*Gordon B. Hinckley* (Ensign, May 1982, 42)

I plead with our people everywhere to live with respect and appreciation for those not of our faith. There is so great a need for civility and mutual respect among those of differing beliefs and philosophies. We must not be partisans of any doctrine of ethnic superiority. We live in a world of diversity. We can and must be respectful toward those with whose teachings we may not agree. We must be willing to defend the rights of others who may become the victims of bigotry. —*Gordon B. Hinckley* (Ensign, May 1995, 71)

Never before has the Church had a better reputation than it has now. This is because of you, my brethren and sisters. The opinions of people concerning us for the most part arise out of personal experiences. It is your friendliness, your concern for others, and the good examples of your lives that result in the opinions held by others concerning the Latter-day Saints. —*Gordon B. Hinckley* (Ensign, Nov. 1997, 4)

The knowledge explosion of which the world is so proud is not of man's creation. It is his discovery of portions of the unlimited knowledge and information which is part of God's knowledge. How we use it is determined by whether we are of the eternal kingdom of God or a part of the temporary understanding of the world. The question is simply this: are we seeking to find our place in the world in the realm of worldly thought, or are we seeking to find our place in the unchanging kingdom of God? —*Howard W. Hunter* (CR, Oct. 1973, 65-67)

We live in a world of temptation—temptation that seems more real and oppressively rampant than any since the days of Noah. Are we remaining faithful in such a world? Every individual in the Church should ask, "Am I living so that I am keeping unspotted from the evils of the world?"—*Howard W. Hunter* (Ensign, Nov. 1976, 17-19)

The restored gospel of Jesus Christ can be a dynamic, moving influence, and true acceptance gives us a meaningful, religious experience. One of the greatest strengths of the Mormon religion is this translation of belief into daily thinking and conduct. This replaces turmoil and confusion with peace and tranquillity. —*Howard W. Hunter* (WMJ, 25-26)

The world needs the gospel of Jesus Christ. Those who are filled with the love of Christ do not seek to force others to do better; they inspire others to do better, indeed inspire them to the pursuit of God. We need to extend the hand of friendship. We need to be kinder, more gentle, more forgiving, and slower to anger. We need to love one another with the pure love of Christ. May this be our course and our desire. —*Howard W. Hunter* (WMJ, 174)

Great nations are never conquered from outside unless they are rotten inside. Our greatest national problem today is erosion, not the erosion of the soil but erosion of the national morality. —*Ezra Taft Benson* (ETB, 574)

Sportsmanship is the spirituality in athletics. —*Ezra Taft Benson* (ETB, 437)

We don't need changed programs now as much as we need changed people. —*Ezra Taft Benson* (AWW, 74)

The problems of the world cannot possibly be solved by skeptics or cynics whose horizons are limited by the obvious realities. —*Spencer W. Kimball* (SWK, 487)

Always remember that if this were not the Lord's work, the adversary would not pay any attention to us. If this Church were merely a church of men and women, teaching only the doctrines of men, we would encounter little or no criticism or resistance—but because this is the Church of Him whose name it bears, we must not be surprised when criticisms or difficulties arise. With faith and good works, the truth will prevail. This is His work. There is none other like it. Let us, therefore, press forward, lengthening our stride and rejoicing in our blessings and opportunities. —*Spencer W. Kimball* (Ensign, May 1981, 79)

Property, virtue and life itself are safe only in that land where lawmakers are influenced by and laws are made and enforced and obeyed in conformity with the basic moral standards found in the holy scriptures. —*Harold B. Lee* (DSL, 7)

Sometimes it is the mark of distinction to have men of ill repute not say good things about you. —*Harold B. Lee* (YLW, 13-14)

The great danger in any society is apathy and a failure to be alert to the issues of the day, when applied to principles or to the election of public officials. —*Harold B. Lee* (YLW, 190)

All churches teach some truth, whether they profess belief in Confucius, Buddha, the Greek and Roman gods, or anything else; otherwise their churches would not endure a month. The fact that they teach some truth does not make them the Church of God. There is but one Church of God. —*Joseph Fielding Smith* (DS3, 271)

I do not know that there was ever a time in the history of mankind when the Evil One seemed so determined to take from man his freedom. —*David O. McKay* (CR, Oct. 1965, 7)

Our religion is not a cloak to wear on Sunday and be hung in the closet for the rest of the week; neither is it something for nations to parade on certain occasions and then to wrap up in mothballs to await another occasion.
Men today are rapidly classifying themselves into two groups: believers and nonbelievers. —*David O. McKay* (CR, Apr. 1962, 125)

The Lord help us to be able to prove to the world that the restored gospel is just what the world today is longing for; and when they see it, may they know, as you know and as I know, that the everlasting gospel is a light to the world. May it ever be a light to the nations, a guiding solution of all the world problems. —*David O. McKay* (CR, Apr. 1963, 99)

I fear that the Latter-day Saints, in many cases, are blinded by their own vanity, by their desire to be what the world is; and we have been told in such plain language by our Heavenly Father that we cannot live as the world lives and enjoy his Spirit. —*George Albert Smith* (CR, Apr. 1929, 30)

What is our difficulty, brethren and sisters? It is that men refuse to hear what the Lord has said. They refuse to pay attention to his wise counsel. They absolutely neglect to give credence to the things that he teaches us, and he will not be mocked. He gives us the advice and the counsel that we need, but he will not compel us. But if we refuse we lose our opportunity, and it passes away from us, in many cases to return again no more forever. —*George Albert Smith* (CR, Apr. 1933, 71)

Every faithful Latter-day Saint believes, beyond a shadow of doubt, that to each individual the free exercise of conscience, the right and control of property, and the protection of life are inherent rights of which he should never be deprived. —*Heber J. Grant* (IE, 39:523)

A good motto for young people to adopt, who are determined to delve into philosophic theories, is to search all things, but be careful to hold on only to that which is true. The truth persists, but the theories of philosophers change and are overthrown. What men use today as a scaffolding for scientific purposes from which to reach out into the unknown for truth, may be torn down tomorrow, having served its purpose; but faith is an eternal principle through which the humble believer may secure everlasting solace. It is the only way to find God. —*Joseph F. Smith* (IE, 14:548)

The gospel that we have received from the beginning is a gospel of persecution and a gospel of sacrifices. It is a gospel and work that requires the utmost diligence in order that we may receive that power, that faith, and that intelligence from the Almighty to such an extent that we may be fully prepared to cope with all the difficulties that may beset our path. —*Lorenzo Snow* (LS, 22)

The Lord has never sent a message to the inhabitants of the earth but what it has been despised, in a great measure, by most of them. As it was in the days of Noah and Lot, so shall it be in the days of the coming of the Son of Man. —*Wilford Woodruff* (WW, 16)

Mormonism is an enigma to the world. . . . Philosophy can not comprehend it; it is beyond the reach of natural philosophy. It is the philosophy of heaven; it is the revelation of God to man. —*John Taylor* (GK, 5)

We have, however, enough to do in attending to the duties of our priesthood and calling without troubling ourselves with the follies and foibles of those who are not of us. As I have already said they do not profess what we do. We profess to be governed by high principles and nobler motives, and by more exalted ideas. Let us try and live up to our profession. —*John Taylor* (GK, 314)

The world will not receive the Gospel, unless they can have it on their own terms, and will persecute the few that do receive it. —*Brigham Young* (BY, 226)

There are as honest men in other churches as there are in ours. —*Brigham Young* (BY, 423)

A child can tell you the truth, in child-like language, while falsehood requires the lawyer and the priest to tell it to make it at all plausible; it requires a scholastic education to make falsehood pass for truth. —*Brigham Young* (BY, 330-331)

Every time you kick "Mormonism" you kick it upstairs; you never kick it downstairs. The Lord Almighty so orders it. —*Brigham Young* (BY, 351)

If I now had in my possession one hundred million dollars in cash, I could buy the favor of the publishers of newspapers and control their presses; with that amount I could make this people popular, though I expect that popularity would send us to hell. —*Brigham Young* (BY, 352)

The Lord deals with this people as a tender parent with a child, communicating light and intelligence and the knowledge of his ways as they can bear it. The inhabitants of the earth are asleep; they know not the day of their visitation. The Lord hath set the bow in the cloud for a sign that while it shall be seen, seed time and harvest, summer and winter shall not fail; but when it shall disappear woe to that generation, for behold the end cometh quickly. —*Joseph Smith, Jr.* (STJS, 340)

I say, in the name of the Lord, that the kingdom of God was set up on the earth from the days of Adam to the present time, whenever there has been a righteous man on earth unto whom God revealed His word and gave power and authority to administer in His name. —*Joseph Smith, Jr.* (STJS, 305)

Where did the kingdom of God begin? Where there is no kingdom of God there is no salvation. What constitutes the kingdom of God? Where there is a prophet, a priest, or a righteous man unto whom God gives His oracles, there is the kingdom of God; and where the oracles of God are not, there the kingdom of God is not. —*Joseph Smith, Jr.* (STJS, 306)

What will become of the world, or the various professors of religion who do not believe in revelation and the oracles of God as continued to His Church in all ages of the world, when He has a people on earth? I tell you, in the name of Jesus Christ, they will be damned; and when you get into the eternal world, you will find it will be so, they cannot escape the damnation of hell. —*Joseph Smith, Jr.* (STJS, 307)

I will illustrate it by an old apple tree. Here jumps off a branch and says, I am the true tree, and you are corrupt. If the whole tree is corrupt, are not its branches corrupt? If the Catholic religion is a false religion, how can any true religion come out of it?—*Joseph Smith, Jr.* (STJS, 423)

88. BLESSINGS AND CHALLENGES IN TODAY'S WORLD

You and I are experiencing the profound and wonderful blessings of the dispensation of the fullness of times. In this day and time there has been restored to the earth all of the principles, powers, blessings, and keys of all previous dispensations. By certain and clear and unequivocal revelation there has come knowledge of the living reality of God our Eternal Father and His Beloved Son, the Savior and Redeemer of the world. —*Gordon B. Hinckley* (Ensign, May 1992, 70)

The magnetism of television and radio is in the accessibility of their mediocrity. Lovely is not an adjective to describe most of their products. The inventors of these wonders were inspired by the Lord. But once their good works were introduced to the world, the powers of darkness began to employ them for our destruction. —*Ezra Taft Benson* (ETB, 325-326)

As Latter-day Saints, we have been driven, mobbed, misunderstood, and maligned. We have been a peculiar people. Now we are faced with world applause. It has been a welcome change, but can we stand acceptance? Can we meet the danger of applause? In the hour of man's success, applause can be his greatest danger. —*Ezra Taft Benson* (ETB, 369)

We must be careful that we do not trade freedom for security. Whenever that is attempted, usually we lose both. There is always a tendency when nations become mature for the people to become more interested in preserving their luxuries and their comforts than in safeguarding the ideals and principles which made these comforts and luxuries possible. —*Ezra Taft Benson* (ETB, 600)

We live in a corrupt world where most of the things we think we want can be purchased with money or obtained through political power, but we also live in a wonderfully good world where the things which really bring us unbounded joy may still be had in rich abundance if we are willing to pay the price, and that price is expressed not in money but in effort. —*Spencer W. Kimball* (SWK, 353)

As members of Christ's true church we must stand firm today and always for human rights and the dignity of man, who is the literal offspring of God in the spirit. —*Spencer W. Kimball* (Ensign, May 1974, 4)

The dispensation in which we live is intended to be a demonstration of the power and effectiveness of the gospel of Jesus Christ to meet these everyday problems here and now. —*Harold B. Lee* (SHP, 278)

We find a tendency of some in our Church schools and seminaries and institutes to challenge, under the guise of so-called academic freedom, the doctrinal purity and Church standards. Beware! . . . Faith was never built by providing the dissenters with a forum to criticize the Church, its institutions, and its authority. —*Harold B. Lee* (YLW, 7)

All will admit that we are living in a most wonderful age, the greatest in many respects this world has ever seen. . . . The great discoveries, inventions, the pouring out of learning, theory and principle both true and false, by which many are deceived, are signs and wonders which are given us and which we should heed. The airplane swiftly winging its way through the heavens; the radio bringing to us the voices of men from all parts of the earth; the great engineering and mechanical undertakings which bring the many conveniences to man; the building of skyscrapers and the harnessing of electricity and making it work in its various forms; the great medical discoveries and surgical skill with the thousand and one other great wonders, have all been given through the will and power of God. —*Joseph Fielding Smith* (CN, Sept. 26, 1931, 7)

There are two ways to stem criminality. One is by united, concentrated public opinion. The other, and more effective, is by personal contact. There are many in this audience who can look back with gratitude to the visit of some kind man, somebody who put his hand on our shoulder and said: "Don't do that," or "I commend you for not doing this, my boy." Some word of commendation, some gentle hand led you back into the path that has given you the success which you have attained. Personal influence—we must not lose sight of it!—*David O. McKay* (CR, Apr. 1931, 82)

The paramount need in the world today is a clearer understanding by human beings of moral and spiritual values, and a desire and determination to attain them.

Never before in the history of the world has there been such a need of spiritual awakening. Unless there is such an awakening, there is danger of catastrophe among the nations of the world. —*David O. McKay* (CR, Oct. 1953, 8-9)

It is often said that the Church is the greatest thing in the world, and it is!—*David O. McKay* (CR, Apr. 1968, 144)

We ought to regard these inventions [airplanes, radio, television] as blessings from the Lord. They greatly enlarge our abilities. They can indeed become blessings if we utilize them in righteousness for the dissemination of truth and the furtherance of the work of the Lord among men. The great challenge facing the world today lies in the use we make of many of these inventions. We can use them to destroy, as we have sometimes done, in the past, or we can utilize them to enlighten and bless mankind, as our Heavenly Father would have us do. —*George Albert Smith* (SGO, 41)

Nations have risen and triumphed when they have operated along righteous lines. Governments have succeeded and flourished when they have kept the commandments of God; and, on the contrary, the greatest nations that the world had seen up to the time this nation was born, have risen to a pinnacle by works of righteousness, and have fallen to the depths of degradation because they have violated the laws of our Heavenly Father. —*George Albert Smith* (SGO, 168)

There are two influences in this world that have been from the beginning; the one is constructive and uplifting—the other is destructive and debasing. We are all subject to our environments, but we have our free agency and can determine for ourselves which of the influences shall motivate our lives. —*George Albert Smith* (SGO, 201-202)

We live in a great and wonderful age. The glory of this century is beyond that of any other century; but I feel that we are in just as great danger as were those who lived in the days of Noah. . . . We are in as great danger as any nation that has ever lived, because God has given us more than any other nation, and if in arrogance and in pride we turn aside from the Father of us all, and in our carelessness and indifference towards sacred things we spend our lives for the things of this world, it will not be very long until the chastening hand of an all-wise Father may come upon us as a nation, and we be counted as the nations of the past, among those that have withered away. —*George Albert Smith* (CR, Oct. 1928, 94)

The truth is, we are not strangers to hatred; and the contempt of the world has been our lot so much that we have no reason to be discouraged when it comes, even in violent forms. The danger lies not so much in our own peculiarity as in the disposition of many of our people to court popularity at all costs, as if it were something devoutly to be wished for. —*Joseph F. Smith* (GD, 340)

Trials are necessary to the perfection of mankind, as friction is necessary to separate the dross of human judgment from the pure gold of divine wisdom. —*Joseph F. Smith* (PC, 149)

The Latter-day Saints . . . believe that God rules in the fire, the earthquake, the tidal wave, the volcanic eruption, and the storm. . . . We believe that his judgments are poured out to bring mankind to a sense of his power and his purposes, that they may repent of their sins and prepare themselves for the second coming of Christ to reign in righteousness upon the earth. —*Joseph F. Smith* (LPS, 234-235)

But it need not surprise us that difficulties and storms arise—that we see hurricanes playing about us—that we see war-clouds gather thick and fast about us; this need not be surprising. Where there is no trial there can be no deliverance; where there is no temptation, the power of God cannot be made manifest to any great extent. —*Lorenzo Snow* (LS, 122)

The misery and evils which now exist throughout the world have got to be corrected, in a great measure, through the power of God, before the kingdoms of this world will become the kingdoms of God and his Christ. It is a great and mighty work to establish the kingdom of God on the earth, that the law may go forth from Zion to rule the kingdoms of the world. The light, knowledge, truth, and wisdom to do this has got to come through the Holy Priesthood, which is the government of God upon the earth. —*Wilford Woodruff* (WW, 185)

Calamities and troubles are increasing in the earth, and there is a meaning to these things. Remember this, and reflect upon these matters. If you do your duty, and I do my duty, we'll have protection, and shall pass through the afflictions in peace and in safety. . . . It's by the power of the gospel that we shall escape. —*Wilford Woodruff* (WW, 230-231)

There is a terrible time approaching the nations of the earth, and also this nation, worse than has ever entered into the heart of man to conceive of—war, bloodshed, and desolation, mourning and misery, pestilence, famine, and earthquakes, and all those calamities spoken of by the prophets will most assuredly be fulfilled. —*John Taylor* (GK, 237)

The judgments will begin at the house of God. We have to pass through some of these things, but it will only be a very little compared with the terrible destruction, the misery, and suffering that will overtake the world who are doomed to suffer the wrath of God. It behooves us, as the saints of God, to stand firm and faithful in the observance of his laws, that we may be worthy of his preserving care and blessing. —*John Taylor* (JD, 21:100)

We have all kinds of fish in the Gospel net. —*Brigham Young* (BY, 444)

There is not a single condition of life that is entirely unnecessary; there is not one hour's experience but what is beneficial to all those who make it their study, and aim to improve upon the experience they gain. What becomes a trial to one person is not noticed by another. —*Brigham Young* (JD, 9:292-293)

The time is coming when a good man will be more precious than fine gold. —*Brigham Young* (BY, 111)

You may remember it and lay it to heart, and if you wish, write it in your journals that some of the best spirits that have ever been sent to earth are coming at the present time. —*Brigham Young* (BY, 109)

We have the best and the worst. Why the worst? Because the Devil prompts men and women of the meanest and lowest grade to embrace the Gospel and get a foothold in the Kingdom of God to destroy it. —*Brigham Young* (BY, 85)

I explained concerning the coming of the Son of Man; also that it is a false idea that the Saints will escape all the judgments, whilst the wicked suffer; for all flesh is subject to suffer, and "the righteous shall hardly escape;" still many of the Saints will escape, for the just shall live by faith; yet many of the righteous shall fall a prey to disease, to pestilence, etc., by reason of the weakness of the flesh, and yet be saved in the Kingdom of God. So that it is an unhallowed principle to say that such and such have transgressed because they have been prayed upon by disease or death, for all flesh is subject to death; and the Savior has said, "Judge not, lest ye be judged."—*Joseph Smith, Jr.* (STJS, 185-186)

Consider for a moment, brethren, the fulfillment of the words of the prophet; for we behold that darkness covers the earth, and gross darkness the minds of the inhabitants thereof—that crimes of every description are increasing among men—vices of great enormity are practiced—the rising generation growing up in the fullness of pride and arrogance. —*Joseph Smith, Jr.* (STJS, 59)

If there was anything great or good in the world, it came from God. —*Joseph Smith, Jr.* (STJS, 278-286)

89. CHURCH AND COUNTRY

Patriotism evidently is gone from the hearts of many of our youth. . . . We shall not build love of country by taking away from our youth the principles which made us strong—thrift, initiative, self-reliance, and an overriding sense of duty to God and to man. . . . How we need to kindle in the hearts of youth an old-fashioned love of country and a reverence for the land of their birth. But we shall not do it with tawdry political maneuvering and enormous handouts for which nothing is given in return.

Love of country is born of nobler stuff—of the challenge of struggle that makes precious the prize that's earned. —*Gordon B. Hinckley* (CR, Oct. 1965, 52-53)

I am not one to advocate shouting defiantly or shaking fists and issuing threats in the faces of legislators. But I am one who believes that we should earnestly and sincerely and positively express our convictions to those given the heavy responsibility of making and enforcing our laws. . . . We are not likely to get that which we do not speak up for. —*Gordon B. Hinckley* (BTE, 55-58)

In the present day of unrest, the question might appropriately be asked, what do we owe to Caesar? To the country in which we live? We owe allegiance, respect, and honor. Laws enacted to promote the welfare of the whole and suppress evil doing are to be strictly obeyed. We must pay tribute to sustain the government in the necessary expense incurred in the protection of life, liberty, property, and in promoting the welfare of all persons. —*Howard W. Hunter* (CR, Apr. 1968, 65-66)

Rarely in the annals of human history has a nation of free people been more careless of their liberty than we Americans. We take our precious God-given freedom for granted. —*Ezra Taft Benson* (ETB, 579)

Patriotism is trying always to give more to the nation than we receive. It is selfless service. —*Ezra Taft Benson* (ETB, 589)

The fact that our Founding Fathers looked to God for help and inspiration should not surprise us, for they were men of great faith. These men had been raised up specifically by the Lord so they could participate in the great political drama unfolding in America. —*Ezra Taft Benson* (ETB, 599)

We need to keep before us the truth that people who do not master themselves and their appetites will soon be mastered by government. —*Ezra Taft Benson* (ETB, 668)

How then can we best befriend the constitution in this critical hour and secure the blessings of liberty and ensure the protection and guidance of our Father in Heaven?

First and foremost, we must be righteous. . . .

Second, we must learn the principles of the Constitution in the tradition of the Founding Fathers. . .

Third, we must become involved in civic affairs to see that we are properly represented. . . .

Fourth, we must make our influence felt by our vote, our letters, our teaching, and our advice. —*Ezra Taft Benson* (Ensign, Nov. 1987, 6)

Father, bless their deliberations that they may always obtain facts and consider them in proper perspective, . . . and that they may always measure every issue by the yardstick of righteousness and weigh it by the scales of justice and ask themselves in every case, "How would my Lord and Master vote on this issue, were he a legislator here?"—*Spencer W. Kimball* (SWK, 404)

To those of you who are citizens of the United States: I wish to urge you and your family members of voting age to go to the polls in large numbers and vote for the strongest, finest people who are certain to do the most to safeguard the rights and freedoms of this nation. We do not endorse any candidates, but we hope you will vote for good men and women of character, integrity, and ability. You are to be the judge. —*Spencer W. Kimball* (CR, Nov. 1980, 45)

A society in which men recognize no check upon their freedom soon becomes a society where freedom is in possession of only a few who lust for power and domination. —*Harold B. Lee* (DSL, 218)

To the membership of The Church of Jesus Christ of Latter-day Saints, the Constitution of the United States is as a tree of liberty under whose coiling branches one might find a haven from the scorching sun of turmoil and oppression and have his rights protected according to just and holy principles. To them, the constitution was established by the hands of wise men whom God raised up for this very purpose, and they devoutly believe that if it should be in danger of being overthrown, their lives, if need be, are to be offered in defense of its principles. —*Harold B. Lee* (YLW, 175-176)

True patriotism was not merely refraining from breaking the law, but was to be evidenced by a constant and courageous effort on the part of each to render service to his community and to his fellowmen. —*Harold B. Lee* (YLW, 178)

This is a great nation; this is a great country; this is the most favored of all lands. While it is true that there are dangers and difficulties that lie ahead of us, we must not assume that we are going to stand by and watch the country go to ruin. . . .

We should be finding what is right about American and should be speaking optimistically and enthusiastically about America. —*Harold B. Lee* (YLW, 341-342)

True patriotism, then, and pursuit of happiness are almost synonymous as they were understood by our early patriots—and it meant to do God's will. —*Harold B. Lee* (HBL, 619)

It is true that a country cannot get ahead of its religion. The higher our ideals, the nearer we observe divine law and the stronger are our spiritual forces. No Christian can forsake the divinity of Jesus Christ and not suffer. —*Joseph Fielding Smith* (CR, Apr. 1943, 15)

Notwithstanding all the warnings the Lord has given us, we are rushing madly, headstrong, to destruction, preparing ourselves if you please for the burning. . . .

So I say I am troubled; I am concerned over this nation; I am concerned over the nations, because of the wickedness of the people. I can see evil in the trend of the times. I can see anarchy ahead of us. If we are going to permit men, in organized form, to desecrate the sacredness of the laws of this country and the Constitution of this country; if we are going to permit them, in the spirit of anarchy, to take possession of that which does not belong to them, without protest, we are going to reap the whirlwind, just as surely as we live. —*Joseph Fielding Smith* (CN, May 8, 1937, 5)

Every man must stand to be judged according to his works, and the Lord will also judge the nations according to their works. —*Joseph Fielding Smith* (CN, Feb. 6, 1932, 5)

Any member of this Church who will not sustain the established laws of the land is not only disloyal as a citizen of the government, but he is disloyal to his Church and disloyal to God. —*Joseph Fielding Smith* (CN, Feb. 6, 1932, 8)

Jesus influenced individuals, knowing that if the individual is pure, strong, a thousand individuals would make a strong community, and a thousand communities would make a strong nation. —*David O. McKay* (CR, Oct. 1958, 91)

A clean man is a national asset. A pure woman is the incarnation of true national glory. A citizen who loves justice and hates evil is better than a battleship. The strength of any community consists of and exits in the men who are pure, clean, upright, and straightforward, ready for the right and sensitive to every approach of evil. Let such ideals be the standard of citizenship. —*David O. McKay* (CR, Apr. 1965, 8)

Honesty, sincerity of purpose, must be dominant traits of character in leaders of a nation that would be truly great. —*David O. McKay* (CR, Apr. 1964, 6)

Unwise legislation, too often prompted by political expediency, if enacted, will seductively undermine man's right of free agency, rob him of his rightful liberties, and make him but a cog in the crushing wheel of regimentation. —*David O. McKay* (CR, Oct. 1965, 8)

The Church, out of respect for the rights of all its members to have their political views and loyalties, must maintain the strictest possible neutrality. —*David O. McKay* (CR, Apr. 1966, 109)

The position of this Church on the subject of Communism has never changed. We consider it the greatest satanical threat to peace, prosperity, and the spread of God's work among men that exists on the face of the earth. . . .
Communism debases the individual and makes him the enslaved tool of the state, to which he must look for sustenance and religion. Communism destroys man's God-given free agency. —*David O. McKay* (CR, Apr. 1966, 109-110)

The Constitution of the United States of America is just as much from my Heavenly Father as the Ten Commandments. —*George Albert Smith* (CR, Apr. 1948, 182)

When our Father in Heaven inspired men to write the Constitution and give unto us the great charter that vouchsafed to us the liberty we enjoy, he did it in order that men might develop and be free, as the gospel of Jesus Christ intends that all men shall be. So the government of the United States was begun under the direction of our Father in Heaven, as declared by his own word, to be an example unto the nations of the earth. —*George Albert Smith* (SGO, 169)

The Constitution and the laws that have been enacted under its provisions are calculated to ensure liberty, not license, to all who dwell here. —*George Albert Smith* (SGO, 169)

It is your duty and mine to remember in our prayers the President of the United States of America, to remember the men who represent us in the Congress of the United States, to remember the executives of the states of the nation, and to pray for them that they might have divine aid. —*George Albert Smith* (CR, Oct. 1945, 174)

I was in a meeting, not very long ago, where a group of Boy Scouts stood and sang, "God Bless America," and they sang it beautifully, and all the time they were singing I asked myself the question, "How can he bless America until America repents?" Every great blessing that we desire is promised us by our Heavenly Father on condition that we honor him and keep his commandments. Praying is not sufficient. Not only must we pray but we must live to be worthy of the blessing. —*George Albert Smith* (CR, Apr. 1948, 184)

No man is a faithful member of this Church, in good standing, who refuses to sustain the law of the land. . . . The Lord directs that we seek after good men and great men, and that we pray for and sustain them in order that the laws that are enacted for our government may be such as he would be pleased to endorse. —*George Albert Smith* (CR, Oct. 1924, 47-48)

In no other nation under heaven could the Church have been organized and gone forward as we have in this nation. The rounding of the United States was not an accident. The giving to us of the Constitution of the United States was not an accident. Our Heavenly Father knew what would be needed, and so he paved the way to give us the Constitution. It came under the influence of prayer, and he guided those who framed that wonderful document. —*George Albert Smith* (CR, Apr. 1947, 163)

Allow me to announce that from the day of Joseph Smith to this identical day, the leaders of this people have had absolute respect, love, and reverence for their country. Allow me to announce further that we are patriotic Americans to the core. . . . We believe absolutely in the inspiration of God to the men who framed our constitution. —*Heber J. Grant* (CR, Oct. 1919, 33)

I know that any ruler who claims to be the representative of Almighty God who would take away the liberties of his fellow men, is not a representative from God. You can draw your own conclusions whom he does represent. —*Heber J. Grant* (CR, Apr. 1918, 24)

I pray for our country and ask the Lord to bless those who preside in the nation; in the states, in the cities, and in the counties. I pray God to inspire the people that they will obey His commands, and elect good men to office; that they will bury their political differences and seek for good men to hold office, and not men who connive with those who are breaking the laws of our country. It is one of the Articles of our Faith to obey and uphold the laws of the land. May God help us to do it. —*Heber J. Grant* (CR, Apr. 1928, 121)

I believe absolutely in the best men for the office. I believe in honest, upright, good men being chosen to occupy places and positions in the state and in the Church. —*Heber J. Grant* (CR, Oct. 1922, 5)

Any Latter-day Saint who sustains or votes for a man to be governor of a state who has ridiculed in print the Savior of the world is doing that which I as president of the Church hereby condemn. —*Heber J. Grant* (CR, Oct. 1934, 131)

To be a true citizen of a great country takes nothing from, but adds to, individual greatness. While a great and good people necessarily adds greatness and goodness to national life, the nation's greatness reacts upon its citizens and adds honor to them, and insures their welfare and happiness. —*Joseph F. Smith* (GD, 411)

A good Latter-day Saint is a good citizen in every way. —*Joseph F. Smith* (IE, 6:382)

It startles men when they hear the elders of Israel tell about the kingdoms of this world becoming the kingdom of our God and his Christ. They say it is treason for men to teach that the kingdom Daniel saw is going to be set up, and bear rule over the whole earth. Is it treason for God Almighty to govern the earth? Who made it? God, did he not? Who made you? God, if you have any Eternal Father. Well, whose right is it to rule and reign over you and the earth? It does not belong to the devil, nor to men. It has never been given to men yet; it has never been given to the nations. It belongs solely to God and he is coming to rule and reign over it. —*Wilford Woodruff* (WW, 146)

We consider that we have been blessed as a nation in possessing the freedom and privileges guaranteed by the Constitution of the United States. They have been a rich legacy from our fathers. We consider our form of government superior to any other on the earth. It guarantees to us "life, liberty and the pursuit of happiness." . . . Still, I have many times thought that we, as American citizens, have not prized the gifts and blessings guaranteed to us by the Constitution of our country. For the last few years, especially, the Constitution at times has been looked upon as a matter of the smallest consequence. In some respects, however, it has been a blessing to us as a people, and it is to the whole nation, as far as it is carried out. But in order to fully receive its blessings we have to honor its precepts. —*Wilford Woodruff* (WW, 186)

In all the history of the dealings of God with man this one principle, sooner or later, has manifested itself: that virtue exalteth a nation, while sin is a reproach to any people. You will see that this has been manifested in the history of all nations under heaven—in their rise and progress and prosperity, and in their fall and decline and in their final overthrow and destruction. You will find in every instance that sin, error, darkness, falsehood, wrongdoing, have laid the foundation of the overthrow of every nation and city under heaven from the foundation of the world until the present time. —*Wilford Woodruff* (WW, 187)

We declare that there is nothing in the ceremony of the endowment, or in any doctrine, tenet, obligation or injunction of this Church, either private or public, which is hostile or intended to be hostile, to the government of the United States. On the contrary, its members are under divine commandment to revere the Constitution as a heaven-inspired instrument and obey as supreme all laws made in pursuance of its provisions. . . .

We claim no religious liberty that we are unwilling to accord to others. We ask for no civil or political rights which are not granted and guaranteed to citizens in general. We desire to be in harmony with the government and people of the United States as an integral part of the nation. —*Wilford Woodruff* (WW, 194-195)

Now, the world is terribly afraid that the Presidency of this Church shall say something to somebody about politics; and even some of the elders of Israel appear very much afraid that they will get some counsel on these things. What are they thinking about? Politics should never turn the heart of any man bearing the Holy Priesthood from his brethren or from the cause of God. Let him enjoy his politics, and vote for whom he chooses . . . It makes no difference to me what a man's politics is: he has a right to enjoy his own political ideas; but let this people realize that they are Latter-day Saints and are held responsible before God for the course they pursue. —*Wilford Woodruff* (WW, 204)

The worst wish we have for the human family is that the principles enunciated in our Constitution may reverberate the wide earth, and spread from shore to shore until all mankind shall be free. —*John Taylor* (GK, 295)

When the people shall have torn to shreds the Constitution of the United States, the elders of Israel will be found holding it up to the nations of the earth and proclaiming liberty and equal rights to all men, and extending the hand of fellowship to the oppressed of all nations. —*John Taylor* (JD, 21:8)

The elders of Israel begin to understand that they have something to do with the world politically as well as religiously; that it is as much their duty to study correct political principles as well as religious, and to seek to know and comprehend the social and political interests of man, and to learn and be able to teach that which would be best calculated to promote the interests of the world. —*John Taylor* (GK, 297-298)

We would to God that our rulers would be men of righteousness, and that those who aspire to position would be guided by honorable feelings to maintain inviolate the

Constitution and operate in the interest, happiness, well-being, and protection of the whole community. —*John Taylor* (GK, 298)

We have no fault to find with our government. We deem it the best in the world. But we have reason to deplore its maladministration, and I call upon our legislators, our governors and president to pause in their careers and not to tamper with the rights and liberties of American citizens, nor wantonly tear down the bulwarks of American and human liberty. God has given to us glorious institutions. Let us preserve them intact and not pander to the vices, passions, and fanaticism of a depraved public opinion. —*John Taylor* (GK, 311)

The government of heaven, if wickedly administered, would become one of the worst governments upon the face of the earth. No matter how good a government is, unless it is administered by righteous men, an evil government will be made of it. —*Brigham Young* (BY, 147)

There is no other platform that any government can stand upon and endure, but the platform of truth and virtue. —*Brigham Young* (BY, 355)

Are we a political people? Yes, very political indeed. But what party do you belong to or would you vote for? I will tell you whom we will vote for: we will vote for the man who will sustain the principles of civil and religious liberty, the man who knows the most and who has the best heart and brain for a statesman; and we do not care a farthing whether he is a whig, a democrat, a barnburner, a republican, a new light or anything else. These are our politics. —*Brigham Young* (BY, 358)

It was observed this morning that the Government of the United States was the best or most wholesome one on the earth, and the best adapted to our condition. That is very true. —*Brigham Young* (BY, 359)

When the Constitution of the United States hangs, as it were, upon a single thread, they will have to call for the "Mormon" Elders to save it from utter destruction; and they will step forth and do it. —*Brigham Young* (BY, 361)

We want men to rule the nation who care more for and love better the nation's welfare than gold and silver, fame, or popularity. —*Brigham Young* (BY, 364)

It is our duty to concentrate all our influence to make popular that which is sound and good, and unpopular that which is unsound. 'Tis right, politically, for a man who has influence to use it. . . . From henceforth I will maintain all the influence I can get. —*Joseph Smith, Jr.* (HC, 5:286)

[T]he Constitution of the United States is a glorious standard; it is founded in the wisdom of God. It is a heavenly banner; it is to all those who are privileged with the sweets of liberty, like the cooling shades and refreshing waters of a great rock in a thirsty and weary land. It is like a great tree under whose branches men from every clime can be shielded from the burning rays of the sun. —*Joseph Smith, Jr.* (STJS, 168)

If, then, we admit that God is the source of all wisdom and understanding, we must admit that by His direct inspiration He has taught man that law is necessary in order to govern and regulate His own immediate interest and welfare; for this reason, that law is beneficial to promote peace and happiness among men. —*Joseph Smith, Jr.* (STJS, 68-69)

90. THE CHURCH IN A FALLEN WORLD

Is there relevancy in Jesus for our time? The world never needed more urgently the power of his example; the world never needed more desperately the vitality of his teachings. —*Gordon B. Hinckley* (CR, Apr. 1969, 61)

It is not always easy to live in the world and not be a part of it. We cannot live entirely with our own or unto ourselves, nor would we wish to. We must mingle with others. In so doing, we can be gracious. We can be inoffensive. We can avoid any spirit or attitude of self-righteousness. But we can maintain our standards. —*Gordon B. Hinckley* (BTE, 27)

We have a responsibility and a challenge to take our places in the world of business, science, government, medicine, education, and every other worthwhile and constructive vocation. We have an obligation to train our hands and minds to excel in the work of the world for the blessing of all mankind. —*Gordon B. Hinckley* (BTE, 27)

Reformation of the world begins with reformation of self. —*Gordon B. Hinckley* (BTE, 55)

We in America are saddled with a huge financial deficit in our national budget. This has led to astronomical debt.

But there is another deficit which, in its long-term implications, is more serious. It is a moral deficit, a decline in values in the lives of the people, which is sapping the very foundation of our society. It is serious in this land. And it is serious in every other nation of which I know. —*Gordon B. Hinckley* (Ensign, Nov. 1993, 54)

I believe we can be modern and enjoy the fruits of a modern world and its high standard of living, and I believe we can have the benefits of modern scholarship and scientific advances without turning to the theories of the modernist. I believe the principles of the gospel announced by the Savior in his personal ministry were true when they were given and are true today. Truth is eternal and never changing, and the gospel of Jesus Christ is ever contemporary in a changing world. —*Howard W. Hunter* (CR, Oct. 1973, 67)

There is a great difference between ethics and religion. There is a distinction between one whose life is based on mere ethics and one who lives a truly religious life. We have a need for ethics, but true religion includes the truths of ethics and goes far beyond. True religion has its roots in belief in a supreme being. Christian religion is based upon belief in God the Eternal Father and in his son Jesus Christ and in the word of the Lord as contained in scripture. Religion also goes beyond theology. It is more than just belief in Deity; it is the practice of that belief. —*Howard W. Hunter* (WMJ, 176-177)

Are we not our own worst enemy with our declining moral standards, our increasing selfishness, the constant search for pleasure, the piling on of luxury upon luxury for the sake of softer and softer living and the possession of a hollow, vacillating national purpose? The battleground is in our hearts, in our intellects, in our homes and our communities—and the war goes relentlessly on. —*Ezra Taft Benson* (ETB, 391)

Never have the forces of evil been so insidious, widespread, and enticing. Everywhere there seems to be a cheapening, weakening, downgrading of all that is fine, good, and uplifting—all aimed at our youth, while many of their parents are lulled away into a false security as they enjoy their comfortable complacency. —*Ezra Taft Benson* (ETB, 409)

I do not believe the greatest threat to our future is from bombs or guided missiles. I do not think our civilization will die that way. I think it will die when we no longer care—when the spiritual forces that make us wish to be right and noble die in the hearts of men. —*Ezra Taft Benson* (ETB, 590)

Decaying cities are simply a delayed reflection of individuals suffering under a decadent attitude. —*Ezra Taft Benson* (ETB, 645-646)

The Lord works from the inside out. The world works from the outside in. The world would take people out of the slums. Christ takes the slums out of people, and then they take themselves out of the slums. The world would mold men by changing their environment. Christ changes men, who then change their environment. The world would shape human behavior, but Christ can change human nature. —*Ezra Taft Benson* (Ensign, July 1989, 4-5)

To hear the population explosion experts talk and write—those people who think themselves so wise—they would depopulate the earth so that the few left would roll in luxury rather than that all the Lord's children could come to earth and have a body and mortality and the good things of the earth. —*Spencer W. Kimball* (SWK, 213)

Important as it is, building stronger homes is not enough in the fight against rising permissiveness. We therefore urge Church members as citizens to lift their voices, to join others in unceasingly combating, in their communities and beyond, the inroads of pornography and the general flaunting of permissiveness. —*Spencer W. Kimball* (CR, Nov. 1977, 4)

The home, the school and the church must bend their energies toward ways of prevention and constructive building rather than to be merely detectives of crime after the act has been committed. —*Harold B. Lee* (DSL, 19)

The greatest weapon against all untruth, whether it be in science, so-called, or in the philosophies of the world, or in communism, or what not—the greatest weapon is the truth of the gospel of Jesus Christ, which preached in power will be a bulwark against these false ideas in the world today. —*Harold B. Lee* (SHP, 288-289)

Where else can you go for guidance? Where is there safety in the world today? Safety can't be won by tanks and guns and the airplanes and atomic bombs. There is only one place of safety and that is within the realm of the power of Almighty God that He gives to those who keep His commandments and listen to His voice, as He speaks through the channels that He has ordained for that purpose. —*Harold B. Lee* (SHP, 383)

The salt that has lost its savor is the Christianity that is worldliness under a different name. —*Harold B. Lee* (YLW, 12)

The saints are peculiar. This is true of them both regarding their habits and their religious belief. If they are true to their faith, they cannot help being different from other peoples. Their religion requires it of them. —*Joseph Fielding Smith* (CN, May 2, 1931, 2)

The world today is full of vain philosophy, full of doctrine that is not of the Lord, full of false conclusions, ideas and theories that were not a part of the gospel in the days of the Son of God, and hence are not a part of it now, but on the contrary are in absolute contradiction of the truth. There are fewer, in my judgment, among the Christian peoples, who believe in the Son of God as the Redeemer of the world. The tendency has been, during all these years, to get farther away from the principles of the gospel as they are contained in the holy scriptures. —*Joseph Fielding Smith* (CR, Apr. 1917, 59-60)

If we are living the religion which the Lord has revealed and which we have received, we do not belong to the world (John 17:14-16). We should have no part in all its foolishness. We should not partake of its sins and its errors—errors of philosophy and errors of doctrine, errors in regard to government, or whatever those errors may be—we have no part in it. The only part we have is the keeping of the commandments of God. That is all, being true to every covenant and every obligation that we have entered into and taken upon ourselves. —*Joseph Fielding Smith* (CR, Apr. 1952, 26)

The chief tragedy in the world at the present time is its disbelief in God's goodness and its lack of faith in the teachings and doctrines of the gospel. —*David O. McKay* (CR, Apr. 1940, 115)

Truly, from the standpoint of enhancing efficiency and progress, the Church of Jesus Christ has that form of government which the nations today are seeking.
This is because it is patterned after that order which Christ himself established. —*David O. McKay* (CR, Apr. 1930, 81)

I am grateful for membership in a church whose religion fits men for the struggle with the forces of the world and which enables them to survive in this struggle. —*David O. McKay* (CR, Apr. 1914, 87)

This is our country, our Heavenly Father gave it to us, and he expects each of us to show our appreciation of our birthright by helping in every possible way to purify society, and to develop those traits of character, and those virtues, that will enrich the community and prepare an environment for those who are now growing up and those who are yet unborn. —*George Albert Smith* (SGO, 167)

It is our duty to set the example; it is our duty to hold aloft the banner of truth. It is our duty to encourage our Father's children to listen to his advice and counsel and so adjust our lives that, wherever we are, we will find the spirit of God burning within our souls and our influence being felt for good. —*George Albert Smith* (CR, Oct. 1947, 166)

This Church stands in no danger from opposition and persecution from without. There is more to fear in carelessness, sin and indifference, from within; more danger that the individual will fail in doing right and in conforming his life to the revealed doctrines of our Lord and Savior Jesus Christ. If we do the right, all will be well, the God of our fathers will sustain us, and every opposition will tend only to the further spread of the knowledge of truth. —*Joseph F. Smith* (IE, 6:625)

Satan is a skillful imitator, and as genuine gospel truth is given the world in ever-increasing abundance, so he spreads the counterfeit coin of false doctrine. Beware of his spurious currency, it will purchase for you nothing but disappointment, misery and spiritual death. —*Joseph F. Smith* (LPS, 21)

I would fear very much for our safety if we had fallen into a condition where the devil ceased to be concerned about us. —*Joseph F. Smith* (LPS, 24)

By and by the nations will be broken up on account of their wickedness. . . . [T]hey will destroy themselves with their wickedness and immorality. They will contend and quarrel one with another, state after state and nation after nation, until they are broken up, and thousands, tens of thousands, and hundreds of thousands will undoubtedly come and seek protection at the hands of the servants of God. —*Lorenzo Snow* (JD, 14:309)

I will say that this nation, and all nations, together with presidents, kings, emperors, judges, and all men, righteous and wicked, have got to go into the spirit world and stand before the bar of God. They have got to give an account of the deeds done in the body. Therefore we are safe as long as we do our duty. —*Wilford Woodruff* (WW, 212)

Did you ever know the Lord to bring his judgments upon any nation, from the days of Adam in the Garden of Eden until the present time, before he had warned them of their sins? No; the Lord has always warned the people before he has punished them for their wickedness. —*Wilford Woodruff* (WW, 223)

Do I delight in the destruction of the children of men? No. Does the Lord? No. He gives them timely warning, and if they do not listen to his counsel, they must suffer the consequences of their wicked acts. —*Wilford Woodruff* (WW, 223)

I do not believe there was ever a generation of men who inhabited the earth who were more wicked, or who were practicing greater abominations, or who were sinning against greater light and knowledge, or who had a greater flood of judgments proclaimed against them by the word of the Lord, than the generation in which we live. Therefore, as Saints of the living God, who hear the Holy Priesthood, we shall be under condemnation if we do not lift up the warning voice against the evils and abominations which exist, so far as we have opportunity. —*Wilford Woodruff* (WW, 228)

I want to see the Latter-day Saints live their religion, keep their faith and do their duty, and trust in God. And if men persecute you for the sake of your religion, what can you do? You can go to God, and make your wants known to him; and that is our duty as Latter-day Saints. —*Wilford Woodruff* (WW, 231)

Lucifer, the Son of Morning, does not like the idea of revelation to the Saints of God, and he has inspired the hearts of a great many men, since the gospel was restored to the earth, to make war against us. But not one of them has made anything out of it yet—neither glory, immortality, eternal life, nor money. No man or people ever did make anything by fighting against God in the past, and no man or people will ever make anything by taking that course in the future. —*Wilford Woodruff* (WW, 238)

But what have we to do with the people of the world? . . . And it is his [the Lord s] business to deal with the nations of the earth at the present time and not ours, further than we are directed by him. What is the mission that we have to perform to this nation? It is to preach the gospel. —*John Taylor* (GK, 329)

We are called of God to be an upright people, a virtuous people, an honorable people. We are called upon to maintain correct principles, and to introduce them among the peoples of the earth, and especially among the people of this nation. —*John Taylor* (GK, 310)

Let us now notice our political position in the world. What are we going to do? We are going to possess the earth. Why? Because it belongs to Jesus Christ, and he belongs to us, and we to him. We are all one, and will take the kingdom and possess it under the whole heavens, and reign over it for ever and ever. Now, ye kings and emperors, help yourselves, if you can. This is the truth, and it may as well be told at this time as at any other. —*John Taylor* (GK, 313)

The proper mode of government is this—God first speaks, and then the people have their action. It is for them to say whether they will have his dictation or not. They are free; they are independent under God. —*John Taylor* (GK, 321)

We talk sometimes about the world, we Latter-day Saints, and we are very flippant in referring to their follies and foibles. We have enough follies of our own; and I often very much question whether they do not live as near to their religion as we do to ours. "How is that," says one. "We are a much more moral people than they are." We ought to be. We make greater professions than they do. They do not talk about having revelation. They do not talk about having any special mission to the nations of the earth, and we do. They do not talk about any celestial glory, and know nothing about it. We profess to know a little about it. They do not aim at a celestial glory, for they do not know what it is. —*John Taylor* (GK, 327)

Anything that is impure must, sooner or later, perish; no matter whether it is in the faith and practice of an individual, town, nation, or government. That kingdom, principality, power or person that is not controlled by principles that are pure and holy must eventually pass away and perish. —*Brigham Young* (BY, 227)

God is at the helm of this great ship, and that makes me feel good. When I think about the world, and the enemies of the cause of God, I care no more about them than I do for a parcel of mosquitoes. All hell may howl, and they may run up and down the earth and seek whom they may destroy, but they cannot move the faithful and pure in heart. Let those apostatize who wish to, but God will save all who are determined to be saved. —*Brigham Young* (BY, 86)

Those who cannot endure persecution, and stand in the day of affliction, cannot stand in the day when the Son of God shall burst the veil, and appear in all the glory of His Father, with all the holy angels. —*Joseph Smith, Jr.* (STJS, 56)

Impressed with the truth of these facts what can be the feelings of those who have been partakers of the heavenly gift and have tasted the good word of God, and the powers of the world to come? Who but those that can see the awful precipice upon which the world of mankind stands in this generation, can labor in the vineyard of the Lord without feeling a sense of the world's deplorable situation? . . . [W]ho but such can realize the importance of a perfect walk before all men, and a diligence in calling upon all men to partake of these blessings?—*Joseph Smith, Jr.* (STJS, 60)

Other attempts to promote universal peace and happiness in the human family have proved abortive; every effort has failed; every plan and design has fallen to the ground; it needs the wisdom of God, the intelligence of God, and the power of God to accomplish this. —*Joseph Smith, Jr.* (STJS, 283)

This generation is as corrupt as the generation of the Jews that crucified Christ; and if He were here today, and should preach the same doctrine He did then, they would put Him to death. —*Joseph Smith, Jr.* (LPS, 224)

91. ECONOMIC PRINCIPLES

I commend to you the virtues of thrift and industry. In doing so, I do not wish you to be a "tightwad," if you will pardon that expression, or to be a freeloader, or anything of the kind. But it is the labor and the thrift of people that make a nation strong. It is work and thrift that make the family independent. Debt can be a terrible thing. It is so easy to incur and so difficult to repay. Borrowed money is had only at a price, and that price cam be burdensome. Bankruptcy generally is the bitter fruit of debt. It is a tragic fulfillment of a simple process of borrowing more than one can repay. —*Gordon B. Hinckley* (Ensign, March 1990, 5)

Our pioneer forebears lived by the adage "Fix it up, wear it out, make it do, or do without."

Reasonable debt for the purchase of an affordable home and perhaps for a few other necessary things is acceptable. But from where I sit, I see in very vivid way the terrible tragedies of many who have unwisely borrowed for things they really do not need. —*Gordon B. Hinckley* (Ensign, Aug. 1992, 2-7)

The price you pay for "something for nothing" may be more than you can afford. —*Ezra Taft Benson* (ETB, 262)

The revelation to produce and store food may be as essential to our temporal welfare today as boarding the ark was to the people in the days of Noah. —*Ezra Taft Benson* (CR, Nov. 1980, 33)

Inspired leaders have always urged us to get out of debt, to live within our means, and to pay as we go—and this is sound advice for governments as well as individuals. History teaches that when individuals have given up looking after their own economic needs and transferred a large share of that responsibility to the government, both they and the government have failed. —*Ezra Taft Benson* (ETB, 289)

A nation can hang itself on the gallows of excessive public debt—and the United States is no exception. —*Ezra Taft Benson* (ETB, 291)

Yes, we have traveled a long way down the soul-destroying road of socialism. . . . How did it happen? Men of expediency ascended to high political offices by promising what was not theirs to give, and citizens voted them into office in the hopes of receiving what they had not earned. You can, therefore, see how the violation of one commandment—Thou shalt not covet—has weakened our entire system of government and led to a partial loss of liberty. —*Ezra Taft Benson* (ETB, 692-693)

The most common method of increasing the money supply today is by spending more than is in the treasury, and then merely printing extra money to make up the difference. Technically this is called "deficit spending." Ethically, it is counterfeiting. Morally, it is wrong. —*Ezra Taft Benson* (ETB, 641-642)

The Lord has urged that his people save for the rainy days, prepare for the difficult times, and put away for emergencies, a year's supply or more of bare necessities so that when comes the flood, the earthquake, the famine, the hurricane, the storms of life, our families can be sustained through the dark days. —*Spencer W. Kimball* (SWK, 374)

Encourage the putting aside for a rainy day in individual homes. That means teaching thrift, frugality, and avoidance of debt. Certainly that is a program that we ought to foster everywhere. —*Harold B. Lee* (SHP, 265)

The first real step toward self-sufficiency and true patriotism is taken when a man resolves in his heart not only to be self-sustaining and independent, but also to aid others to be likewise. —*Harold B. Lee* (YLW, 178-179)

Gold, silver, and precious stones, which are called wealth, are of no use to man, only as they enable him to take care of himself, and to meet his necessities here. —*Joseph Fielding Smith* (DS1, 69)

When we quit loving money and get the love of gold out of our hearts and the greed and selfishness, and learn to love the Lord, our God, with all our hearts, and our neighbor as ourselves, and get on our knees and learn to pray and repent of our sins, we will have prosperity, we will have peace, we will have contentment. —*Joseph Fielding Smith* (CN, May 4, 1935, 6)

Latter-day Saints should avoid affiliation with any committee, any group, any union that would, through coercion or force, deprive a person of the free exercise of his or her freedom of choice. It is understood, of course, that any person is free to join a union, when to do so favors his best interests; but no one should be compelled to join, or be deprived of any right as a citizen, including the right to honest labor, if he chooses not to become a member of a union or specially organized group. —*David O. McKay* (CR, Apr. 1940, 118)

The game of life is fascinating, and when men enter it, they enter to win. To win becomes the sole aim of life. The merchant, for example, wishes to succeed, no matter what it costs, though it be honor itself. The politician (not the statesman) enters the political world to satisfy his ambition, regardless of serving the community or his country. Thus, men lose sight of the high things of life; worldly things crush the spiritual light flickering within the soul. —*David O. McKay* (GI, 514)

There are many people who are born tired and never get rested. There are any number of people who just naturally have no conception of self-independence. Our country today is in a terrible condition on that account principally. —*Heber J. Grant* (GS, 108)

I say that, to my mind, a provision in a labor union is all wrong that favors boycotting and the laying down of tools or the quitting of employment because a non-union man obtains employment while exercising his God-given right to stay out of a union. Men who have that kind of rule have a rule that is in direct opposition to the laws of God. —*Heber J. Grant* (CR, Oct. 1919, 13-14)

If a person owned what he had and did not have to pay interest, and only bought as he had the money to buy, the majority of people would be in reasonably comfortable circumstances. —*Heber J. Grant* (GS, 112)

Keep your possessions free from debt. Get out of debt as fast as you can, and keep out of debt, for that is the way in which the promise of God will be fulfilled to the people of his Church, that they will become the richest of all people in the world. —*Joseph F. Smith* (CR, Apr. 1915, 11)

All this rage about success simply indicates the gross materialism of the age in which we live. . . . Certainly nothing is more fatal to our well being than the notion that our present and eternal welfare is founded upon the wealth and honors of this world. —*Joseph F. Smith* (GD, 124-125)

Men and women of wealth, use your riches to give employment to the laborer! Take the idle from the crowded centers of population and place them on the untilled areas that await the hand of industry. Unlock your vaults, unloose your purses, and embark in enterprises that will give work to the unemployed, and relieve the wretchedness that leads to the vice and crime which curse your great cities, and that poison the moral atmosphere around you. —*Lorenzo Snow* (LS, 63)

[T]here should be no unjust competition in matters that belong to the Latter-day Saints. That which creates division among us pertaining to our temporal interests should not be. —*Lorenzo Snow* (LS, 181)

In every age of the world the Saints of God have been obliged to be united. Babylon may divide; the inhabitants of the earth may have all the division they wish for; but they will all receive the results of that disunion, and have done all the way through. . . . But the Saints of God cannot prosper unless they are united. —*Wilford Woodruff* (WW, 126)

We have to become united as a people in all our labors—in our agriculture, manufactures, and every branch of our temporal labors. It is of great importance to the Latter-day

Saints that they should unite together on the principle of cooperation. —*Wilford Woodruff* (WW, 169)

It is suicidal for any people to import ten dollar's worth of products while they export only one, and it is a miracle and a wonder to me that we have lived as long as we have under this order of things. —*Wilford Woodruff* (WW, 171)

I do not find fault with a man getting rich, I find fault with our selling the kingdom of God, our birthright, selling the gospel and depriving ourselves of eternal life, for the sake of gratifying the lusts of the flesh, the pride of life and the fashions of the world; and setting our hearts upon these things. —*Wilford Woodruff* (WW, 173)

As for riches and wealth, I do not want them if they will damn me. I would like to have enough to clothe, shoe and feed my wives and children, and to make them comfortable, if I can get it honestly before the Lord; but I would rather myself and them all be in poverty than to have wealth and be destroyed. Riches are dangerous unless we can use them so as not to destroy us; if we cannot use them to the glory of God and for the building up of his kingdom, we are better without them. —*Wilford Woodruff* (WW, 173-174)

Money is not to be compared with intelligence. —*John Taylor* (GK, 275)

He must be a fool who would barter away eternal life, thrones, principalities, and powers in the eternal world for the paltry trash which exists in the shape of wealth and worldly honor; to let go his chance of heaven and of God, of being a king and priest unto him, of living and reigning forever, and of standing among the chiefs of Israel. I cannot help calling such men fools, for they are damned now in making such a choice, and will be hereafter. —*John Taylor* (GK, 314)

[D]on't relieve the idle, for relieving those who are able but unwilling to work is ruinous to any community. —*Brigham Young* (BY, 217)

If you wish to get rich, save what you get. A fool can earn money; but it takes a wise man to save and dispose of it to his own advantage. —*Brigham Young* (BY, 292)

The riches of a kingdom or nation do not consist so much in the fulness of its treasury as in the fertility of its soil and the industry of its people. —*Brigham Young* (BY, 297)

Our wants are many, but our real necessities are very few. Let us govern our wants by our necessities, and we shall find that we are not compelled to spend our money for naught. —*Brigham Young* (BY, 297)

To be prudent and saving, and to use the elements in our possession for our benefit and the benefit of our fellow beings is wise and righteous; but to be slothful, wasteful, lazy and indolent, to spend our time and means for naught, is unrighteous. —*Brigham Young* (BY, 303)

A man who will run into debt, when he has no prospect of paying it back again, does not understand the principles that should prevail in a well regulated community, or he is wilfully dishonest. —*Brigham Young* (BY, 304)

What comes of litigation? Poverty and degradation to any community that will encourage it. Will it build cities, open farms, build railroads, erect telegraph lines and improve a country? It will not; but it will bring any community to ruin. —*Brigham Young* (BY, 197)

It may be said that we shall always be poor without commerce; we shall always be poor with it, unless we command it; and unless we can do this, we are better without. —*Brigham Young* (BY, 299)

Are our merchants honest? I could not be honest and do as they do; they make five hundred percent on some of their goods, and that, too, from an innocent, confiding, poor, industrious people. —*Brigham Young* (BY, 300)

92. WAR

I deeply appreciate those who have sacrificed their lives for the cause of human liberty. I hate war, with all its mocking panoply. It is a grim and living testimony that Satan, the father of lies, the enemy of God, lives. War is earth's greatest cause of human misery. It is the destroyer of life, the promoter of hate, the waster of treasure. It is man's costliest folly, his most tragic misadventure. —*Gordon B. Hinckley* (Ensign, March 1971, 20)

Lust has been the motivating force of the wars that have afflicted and desolated the world. One nation has coveted another's territory or property or has attempted to force its will or way of life upon another . . . History is a repetitious recital of international and wanton destruction of life and property. Today is no different from the yesterdays. —*Howard W. Hunter* (WMJ, 28)

An ounce of energy in the preservation of freedom is worth a ton of effort to get it back once it is lost. —*Ezra Taft Benson* (ETB, 657)

O foolish men who think to protect the world with armaments, battleships, and space equipment, when only righteousness is needed!—*Spencer W. Kimball* (SWK, 416)

It is my conviction that the devastating scourge of war in which so many are slain, many of whom are no more responsible for the causes of the war than are our own boys, is making necessary an increase of missionary activity in the spirit world and that many of our boys who bear the holy priesthood and are worthy to do so will be called to that missionary service after they have departed this life. —*Harold B. Lee* (YLW, 197)

All through the ages some of the righteous have had to suffer because of the acts of the unrighteous, but they will get their reward. Many of those who are taken in these days of battle are called because they are needed for work on the other side. —*Joseph Fielding Smith* (DS3, 37)

Yes, the causes of war are vanity, selfishness, unjust commercialism, unrighteousness, and other things contrary to the spirit of the gospel of Jesus Christ. —*David O. McKay* (CR, Oct. 1914, 88-89)

There are some things which man should hate—he should hate injustice; hate hypocrisy; hate wickedness in all its forms; but never hate mankind. —*David O. McKay* (GI, 280)

We see that war is incompatible with Christ's teachings. The gospel of Jesus Christ is the gospel of peace. War is its antithesis and produces hate. It is vain to attempt to reconcile war with true Christianity. —*David O. McKay* (GI, 285)

There are, however, two conditions which may justify a truly Christian man to enter—mind you, I say enter, not begin—a war: (1) an attempt to dominate and to deprive another of his free agency, and (2) loyalty to his country. Possibly there is a third, viz., defense of a weak nation that is being unjustly crushed by a strong, ruthless one. —*David O. McKay* (GI, 286)

The most ominous threat to the peace and happiness of mankind in this the twentieth century is not the probable misuse of the atomic bomb, but the dwindling in men's hearts of faith in God. —*David O. McKay* (IE, 50:507)

If the people who dwell on this earth were obedient to the loving advice of our Heavenly Father, that has been given through his servants down through the ages, instead of war, rapine and murder, we would have peace, prosperity and happiness. There is no way for us to enjoy the blessings of our Heavenly Father but by obedience to his counsel. —*George Albert Smith* (SGO, 203)

The world will soon be devastated with war and carnage, with plague and all the distresses that the Lord has promised unless they repent; but he has indicated that they will not repent, and distress must come. —*George Albert Smith* (CR, Apr. 1937, 36)

We affirm that all international controversies may be settled by pacific means if nations will but deal unselfishly and righteously one with another. We appeal to the leaders of all nations and to the people themselves thus to mend and adjust their differences, lest the vials of God's wrath be poured out upon the earth, for He has said He will visit His wrath upon the wicked without measure. —*Heber J. Grant* (CR, Oct. 1939, 8)

I want every Latter-day Saint soldier to get down on his knees and pray God to help him to lead a clean life, and to preach the gospel while he is in the army. The army, as a rule, is a demoralizer of the morals of men, to a very great extent. They think: "Oh, well; we are going to be killed anyway—let's have a h—l of a good time." Do not wish for any such good time; there is no good time anywhere for any human being except by doing good and doing right. There is a peace, a joy, and a happiness that comes from doing right that nothing else can compare with. —*Heber J. Grant* (GS, 149)

I don't want you to think I believe that God has designed or willed that war should come among the people of the world, that the nations of the world should be divided against one another in war, and engaged in the destruction of each? God did not design or cause this. It is deplorable to the heavens that such a condition should exist among men, but the conditions do exist, and men precipitate war and destruction upon themselves because of their wickedness, and that because they will not abide in God's truth, walk in his love, and seek to establish and maintain peace instead of strife and contention in the world. —*Joseph F. Smith* (GD, 3)

I repeat, there is but one remedy that can prevent men from going to war, when they feel disposed to do it, and that is the Spirit of God, which inspires to love, and not to hatred, which leads unto all truth, and not unto error, which inclines the children of God to pay deference to him and to his laws and to esteem them as above all other things in the world. —*Joseph F. Smith* (GD, 418)

Barbarism of the past should be buried. War with its horrors should be but a memory. The aim of nations should be fraternity and mutual greatness. The welfare of humanity should be studied instead of the enrichment of a race or the extension of an empire. —*Lorenzo Snow* (PC , 169)

The welfare, happiness, exaltation, and glory of man are sacrificed at the shrine of ambition, pride, covetousness, and lasciviousness. By these means nations are overthrown, kingdoms destroyed, communities broken up, families rendered miserable, and individuals ruined. —*John Taylor* (GK, 300)

Why is it that thrones will be cast down, empires dissolved, nations destroyed, and confusion and distress cover all people, as the prophets have spoken? Because the Spirit of the

Lord will be withdrawn from the nations in consequence of their wickedness, and they will be left to their own folly. —*John Taylor* (GK, 300)

Of one thing I am sure; God never institutes war; God is not the author of confusion or of war; they are the results of the acts of the children of men. Confusion and war necessarily come as the results of the foolish acts and policy of men; but they do not come because God desires they should come. If the people, generally, would turn to the Lord, there would never be any war. —*Brigham Young* (BY, 366-367)

93. THE SCRIPTURES

We all do a lot of studying, but most of us don't do much meditation. We don't take time to think. I'd like to suggest that next fast day . . . everybody in this hall set aside an hour or two. Sit by yourself. Go in the bedroom and lock the door. Go out in the yard under a tree. Go in your study if you have one and shut the door, and think about yourself and your worthiness. . . .

"Ponder." What do we mean by "ponder"? Well, I think it simply means kind of quietly thinking things through. Ponder what you have read. Ponder your life. Are you worthy, are you living the commandments?—*Gordon B. Hinckley* (CN, Jan. 6, 1996, 2)

There may be so very much our Father in Heaven would like to give us—young, old, or middle-aged—if we would but seek his presence regularly through such avenues as scripture study and earnest prayer. Of course, developing spirituality and attuning ourselves to the highest influences of Godliness are not an easy matter. It takes time and frequently involves a struggle. —*Howard W. Hunter* (WMJ, 120)

Where could there be more profitable use of time than reading from the scriptural library the literature that teaches us to know God and understand our relationship to him?—*Howard W. Hunter* (CR, Nov. 1979, 64)

It is certain that one who studies the scriptures every day accomplishes far more than one who devotes considerable time one day and then lets days go by before continuing. Not only should we study each day, but there should be a regular time set aside when we can concentrate without interference. . . .

It would be ideal if an hour could be spent each day; but if that much cannot be had, a half hour on a regular basis would result in substantial accomplishment. A quarter of an hour is little time, but it is surprising how much enlightenment and knowledge can be acquired in a subject so meaningful. The important thing is to allow nothing else to interfere with our study. —*Howard W. Hunter* (CR, Nov. 1979, 64)

We should make daily study of the scriptures a lifetime pursuit. —*Ezra Taft Benson* (CR, Nov. 1986, 47)

Often we spend great effort in trying to increase the activity levels in our stakes. We work diligently to raise the percentages of those attending sacrament meetings. We labor to get a higher percentage of our young men on missions. We strive to improve the numbers of those marrying in the temple. All of these are commendable efforts and important to the growth of the kingdom. But when individual members and families immerse themselves in the scriptures regularly and consistently, these other areas of activity will automatically come. Testimonies will increase. Commitment will be strengthened. Families will be fortified. Personal revelation will flow. —*Ezra Taft Benson* (Ensign, May 1986, 80-81)

I find that when I get casual in my relationships with divinity and when it seems that no divine ear is listening and no divine voice is speaking, that I am far, far away. If I immerse myself in the scriptures the distance narrows and the spirituality returns. I find myself loving more intensely those whom I must love with all my heart and mind and strength, and loving them more, I find it easier to abide their counsel. —*Spencer W. Kimball* (SWK, 135)

I ask us all to honestly evaluate our performance in scripture study. It is a common thing to have a few passages of scripture at our disposal, floating in our minds, as it were, and thus to have the illusion that we know a great deal about the gospel. In this sense, having a little knowledge can be a problem indeed. I am convinced that each of us, at some time in our lives, must discover the scriptures for ourselves—and not just discover them once, but rediscover them again and again. —*Spencer W. Kimball* (Ensign, July 1985, 4-5)

I say that we need to teach our people to find their answers in the scriptures. . . . But the unfortunate thing is that so many of us are not reading the scriptures. We do not know what is in them, and therefore we speculate about the things that we ought to have found in the scriptures themselves. I think that therein is one of our biggest dangers of today. —*Harold B. Lee* (Ensign, Dec. 1972, 2)

Do you have a daily habit of reading the scriptures? If we're not reading the scriptures daily, our testimonies are growing thinner, our spirituality isn't increasing in depth. —*Harold B. Lee* (HBL, 152)

Let there be study of the scriptures at least thirty minutes of each day. At an early morning hour, or at late night, as best suits your schedule, allow yourself an hour of prayerful meditation where you can tune in with God and discuss with Him problems that are too much for human understanding, too great for human strength. —*Harold B. Lee* (HBL, 152)

If a man will permit reason to guide him in the path of common sense, he will be forced to conclude that there is no justification for the belief that all scripture is enclosed within the cover of the Holy Bible. Such a doctrine closes the mouth of the Almighty, denying him power to speak. Nor can it be consistently stated that there is no need for further revelation. —*Joseph Fielding Smith* (CN, June 20, 1931, 2)

It is wrong to take one passage of scripture and isolate it from all other teachings dealing with the same subject. We should bring together all that has been said by authority on the question. —*Joseph Fielding Smith* (DS2, 95)

It makes no difference what is written or what anyone has said, if what has been said is in conflict with what the Lord has revealed, we can set it aside. My words, and the teaching of any other member of the Church, high or low, if they do not square with the revelations, we need not accept them. Let us have this matter clear. We have accepted the four standard works as the measuring yardsticks, or balances, by which we measure every man's doctrine. —*Joseph Fielding Smith* (DS3, 203)

I wish that all the people of the world—all our Father's children—could understand the scriptures that have been given to us by the Lord and preserved by the Lord and preserved by his servants. They are replete with assurance of the resurrection and eternal life. —*George Albert Smith* (SGO, 69)

What mattereth it though we understand Homer and Shakespeare and Milton, and I might enumerate all the great writers of the world; if we have failed to read the scriptures we have missed the better part of this world's literature. —*George Albert Smith* (CR, Oct. 1917, 43)

Do not trust in yourselves, but study the best books—the Bible and Book of Mormon—and get all the information you can, and then cleave to God and keep yourselves free from corruption and pollution of every kind, and the blessings of the Most High will be with you. —*John Taylor* (GK, 240)

We believe that God condescended to speak from the heavens and declare His will concerning the human family, to give them just and holy laws, to regulate their conduct, and guide them in a direct way, that in due time He might take them to Himself, and make them joint heirs with His Son. But when this fact is admitted, that the immediate will of heaven is contained in the Scriptures, are we not bound as rational creatures to live in accordance to all its precepts? Will the mere admission, that this is the will of heaven ever benefit us if we do not comply with all its teachings? Do we not offer violence to the Supreme Intelligence of heaven, when we admit the truth of its teachings, and do not obey them?—*Joseph Smith, Jr.* (STJS, 66-67)

Search the scriptures—search the revelations which we publish, and ask your Heavenly Father, in the name of His Son Jesus Christ, to manifest the truth unto you, and if you do it with an eye single to his glory nothing doubting, He will answer you by the power of His Holy Spirit. You will then know for yourselves and not for another. You will not then be dependent on man for the knowledge of God; nor will there be any room for speculation. No; for when men receive their instruction from Him that made them, they know how He will save them. Then again we say: Search the Scriptures, search the Prophets and learn what portion of them belongs to you. —*Joseph Smith, Jr.* (STJS, 16-17)

From what we can draw from the Scriptures relative to the teaching of heaven, we are induced to think that much instruction has been given to man since the beginning which we do not possess now. This may not agree with the opinions of some of our friends who are bold to say that we have everything written in the Bible which God ever spoke to man since the world began, and that if He had ever said anything more we should certainly receive it. But we ask, does it remain for a people who never had faith enough to call down one scrap of revelation from heaven, and for all they have now are indebted to the faith of another people who lived hundreds and thousands of years before them, does it remain for them to say how much God has spoken and how much He has not spoken?—*Joseph Smith, Jr.* (STJS, 74-75)

I have a key by which I understand the scriptures. I inquire, what was the question which drew out the answer, or caused Jesus to utter the parable?—*Joseph Smith, Jr.* (STJS, 312)

94. THE BIBLE

The Bible provides the foundation of our faith: The Old Testament gives the word of Jehovah through His ancient prophets; the New Testament sets forth, in language beautiful and moving, the matchless life and sacrifice of the Savior of mankind. —*Gordon B. Hinckley* (Ensign, Apr. 1983, 4)

It is only as we forsake the traditions of men and recover faith in the Bible, the truth of which has been fully established by recent discovery and fulfillment of prophecy, that we shall once again receive that inspiration which is needed by rulers and people alike. —*Harold B. Lee* (HBL, 158-159)

The Holy Bible has had a greater influence on the world for good than any other book ever published. . . . The reason for the Bible's great influence for good is because it is inspired and contains the word of the Lord delivered to his prophets, who wrote and spoke as they were moved upon by the Holy Ghost, since the world began. —*Joseph Fielding Smith* (CN, Jan. 2 1937, 1)

We are all aware that there are errors in the Bible due to faulty translations and ignorance on the part of translators; but the hand of the Lord has been over this volume of scripture nevertheless, and it is remarkable that it has come down to us in the excellent condition in which we find it. —*Joseph Fielding Smith* (DS3, 191)

We are called a peculiar people because, perchance, we thoroughly believe and obey the Gospel of Jesus Christ. Our peculiarity lies very largely in the fact that we believe the Old and New Testaments actually contain the word of the Lord, as far as they have been translated correctly. —*George Albert Smith* (CR, Oct. 1905, 26)

The Old and New Testaments contain the teachings of our Heavenly Father. I admonish you, O Israel, search the scriptures; read them in your homes; teach your families what the Lord has said, and let us spend less time in reading the unimportant and often harmful literature of the day and go to the fountain of truth and read the word of the Lord. —*George Albert Smith* (CR, Oct. 1917, 41)

The Bible, as all other books of Holy Writ, to be appreciated must be studied by those spiritually inclined and who are in quest of spiritual truths. —*Joseph F. Smith* (GD, 46)

The whole Christian world professes to believe the Bible, and perhaps they do when it is shut. But open the Bible and read the declarations contained therein, concerning the last dispensation of the fulness of times, and where is the man who believes them? You cannot find one, and it requires faith even among the Latter-day Saints to believe the revelations of God, and to prepare themselves for those things which await the world. —*Wilford Woodruff* (WW, 48-49)

If you profess to believe in the Bible when shut, believe it when open, and practice its principles. —*John Taylor* (GK, 308)

I believe the words of the Bible are just what they are; but aside from that I believe the doctrines concerning salvation contained in that book are true, and that their observance will elevate any people, nation or family that dwells on the face of the earth. . . . Follow out the doctrines of the Bible, and men will make splendid husbands, women excellent wives, and children will be obedient; they will make families happy and the nations wealthy and happy and lifted up above the things of this life. —*Brigham Young* (BY, 125)

It has been proclaimed that there is a great difference between us and the Christian world. . . . The difference arises from the fact that we believe this Bible, wide open, from genesis to Revelations. They believe it, sealed up, never to be opened again to the human family. They believe it shut, we believe it open; they believe it in silence, we believe it proclaimed on the hose top. —*Brigham Young* (JD, 15:41)

The book of Revelation is one of the plainest books God ever caused to be written. —*Joseph Smith, Jr.* (STJS, 323)

95. THE BOOK OF MORMON

To a world wavering in its faith, the Book of Mormon is another testament and powerful witness of the divinity of the Lord. —*Gordon B. Hinckley* (Ensign, Apr. 1983, 4)

I should like to make a request and offer a challenge to members of the Church throughout the world and to our friends everywhere to read the Book of Mormon. Then I should like to challenge each one to put to the test the words of the prophet Moroni, written as he completed his record fifteen centuries ago. —*Gordon B. Hinckley* (BTE, 100-101)

I know the Book of Mormon is true. You just have to read it. You only have to read it, prayerfully, and you'll know it is true. It speaks for itself. It is its own greatest testimony of its truth. And the marvelous thing is, every time you read it you see things you never saw before. Read it. I know it's true. —*Gordon B. Hinckley* (CN, Jan. 6, 1996, 1)

To those who may not be familiar with the Book of Mormon but are sincerely seeking truth, reading it will have a profound effect on your life. It will expand your knowledge of the way God deals with man and will give you a great desire to live in harmony with his gospel teachings. It will also provide for you a powerful testimony of Jesus. —*Howard W. Hunter* (Ensign, May 1983, 16)

Social, ethical, cultural, or educational converts will not survive under the heat of the day unless their taproots go down to the fullness of the gospel which the Book of Mormon contains. —*Ezra Taft Benson* (AWW, 6)

The Book of Mormon brings men to Christ through two basic means. First, it tells in a plain manner of Christ and His gospel. It testifies of His divinity and of the necessity for a Redeemer and the need of our putting trust in Him. It bears witness of the Fall and the Atonement and the first principles of the gospel, including our need of a broken heart and a contrite spirit and a spiritual rebirth. It proclaims we must endure to the end in righteousness and live the moral life of a Saint.

Second, the Book of Mormon exposes the enemies of Christ. It confounds false doctrines and lays down contention. It fortifies the humble followers of Christ against the evil designs, strategies, and doctrines of the devil in our day. The type of apostates in the Book of Mormon is similar to the type we have today. God, with his infinite foreknowledge, so molded the Book of Mormon that we might see the error and know how to combat false educational, political, religious and philosophical concepts of our time. —*Ezra Taft Benson* (AWW, 3)

We do not have to prove the Book of Mormon is true. The book is its own proof. All we need to do is read it and declare it. The Book of Mormon is not on trial—the people of the world, including the members of the Church, are on trial as to what they will do with this second witness for Christ. —*Ezra Taft Benson* (AWW, 13)

The time is long overdue for a massive flooding of the earth with the Book of Mormon for the many reasons which the Lord has given. In this age of electronic media and mass distribution of the printed word, God will hold us accountable if we do not now move the Book of Mormon in a monumental way.

We have the Book of Mormon, we have the members, we have the missionaries, we have the resources, and the world has the need. The time is now! —*Ezra Taft Benson* (Ensign, Nov. 1988, 4-5)

I challenge the homes of Israel to display on their walls great quotations and scenes from the Book of Mormon. . —*Ezra Taft Benson* (Ensign, Sept. 1988, 5-6)

[W]e see in the Book of Mormon the dangers of materialism and setting our hearts on the things of the world. Can anyone doubt that this book was meant for us and that in it we find great power, great comfort, and great protection?—*Ezra Taft Benson* (Ensign, Jan. 1992, 7)

There is nothing better that we can do to prepare ourselves spiritually than to read the Book of Mormon. Many doctrines of the Bible that are only partially covered there are beautifully explained in the Book of Mormon, the Doctrine and Covenants, and the Pearl of Great Price. —*Harold B. Lee* (HBL, 155)

If one wants to get close to God, he can do it by reading the Book of Mormon. —*Harold B. Lee* (HBL, 155)

So far as we are concerned, the best evidence in the world of the truth of the Book of Mormon is the Book of Mormon itself. —*Harold B. Lee* (HBL, 156)

It seems to me that any member of this Church would never be satisfied until he or she had read the Book of Mormon time and time again, and thoroughly considered it so that he or she could bear witness that it is in very deed a record with the inspiration of the Almighty upon it, and that its history is true. . . .

No member of the Church can stand approved in the presence of God who has not seriously and carefully read the Book of Mormon. —*Joseph Fielding Smith* (CR, Oct. 1961, 18)

The Book of Mormon is a sacred record containing information that is found in no other book. The Lord has commanded us to share with all his children the truths of the everlasting gospel. Distributing the Book of Mormon is a most important duty. —*George Albert Smith* (SGO, 100)

The Book of Mormon consists largely of the teachings of the prophets who, from age to age, taught the gospel to the people of ancient America. —*George Albert Smith* (CR, Apr. 1916, 46)

The Book of Mormon is in absolute harmony from start to finish with other sacred scriptures. There is not a doctrine taught in it that does not harmonize with the teachings of Jesus Christ. . . . There is not a thing in it but what is for the benefit and uplift of mankind. It is in every way a true witness for God, and it sustains the Bible, and is in harmony with the Bible. —*Heber J. Grant* (CR, Apr. 1929, 128-129)

The Book of Mormon is the great, the grand, the most wonderful missionary that we have. —*Heber J. Grant* (CR, Apr. 1937, 126)

Men have been opposed to the Book of Mormon because it was a new Bible. The poor fools did not know that wherever there was a true Church there was revelation, and that wherever there was revelation there was the word of God to man and materials to make Bibles of. —*John Taylor* (JD, 5:266)

There is not another nation under heaven, in whose midst the Book of Mormon could have been brought forth. —*Brigham Young* (BY, 109)

Here is the Book of Mormon. We believe it contains the history of the aborigines of our continent, just as the Old Testament contains the history of the Jewish nation. In that book we learn that Jesus visited this continent, delivered his Gospel and ordained Twelve Apostles. We believe all this, but we do not ask you to believe it. What we do ask is that you will believe what is recorded in the Holy Bible concerning God and his revelations to the children of men. Do this in all honesty and sincerity, then you will know that the Book of

Mormon is true. Your minds will be opened and you will know by the vision of the Spirit of God that we teach the truth. —*Brigham Young* (BY, 109)

I wish to mention here, that the title-page of the Book of Mormon is a literal translation, taken from the very last leaf, on the left hand side of the collection or book of plates, which contained the record which has been translated, the language of the whole running the same as all Hebrew writing in general; and that said title-page is not by any means a modern composition, either of mine or of any other man who has lived or does live in this generation. —*Joseph Smith, Jr.* (STJS, 13)

Take away the Book of Mormon and the revelations, and where is our religion? We have none. —*Joseph Smith, Jr.* (STJS, 86)

I told the brethren that the Book of Mormon was the most correct of any book on earth, and the keystone of our religion, and a man would get nearer to God by abiding by its precepts, than by any other book. —*Joseph Smith, Jr.* (STJS, 220)

96. DOCTRINE AND COVENANTS

The Doctrine and Covenants is unique among our books of scripture. It is the constitution of the Church. —*Gordon B. Hinckley* (Ensign, Jan. 1989, 2)

The Doctrine and Covenants is a glorious book of scripture given directly to our generation. It contains the will of the Lord for us in these last days that precede the second coming of Christ. It contains many truths and doctrines not fully revealed in other scripture. —*Ezra Taft Benson* (AWW, 28)

This Doctrine and Covenants contains the word of God to those who dwell here now. It is our book. It belongs to the Latter-day Saints. More precious than gold, the Prophet says we should treasure it more than the riches of the whole earth. I wonder if we do? If we value it, understand it, and know what it contains, we will value it more than wealth; it is worth more to us than the riches of the earth. —*Joseph Fielding Smith* (DS3, 199)

I wish that I had the ability to impress upon the Latter-day Saints the necessity of searching the commandments of God—the revelations from the Lord, the Creator of heaven and earth—as contained in the Doctrine and Covenants. If we as a people would live up to those wonderful revelations that have come to us, we would be a bright and shining light to all the world. —*Heber J. Grant* (CR, Oct. 1927, 4)

97. TEACHINGS OF LATTER-DAY PROPHETS

It is the present living prophet who is our leader, our teacher. It is from him we take direction in the modern world. From all corners of the earth we who sustain him as a prophet of the Lord, express our appreciation for this source of divine guidance. We are grateful for his life, his example, his teachings, his leadership. —*Howard W. Hunter* (Ensign, Oct. 1963, 101)

May we cherish God's revelations more than man's reasoning and choose to follow the prophets of the Lord rather than the precepts of men. —*Ezra Taft Benson* (ETB, 143)

The most vital words that you can read are those of the Presidents of the Church—particularly the living prophet—and those of the Apostles and prophets. —*Ezra Taft Benson* (ETB, 302-303)

The living prophet is more important to us than a dead prophet. The living prophet has the power of TNT. By that I mean "Today's News Today." God's revelations to Adam did not instruct Noah how to build the ark. Noah needed his own revelation. Therefore, the most important prophet, so far as you and I are concerned, is the one living in our day and age to whom the Lord is currently revealing His will for us. —*Ezra Taft Benson* (ETB, 335)

Prophets say the same things because we face basically the same problems. Brothers and sisters, the solutions to these problems have not changed. It would be a poor lighthouse that gave off a different signal to guide every ship entering a harbor. It would be a poor mountain guide who, knowing the safe route up a mountainside, took his trusting charges up unpredictable and perilous paths from which no traveler returns. —*Spencer W. Kimball* (CR, Nov. 1975, 4)

The fact that I was not born in the times of spiritual darkness in which the heavens were silent and the Spirit withdrawn fills my soul with gratitude. Truly, to be without the word of the Lord to direct us is to be as wanderers in a vast desert who can find no familiar landmarks, or in the dense darkness of a cavern with no light to show us the way to escape. —*Spencer W. Kimball* (Ensign, July 1985, 4)

If you want to know what the Lord has for this people at the present time, I would admonish you to get and read the discourses that are delivered at general conference; for what the Brethren speak by the power of the Holy Ghost is the mind of the Lord, the will of the Lord, the voice of the Lord, and the power of God unto salvation. I am sure all who listen, if they are in tune, feel the sincerity and the deep conviction from those who speak so appropriately and so effectively. —*Harold B. Lee* (SHP, 183)

Now, we may take the Bible, the Book of Mormon, and Doctrine and Covenants, and we may read them through, and every other revelation that has been given to us, and they would scarcely be sufficient to guide us twenty-four hours. We have only an outline of our duties written; we are to be guided by the living oracles. —*Wilford Woodruff* (WW, 47-48)

We have got to follow the oracles of heaven in all things; there is no other way but to follow him God has appointed to lead us and guide us into eternal salvation. He is either delegated from heaven to do this, or he is not; if he is, we will follow his counsel; if he is not, then we may kick up our heels, and every man help himself the best way he can. —*John Taylor* (GK, 249)

The Book of Mormon is good, and the Doctrine and Covenants, as land-marks. But a mariner who launches into the ocean requires a more certain criterion. He must be acquainted with heavenly bodies, and take his observations from them, in order to steer his barque aright. Those books are good for example, precedent, and investigation, and for developing certain laws and principles. But they do not, they cannot, touch every case required to be adjudicated and set in order. —*John Taylor* (GK, 34)

I have never yet preached a sermon and sent it out to the children of men, that they may not call scripture. —*Brigham Young* (JD, 13:95)

With us the Bible is the first book, the Book of Mormon comes next, then the revelations in the book of Doctrine and Covenants, then the teachings of the living oracles, yet you will find, in the end, that the living oracles of God have to take all things of heaven and earth,

above and beneath, and bring them together and devote them to God, and sanctify and purify them and prepare them to enter into the Kingdom of heaven. —*Brigham Young* (BY, 126)

I never told you I was perfect; but there is no error in the revelations which I have taught.
—*Joseph Smith, Jr.* (STJS, 415)